Popular Science

HOMEOWNER'S ENCYCLOPEDIA

FULLER & DEES

TIMES MIRROR

New York • Los Angeles • Montgomery

© Fuller & Dees MCMLXXIV
3734 Atlanta Highway, Montgomery, Alabama 36109

Library of Congress Cataloging in Publication Data
Main entry under title: Popular Science Homeowner's Encyclopedia

1. Dwellings — Maintenance and repair — Amateurs' manuals. 2. Repairing —
Amateurs' manuals. 3. Do-it-yourself work. I. Title: Homeowner's encyclopedia.
TH4817.3.P66   643'.7'03   74-19190
Complete Set ISBN 0-87197-070-8
Volume II ISBN 0-87197-072-4

Popular Science

HOMEOWNER'S ENCYCLOPEDIA

Dead Load

Dead load, the stationary weight of the various parts of a house structure, must be figured in order to estimate the strength of the foundation prior to construction. Dead load is computed in pounds per square feet and should include the weight of seemingly unimportant loads such as roof shingles and household furniture. *SEE ALSO FLOOR CONSTRUCTION.*

Decibel

Decibel is a unit for measuring the intensity of sound. It is usually gauged in relation to the capacity of the human ear. The normal ear can differentiate nearly 130 decibels.

Deciduous

Deciduous is a term that defines those shrubs, vines and trees which shed their leaves in the winter. Most broad-leafed trees like sweet gum, maple, pecan and oak are deciduous. Hydrangeas, forsythias, spirea and varieties of azaleas are deciduous shrubs. The more common leaf-shedding vines are wisteria, bittersweet, Boston ivy and kudzu. Ground covers, which resemble coarse lawns, are used on steep banks and in heavily shaded areas where grass will not grow. There are available in deciduous varieties like bishops weed, bugle weed, cotoneaster and barren wort. Most of these as well as the deciduous trees, shrubs and vines generally change their color to brown, yellow, orange or red in the fall before shedding in the winter. *SEE ALSO LAWNS & GARDENS.*

Deck Faucet

A deck faucet, used for a kitchen or bathroom sink, is equipped with two handles and valves through which both hot and cold water flow. Parts of this faucet include a large top screw, the handle, packing nut or bonnet, sleeve, spindle or stem, washer and a large bottom screw.

The faucet washer, made of either plastic or rubber, is attached to the spindle or stem. When a deck faucet fails to provide water, a faulty washer is usually the problem, since the washer twists each time the handle is turned. However, washers may be easily replaced.

The faucet handle is attached to the top portion of the stem. Deck faucets vary in sizes from four to six to eight inches between stems. *SEE ALSO FAUCET.*

Decks & Deck Construction
[SEE WOOD DECKS.]

Decorating

The first consideration in decorating a home should be the people who live in it. For best results, make a master plan. Perhaps you live alone. Perhaps there are small children or teens, or possibly a grandparent lives with the family. The needs of each, individually and collectively, must be considered.

MAKING THE MASTER PLAN

To begin, write the names of each member of the family on a separate sheet of paper. Then list the traits, needs, hobbies, likes and dislikes of each person. One sheet may look like this: "Dad. informal, active, brings work home from office, assistant scoutmaster, hosts his card game every five weeks, builds model ships, reads, likes comfortable, over-stuffed chairs, favorite color is blue, and dislikes clutter, loud music, and the color violet."

When all the sheets are finished, bring the whole family into the planning. Everyone working

together can offer suggestions and agree to compromises. More important, this is an opportunity to build enthusiasm and cooperation for the project.

Here are some of the questions to consider in planning: *What is your family's lifestyle?* If you live a formal, contained life, your plans will be drastically different from those of an informal, casual family. If you and your family are active people always on the go, you will want to consider making your home easy to care for. If you entertain often, the comfort of your guests deserves a place in your plans. Many families have a mixture of lifestyles. A formal living and

dining room can be balanced with a very informal family room and kitchen eating nook.

What are the individual needs of your family? An elderly or ill person or a young baby will need a quiet room. The safety of young children would be of paramount importance in planning storage and room accessories. Do not forget to protect precious possessions from young children, either. Everyone should have a place to withdraw from the activity of the household, whether it be a bedroom, a den, or a basement. Some family members will need room to pursue their hobbies. Even if there is not a separate room available, space can usually be found for

Tasselled pillows provide additional seating for television viewing in this informal family room.

Courtesy Ethan Allen

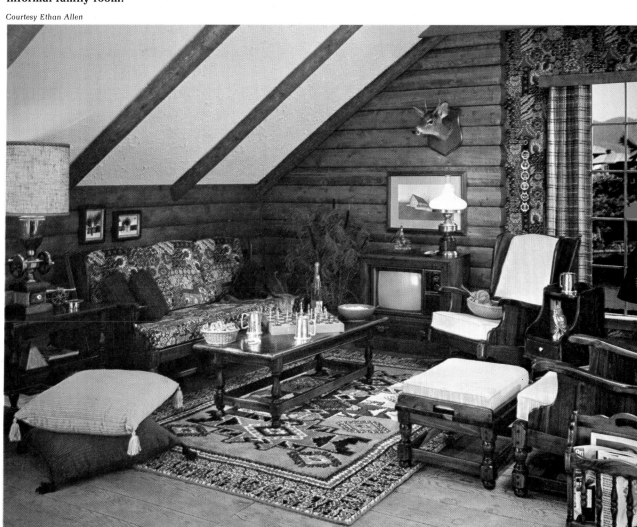

sewing, model building, oil painting, and other interests. Students will need a place to study.

What are the collective needs of the family? Every family does something together, even if it is only eating or watching television. If television is important to the family, provide adequate seating in the television room. That room may be the living room, den or family room, and the seating may be simply large pillows for lounging on the floor. If the whole family seldom gets the chance to dine together, you can save a lot of time by providing for a small eating area or counter in the kitchen.

How should you plan for guests? For parties and get-togethers, plan areas that can be used effectively: a convenient space for a game table, an expandable dining facility, comfortable conversation clusters. If you have overnight guests, consider hideaway beds and rooms that do double service, such as a den-guest room.

How much can and will you spend? The family budget will determine the answer to this question. If decorating gets but a few dollars a week, you can still begin. Do not plan any immediate major expenditures. Complete the plan as money allows. Even if money is no consideration, gradual decorating will give a chance to judge the total effect and make changes as necessary.

Family discussions should have built a complete master plan. Now translate these general guides into specific plans.

DECORATING STYLE

The main concern in any decorating plan is that the home be comfortable. Everyone believes in comfort and wants it, but comfort means different things to different people. No matter how fashionable a room may look, if you are not comfortable in it, it is not the room for you.

How do you know which is your style? It is actually easy to decide after you ask yourself a few basic questions. For example, how do you prefer to entertain? Say you often choose a cookout in the backyard, with guests invited to "come as you are." For family meals, you would much rather eat in the kitchen than in the dining room, which indicates a preference for a casual, informal way of life.

If you are the type of person just described, you will probably feel most comfortable with Early American, French Provincial or other types of simple, sturdy, rustic furniture. You like the look of a polished wood table of maple, oak, knotty pine or chestnut, reflecting colorful ceramic pottery. Braided or hooked rugs, tie-back print curtains, and antique implements add to your picture of the perfect country look. The colors that go best with this type of furniture are the primary colors, red, blue, yellow, and the warm oranges, rusts, and browns.

Do you prefer a more formal lifestyle, with formal dinner parties, elegant clothing, heavy, smooth fabrics such as brocades, silks, damasks, satins? If so, you probably will want to decorate your home in formal fashion, with English and American styles from the eighteenth century.

If you prefer French period styles, choose Louis XV, Louis XVI, or the Napoleonic styles, Directoire or Empire. Oriental rugs, lush carpet, velvet draperies, and crystal chandeliers are perfect accompaniments for such styles.

Perhaps you are a person who likes to experiment with new materials and new ways of doing things. You demand that the furnishings in your home do what they are supposed to do with a minimum of ornamentation and clutter. If so, choose the contemporary style of decor: steel, glass, plastics, anything shiny or translucent; foam rubber or polyurethane foam furnishings, which give the opportunity for irregular, free-form shapes. Consider cardboard or inflatable furniture and rough-textured, hand-loomed fabrics. A complementary color scheme based on black, white, or beige, with accents of brilliant, off-beat colors such as coral or lime, would enhance contemporary decor. Plants, stereo components and abstract sculpture are ideal for living rooms and family rooms.

A fourth choice is called the eclectic style, a style based on personal selection from various

sources. If you are an eclectic, you probably appreciate good design regardless of style or period. You will mix and match decorating styles, colors, moods, and so forth to suit yourself. You may choose a Boston rocker and an Indian rug by the fireplace, while your dining area has a butcher block table and chrome-and-leather chairs. As long as you follow the principles of good design, which are discussed later, an eclectic room can be as attractive as one done in a set style.

COLOR

Color sets the mood and often alters the perception of size and shape. Therefore, the selection of color or colors is one of the major decisions to make in the Master Decorating plan. Magazine illustrations, manufacturers' brochures, and even other people's homes will provide help in making color decisions.

Color and Personality

Different people like different colors. Not surprisingly, scientists have found a relationship between color and personality.

Yellow is the brightest of all colors. People who like yellow are spontaneous and enthusiastic, expansive and forward-looking.

This high-rise living room uses a monochromatic background to create a sense of serenity. The important painting is the sole wall decoration.

Window Shade Manufacturers Association.

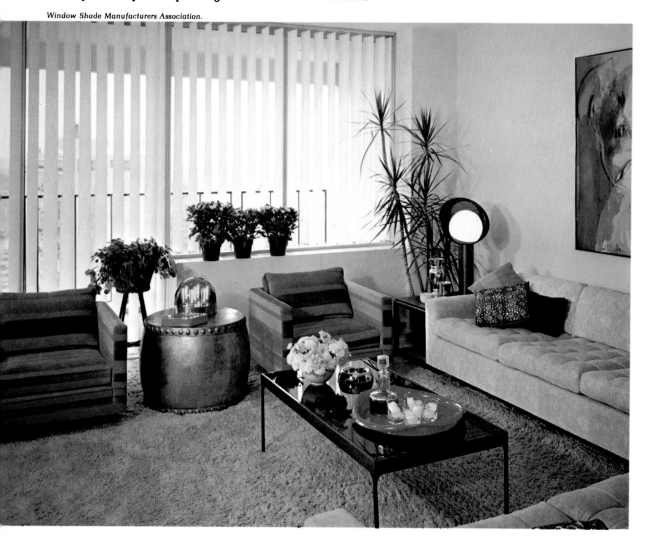

Green is the color of constancy and firmness. People who favor green, are persistent and like to assert themselves. They resist change, preferring to build on what is already there.

Blue is the color of peace and rest. People that like blue, are settled and secure. They enjoy harmony and balance, and are sensitive and sympathetic.

Red is a pulsating, vital color. It exudes power and drive. People that prefer red like to live dynamically and experience life fully.

Violet is a mystical color. As a blend of red and blue, it incorporates blue's security with red's impulsiveness. A person who prefers violet is probably artistic and sensitive.

Brown, which is a shade of orange, suggests warmth and home. A person that prefers brown, prefers coziness to adventure.

Color and Mood

Color not only expresses personality; it greatly influences mood. A party in a room decorated mainly with red and yellow would tend to be lively, while a party in a green and blue room could be expected to be more relaxed. When you select a color for a room, take into consideration the people who use the room and the activities that normally occur in that room.

Remember when choosing a color that the family will probably have to live with it for a long time. Do not choose a fad color unless someone really likes it. It may quickly become tiresome. Few things date decorating more than a fad color now out of style.

The Properties of Color

When selecting a color, be aware of its variations and relationships with other colors. Someone who likes red, but would never dream of painting a living room that color, should consider pink (a mixture of red and white), rose (red and gray), maroon (red and black) or even russet (red and orange).

An understanding of the properties of color is needed to work effectively with it. A knowledge of pigments, basic colors, the color wheel and related topics is needed for the skillful use of color in decorating.

Pigments

Pigment is what gives an object its color. An object with green pigment absorbs all colors except green. An object without pigment, a white one, absorbs none. A black object, one with all pigments, absorbs all colors.

The Basic Colors

Red, yellow, and blue are primary colors, which means that no other colors can be mixed together to get red, yellow, or blue. But by mixing primary colors in different combinations, a home decorator can make any other color.

Any two primary colors mixed equally form a secondary color. There are three secondary colors: red and yellow make orange; yellow and blue make green; and blue and red make violet.

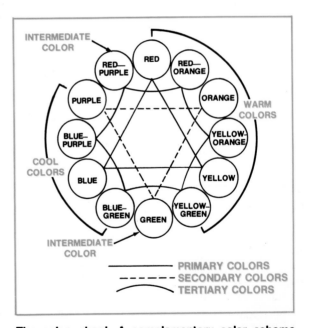

The color wheel. A complementary color scheme produces a set of warm and cool colors that intensify each other when placed in proximity. Use of tints or shades will moderate this effect. An analogous harmony is made up of colors having a common element — the yellow in yellow-orange and yellow-green. Here, different values and intensities will avoid a monotonous effect.

A secondary color mixed equally with one of the primary colors used to make it, will form a tertiary or intermediate color. Green mixed with blue yields aqua or turquoise.

The Color Wheel

The primary, secondary, and tertiary colors can be arranged in an order called a *color wheel*. The thousands of different colors found in the world all have their basis in the color wheel. The basic colors can be varied infinitely by mixing them with black, gray, white or different colors on the wheel.

Color Terms

Mixing a color with black results in a *shade*. Mixing a color with white results in a *tint*. The darker the shade or the lighter the tint, the less intense the color. The highest intensity of a color is its pure state. *Intensity* is the comparative dullness or brightness of a color.

You can neutralize a color in its pure, shaded, or tinted form by adding gray or a complementary color. The more vivid the color, the higher its *saturation* is said to be.

Brilliance is a comparative judgment of colors to variations of gray. Red is a more brilliant color than brown, which is in turn a more brilliant color than pale yellow.

The harmonious relationships of colors on the color wheel have names. If you look at the color wheel, you will see that red is opposite green. Red is the complement of green; red and green are *complementary* colors. Yellow-orange and yellow-green are next to yellow. These colors are related or *analogous*.

Colors also have warmth and coolness. Red, orange, and yellow are warm colors. They remind you of fire, sun, heat. Green, blue, and violet are cool colors. They remind you of ice, water and winter.

In choosing colors for a room, bear in mind the room's use and its location. A blue bathroom could make baths seem chilly. A red and orange kitchen, while cheerful and cozy in winter, may seem like a furnace in summer.

Choosing Your Color Scheme

Assume the main colors have been selected. Now they must be put into schemes or harmonious color relationships. There are two principal color schemes: *complementary* and *analogous*.

A complementary scheme uses complementary colors (colors opposite each other on the color wheel). A complementary color scheme is always a combination of a warm color and a cool color.

An analogous scheme uses colors next to each other on the wheel, thus such a color scheme is usually either warm or cool. To moderate the color temperature, use colors complementary to your scheme in small areas and accessories.

A third system is based on a variation of the analogous color scheme. This scheme uses shaded, tinted and neutralized variations of one color. One possible combination is blue, powder blue and navy blue. A monochromatic scheme is usually too austere and formal for most tastes. If you use one, be sure to use complementary-colored accents.

Colors are seldom used in their pure state. If blue is your main color in a complementary color scheme, use shades and tints of blue with shades and tints of orange. Brown wood is a shade of orange if it is dark and a tint of orange if it is light or natural.

Remember to vary the intensity of colors as well as their brilliance in a color scheme. If you paint your breakfast nook vivid yellow, you may bring it back to earth by adding pale tints of yellow-orange and dark shades of yellow-green.

Color, Size, and Shape

Use color to alter the apparent size and shape of a room to the eye and to de-emphasize unwanted features. Color can also be used to create an impression of spaces in a small house or apartment.

The basic rule for altering apparent dimensions of a room is the following: warm colors and dark colors reduce, cool colors and light colors expand. A high ceiling painted with a dark shade will not seem as high as it actually is. Conversely, to make a ceiling seem high, paint it white or a very pale tint. You can use the same effect to expand or reduce the apparent dimensions of a room. Even the shape of a room can be altered. If you want a rectangular room to seem square, paint the end walls a dark warm color.

A small room will look larger if you paint the woodwork, windows and doors the same color as the walls. Using the same color as the surrounding area also minimizes unwanted or ugly architectural features such as radiator covers. The impact of a piece of large, bulky furniture is similarly reduced by blending it with its surroundings. Conversely, to emphasize certain features of your home, such as beams or half-framing, be sure to paint them a color that contrasts with the surroundings.

A small house or apartment can be made to look spacious and open by using the same color or color scheme throughout. A light tint used on all the walls will blend the rooms into a unified whole.

ELEMENTS OF DESIGN

After working out the master plan for decorating and deciding on the style and color, begin considering design. While choice of style and colors is subjective and depends on personal preference, choice of design is objective. That is, certain things make up good design and others do not. A person is attracted and pleased by good design, and displeased by bad design. The elements that make up design are *line, form* and *composition*.

Line

Design begins with line because line determines form (or shape). In interior design line is what makes an overstuffed sofa look comfortable and a tall grandfather clock appear stately and reliable. People cannot help having an emotional reaction to line, so it is important to consider the desired effect, which can be achieved simply by noting and utilizing the way line influences mood.

Horizontal lines are restful. They invite the eye to "stretch out," and give a feeling of calmness and informality. A room in which the sofa, chairs, tables, and fabric patterns are primarily horizontal in line is an easy room in which to relax.

Vertical lines are formal. They lead the eye to "straighten up," and give the viewer an impression of stability and dignity. A tall china cabinet, high-backed chairs, and vertically striped wallpaper will give a room a feeling of regularity and conventionality.

Diagonal lines are active and disturbing. They should be used with care in decorating. Their effect comes from the fact that they seem to defy gravity, thus they keep the eye "unsettled." Diagonal lines are best used only as accents, such as in an area rug or in the upholstery of one piece of furniture. A room full of diagonals can only give an effect of busyness and dizziness.

Curved lines may be controlled or free-form. Both are graceful; but they differ in their applications. Controlled curves have a lighthearted look. They are exemplified in the carved and shaped French baroque and rococo styles of the eighteenth century, in some Victorian furniture and in the bentwood and wicker pieces first produced at the turn of this century. Free-form curves are strictly contemporary. They have a flowing, unrestricted natural look. Frequently they are used in furniture made of new materials such as foam and plastics. Free-form curves appearing in sculpture, rugs or wall hangings lend a casual air to a room.

Form

Lines make up forms. Straight lines make squares, rectangular or oblongs, and triangles. Curved lines make circles, ovals, and ellipses.

Squares make people think of sturdiness and strength. However, only one form in a room is usually undesirable. A square room furnished with square tables and chairs would have a static

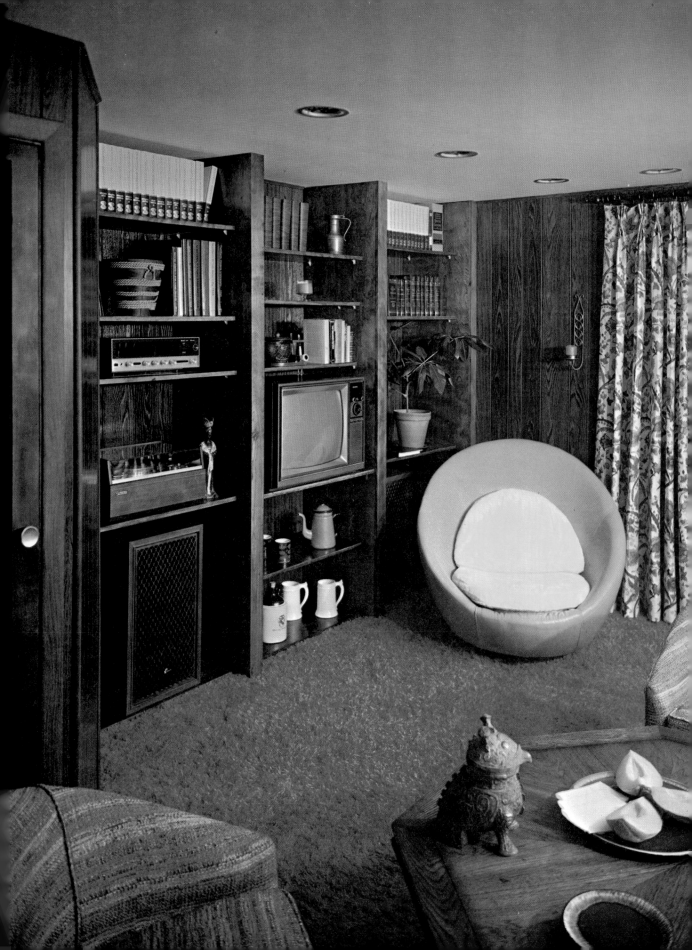

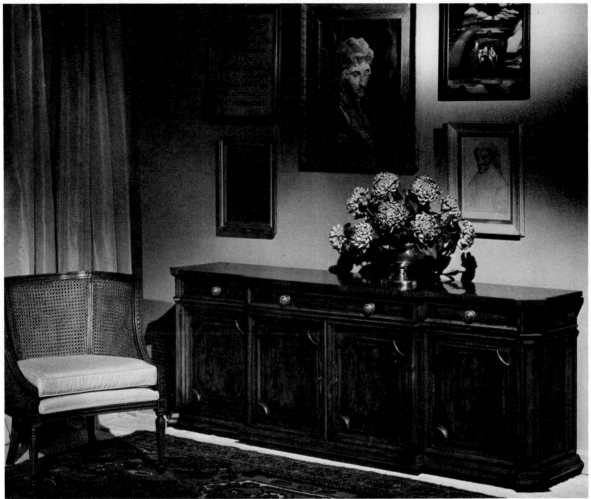

Courtesy of The Karges Furniture Company, Inc.

In developing a wall grouping, consider the grouping and major pieces of furniture along the wall as one decorating unit.

feeling. To add a sense of motion and variety, choose ceiling-to-floor draperies, large, round pillows or hassocks on the floor, or use free-form-curve patterned accents.

The oblong or rectangle is an elongated form of the square. The oblong was judged the form most pleasing to the eye in ancient Greece. The most famous Grecian buildings, such as the Parthenon, are based on a mathematical ratio

Masonite Corporation

This handsome shelf arrangement houses a television set, stereo components, books, and a favorite collection. Soft, recessed lighting and comfortable seating make this a popular entertainment center.

called the "golden oblong." Ideally, this is a ratio of two units to three units, three units to five units, five to eight, eight to thirteen, and so on. In practice, you can apply this ratio by hanging a 3-foot-wide rectangular painting above a 5-foot-wide oblong sofa. Try to group, for example, two objects (such as chairs) with three objects (such as two tables and a sofa), rather than grouping two-and-two.

Triangles suggest unity and balance, and are often used in corners. An L-shaped sofa with a coffee table defines a specific area in a room. Triangular corner tables can enliven a room by suppressing a feeling of boxiness. Triangular end tables will modify the starkness of a

straight-lined sofa. Circles offer the eye a pleasant contrast to the straight forms of most pieces of furniture. For example, introduce a curved-back chair into a room that appears full of right angles. Round accessories, such as tables, mirrors, pictures, pillows, large candy dishes or ashtrays, may be just what is needed to bring life to a room that looks unbearably solemn.

Ovals or ellipses can serve much the same function as circles. In a rectangular dining room, for example, an oval table may look best.

Composition

Grouping different parts to achieve a unified whole creates a composition. When the goal is an attractive, comfortable home, the task can be made a great deal easier by following a few simple rules. These are the same rules that guide an artist in the composition of a painting or a musician in composing a symphony. There are five of these rules, or principles: *harmony, proportion, balance, rhythm,* and *emphasis.*

Harmony

In decorating, harmony comes as a result of consideration, planning and attention to mood.

Always think of the mood which is desired. One can mix periods and styles of furnishings and create an interesting atmosphere that is distinctively personal. All of the individual elements should be compatible, however. They should be in the same mood: formal or informal, heavy and dignified, or light and casual. A few examples will illustrate this point.

Picture a simple, informal Shaker chair placed next to an ornate Louis XV table. The discord would be extreme. It would be better to use the chair with a French Provincial table because the two informal pieces go more naturally together. Next, imagine a sleek, chrome-and-plastic contemporary den with ruffled calico curtains at the windows. This combination would be very unpleasant. Instead, maintain the ultra-modern feeling of the den with simple draperies, or perhaps use window shades or screens.

The way objects are placed in a room or accesso-

ries added to it can also create or destroy harmony. One example is a buffet with three decorative plates displayed above it. Arranging the plates step-fashion, each one to the side and slightly above the other, will create an uneven line that is not satisfying to the eye. Remember when arranging anything on a wall that hanging objects must be close enough to the piece of furniture below for the composition to be viewed as a unit. The width of the picture, or group of plates, should be less than the width of the furniture. Also remember that when hanging a group of objects, the spacing between them should be smaller than the size of the objects. Order and cohesion are vital to a sense of harmony.

Use this practical trick to save wear and tear on walls and you: before you pick up a hammer or nail, cut out brown paper shapes the same size and shape as each object to be hung. Tape different arrangements to the wall until you find the one that seems to go best with the space it takes and the furniture below it. Leave the cutouts up for a few days to make sure the family likes the arrangement. After everyone agrees on the arrangement, hang the objects.

Proportion

When parts of a composition exist in good relation to each other and to the composition as a whole, the composition has good proportions. Apply this principle to the wall arrangements just discussed. Apply it to any articles of furniture considered for purchase or any room about to be decorated. Think about a lamp, for example. If the shade is too large for the base, the lamp will look top-heavy. If the shade is too small, it will look bottom-heavy. Rely on your eye to tell when objects are in proportion to each other.

A room with a pleasing ratio in length, width and height has good proportions. The windows, doors, fireplace or other built-in features would have to be in a pleasing ratio to the whole room. The ideal is once again the "golden oblong" mentioned under form. Unfortunately, many builders do not abide by the Greek law of proportion, so part of the decorating task may be to

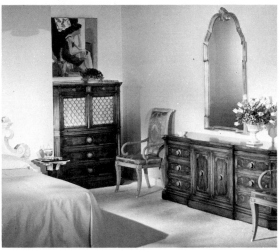

Courtesy of The Karges Furniture Company, Inc.

The balanced arrangement of dresser and chairs is typical of the symmetrical balance that is used in most formal decorating.

give the illusion of good proportion to a less-than-perfect room. But you can keep the ideal ratio in mind when you look for tables, mirrors, rugs, television sets and other rectangular objects with which you furnish your home.

Balance

Two parts of a composition are balanced when a state of equality, or equilibrium, exists between them. In decorating there are two kinds of balance: symmetrical or formal balance and asymmetrical or informal balance. Either type can be achieved with any style of furniture.

Symmetrical balance is what results when both halves of a composition are just alike. This may be seen in a fireplace with matching bookcases on either side, in the facade of a Georgian house with identical pilasters and windows on both sides of a central entrance, or in a crystal pitcher surrounded by eight identical glasses. In this type of formal balance, one side of the composition is a reflection of the other. The effect is attractive, but it is best to use it sparingly. An entire house arranged symmetrically may tend to take on a military stiffness.

Asymmetrical balance is what results when both halves of a composition are in balance although they are not at all alike. Informally balanced ar-

rangements are used a great deal in homes today. They seem to be part of the general trend toward less rigidity and more casualness in living as well as in decorating.

A person's eye is the best judge of what makes a good informally balanced design. Remember how the bigger child always had to sit closer to the center of the see-saw or teeter-totter so the board would balance? The same principle applies to informal balance, but in this case *bigger* means larger, heavier, more brightly colored, irregularly shaped, or in *some* way more noticeable. Suppose the task is to arrange a vase of spring flowers and a large, shiny copper bowl on a mantel. Put the bowl nearer to the center, because its visual weight is greater than the vase of flowers.

Rhythm

Rhythm is the repetition of accents at regular or irregular intervals. Accents are motifs or features of design that help hold together the varied elements of a composition. The composition may be a single object such as a lighting fixture, or it may be an entire room full of furniture.

When a feature such as a color, a form, an abstract motif, or a concrete object appears over and over in a composition, a pattern emerges. The eye follows the feature from one occurrence to the next, and the viewer becomes more interested as he continues to look at the object or the room. The elaborate, endlessly repeated woven patterns of oriental rugs are a good example. Sometimes repetition can be overdone, as in a kitchen where *everything* — floor, counter tops, curtains, table — is covered with Delft tile. Remember that rhythm is based on accents, not abundance, and that the idea is to add interest, not boredom, to the home.

Emphasis

What makes some rooms exciting and others dull? What is it about the finished look of a room that makes people exclaim in one case, "You must see what Connie and Bill have done to their living room!" and remark in another, "Well, Doris and Henry spent a lot of money, but something is missing." Chances are, that hard-to-pin-

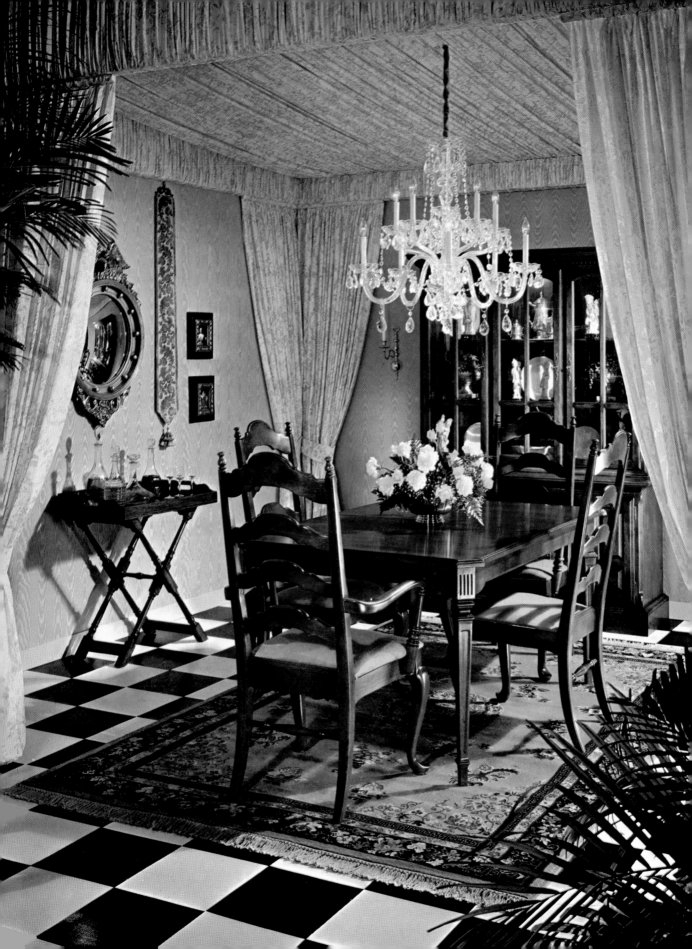

down something is a matter of emphasis. Whether it is called emphasis or focal point or center of interest, every well-decorated room should have one feature that draws the visitor's attention.

In some fortunate cases the focal point comes with the house or apartment. It may be a handsome fireplace or a quaint Franklin stove, a built-in antique china cupboard, or a picture window that frames a spectacular view of the mountains, the ocean, or a city skyline. All that is needed then is to arrange the furniture with the center of interest always in mind.

Most of the time, however, the dominant feature will have to be provided. An exciting painting or piece of sculpture is always good and not always expensive. Paint supergraphics right on the walls, or hang up lengths of vividly colored or patterned textiles. A striking area rug will focus interest anywhere it is placed; so will an unusual lighting arrangement, or a miniature jungle of luxuriant tropical plants. Remember that emphasis is not an example of "the more the merrier." One major center of interest per room is usually enough.

TREATMENT OF SURFACES

A home is a lot more than the walls that surround and the floor beneath, but these two surfaces require much thought and care when decorating.

One can always slipcover a sofa or move a disastrous lamp to another room (or the attic), but if walls and floors do not turn out the way you wanted them, you may have to live with the results for quite a while. It really pays to examine the numerous possibilities in wall and floor coverings that exist today. Both basic materials and "cover-ups" are legion. The way to treat walls and floors is limited only by a person's imagination and budget.

Courtesy of Ethan Allen

Shirred and draped fabric create the effect of a tent for this cheerful yet formal dining room.

Textures

One of the more noticeable qualities of floors and walls is texture. Floors may be grooved wood, shiny slate, inlaid tile, plush carpet, etc. Walls may be smooth plastic, rough brick, pebbly adobe, velvet-flocked paper, etc. Texture is of importance in the decorating plan because it greatly affects the mood of a room.

Rough, natural materials, such as bamboo, willow, rattan and hemp are generally made into coarsely woven objects and fabrics. They impart a country look to rooms in which they predominate. Fabrics such as velvet, brocade and satin, and shiny polished woods are luxurious. They are used best in formal settings. Sensuous "skin" textures, such as suede, furs, and leather go especially well with contemporary decor.

Texture always affects color. Rough textures seem to "heat up" the atmosphere of a room; smooth textures "cool down." Red plush looks warmer than red linen. Blue satin is much cooler than blue corduroy. This is a good point to bear in mind when decorating a summer home, for example. Conversely, in a weekend ski retreat, cover the floors and furniture with rough, wooly finishes. However, the most effective use of texture is to spark contrast. Plan on at least one nubby rug in the beach house, or a smooth leather couch at the ski lodge, to preserve contrast.

Texture can be used to bring out a room's good points and conceal its weak ones. A close ally of texture, especially in helping to achieve this objective, is *pattern*. In some rough-finish materials and fabrics the pattern may be defined by the texture. In other cases, pattern dominates texture and exerts its own influence on a decorating scheme. Strong textures and patterns, by minimizing or concealing the architectural features of a room, may minimize the visual effects of poor proportions, badly placed doors, awkward heating units, etc.

Floors

Most floors are made of wood. If older floors are scarred beyond economical refinishing, they may be covered with hard surface wood flooring that is prefinished and simple to install. You may

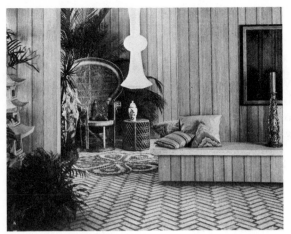

Masonite Corporation

An Oriental theme can be effectively carried out by a few well-chosen pieces, as in this family room. Here, the brick-patterned vinyl floor and the vertical lines of the wall treatment help achieve the open feeling. Exotic touches are in the accessories: rice paper hanging lamp, Ming statue, altar candlesticks and the oriental painting.

choose rustic looking tongue-and-groove planks, or large or small parquet tiles. Both come in a wide range of colors and textures. If you happen to have solid oak floors that are in good condition, you may wish to simply refinish them and show them off with appropriate rugs. Wood floors, though expensive, are very durable.

Other natural floor coverings are frequently used in modern homes. Stone of various kinds is extremely good-looking and durable. Marble, slate or flagstone will serve well in a den. For an Early American, French Provincial or any but the most formal dining area, bricks or tiles are ideal. They are available in a wide range of colors, textures, and styles. Baked, waxed, painted or plain, they can be set in any pattern you desire. For a more elegant look, you may try a terrazzo mosaic floor. Any of these non-wood materials would be especially suitable for a foyer or entrance hall. Umbrella puddles or tracked-in mud could be easily wiped up without leaving a trace.

The materials called resilient floor coverings have come a long way from the old-fashioned speckled linoleum kitchen floor. Linoleum is still a good choice for kitchen floors, but it is now made in so many fashionable colors and patterns that it may be appropriate for any room in the house. The many types of resilient floor coverings are versatile and practical in addition to being attractive. They are easy to install, and the home craftsman can create almost any design effect.

Solid vinyl comes in tiles or sheets resembling every natural surface, as well as in unique patterns and colors. It is initially more expensive than some other synthetic floorings, but its nonporous quality and resistance to grease, moisture, and alkali and ease of care make it a practical, as well as a fashionable, choice. Vinyl-asbestos is next in quality and is generally similar in style. It can be installed even over radiant-heated floors. Asphalt tile is least expensive. It is fireproof and moisture-resistant and can be made grease-proof. However, it cracks easily and is noisy to walk on.

Two types of resilient floor covering tiles are made of natural materials: rubber and cork. Rubber is quiet, easy to maintain, and comes in a number of "marbled" colors. Cork tile is limited to several attractive shades of brown. It is very quiet and gives an interesting effect, but it dents easily.

Most people are accustomed to thinking of one type of flooring per room, all wood, all vinyl or all brick. But by mixing similar or contrasting materials in original ways, you can create very distinctive rooms. Be sure to get a group of samples and try them out before you buy.

A third possibility is soft floor coverings, rugs and carpets. Rugs are used in conjunction with natural or resilient flooring. Wall-to-wall carpeting, on the other hand, makes what is underneath unimportant, since the basic flooring material is entirely covered. With both rugs and carpeting, use padding for better feel and longer wear. Total-floor carpeting tends to make rooms look larger since no border or other-colored surface distracts the eye. Room-size rugs and area or accent rugs leave part of the floor exposed. They draw attention to walls and furniture, and can make a room appear smaller.

Soft floor coverings require much care. They must be vacuumed frequently and cleaned regularly. However, rugs and carpets provide warmth, absorb sound, add textural interest and furnish beauty in a room. The variety of soft floor coverings is almost endless.

Walls

Depending on what is done, walls can surround and enrich home life, or enclose and restrict it. The effect depends entirely on the way they are decorated. With forethought and originality, walls can coordinate the arrangement and style of a room and give it a spacious or intimate at-mosphere. When planning wall treatments, include the other peripheral features of the room. Ceilings, windows, doors and fixtures are all part of the total visual effect.

The easiest way to make walls the desired color is to paint them. Paint is easy to apply, easy to keep clean, economical and practical. Indoor paint is of two types: oil-base, thinned with tur-pentine, and latex-base, thinned with water. Either type comes in three finishes: flat, semi-gloss and gloss (enamel). You can choose the finish to get a particular effect. For example, because light bounces off shiny surfaces, a dark-colored wall will stand out more in a flat finish.

Strict attention to detail creates the relaxed formality of this French Provincial dining room. Light colored paneling hides an entire wall of storage.

Masonite Corporation

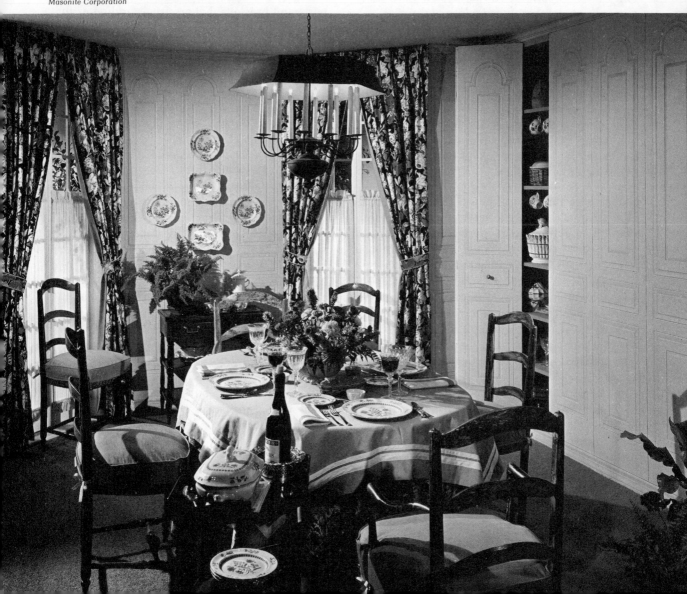

Decorating

Vary the apparent shape of a room with paint. Remember that bold colors advance and pale colors recede. To make a long and narrow room seem wider, paint the end walls a brighter color than the side walls. To make a square room seem to take on the ideal oblong shape, paint one or two walls darker than the others. To make a ceiling appear lower, paint it darker than the walls. To make a ceiling appear higher, paint it white.

A large design is especially good for diverting the eye away from structural defects. This is one of many reasons why people like to use wallpaper. There are wallpapers that fool the eye by seeming to hide another design behind the dominant one. Mural papers cover an entire wall with an interesting scene. Wallpaper also simulates various textural effects including stone, brick, leather, wood, cloth and metal.

For actual texture, use fabric on walls. Felt and burlap are available with a paper backing usable with ordinary wallpaper paste, but it is easy to hang almost any textile using fabric paste. Give a teenager a bedroom wall of real faded blue denim. Line a Scotsman's study with his clan tartan. Some vibrant and unique prints, such as those made by Marimekko of Finland, are available only in fabrics.

Some materials mentioned in the section on Floors can also be used on walls. Ceramic tiles, vinyl tiles, cork and leather come readily to mind. Many people who collect prints, paintings or photographs have discovered that smooth carpeting makes an ideal background for a wall display. The texture hides nail holes, and parts of the collection can easily be removed or changed. Carpeted walls make sense for the stereo buff or the musician, too, because they provide an excellent sound-absorbing surface.

Another good material for wall decor is wood. From old French wall paneling to the pre-cut paneling available today, walls of wood give a rich, warm look to a room. Different woods evoke different atmospheres. Heavy, dark oak or mahogany paneling is reminiscent of antiques and elegance. Wormy chestnut or knotty pine gives the atmosphere of a casual life, such as that of a hunting lodge. Smooth cherry or fruitwood

recalls the homespun charm of Early Americana.

Storage Walls

All the treatments discussed so far deal with ways to make walls a decorative feature of the room. Walls can also be useful. A current and practical feature of many living rooms, dens and studio apartments is the storage wall. Unlike the long row of closets its name implies, the storage wall can be an integral and interesting part of any room.

Handsome units of furniture have been designed to house desks, drawers, shelves, cabinets, bars and buffet surfaces. The units are generally interchangeable and adjustable, with upright supports and brackets that are free-standing or that attach to the wall. While the storage wall idea is definitely contemporary, the component pieces are made in rustic and period styles as well. Such a wall may be the simple answer to storage and display space needs.

Windows

Shutters, shades, screens, curtains or draperies provide privacy and decoration for windows in the home. Before deciding which window coverings are best, consider the following: Do you live on a crowded city street or a quiet country lane? Is the climate moderate, or must you rely on heating or air conditioning at all times? Do you have a view of a shimmering sunset or of the building wall next door? Are you willing to wash and iron ruffled curtains, or do you insist on the ultimate in practicality? The answers to these questions will determine the best window treatment needed.

Roller shades are a simple and economical cover-up. They can be made to fit almost any window, and they come in a wide variety of colors and materials.

Shades that match draperies, wallpaper, or upholstery add a custom touch to any room. Simply have the same fabric laminated to the shades. Shades can be mounted on the bottom of a window and pulled up instead of down. These

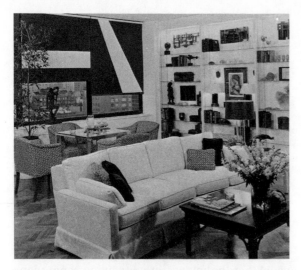

Window Shade Manufacturers Association.

Strong architectural content was given a square room with a window wall by playing off a stark white, glass-shelved wall against a stunning window treatment. Dark brown shades, hung within the frames to accent the sharp lines, are painted with a smashing white design. Diffused lighting, see-through quality of shelving and table tops, and careful control of pattern give the room its airy quality.

shades offer an unusual solution for oddly shaped windows.

Two variations on the roller shade are popular because they add textural interest to a wall. Roman shades hang straight but, when raised, fold into horizontal accordion pleats. They look equally handsome in solid colors, patterned or vertically striped fabric. Austrian shades hang in gathered, scalloped panels that flounce when they are raised. Austrian shades made of silk and trimmed with fringe are especially beautiful in a formal room setting. Both Roman and Austrian shades work particularly well on tall windows.

Venetian blinds require more maintenance than shades, but they do permit you to regulate light and control the flow of air. Blinds are available in wide or narrow steel, aluminum, or wood slats in many colors. On very large windows you may consider using vertical blinds.

Other window treatments that give an airy look and obstruct light in varying degrees include

bamboo blinds and strings of beads in wood, crystal, plastic, or cork. These are used more for ornament than for privacy.

Shutters provide privacy and decoration. They are well suited for city apartments because they allow light and air but shut out all or part of the view. You may also look into the possibility of installing a custom-fitted grille, lattice or trellis, all particularly effective used in conjunction with growing plants.

Plants often make beautiful coverings for windows. Mount adjustable glass shelves across windows and arrange leafy plants in earthen or colorful ceramic pots along the shelves.

Curtains and draperies are the most versatile window coverings. They are not limited to the size of the window frame, so they can be planned to cover intervening wall areas and tie together various elements of decor. Choose curtains to harmonize or to contrast with prevailing colors in a room.

Curtains may be sheer and hang directly in front of the glass to permit seeing out; they may be heavier or lined to be drawn for privacy; or they may be decorative draperies or overcurtains, used purely for ornament.

To make a small room seem larger, match draperies to the walls. For a dramatic effect in a large room, use a colorful pattern that picks up a predominant tone in the furnishings. Keep in mind the principles of design and color.

LIGHTING

Good artificial lighting contributes a great deal to the comfort and appearance of a home. There are a number of factors to consider. Lighting must be adequate for the activity it serves and yet not be glaring. Brighter light is obviously needed for reading a book than for eating. It is better to have a lamp focused directly on the work area to sew, read, write or use tools, than to have only the general illumination of a large overhead bulb.

Light is also necessary for safety. You should have easily accessible light switches inside the

doorway of every room, including the basement and attic. These switches can control not only overhead lights but also lamps plugged into specially wired wall outlets. It is also very helpful to have lights in closets. Switches that work automatically as the door is open or closed are convenient.

Direct and Indirect Illumination

Direct light, which comes in a straight line from the bulb, is necessary for detail work. In addition to being used for working or reading, direct light from spotlights can be used to illuminate objects of art and architectural features. Indirect light, which is reflected light, is used for general illumination. Lights hidden in cornices are a good example.

The appropriate choice of lighting will usually combine indirect and direct light. Table lamps properly placed provide both. The lampshade reduces glare at normal eye level. Reading is aided by the direct light from under the shade while light above the shade is reflected from the walls and ceiling.

Fluorescent and Incandescent Light

Although fluorescent light was once popular, experience has shown that it is generally unsuitable for home use. While it is economical to use, fluorescent light changes the apparent color of its surroundings. Even recent improvements have failed to prevent these color changes. Skin tones look unflatteringly pastry. If you have fluorescent lights, relocate them to the laundry room or garage.

Incandescent light, the standard light for the home, is a warm, complimentary light. Incandescent bulbs are available in a multitude of shades, shapes and colors. Experiment with different shades of "white" lights. These shades range from a cool white to rosy pink. Different rooms may call for different colors, warm shades for bedroom or bathroom and cool shades for den or sewing room. Variously shaped bulbs lend interest to light fixtures. The familiar flame-shaped bulb is suitable not only for chandeliers but also for sconces and candelabra lamps. Colored bulbs are infrequently used in the home, but they can be used to set a mood for a party.

Permanent Fixtures and Lamps

Some rooms lend themselves to permanent fixtures, others to lamps. Still others benefit from a combination. The kitchen, dining room, bathroom and halls usually have permanent overhead lamps for general illumination. The living room, bedroom, and den frequently have lamps to permit selective lighting. The choice depends on personal preference and requirements.

FURNITURE AND ROOM ARRANGEMENT

A piece of furniture should "belong" in a room. Its size, shape and features should harmonize with the room and with the other pieces of furniture in the room. A ten-foot, L-shaped, modish couch hardly belongs in your living room plans if the room is small and the other furniture formal. A small, graceful Chippendale chair would look out-of-place in a large room filled with weighty Mexican furniture.

Furniture and Scale

When selecting furniture you must keep in mind the size of its intended room. Petite pieces of furniture make a large room appear empty or sparsely decorated. in a small room the same piece would lend a desired feeling of spaciousness. This aspect of furniture, its size in relation to the size of a room, is called *scale*. Furniture should always be in scale to a room.

Furniture and Proportion

A second aspect of furniture is proportion, the relation in size of one piece of furniture to the other pieces. A round table of normal height would be in better proportion to three tall ladderback chairs than would a squat, square coffee table. Similarly, a small, formal loveseat would all but disappear if it were flanked by large end tables with massive lamps.

Furniture and Balance

Another important aspect of furniture is balance, the selective distribution of furniture within a room according to the furniture's impact. The impact of furniture is derived from its size, color, style, texture, pattern and material. A good room arrangement will incorporate a harmonious

balance. You should blend the different features of furniture so that no one part of the room will seem to weigh down the whole room. If all bright-colored furniture is placed in one grouping, the rest of the room will seem dull. Check with a judicious eye for balance in texture and pattern throughout the room. A sleek vinyl sofa grouping should be balanced with other glossy items. Wood, chrome, iron or other similar material should not be clustered in one area. Heavy or dominant objects against a wall should be balanced with objects of similar weight on the opposite wall. A large wooden table at one end of a room can be balanced with a china cabinet or wooden shelves at the other.

THE FLOOR PLAN

A floor plan will help you visualize a furniture arrangement, thus saving much back-breaking labor pushing heavy furniture around. A floor plan is also an invaluable aid when purchasing new pieces of furniture.

When using a floor plan, be sure to keep the scale consistent. If the outline of the room is drawn to $1/4''$ scale, the furniture should be drawn to this scale also. This will give a realistic view of the actual room space.

Carefully measure the rooms to be decorated and transfer these measurements to $1/4''$-scale graph paper, using each square as one square foot. Be sure to indicate all doors and the direction in which they open, all windows, radiators or heat vents and other architectural features such as fireplaces, built-in bookcases, and wall niches. It is also helpful at this time to measure the height of doors, windows, ceilings and such features as chair moldings and window ledges. Write these measurements in the margins of the floor plan. These figures then will be readily available and will remind you to think in three-dimensional terms when trying various arrangements on the floor plan. Before starting the floor plan, consider the activities the room will contain, the room's focal points and its traffic patterns.

The Activities in a Room

A good floor plan will accommodate a setting for all normal uses of a room and will adapt easily for less frequent activities. If a living room must function as television room, library and social room, attempt to arrange it so that these functions all have a place. Ideally, distinct uses should have distinct areas, but arrangement can make some areas multipurpose. For example, a table for writing can double as a game table. The game table chairs can be easily rearranged to enlarge a conversation area or a television area.

The Focal Points of a Room

A focal point in a room is any area that draws the eye and interest. Some rooms have a natural focal point, such as a fireplace or a picture window with an interesting view. In other rooms, the focal point may be a large mirror, a picture or a crystal chandelier.

Use the natural focal points of a room in arranging furniture. The most common example of this is a conversation area of sofa, chairs and tables before a fireplace. An attractive bay window can serve as an elegant backdrop for a small conversation or dining area. If a room does not have a natural focal point, try to create one. A collection of paintings over a sofa, a bright-hued area rug under a desk, or a cluster of large plants near a conversation area can be used to draw the eye and define the area.

Traffic Patterns

On the room outline, lightly pencil in arrows to show the flow of traffic. These arrows should show the most direct route from one entrance to another, if that is a frequent path of traffic. When trying various arrangements, allow for these paths as much as possible.

Rearranging or adding furniture in a room will create new traffic patterns. It is not wise to create patterns that interfere with normal activities. People tend to take the shortest route when moving into, within or through a room. It would be unwise to place a study area on a major traffic lane in a room. A quiet corner would be more suitable. If a traffic lane isolates a small corner of a room, you should use that corner for storage, perhaps in the form of a cupboard or chest.

Traffic lanes should be at least three feet wide. A coffee table should be fifteen to eighteen inches from a sofa or chairs. Try not to crowd furniture next to doors unless, of course, the door is very wide. Leave adequate space around the front door, since people arriving or leaving cluster around this door.

Arranging the Room

Once the room's focal points and traffic lanes are determined, try different furniture arrangements on the floor plan. Position the large, bulky items first, such as large sofas or a piano. Large bookcases and tables should be arranged next. Then arrange chairs, tables, desks and lamps. Finally, position small articles, such as magazine racks, hassocks and larger plants. The placement of larger pieces indicates the best position for smaller ones, some because they are necessary, others because they seem natural. A night table goes by the bedside, a chair with a desk, but hassocks and magazine racks are nomadic. Place them where they seem most natural.

When working on floor plans, think in three dimensions. A pleasing effect on paper can be disastrous when transferred to an actual room. Think in terms of scale, balance and proportion. Do not obstruct windows needed for light and ventilation. If trying to achieve a private nook, such as a study area, taller items such as bookcases, screens and room dividers define the area much better than just a desk or table.

Purchasing Furniture

While working with a floor plan, a certain piece of furniture may become necessary. Perhaps you want to replace one or two pieces, or all of your furniture. When shopping, do not forget to take the plan and a tape measure. Furniture in a display room will look much different when it is in the home. Measure a piece of furniture carefully to be sure that it fits where planned.

Accessories

Accessories add the finishing touches to a room. They include vases, ashtrays, pictures, sculpture, clocks, candles, figurines, music boxes, antique spoons and anything else that may be displayed. Some of the most enjoyable decorating time will probably be spent in acquiring and finding ways to display these smaller items. Accessories can show off a hobby, such as needlepoint, model making or decoupage. They can reflect a scholarly interest in antique maps or pre-Columbian artifacts.

Accessories are accents. They add a touch of visual excitement and personality to any setting. Use accessories to provide dramatic contrast in color, shape or texture, such as raspberry linen place mats in a cool blue and white enamel-and-plastic dining room. If a living room has predominantly square lines, use several large round pillows to break the visual monotony. In a family room where all the furnishings are sleek and contemporary, an old-fashioned crocheted afghan would be a strong visual accent.

PLANNING SPECIFIC ROOMS

The Living Room

The living room is the hub of the household. It is the room most seen by guests. It is the room that gets the most attention and expenditure in decorating. The living room should be inviting. It should be alive, yet comfortable and conducive to its many possible activities: conversation, television, reading, study, entertaining, lounging. An alive room is visually exciting. It reflects the interests and tastes of the family. A comfortable room, a room conducive to activity provides arrangements free from unnecessary interference, yet invites easy participation in the life of the room. Try to avoid stringing furniture along the walls, leaving the center of the room empty.

Choose the color scheme and style of the room to suit the preference of the family. This usually involves some compromise. The living room is everyone's room. Every living room should have at least one conversation cluster. This group should become part of the room's main focal point. The simplest group consists of two seats, one of which is usually a sofa. They should be arranged so that eye contact can be made comfortably. The seats either face each other or are at angles to each other. The basic group also has at least one table for candy dishes, ashtrays, magazines and so forth. Light sufficient for read-

ing is also necessary. Light can be provided by a table lamp, floor lamp, or a wall or ceiling light.

The size and features of your basic conversation group are limited only by available resources and imaginative good taste. Even if you often have large parties, it is better to have several smaller conversation groups than to have one large, more public area. A smaller group, perhaps only two chairs and a table, also provides a setting for private conversation.

Provide in your living room for entertainment (television, stereo, card or game table), work and study (desk and chair), and storage and display (bookcases, shelves, cabinets). Conversation groups often double for entertaining and less frequently for work and study. Television has been known to stifle conversation and study. If the living room is used frequently as a bedroom, plan your arrangement so that a convertible sofa can be made into a bed without too much inconvenience. You should plan for an out-of-the-way place to store any displaced chairs and tables. You may wish to work a screen into your living room plans, so that it can be used at night for privacy. Screens and room dividers are also useful in large and L-shaped rooms to separate different areas and activities.

The Dining Room

A pleasant ambiance, or atmosphere is the feature to strive for in the dining room or dining area. Chairs should be padded for long periods of sitting. Everyone should have enough room to loosen up and relax. The temperature should be slightly cool, and the color scheme should be pleasing and restful. Provisions for easy service and clean-up will add to the leisure of dining.

THE BASIC DINING ROOM

The dining table is almost always the focal point of the dining room. If the room has some other strong focal point, such as a hearth or an exciting view, balance or blend your furniture arrangement to make the most of both features. A china cabinet on the opposite side of the table may achieve balance with a hearth. Moving the table close to or even touching the window can blend your arrangement into a unified whole. Reserve

chairs should be placed along the walls, if they are not stored or used in other rooms. Avoid placing them in the corners because they tend to create unpleasant diagonals.

The Table

There are dozens of different types of dining room tables available. Select a style that harmonizes with the room, especially if the dining area is an extension of the living room or kitchen. The table should be in proportion to the room. While most tables are rectangular, the adaptability of the round table or graceful curves of the oval table may enhance the atmosphere. Round tables also offer more seating room. Pedestal tables eliminate legs and create comfortable seating arrangements.

Whatever style and shape you select, the number of family members and the table's everyday use will determine the size of the table. Expandable tables with drop leaves, movable leaves, self-extension or console construction are especially handy for entertaining guests.

Serving and Storage

Buffets, breakfronts and servers all assist in presenting and serving food. Some counter area, even if it is only a shelf, should be convenient to the kitchen. You will want to provide some pro-

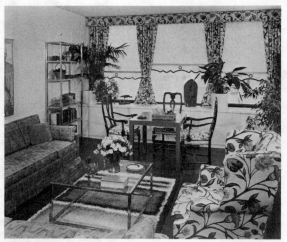

Courtesy Window Shade Manufacturers Association

Repetition of a print fabric in window treatment and upholstery provides a unifying element in this attractive provincial living room.

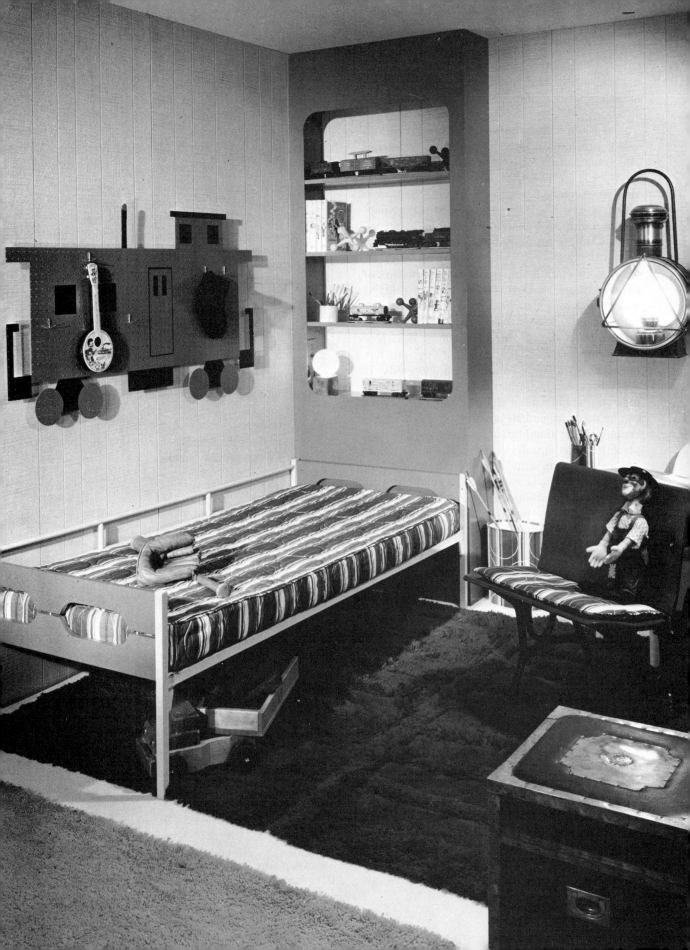

tection to furniture surfaces if they are vulnerable to damage from spills or dropped dishes. Storage space should be handy to the table for setting and for course changes.

Color

Use a cheerful color scheme in your dining area. Avoid bright, distracting colors or patterns. Violet and off-shades of green have been found to be appetite-depressants. Accent your room with appropriate accessories, such as antique or unusual platters, silver and glassware.

FAMILY ROOMS

A family room can be a recreation room, a study, a den, a sewing room or all of these and more. Leave adequate playing space around objects such as ping-pong and pool tables. Consider a permanent dance floor, especially if you have teenagers. To show films or slides you will need a projection area and a space to stand or hang the screen. Remember that a light-colored wall can serve as a screen. If the family library is located here, provide reading areas with sufficient light. Although useful throughout the house, built-ins and storage walls are especially practical in the family room. They help organize the many items used in the room: stereo, records, tapes, games, sewing equipment, hobbies and craft materials.

BEDROOMS

Bedrooms are personal rooms. They do not have to be shared with the whole family. They should, therefore, accommodate personal tastes and activities. The basic furniture of the bedroom is the bed, the night table and a lamp. Dressers, mirrors, wardrobe and chests should be provided for grooming and storage.

Forethought in decorating a child's bedroom can make life more pleasant for the whole family. If a room pleases a child, he or she will spend more time in it and less time underfoot.

Children love bright colors, so use them lavishly. Pictures and large patterns appeal to their imagination.

A child's room should be furnished with durable, easy-to-clean materials, but it is not

necessary to resort to only hard, flat surfaces. Washable rugs, draperies, and acoustical tile ceilings help absorb excessive youthful clamor. Encourage children to be neat by providing plenty of easy-to-use storage for clothes and toys. Low hooks will hang more clothes than hooks a child needs a chair to reach. Lots of shelves keep clutter off the floor and provide display space for favorite toys, dolls, rocks, shells and other childhood treasures. A comfortable desk and chair encourage the young student. A child's room should change as he or she grows. Rock collections give way to rock albums. If more than one teenager uses a room, provide privacy by using dividers or screens. Active play areas are no longer needed, so bunkbeds can be dismantled and moved to opposite sides of the room.

An adult bedroom can be a haven from the activity of the house. Comfortable chairs and a desk or table can be used for reading, sewing, work from the office, letter-writing or a cozy breakfast. In the shared bedroom, separate nightlights are an absolute necessity. The only restriction on the mood of the bedroom is that it be restful. Yards of soft, luxurious satin; hard, sleek chrome; fourposter bed; water bed — the decor is decided by the imagination of the individual.

Deep Well Pump

A deep well pump brings water to the surface by means of a piston. Deep wells are usually found in areas having small amounts of surface water. Normally isolated below a layer of impenetrable rock, water for a deep well is located 100 feet or more below ground level. Filtration takes place as the water seeps through the layers of rock and other materials until it reaches a strata of water-bearing material.

The pump itself is suspended by long, wooden sections of rod joined to match the lengths of the pipe in which it is centered. Since wood suspended in water is practically weightless, a relatively low-powered motor can raise and lower the piston a hundred feet or more. The

major disadvantage is the difficulty to repair the pump. The entire pipe must be hoisted out and dismantled section by section to repair it. *SEE ALSO PUMPS.*

Deep Wells

Deep wells are wells with a depth of 100 feet or more. The drilling depth depends on the location of the level of the aquifer or water-bearing strata. This strata is usually located beneath an impenetrable layer of rock or solid matter. This depth indicated that the water has undergone a considerable filtration process before it reaches the aquifer.

Wrought iron pipe with a diameter of six to eight inches is used as a well casing to seal the well and prevent contamination by surface water. Within this pipe one or possibly two smaller pipes carry the water from the water-bearing strata. Pumping is usually necessary to bring the water to ground level, although the artesian well requires no pumping since the water pressure in the aquifer is great enough to force the water up and out of the well. An artesian well usually occurs when the water source supplying a deep well comes from surrounding high ground. *SEE ALSO WELLS & SEPTIC TANK SYSTEMS.*

Defensive Driving

[SEE DRIVING SAFETY & AUTOMOBILE INSURANCE.]

Dehumidifiers

The dehumidifier is an entirely different type of appliance than a humidifier in terms of operation. The dehumidifier is a refrigeration appliance which uses a compressor, evaporator and condenser just like any other of its type. It has nothing directly to do with heating or cooling, however. It is solely intended to remove

moisture from the air, preferably without raising or lowering the temperature to any extent.

Be sure to unplug the dehumidifier to turn power off before removing any panels for inspection, testing or repair.

In a dehumidifier a compressor pumps refrigerant to the evaporator which is designed to operate at a temperature somewhat above the freezing point. (Many dehumidifier evaporators tend to ice during the first thirty minutes or so of operation on a cool day). The condenser is located immediately adjacent to and behind the evaporator. A fan forces air across these coils at all times when the unit is operating. When evaporator coils become chilled, moisture tends to condense on the coil like it does on a glass of iced tea. The air temperature is lowered somewhat, also. To avoid damp air leaving the dehumidifier, the condenser is placed in-line to help reheat it back to normal room temperature. A drain or collector coil is placed underneath the evaporator. The drain pan may channel the water to a collector pan underneath the

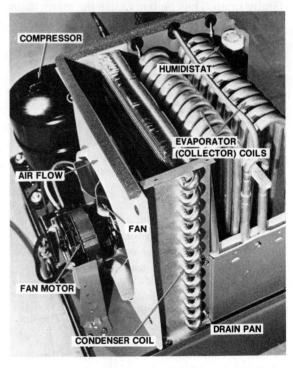

With the cabinet removed, components are easily located and visible.

dehumidifier, which must be removed and emptied as the dehumidifier becomes full.

An adjustable humidistat is often used on the dehumidifier. This is a device much like a thermostat that is sensitive to moisture levels rather than temperature. Some of these humidistats have controls that are marked at various levels of humidity. Others are marked with notations such as more dry and less dry. The levels are not critical. Usually the control can be adjusted to compensate for differences between calibration and the actual moisture level.

Many dehumidifiers use a de-icer control to limit the amount of frosting that can occur on the evaporator coil. If the coil becomes heavily iced, the de-icer, a simple bimetal thermostat, will then turn the compressor off while the fan continues to run, allowing the coil to defrost. Dehumidifiers should not be operated at temperatures below 65 degrees.

A dehumidifier simply requires that you place it and set the humidstat to the level of moisture that you want to maintain in a particular area. But there are ways to use one wisely that can widely affect the results obtained: Begin by eliminating all areas where moisture can enter the house. Make a habit of using the vent fan in the kitchen. Use the vents in the bathrooms, particularly those above showers and tubs. Be sure that your clothes dryer is vented to the outside of the house. If your home has a crawl space, consider placing strips of four-mil polyethylene over the ground area. Don't cover the ground area completely. By leaving some space between the strips near the foundation you have a means of controlling the amount of moisture entering the home. This is an important factor in moisture control.

Determine the areas of excessive moisture in your home. Mildew and mold under carpet, rugs and furnishings are indications that the problem exists. Wooden materials that absorb moisture can warp. Metal equipment can become rusty and an unpleasant musty odor can prevail. The dehumidifier can usually remedy these problems, at least to a large extent.

A dehumidifier covers only a limited area, but by moving it from space to space for a day or two at a time you can usually cover a household with one unit. If there is a problem in a particular area, move the appliance to that area for a few days. Then go on to other areas of the home, establishing a rotating schedule.

One factor to consider in locating a dehumidifier is a means of disposing of the condensate water. While most portable units do have self-contained collector pans, the pans are seldom large enough to contain the amount of water the unit can remove during wet or damp weather. In some cases, a garden hose can be attached to carry the water outside. If you use a garden hose to drain the condensate from the dehumidifier, be sure that there are no kinks in it and that it slopes gradually to the outlet, which should be low enough to allow proper drainage. Other possible applications are to place the dehumidifier over a sink outlet or a floor drain.

The water that comes from the dehumidifier can be useful, particularly if you live in a hard water area. Since it contains no minerals, it is excellent for use in steam irons or automobile batteries. Strain the water to remove any lint before using it for these purposes.

Remember that the area to be dehumidified must be isolated from outside areas as much as possi-

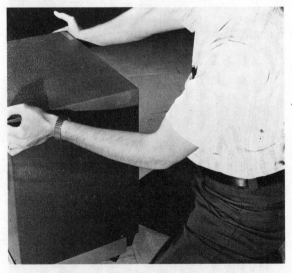

With the end panels removed, screws in cabinet can be loosened and cabinet lifted away from dehumidifier.

ble. Otherwise, the infiltration will be as much as the moisture that you are removing.

To disassemble dehumidifiers, be sure that it is unplugged, then examine the two end panels. These are often held in place by two screws at the bottom and clips at the top, or by pins which will allow the panels to be pulled away at the bottom and then snapped loose at the top. With the end panels removed, look for screws along the bottom of the envelope-type cabinet. When these screws are removed, the shell can be lifted off, exposing all components of the dehumidifier.

The refrigeration system for the dehumidifier is checked very much like any other refrigeration appliance. The controls can be easily tested with a continuity tester, but the symptoms will give you an idea of the problem too. For example, a faulty humidistat will shut off all power to the compressor and the fan motor. A defective de-icer (if the unit is so equipped) will shut off only the compressor, not the fan motor.

To check the accuracy of a humidistat that is calibrated by the percent of relative humidity, simply place the dehumidifier outdoors for

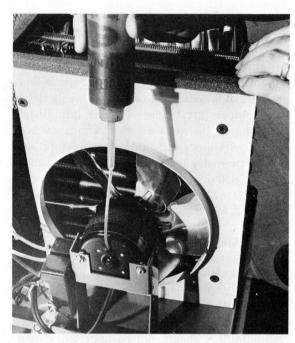

If oil ports are provided in fan motor, apply a couple of drops of SAE 20 oil.

several hours. Determine from the weather bureau the prevailing relative humidity and adjust the control to this level. An adjustment, usually in the form of a screw, is provided on most of these controls for calibration.

The collector and condenser coil of the dehumidifier should be vacuumed at least once each season. After vacuuming, wipe the condenser coil with a clean cloth. If oil ports are provided on the fan motor, use a few drops of SAE 20 non-detergent oil or the lubricant recommended by the manufacturer. If the fan has no oil ports, it is still wise to wipe away any lint that may have been left on the motor shaft. Scrub the collector pan and the storage container with household ammonia diluted in water several times during the course of each season to prevent the growth of algae and mold.

If the dehumidifier seems to be noisy, remove the cabinet and check the tubing. Also, check the compressor mount, the fan motor mounts and the point where the fan blade attaches to the motor shaft. Looseness at any of these points can cause an unusual noise. If tubing is touching, move the two points carefully apart, being

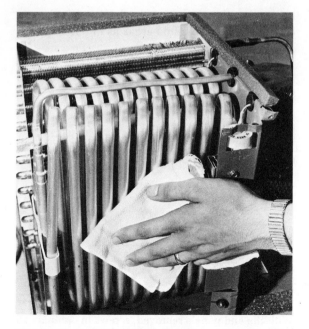

Clean collector coil with cloth and vacuum away lint at beginning of each season.

careful not to bend or damage any of the tubing. Vibration between two pieces of tubing over a long period of time can actually rub a hole in the tubing, requiring a system repair to remedy the failure.

Some models have an overflow switch to shut off the unit if the pan becomes full. Sometimes this is a float type switch; at other times, a diaphragm pressure switch similar to that found on an automatic washer is used. Check the

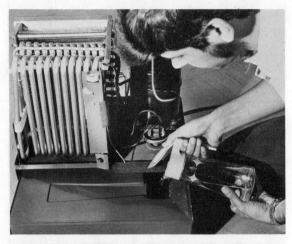

The overflow switch can be tested by pouring water into the container and checking to see that switch turns off before the container overflows.

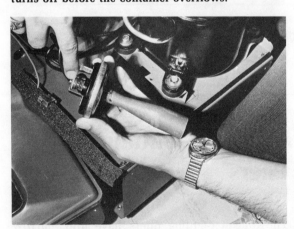

A pressure-type overflow switch is adjusted by turning a screw.

linkage of the float switch occasionally to make sure that it is turning the unit off. Often an indicator light is provided to show when the overflow switch has the dehumidifier turned off.

If the dehumidifier fails to run, a blown fuse or power cord can also be at fault.

Demountable Joints

Demountable joints are joints which have two metal parts that, when interlocked, create a solid joint that may be repeatedly taken apart or put together without the aid of tools. These joints are commonly used to join side rails to head and foot boards in bed frames. *SEE ALSO FURNITURE MAKING.*

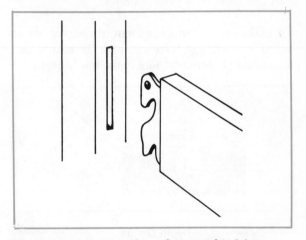

Hooks slip into slot to form demountable joint.

Dentil

A dentil is one of a series of small, rectangular blocks that are equally-spaced in a horizontal molding. *SEE ALSO MOLDING & TRIM.*

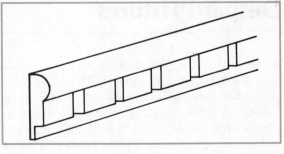

Dentil

Depth Gauge

A depth gauge is a narrow ruler which has a movable clamp that marks the distance and measures the depth of a hole. Another simpler form of a depth gauge is a rectangular-shaped structure that is flatly placed on the surface over the hole that has been drilled. To measure the hole's depth, slide the scale through it until the gauge stops at the end of the hole. These gauges may be clamped on auger bits and twist drills to stop the tools when the bit or cutting edge of the tool has reached a pre-set depth.

To make your own gauge, cut a piece of scrap wood long enough to reach from the chuck, the attachment holding the tool in the machine, to the

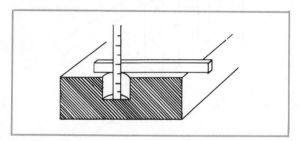

Depth Gauge

correct point on the bit. Then drill through the scrap, leaving it on the bit, facing the chuck. When the bit has reached the pre-set depth, the wood acts as a stop. These gauges are especially helpful when boring many holes to the same depth, such as in dowel work. *SEE ALSO HAND TOOLS.*

Despard Fixtures

A Despard fixture is a locking plate which fits over a single outlet receptacle. The plate commonly has three holes to take either individual outlets, switches, pilot lights or night lights in any desired combination. Combinations might include two outlets plus a night light or an outlet with a switch and a pilot light. Named after Vic-

tor Despard who pioneered it, a Despard fixture is usually referred to as a 3-opening Despard. *SEE ALSO SWITCHES & OUTLETS.*

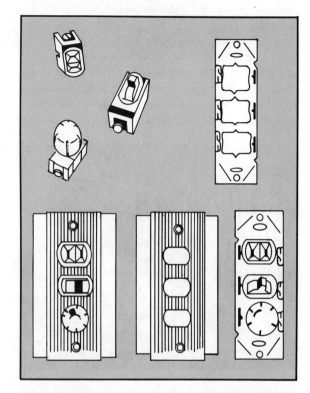

Despard fixtures permit the combination of three devices.

Developing
[SEE PHOTOGRAPHY.]

Diagonal-Cutting Pliers

The diagonal-cutting pliers have thin, narrow noses that can reach into tight spots to nip wires and perform other operations that a larger nosed plier could not perform. Since the diagonal slant of the cutting surface makes it possible to nip wires without the handle getting in the way, they excel in cutting. This tool is extremely useful to the electrician. *SEE ALSO HAND TOOLS.*

Diagonal Sheathing

Diagonal sheathing is a technique of covering an exterior wall with boards to add rigidity to the wall. The boards are fastened to the wall framing at a 45 degree angle, making each board a brace. *SEE ALSO WALL & CEILING CONSTRUCTION.*

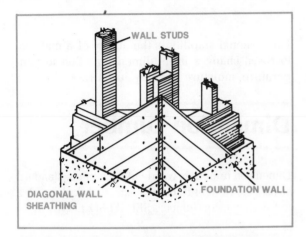

Diagonal Wall Sheathing

Diameters of Pipes

Precise diameter sizes of pipe, unlike nominal or stated sizes in lumber that are consistently larger than actual dimensions, may be larger or smaller than the nominal size, depending upon the particular size and kind. Although pipe is generally measured according to inside diameter, most charts size pipe by the actual outside diameter. Since methods of sizing do vary, brands should be double checked when size factor is important. *SEE ALSO PIPE SIZES.*

Dies & Taps

Dies are round, square or hexagonal tools that fit over a piece of bolt, rod or pipe to cut external threads. Made of steel, dies have internal threads with flutes that form a cutting edge which is ground slightly on one side for easy starting. To use a die, file a slight bevel on the edge of the rod or pipe to be threaded and clamp it in a vise, beveled end up. Secure the die in the die stock or holder and place it evenly over the end of the work. Pressing downward, turn the stock to the right till the threads bite. After making a few threads, remove the die stock and use a square to check for even alignment. If the threads are leaning to one side, this may be corrected by applying pressure in the opposite direction as the die is turned. Continue the threading and keep the threads oiled. After the thread has been started, downward pressure may be stopped and the die will cut by itself. Reverse the direction of the die after each half turn to remove metal chips.

Taps are similar to dies, except they cut the internal threads in rods, bolts, pipes and steel. Taper taps have threads that gradually taper at one end and are used for cutting threads through open holes. To thread a partially open hole, start with a taper tap and finish threading with the plug tap. To thread to the bottom of a closed hole, three taps — taper, plug and bottoming — will be needed. To make the threads, drill a hole slightly smaller than the outside diameter of the tap. Insert the tap and check it for squareness with the work surface. Then, using a tap wrench, apply downward pressure and begin threading.

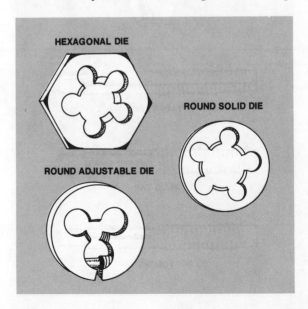

409

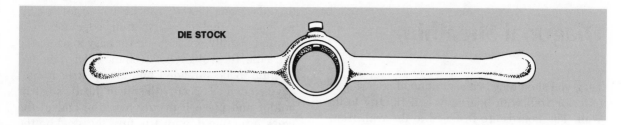

DIE STOCK

Lubricate the threads with oil and back off on the tap every two or three turns to release metal chips.

Dies and taps are available in different sizes and shapes to provide a good fit. Some metalworkers find these tools useful not only in threading pipe and rod, but also in repairing or making bolts. *SEE ALSO METALWORKING TOOLS.*

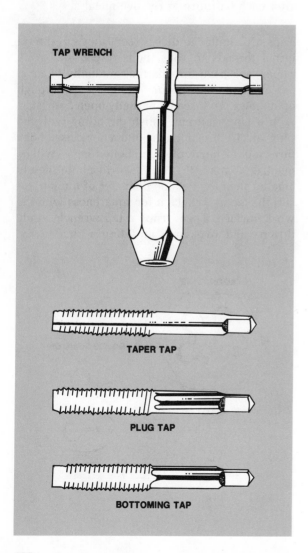

TAP WRENCH

TAPER TAP

PLUG TAP

BOTTOMING TAP

Dimensional Stability

Dimensional stability is the ability of a material to resist changes in its dimensions due to temperature, moisture and physical stress.

Dimension Lumber

Dimension lumber is wood cut to common standard sizes used in light framing, joists, and decking. A 2 x 4 is dimension lumber. *SEE ALSO LUMBER.*

Dimmer Control

A dimmer control is a light control switch that adjusts incandescent light to any desired level of intensity. In the small size, it fits into an ordinary

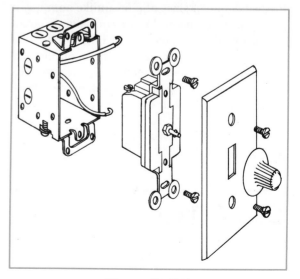

Dimmer Control

switch box and is connected like a toggle switch. A dimmer control switch for higher wattage requires a larger box. A dial control replaces the usual switch lever. Other specialized dimmer control switches can be used in place of lamp sockets and cord switches.

To install, turn off household power and remove plate and light switch; connect the black wire and white wire to the dimmer switch (in off position). Then push dimmer switch into switch box; replace screws in wallplate, attach dial control knob and turn power on. *SEE ALSO SWITCHES & OUTLETS.*

Dining Room
[SEE DECORATING.]

Direct Current

Direct current (DC) is electric current that flows continuously in the same direction, as opposed to alternating current (AC), which reverses flow direction 60 times a second. *SEE ALSO ELECTRICITY.*

Discharge Pipe

The large pipe found between the toilet tank and the bowl is called a discharge pipe. It is connected at each end with slip joints which are rubber-sealed. Once the toilet has been completely flushed, this pipe is empty. *SEE ALSO DRAINAGE SYSTEMS.*

Disc Sander & Polisher
[SEE PORTABLE POWER TOOLS.]

Disc Valve Faucet

The disc valve faucet is a one-handle, washerless faucet composed of discs, which allow hot and cold water to mix. Its handle is moved laterally to control the water's temperature and up and down to control the rate of flow. Included in the disc valve faucet are the stem pivot, stem stop, two large screws which hold the unit together and a cartridge body which contains the discs. There is a movable top disc, which acts simultaneously with handle movement, and a bottom disc which is stationary. Also attached to the cartridge body are cold and hot-water inlet seals and a larger outlet seal, all made of rubber. To replace the rubber seals, which may deteriorate with the use of hard water, the entire unit must be taken apart. Other parts of the faucet should never wear out.

O-Ring disc valve faucets, commonly used in modern showers, contain an alignment of discs which match or mismatch to control the water flow. O-Rings make up the inner spindle or stem and may be easily repaired. If an O-Ring is malfunctioning, it may be turned over and restored to proper working order. To remove the spindle, the faucet handle and keeper ring should be taken off. Often it is easier to remove the entire operating core of a disc valve faucet and buy an identical replacement for it.

There are other types of one-handle disc valve faucets which have complex parts like steel-ball encapsulations, eccentrics and cams. These parts work together to blend hot and cold water. *SEE ALSO FAUCET.*

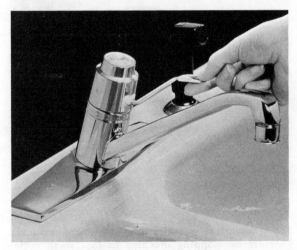

Courtesy of Kohler Company
Disc Valve Faucet

Dishwasher Repair

Automatic dishwashers not only save many hours previously spent washing dishes but they often require less hot water than hand dishwashing. Because they can withstand hotter water and stronger concentrations of detergents than hands can, dishes are better sanitized than even the most thorough hand dishwashing can do.

Remember: always unplug or disconnect the dishwasher before attempting any repairs, checks or inspections. Watch out for sharp edges behind sheet metal panels, and use tools correctly and safely.

Dishwashers require a minimum water temperature of 140 degrees to provide good washing results since dishwasher detergents dissolve and perform properly at that temperature. Also, the greases left by foods cannot be made soluble and washed away at lower temperatures. To check the water temperature, allow the dishwasher to fill with water as if washing a load of dishes. Let it go through the first cycle and enter the main wash cycle. Take a candy thermometer, meat thermometer or other thermometer that is

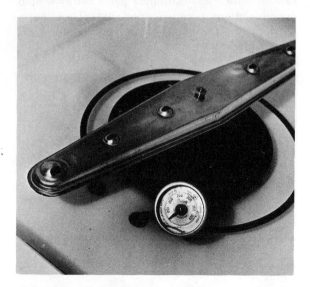

The temperature of water in dishwasher is critical. Measure by stopping machine in first wash cycle and inserting candy or meat thermometer. It should read at least 140 degrees.

graduated between 100 and 200 degrees. Turn off the machine, open the door and measure the water temperature. If it is lower than 140 degrees, the dishwasher is not washing efficiently. Another quick check to determine if this condition exists with a dishwasher is to run a finger along the lower corners of the cabinet of the front-loader just outside the gasket area. The presence of a greasy, oily film here suggests that the water temperature is not hot enough.

Correct this condition by raising the water temperature at the hot water heater. Remember that the water temperature will drop with each foot of line between the dishwasher and the heater; therefore, it may be necessary to set the heater at a higher temperature to deliver 140 degree water at the dishwasher. In addition, allow the water to run in the kitchen sink until it becomes hot before starting the dishwasher.

DETERGENTS

Dishwasher detergents are entirely different from those used in automatic washers and for hand laundry. They are highly alkaline and extremely concentrated, so their shelf life is short and they are therefore not available in the large bulk sizes as is laundry detergent. Dishwasher detergents will not keep for a long period of time once the foil wrapper is broken. Closing the special sealing spout helps to keep out moisture and the detergent fresh. Be sure to keep all dishwashing detergents out of the reach of children.

Often the cause of dishwasher cleaning problems is the detergent. No one detergent is best; however, use only those detergents formulated specifically for automatic dishwashers. There is usually one or more brands whose formulations work better in a particular water supply. Try several brands to find the one which provides spot-free washing results.

If there is any doubt about the condition of a box of detergent, first check to see if it has become caked. If so, it is not capable of doing its job. To test further, try the two-by-two test. Dissolve two teaspoonfuls of detergent in a glass of hot tap water, (140 degrees or more), and stir it for two

minutes. If a gritty residue remains, the detergent should be discarded.

TYPES OF DISHWASHERS

There are two major types of dishwashers in use today. One of these uses an impeller, a bakelite blade that sits directly on top of the motor shaft projecting through the bottom of the tub. Its spinning action picks up the water and forces it out at speeds of over 100 miles an hour. Therefore, the blade tips are critical areas. If you have an impeller-type dishwasher, make sure that these tips haven't become chipped or worn down over a period of time. A chipped blade can change the water pattern and reduce washing results.

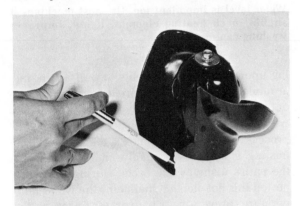

The impeller in this dishwasher is a critical part. The edges of the blade must not be nicked or worn, or improper spray patterns will result.

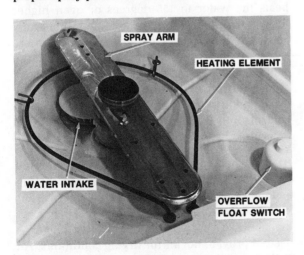

Be sure spray arm turns freely on dishwasher. It may be necessary to adjust housing to obtain freedom of movement.

Most newer machines use spray arms to get the water to the dishes and scrub the soil away. The spray arm is just what its name implies. It is an arm that is perforated with holes which have been precisely engineered and placed. These serve to provide a pushing action that makes the arm revolve and provides the highest possible water force as the water strikes the dishes. The arm perforations are aimed so as to strike every square inch within the machine. On most of the better models two-level spraying is provided by using a spray in the top or middle of the machine under the upper rack in addition to the spray in the bottom of the machine.

The force necessary to push the water through these spray arms comes from a high speed pump which is usually attached directly to the motor shaft. In some instances these motor-and-pump assemblies are located under the machine without a direct connection to the tank. In other cases the motor is suspended under the bottom of the tank, with the pump in the sump at the very bottom. Often filters are used to keep heavy food particles from reaching the pump. Others use a macerator blade to help grind up food particles and flush them away.

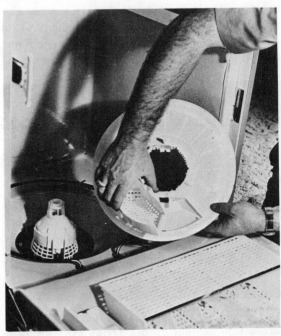

The filter in this machine keeps heavy food particles from reaching the pump.

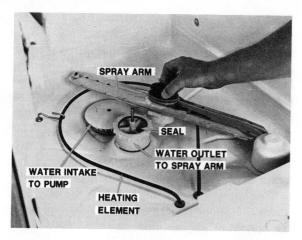

The pump is located under the tub of this dishwasher. Note the large opening from tub into pump. The heating element is used to maintain water temperature during wash and to heat air in drying cycle.

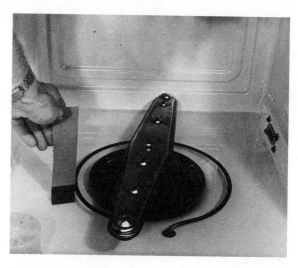

Water level is important too. On most machines it should reach heating element. If not, improper washing can result.

The drain system on a dishwasher is operated either by the action of a solenoid or by reversing the direction of motor rotation. In either case, water is discharged into a drain line which carries it away. A number of washes and rinses are usually provided in the course of each wash cycle.

At the end of the washing and rinsing action, a drying cycle is carried out using a heating element which heats the air within the tank to evaporate the moisture which remains. Some machines use a convection drying system, rely-

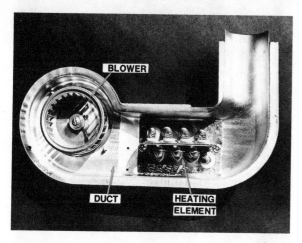

Duct heater in this dishwasher heats air that is forced into cabinet during drying cycle. Blower assembly helps circulate air through cabinet on drying cycle, providing faster drying action.

ing upon natural air currents to pull air in and around the dishes and to circulate the moist air out and into the room. Others use a small fan within the compartment to speed up the drying process by pulling air across the dishes. The heating element is normally energized during the entire dishwashing cycle. During the wash period this hot element maintains the water temperature, preventing a temperature drop as the water is circulated through the machine.

Some machines feature a sanitizing cycle which heats the water to 155 degrees or even higher during the final rinse. Sanitizing is generally considered to be the condition where there are no more than 100 bacteria per dish. In the sanitizing cycle, a thermostat assumes control from the timer. The thermostat prevents the timer motor from operating and advancing the control until the machine has reached the predetermined sanitizing temperature.

At least one manufacturer uses an additional heater mounted in the air duct between the fan and the dryer. The heater within the dishwasher is used to maintain water temperature and for the sanitizing cycle; the external duct heater is used to provide hot air for drying conditions. An indication whether your machine is operating under proper water temperature conditions can come from the sanitizing cycle. The temperature

is usually increased at about one degree per minute of operation during the sanitizing delay. On a 155-degree sanitizing cycle, if the water temperature was only 125 degrees this would mean that a 30 minute delay would be necessary. If this happens when you use the cycle, there is a good possibility that the water temperature reaching the dishwasher may be too low. Some people do not use their sanitizing cycle because of the long delay. The problem is not within the dishwasher at all but rather in the water supply. When this temperature problem is corrected, not only will the sanitizing cycle operate without inconvenience, but also dishwashing results are greatly improved.

TROUBLESHOOTING

When attempting to repair a dishwasher, be sure to turn off the power supply or unplug the machine before starting work. Also, be sure to be careful of sharp edges within the machine when inspecting or checking it.

Dishwashers contain a water inlet valve, very similar to those found on automatic clothes washers. The primary difference is that this is a single-port valve since only hot water is used in dishwashers. If there is a low buzzing sound but no water comes into the machine, be sure to check to see if the filters are clean. The filters are found at the point where the water line attaches to the inlet valve. If the filters are not clear, remove them and brush them out under a faucet using an old toothbrush. In the case of portable dishwashers, be sure that the faucet is turned on and that the aerator on the faucet is not clogged.

If water fails to turn off, the inlet valve has to be disassembled. Remove the toe panel after unplugging the machine and turning off the water supply. Remove the water line from the inlet valve. Next, remove the coupling or bracket that holds the valve in place and remove the two wires from the solenoid. Since this is a single-port valve, it will not be necessary to mark the two wires that connect to the solenoid. With the solenoid out of the machine, remove the three screws that hold the electrical coil to the body of the solenoid. Remove all internal parts that come in contact with water and flush them out with

running water. Reassemble the valve. The water should shut off now when the sump has filled. Be sure to clean out the filter screens while the valve is apart.

If a machine fails to pump water out, check the pump filter first, if the machine has one. If it is clogged, rinse it out. If this doesn't remedy the problem, it will be necessary to remove the top of the pump. Unplug the dishwasher and mop out the water in the sump or the bottom of the tub with a large towel. With the pump cover removed, grasp the impeller to see if the pump turns freely. If not. look for a foreign object such as an olive pit or broken piece of glass that may have lodged in the pump. When disassembling the pump, watch for small brass spacers or shims. Be sure to reinstall these in exactly the same order in which they were removed. If the blades on a metal impeller are sheared by a foreign object in the pump, be sure to count the number of blades on the new replacement impeller. Be sure that all of the old ones are retrieved from lines and the pump housing when the new impeller is installed; otherwise the blades will find their way back into the pump and ruin the new one.

Remember that the pump in a late model dishwasher serves both to recirculate the water through the spray arm that washes the dishes, as well as pumping the water from the machine at the end of a cycle. If the machine runs, but doesn't seem to be cleaning correctly, check the filter and pump unit. Some dishwashers use one pump for circulating the water during wash and a separate pump to drain the water from the machine. Others may use no pump at all for draining, utilizing a dump valve which is simply a solenoid-operated valve placed in the drain line. Upon command from the timer, the solenoid simply opens the valve, permitting the water to flow out the gravity drain. There is little to go wrong with this valve unless the solenoid fails or unless it binds in some manner.

If dishes are not cleaning as they should, yet the machine seems to operate satisfactorily, be sure that it is loaded correctly. This is a critical factor since the dishes must be placed so the water can strike them with full force. This is true whether

415

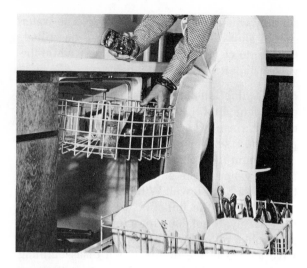

Loading is critical on newer dishwashers. Dishes must be placed so they don't block water flow from spray arm.

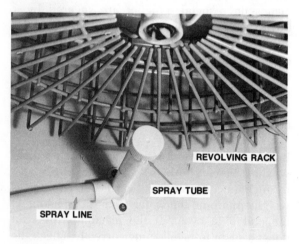

REVOLVING RACK

SPRAY TUBE

SPRAY LINE

Revolving racks must be completely in position. Spray arm or tube furnishes water to rack or water is directed to cause rack to rotate when loaded properly.

your machine uses an impeller or a spray arm to circulate the water. Follow the manufacturer's instructions when loading. Be sure that the dishes are not nesting within each other, preventing water from flowing between them. Also, be sure that a large pan or other utensil does not block water from other dishes.

Other causes for poor washing results include low output pressure from the pump. This will usually be noticed during the drain cycle. A clogged filter previously mentioned can cause

this problem, or a stuck spray arm can also keep water from circulating well. Sometimes an arm doesn't revolve freely after it becomes hot or wet. If you suspect this, let the machine run during part of the wash cycle. Then turn it off, open the door and spin the spray arm by hand. If it does not turn freely, there is a good chance that it is causing a problem with your washing results. Revolving racks that are not fully in position or that are binding or dragging can also result in poor washing within that particular rack area.

If you have a leak from your dishwasher, try to determine exactly where it is coming from at the time you notice the leak. Turn off the machine, turn off all power and remove the toe panel and look underneath it. On some machines it is necessary to remove an outer door panel before the toe panel can be loosened. Usually, only a few screws hold the upper panel in place. When you locate the position of the leak immediately after it occurs, it should be easy to pinpoint the component that is causing the problem. Often tightening a loose hose clamp is all that is necessary to bring about a cure.

Leaks can occur around door seals, particularly with front loading machines. Some of these can be hard to locate. Some things to look for are splits and seams in spray arms that cause turbulence in the washer, allowing it to splash over

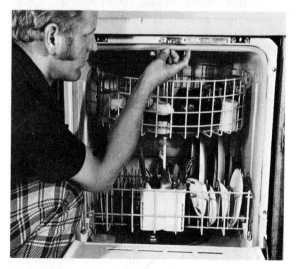

Check door gaskets carefully. If they are hardened or torn they will let the machine leak around door area.

a dam that is built into the front of the door. Poorly sealing or hardened gaskets can be at fault. These hardened gaskets usually appear to be in good condition, but are no longer soft enough to provide a good seal around the door when it is closed. Improper use of detergents or the wrong type of detergent can cause sudsing or foaming conditions which invariably lead to leaks. If your dishwasher has a wetting agent dispenser, it is designed to inject only a few drops of the fluid into the water during a particular cycle. If the dispenser is faulty and is allowing a large amount of wetting agent to flow into the water, foaming conditions that cause leaking can result.

The water fill on automatic dishwashers is usually controlled by the timer itself. A small washer with an orifice formed into its center acts as a regulator within the inlet valve, allowing only a certain amount of water to flow. This flow is regulated regardless of water pressure so long as it is within limits (from 20 to 100 pounds per square inch). After a certain number of seconds, the timer shuts the water supply off.

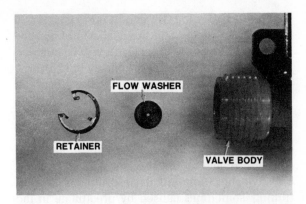

Flow washer from dishwasher valve helps regulate amount of water that enters machine. The valve and strainers require same attention as those found on automatic washers.

Inside the tub on many models is a float which is actually an overflow protector. If the water rises to a limit that raises the float off its seat, it opens a switch which shuts off the water supply, even though the timer may still call for more water. The water in an automatic dishwasher should just cover the heating element. Usually this will also mean that it is just beginning to lift the float, if it is so equipped. To check the level in your washer, allow the machine to fill during the wash cycle. Then shut it off and open the door. If

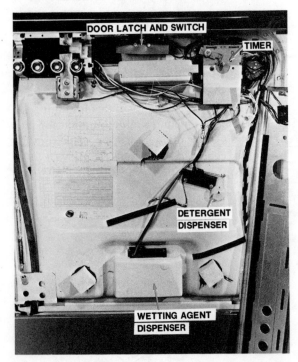

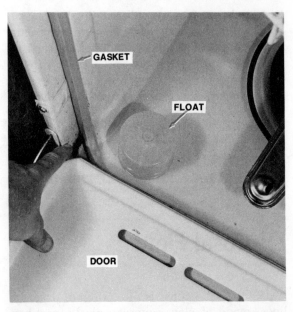

The float switch controls water in case valve allows too much to enter. All linkages to the switch should be free. Greasy film on liner seen in corners is an indication that water temperature is too cool.

it appears that a low-fill condition exists, it is a good idea to check with the dealer to obtain the exact specifications for water flow for your particular machine. If it is a portable model it is easy to check the amount by simply catching the drain water in gallon containers when the machine pumps out.

Often the glassware is a good indication of the type of problem involved when a fault occurs in a dishwasher. Some of those problems include filming, sometimes caused by precipitate in the detergent or by a silicate buildup from the water itself. This film is usually not permanent, but another similar-appearing condition can be permanent. This is called soft water etching, and is particularly likely to occur on better quality glassware. If your dealer or servicing agent cannot advise you about prevailing local water conditions, approach this possibility with caution. Wash only one piece of fine glassware over a period of several washings and observe any filming which might occur. This situation can also occur even with handwashing, but the higher temperatures and stronger detergent compounds involved with automatic dishwashers makes the symptoms develop more quickly.

Dishwashers of today will handle any reasonable loading with little problem. Simply rinse the dishes off under running water (never rinse them in water containing hand dishwashing detergent) and place them properly in the rack. Many manufacturers recommend only that you scrape away major food deposits before loading.

Disposal
[SEE GARBAGE DISPOSAL REPAIR.]

Disposal Field

A disposal field consists of a group of drainage lines, made of clay, concrete, plastic or fiber, which radiate from the distribution box. These pipes are loose-jointed or perforated to allow seepage of the effluent into the ground. To pre-

vent excessive seepage at pipe ends, they may be closed with a masonry block or filled in with six inches of gravel. The disposal field should be located several feet away from the septic tank to avoid having a concentration of effluent around it. *SEE ALSO SEPTIC SYSTEMS.*

Distribution Panel

The distribution panel contains the fuse or circuit breaker panels and acts as a point of "distribution" for the individual circuits. The distribution panel is located in the service entrance. *SEE ALSO ELECTRICAL WIRING.*

Divider

A divider is a vertical or horizontal member used as a partition in a cabinet, drawer or chest. Dividers are commonly made of hardboard or plywood, and are fitted into dado cuts made in the sides or top and bottom members of a cabinet. The correct location of these cuts should be determined prior to assembly so that they will match and the dividers will be straight. Metal channels which hold the dividers can be hammered into the piece as substitutes for dadoes. A front frame is sometimes added to hide the cuts of channels if the dividers can be seen from the front of the cabinet. *SEE ALSO KITCHEN DESIGN & PLANNING.*

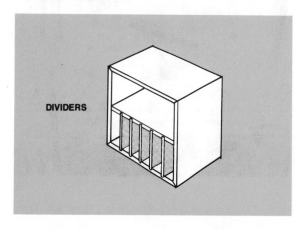

DIVIDERS

Dividers

The wing divider has two steel legs and a quadrant-shaped "wing" that runs from one leg through a slot in the other. The slotted leg has a screw that is used to lock the quadrant in different positions. To use a wing divider, set the approximate spacing and lock it with the screw. Then, use it as you would a compass for scribing circles, dividing lines and arcs and locating the center of a circle.

Angle dividers are double bevels made of wood, steel or other alloys, used in dividing angles for mitering, in finding the center of angles formed at corners and joints; and when used in conjunction with a T-bevel, can transfer angles from one surface to another. An angle divider's blade can also be used as a try square for checking corners and joints. Most models can be locked in different positions for accurate measuring. *SEE ALSO HAND TOOLS.*

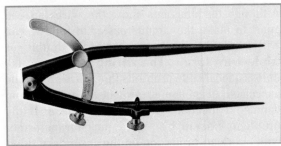

Courtesy of The Stanley Works

Wing Divider

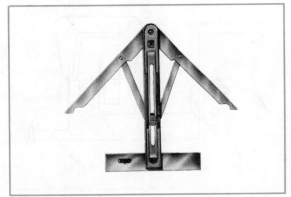

Courtesy of The Stanley Works

Angle Divider

Docking Saw

The docking saw, a rugged, skew-backed saw, derives its name from its primary use around boat docks. It is also a favorite tool among farmers and mine workers. Typically, the blade is 30-inches long and has four-and-one-half points. *SEE ALSO HAND TOOLS.*

Dolly

A dolly is a square or rectangular platform made of wood or steel with four casters attached to the bottom. A dolly can be used for moving heavy objects around the house and for transporting cleaning items from room to room. Mechanics often use dollies for rolling themselves under automobiles in order to work on them.

Door Antiquing
[SEE ANTIQUING.]

Doorbells, Chimes & Buzzers

Doorbells, chimes and buzzers, all signaling devices, are sound systems found in most well-equipped homes. Although all are used to announce someone's arrival, the tones produced are quite different. Normally, a doorbell makes a ringing sound while a humming noise is characteristic of a buzzer. Chimes, on the other hand, emit notes made by a musically tuned set of bells.

In the past, the doorbell was usually operated by two or four dry-cell batteries providing a total of either 3 or 6 volts. Many of the older models are

still operated that way. Today's doorbells and buzzers commonly operate on 10 volts, and chimes on 16 volts. Whatever the voltage required, you can buy a transformer to supply it, as it will be stocked by the same dealer who handles the bell or chime. If you replace an old transformer-operated doorbell or buzzer with a chime unit, you will undoubtedly have to replace the transformer also, as the old doorbell very likely operated at about 6 volts.

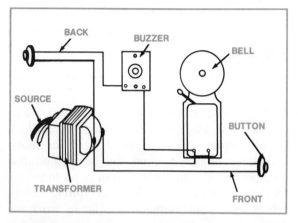

Wiring for doorbell and buzzer. Buzzer signals back door, bell signals front.

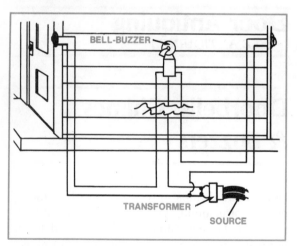

Path of wiring from doors to basement transformer and bell-buzzer unit.

Often no bigger than your first, the transformer is a small unit. For higher-voltage chime units, however, it is usually larger. This transformer reduces the 120-volt household current to which it is permanently connected to the low-voltage current on which doorbells and chimes operate.

Since the reduced voltage is not strong enough to shock you, it is safe to work on a chime or bell system without shutting off the power.

If you are planning to install a completely new bell or chime system, buy all of your materials at the same source to assure voltage matching. (You will need to measure for the length of wire needed.) In many cases the entire system is sold as a kit with enough wire to take care of the average installation. If you buy a kit, it pays to measure your wiring run in advance in case the length of wire provided is not enough. It is much handier to buy the length of wire required at the outset than to have to buy it during the job.

WIRING A DOORBELL

To trace the path of the current, consider the transformer as the source, the doorbell button as the switch, and the chime or bell as the outlet. To provide a single front-door button or various front- and rear-door arrangements, as shown by the diagrams, you have a choice of lead bell wire in single-, double-, and triple-wire form.

Although the diagrams show the wires spaced apart to make the circuits easier to follow, you will usually be able to use one of the double- or triple-wire forms. The wiring is run "as is" unless a local code prohibits this. Care should be exercised, of course, to protect the wiring from damage in locations where it might occur. If any problems exist in this regard, pick a transformer with overload protection on the secondary (low-

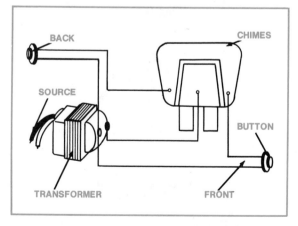

Wiring for one- and two-note chimes, one note for back door, two for front.

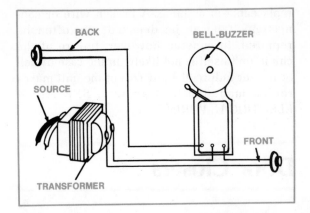

Combination bell and buzzer unit provides separate signal for front and back doors with simplified wiring. Unit has three terminals.

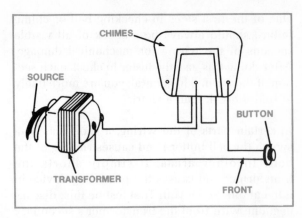

Wiring for one- and two-note chimes, front door only.

voltage) wiring. This is built into many quality transformers now. With this type the current is cut off in the secondary when trouble occurs.

Note that a separate buzzer for the back door and a bell for the front can be used. You can also buy a combination bell and buzzer. Note that the single units have three terminal screws. Connect them as shown in the diagrams.

INSTALLING NEW CHIMES

Having located the transformer, check to see if both the chimes and transformer operate on the same voltage. Labels give this information. A variety of voltage levels with separate terminals marked for each are provided by many transformers. Be sure to use only those suited to your specific need.

Run the wires from the transformer through the house to the chime unit. Then, connect them to the entrance button and correct terminals. On more modern types, a single chime unit can be used with different signals for front and back doors — two or more chimes for the front, one for the back. The difference depends on the make and model. Connect them as shown in the diagrams.

Whether you are installing a bell or chime, be sure to locate it where its sound is most likely to reach you anywhere in the house. Remember that the wiring is simple when compared to regular house wiring and that it can be led safely over

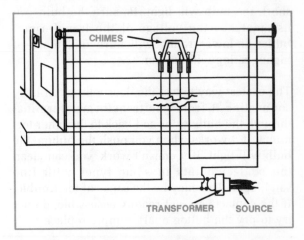

Four-note chime units can sound single note for back door, as many as eight notes for front.

its course without the work involved in 120-volt work. Keep in mind, too, that even though a particular chime may have provision for an elaborate hook-up, you can usually use it in a simple single-button front-door system.

TESTING FOR DOORBELL OR CHIME FAILURE

To find the cause of bell or chime failure, simply use a low-voltage circuit tester. In most cases the failure occurs at the doorbell button because of mechanical (usually spring-metal) failure or because corrosion from weather has affected the contact areas. In some cases, the bell will fail to ring at all. In others, it may continue ringing after the button is released. In the latter case, remove one of the wires from the secondary terminal screws.

One of the first steps in checking bell or chime failure should always be a check of all visible sections of the wiring for mechanical damage. After doing this, use the tester to check each section of the wiring. In general, you are more likely to find a break than a short.

In certain parts of the wiring, a short acts as a switch (or bell button) and causes ringing of the bell. In other areas, it simply shorts the transformer and causes the protecting device in it to cut out. So let your first test be this: disconnect one wire from the transformer's secondary screw terminals and touch your tester to the terminal and the disconnected wire. If there's a short, the bulb will light. Be sure the bulb you use matches the voltage of the transformer. Bulbs of lower rating will burn out, those of higher rating will be dim.

The easiest way to test the doorbell button is by connecting it from one transformer terminal through the bulb tester and back to the other terminal. If it works when you push the button, the bulb will light. If it doesn't work, you can clean the contact points in some types with fine sandpaper. This may be the cause of the trouble. If the contacts are not readily accessible, do not try to pry the button apart. Simply replace it.

If the button proves sound and the trouble appears to be at the bell or chime, check the terminal connections. Vibration sometimes loosens them. If the problem is in the chime or bell unit, the chance of repairing it depends largely on the individual make and model. A burned out solenoid (not common) may or may not be replaceable in a chime. A broken wire or connection, if it can be detected, can often be repaired. In general, however, failure of the chime unit itself is not likely. In the case of bell or buzzer failure, the low cost of the unit makes replacement the best answer. *SEE ALSO ELECTRICAL WIRING.*

Door Closers

Both pneumatic and hydraulic door closers control the closing of a door. Door closers automatically close a door, prevent the wind from opening it, keep the door from opening too far and damaging the hinges and provide a smooth closing of the door. Screen, storm and other exterior doors are usually equipped with a closer, but some office buildings also have them on interior doors. The rate of speed at which a door closes is determined by a screw on the pneumatic closer and a slotted cylinder on the hydraulic varieties. However, no matter what speed is selected, the last three closing inches move more rapidly to insure that the door will close completely.

Before installing a door closer, be sure that the door does not bind, that it swings freely in any position and that accessory hardware is in place, securely fastened and will not impede the action of the door's closing. Because hydraulic and pneumatic door closers are installed differently, it is best to follow the manufacturer's instructions.

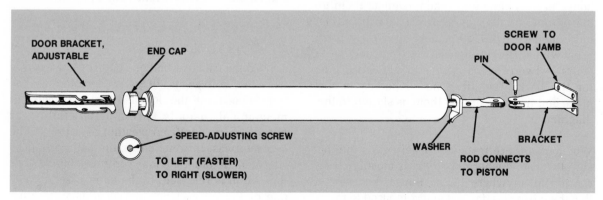

Pneumatic Door Closer

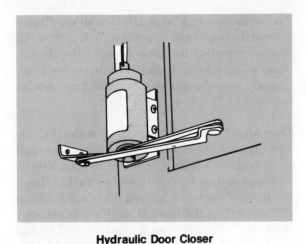

Hydraulic Door Closer

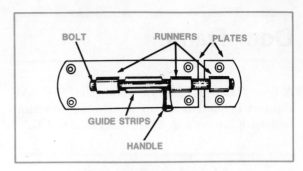

Barrel bolt in lock position

Door Fasteners

Door fasteners, in addition to door locks, are designed to provide extra protection against possible break-ins. Metal barrel bolts and brass chain fasteners are the two most widely used, and both are easily installed.

BARREL BOLTS

Barrel bolts consist of a round, slender bolt and two metal plates equipped with cylindrical runners which hold the bolt so that it may slide back and forth without losing its alignment. To install a barrel bolt, grasp the handle of the bolt and slide the bolt to the left of the longest rectangular plate. Then, push the handle down so that it is resting between the far left runner and the lower metal guide strip. Place the plate close to the edge of the door and fasten it at each corner with screws. The shorter plate fits on the side of the door facing and should be perfectly aligned with the first plate before securing with screws at the center of the upper and lower edges.

To place the bolt in the locked position, lift the bolt handle, slide the bolt through the first two runners on the longest plate, and into the runner on the second plate so that a bridge is formed between the two plates and across the door opening. Push the handle down so that it is locked between the second runner and the guide strip. To unlock the bolt, reverse the procedure.

CHAIN FASTENERS

Chain fasteners have a slotted plate for the chain to slide in and a second plate which holds the chain when it is not in use. One end of the chain is fastened to the second plate and the other end has a knob that slides in the slotted plate. To install chain fasteners, place the slotted plate horizontally next to the door edge and drive a screw in each of the three or four screw holes. The second plate is placed vertically on the door facing with its top edge, which contains the chain holder, even with that of the slotted plate. This plate is secured with one, two or four screws depending on the fastener chosen. To put the chain fastener in locked position, take the knobbed end of the chain, place it in the left side of the slot and slide it to the right end of the plate. The fastener is unlocked by reversing this operation.

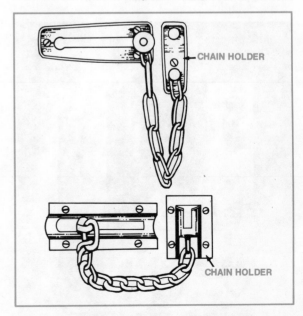

Two types of chain fasteners in locked position.

Door Frame

A door frame is made of wood parts that add support to, and form an interior or exterior enclosure for, a door. *SEE ALSO FRAMING.*

Door Knobs & Knockers

Door knobs and knockers not only serve a purpose, but also add beauty to a home if the correct styles and colors are chosen. Both knobs and knockers are made of either brass, aluminum, metal or other alloys and are available in many shapes, sizes, textures and finishes. Knobs and knockers should be selected according to the architecture of the house. The size of the home should be kept in mind, too, especially when choosing knockers. A large, heavily ornamented knocker would overpower a small home with a single door. This type knocker is best for tall, wide or double doors. Simply designed small knockers are more commonly used on apartments, cottages and mid-size homes.

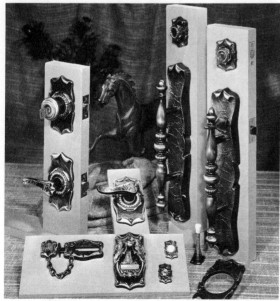

Courtesy of Amerock Corporation

An escutcheon can be installed with or slipped around the door knob to decorate and protect the area surrounding the knob. Most knobs already come with a simple, round escutcheon, but since they are interchangeable, the escutcheon can be matched to the theme of the door.

Door knobs are available with or without locks, and dummy knobs are used when only a pull knob without a latch is required to open a door. One type of door knob is locked by pushing in on the interior knob and turning it to the right till it catches. When the knob is in this position, the door can be closed from the outside and locked until opened with a key. Other types of knobs are locked by pushing in a button at the center of the interior knob. Many of these can be released by inserting a pin through a hole in the knob to prevent small children from becoming locked in. A locking door knob should be chosen for its convenience since it generally has no affect on the house decor.

Door Lock Installing

Door lock installing is a simple process when clear concise steps are followed. There are three basic locks: rim, called night locks or latches, cylindrical and mortise. The tubular lock is a division of cylindrical locks.

INSTALLING A RIM LOCK

A rim lock is one of the easiest to install. Because it requires less woodworking, the installation can be accomplished in six steps.

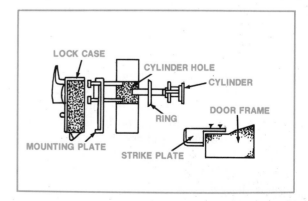

1. Mark the location for the key cylinder.

2. Drill a hole for the cylinder.

3. Fasten the cylinder to the mounting plate with connecting screws cut to match the door's thickness.

4. Fit the lock case to the mounting plate making certain that the connecting bar enters the lock mechanism.

5. Position the strike plate on the door jamb so the latch bolt matches the strike plate opening.

6. Cut a mortise for the strike plate and mount the plate on the jamb with screws.

INSTALLING A CYLINDRICAL LOCK

The installation of a cylindrical lock is a more complicated procedure. It involves woodworking on three surfaces. The installation can be completed in eleven steps.

1. Mark the center of the hole for the lock on the door face and the center of the latch bolt hole in the edge by using the template provided in the lock kit.

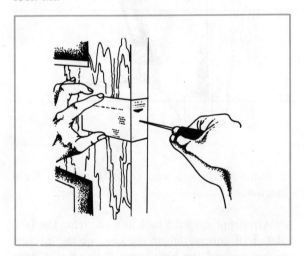

2. Use a 2¹/₈ inch expansive bit or hole saw to drill a hole. Stop drilling when the bit breaks the surface and begin drilling the other side.

3. With the ¹⁵/₁₆ inch bit at a right angle to the door edge, drill until it reaches the large hole.

4. After inserting the latch bolt in order to mark the dimensions of the plate, remove the bolt and chisel the wood until the plate will fit flush with the edge.

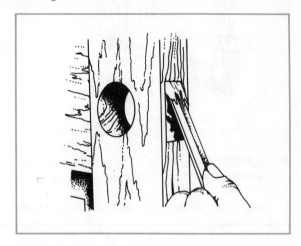

5. Reposition the latch bolt in the chiseled groove and fasten securely to the edge with the supplied screws.

6. While pushing in the latch bolt and checking to see that stems are correctly placed through the latch holes, insert the exterior knob.

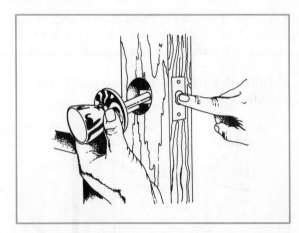

7. After inserting the interior knob and rose, and aligning screw guides and stems, push the knob and rose flush to the door and secure them with screws.

8. Locate the position of the strike plate with the template on the jamb.

9. Using a ¹⁵/₁₆ inch drill bit, make a ¹/₂ inch hole in the jamb.

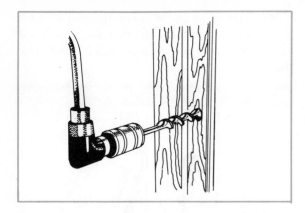

10. Mark the dimensions of the strike plate and chisel out the jamb until the plate fits flush.

11. Insert the strike plate and securely fasten with screws.

INSTALLING A MORTISE LOCK

A mortise lock is one of the older types of locks. Installing a mortise lock is not as complicated as cylindrical lock installation, although woodworking is involved. Nine steps should be followed.

1. Use the template to mark the location of the center of the cylinder hole and the spindle which should be located 36 inches above floor level.

2. Drill holes in the door face as specified by the manufacturer.

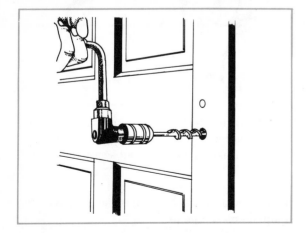

3. Also drill a series of closely located holes in the door edge. They should be drilled to the

depth of the lock and $1/16$ inch wider than the lock body.

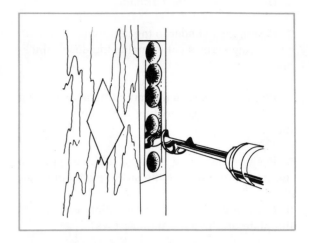

4. After removing the wood between the holes in the door edge, insert the body of the lock into the opening and trace the outline of the face plate on the door edge.

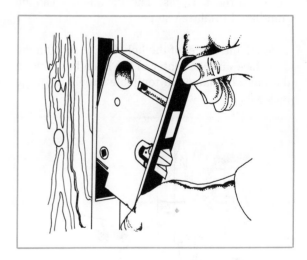

5. Remove the lock and chisel the wood for a mortise.

6. After replacing the lock and securing the face plate with screws, attach the knob on the interior door face and the handle on the exterior door face.

7. Matching the position of the strike plate to the lock, mark the location of the plate on the door jamb.

8. Chisel holes to receive the latch and the dead bolt.

9. Fasten the strike plate with screws.

Door Painting

[SEE PAINTS & PAINTING.]

Doors

Doors are used to prevent or permit entry to a building or room. Most doors swing on hinges, although sliding, folding and pocket doors have become popular because they take up less space. Door frames may be made of wood, as are flush and panel doors, or metal, as sliding or screen doors. Glass or plastic panels are often added to let in light or create a decorative effect. Most doors are factory-produced and come ready to install.

FLUSH & PANEL DOORS

Doors may be classified according to type, size, placement and function. The two general types of doors are flush and panel. Flush doors consist of a wood frame with material sheets on both sides and no paneling or molding as trim. Panel doors, also called stile-and-rail doors, have stiles and rails with one or more panels. Rails are horizontal sections grooved to hold panels, while stiles are vertical sections. Mullions are the bars dividing the panels.

DOOR SIZES

The largest door in a house is usually the garage door, with a minimum width of eight feet and height of 6'4'' in residential garages. A two-car garage is usually 16 feet wide. Exterior doors of homes are usually 6'8'' or sometimes seven feet high with widths of three feet for main entrances and 2'8'' and 2'6'' for rear and service doors. Specifications for interior doors range from widths of two feet for closets and bathrooms to 2'6'' for bedrooms, with heights of 6'8''.

DOOR TYPES

The function and placement of a door partially determines the particular type of door to be used. Most front entrance doors are focal points and should be attractively suited to the architecture of the building. Because swinging, hinged doors require room to open, folding and sliding doors are used in areas where space is a problem. Storm and screen doors are used at front or rear entrances to let light or air in while still serving as protective shields against weather, insects, etc. Decorative doors, such as Dutch and basket weave doors, are selected to fit a particular need or design.

HAND OF A DOOR

The hand of a door is determined from a position outside an entrance door and on the hall side of an interior door. If the door hinges are on the left side of the door and it opens inward, it is a left-hand door. The hinges of a right-hand door are on the right and the door opens inward. A left-hand reverse door has the hinges on the left and the door opens outward. If the hinges are on the right and the door opens outward, it is a right-hand reverse. This information is needed when selecting handed locks.

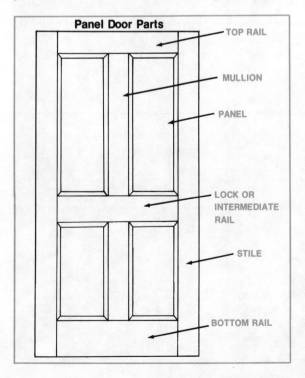

Panel Door Parts

TOP RAIL

MULLION

PANEL

LOCK OR INTERMEDIATE RAIL

STILE

BOTTOM RAIL

DOOR INSTALLING

There may be times when the homeowner will want to either replace an old door or, in the process of remodeling, install a new door. A door must have at least ¹/₂ inch clearance above the finished floor or carpet. In order to properly fit the door, set it into the jamb or frame so that it is square or plumb. Mark the locations of hinges and knob. Remove the door from the jamb, install the hinges and set the door back into the opening. Fasten the hinge to the jamb, making sure that the door swings freely. The knob and lock should be installed after the door has been hung.

This remodeling door comes with frame and weather-stripped stops and sill.

Courtesy of The Stanley Works.

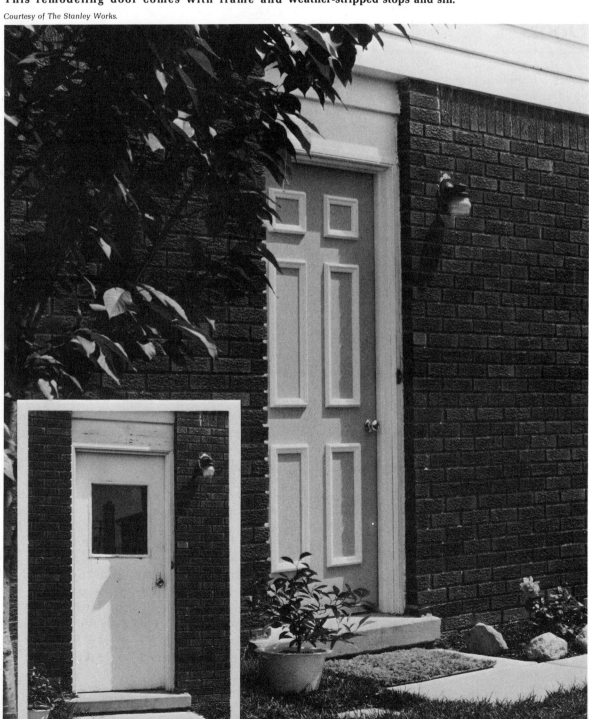

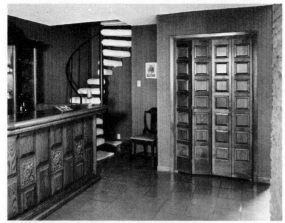

Courtesy of Ideal Company

Folding Doors

COMMON DOOR REPAIRS

Doors require frequent repairs due to their constant use. The most common problem is sticking, often caused by warping and shrinking. A door will stick when the weather becomes humid and the wood expands. The easiest way to cure a sticking door is to move or adjust the hinges. There is a general rule to follow when repairing a sticking door. If the door sticks on top, put a piece of cardboard or other material, called a shim, behind the bottom hinge. A shim should be put on the top hinge if the door sticks at the bottom.

Another method of repairing sticking doors is planing. Plane a small amount off at a time on the hinge side because it is less conspicuous and

does not involve the lock. If the door has to be heavily planed, take it off the hinges. Sometimes a simple lubrication using spray lubricant or a lube stick will stop a door from sticking.

To stop a door rattle, felt may be attached to the top of the door stop. If the door does not latch, filing the strike plate may help. Weather stripping may have to be replaced to keep a tight fit.

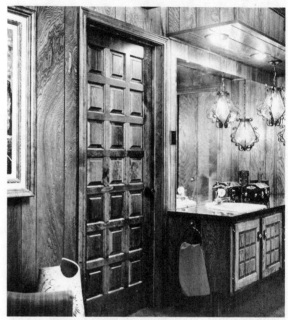

Courtesy of Ideal Company

Panel Door

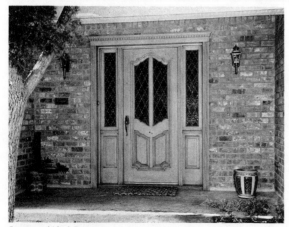

Courtesy of Ideal Company

Traditional Design

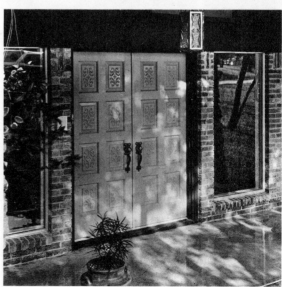

Courtesy of Ideal Company

Double Doors

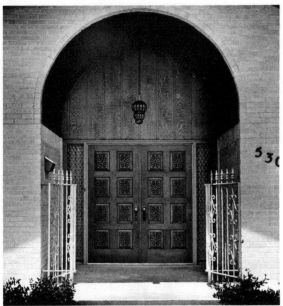

Couresty of Ideal Company

Residential Entrance

Door Stop

Door stop is a molding that attaches to a door frame jamb, providing a raised surface to prevent the door from swinging through. It is installed so that it tapers away from the door. *SEE ALSO MOLDING & TRIM.*

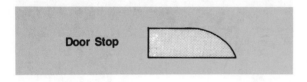

Door Trim

Door trim is the exposed finished wood around a door. The style of trim chosen depends mostly on the homeowner's taste and the architecture and room design of the house. Trim may have simple lines and a flat surface, or a scrolled pattern with carvings. Generally, the door casing and the door are purchased together and inserted to form one piece so the door and trim

match. Use headless finishing nails when installing door trim. *SEE ALSO MOLDING & TRIM.*

Dormer Construction

When a growing family requires more living space, the attic is a natural place to look. Unfortunately, most attics are rather dismal places, with only a window at each end to provide ventilation and natural light. And, especially in story-and-a-half homes, the sharply pitched roof may limit ceiling height. The addition of a dormer solves these problems.

TYPES OF DORMERS

A dormer is a projection from a sloping roof, with a vertical wall in which a window or windows can be installed. There are two basic types: *gable dormers,* normally with a single window and a peaked roof, and *shed dormers,* usually with a flat, sloping roof and extending the width of the room, and often of the entire house. Within these two definitions are many variations. Gable dormers may be built with hip roofs and, sometimes, flat roofs. In some instances, a shed dormer may have a gable roof. The type of dormer you build will depend on the space needed, the planned interior layout and the architectural style of the house.

PLANNING A DORMER

Gable dormers can be installed on either the front or the back of your house, and will usually add an attractive design element to an otherwise uninteresting roofline. Shed dormers are generally less attractive and are seldom used in the front of the house, but there are exceptions.

Gable dormers should be spaced so that they give a pleasing proportion to the home's elevation. In most cases, this means equidistant from the ends of the roof when there are two dormers. When there are more than two, intermediate dormers should be equally spaced between the outer ones for a symmetrical appearance. The dormers can be built out to the roof edge or be

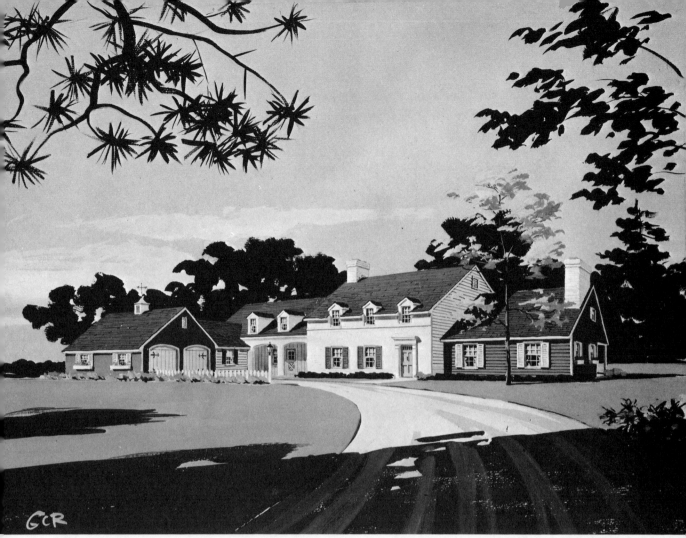

This large home illustrates the usage of gable dormers. The three dormers in the main roof are equally spaced. In the wing at the left, two dormers provide the needed light and ventilation for a spacious bedroom-dressing-bath area.

set back into the roof, but they should all be the same depth.

Shed dormers can be as wide as you wish, up to the full width of the house. The major advantage of this type of dormer is the increased headroom it gives to the entire attic. Most often, shed dormers extend from the roof peak. Like gable dormers, they can be built out to the edge of the roof or set back; this will be largely a matter of appearance, as well as space requirements. As a rule of thumb, narrower shed dormers look better if they are set back from the roof edge.

If your home has a hip roof, you can build a shed dormer the width of the roof peak. Or you can build gable dormers into either front or sides to provide light and ventilation for an attic room.

When you have decided on the appearance of your dormer addition, make a simple drawing showing all framing members. Wall framing is conventional 2 x 4 stud construction. Roof framing for most gable dormers is also of 2 x 4s. Larger shed dormers will require 2 x 6 rafters and ceiling joists and, where the span is exceptionally great, 2 x 8s. For shed roofs, allow a pitch of at least one inch per foot. Where pitch is minimal, roll roofing is preferable to asphalt shingles. Use the drawing to estimate material needs, including plywood or tongue-and-groove sheathing, roofing and siding to match the rest of your home.

There is one more important step that must be taken before you start the actual work on the dormer addition. Just as with any other major

431

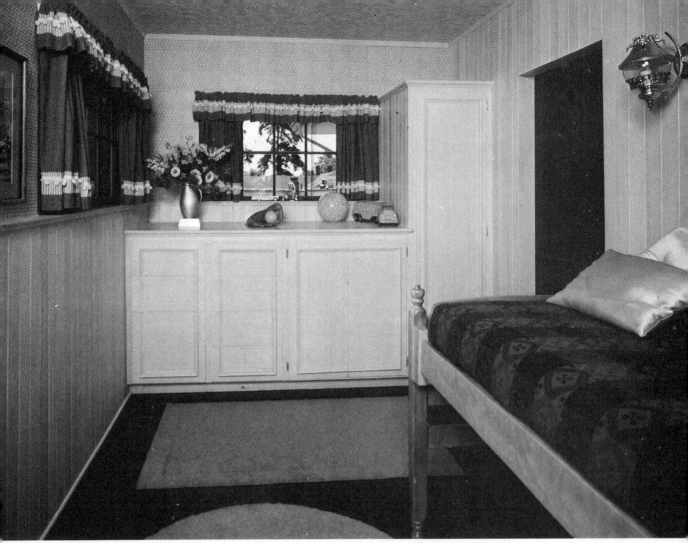

A shed dormer on the back of a small story-and-a-half home added enough space for this youngster's bedroom. Built-ins make the most of the available footage.

home alteration project, you must first check with your local building department to see if there are any special restrictions or requirements concerning the type of addition you intend to construct. The building code may specify certain lumber sizes for joists, rafters and other structural members, as well as maximum allowable spacing of these members. You may also be required to obtain a building permit for the project; however, this is normally a simple formality.

BUILDING A GABLE DORMER

The dormer opening must be flanked by rafters. If existing rafters are not located where the opening will be cut, install new ones, nailing to the ridge beam and the wall plate.

The opening can be cut from inside the attic. Carefully measure and mark the area of the cut. Drill a starter hole alongside the rafter, then cut through the roof sheathing with a keyhole saw to begin the cut, and finish with a crosscut saw or a power utility saw. (Be forewarned that, since you will be cutting through asphalt roof shingles at the same time, the saw blades will suffer.) Cut across the opening at top and bottom (this step is not necessary if *roofers,* tongue-and-groove boards, are used for sheathing rather than plywood), but do not cut through the rafters. Knock out the roof sheathing. Salvage as many shingles as possible for later use; these will provide a match for the existing roof.

Make a temporary support for the ridge beam by

wedging a post of doubled 2 x 4s between the floor and the ridge, centering it on the dormer cutout. The post should be placed over a floor joist and above the main bearing wall of the house; in most story-and-a-half designs, this wall is directly below the ridge beam.

Saw through rafters at the top of the roof opening, cutting them off at a 90-degree angle. Saw through rafters at the lower end of the roof opening, cutting them at a plumb (vertical) angle. Nail a header, the same size as the rafters (usually 2 x 6), between the flanking rafters at the top of the opening, and nail through this into the cut-off ends of the rafters. Nail a second header to the first and to the flanking rafters. Nail a header at an angle between the flanking rafters and to the plumb-cut ends at the lower end of the opening. Since this header will also serve as a sill for the window framing, it must be made $1/2$ inches wide (the width of the 2 x 4 framing members). Nail $1/2$ inch spacers (scrap wood or plywood) to the face of the header, then nail a second header to the first and to the flanking rafters to make this $3^1/2$ inch width. Now nail a second rafter alongside the flanking rafter at each side to complete the opening.

Assemble the side walls on the floor, nailing 2 x 4 studs between bottom and top plates. Lift the framing assembly into position and nail to the floor and to the flanking rafters, after first checking with a level to make sure studs are perfectly vertical. Nail the 2 x 4 front plate on top of the side frames. Double both the side and front plates to form a dovetailed corner, securely locking the structure. Nail studs between the top plate and the bottom header to frame the opening for the window.

Cut one end of the 2 x 4 dormer ridge beam at an angle to fit against the header at the top of the roof opening. Nail the ridge beam to the header, with the other end resting on a stud nailed to the front top plate. Check with a level to make sure the ridge beam is perfectly horizontal. Cut two front rafters and nail into place between the wall plates and the ridge beam.

Measure and cut two valley rafters. (These will require compound cuts; they can be laid out with

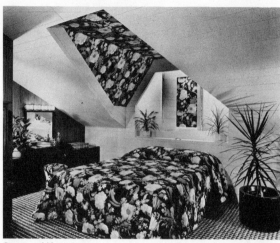

Courtesy of Masonite

The gable dormer built into the front of this attic becomes a focal point of the room's decor, as well as providing adequate ventilation and headroom in the sleeping area.

a framing square or by the trial-and-error method.) Nail valley rafters in place.

Cut and install remaining full dormer rafters, spaced on 16-inch centers. Cut the dormer jack rafters, measuring each one individually, and nail between the dormer ridge beam and the valley rafters. Cut the jack rafters to fit between the main roof ridge beam and the valley rafters and nail in place.

Cut and fasten both the gable studs and studs to fit below the window opening. Nail ceiling joists inside the gable to complete the framing. The support under the ridge beam may now be removed. Nail sheathing to the walls and roof of the dormer, and fill in the main roof around the top of the dormer where original sheathing was removed. (*Nailers,* boards fastened alongside the rafters, may have to be provided to back up the sheathing patches.)

Nail metal apron flashing at the base of the dormer, extending up the dormer wall at least 6 inches (or up to the window opening), over the first course of roof shingles below the dormer and under the next course of shingles at the sides of the dormer. Place individual pieces of flashing or shingle tin under subsequent shingle courses, with each piece over-lapping the one below it. The flashing should be bent sharply so

433

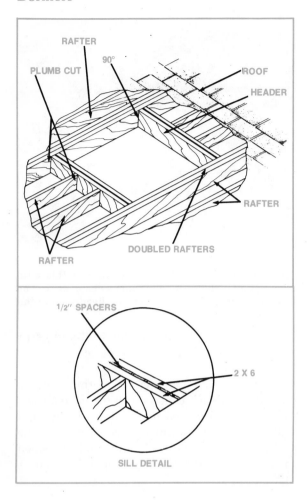

then nail securely. Attach felt paper to the outer walls of the dormer, starting at the bottom. Finish the walls with siding to match the body of the house, overlapping the flashing and butted tightly against the window frame.

Staple batt insulation between the studs, around the window and between the ceiling joists of the dormer. Cover the dormer walls with gypsum board or paneling to complement the decor of the attic room.

BUILDING A SHED DORMER

Construction of a shed dormer is somewhat more complex because of its larger size. Existing rafters cannot be cut until a new structure is in place. And, since you are literally raising the roof, you must be sure to enclose the area quickly, or to take some measures to protect it from inclement weather.

If you can muster a crew of willing workers (not necessarily professionals, but reasonably dextrous), you should be able to have your shed dormer erected and enclosed in a day (a sunny day, of course, with no precipitation in the forecast).

As with a gable dormer, the shed dormer must be flanked by rafters at each end. If none are so located, install new rafters as required, nailing to the ridge beam and the wall plate. Snap a chalkline on the attic subfloor where the new wall is to be located. Select a straight piece of 2 x 4 lumber and secure it to the floor along this line with 12d nails driven into floor joists. (This step does not apply if the shed dormer is to extend to the outside wall of the house; in this case, the new framing members are fastened directly to the existing wall plate.) Select another straight piece of 2 x 4 lumber for the top plate and lay it alongside the plate that has been nailed to the floor (or lay it out individually if there is no floor plate). Mark locations of studs simultaneously

that it fits tightly against both the roof and the dormer walls. When the top of the dormer wall is reached, a valley flashing is set over the joint between the main roof and the dormer roof, under the shingles on the main roof. (Flashings are available from building supply stores, or you can have them made to your specifications at a sheet metal shop.)

Cover the roof of the dormer with roofing felt. Install asphalt shingles, matching as closely as possible the original roof shingles. Start the shingle application at the roof edges and work toward the ridge, overlapping joints of the shingles. Fill in shingles where the original roof was cut out, using those shingles salvaged from the original section.

Set the window in its opening. Check with a level to make sure that it is plumb and square,

Courtesy of Celotex Corporation.

Even a large attic like this one benefits from the addition of a gable dormer. The ceiling height is maintained at the window area, allowing installation of a full-length window for maximum natural light.

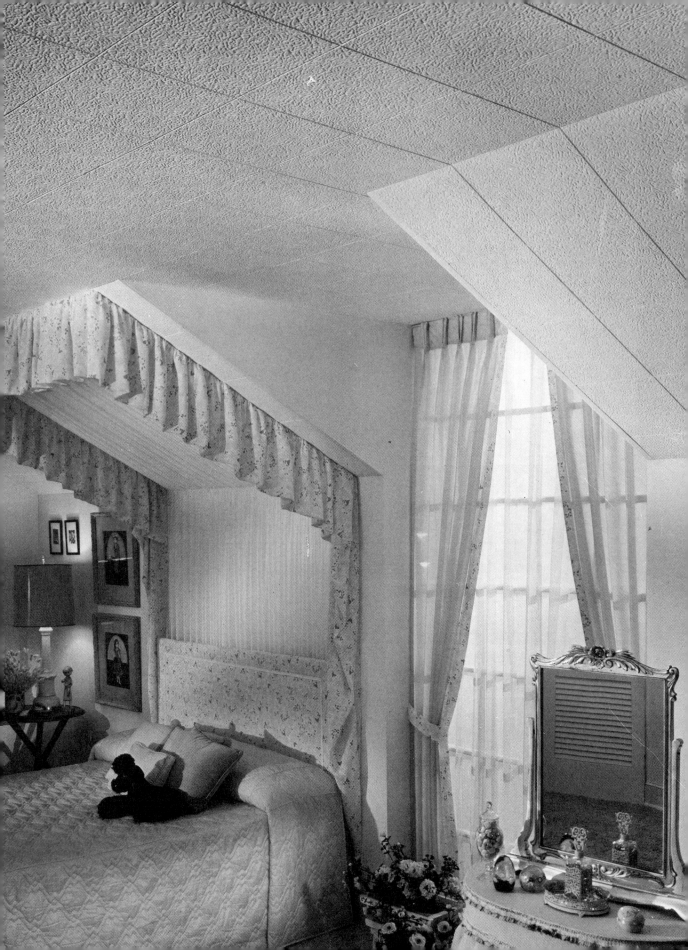

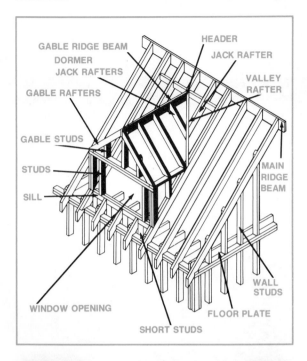

GABLE RIDGE BEAM
DORMER
JACK RAFTERS
GABLE RAFTERS
GABLE STUDS
STUDS
SILL
WINDOW OPENING
SHORT STUDS
HEADER
JACK RAFTER
VALLEY RAFTER
MAIN RIDGE BEAM
WALL STUDS
FLOOR PLATE

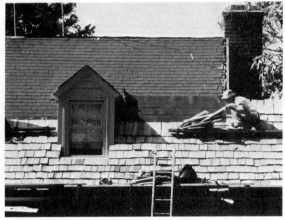

Courtesy of Red Cedar Shingle & Handsplit Shake Bureau

Here, new cedar shingles are being applied over the old roofing. Note how the shingles are cut around the dormer. Flashing at the dormer sides prevents leakage.

on both plates, by placing a framing square across the two 2 x 4s and making a pencil line, then marking an "X" on each plate on the side of the line where the stud is to go. Studs should be immediately adjacent to existing rafters, normally spaced on 16 inch centers.

Cut the required number of studs to length. Cut framing members for window openings, and code them so that you can locate them quickly as

needed. Window framing consists of full-height studs on each side, short studs up to $1\frac{1}{2}$ inch below the opening, a flat 2 x 4 sill between the flanking studs, filler studs inside the opening, a header of doubled 2 x 4s with $\frac{1}{2}$ inch spacers of wood or plywood sandwiched between, and short studs between the header and top plate.

With all preparations made and the work crew assembled, open the roof. Cut along the flanking rafters, drilling a starter hole and using a keyhole saw, then a crosscut saw or a power utility saw. If the roof sheathing is of tongue-and-groove boards, knock them loose from inside. If the sheathing is plywood, you will have to make horizontal cuts before prying loose the panels.

With the roof opened, toenail the studs to the floor plate, placing them on the X-marked sides of the pencil lines; use five 8d nails at each stud. Nail the top plate to the studs, again following the pencil marks, using two 12d nails through the plate into each stud. Similarly assemble the side walls of the shed dormer, nailing to the flanking rafters and dovetailing the top plates into the main wall plates as in ordinary wall construction. Check frequently with a level to make sure that the work is plumb and square.

Have one or two of the workers complete framing the window openings, while the rest install ceiling joists. These are toenailed to the top of the wall plate and fastened at the other end to rafters on the opposite side of the ridge beam. Nail 1 x 2s across the tops of the joists to tie them all together.

Set two new end rafters in place immediately alongside the flanking rafters and nail to the ridge beam, the flanking rafters and the top plate of the new wall, using 12d or 16d nails. Next fasten remaining rafters in place, but do not nail to existing rafters, only to the ridge beam and the plate. With joists and new rafters in place, nail existing rafters to the new studs, then cut them off flush with the insides of the studs and pry or cut them loose from the ridge beam.

Starting at the edge of the new roof, nail sheathing across the rafters, overlapping the ends of the rafters by at least the thickness of the

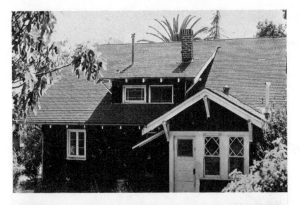

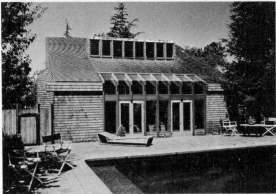

Courtesy Red Cedar Shingle & Handsplit Shake Bureau

This 1914-vintage home with its small shed dormer was completely transformed with new siding, lots of glass and a multi-windowed dormer to open up the second floor for modern living.

wall sheathing and a fascia board (or more, depending on the amount of roof overhang in your design). Cover the sheathing with 15-pound felt, lapping the first piece over the edge of the sheathing. Cover the felt with roll roofing, overlapping the strips 2 inches and applying roofing cement along all seams and over nail heads. The last strip of roofing will be under the existing ridge cap. (If the shed dormer starts below the peak of the roof, metal flashing must be inserted under the old shingles and over the new roof.)

Apply sheathing to the dormer walls. Cover the sheathing with building felt. Install the windows, checking carefully with a level for proper positioning. Install flashing along the front wall of the dormer, over the existing shingles. Install individual strips of flashing under roof shingles along the sides of the dormer, with each piece overlapping the one below it. With the shed

dormer now effectively weatherproofed, you can proceed at a more leisurely pace to install siding to match or complement the rest of the house.

Inside, do all electrical wiring before enclosing the walls. Staple batt insulation between wall studs and between ceiling joists. Finish the walls with gypsum board, paneling or other material to match the rest of your new attic room.

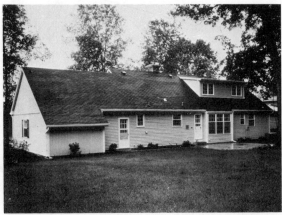

Courtesy of Mastic Corporation

A narrow shed dormer set back into the roof of this story-and-a-half home provides sufficient headroom for an added bedroom and bath.

A DO-IT-ALL-YOURSELF DORMER

If you are unable to find enough capable help for a one-day roof-raising, or if for some reason you prefer to stretch the job over a longer period of time, there is another method of adding a shed dormer without having to be concerned about the weather. You can build the new dormer with the old roof still in place, then remove the old roof from inside at your leisure. This involves making a number of small holes in the old roof, but these can be covered with lumber or plywood scraps and tarpaper when rain clouds appear or when you leave the job for a few days.

If the outer wall of the dormer will be directly over the wall of the existing house, simply remove the lower roof boards or plywood sheathing up to the wall plate. If the dormer wall is to be set back into the roof, you will have to lay down a floor plate (as in the conventional shed

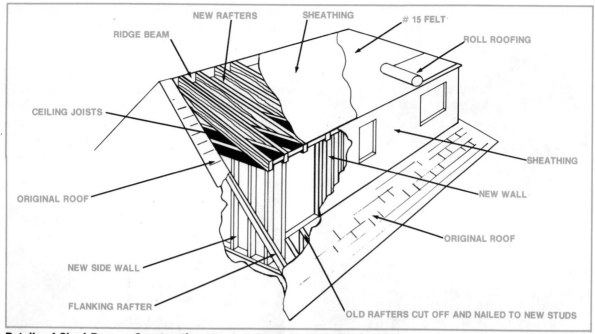

Details of Shed Dormer Construction (Dormer Set Back From Roof Edge)

dormer construction discussed previously) and cut individual holes through the roof for each stud. This will require some careful measuring and mathematics, but it allows you to do the job with a minimum of assistance (albeit an extra expenditure of your time).

Erect the end studs and a few intermediates (at four foot intervals will be adequate), toenailing the studs to the floor plate or nailing to the wall plate alongside the joists; in the latter case, where the new wall is directly over the old, do not nail into the existing rafters—these will be removed later.

Nail a top plate across the studs, using temporary braces nailed to the roof to keep the structure perfectly plumb. Nail doubled top plates for the side walls of the dormer to the top plate and, through holes cut in the roof, to the rafters that flank the dormer. Dovetail side-wall plates with a double plate on the dormer's long wall to lock the structure together.

Complete the stud framing of the long wall, framing around windows in the conventional manner discussed previously. Remove roof boards or cut away plywood sheathing along the

peak of the roof where the dormer will be built. Attach dormer rafters at each end by toenailing to the new wall plate and the existing ridge beam, as well as to the flanking rafters. Fasten intermediate rafters, nailing to the plate and the ridge beam but not to the existing rafters, which will be removed.

With all rafters secured, install roof sheathing and roofing as in conventional dormer construction. This will provide a considerable degree of protection for the old roof. But if a storm threatens, you can still cover cut-open areas of the roof with tarpaper, held down by batten strips.

To install framing for the end walls of the dormer, cut out only those portions of the old roof between the existing rafters where the end walls will be. Nail a floor plate directly beneath the already fastened top plates, and toenail studs between the two plates.

Install sheathing, windows, felt, flashing and siding as in conventional construction. With the new dormer now entirely enclosed, the remainder of the work is done from inside the attic.

Remove the old roof sheathing; you will probably have to cut it into manageable sizes before knocking it loose from the rafters. A pinch bar or wrecking bar is a help in prying up the sheathing.

Install ceiling joists (2 x 6s unless the span is quite short), nailing them to the plate and the new rafters at one end and to the existing rafters on the opposite side of the ridge beam at the other. With all the joists in place, you can proceed to remove the old rafters in the dormer area. If the dormer wall is not built over the outer wall of the house, first nail the rafters to the studs of the new wall. Then cut rafters flush with the insides of the studs. Pry rafters loose from the ridge beam with a wrecking bar. Complete the inside of the attic room as above.

CHIMNEYS AND OTHER OBSTRUCTIONS

Often a chimney, a vent pipe or an exhaust vent will protrude through the roof in the area where the dormer is to be built. This is particularly true of shed dormers in the rear of the house, where most such obstructions are located.

In the case of a chimney, it is relatively simple to box around. This is done by fastening headers between the rafters on each side of the chimney, similar to the headers between the existing rafters around the chimney that will be removed. The interrupted rafters are then toenailed to the headers. Most building codes require a clearance around the chimney, usually about 2 inches between the masonry and any wood structural members. This space is covered over with flashing. The flashing should extend into the masonry joints of the chimney. If the chimney needs repointing, insert the flashing into the joint before mortaring. Otherwise, cover the chimney-flashing joint with asphalt compound. Sides and rear of the flashing are placed under the roofing; the front is on top of the roofing. Cement all around the flashing with asphalt roofing compound.

The height of a chimney is determined by the highest point of the roof. Since you will not be raising this highest point, it will not be necessary to add to the chimney's height. However, in the case of vent pipes and exhaust vents, it may be necessary to add piping or metal ductwork to bring these above the new roof level. Just how this is done will depend on the nature of the pipe or duct to be lengthened. Where these items go through the new roof, flashing must be used. Special flashings for such purposes are available at building supply stores; exhaust vents often have flashing collars which are fitted into the roofing just as regular flashing.

Double Coursing Side Walls

Double coursing side walls is a roofing technique of laying two layers of shingles on the sidewall direction of the roof for sturdier construction. The shingles of the second layer are staggered so that the joints do not fall directly on top of the joints of the first layer. *SEE ALSO SHAKES & SHINGLES.*

Double Header

A double header is used in rough framing for extra support. It is two pieces of lumber which run perpendicular to the joists and are placed either

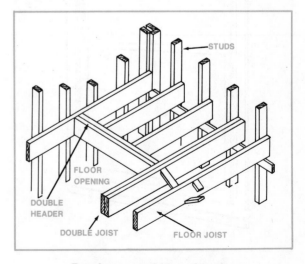

Framing around Floor Opening

at the top and bottom of a window or at the top of a door opening. *SEE ALSO WALL & CEILING CONSTRUCTION.*

Double-Hung Window

A double-hung window has two sashes which slide vertically and are controlled by springs or weights. The upper sash slides down on the outside while the lower sash slides up on the inside. Regulating these sashes are pulleys with cords and weights or springs. Screens and storm sash are on the outside of a double-hung window and do not interfere with the window's operation.

Double-hung windows are popular because they are inexpensive, easy to operate and suitable for almost any architectural design. Most are made of wood, although aluminum ones are manufactured.

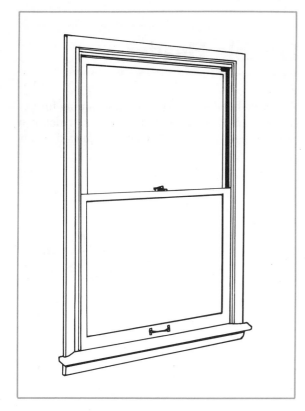

Double-Hung Window

Double Joist

A double joist consists of two beams placed side by side for additional support in framing under floors or ceilings. When a partition runs parallel to the joists, double joists are used under it. They are called trimmers when used around openings in the floor frame for stairways and fireplaces. *SEE ALSO FLOOR CONSTRUCTION.*

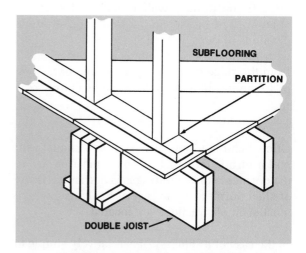

Partition supported by double joist.

Double Plate

A double plate is used in framing for extra support under rafters and joists. Both pieces of the

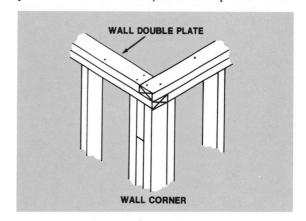

Lap double plate joints at corners.

double plate should be long and straight and held together by 10d nails spaced 16 inches apart and near both ends. Joints for upper plates should be at least four feet from joints on the lower plates. These double plates also help secure the wall frame. *SEE ALSO WALL & CEILING CONSTRUCTION.*

Double-Pole Switch

The double-pole switch opens or closes the circuit in two wires simultaneously. It makes or breaks contact in both the hot or live wire and the ground wire. A single-pole switch breaks or completes the circuit only in the hot wire. Double-pole switches are sometimes used indoors to control outside lighting. *SEE ALSO SWITCHES & OUTLETS.*

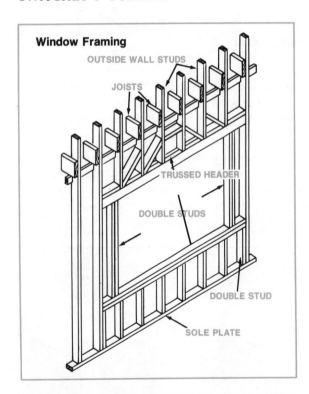

Window Framing

OUTSIDE WALL STUDS

JOISTS

TRUSSED HEADER

DOUBLE STUDS

DOUBLE STUD

SOLE PLATE

Double Stud

A double stud provides support that is missing in framework because of openings, such as win-

dows and doors. In addition to necessary support, double studs also eliminate vibrations when a door is closed. *SEE ALSO WALL & CEILING CONSTRUCTION.*

Douglas Fir

Douglas fir is a strong, pliable softwood that is grown on the Pacific Coast from Oregon north through British Columbia. It is yellow in color with reddish markings. The grain is straight and close, with heavy contrast between spring and summer growth. Douglas fir is used primarily for framing, trim, doors and veneers. This wood machines and sands poorly and is seldom used for finish. *SEE ALSO WOOD IDENTIFICATION.*

Dovetail

The dovetail is a strong joint primarily used in furniture construction. Various kinds of dovetails include the single dovetail, the through dovetail, the lap dovetail, the multiple dovetail and the blind dovetail.

The single dovetail is constructed by first marking and cutting the pin, which is the flared tenon at the end of the board, with either a fine-toothed backsaw, a sabre saw or a dovetail saw. Softwood pins should be angled one inch for each $1/6$ inch, and hardwood pins should be angled one inch for each $1/8$ inch. Mark the pin shape on the end of the board to be joined with a pencil or knife to achieve a precise cut. Saw down the cutout shoulders of the dovetail and cut the middle of the waste to aid in chiseling. Make sure the joint fits correctly, then glue and clamp it. Remove any excess glue so that the amount of sanding is reduced.

The single dovetail can also be cut by using a jigsaw with a tilt adjustment. Place the blade of the saw vertically when cutting the pin and mark the pin shape on the second board end. Adjust the table tilt to the angle which is marked and cut in-

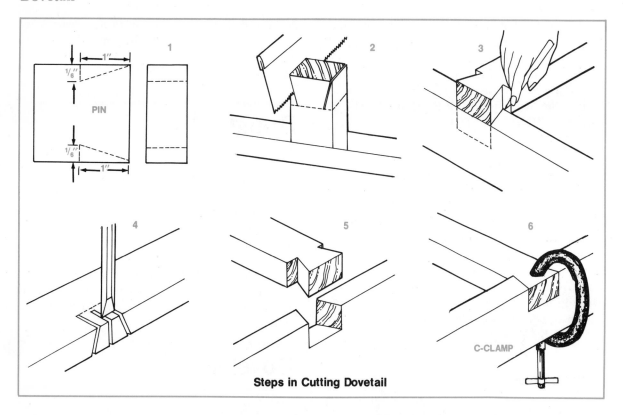

Steps in Cutting Dovetail

ward. Then chisel out the waste material. A router with a dovetail bit may be used to cut small dovetails and multiple varieties quickly.

The through dovetail, which is the most durable and decorative corner joint, is used extensively for drawer backs and other cabinetwork. The "through" is basically a type of joining rather than an actual joint. Through dovetails may be either single or multiple.

Lap dovetails provide a neat edge when joining drawer and bookcase fronts, since one end of the joint laps over the other. In this joint, the sides must be cut and planed to the length of the drawer, minus the lap thickness. The front should be cut and planed to the size of the area it is to fit.

The multiple dovetail is formed and used much the same way as the single, except that more joining parts are cut. Because of the additional dovetails, the multiple joint has more holding power than the single.

A blind or secret dovetail joint is used primarily

on high quality furniture. When this joint is cut and fit properly, it is not visible because the joining parts are hidden by an overlap in the wood. *SEE ALSO FURNITURE MAKING.*

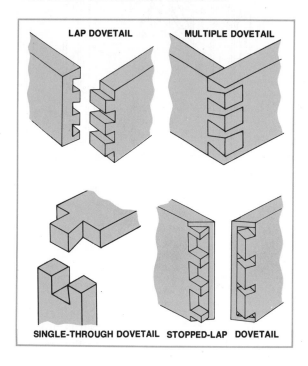

LAP DOVETAIL   **MULTIPLE DOVETAIL**

SINGLE-THROUGH DOVETAIL   **STOPPED-LAP DOVETAIL**

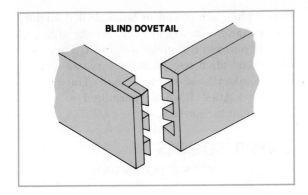

BLIND DOVETAIL

Dovetail Saw

The dovetail saw, a smaller version of the back-saw, ranges in blade length from about 8″ to 12″ with 15 points per inch. As the name implies, it is designed for precision dovetail joint work. Although sometimes called a cabinet saw, this tool is also useful for making models, toys and other small-scale, finely detailed projects. *SEE ALSO HAND TOOLS.*

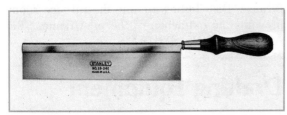

Courtesy of The Stanley Works

Dovetail Saw

Doweling Jig

A doweling jig is a device which enables the handyman to drill a series of holes exactly alike at the exact same distance apart. The jig comes equipped with a set of interchangeable guides to match bits which range from $3/16$″ to $1/2$″.

A doweling jig is indispensable in the making of doweled joints, without the help of a drill press. It allows the handyman to align the holes with

the precision needed to form the joint. *SEE ALSO PORTABLE POWER TOOLS;*

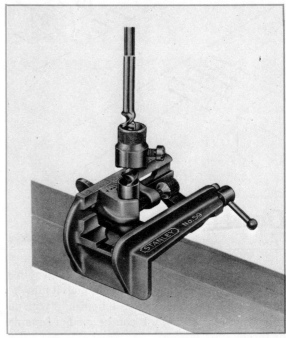

Courtesy of The Stanley Works

Doweling Jig

Dowel Joint

A dowel joint is made when two pieces of wood are joined by dowels. More specifically, it is a butt joint with dowels in both sides. Used in good furniture and carpentry where an un-marred surface is important, dowel joints secure the wood pieces with no visible fastener. These invisible joints are called blind dowel joints. The receiving holes are made slightly longer than the dowel to accommodate the glue and slightly narrower for a tight fit. *SEE ALSO FURNITURE MAKING.*

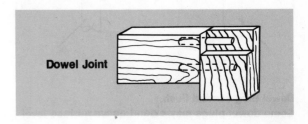

Dowel Joint

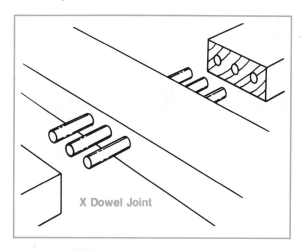

X Dowel Joint

Dowel Plug

A dowel plug is used to strengthen glued joints and to aid in their alignment. Although it may be any shape, a dowel plug is usually round with all edges slightly rounded. It can be made of maple or birch.

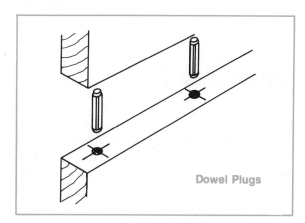

Dowel Plugs

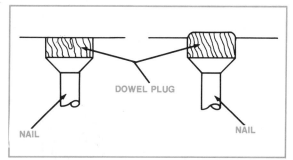

DOWEL PLUG

NAIL

NAIL

Dowel plug sanded flush.
Some dowel plugs may extend above surface level.

Dowel plugs are placed in holes drilled slightly longer than the dowel to allow for the glue and slightly narrower to make a tight fit. They may secure and align two joints or serve as a cover for a sunken head screw or nail. These plugs may be sanded flush or permitted to extend higher than the surface.

Downspouts
[SEE GUTTERS & DOWNSPOUTS.]

Draft Diverter

A draft diverter is used to prevent the pilot flame in a gas heating unit from being extinguished. A draft diverter appears as a funnel within a funnel, with a small space in between them. Air flows easily from the large portion of the funnel through the smaller part, but this movement is hindered when air flow is reversed, such as in a downdraft. When this occurs, air is dispersed through the spaces between the funnels and into the furnace room, instead of blowing into the furnace. Distributing air into the furnace room prevents the extinction of the pilot flame. *SEE ALSO HEATING SYSTEMS.*

Drafting Equipment

A basic set of drafting equipment includes a drawing board, a T-square, triangles, a protractor, a compass, a French curve, an architect's scale, drawing pencils and sandpaper pad, ruling pen, erasers and drawing paper. With this equipment, the home craftsman can turn out professional-quality plans for use in his shop.

Drafts, Heating Unit
[SEE HEATING SYSTEMS.]

Drainage Fields
[SEE SEPTIC SYSTEMS.]

Drainage Pipe

Drainage pipe carries liquids and waste away from the building. Sometimes made of the same materials, drainage pipe mainly differs from water-supply pipe in that it does not have to withstand high pressure. Separated into two types, drainage pipe is classified as indoor and outdoor pipe.

INDOOR PIPE

The indoor pipe types are copper and cast-iron. Copper pipe is thinner, lighter, easier to solder and less expensive than cast-iron. Cast-iron is heavy and extremely durable.

OUTDOOR PIPE

Outdoor drainage pipes include fiber, clay, vitrified and concrete tile. Available in short sections, these pipes are placed in a trench with an opening between each section. Roofing or tar paper is placed over the spaces to prevent soil from filling them when the trench is filled. When this pipe drainage field is attached to a waste liquid drainage system, liquids seep into the ground through the open joints.

Made from coal-tar elements in the better grades, fiber pipe is available with evenly spaced perforations in the side of the pipe to increase drainage. Clay tile is yellowish or red while vitrified tile is reddish-brown in color. Concrete tile is the lowest priced of the tiles. *SEE ALSO PLUMBING MATERIALS.*

Drainage Systems

A home drainage system includes all of the piping and accessories that carry liquid and solid wastes from the building. The design and construction of the drainage system is undoubtedly more important than the design and construction of the water distribution system because the waste matter within the drainage system may harbor disease micro-organisms, such as those responsible for cholera and dysentery. In addition, the decomposition of the organic wastes in the pipes generates gases that are either poisonous or explosive, or both.

Each fixture in a house is drained by a separate *fixture drain*. These drain lines usually lead to a common *branch drain* (or waste stack) that carries the liquid wastes to the main *building drain*, which in turn carries the wastes to the *building sewer*, which is that part of the drainage system that lies outside the house.

The branch drains may or may not discharge their wastes into a *soil stack*, which is a separate pipe into which is discharged the solid wastes from the water closet; whether the branch drain does discharge into the soil stack depends on the size and layout of the plumbing system. Also included in the drainage system are *traps* and *vent pipes* (or *vent stacks*), the functions of which are described below. (Note: The term "stack" is used for any vertical drain line in a house drainage system.)

FIXTURE DRAINS

The fixture drains conduct liquid wastes from the individual fixtures to a branch drain (or waste stack). The minimum size of each fixture drain pipe is specified by local building codes according to the amount of water used in the fixture. Typical minimum pipe sizes are as follows:

Branch Drain (Waste Stack)	$1^1/_2$ in.
From Fixtures:	
Water Closet	3
Floor Drains, Shower Stall	2
Bathtub, Dishwasher, Kitchen Sink,	
Laundry Tub	$1^1/_2$
Lavatories	$1^1/_4$

Trap

Each fixture drain line has in it a trap that is located as close to the fixture as possible. Water closets usually have their own built-in traps. Traps are either S-shaped or P-shaped, depending on the way in which the drain line connects to its branch drain. The lower curve of the trap is sized to hold between 2 inches and 4 inches of water.

The purpose of the water in the trap is to seal off the drainage system and prevent sewer gases from making their way out of the system and into the house. These gases include methane, hydrogen sulfide, carbon monoxide, acetylene, ammonia, and carbon dioxide, among others. Methane, hydrogen sulfide, carbon monoxide, and acetylene are potentially explosive. Hydrogen sulfide and carbon monoxide can be poisonous. All of the gases can be asphyxiating in sufficient concentrations. The importance of properly installing the traps is obvious.

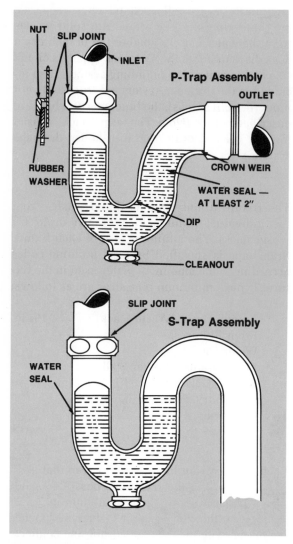

Each fixture must have a trap installed in its drain line. The two main types of trap are P-traps and S-traps, as illustrated.

VENT LINES (VENT STACKS)

It is possible, however, that a buildup of pressure within the drainage system will force the sewer gases past a trap and into the house. To prevent this from occurring, each fixture drain is also vented to the atmosphere, either through its own vent line or through a common vent line that serves several fixtures. The vent line (or lines) extends through the roof of the house by 6 to 8 in. The vent line may also be connected to the soil stack.

Soil Stack

A water closet must always be connected directly to its own soil stack, which will carry the solid wastes discharged from the water closet to the building drain. However, there is nothing that prevents a soil stack from also serving as the branch drain for other fixtures if the fixtures form a convenient group, as usually happens with the fixtures in the same bathroom. A soil pipe may also be connected to several water closets, if the water closets are located one above the other on different floors of a house. The minimum size of the soil stack is usually specified by local building codes; it is usually 3 or 4 in. in diameter. Soil pipes are usually made of cast iron and they are joined by bell-and-spigot connections.

BUILDING DRAIN

As much as possible, all of the drainage system consists of pipes (or stacks) that drop vertically through the walls of the house with a minimal number of bends until they connect to the main building drain located in the cellar or under the house. In fact, the building drain is, or should be, the only horizontal pipe in the entire house drainage system, and even the building drain isn't perfectly horizontal. It slopes at the rate of $1/8$ inch to $1/4$ inch per foot in order that the wastes can flow by gravity toward the house sewer. The degree of slope depends on the size of the piping, the larger pipes requiring less of an angle than the smaller pipes.

The building drain is usually made of extra heavy cast-iron piping joined by bell-and-spigot connections. The usual pipe size for houses is 3

or 4 inches. Just before the building drain leaves the building, a main trap is installed in the line to prevent sewer gases generated in the house sewer from entering the house drainage system.

CLEANOUTS

Because the main building drain is laid horizontally, it is possible for solid wastes to collect inside the pipe and thus restrict the discharge of wastes from the pipe. The building drain, therefore, always has at least one cleanout installed in it, usually at the end of the line where it connects with a waste stack or soil stack.

A cleanout is a fitting with a removable plug. To clear away any obstruction within the pipe, the plug is removed and a plumber's *auger,* or snake, is inserted into the pipe to scour away any solid matter in the pipe. The snake pushes the waste matter before it until this matter has been pushed into the house sewer. This process is aided by running water obtained from a hose inserted into the cleanout hole.

FLOOR DRAINS

Floor drains are usually installed in the cellar and laundry rooms, to drain away any water that may collect. The floors, of course, should slope toward the drain. The drain is usually covered with a removable grating that is flush with the floor. Each floor drain line should have a trap installed in it. Vent lines are usually unnecessary since any sewer gases in the lines tend to rise to the top of the house.

The size of the vent piping is usually specified by local building codes. The pipes are usually the same diameter as the drain lines they vent, though the minimum size for any vent line is usually specified to be 1^1/$_2$ inches and 3 inches for soil stack vents. If the drain pipe should be smaller than 1^1/$_2$ inches, the size of the vent pipe must be increased to at least 1^1/$_2$ inches before it pierces the roof. The reason for increasing the size of the vent lines is that the moist air within the drainage system is liable to freeze on the inside of the pipes during cold weather. If the frost buildup is excessive, the vent pipes may be frozen completely shut. If this happens, the vent system is entirely inoperative.

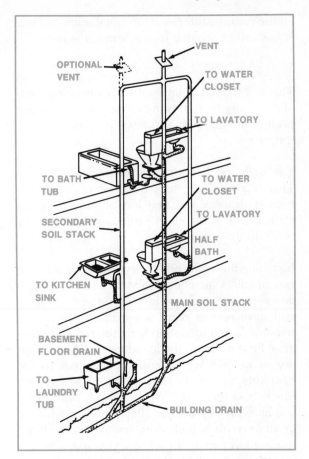

A vent-pipe circuit.

Drainpipe Leaks
[SEE PIPE LEAKS.]

Drains, Clogged
[SEE CLOGGED DRAINS.]

Draperies, Automatic
[SEE AUTOMATION.]

Drapery Hardware

There are four basic types of drapery and curtain rods. Each has several variations, depending

on the manufacturer, but the installation and use is basically the same for each manufacturer.

THE SASH ROD

This is a flat rod to be used for sheers, door curtains, or any type curtain or drapery with a short projection that has a runner to slide the rod through.

The sash rod has about a one-inch projection. This is a good rod to use for sheers behind a regular drapery rod that has already been installed. Due to the short projection, the drapery will still draw freely.

Installing the sash rod is very simple. There are two brackets for door windows and small windows up to 48 inches wide. The larger windows will have one or more supports to screw into window facing or wall to keep the rod from sagging. First measure the length of the sheer drapery or curtain which will regulate where the brackets are to be placed. There are two brackets, a left and a right bracket. Make sure you have the bracket that fits the side of window or door with which you are working. Each bracket has two small screws. If you are installing in sheetrock, instead of the screws, you should use plastic anchors.

THE BRASS ROD

Due to the shape of the end brackets the brass rod is one of the most difficult to install. The brass rod is used for a decorator look at the top of the drapery.

Brass rod brackets have a small flat section at the bottom of the bracket, with a hole for the bottom screw. The flat section starts to protrude forward; *this is the most important point of the brass rod*. The point where the bracket starts to protrude forward is the place to mark. This is the point where the top of the drapery will hang when the rod is placed in the bracket.

The bracket has two screws (top and bottom) and a rosette set screw. The set screw has to be loosened before the brass rod can fit the bracket. The rod has a small hole on each end that has to fit the bracket at that point, then tighten the ro-

sette-type set screw. The rod then will be locked in place.

The rod has a set number of rings that come with the rod, as well as the *master glides*. These master glides are the two pieces that make the drapery open, shut and overlap at the center. (If the drapery closes only in one direction, then there will be only one master glide.)

To figure the number of brass rings needed for a particular drapery, count the drapery pins and subtract six, if you have a two-way draw drapery. If you have a one-way draw drapery you will need three less rings than you have pins. The reason for this is, that on each of the drapery rods you will place two pins in the master glide, and one in the bracket. The one that fits in the bracket is called a return. If your drapery has four or five-inch return, you can adjust the projection of the bracket to compensate for this by loosening the screw on top of the protruding section of the brass rod allowing it to move forward or backward. The pin in the return of the drapery will fit in a small hole on the bottom protrusion of the bracket. There should always be one brass ring to the left and right on the end brackets.

After these rings have been placed, then the finial can be placed on the rod. The finial is the dome-looking hollow piece of brass. There are two of these for each rod. Make sure you have the right and left finial on the correct sides. One has a larger opening than the other because one side of the rod is slightly larger. There will also be extra supports for longer rods.

TRAVERSE

The traverse rod is very simple to install, and is the most widely used type of rod. A traverse rod is used with a plain pleat top or with a decorative over treatment such as a cornice, valance, or swag.

A traverse rod will come equipped with two brackets, a left and right. Be sure these are installed on the correct side of the window. Each bracket will have three screws and when installing in wood, the screws are all that will be necessary. Installing in sheetrock you will, as

with other rods, need the plastic anchors to prevent the screws from pulling out of the sheetrock.

Measure the length of drapery and place the top of the bracket at the length you want the drapery to hang. This rod also has two master glides and two returns. The projections of the returns can be adjusted by loosening the screw on the side of the bracket. There will be extra supports to keep the rod from sagging on wider windows. These are very simple to place in position. The support on this rod snaps over the rod with the flat part of the projection above the rod. The supports have two screws, and again the fastener must suit the wall material.

All types of traverse rods have a lock on the back of the left master glide. This lock is a little *T* shape on point of metal that points down toward the floor. After the drapery is in place with the master glide meeting at the middle of the window, pull the drapery cord (which is looped above the lock) out and over the lock, placing the cord between the lock and rod. This will keep the drapery from sliding to the left or right, and will always meet at the center of the window.

CURTAIN ROD

This rod is used when you do not want a drapery to traverse or draw. Use the curtain rod for a stationary drapery on which tie backs will be used. This rod can be bought as a single or double. When the double rod is used, the back rod is for the curtain, drapery or sheer. The front rod is used for a valance or over-treatment. You can use a pleated drapery, a curtain with pins or a run-on-the-rod type curtain on a stationary curtain rod.

This rod is installed very much like the sash rod. It has a left and right bracket and the top of the bracket will be placed where the top of the curtain or drapery will hang. The rod has a small hole on top of each return, which is part of a one-piece rod. The brackets have a point that fits into the rod return. The rod must be tilted slightly upward to let the points of the brackets fit into the hole on each end of the rod return. Then pull the rod down over the points of the brackets.

Drawer Construction
[SEE FURNITURE MAKING.]

Drawknife

The drawknife is for removing large amounts of unwanted wood stock before planing. It has a thin blade, generally 10- to 12-inches long, with wooden handles at either end running at right angles to the blade. To operate a drawknife, pull it toward you along the woodgrain; depth is determined by the angle at which it is held. The drawknife will take off more wood than a plane, but it is harder to control. *SEE ALSO HAND TOOLS.*

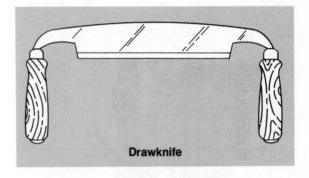

Drawknife

Drills

Hand and power drills are used for making holes in wood, metal and masonry work. Push and hand drills are good for accurate, slow drilling, primarily in wood and metal. Power drills can be controlled by an experienced worker to quickly make accurate holes not only in wood, plastic and metal, but in concrete and masonry, also. While both hand and power drills have assorted bits for boring holes of different sizes, some power drills have attachments for converting the drill into a circular saw, sabre saw, drill press, plane and sander. *SEE ALSO HAND TOOLS; PORTABLE POWER TOOLS.*

Drill Press

To buy a drill press based only on the need to drill holes is no longer realistic. If you use good techniques and choose wise accessories and jigs, the drill press can become one of the most versatile tools in your wood-working shop. Furthermore, it can easily become the second most important piece of equipment in your home workshop.

Its essential mechanism is a spindle that has a gripping device at the free end. In most cases, a key-operated, three-jaw chuck is used; but there are times when a substitution is necessary. Such a substitution can be needed when you are using mortising bits and chisels, which require special holding items, or when you are using router bits,

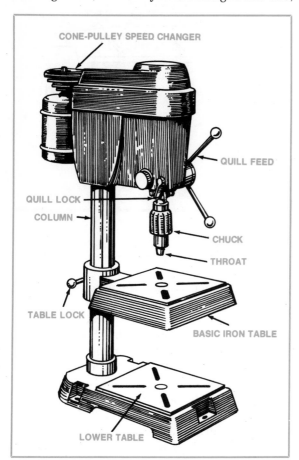

Basic parts of the drill press

which develop sufficient side thrust to warrant a special kind of chuck.

The *head* of the tool is composed of all the parts attached to the top of the column. The *table* is movable vertically, may be swung aside and, on some units, can be tilted. The *quill* houses the spindle and is moved downward by means of the *feed lever.* The return of the quill to normal position is done automatically through a spring action. There is usually an adjustment procedure so this action can be strengthened or weakened. Normally, the quill should return smoothly and without great shock.

It's possible to lock the quill in any extended position or to limit its extension through the use of the *depth stop,* almost always located on the outside of the quill housing. Cone pulleys allow you to select speeds. The more expensive drill press can have a built-in, variable speed mechanism.

The *base* of the drill press is the table-like casting on which the unit stands. The length of the *column* determines whether the drill press is a *bench model* or a *floor model.* The capacity of a drill press defines the distance from the column to the spindle center and from the chuck to the base. When the capacity is specified as 15″, the column-to-spindle distance is 7½″, which permits you to drill in the center of a 15″ wide board.

Adjustments on a drill press are mostly operational; the tool has to be accurate to begin with. If the table is adjustable, then you should check to see, when it is in normal position, that the angle between it and the spindle is 90°. One way to do this is to insert a length of ½″ drill rod in the chuck and then work with a square to achieve the correct angle.

Typical Drill-Press Tools

The most common drill-press tools are those you will use to form holes. These can range from the smallest twist drill to good-size fly cutters. Although you will use twist drills quite a bit, they really don't do the very best job in wood. They have to be used simply because no other

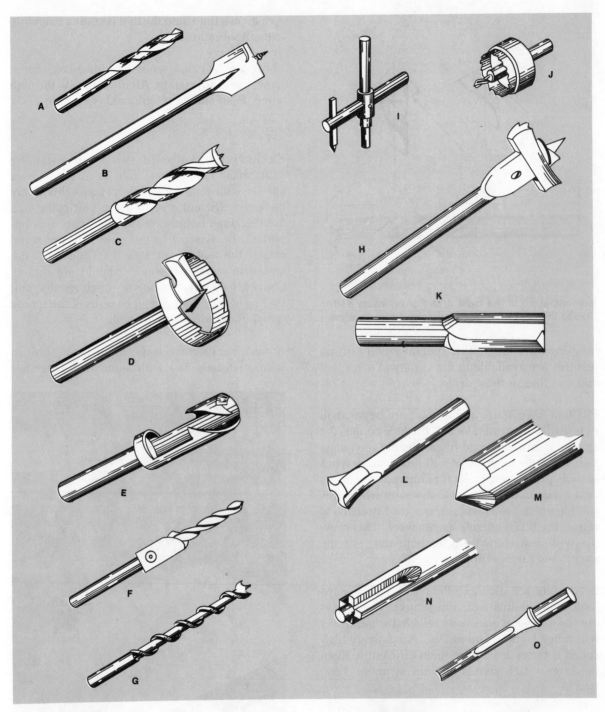

Typical drill-press tools
  A. twist drill
  B. spade bit
  C. spur machine drill
  D. multi-spur machine bit
  E. plug cutter
  F. twist drill w/adjustable countersink attachment
  G. solid-center bit

H. expansive bit (w/brad point)
I. fly cutter
J. hole saw
K. router bit
L. dovetail cutter
M. countersink
N. counterbore (w/pilot)
O. mortising chisel

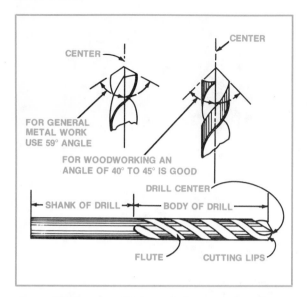

Nomenclature of the twist drill. For optimum performance in wood the point angle should be as shown.

In the diagram:
CENTER — CENTER
FOR GENERAL METAL WORK USE 59° ANGLE
FOR WOODWORKING AN ANGLE OF 40° TO 45° IS GOOD
DRILL CENTER
SHANK OF DRILL — BODY OF DRILL
FLUTE — CUTTING LIPS

hole-forming tools with special wood-cutting features are available in the variety of sizes that you can find in twist drills.

Bits that have spurs and a point are better than twist drills. The point locates the hole center; the spurs cut through wood fibers cleanly so you get a smooth hole to exact size. Flutes in these types of tools provide channels for chip removal so it's never wise to bury the bit to the point where this can't happen. On most jobs, it's good practice to retract the bit frequently as you work. This practice will clear chips from the hole and keep the cutter cool to prevent burning.

Spade bits are also excellent tools. They have long, sharp points and slim shanks. The blades are flat and good ones have relieved edges. A set will range from $1/4''$ up to $1^1/2''$. A relatively high speed is necessary to use them efficiently. Even the largest size should be run at about 1,500 rpm's.

When you want to drill large holes, you can think in terms of fly cutters and hole saws. The fly cutter is an adjustable item that rotates a vertical bit at the end of a horizontal arm. Slow speed is essential. Clamp the work and keep your hands clear as you start the machine at the slowest speed. If you have variable speeds, you can pick

up a bit at a time until the tool is cutting smoothly without vibration.

There are various types of hole saws, some fixed, some adjustable. All of them saw through wood. Feed should be minimal, speed slow.

Speeds and Feed

Excessive speeds on some tools can be dangerous. The general rule is to use slower speeds with larger tools. Sometimes this is not the most efficient way to use a particular tool, but it is done because the safety factor is as important. Be aware that the most efficient setup causes the tool to cut steadily. Unless it's designed to work that way, it should not scrape. Chatter, excessive vibration, rough results, and stalling of the motor can all be signs of the wrong speed, the wrong feed, or both.

At the other extreme, a speed that is too slow on some materials and with some tools, together

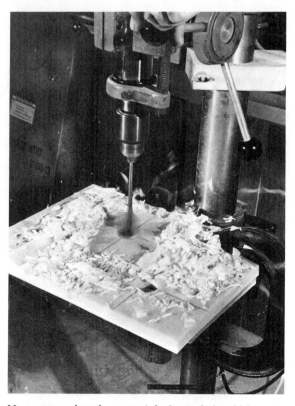

No matter what the material, the tool should be cutting constantly, taking a smooth, even bite. Correct speed and feed accomplish this easily.

with a hesitant feed, can cause the tool to rub, which won't do anything but dull the cutting edges. A slow speed with heavy feed can make the tool dig in, which can stall the motor or even cause breakage of the cutting edges.

There is an ideal speed and feed for any tool and any material, but drill speed charts should be used only as a general guide. Most importantly, the tool should be cutting steadily, smoothly and without excessive vibration, no matter what the material. Increasing or decreasing rpm's can even be justified by differences in boards from the same species.

Feed is the amount of pressure you apply to control penetration. It goes hand in hand with speed, and the best general rule to follow again is to keep the tool cutting, taking a bite evenly and without strain.

When doubt exists, always start at a slow speed. Increase the speed to the point where the situation is as ideal as you can make it.

Work Support

When the underside of the piece you are drilling doesn't matter, you can rest the work directly on the table and drill through when the table opening is aligned with the spindle. It really isn't a bad idea to use a scrap block between the work and the table, no matter what the job. The scrap block will protect the table and provide backup so the cutting tool will not splinter the underside of the work as it emerges.

It's permissible to hold the work by hand if the work size permits and the hole size is not excessive. Often, on long work, you can brace one edge of the work against the drill-press column, and this setup is sufficient to counteract any twist caused by the cutting.

Don't hesitate to use clamps to lock the work to the table. Using clamps provides a guarantee that, should the cutter grab in the hole particularly at the breakout point, the work will not be twisted out of your grasp. Such a possibility should be considered if you wish to avoid having your fingers rapped.

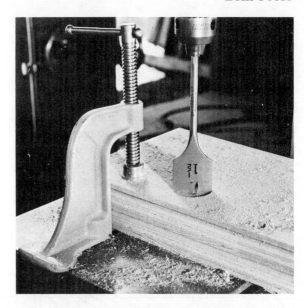

Clamping the work makes a lot of sense when forming large holes. It is good for both safety and accuracy. This type of clamp is made especially for drill-press work. It locks through the table slots and so may be positioned just about anywhere in relation to the work.

Many times, a fence, in addition to being a guide, acts as a safety mechanism. The fence doesn't have to be more than a straight piece of wood clamped to the table in position to gauge the edge distance of the hole. With such an item in place, any twisting force exerted by the drill will be taken by the fence, not your hands.

Drilling to Exact Depth

Drilling exactly to a predetermined depth can be done in one of two ways.

Set the work on the table and extend the drill so that its point contacts the work. Then set the nuts on the stop rod the additional amount needed to achieve the hole depth.

Another possibility is to make a mark on the side of the work to indicate hole depth. Extend the quill so the drill point touches the mark and set the stop-rod nuts accordingly.

After you have set up in one of these two ways, you can drill any number of holes knowing that each will be to the same depth.

Work Layout

Be careful and accurate when you are measuring and marking lines. The pencil you use should be about 3H and should always be sharp.

The easiest and most accurate method of marking a hole location is to draw intersecting lines that tell you the center of the hole. Puncture this point with an awl and position the point of the drill there. A combination square can be used to draw lines at right angles to an edge and may

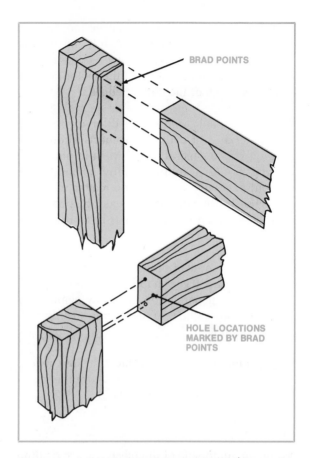

By tapping in brads at location points and then snipping off the brad heads, one part can be pressed against another to get the correct mating locations.

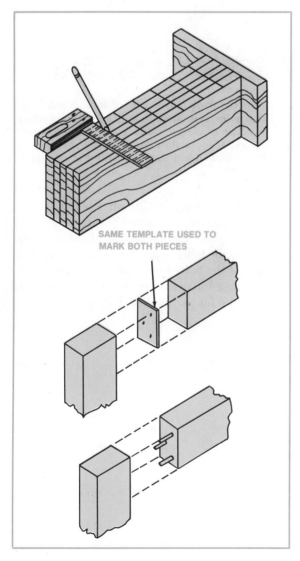

Drilling accuracy depends greatly on careful layout. When the same marking is required on many pieces, it pays to make a template instead of laying out on each part.

also be used as an edge-marking gauge. Dividers (or a compass) do a good job when it is necessary to pick up a dimension from one piece (or a drawing) so you can carry it to another. Dividers are also a good tool to use when you wish to divide a line into a number of equal spaces.

What you do depends on the job and whether you have one piece to be drilled or a number of pieces to be drilled alike. Templates can be used. You can make these of stiff cardboard, hardboard, plywood or even sheet metal if the long-term use justifies it. Some pieces of hardware, such as a hinge, hasp or drawer pull, provide their own template.

An often-used trick to use when ordinary layout proves impractical or too time consuming is to insert headless nails in appropriate locations in

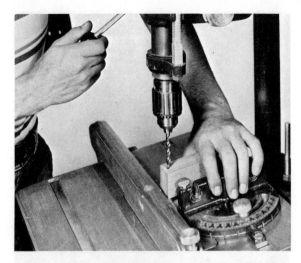

When rip fence and miter gauge are part of the table, they can be used to form jigs. Lacking such accessories, substitute wood pieces to accomplish similar chores.

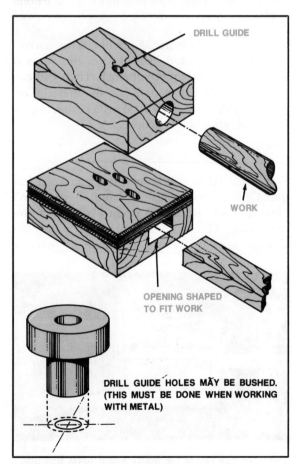

When needed fixtures can be designed to guarantee accurate placement of holes. Such items should be made only when the quantity of work justifies it.

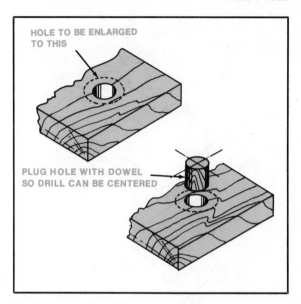

When a drilled hole must be enlarged, plug the original hole to center the bit for the new drilling.

one of the pieces. When this piece is pressed against the mating part, the nails provide drill location points.

To mark hole locations on a series of boards that will be joined edge-to-edge by doweling, align the board edges and butt them surface to surface. Mark hole locations on one edge and carry the line across all pieces by using a square.

Use a fence as a guide whenever you must drill a series of holes with a common center line. Such a fence can be two pieces of wood joined to form an L-shape. C-clamps can then be used as stops to positon any number of pieces that require the same hole in the same place. When you can use a fence and a miter gauge, any number of setups can be created to position work for drilling. In fact, pieces of wood can be used on any drill press as substitutes for built-in accessories.

Auxiliary Tables

Such tables can serve dual purposes. They are instantly available setups for, in one case, drum sanding, which is a very good drill-press application; and they are handy tool shelves when work is being done on the regular drill-press table. A one-piece table is probably more convenient for a small drill press while a split-table

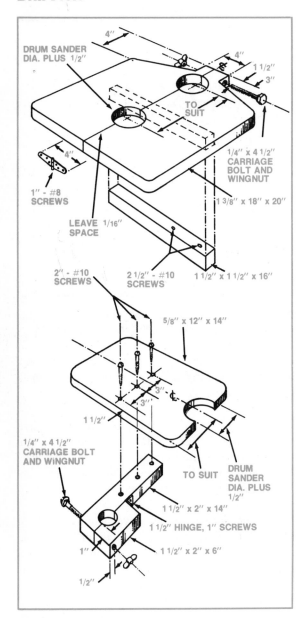

DRUM SANDER
DIA. PLUS 1/2"

4"

4"

1 1/2"

3"

TO SUIT

1/4" x 4 1/2"
CARRIAGE
BOLT AND
WINGNUT

4"

1" - #8
SCREWS

1 3/8" x 18" x 20"

LEAVE 1/16"
SPACE

2" - #10
SCREWS

2 1/2" - #10
SCREWS

1 1/2" x 1 1/2" x 16"

5/8" x 12" x 14"

3"

3"

1 1/2"

1/4" x 4 1/2"
CARRIAGE BOLT
AND WINGNUT

TO SUIT

DRUM
SANDER
DIA. PLUS
1/2"

1 1/2" x 2" x 14"

1 1/2" HINGE, 1" SCREWS

1"

1 1/2" x 2" x 6"

1/2"

Construction details of a similar table that might be more convenient for a smaller drill press. It is also good for drum sanding but the design makes it necessary to stay on one side of the drum as the work is done.

model will go with almost any tool. Either would be easy to scale to suit your equipment.

In either case, the attachment design is a split-clamp arrangement. A turn of a wing nut enables you to position the accessory anywhere, vertically or horizontally. The clamps must lock tightly on the drill-press column. If you have a

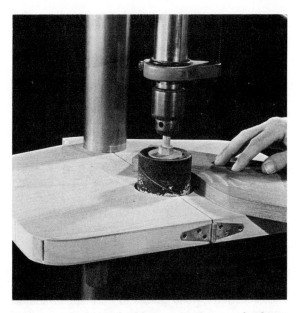

Easy-to-make hinged table permits the use of a drum sander.

hole saw or a fly cutter that will cut the correct size hole, it's a good idea to form the support arms from a single piece of stock. Then you can cut on the hole center line, and the material removed by the saw cut will be just enough to give you good, split-clamp action.

Column Storage Rack

Drill-press work will be easier if you keep frequently used tools close at hand so you don't have to walk, stretch or stoop every time you need one. That's the objective of a column storage rack. It is not a substitute for a large

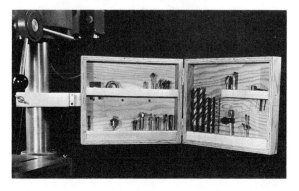

The case has space for many small tools but don't outfit it haphazardly. Instead, lay out small tools used frequently and design holders to use the space efficiently.

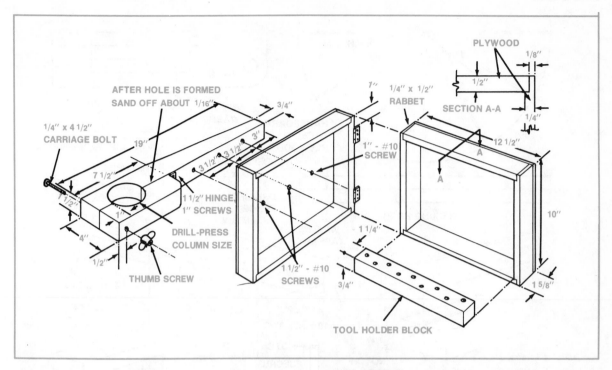

Construction details of the case. Note that it is made as a unit and then cut in half to make the two parts.

cabinet, but if you analyze your work and outfit the case to suit your needs, you'll find it a big help.

The split-clamp lock described for the auxiliary tables also applies to this storage case. You might be able to mount both the case and a table without critically reducing the distance between the spindle and the table proper.

Two Advanced Jigs

A couple of very professional jigs will be described here even before the main material about drill-press work is given. It seems a good way to demonstrate immediately how flexible the drill press can be. Also, a good many of the operations will be done on these jigs rather than on commerical units you might have to spend a lot of money for.

Make a decision on which of the two jigs will be most useful to you. You might base your decision on particular operations. Jigs like these are what make the drill press flexible. Otherwise, it wouldn't be useful for anything but drilling holes.

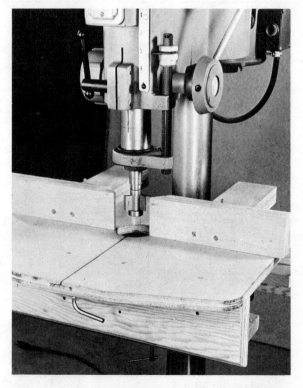

Advanced jig #1. Here it is set up in the shaping mode. Other applications will be shown as we go along.

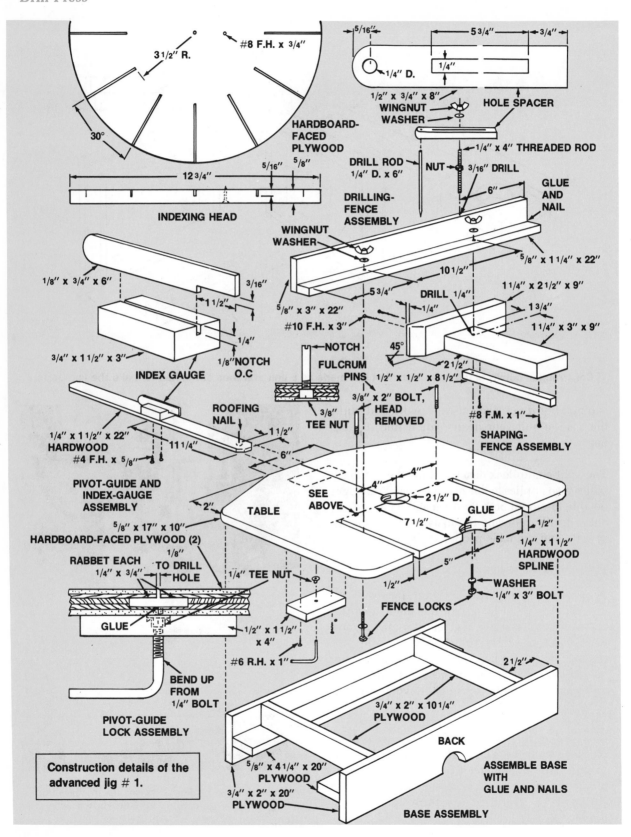

#8 F.H. x 3/4''

3 1/2'' R.

30°

HARDBOARD-
FACED
PLYWOOD

5/16''   5/8''

12 3/4''

INDEXING HEAD

5/16'' — 5 3/4'' — 3/4''

1/4'' D.

1/4''

1/2'' x 3/4'' x 8''   **HOLE SPACER**

WINGNUT
WASHER

1/4'' x 4'' THREADED ROD

DRILL ROD   **NUT**   3/16'' DRILL
1/4'' D. x 6''

DRILLING-
FENCE
ASSEMBLY

6''   **GLUE**
AND
NAIL

WINGNUT
WASHER

5/8'' x 1 1/4'' x 22''

1/8'' x 3/4'' x 6''

3/16''

1 1/2''

1/4''

3/4'' x 1 1/2'' x 3''

1/8'' NOTCH
O.C

INDEX GAUGE

5/8'' x 3'' x 22''
#10 F.H. x 3''

5 3/4''

10 1/2''

DRILL 1/4''

1/4''

45°

1 1/4'' x 2 1/2'' x 9''

1 3/4''

1 1/4'' x 3'' x 9''

2 1/2''

1/2'' x 1/2'' x 8 1/2''

#8 F.M. x 1''

NOTCH
FULCRUM
PINS

3/8'' x 2'' BOLT,
HEAD
REMOVED

SHAPING-
FENCE ASSEMBLY

ROOFING
NAIL

1 1/2''

3/8''
TEE NUT

1/4'' x 1 1/2'' x 22''
HARDWOOD
#4 F.H. x 5/8''

11 1/4''

6''

PIVOT-GUIDE AND
INDEX-GAUGE
ASSEMBLY

2''   **TABLE**

SEE
ABOVE

4''

4''

2 1/2'' D.

7 1/2''

GLUE

1/2''

5''

5''

1/4'' x 1 1/2''
HARDWOOD
SPLINE

1/2''

WASHER

1/4'' x 3'' BOLT

5/8'' x 17'' x 10''
HARDBOARD-FACED PLYWOOD (2)

RABBET EACH
1/8''
TO DRILL
1/4'' x 3/4''   **HOLE**

1/4'' **TEE NUT**

GLUE

1/2'' x 1 1/2''
x 4''

#6 R.H. x 1''

FENCE LOCKS

BEND UP
FROM
1/4'' BOLT

PIVOT-GUIDE
LOCK ASSEMBLY

2 1/2''

3/4'' x 2'' x 10 1/4''
PLYWOOD

BACK

5/8'' x 4 1/4'' x 20''
PLYWOOD

3/4'' x 2'' x 20''
PLYWOOD

ASSEMBLE BASE
WITH
GLUE AND NAILS

BASE ASSEMBLY

Construction details of the
advanced jig # 1.

One jig is basically a table attached to a base that is secured to the regular drill-press table with two C-clamps. The table hole centers under the drill press spindle and permits the use of drum sanders and three-lip shaper cutters. Individually adjustable fences are used for shaping straight line work. Fulcrum pins support curved work that must be shaped freehand.

This jig has a drilling fence that can be used in place of the shaping fences for drilling holes at equal distances from the edge of the work. A built-in spacer can be used to automatically gauge the distance between holes. It is organized for a pivot guide for rotational passes against a cutter and has an indexing head. These and other features have prompted it to be called the "Woodworking Champ of any Shop."

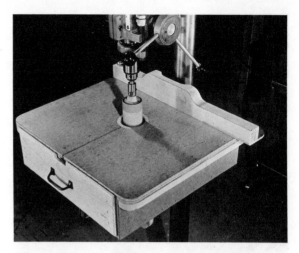

Advanced jig #2 will align automatically if the back cutout is made carefully and the clamp ledge installed accurately. Built-in drawer has ample room for storage.

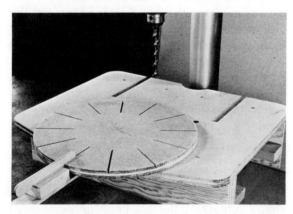

The indexing head mounts on the pivot pin. Since this pin must go through the indexing head in order to hold the workpiece, keep several lengths of roofing nails on hand for different jobs.

Once made, the jig becomes a lifetime tool so it makes sense to construct it accurately to begin with. Start by making the base assembly, checking its dimensions against the size of the table on your drill press. The only change that might be necessary is a reduction or increase in the overall width. Once the base is assembled, you can add components. If you are a beginner, it would be wise to pause after the basic table construction. You can add other items to it after you have become more involved in drill-press work.

A second jig contains a drawer that provides for storage of tools that you use with the tool. This

design evolved from simpler version that was made for drum sanding and drum-sander storage. The drill press is a great tool for such work, but the regular table just won't do. For rotary sanding only, you could get by with nothing more than an inverted, U-shaped structure; holes at the top allow the drum to pass through.

Since the same general construction serves for other rotary tools, it is logical to provide for different size table inserts.

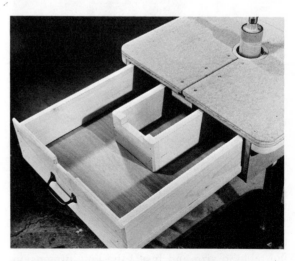

The drawer back has a peculiar shape because it must clear the cutter and keep waste out. The pocket so created collects a good percentage of waste from the drill and, so captured, it is easy to clean away.

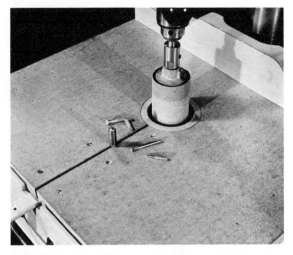

Different types of guides, all designed around store-bought 10-32 screws, lock into the aluminum slide and facilitate sanding and cutting operations. Polish guides with emery cloth.

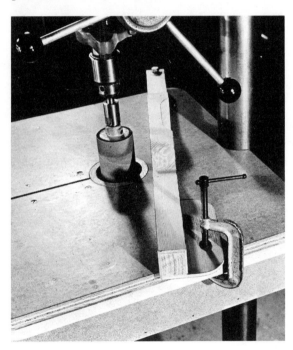

The pivoting fence is as functional as any more elaborate parallel type. Make the hole for the pivot bolt a fairly tight fit. A C-clamp at the free end provides security for the setting.

Critical construction points of this jig follow. Cut the table to size and bisect the long dimension with an accurate center line. On the center line at the rear of the table, make an accurate half-circle cutout to fit the column.

With the table in place, use the drill press to form a small hole on the center line. This hole is the center of the table opening.

Work on a table saw to form the slot and the groove for the slide. The slide should not fit loosely; provide for a good fit even if it means having to exert a little pressure to move the slide to and fro. Shape one end of the slide support to conform to the table opening.

Shape and attach the rails with glue and screws that are driven up through the underside. The rails provide location points for the case sides which you can attach after forming the rabbets along the bottom edge.

Cut the case bottom to size and assemble, without gluing, what you have done so far. Put the unit in place on the drill press with the center line exactly so and scribemark the location of the front edge of the regular drill-press table so you will know exactly where the dado for the clamp ledge must go. This factor is critical for automatic jig alignment; therefore, take the time needed to do it correctly.

A point about the drawer is its peculiar shape at the back. This design prevents the drawer from becoming a receptacle for dust and chips. The U-shape actually collects a good percentage of waste which is easily brushed out or vacuumed away.

How to Drill for Wood Screws

Normally, two holes are required for a wood screw. These holes permit the screw to be driven and allow for maximum holding power. The body hole equals the screw gauge; the smaller lead hole provides entrance for the screw end.

A good procedure is to drill lead holes first and then open up the top portion to body-hole size. Countersinking is done so flat-head screws can be driven flush. Control the countersink depth by using the stop rod. On hardwoods, countersink to the full depth of the screwhead. On softwoods, stay on the minus side. The screw will pull flush as you finish driving.

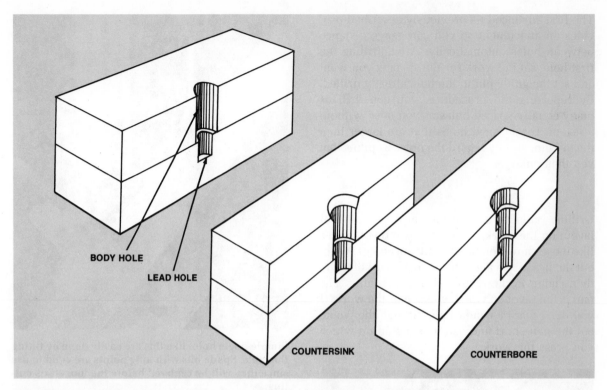

BODY HOLE

LEAD HOLE

COUNTERSINK

COUNTERBORE

Nomenclature of holes required for screws is shown when screw-heads must be flush. Use a counterbore when the screw is set below the surface and then in these cut-away drawings. A countersink is used concealed with a plug.

When you are driving very small screws in soft-wood, you can often simply make a starting hole with an awl. It's also possible to do this with some hardwoods. Make a judgment after testing with one or two screws.

A counterbore is required when the fastener head must be set below the surface. The counter-bore is no more than a shallow hole sized to suit the head of the screw or bolt. Special counter-boring tools are available, but you can form the counterbore first, using a spade bit or something similar instead, and then do the lead and body holes.

Such holes are often sealed with plugs cut from the same type of wood. Special tools for cutting out such plugs are available, and they will be discussed in the section on plug cutters.

Equi-Spaced Holes

A simple way to equally space holes is to pencil mark the distance between the holes and to use a

fence to establish edge distance. The fence doesn't have to be more than a straight piece of wood clamped to the drill-press table. The dis-tance from it to the drill point must equal the edge distance required for the job.

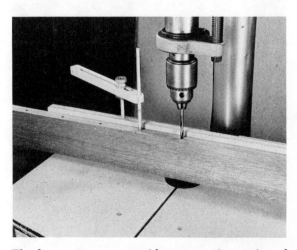

The fence accessory provides automatic gauging of equally spaced holes. The pin seats in each hole drilled to position the work for the next one.

The first advanced jig previously described provides an attachment so you can gauge distance between holes automatically. After drilling the first hole, set the work for the spacing you want and set the guide pin in the hole already drilled. By repeating the procedure, you can drill as many equally-spaced holes as you need without a layout. If you need holes that are larger than the ¼" pin, simply regard the holes as pilots that you then enlarge.

Radial Holes

Drilling radial holes can be simply a matter of layout on the work, or you can use pivot guides like those shown on the two advanced jigs. Without the jigs, drive a nail through a board that you then clamp to the regular drill-press table. The nail is the pivot on which you center the work. If you don't want a center hole through the wood, cut the nail short and use it as a stud on which you press the work.

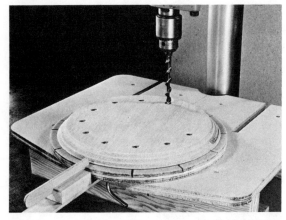

Within its limits (the number of slots that are cut) the indexing head automatically positions the work for the various radial hole locations.

Edge holes are different. On a conventional drill press, you tilt the table so its surface is on a vertical plane and clamp the work to it. If the work is round, you can make a V-block. Be sure to line up the center of the "V" with the point of the drill.

Angular Drilling

Three kinds of off-vertical holes can be drilled; the position of a chair leg in each type of hole

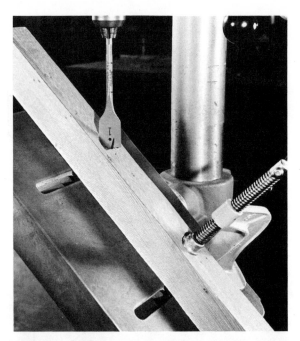

Simple-angle holes like this are easily done by tilting the table. Spade bits with long points are good to use since they will be centered before the tool starts cutting.

best illustrates each type of angle. At a simple angle, the leg tilts in one direction. The angle is obvious when you view it from one side. The equal compound angle has the leg tilting the same amount in two directions. The angle will be the same whether you view the leg from the front or the side. With an unequal compound angle, the leg tilts two ways but a greater amount in one direction. The angle viewed from the front is different than the angle viewed from the side.

When the work size permits, the simple angle is done by tilting the drill-press table. If this is not feasible, then you must leave the table in normal position and use a height block under one edge of the work. Size the height block to give you the angle you want.

The equal compound angle is popular. It has some overall factors that are interesting and that can make many jobs easier to do. If you mark perpendicular diameters on a circular piece of wood or corner-to-corner lines on a square piece of wood and then drill simple angles with the layout lines in line with the spindle, you will

have a compound angle position for what you insert in the hole.

What makes many of these jobs difficult is not the operation but the size of the workpiece. However, you can facilitate matters through careful designing. Let's assume you have a round or square table on which you wish to splay the legs. Picture the understructure as legs attached to two crosspieces. If you drill simple angles at the end of each crosspiece and then assemble the crosspieces with a centered half-lap joint so that they are at right angles, what you inset in the holes will be equally splayed about the table.

On all angular drilling, be aware that the side of the cutter may contact the work before the point does. This can lead to wandering of the drill unless you make contact with an extremely slow feed until the drill is firmly positioned. On extreme angles, it pays to use a leveling block which will provide a flat for the drill to enter.

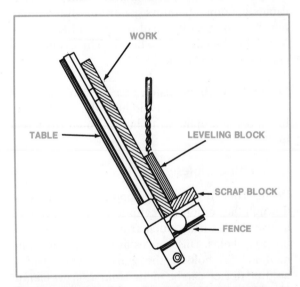

On an extreme angle, where the side of the bit will make contact before the point, use a leveling block to keep the bit stable and prevent it from wandering.

Large Holes

What is a large hole? You might say it's anything above the maximum size you can do with a space bit, which is 1¹/₂″. Going above this measurement is a question of having the tool that will do the job. Fly cutters provide a good solu-

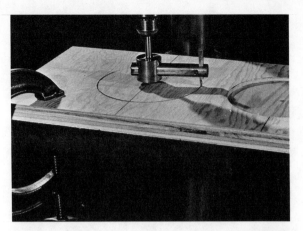

A fly cutter can be used for holes up to 6″ in diameter. Keep feed and speed at a minimum and always clamp the work securely. Never place hands near the cutting area.

tion because you can bore any size hole between the minimum and maximum settings. Fixed hole saws can be used, but being equipped for anything can be expensive; few, if any, of the adjustable types go above approximately 3″. Fly cutters can produce up to a 6″ diameter. You might regard the job as a piercing assignment for a jigsaw or a sabre saw.

There is a drill-press solution with the appropriate technique and jig. However, the chore is really a routing operation. A center hole drilled in the work is placed over the dowel pin in the adjustable jig. The jig is secured to gauge

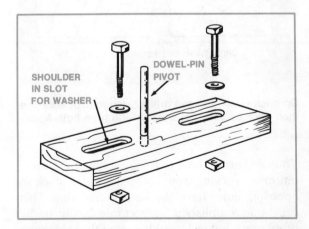

The jig that permits a router bit to be used for cutting extra large holes is shown here. A center hole drilled in the work fits over the dowel pivot. The work is then rotated against the direction-of-rotation of the cutter.

the radius of the hole, and then the work is rotated so the ¹/₄″ router bit forms a circular groove. On thick work it may be necessary to rotate the work several times, cutting a bit deeper after each pass.

Large hole forming calls for maximum security for the work and ample clearance for your hands. Position the work and then clamp it solidly to the drill-press table. Use a slow feed and a slow speed. The outboard, cutting end of a fly cutter can be just a blur even at slow speeds, so keep your hands well away.

Deep Holes

The maximum depth of a hole you can drill is limited by the maximum extension of the quill regardless of the length of the drilling tool. When, for example, quill extension is 4″ and the bit is 6″, you can get the full cut by drilling 4″ first, then raising the table so the bit is in the hole that extra 2″ and drilling again.

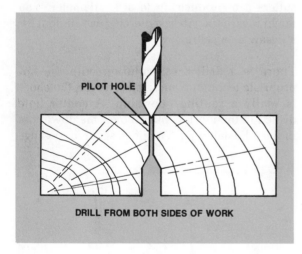

On thick stock, you can drill a through pilot hole and then open up to full size by drilling from both ends.

You can form a hole that is two times the maximum by working from both sides of the stock so opposing holes have the same center line. This can be accomplished by accurate layout or by providing a hole-size guide pin on the table over which the work can be placed after the first hole is formed. This technique positions the work accurately for drilling from the opposite side.

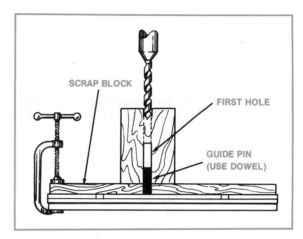

Set up to drill accurately from both ends of the work in order to double hole depth. In this case the guide pin is secured in a board that is clamped to the table after pin and bit have been aligned.

Extension bits can be used for very deep holes, but they are not too usable on bench model machines because of the limited chuck-to-base capacity. Some operators get around this limitation by swinging the drill-press head so it projects over the edge of the bench. Thus, they get a chuck-to-floor capacity.

Be careful with extension bits because they can whip. Use a slow speed and have the point of the bit embedded in the work before you turn on the tool.

Concentric Holes

Picture concentric holes as longitudinal openings through the center of a cylinder. The techniques to use don't differ much from those described for deep holes. Differences arise, sometimes, in methods for holding the work. A very useful holding device can be made from a screw clamp merely by cutting matching "V's" in the jaws. This permits round work to be gripped securely. If the screw clamp is large enough, one of its handles can be braced against the drill-press column to counteract any twist created by the cutting action. Further security is achieved by using a C-clamp to lock the screw clamp to the drill-press table.

If you have an adjustable lathe chuck, it makes a fine holding device for concentric drilling

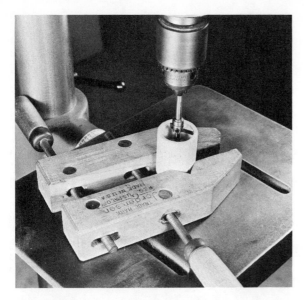

Screw clamp with matching Vs cut in its jaws makes holder for concentric drilling of either round or square stock. Handle of clamp is braced against column to counteract twist of the cutter.

because it is heavy enough to provide very good support. Even tubing can be gripped for drilling should the I.D. be too small for your needs.

The Countersink

The countersink is a tool that forms an inverted cone to seat the heads of flat-head screws flush with adjacent surfaces. They are available with different bevel angles to suit the fastener. All wood screws require one angle; machine screws require another.

When you need a number of countersunk holes, it's best to set the drill-press stop rod to control depth. This method is theoretically wrong, but a countersink is often used to form the seat for the screw head and also a counterbore for a plug to hide the screw. This means going deeper with the countersink than you need to go for the screw head alone. Consider two factors. Be sure you have a plug-cutting tool that matches the O.D. of the countersink. Be aware that you are burying the countersink more than you should so retract frequently to clear waste from the hole and thus avoid burning the tool and/or the work.

Countersinking in thin sheet metal calls for a "dimpling" procedure. Using a countersink in

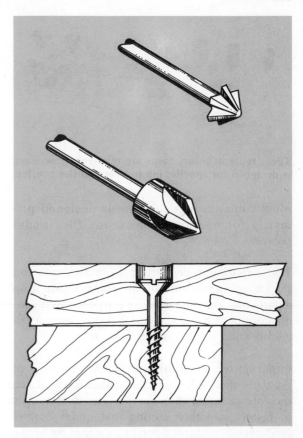

There are many styles of countersinks but they all make inverted cone depressions so screw heads can be set flush.

normal fashion would simply form a sloppy hole for the screw head. To get around this, shape the end of a hardwood dowel so it matches the angle of the countersink you need. Use the countersink in a backup block. Chuck the dowel and use it like a press to form the metal into the countersink shape. Success depends greatly on the gauge and the softness of the metal. It works fine on do-it-yourself aluminum. Using a slow speed and putting a dab of paste wax on the end of the dowel are also helpful.

Rotary Rasps

Rotary rasps are little tools; but when you use them on a drill press, you can do good-sized jobs. Such jobs include making joints, doing shaping and pattern forming or accomplishing pesky short-run chores, especially on small pieces that might be difficult to handle by other means.

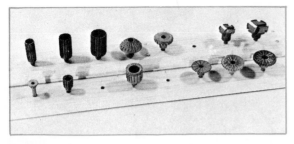

These types of rotary rasps are relatively new. Each is designed for specific job but capabilities overlap.

Most common types are rasps designed primarily for use as rough-cutting files under power.

The imported types differ from the common rasp image in that each of the units is meant to do a particular job. The primary purpose usually indicates the shape of the tool, but imagination can lead beyond the single application.

Imported types cut differently, too. On most of the tools, the teeth are like raised chisel edges so they shave rather than scrape. This action leads to faster, smoother cutting that under correct feed-speed conditions produces edges requiring little additional attention. To get the most out of these imported rotary rasps you should have a couple of easy-to-make jigs.

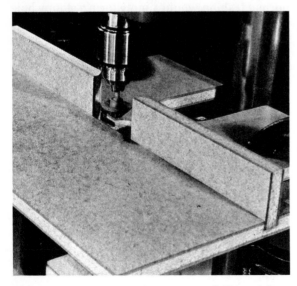

Best way to use the rotary rasps on a drill press is to make a special table and some other simple guides that are used along with it.

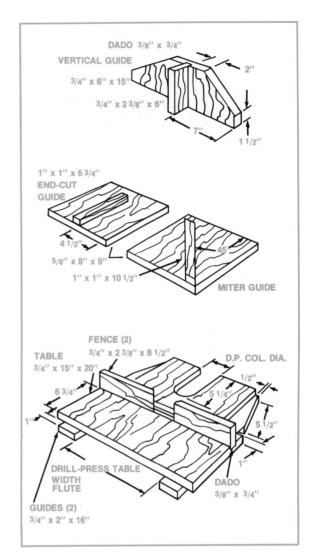

Construction details of rotary rasp table and some guides that make it easy to do accurate cutting.

When you make the end cut, miter and vertical guides, check your cuts with a square and be sure the blocks that will be used to position the workpieces are exact.

Very high speeds, especially in hardwoods, can cause burning and in soft, gummy woods can clog the teeth quickly. Moderate speeds plus light feed pressure will help keep the teeth sharper, longer.

When you use a shape that must be buried in the work, regard it as a drill, retracting frequently to remove waste.

Don't try to cut too deeply. As an example of how much material the tool can remove in one pass, figure a groove about $1/4''$ wide by $3/8''$ deep in pine as an approximate standard.

Even under ideal conditions, the teeth will clog; but you can clean them easily with the same kind of brush you use on your hand files. For problem clogging, first dry-brush the tool and soak in paint thinner for a minute or two; then brush again.

Shaping on a Drill Press

The drill press makes a good shaper if you are aware of two limiting factors. The highest speed doesn't match the rpm's you can get from an individual machine; the spindle is above the table instead of being under it. Since you can compensate for lack of speed simply by slowing up the feed and since the above-the-table spindle position is not critical for the bulk of shaping work, you can get along quite well.

The drill press does require a shaping table accessory. This accessory can be a commercial unit you buy or an attachment you make to use with the advanced jig. Beyond this, you need an adapter to use in place of the regular chuck, depth collars that are used on the adapter and the cutters themselves.

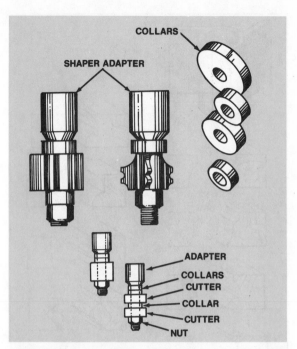

Collars are used to control depth of cut. This is more essential with freehand shaping than when shaping against a fence. Collars may be used over, under or between cutters.

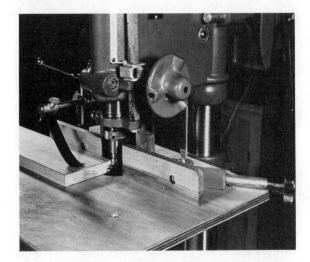

Typical setup for shaping on a drill press using commercial accessories. Auxiliary table bolts to the regular table. Fences are individually adjustable. Such units are available for most any drill press.

Several general rules apply when using the drill press as a shaper. Always use the fastest speed you have. Work against a shaper fence whenever possible. Try to keep the cutting tool under the work. One reason is for safety; the other is to guard against gouging the work should you lift it accidentally during the pass. Feed the work into and against the rotation of the cutting tool. Hold hands away from the cutting area and try to feed so fingers are hooked over work edges to guard against slippage. Don't force the work; make all passes with a slow, steady feed. Don't try to shape pieces that are too small to be held safely.

The one-piece, three-blade cutter is the most practical type of tool for homeshop use. Like molding head knives, these may be designed for full profile cuts to produce a specific shape or they may be combination cutters where you use part of the edge to achieve a form.

Straight pieces should be shaped against a fence. When only part of the edge is removed, the fences are set on the same plane. When the entire edge of the stock is cut away, then the out-

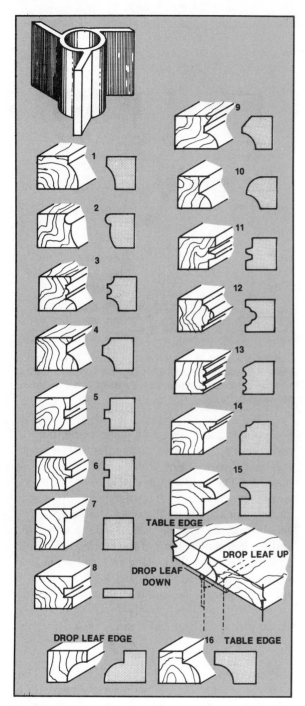

Typical profiles that are available in three-lip shaper cutters.

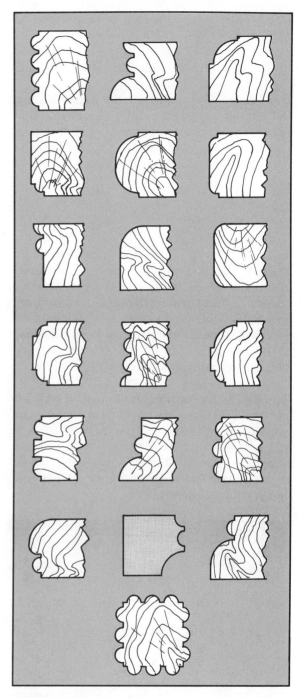

Important factor in three-lip shaper cutter use. All of the designs shown here were done with a single combination quarter-round and bead cutter. Variations made possible simply by changing relationship of work and cutter.

feed fence is brought forward an amount that equals the depth of cut. Both practices allow the work to have full support both before and after the cut.

Freehand shaping, necessary when the work has an inside or outside curve, is done against

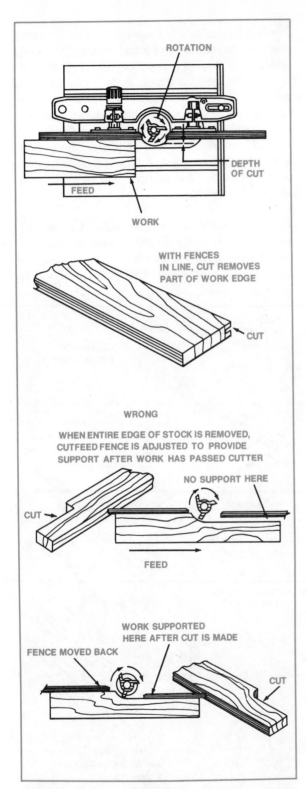

ROTATION

DEPTH OF CUT

FEED

WORK

WITH FENCES
IN LINE, CUT REMOVES
PART OF WORK EDGE

CUT

WRONG

WHEN ENTIRE EDGE OF STOCK IS REMOVED,
CUTFEED FENCE IS ADJUSTED TO PROVIDE
SUPPORT AFTER WORK HAS PASSED CUTTER

NO SUPPORT HERE

CUT

FEED

WORK SUPPORTED
HERE AFTER CUT IS MADE

FENCE MOVED BACK

CUT

Some of the important points regarding fence alignment when doing shaping operations are shown here.

fulcrum pins. These pins are vertical "dowels," one on each side of the cutter. To start the cut, brace the work against the infeed pin and gradually move it forward to make contact with the cutter. You can still hold against the infeed pin as you continue to make the cut. As you near the end, swing the work to brace against the outfeed pin and finish the job. On all such jobs, collars are used on the adapter together with the cutter to control depth of cut.

Routing

Routing is done with special bits, best secured to the spindle with a router chuck. Many of the rules described for shaping apply to router work, especially the advice about speeds and feed.

Router bits don't have to be straight-shank affairs. Many are available that will produce shaped edges, even dovetail slots. If you are going to set up for both shaping and routing, you want to be careful that you don't duplicate coverage.

Routing cuts are smoothest when you work with the grain of the wood. Cross-grain cuts, especially when they must be straight, are the most difficult to do. Use a fence or guide for either type of cut.

For much cross-grain work, it's best to prepare a special setup. This is an auxiliary table with a fence guided by rails that move along opposite edges. The idea is to guide the work so the line of cut is at right angles to the work edge.

When doing freehand routing, you must be very careful to hold the work firmly as you guide it. Cutting action will vary with differences in grain structure, and it's quite easy for the work to move away from the line you are trying to follow. The deeper you try to cut in one pass, the more obvious the movement away from the line will be.

Pattern routing is a way to do intricate shapes with good guarantee of accuracy. It is also a good method to use when you require many similar pieces.

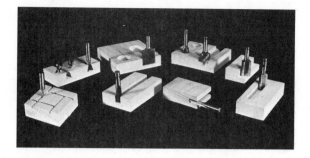

Router bits come in various shapes and sizes. All of them should be run at the highest speeds possible.

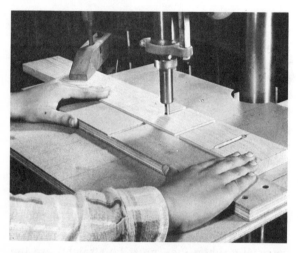

This sliding fence, used on the router table, permits feeding the work at right angles to the cutter. To guarantee a straight cut, clamp the work to one of the fence guides (notice the clamp in upper left corner of photo).

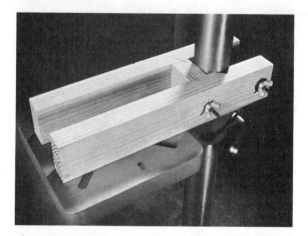

Make the base for the table from stock 2 x 4s V-notched at the rear to fit the drill-press column. After the base is made, clamp it in place with the set screws and then attach the table.

For this type of routing, secure a router bit-sized post in a board that you attach to the drill-press table so the post is exactly aligned with the cutter. Cut the pattern you wish to reproduce in a piece of plywood or hardboard. The pattern is tack-nailed to the work and situated over the post. Bring the cutter down to the depth you want. Move the work and pattern so the pattern is constantly bearing against the post. Since the post and cutter are in line, you duplicate the shape of the pattern.

To rout parallel to a curved edge, you need a guide that will maintain the correct distance between work edge and cutter. The guide can be a pointed piece of wood that you clamp to the

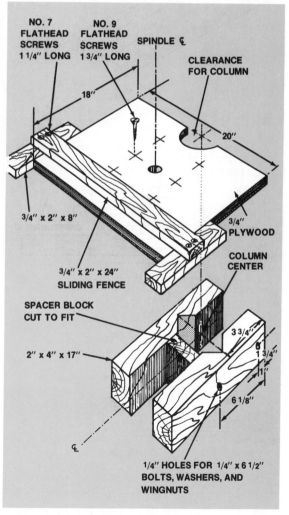

Construction details of the router table and the special fence.

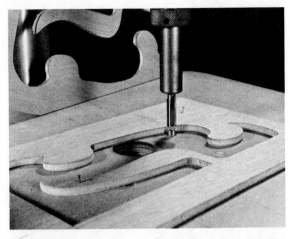

The essence of pattern routing is shown here. The pattern rides a pin that is set in a table (or a board) directly in line with the router bit. The work is tack-nailed to the pattern . . .

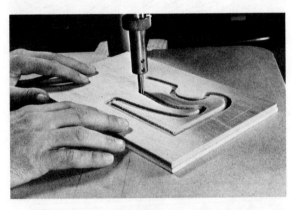

. . . and, as the pattern rides the pin, the shape is duplicated in the work above it. Best way to align the pin is to drill its hole with the router bit to be used for the job.

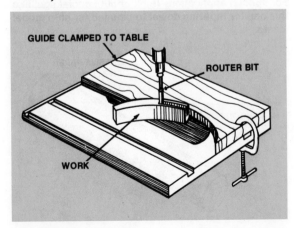

GUIDE CLAMPED TO TABLE

ROUTER BIT

WORK

Specially shaped board is helpful for "odd" shaped pieces that would be difficult to control.

regular table or nail to a board that is then clamped to the table. It can also be the more sophisticated version designed for use with the second advanced jig.

V-blocks, semi-circular guides or specially made shapes that are made to fit the work can be used advantageously.

Drum Sanding

A drum sander is the tool to use for many edge-smoothing operations, and the drill press is a fine tool to use it on. Since the regular drill-press table won't do for this technique, you can make an auxiliary table with a U-shaped cutout. Thus, the drum can be situated so its bottom edge is below the work that rests on the new table, and the entire edge of the work can be brought to bear against the drum. This setup also assures a right-angle relationship between work and drum so the sanded edge will be square to adjacent surfaces.

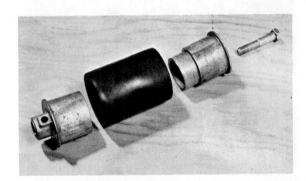

Basic drum sander assembly. Taking up on the nut with the parts together, expands the rubber sleeve to grip the abrasive band that is placed over it.

While this primitive jig is appropriate as a quick solution, it is not ideal since it doesn't allow for use of all the abrasive surface. An improvement would be to elevate the auxiliary table so the drum could be set higher or lower at will. This feature is possible with the advanced jigs.

To do pattern sanding, you can make a guide to match the diameter of the drum. This guide is attached to a board, and the board is clamped to the drill-press table so the guide is in perfect alignment with the sander. Correct alignment

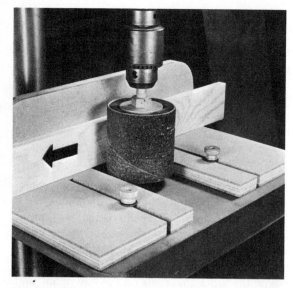

This L-shaped jig locks with bolts that are pushed through the slots in the regular drill-press table. Be sure the vertical piece is perpendicular to the table surface.

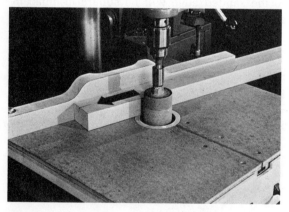

Edges can be sanded in fine style when the work is run between the drum sander and a fence. Don't try to remove a lot of material in one pass.

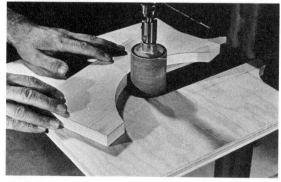

Best way to use a drum sander is to establish a setup so work can be held flat while its edge is smoothed.

can be accomplished by using the second jig to make a special insert which is secured to the guide.

To use the guide, shape one piece of work as a pattern and cut the others roughly to shape. The rough pieces are tack-nailed to the pattern. Since the pattern rides the guide, the drum sander cuts down the rough pieces to match the pattern.

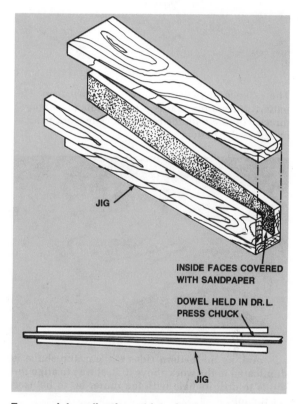

For special applications think about special jigs, like this one for tapering dowel to be used for ship model masts.

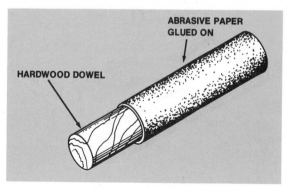

Make special size drum sanders by gluing abrasive paper around a length of dowel.

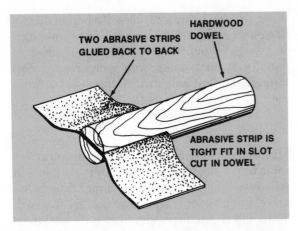

Make a flap wheel by inserting strips of sandpaper in a slot cut in a dowel. Such a flexible sander can be used on odd-shaped pieces or to smooth small holes and plastics.

Decorative Work

You can do luxurious carving, as well as create such items as drawer fronts and door pulls with a custom look, on your drill press.

Much is done with a fly cutter that has a sloping bit rather than a vertical cutter. As the tool is fed, its pilot drill makes a center hole and the blade makes a circular recess with a sloping bottom. When a second cut is done close enough to over-lap the first, new angles and interesting patterns result. The cutter is available in two sizes. Since both have adjustable bits, a wide range of designs is possible.

This kind of decorative work can be done on almost any wood, but stock such as maple and birch is best to use.

Work with a ruler and compass to plan designs. Mark centers accurately and drill pilot holes first, either by working with a similar size bit or by taking the cutting blade out of the tool and using the pilot drill alone.

Always clamp the work and run the drill press at a slow speed. Do larger circles first and use the quill stop to control depth of cut. As with all fly cutters, keep hands away from the cutting area. Use a slow feed; and when the tool is at full depth, hold it there a second or two. A burnishing effect results that helps produce a smooth finish.

You can increase speed as you decrease the hole diameter. If the wood you are using leaves a rough nap, try dampening the wood after the initial cuts. When it dries, make a very light

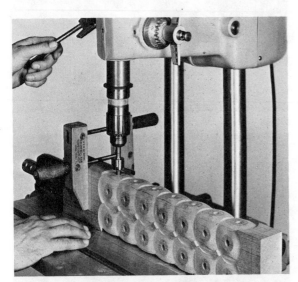

Uniform cuts on four sides with the fly cutter can result in attractive lamp bases, railings, posts, etc. Use the quill stop to control cut-depth. Clamp the work securely and be accurate with layout.

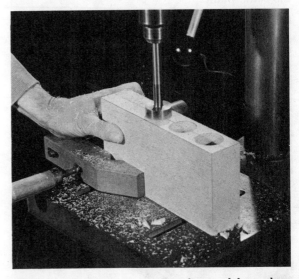

Clamp two similar pieces together and bore deep holes on the joint line. Separate the pieces and strip cut to produce slats that can be joined edge-to-edge for open work panels.

smoothing cut to remove the fuzz raised by the moisture.

The pilot-drill holes can be left open for a lacy effect; or they can be plugged with dowels, discs or buttons. Such pieces can have a contrasting tone. While the finished jobs can be spray painted, natural finishes seem more appropriate, especially on hardwoods.

Decorative effects can be achieved by drilling on the center line of two boards that are clamped together. After the boards are strip-cut, the slats can be joined edge-to-edge to form fancy, pierced panels.

Sometimes, simply a pattern of overlapping holes can create a special design. Mortising bits and chisels can be used to pierce stock that is then cut into slats.

V-Block Work

V-blocks make excellent holders for drilling diametrical holes through cylinders and tubes. The V-shape is formed with saw cuts; the holder is clamped to the drill-press table so the point of the bit is on the V's center line. The result is that the longitudinal diameter of the work is put on the same plane.

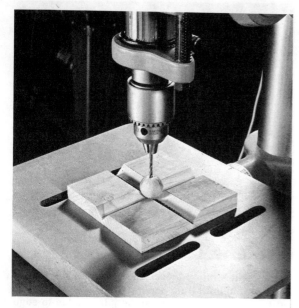

The intersection of two V-cuts makes a good holding situation for drilling into or through, ball shapes.

When drilling a series of holes, it's best to draw a line on the work to help keep you from rotating it as you go. When the job calls for a series of equally spaced holes, you can drive a nail through the first hole drilled: the distance from the nail to the bit equals the hole spacing.

Mortising

Mortise-and-tenon combinations account for some of the strongest and most durable joints in woodworking. The closest competition is the dowel joint, but only when two dowels are used. Twin dowels are necessary to gain the anti-twist strength that a tenon in a mortise provides automatically.

The tenon is an easy table-saw job, but the mortise sometimes puzzles the beginning craftsman. The mortising bit forms a hole much like a drill bit, but it is encased in a square, steel sleeve that

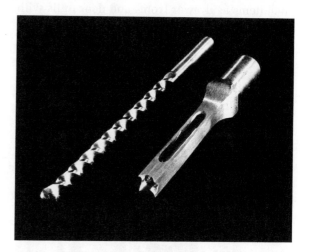

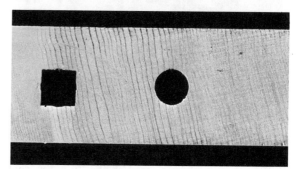

The mortising bit and chisel set does two things. The bit forms the round hole to remove most of the waste — the chisel cuts away the remaining corners to produce the square hole.

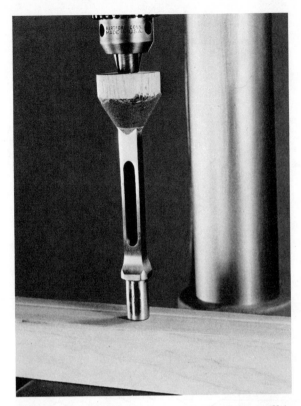

Chisels must be sharp, since pressure of the quill is the only push behind them. An emery wheel makes a good sharpening tool. Make one by shaping a cone to match the chisel bevel. Glue on emery paper and then use as shown here. Just a light touch is required.

is really a four-sided chisel. The job of the chisel is to clean out the corners left by the bit, and the result is a square hole. Since one side of the chisel is slotted, waste chips can escape.

In order to use the chisels, you must have a special casting that locks in some fashion to the end of the quill. Usually, this component is part of a kit you buy that includes a special fence and a hold-down.

Two factors apply no matter what your equipment is. The chisel must be square to the fence so cutting will be done parallel to the work edge. There must be at least $1/32''$ — but no more than $1/16''$ — clearance between the spurs on the bit and the cutting edge of the chisel. Keep this clearance to a minimum but not so tight that you create excessive friction between bit and chisel. Not enough clearance will result in overheating

and damage to the tools. Too much clearance is needless and can result in large waste chips that may clog inside the chisel.

The larger the chisel, the slower the speed should be, especially in hardwoods. For chisels up to $1/2''$ size, use a speed range of 1,700 rpm's to 3,500 rpm's in softwood and a maximum of about 2,000 rpm's in hardwoods. These rules apply best under ideal conditions. There are differences in softwoods and hardwoods, even in boards cut from the same tree. You must also consider whether you are cutting across the grain, with the grain or into end grain.

Regard these rules as generalizations and break them according to how the cut is going. Stay away from excessive feed pressure; although a feather touch won't work since the chisel cuts under quill-feed pressure only. The rate of feed and speed are probably correct when the waste chips move smoothly up the flutes of the bit and easily out through the escape slot in the chisels. Retracting can also help to keep things going

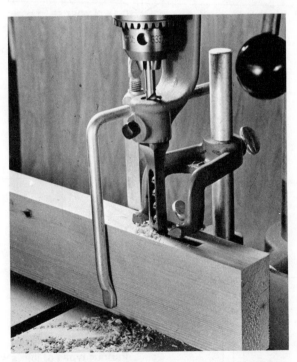

Typical mortising setup on a drill press. Special casting attaches to the end of the quill and is used with the regular chuck. U-shaped foot holds the work down, L-shaped rod keeps it against the fence.

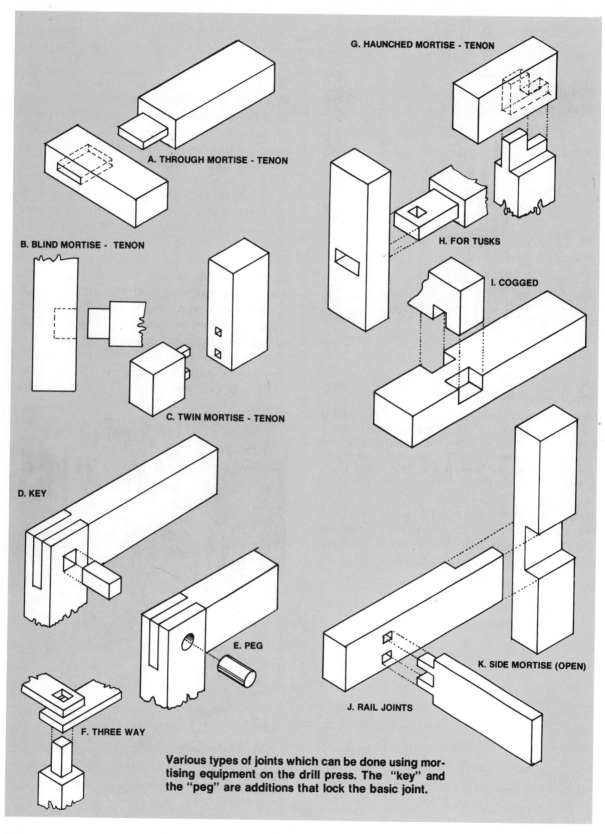

G. HAUNCHED MORTISE - TENON

A. THROUGH MORTISE - TENON

B. BLIND MORTISE - TENON

H. FOR TUSKS

C. TWIN MORTISE - TENON

I. COGGED

D. KEY

E. PEG

F. THREE WAY

J. RAIL JOINTS

K. SIDE MORTISE (OPEN)

Various types of joints which can be done using mortising equipment on the drill press. The "key" and the "peg" are additions that lock the basic joint.

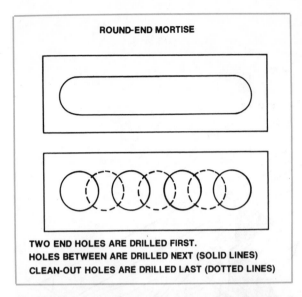

ROUND-END MORTISE

TWO END HOLES ARE DRILLED FIRST.
HOLES BETWEEN ARE DRILLED NEXT (SOLID LINES)
CLEAN-OUT HOLES ARE DRILLED LAST (DOTTED LINES)

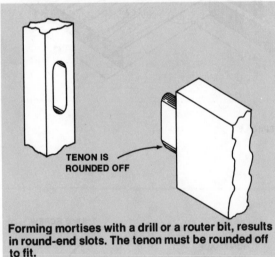

TENON IS
ROUNDED OFF

Forming mortises with a drill or a router bit, results in round-end slots. The tenon must be rounded off to fit.

Special Mortising Jig

You don't have to restrict mortising to square stock. If you make a V-jig accessory to replace the conventional fence arrangement, you can form square cavities on round stock or on the corners of square pieces. Operational considerations don't change, and you use all the items that normally attach to the quill.

These procedures make it possible to mortise rails into round legs, to attach corner-to-corner stretchers or rails when square legs are used and to install shelves on round posts by forming radial mortises.

When you make the jig, be careful of the dimension from the center of the "V" to the back edge of the jig. It should equal the distance from the center of the spindle to the back edge of the table to easily achieve alignment each time the jig is used.

When you use the jig be sure that the spindle and "V" have the same center line and that the chisel is square. Place your work in the "V" and trap it with the hold-down. Similar cuts on multiple

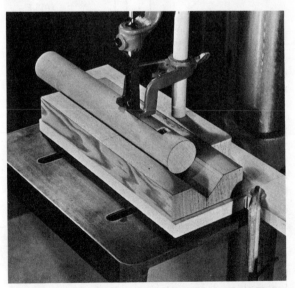

Working in the round is no trick at all if mortising equipment and a V-jig developed for the purpose are used. Place the round work in the V and secure it with the hold-down. Proceed with cutting in normal fashion making end cuts first and then cleaning away the stock between.

well. Control the depth of blind mortises by using the quill-feed stop rod.

There is some splintering where the chisel breaks through. This is minimized by using a scrap block under the work; for a perfect job, work on stock that is slightly thicker than the part needed. After mortising, do a light shaving cut on the table saw to remove the imperfections.

When you get to the tenon, don't size it so it must be wedged into the mortise or cut it too long. There must be room for excess glue. Keep the tenon shorter by about $1/16$'' or chamfer its end.

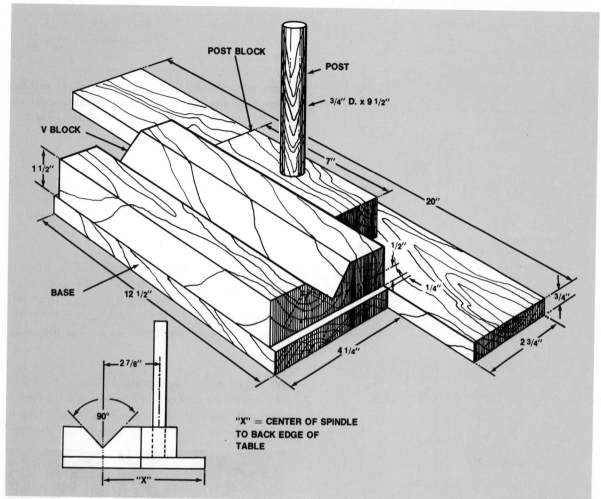

POST BLOCK

POST

3/4" D. x 9 1/2"

V BLOCK

1 1/2"

BASE

12 1/2"

7"

20"

1/2"

1/4"

3/4"

2 3/4"

4 1/4"

2 7/8"

90°

"X" = CENTER OF SPINDLE
TO BACK EDGE OF
TABLE

"X"

Construction details of a V-jig and design for a hold-down to make at home.

pieces can be gauged easily by tack-nailing a stop block across the "V." The same idea applies when you do radial mortising. Alignment of repeat cuts when forming slots is controlled by drawing a longitudinal line on the work after you have formed the first cavity. Thereafter, keep the edge of the chisel on the line.

Concentric mortises are feasible if you devise a means of holding the work in relation to the cutting tool. Mortising equipment can also be used for making large interior cutouts in panels of wood or other materials. Unlike drilled holes, the mortises give the cutouts square corners. After the cuts are made, make straight cuts along the sides of the cutout by working on the table saw.

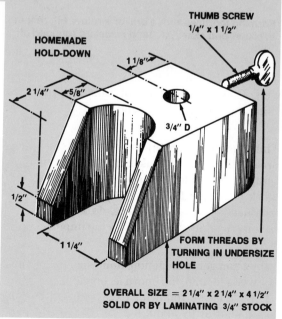

THUMB SCREW
1/4" x 1 1/2"

HOMEMADE
HOLD-DOWN

1 1/8"

2 1/4"

5/8"

3/4" D

1/2"

1 1/4"

FORM THREADS BY
TURNING IN UNDERSIZE
HOLE

OVERALL SIZE = 2 1/4" x 2 1/4" x 4 1/2"
SOLID OR BY LAMINATING 3/4" STOCK

Spiraling Dowels

Drill a horizontal hole through a block to fit the dowel being grooved. Drill a vertical hole through the surface of the block until it meets the horizontal hole. The vertical hole is for the router bit that will do the cutting. Run the drill press at high speed and push the dowel through the horizontal hole. After you make contact with the router bit, rotate the dowel as you continue to feed it through. This is a good way to do grooves for gluing in any common dowel.

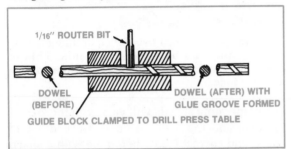

How to cut spiral grooves in dowels. A special guide block is required for each size dowel you wish to treat this way.

Plug Cutters

Concealing a screw or bolt hole with a plug cut from an ordinary dowel that you buy in the local hardware store is not the best method to use. Such items are not always accurate, and you can't find them in all kinds of wood. It would be too much to expect that the grain of the plug would match that of the wood you are using. Plug cutters are good solutions to this little headache since you can cut plugs from the same material you are working with and match the grain so closely that the plug would be hard to find.

The plug cutter used in the drill press can also make dowels. Length is limited to about two inches, but this is long enough for dowel joints. You can use scrap pieces of lumber as stock; and since hardwood dowels are not inexpensive this alone helps justify the cost of the tool.

In addition to forming plugs and dowels of wood, the plug cutters can be utilized to form integral tenons whether the stock is square or round.

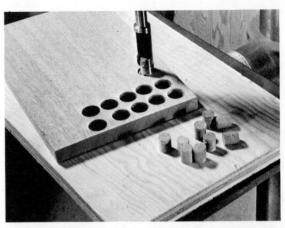

Crossgrain plugs cut from the same material as the project are not easily seen when they are used to fill screw or bolt holes. The grain direction, even the tone can be matched when the work is carefully done.

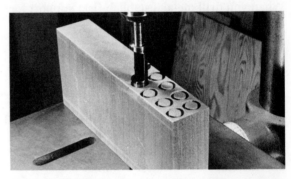

This type of plug cutter is strictly for drill-press use. It will cut plugs or short dowels as shown here. They are cut in the end grain of the wood so the dowel will have a strong cross-section. Run between 1,200 rpms and 1,800 rpms. Feed slowly and retract frequently.

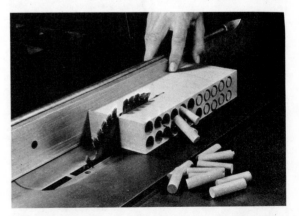

Free the dowels by making a saw cut. Determine dowel length by this cut. Don't make this kind of cut so the loose dowels will be between the saw blade and the fence.

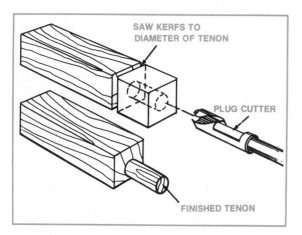

The idea is to saw kerfs to match the diameter of the tenon and then to plug-cut to meet the kerfs.

Metal Drilling Techniques

When you drill metal, establish firm support for the work as close to the cutting area as possible. You can place work directly on the table. Center the bit over the table hole or place a scrap block under the work as you do when drilling wood. Parallel supports are often used under the work, but it's an error to separate them·very much. Metal drilling develops considerable twisting action especially when the drill breaks through. Therefore, keep the work clamped at all times or provide stops that will do a similar job.

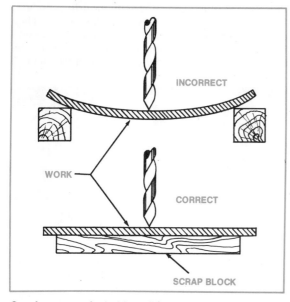

Good support is achieved by using a scrap block under the work. When using parallel supports, keep them close to the cutting area.

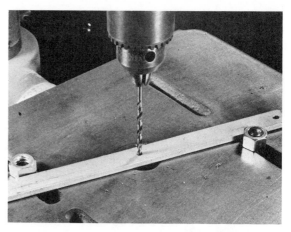

Good way to counteract twist when drilling metal is to use a nut-and-bolt setup like this. This is especially good when a number of similar pieces must be done.

Good operating speeds will vary with the size of the drill and the material being worked. Good speed and correct feed when done with a sharp cutter will curl a ribbon of metal out of the hole. The bit should cut constantly or you will merely rub the metal, accomplishing nothing but dulling the tool. The feed refers to how strongly you bring the cutting tool to bear.

Some suggested lubricants to use on various kinds of non-wood drilling include dry or paraffin oil and lard oil.

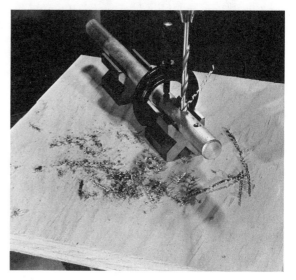

Good metal drilling calls for maximum work security and a feed-speed combination that causes the waste to emerge as a twisting ribbon.

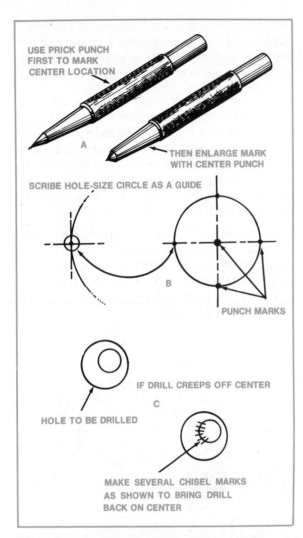

USE PRICK PUNCH FIRST TO MARK CENTER LOCATION

A

THEN ENLARGE MARK WITH CENTER PUNCH

SCRIBE HOLE-SIZE CIRCLE AS A GUIDE

B

PUNCH MARKS

HOLE TO BE DRILLED

IF DRILL CREEPS OFF CENTER

C

MAKE SEVERAL CHISEL MARKS AS SHOWN TO BRING DRILL BACK ON CENTER

Hole locations should be marked with a prick punch and then indented further with a center punch. This is not too critical on very small holes.

Twist drills are available in fractional, letter or number sizes. Since you probably won't be completely equipped with all three, you can work from a chart of decimal equivalents to select a size that comes close to what is called for.

Work with a sharp scriber to do layout work. On some metals a scribed line doesn't show clearly. In addition, it's often poor practice to incise the line, so surface-coaters are used. By using these and scribing lightly, you can do layout work without cutting into the metal surface.

Always use a prick punch to mark hole centers. In addition, a center punch can be used to form a

slight well into which you seat the drill point when you start drilling. Without it, especially on round surfaces, the drill point can wander off the mark.

You can work with extreme precision if you use the prick-punch mark as the center for scribing the hole size you want. The scribed circle is a guide to tell you if the drill is moving off-center. To get to a $1/2''$ hole, it isn't uncommon to start at $1/16''$ or $1/8''$ and then work up through several other sizes to get to the final $1/2''$.

A sure way to locate work so the hole mark is centered exactly with the drill is to work with a centering pin. This doesn't have to be more than a short length of $1/8''$ or $1/4''$ drill rod sharpened at one end. In practice, you secure the pin in the chuck and lower it so the point engages the center-punch mark. Then you clamp the work and substitute the drill for the pin.

Tapping

The drill press may be used to overcome the difficulty of keeping a tap square to the work. Any of the three kinds of taps, when secured in the drill-press chuck, will be square to the work surface throughout the job.

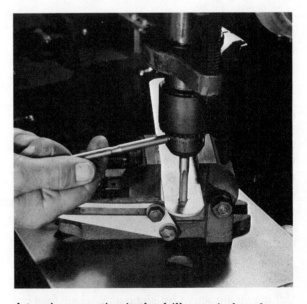

A tapping operation in the drill press is done for accuracy — it is never done under power, not in the home workshop anyway. Tapping is done by turning the chuck by hand.

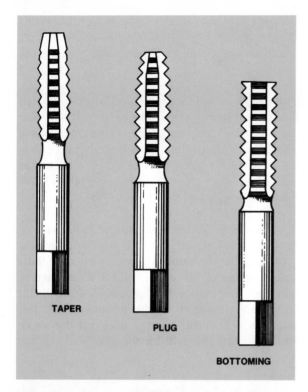

TAPER

PLUG

BOTTOMING

When threading a hole that is clear through the material, use the "taper" or "plug" tap. When the hole does not go through, start the job with the "taper", use the "plug" to the bottom of the hole, finish up with the "bottoming" tap.

However, tapping is never done under power. The drill press merely assures squareness; the tapping is done by turning the chuck by hand as you apply very light feed pressure. To do this, use a short length of metal rod (or a suitable bolt) in the chuck holes normally used by the chuck key.

The tap works by cutting metal. To remove waste, turn the chuck to the right about one-fourth turn for every half turn to the left. Use a drop of oil on the tap as you go. Be careful when withdrawing the tap. Keep some feed pressure as you continue to turn the chuck to the right until the tap is clear.

Spot Polishing

Getting an attractive finish on a metal surface by "grinding" overlapping spots is spot polishing: The tools can be made as shown in the accompanying drawing. The abrasive you use can be judged in relation to the hardness of the metal. A plain rod can be used when a mixture of emery dust and light oil is applied to the work. Abrasive paper or steel wool can be worked dry.

Always do some test work first on scrap stock. Use a fence so you can move the work in a straight line and try to overlap the spots evenly. Feed pressure should be very light; and speed must be judged on the basis of the abrasive, the material being worked and the results you are getting. Start at a slow speed and increase the speed gradually to what does the job you want.

When you make the tools, be sure that the working end will bear flat against the work. *SEE ALSO BAND SAW; BENCH GRINDER; JIGSAW; JOINTER; LATHE; RADIAL ARM SAW; SHAPER; STATIONARY BELT & DISC SANDER; TABLE SAW.*

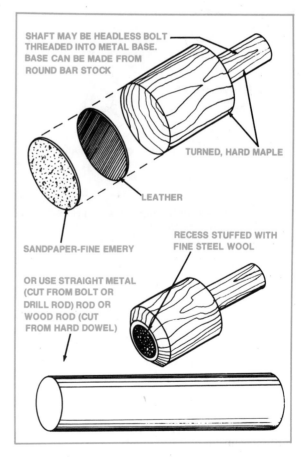

SHAFT MAY BE HEADLESS BOLT THREADED INTO METAL BASE. BASE CAN BE MADE FROM ROUND BAR STOCK

TURNED, HARD MAPLE

LEATHER

SANDPAPER-FINE EMERY

RECESS STUFFED WITH FINE STEEL WOOL

OR USE STRAIGHT METAL (CUT FROM BOLT OR DRILL ROD) ROD OR WOOD ROD (CUT FROM HARD DOWEL)

Spot polishers to make and use in the drill press. Such an operation is often referred to as "damaskeening".

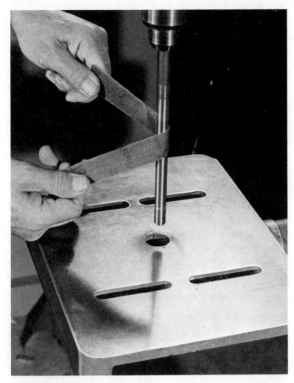

To polish rods, chuck in the drill press and apply an abrasive strip as shown here. Work down through progressively finer abrasive and end up with steel wool for a professional looking finish.

Drip Cap

Drip cap is a molding placed on the top exterior side of a door or window that allows water to drip beyond the outside of the frame. *SEE ALSO MOLDING & TRIM.*

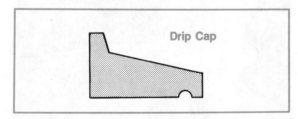

Drip Cap

Drip Edge

A drip edge is a strip of metal which runs along the edges of a roof to provide proper water drainage. The more common type of drip edge extends back from the roof approximately three inches, and is placed between the sheathing and underlayment. Another form of a drip edge is a strip of metal placed between the underlayment and the shingles. After the strip is laid on the roof surface, it is bent down over the edge so water may drip free of underlying cornices. *SEE ALSO ROOF CONSTRUCTION.*

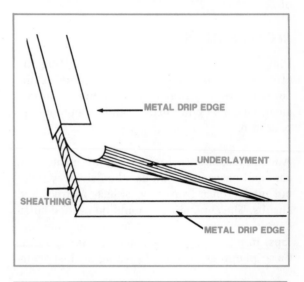

Drip Groove

A drip groove is a small hollowed out section on the under side of a window sill or wood or metal drip cap that causes water to drip off before reaching the face of the wall. *SEE ALSO MOLD-ING & TRIM.*

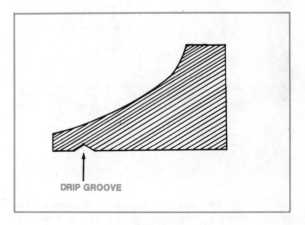

Drip Cap

Driveways

Driveways are areas used for driving a car from the street to its parking area. A driveway should be located where it is both useful to the car owner, and does not detract from the appearance of the home.

REQUIREMENTS

Planning a new driveway, or evaluating the effectiveness of an existing one, requires the consideration of four requirements: adequate clearance, size and surface, and acceptable appearance.

Adequate clearance for a driveway means that cars and passengers can use the driveway without interference from such objects as trees and shrubs. These plantings should be pruned sufficiently so that they will not scrape car sides and tops. In addition, people should be able to pass these plantings without brushing against them.

To avoid creating a blind spot and a potentially hazardous area, no large shrub or tree should be located near the curb at the end of a driveway.

Adequate size for a driveway means a 10 foot width with an absolute minimum of 8 feet. The additional 2 feet recommended provides space around the car to enable passengers to dismount and walk around the car. This space is most convenient where the lawn is wet or muddy. The ten foot width also insures that delivery vans and other vehicles will be able to use the driveway without damaging the lawn.

An adequate surface for a driveway is one that provides traction for a car in all weather, does not hold and puddle water, does not track into the house or car and is relatively maintenance free. The more common surfacing materials are reinforced concrete, blacktop or asphalt, and gravel.

Acceptable appearance for a driveway is best described as least obtrusive. If turnaround areas and spaces for off-street parking are to be provided in a relatively cramped suburban lot, careful landscaping should minimize the mass of paving. Materials that blend with the architecture of the house should be used whenever possible.

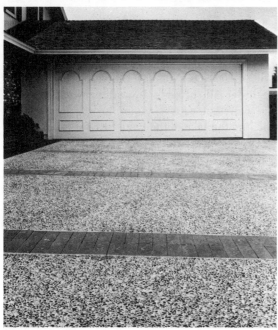

Courtesy Portland Cement Association

Exposed aggregate and brick may be combined for an unusual driveway treatment. Note how the driveway slopes away from the house to provide drainage.

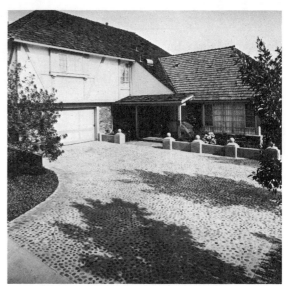

Courtesy Portland Cement Association

Exposed aggregate and brick edging combine to provide a welcoming forecourt for this house.

PLANNING

Graph paper and tissue or tracing paper are the basic tools in planning a driveway. Draw the scaled dimensions of the house and lot on the graph paper. Cover that drawing with the tissue paper and sketch in possible routes for the driveway. If lot space is available, experiment with turnaround areas, off-street parking, and planting areas. If turnaround areas or right-angle turns are necessary in the laying out of a driveway, a minimum radius of 20 feet should be used. Once a paper plan has been made, the driveway should be staked out on the lot for a practical check of the dimensions. Ideally, assuming the ground is dry and firm, an automobile should be driven up and down the proposed driveway, testing clearances, curves and other features of the proposed design.

SURFACING MATERIALS

A driveway should be surfaced with some material that will ensure its being passable in all weather. The three most common utilitarian surfacing materials are gravel, asphalt, and concrete. Some of the more decorative materials available are soil cement, brick, paving stones and wood.

Gravel is possibly the least expensive of the utilitarian materials. It is also possibly the least durable. The advantages of gravel are its low cost and natural look, which enables it to blend with the landscape more easily than a wide expanse of asphalt or concrete. Unfortunately, gravel has several disadvantages. First, it is not a permanent surface. After a period of use, a new load of gravel must be spread on the driveway to renew the all-weather surface. Second, a gravel driveway can be used only as a driveway. Asphalt or concrete driveways may also be used as hard-surfaced play areas for children. Such activities cannot be carried out on gravel. Third, gravel is noisy. Driving on gravel generates noise inside and outside the automobile.

Asphalt, or blacktop, a more expensive surfacing material than gravel, is relatively permanent. It can provide a multi-use play area for children and if laid properly it will shed water, and will not wash away, as gravel will. It does have cer-

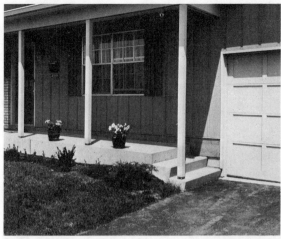

Courtesy Portland Cement Association

An asphalt driveway blends well with rustic or traditional architecture.

tain disadvantages. In extremely hot weather the surface may become soft and tacky, and as it is a dark color, asphalt will hold and retain heat. If the driveway is next to living areas of the house, this retained heat may be uncomfortable and may also increase home cooling costs. Blacktopped driveways require rapid attention to cracks and breaks in the surface, or the material will wear away and a deep pothole will result.

Reinforced concrete laid upon an adequate bed of gravel or crushed stone is probably the most durable and versatile surfacing material for a driveway. Concrete contains the advantages of blacktop without the disadvantages. Two disadvantages to concrete are its initial cost and its utilitarian appearance. If blacktop and gravel maintenance and repair costs are deducted from the initial cost of a concrete driveway, the cost is not nearly as excessive. Also, costs may be reduced by pouring driveway strips and filling the center strip with sand, gravel, or crushed stone. This strip design also helps to change the utilitarian appearance of concrete. Other ways that help are to pour the driveway as a series of large blocks, color the concrete, or use exposed aggregate in the driveway.

Soil cement may be used in naturalized, or rustic settings to provide a hard surfaced area that will blend well with the natural surroundings. Soil cement drives work well with natural looking planted areas.

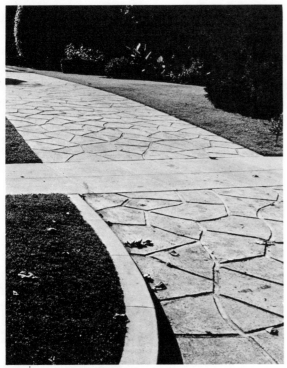

Courtesy Portland Cement Association

a poured concrete driveway may be tooled to resemble flagstones.

Brick, laid over a concrete base, makes a rather formal drive. If combined with off-street parking or a loop driveway, an area closely resembling an eighteenth century French or English forecourt may be created. Paving stones, salvaged from municipal repaving efforts, may also be used to create a formal forecourt area.

Wood rounds or strips, of either pressure-treated or decay-resistant woods, may be used to create a rustic and different driveway area. Wood paving materials, while providing a unique landscaping opportunity, are relatively high-maintenance items.

DRIVEWAY REPAIR

The more permanent surfacing materials, concrete and asphalt, will occasionally be in need of patching and repair. Even though the materials are dissimilar, the patching processes are similar in terms of cleaning out the broken area, and in tamping the patching material.

To patch concrete, all loose and broken pieces of concrete must be removed from the damaged area. Use a chisel and mallet to undercut the edges of the hole to provide a ledge to which the patching material can adhere. Roughen the bottom of the area with the chisel also (The basic idea is to provide a lip and rough surface to give the patch as much gluing area and support as possible). Safety goggles should be used to protect the eyes from flying concrete chips.

Sacks of prepared dry concrete provide the easiest method of obtaining patching material. After cleaning the damaged area of all loose concrete and concrete dust, sponge and hose down the patch area. Since the concrete patch will not adhere to dry concrete, the damaged area must be slightly damp. Remove all standing water before patching. Butter all surfaces of the damaged area with a mix of portland cement (about the consistency of creamy cake frosting), then fill the cavity with the patching mix. Tamp the patching material thoroughly, making sure there are no air cavities within the patch. Mound slightly to allow for shrinkage. Smooth lightly with a wooden float, then, as the concrete begins to set up, finish the surface to match the texture of the existing driveway. Allow to cure for 6 days before driving on the patch.

Asphalt driveways may also be patched with prepared mix available at building supply stores. Dig out the damaged blacktop until edges of solid·asphalt are formed. If the hole is quite deep, use gravel or sand to fill within 4 inches of the surface. Fill the remaining space with the prepared mix, cutting through the patching material with a shovel to prevent voids or air pockets. The patching material should be tamped while the repair is being made. Use a 3 foot piece of 2 x 4, 4 x 4, or 6 x 6 lumber and pack the material firmly in place. Tamp as each inch of patching material is laid down, or wait until the last inch of patching material is about to be placed in the hole. After firmly tamping, add about 1½ inches of patching material (mound about ½ or 1 inch above the driveway surface). Roll this material level with the surface, or pack flat with either the flat of the shovel, or the lumber tamper. Driving the car over the patch several times will firm the material well. Add

additional patching material as necessary to level the area. Spread a thin layer of sand over the fresh patch to provide a track-free surface. *SEE ALSO CONCRETE.*

Driving Safety & Automobile Insurance

DRIVING SAFETY

Nearly 60,000 people die annually on U. S. highways, as pedestrians, bicyclists, or drivers. The cost alone reaches $50 billion. Seat belts have the potential to keep 15,000 people alive each year, but the belts have largely been ignored. Available to 80 percent of vehicle occupants, seat belts are used only 20 percent of the time.

Auto seat belts have been mandatory equipment on all new U. S. cars since 1964. In a crash, properly worn seat belts lessen injuries resulting from being bounced around a car interior. Moreover, shoulder belts, mandatory since 1968, restrain the upper torso in a crash, preventing head-on body collisions with the steering column or dashboard. Belts enable a driver to stay behind the wheel, make emergency maneuvers, and keep other occupants from being thrown out of the vehicle.

In a study of 28,000 highway crashes, none of 9,345 occupants wearing seat/shoulder belts were fatally injured, even in crashes up to 60 mph (94kph). Yet nonbelted occupants were killed at speeds low as 12 mph (19kph).

Seat belts should be fastened low over the hips and tightened until just snug. Nontensioning shoulder belts should be adjusted so that when the driver is seated, he can fit a clenched fist between the chest and the belt. Tensioned inertia-reel belts are self-adjusting.

Defensive Driving

Defensive driving is defined as piloting a car to minimize risk to yourself by anticipating the actions and errors of other drivers. As a defensive driver, strive for perfection by staying alert, keeping ahead of the traffic situation, maintaining the correct distance between you and the car ahead and by adjusting your speed to driving conditions. Drive according to weather, road surface, lighting, traffic, car and your own mental and physical condition at the time. When a hazard is spotted on the road ahead, slow down. Check side and rear-view mirrors frequently. As a defensive driver, study what to do in emergencies and always be mentally prepared for one.

Be aware of the braking and traction capabilities of your car under various conditions. Most drivers do not realize the full emergency steering potential of their cars. Fast maneuvering and prudent use of the brake can reduce the risk of collisions due to locked brakes. Rather than panic on the brake pedal, pick out a safe escape route along the shoulder, into a field, across a ditch or up a hill. Avoid hitting concrete abutments, bridge supports, power poles, and any trees more than 8 inches (200 mm) in diameter, all of which can prove fatal in collision.

The faster your car is moving, the more following distance it will take you to stop. On a dry, level pavement, the average car takes 75 feet (22.9m) to stop from 30 mph (48kph). At 60 mph (94kph), the car travels nearly 275 feet (84m) before stopping. Adjust your following distance behind other cars to suit speed. In rain, snow, and other adverse conditions, allow a greater time interval.

Skid Control

To regain control of a car in a skid, steer into the skid, avoiding both the brake and the gas pedals. Stomping the brake pedal, a natural instinct in a skid situation, will negate all steering effort. Do not use either the gas or the brake pedal until the car is under control.

Great Escapes

If the brakes fail, first try pumping the brake pedal. If this doesn't produce a slowing action, apply the parking brake and shift to a lower gear. If you lose your brakes on a long mountain grade, it may be necessary to sideswipe an embankment or drive into a grove of small trees to stop the car.

487

If the accelerator pedal sticks, turn off the ignition quickly and brake to a stop. Be prepared for the loss of power steering and power brakes.

If a tire blows out, maintain a firm grip on the steering wheel while gradually slowing down. Panic braking may send the car out of control. Pull far off the road on the shoulder to change the tire.

AUTOMOBILE INSURANCE

Auto insurance coverages are available in the following: bodily injury liability, property-damage liability, collision, medical payments, comprehensive, emergency road service, car rental, and uninsured motorist.

Both property-damage liability and bodily injury liability coverages protect you up to a specified dollar limit from claims for property damage and for injury to others. A 25/50/10 policy will pay $25,000 to one injured person, a maximum of $50,000 for all injuries in any one accident, plus $10,000 for property damages from that accident.

Medical-payments coverage generally pays the medical bills of anyone who is injured in an auto accident, regardless of fault. This coverage also has limits. Thus, hospital-doctor bills are paid without waiting for lengthy liability proceedings. A special coverage, called death indemnity, dismemberment and loss of sight, pays a specified sum if the insured dies or is seriously injured because of an auto accident. Disability insurance coverage pays regular sums if the insured is disabled and cannot work following an accident. It may also be called loss-of-income coverage.

Comprehensive coverage reimburses for loss or damage to your car by theft, natural disaster, riot, fire, and most other catastrophic events that are out of your control. It also pays for broken windows and items lost or damaged while inside your car. Some comprehensive coverages have deductibles to eliminate small claims.

Collision insurance pays for repairs to your car in an accident where you are liable for your own damages. It usually has a deductible amount,

which means that in the event of a collision, you pay something toward any repair. The company pays everything more than the deductible up to the total value of the car. The larger the deductible amount, the lower the premium. Collision coverage is often required by the lender if a car is financed. The lender will ask for a proof of loss policy. In case of loss, the insurance company will pay the lender.

Accidents

1. Stay at the accident scene. It's unlawful to leave without permission.
2. Turn off the ignition switch. Don't smoke.
3. Ask a passing motorist to call the police.
4. Don't move the injured unless it is necessary to protect them from fire or traffic. Don't give any first aid that you are not qualified to administer.
5. Station someone down the road to slow traffic and prevent further accidents. Set out flares if you have them.
6. Get names, addresses and license numbers of all parties involved in the accident, plus witnesses.
7. Don't admit responsibility for the accident and don't encourage others who were involved to do so. It can void insurance coverage. Don't say anything you wouldn't want repeated in court.
8. Give other parties the name and address of your insurance agent. Call your agent immediately afterward.
9. Write down the details and all the facts of the accident — everything you can recall. Diagram it on paper. File a state accident report, if required.

Rating

Insurance rates are determined partly by the age, sex, occupation and marital status of drivers in the family. The intended use of the car and the area in which you live has a bearing, too. Most companies use a point system to determine your insurance rating. According to the severity and number of accidents you have had, points are added to the rating. Having no points entitles you to a 15 percent good-driver discount; 1 point puts a 5 percent surcharge on your premium; 2 points, 50 percent surcharge; 3 points, 100 percent surcharge. Having 4 or more points means that

you will have to pay a 150 percent surcharge. Three years of perfect driving will eliminate the latter.

Beyond this, especially high-risk drivers are given an *assigned-risk* category. Auto insurance companies are required by state law to accept a quota of assigned-risk drivers each year. Though assigned-risk premiums are much higher than normal ones, it is still a losing proposition for them.

Company and Agent

There are two kinds of auto insurance companies: direct-writing and agency companies. Select the company first. Choose a financially strong, well-managed one that operates throughout the nation. Also, choose a company with a reputation for paying its claims fairly and promptly, and for not canceling policies without good reason.

An insurance company's financial strength can be checked at your local library in a book called *BEST'S INSURANCE REPORTS* for property-liability companies. Insist on a rating of A+ (excellent) in financial stability.

Company chosen, probably the best way to select an agent is to ask friends, neighbors, and co-workers. General agents, making up what is called the American agency system, each represent several insurance companies. They will place your insurance with whatever company they feel is best, unless you ask for a particular one.

No-Fault Coverage

No-fault auto insurance is a different kind of coverage. It departs from conventional auto insurance in that each policyholder is reimbursed for medical and hospital cost by his own insurance company. Not all no-fault includes repair or replacement of cars and property. No consideration is given to whose fault the accident was. This is supposed to save over the present system by cutting out court, lawyer, claims adjuster and legal costs in proving fault.

Drop Cloth
[SEE PAINTS & PAINTING.]

Drop Siding

Drop siding is a final protective covering applied to the outside walls of a building. It is composed of horizontally laid boards, which are nailed to the wall sheathing or directly to the house frame. Drop siding boards are interlocked by tongue-and-groove joints. They are generally one inch thick and six inches wide, and are milled in various shapes and patterns. *SEE ALSO SIDING.*

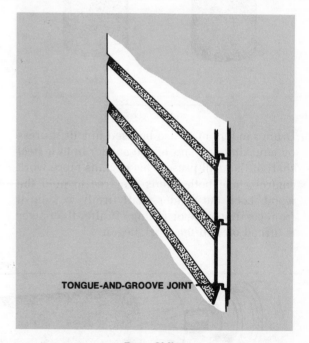

TONGUE-AND-GROOVE JOINT

Drop Siding

Drum Sander

A drum sander is any sander which has a steel cylinder to which sandpaper is attached for smoothing wood surfaces. The most common drum sander is operated by attaching the drum

to a special bit and inserting it in a power hand drill. These sanders usually range in sizes from one-half to two inches in diameter and have replaceable sandpaper cylinders called sleeves. The sleeves come in different grades of coarseness for rough or fine work. This type of drum sander is used primarily for smoothing narrow, concave edges and sabre-sawed holes. In using the drum sander, move it against the drum rotation so it won't kick into a more rapid motion and cause a temporary loss of control and damage to the work.

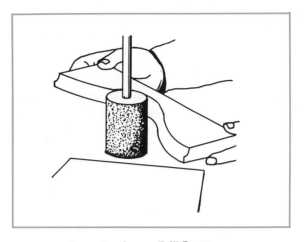

Drum Sander on Drill Press

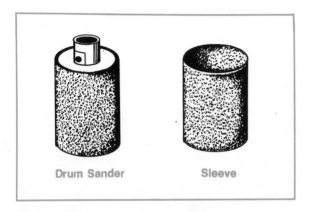

Drum sanders may also be used in a drill press by chucking one end of the sander onto a steel shaft of the drill press. This permits more work control since both hands are free to hold the wood. Lock the sander shaft firmly to keep it from coming loose or falling off after the power is turned on and the work begun.

There are electric-powered machines designed specifically for drum sanding. This tool has adjustable heights and positions for smoothing concave edges, cabriole legs, board surfaces and jointing edges. These drum sanders permit the wood to be worked free hand or by placing it on a surface for additional support. A drum sander of this variety is generally used by professional woodworkers.

A home-made drum sander is a wood cylinder which has a notched wedge in it that can be removed for changing sandpaper. The sander is approximately 15 inches long and is mounted between the centers of a lathe for smoothing wide boards. A table is placed underneath the board for support during sanding.

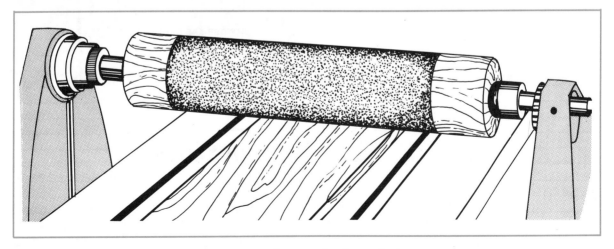

Home-Made Drum Sander on Lathe

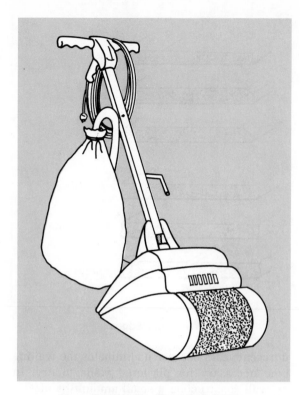

Drum Sander For Floor Refinishing

Drum sanders can also be a large machine for smoothing down and removing varnish from wood floors. This electric sander has a switch to control the speed, a large drum with diagonal slots for changing sandpaper, a dust bag and handles for easy operation. Sanding should be done with the grain at an even pace and the sandpaper should be changed from coarse to fine as the work progresses. This type of drum sander can be rented for flooring projects. *SEE ALSO PORTABLE POWER TOOLS.*

Drum Trap

A drum trap or drum trap with cover is a one piece copper pipe fitting. It has an opening which connects a bathtub drain to the bottom of the fitting. Another feature of this fitting is a side inlet. The top of the drum trap has a plug to prevent water from escaping through it. *SEE ALSO PIPE FITTINGS.*

Drum Trap

Drumming Pipes
[SEE WATER HAMMER.]

Dry Rot

Dry rot is a term used to describe a type of wood decay caused by a water-conducting fungus. The spores of this microscopic, thread-like fungus grow and spread in a damp environment, primarily moist soil. These spores are transported by clothing, shoes or through the air. The fungus becomes visible in timber as a multiple of white mycelium strands. These strands form sheets which sprout tendrils or tubes throughout the wood, which seek moisture for nourishment, causing weakening or destruction of the lumber. The term *dry rot* is actually an inaccurate description of the condition, for the fungus cannot live and cause decay in dry wood, although the wood may be reduced to a dry, powdery form after advanced decay has taken place.

Cellars, stair-supporting timbers, and any lower structure wood members in direct contact with the dirt should be inspected for decay at regular intervals. Roof and bathroom fixtures should also be watched for leaks, and attics should be well-ventilated. Wood that appears spongy and contains open pores may be weakened by dry rot and should be replaced. Lumber that has been pretreated with a chemical preservative is best to use for construction. For maximum protection against decay, the wood should be deeply penetrated with the preservative. This is accomplished through a pressure treatment, which an industrial plant is best equipped to handle. Creosote is a chemical sometimes used to pretreat wood. Because of the strong odor of creosote, Pentachlorophenol and other metallic salts are more often used for wood preservation.

491

However, the homeowner can treat his own lumber with one of the new chemical wood preservatives. These preservatives may be applied to the wood with a brush, but since the chemical must impregnate the lumber as fully as possible, soaking the exposed ends of the wood in the preservative is the recommended method. Some of these modern preservatives are pentachlorophenol, zinc and copper naphthenates, and copper sulfate crystals dissolved in water. These modern preservatives are poisonous to human beings and should be used with caution. They are not, however, dangerous to plant life after they have dried into the lumber. Drainage of moist dirt on the construction site and ventilation of the crawl space or vapor barriers between floors and subfloors are also recommended measures for protection against decay.

To halt the progress of decay, the fungus must be cut off from its source of moisture. Often, the fungus travels to a joist or sill through a wooden brace frame or grading stake or through a tree stump left beneath the house. The fungus may also grow and spread to the sills through dirt fills beneath concrete porch slabs or wood that is set in moistened concrete. Direct contact with wood is not always necessary for the bacteria to get moisture from the dirt. Mycelium strands extending over foundation walls or through cracks in loosely constructed masonry may provide the fungus with nourishment from the soil. If the decay cannot be stopped after all possible sources have been eliminated, a corrosion-proof metal cap, similar to a termite shield, may be placed over the sills or over the top of foundation walls. The soil surrounding foundation walls may be poisoned with a four per cent sodium flouride solution, five gallons for every ten feet of soil, which is the same treatment recommended for termites.

Drywall

Drywall is a construction term which refers to the application of prepared plaster sheets, such as gypsum wallboard, to walls and ceilings. The use of drywall has become increasingly popular

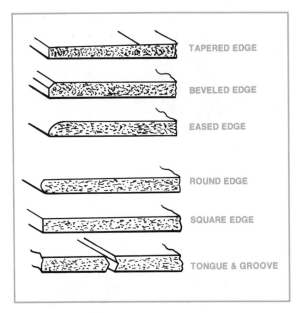

Wallboard Edges

in recent years because it eliminates the waiting time necessary for plastered walls to dry. In drywall construction a small amount of plaster or wallboard joint compound is used to seal the joints and cover nailheads.

One of the basic materials needed for drywall construction is the wallboard itself, sometimes called sheetrock, plasterboard or gypsum wallboard. The wallboard consists of a noncombustible core, often particle board, styrofoam or paper honeycomb, between two sheets of treated, heavy paper. Wallboard panels come in a variety of thicknesses, including $3/8$, $1/2$ and $5/8$ inches, and are usually four feet wide and from six to 16 feet long. The panels are sometimes finished with a decorative or wood grain pattern, although more often wallboard is painted or finished after it is applied. Wallboard edges may be tapered, beveled or grooved to make different types of joints between panels which can be filled with compound to form a smooth wall or ceiling surface.

MEASURING & CUTTING WALLBOARD

Drywall construction requires accurate measuring to insure proper cutting and fitting of the wallboard. To cut the wallboard, score the face side with a sharp knife using a straightedge.

Then cut through the paper, slightly penetrating the core. Place the wallboard over a table edge or sawhorse and snap downward away from the scored side so that the core will break. Cut the paper on the under side. The edges may be smoothed with sandpaper. When cutting a hole in the wallboard, such as an opening for an electrical outlet, measure carefully and mark the design to be cut. Use a drill to put holes in the corners and a compass saw or a coping saw to make the cut.

APPLYING SINGLE LAYERS

Wallboard can be applied in single or double layers. Single layers are applied to the wood framework with panel joints in the side walls located at the center of the studs. Usually wallboard is applied on the ceiling first, with long edges at right angles to studs and joists. This requires either two people or one person using a T-brace to hold up the panels. Side walls are covered by starting at one corner and working around the room. Apply wallboard with joints either parallel or perpendicular to studs depending on which method uses the fewer number of joints. On the individual panels, work from the center out and use cement-coated wallboard nails or drywall nails in various sizes according to the thickness of the panel (usually $1^5/_8$ inches for $^3/_8$ inch or $^1/_2$ inch wallboard and $1^7/_8$ inch for $^5/_8$ inch). Nails should be spaced eight inches apart and $^3/_8$ inch in from edges. Make sure to drive the nail into a stud, using a crown-head hammer to dimple the panel with the final blow. Be careful not to break the surface paper or crumble the core. Joint compound is used to fill the hole and even out the surface around the nail head.

Using a special adhesive is another method of attaching wallboard. The adhesive is applied in a continuous bead to the center of a joist, stud or furring. Nails or braces can be used to temporarily hold the wallboard in place until the adhesive sets.

TAPING JOINTS & CORNERS

After the wallboard has been attached, the next step is taping the joints and corners. Use a wide putty knife or joint knife to press the compound into the joint between wallboard panels. Before the compound dries, put perforated wallboard tape in the joint and press with a trowel so that the cement comes through the holes. After the embedding coat is dry, add two more coats, waiting for each to dry in between, until the joint is sealed and the surface is level. Feather the edges of the joint with each application and sand lightly after the final coat to insure a smooth surface.

Corners must be taped also. Inside corners are done in the same manner as wallboard joints

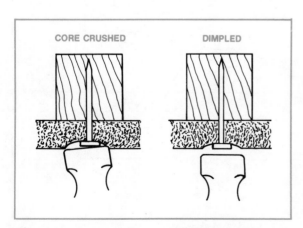

Use crown-head hammer to dimple wallboard.

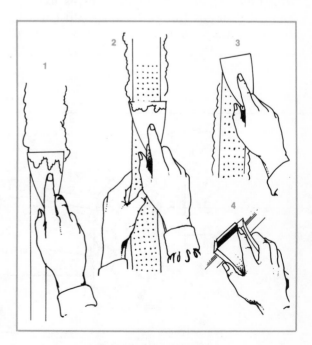

Steps in taping a joint.

with the tape folded to fit in the corner angle. Outside corners are reinforced with a metal corner bead. One type of bead is metal with paper flanges covered with joint compound as are regular joints. Another type is nailed through the wallboard to the frame.

APPLYING DOUBLE LAYERS

Wallboard may be applied in double layers for stronger walls or better sound insulation. The first layer is usually regular gypsum wallboard attached in the usual manner. The second layer is attached to the first by wall joint compound or an adhesive, with joints offset at least ten inches from joints in the first layer. The adhesive is applied either in strips or dabs, making sure the outer layer is sufficiently bonded to the under layer. Use nails or braces to temporarily hold the layers together until the adhesive dries. Fill nail holes with compound. *SEE ALSO WALL & CEILING CONSTRUCTION.*

Dry Well

A dry well is a hole in the ground, usually filled with rocks or gravel, which receives excess water that drains from a building. Most water drains off the outside and roof of a building through gutters and downspouts and when water draining through a downspout is heavy, top soil may wash away. To prevent this wash, a dry well is constructed by digging a hole under the downspout and filling it with old concrete blocks, rocks or stone through which water seeps and soaks into the ground. It should be positioned at least ten feet from the foundation wall.

More complicated dry wells are connected by drain tiles to sewer lines and are walled with concrete blocks or made from a steel drum placed 12 or 18 inches below the ground. The drum is punctured with random drill holes and filled with rocks or blocks. An underground pipe connects the drum to the main downspout. Either a grill or wooden planks may cover the drum before earth is packed tightly around and on top of the dry well.

When water drainage is an extreme problem, several dry wells are used with placement at corners of a building or near downspouts. Before installing a dry well to handle other water drainage problems, such as washing machines, wash basins and tubs, check with the local building code. Some codes will permit all but toilet drainage to empty into a dry well. When kitchen sinks are connected to a dry well, a grease trap should be used. *SEE ALSO GUTTERS & DOWNSPOUTS.*

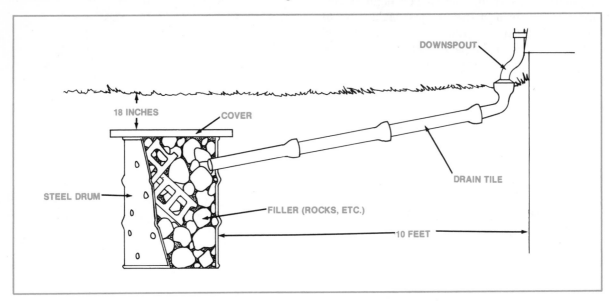

A dry well made of a steel drum.

Dual-Control Lights

Dual-control lights are controlled by switches in two different locations. In this way, lights can be turned on or off from one switch regardless of the on-off position of the other. For example, an upstairs light can be turned on downstairs and then turned off from another switch upstairs. *SEE ALSO SWITCHES & OUTLETS.*

Duct Tape

Duct tape is a special tape used to hold insulation on round ducts to stop heat loss through the duct. This tape may be used in place of staples and can usually be purchased with the insulation.

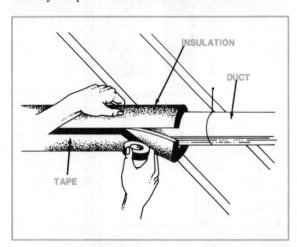

Attaching insulation to a duct.

Ductwork, Warm Air
[SEE HEATING SYSTEMS.]

Dull Rubbing

Dull rubbing is the process of rubbing a high-gloss finished surface with abrasives to achieve a dull glow. When dull rubbing, it is important to rub with the wood grain and use either fine sandpaper or 000 grade steel wool to prevent scratching or cutting the surface. After dull rubbing is completed, wax the surface to protect it. *SEE ALSO WOOD FINISHING.*

Duplex Outlet Receptacle

Duplex outlet receptacles are devices set into or mounted on walls and baseboards to accommodate (or give power to) two plugs at the same time. In their usual form, duplex outlet receptacles have two terminal screws on each side for connection to house wiring and "plaster ears" at each end for mounting in the common outlet or switch box. Rated at 15 amperes, they are available with vertical or T slots.

An adequately wired home should have enough duplex outlets in each room to accommodate all appliances without the use of extension cords. Additional outlets are less expensive to install during initial home construction than when added afterward. *SEE ALSO SWITCHES & OUTLETS.*

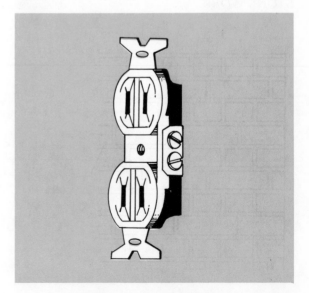

Duplex Outlet Receptacle

Dust & Moisture Proof Receptacle

Dust and moisture proof receptacles are specialized receptacles with obstructed slots that admit plug prongs but close when the plug is removed to prevent the entrance of dust and moisture. Some also have hinged covers which prevent dirt or moisture from entering receptacle slots. Dust and moisture proof receptacles are neither child proof nor weatherproof. *SEE ALSO SWITCHES & OUTLETS.*

Dutch Bond

Dutch bond, also known as English cross bond, describes a pattern of brick laying which is a modification of English bond. Dutch bond has alternating courses or rows of headers, bricks laid crosswise, and stretchers, bricks laid end to end, as does English bond. However, in Dutch bond, two courses of headers and one course of stretchers are laid in between stretchers with coinciding vertical joints. *SEE ALSO BRICK & STONE WORK.*

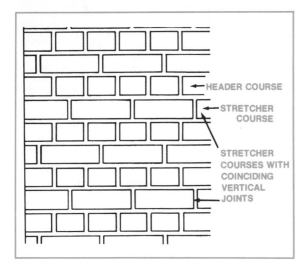

Dutch Bond

Dutch Doors

A Dutch door is a door which is horizontally divided with its two halves swinging in or out on separate hinges. One or both of the halves may contain a window or screen. Most Dutch doors are factory made in standard sizes and come in a complete package including frame, sill, threshold and hinges. When used as exterior doors, Dutch doors usually swing in.

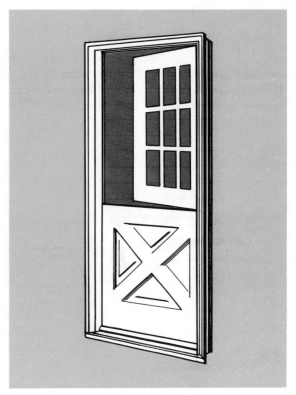

A typical Dutch door.

Dutchman

A dutchman is a piece of material used to hide or cover a defect. An example of a dutchman is a piece of cardboard placed in a window pane to cover a broken or missing section.

Dwell Meter

A dwell meter is a complex testing instrument used by the handyman for normal automobile maintenance work. By indicating the time that the distributor points remain closed, it shows the passage of current in an automobile engine. Most large American cars with V-8 engines have distributors located in such inaccessible places that it is impossible to set the points using an ordinary feeler gauge. *SEE ALSO SYSTEMS, AUTOMOTIVE.*

Easel, Photographic
[SEE PHOTOGRAPHY.]

Eave

Eaves are the lower part of the roof that overhangs the exterior walls. The eave is sometimes called the overhang. *SEE ALSO ROOF CONSTRUCTION.*

Eave Flashing

Eave flashing is a sheet metal strip used for waterproofing and protecting the eaves from melting snow or from backed-up frozen slush in the gutters. It should be installed over the underlayment at least 12 inches from the roof edge and down to and overlapping the metal drip edge. Eave flashing is then covered with roofing shingles. *SEE ALSO ROOF CONSTRUCTION.*

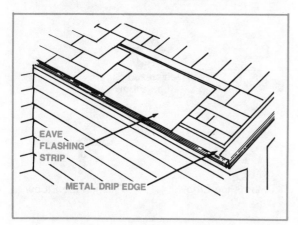

Ebony Wood

Ebony wood is an extremely hard, heavy wood that is found in Africa and Asia. Although referred to as a black wood, ebony wood actually has striped bands of dark brown and salmon pink. One of the main uses of ebony wood is for black keys on a piano. It is also used for inlays, marquetry and small decorative articles.

Ebony wood was used by the Egyptians and Babylonians in the 17th century B.C. They used it with gold, silver and ivory for their court furniture. *SEE ALSO WOOD IDENTIFICATION.*

Edge Nailing
[SEE FASTENERS.]

Edger
[SEE LAWNS & GARDENS.]

Edge Tools

Edge tools are tools which have a sharp edge that is used for chiseling, scraping, smoothing or cutting. Among these are planes, chisels, knives and scrapers.

Probably the most familiar edge tool is the plane. Planes are used in smoothing rough surfaces, grooving and routing. Each one has a different blade angle which is easily adjusted by a nut. The jack plane is a carpenter's favorite because it is small enough for trimming and smoothing

wood, but large enough to make a straight cut over a long board. Block planes are generally six or seven inches long, permitting control with one hand for small jobs, such as smoothing end grain. A rabbet plane is for rabbeting boards and has flat sides at a right angle to the bottom of the plane. Router planes are for removing wood from grooves and dadoes after the sides have been sawed.

Wood chisels are designed to work across or with the grain in removing strips or chips of wood. Standard wood chisels have flat blades ranging in widths from $1/8$ to $1^1/2$ inches and are operated either by hand or striking the handle with a soft-faced hammer or mallet. Cabinet and butt chisels have short blades for accurate work in forming hinge and similar mortises. Spear, round-nose and skew chisels are used in lathe work for forming delicate shapes and patterns.

Cold chisels are used primarily by masons and metalworkers for heavy cutting and shaping. Cape chisels are for chipping narrow grooves; diamond points are designed for cleaning out sharp corners and cutting V-shaped grooves; flat chisels are used for cutting rivets and bars and shearing metal.

Knives are one type of edge tool probably most everyone has. Pocket knives are for cutting, scraping and whittling; putty knives are for scraping paint and applying filler; utility knives are for cutting different materials and linoleum knives are used in cutting linoleum.

Scrapers have thin sharp edges for removing paint, varnish and wood. Hand scrapers are good for working in corners because they have no frame or handle. Pull scrapers have a handle which provides more leverage for removing large quantities of wood. Cabinet scrapers are for smoothing wood in cabinetmaking.

A cornering tool has a straight, flat body that curves in opposite directions at each end. In the center of each curve is a round opening that is used for rounding off sharp edges. *SEE ALSO HAND TOOLS.*

Egyptian Saw

The Egyptian saw, first made by the early Egyptians, has teeth which are pointed backward to cut on the pull stroke. Although most Oriental saws are made this way today, all Western hand saws except the coping saw are devised to cut on the push stroke. *SEE ALSO HAND TOOLS.*

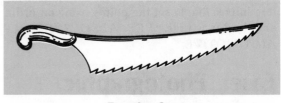

Egyptian Saw

Elbow

An elbow can be a copper tube, copper pipe, galvanized steel, plastic or steel pipe fitting. This type of fitting joins pipe meeting at various angles. An elbow is designed to form bends or turns in the pipe. *SEE ALSO PIPE FITTINGS.*

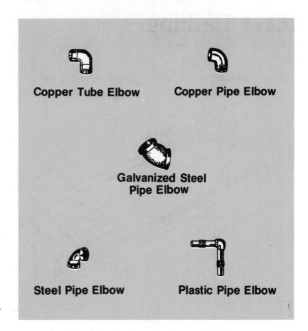

Copper Tube Elbow **Copper Pipe Elbow**

Galvanized Steel Pipe Elbow

Steel Pipe Elbow **Plastic Pipe Elbow**

Electrical Code
[SEE NATIONAL ELECTRICAL CODE.]

Electrical Fuses
[SEE FUSES & CIRCUIT BREAKERS.]

Electrical Hazards

An electrical hazard can be anything from a blown fuse to an inadequately-grounded wiring system. Most electrical hazards can be prevented by knowing where they originate and how to avoid them. Never attempt even a minor repair, like replacing a fuse, without first turning off the main switch, which is located in the fuse panel. This will prevent shock and possible death.

Probably the most common electrical hazard is a blown fuse or a tripped circuit breaker. These are generally caused by an overloaded circuit breaker or motor, or worn insulation causing two bare wires to touch and short. In replacing a fuse, turn off the current, remove the blown fuse and then screw the new fuse in its place, always keeping one hand free or in a pocket. Never use a high-amperage fuse in a lower-amperage socket. This causes overheated wiring in the walls of the house, which could result in fire.

Extension cords, if not properly used, could be the source of an electrical hazard. Overloaded extension cords can overheat, melt the insulation in the cord and possibly cause a fire. An extension cord should never be run under a rug since the abrasion will wear through the insulation and, again, possibly cause a fire. When extension cords show wear near the plug, replace the cord rather than taping it. Worn cords have little (if any) insulation, which can leave loose wires that can touch and cause a short circuit. Never pull a plug from a socket by its cord, as this could cause the wires to loosen from the terminal screws, and eventually form a bad connection. Extension cords should never be used as part of

a permanent wiring system because they are usually light gauge and cannot withstand a lot of electrical power like cable can. A cord of any kind near a heat source, like a radiator or hot-air duct, should be checked often for cracks that will cause the insulation to wear thin and leave bare wire sections touching which again, could create a fire. One of the best ways to avoid using overloaded and extremely long extension cords to reach outlets, is to install new receptacles.

Improperly grounded wiring systems and appliances or lightening rods struck by lightening can cause fuses and circuits to blow and start a fire. Additional grounding wire can be attached to receptacles and run to the original wiring system which will alleviate the first hazard. Lightening rods should either be removed or properly grounded with a neutral wire running from the rod to another metal rod in the ground.

Working with electricity in a damp basement without taking the proper precautions is hazardous. Always use insulated tools, gloves and wear rubber boots. Turning on a light while standing in a filled bathtub can be fatal if a metal portion of an electrical fixture on the "hot" side of the circuit is touched, and the bathtub is on the "grounded" side. Never use an electric fan or any appliance near a tub of water or any other water source. The right amount of water could cause a fatal shock. *SEE ALSO ELECTRICAL WIRING.*

Electrical Symbols

Electrical symbols are used on blueprints to indicate placement of electrical fixtures. Since plans are drawn to scale, symbols are used

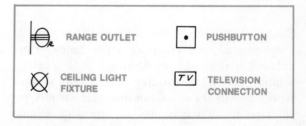

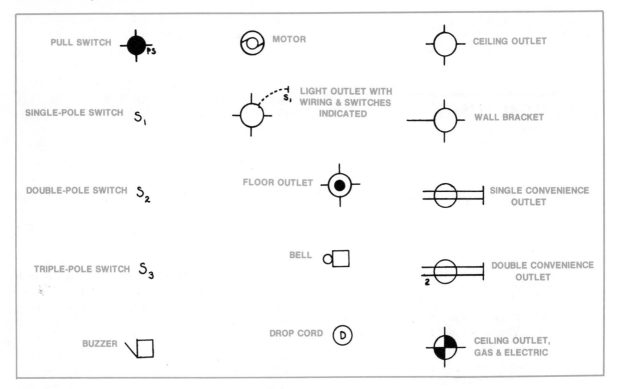

rather than labels or scale drawings for ease in preparing and reading plans. *SEE ALSO BLUEPRINTS.*

Electrical System, Auto
[SEE SYSTEMS, AUTOMOTIVE.]

Electric System Modernization
[SEE ELECTRICAL WIRING.]

Electrical Tape

Electrical tape, or electrician's tape, has a black vinyl plastic outer covering which helps in insulating a wire splice. Although it is used in almost any wire splicing, electrician's tape works best in dry areas. For instance, use electrical tape in switch outlets or any area where

space is minimal. *SEE ALSO ELECTRICIAN'S TOOLS & EQUIPMENT.*

Electrical Wiring

Electrical wiring systems should be planned, installed and properly maintained for prolonged use and safety. This is easily done in a new home, but older homes may require rewiring or repairing to prevent overloaded circuits, blown fuses and fire hazards. The city code will list what cable should be used, if the homeowner may perform the entire job, part of it or none at all. In some cities, a licensed electrician is required only to complete the final hook up.

An electrical system must be properly grounded to prevent blown fuses, shock, overloaded circuits and possible fire. Additional grounding wire, three-prong outlets or three-prong adapters may be used for extra safety.

Wiring for 240 or 120/240-volt combinations necessitates larger wire than regular 120-volt

wiring. Before performing any 240-volt wiring, check the city code for grounding details and inspect the service entrance to determine if it is large enough. A new service panel may be needed when rewiring an old home. After the service panel is replaced, the wiring may be added. Surface wiring is probably the easiest way to install additional circuits in an older home. In this method, the wiring is mounted on the wall surfaces with staples so that drilling and sawing in the house walls are kept at a minimum.

Outdoor wiring systems should be constructed of weatherproof outlets and switches and wire suitable for underground use. Consult the city code for regulations concerning appropriate materials. Underground fused wire is generally run between the outdoor fixture and the wiring system, but in some areas it may be prohibited.

Check the National Electrical Code for approved wiring procedures and techniques before adding or reworking an electrical system. For additional safety, use cables, wires, receptacles and other materials which are endorsed by Underwriter's Laboratories.

Before installing, repairing or rewiring an electrical system, turn off the main switch at the service panel. Wear insulated gloves, rubber boots and use insulated tools when working with electricity, particularly in a damp basement. Test the wiring job before replacing switches and outlets to check for loose connections or other electrical faults. *SEE ALSO WIRING SYSTEMS, ELECTRICAL.*

Electric Blanket Repair

Electric blankets have a soft, flexible resistance wire built into the middle of a dual-layer blanket. When dual controls are used, two of these elements are connected to a common terminal and a separate control switches each off and on independently to maintain proper heat. Within the blanket there are also thermostats which will turn the element off in case of overheating.

The control from the blanket is activated by the temperature within the room. As the room becomes cooler, a bimetal arm tends to hold the contacts closed longer. The control has a compensator heater built into the control body to cause the control to "shortcycle". This eliminates long periods of heating. This compensator heater uses the resistance of the blanket to create a small amount of heat within the control, causing it to cut off sooner than it would otherwise. The temperature of the room determines how long it takes the contacts to reset and turn the element back on. This is the clicking sound that you hear as the control operates when the blanket is in use.

Since most controls have a pilot light built into them, it is easy to tell if power is coming to the blanket when it fails to operate. If the pilot is off, it is a good indication that a fuse has blown or that there is something wrong in the house circuit. If the pilot light burns and the blanket still doesn't operate, check the cords and make sure that all connections are tight.

Lacking a test meter, it is often helpful to use substitution to locate the problem within an appliance like an electric blanket. If you have another blanket or a similar blanket in the home with identical wiring connections, you can remove one control and try it on the other

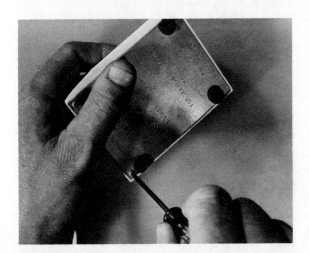

The control base of an electric blanket is usually serviced by removing small screws from the bottom cover. Be sure that blanket is unplugged before loosening this screw.

blanket. Often this will pinpoint the problem quickly. If the fault lies within the blanket itself, it is likely within one of the thermostats or the heating element. It's not advisable to open the blanket to make such a repair. Luckily though, when used according to the manufacturers recommendations and when care is used in washing, blanket problems with the heating element and built-in thermostat seldom occur.

The control is serviceable enough. Unplug it before attempting to inspect it. The bottom cover or back can usually be opened by removing the screws that hold it to the top. This will expose at least a part of the control section and usually the contact section, where the problem often lies. A small amount of wattage is used by these blankets and contacts seldom become burned. However, they can become coated with lint or dust that insulates them. A piece of white bond paper pulled through the contacts several times should serve to polish them enough to restore operation.

If the blanket should overheat, the fault usually lies within the control. If the control is out of calibration or is sticking, you may be able to make some limited adjustment at the knob or on the back of the control itself. If the control has been dropped, there is a chance that the compensator heater (which will be seen as a wire element running across the back of the control

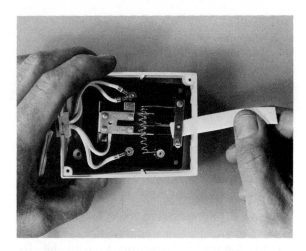

The compensator heater in an electric blanket control helps even out cycles and prevent abrupt temperature changes. Look for loose connections at either end of the compensator.

bimetal) has been bent too close to the bimetal. Spreading it away slightly may remedy the condition. No weight such as a spread, another blanket or even a bedspread should be placed on an electric blanket.

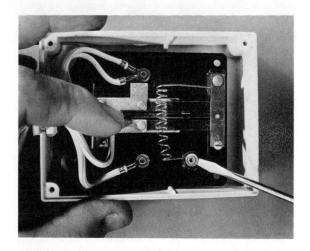

Contacts in an electric blanket control can be cleaned with a small strip of bond paper. Wiping paper lightly across the contact removes grease and lint.

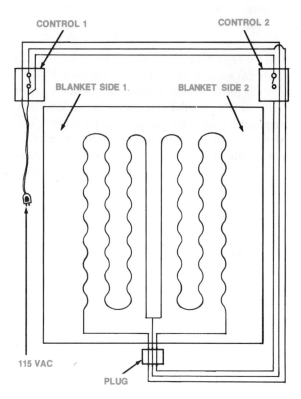

Typical Electric Blanket

If the pilot fails to operate, the problem is likely within the light itself or the resistor which is used in series with it. Small neon lights sold at replacement parts dealers can be soldered in to replace the defective one. If the blanket operates properly but the light does not operate, this repair is usually all that is necessary.

Electric Bug Killer

Flying insects are attracted to an artificially lighted area. A blue light, in particular, seems to be especially attractive to them. That is because the blue light spectrum is rich in ultraviolet radiation. This electric bug killer uses a centrally located blue electric bulb, surrounded by two concentric metal grids made from 2^1/$_2$ inch long wire rods. The rods that make up the outer grid are spaced ^{3}/$_8$ inch apart, while those of the inner grid are separated by only ^{5}/$_{16}$ inch. The grids are aligned so that the vertical rods of the inner one lie opposite the spaces separating the rods of the outer grid.

These two grids are connected to a 1,200-volt step-up transformer, so that a constant high-voltage electrical charge exists between them whenever the killer is plugged in. A flying insect which is drawn toward the blue light has to pass between the inner and outer grids to reach the light. Because of the rod placement, it is very likely that the bug will touch both inner and outer grids at the same time with some part of its body (the wing tips for example) and the bug is electrocuted. The dead insect drops into a convenient snap-out trap which makes disposal a neat and simple matter.

The step-up transformer of the bug killer makes high voltage from conventional 120-volt, 60 cycle alternating current. The transformer consists of two windings of fine, insulated wire, wrapped about a special steel core. The *primary* winding connects to the house current outlet. The *secondary* winding, which has 10 times the number of wire turns on the primary, connects to the inner and outer grids. The two windings are electrically insulated from each other, but are

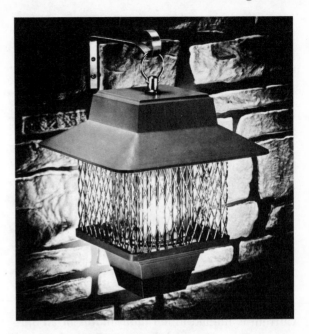

The Electric Bug Killer

linked by electromagnetism. Current flow through the primary winding sets up a strong magnetic field about the steel core. The field rises and falls 120 times a second, in step with the cycle of power line voltage. The changing field cuts through the secondary winding, inducing a voltage 10 times higher, simply because there are 10 times as many wire turns.

The bug that closes the secondary circuit with its body receives the full 1,200-volts available between opposite ends of the secondary winding.

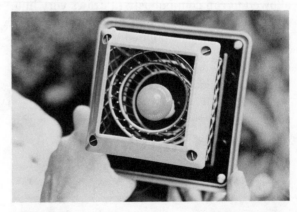

This electric bug killer uses a centrally located blue electric bulb, surrounded by two concentric metal grids made from 2^1/$_2$ inch long wire rods.

503

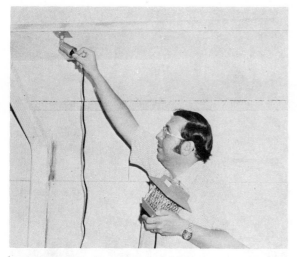

Proper placement is necessary for best results with the Electric Bug Killer.

Current is limited to ten thousandths of an ampere (0.01 amp), which is said not to be lethal to man.

Bug killers will work effectively only if they are properly located. The device should be placed at least 10 feet away from the patio, terrace or pool area that the homeowner wants cleared. Because other lights have some attraction, as does human body warmth and odor, the bug killer should be mounted where there will be minimum competition from interfering factors which can distract the bugs. It is best to leave the unit on continuously once the season starts, rather than turn it on and off. While a bug killer is most effective after dark, it does work during the day as well. If allowed to run continuously (it draws very little current) a bug killer will do a much better job of controlling the insect population by continuously eliminating the egg-bearing females which would otherwise tend to re-populate the area at frequent intervals.

Electric Can Opener Repair

Electric can openers are composed of a cutting wheel, usually stationary and mounted to the housing of the appliance, and a gear or sprocket wheel which holds the can in place and rotates it as the cutting wheel slices the top away. A small shaded pole motor is used to drive the gear wheel, but it must be geared down to gain the necessary torque and reduce the speed to the proper level. These gears are located inside the housing along with the motor.

Many electric can openers have a knife sharpener on one end of the housing. This feature is accomplished by adding a grinding wheel to the opposite end of the motor shaft from the gear train. The housing is slotted so that a knife, when inserted slowly into and pulled through the slot, is held in the correct position to put a hollow-ground edge on the blade.

The sharpener can be a source of problems. When a can opener is disassembled after first being unplugged, vacuum away any metallic particles that are within the housing. This will keep them from being pulled into the rotor of the motor by the small fan which is often used to cool the windings.

Most can opener problems are due to food residue which builds up on the cutter head and sprocket wheel. One or both of these components can usually be removed from the outside of the opener. To clean the heads and wheel remove them and soak them in a solution of hot water and dishwashing detergent for several hours. Then clean them thoroughly with an old toothbrush, which should loosen any remaining residue. Finally put the components back in place.

When the cutter head and sprocket wheel is removed, check closely for signs of wear or damage. If after cleaning, the opener still will not operate properly, the cutter wheel and/or sprocket will likely have to be replaced. When installing new parts be sure and put any spacers or washers in exactly as they were removed. The larger beveled edge of the cutter wheel goes to the inside.

If the can opener will not operate at all, check the receptacle with a table lamp to see that current is

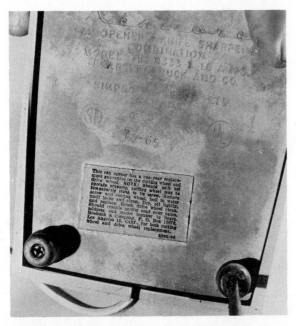

Disassemble a can opener by unplugging it and then removing bottom cover.

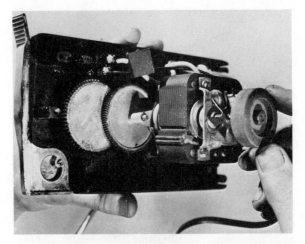

With cover removed, shaded pole motor and drive mechanism are visible. Large gears are necessary to reduce speed and increase power to sprocket gear.

reaching the opener. If this checks okay, unplug it and look carefully at the cord around the plug and the point where it enters the appliance. If this doesn't correct the problem, the unit will have to be disassembled.

To disassemble the can opener, remove the bottom cover. Often the screws that hold it in place are located under or within the rubber feet. With the cover removed, the motor and gearing are visible.

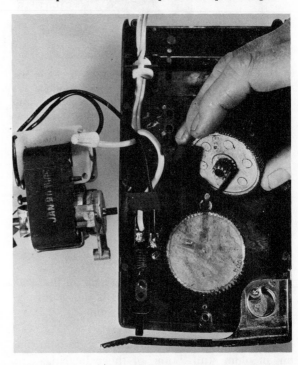

Gears may be removed for replacement when motor is loosened from brackets. To replace upper gear it must be unscrewed from sprocket.

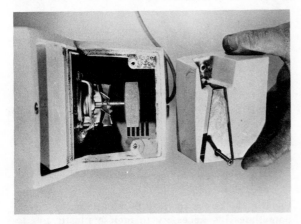

If can opener has a knife sharpener, it is also often necessary to remove the sharpener section cover.

If the can opener makes no sound, look for the switch operated by the handle when a can is in place. To check this, use an empty can inserted upside down in the can opener and pull the handle down (with the power off, of course) just as if you were going to remove the bottom from the can. You should be able to see or hear the switch

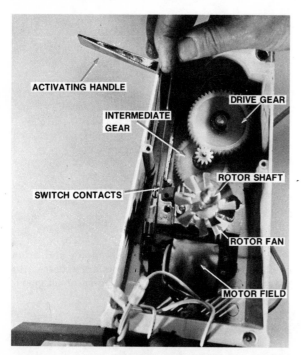

ACTIVATING HANDLE

DRIVE GEAR

INTERMEDIATE GEAR

ROTOR SHAFT

SWITCH CONTACTS

ROTOR FAN

MOTOR FIELD

Switch is actuated by handle on many can openers. Often contacts are visible. On some models, it's necessary to insert an empty can bottom side up, into cutter unit. This should "fool" opener and close switch.

make contact. If not, the switch mounting will have to be adjusted.

If all wiring appears to be okay and there is still no sound, the motor windings are likely open. This won't be visible — you'll have to use a VOM or continuity tester to verify it.

If the unit is noisy, look for damage in the gear train or for a loose fan blade. If the gears are damaged they will have to be replaced.

Often poor performance is due to worn bearings on an older unit. Some of these bearings are made into the front casting. In this event, the entire casting would have to be replaced. After reassembling, check for grounds with a VOM set to the highest resistance scale before using the opener. *SEE ALSO APPLIANCE REPAIR, SMALL.*

Electric Circuit Breaker
[SEE FUSES & CIRCUIT BREAKERS.]

Electric Clocks Repair

Electric clocks usually consist of a gear train driven by a shaded pole or synchronous motor. The hands of the clock are mounted to the extension shafts of the gear train to give the readings of proper movement to indicate the minutes and seconds. In the case of alarm clocks and in clock radios, there is also a buzzer unit which is usually energized by the magnetic field from the motor windings and a switch to turn the radio or even various appliances on and off. The switch and buzzer are operated by cams which are designed into the gear movement.

Often a binding clock mechanism has been caused by an accumulation of lint and dirt. This may even occur under the face of the hands themselves. If this seems to be the case, brush the lint away very carefully with a soft brush. A camel's hair brush, such as those found in photographic stores, is especially handy for this purpose.

The motor unit of a clock is often sealed, but it can often be put back into service if it fails. Sometimes lubricant may have settled to the bottom of the motor causing it to bind. If the motor is free to rotate in its retainer, simply turn it upside down. This will sometimes restore it to operation. If this fails, it is possible to drill or cut

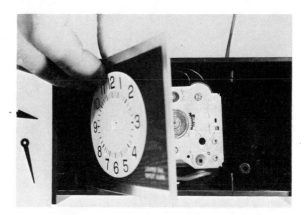

Electric clocks are serviced by removing the cover. Sometimes it's necessary to melt a plastic pin to reach inner workings, or to remove front cover as seen here.

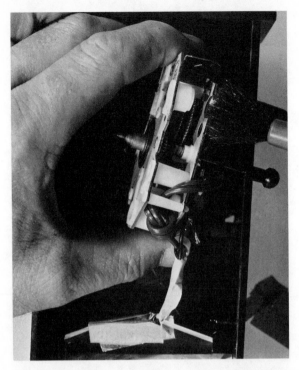

Look closely in gear mechanism and around hands for lint accumulation. Brush away with soft brush if it's found.

a small notch in the motor housing using a hacksaw or drill. Then apply a few drops of light machine oil. When reinstalling the motor, use a piece of tape to cover the hole.

When reassembling a clock, use particular care to see that all hands are in correct position and are not touching either the glass or the face of the clock. If it is necessary to remove the plastic pin

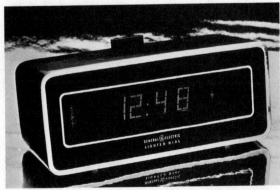

Courtesy of General Electric Company

New digital clocks from GE have "ferris wheel" movement

to enter the clock, use a drop of epoxy when reinstalling the cover. This should hold it in place securely.

Many new clocks are the digital type. Usually these use a flip mechanism to drop a series of plates or a numbered band in position to indicate the time of day. A gear train and motor still accomplishes the job, and most of the same servicing techniques would apply. Look carefully for a binding mechanism in case the digital clock fails to operate. *SEE ALSO APPLIANCES, SMALL.*

Electric Cord Repair

Repairing a lamp cord, extension cord or small-appliance cord of any kind is one of the first electrical tasks many people have occasion to learn. It is comparatively simple to do which perhaps is the reason it is so often tackled blindly and done badly. A poor job will have to be done over again and can offer a distinct hazard of shock or even fire.

If new cord is necessary due to deterioration of insulation or fraying of the covering, the easiest thing to use is No. 18 flat cord. This is the kind sometimes called zip cord. It comes in many colors, in rubber or translucent or transparent plastic covering. It is the kind in which the presence of two conductors is clearly evident. Advantages of No. 18 cord are that it is inexpensive, easily bought and that it can be equipped with a plug, switch or other device in a matter of seconds if a type made for it is selected.

Standard flat cord is not always suitable for a job. You may need a heavier cord for a large lamp or heavy appliance. A fabric-covered cord may be preferred for its appearance, as for a living-room table lamp, for instance. For these other cord types, use some version of the standard plug shown in the photographs.

The shape of plug is an important consideration which is often overlooked. If the plug is likely to remain more or less permanently inserted, or if

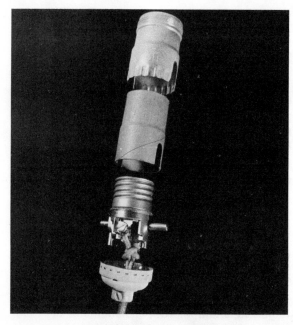

A standard electric socket.

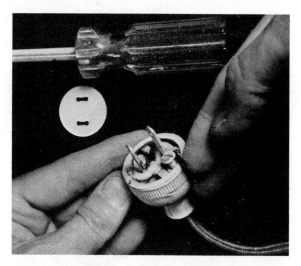

Wiring A Standard Plug

it must go behind a piece of furniture, the prime consideration should be its flatness, so it will be out of the way. For a lamp or other device that will be moved frequently, try to find a plug that can be easily grasped and pulled out without putting stress on the cord. Pulling by the cord, after all, is the thing that most often makes repairs necessary.

PARTS OF A SOCKET

The parts of a standard electric socket are the cap; cord tied with an underwriter's knot; switch; insulation; and the brass or plastic shell. With silk-covered or other round cord, use standard plugs. They have binding posts and require that the ends of the wires be bared. With the usual type of lamp cord, No. 18 parallel, use either the standard plugs or snap-on plugs that make contact without your having to strip wires.

HOW TO WIRE A STANDARD PLUG

Separate the wires for about 3 inches by removing the braid or splitting the covering. Run the cord through the back of the plug, then tie an underwriter's knot as shown below. With a knife held at an angle to avoid cutting wire strands, bare ½ inch of wire and twist strands together. Pull the cord to draw the knot into the plug

hollow. Run each wire around a plug prong and twist around binding post clockwise so that the wire will not loosen when the screws are tightened.

HOW TO WIRE SNAP-ON PLUGS

With this type plug, push wire into the full depth of the jaws. Then squeeze, and push the jaws into the body until the blades click.

Another kind of plug requires that you squeeze the prongs so the inside slips from shell. Push the cord through the cap into the body. Press the prongs together and slip body into shell.

Slit to separate the cord for ¼ inch as at left of picture. Push through hole in side of plug until wire hits other side and stops. Press shut the clamp on top of the plug.

To wire a flat plug, part the cord for ¾ inch and slip it into blade ends. Push blades back into the base of the plug and screw cover back on.

HOW TO TIE AN UNDERWRITER'S KNOT

This knot is a safety device that takes the stress off the copper conductors and puts it on the whole cord, which is far stouter. Use it when wiring lamp sockets and standard plugs with any type of wire. To tie an underwriter's knot, follow the illustration. *(SEE UNDERWRITER'S KNOT.)*

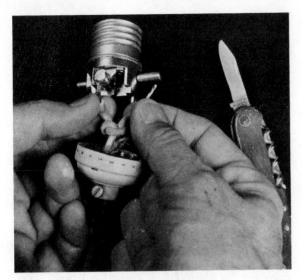

Parts of a Lamp Socket

HOW TO WIRE A LAMP SOCKET

First press with thumb or screwdriver, either beside switch cut-out, or at point (on some sockets) marked *press*, to separate cap from shell. Bring wire through cap. Tie an underwriter's knot. Strip insulation being careful not to cut any copper wires. Loop strands around binding posts clockwise, and then tighten the screws. Reassemble the socket.

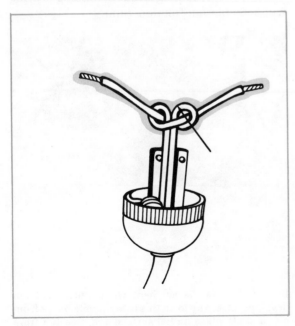

Underwriter's Knot

HOW TO REPAIR A LAMP CORD

To push in a new lamp cord, first remove lamp base or strip back felt so cord will not have to make a right angle. On lamp like this one, with switch in base, note wiring arrangement with solderless connectors.

Protect the cord against wear by taping it at the stress point where it enters lamp base. For the neatest, strongest job, cut electrical tape into ¼ inch wide strips. Mend frayed spots in an old cord with plastic electrician's tape, using narrow strips. Wrap each of the wires separately if there are signs of wear, then the whole cord.

HOW TO REWIRE A LAMP

Cut off the old plug. Take the lamp apart, usually by loosening set screw and unscrewing the parts. Run in the new cord. If the lamp has sharp curves, drop through a weight on a string, using this to pull in the lamp cord and tie underwriter's knot. Reassemble lamp. Where it is necessary (to avoid twisting cord) give the socket about 10 reverse revolutions before engaging with pipe stem. Complete wiring of lamp socket, as directed in the previous section.

Finish assembling the socket and put on new plug, as shown earlier. Protect the new cord, avoiding future repair or replacement, by taping at base and other stress points. Follow the same wiring procedure for 3-way lamps.

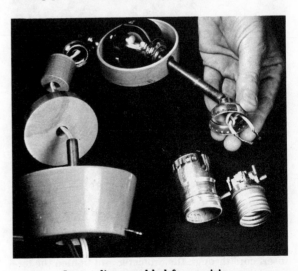

Lamp disassembled for rewiring

HOW TO REPLACE AN IRON CORD

The best answer for an old iron cord with frayed insulation, broken wire or damaged plug is a new one. The first repair step, opening the iron to get at the terminals varies with age and brand of iron. Many require the simple screwdriver removal of cover plate at back.

A cover plate under the body hides the terminals in this iron. The repair cord should be one made for irons, with asbestos insulation, a rubber or plastic plug that is easy to grasp, and brass eyelets.

Where you find no cover plate, opening an iron usually calls for removing the upper part. In buying a replacement iron cord, ask for one with 16-gauge wire, instead of the smaller 18-gauge, if there is a choice.

Unscrew terminal screws to remove the old cord. If terminals are burned or pitted, brighten them with fine sandpaper, and replace terminal screws if possible. Often you will have to pry open a strain-relief clip and slip it off, then pull cord through a rubber cord-protector.

The last main step before completing reassembly usually will be to slip new cord through pro-

tector and slide strain-relief clip up far enough to keep wires slack at terminals, squeezing it tight. Insert terminal screws in eyelets of new cord, tighten, fit cord-protector into place, and install cover plate.

Electric Drill
[SEE PORTABLE POWER TOOLS.]

Electric Fan Repair

Most electric fans use a shaded pole motor to drive the fan blade. Often a small gearbox is connected to one end of the motor, which causes the fan to oscillate on its base by means of a linkage. Often a speed control is used. This can be a small reactor, a transformer-like device that alters the voltage into the motor field.

When a problem arises with an electric fan, it's often due to improper maintenance. Fan blades should be cleaned yearly and the motor bearings lubricated at least once a year where oil ports are provided on the fan motor. Since a shaded pole motor has little starting torque, a binding bearing will keep the fan from operating.

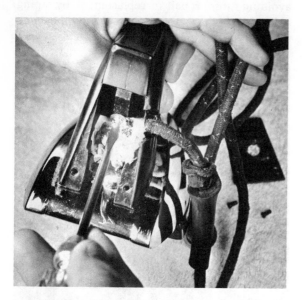

Insert cord through the protector and tighten the terminal screws.

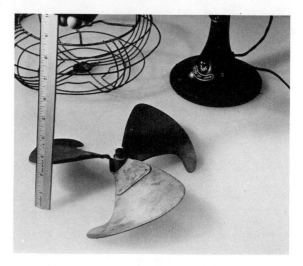

Be sure that fan is not bent when noise problem develops. One way to do this is to remove blade from motor shaft, place on flat surface and measure from highest point at tip of each blade.

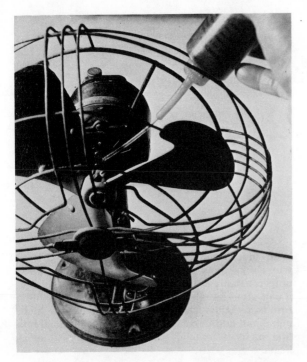

Often problems with electric fans are due to lack of lubrication. If oil ports are provided, apply no more than two drops of SAE 20 non-detergent motor oil twice a year.

Cords can be faulty too, especially in the area of the heads where the cord moves back and forth. To check this, unplug the fan and pull the wiring gently at the point where it enters the fan motor. If this checks okay, inspect the point where it enters the base. Any break in the wiring will likely show up in one of these two areas.

To reach the switch, you'll have to remove the bottom of the base. This is usually held in place by screws which are accessible beneath the housing.

If the fan motor itself seems to be binding, oil the bearings externally by applying two-drops in oil ports or to the motor shaft where it enters the housing. If this doesn't help, the motor may have to be taken apart. Remove or loosen the screw that holds the fan blade to the motor shaft. On many models a small screwdriver will do this. On some others, a small setscrew wrench will be necessary to loosen it. Next, loosen the guard at the motor housing. Both blade and guard can now be removed.

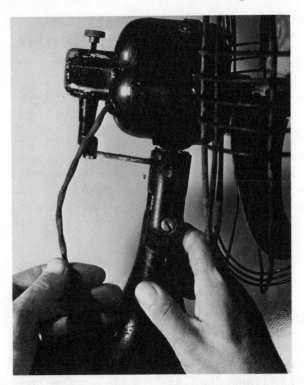

On oscillating fans, be sure to check condition of cord between motor and base unit. If frayed or deteriorated, it should be replaced. Often internal break in cord will prevent motor from operating. If tugging on cord reveals stretch, this is usually cause of problem.

With the blade and guard out of the way, the motor can usually be opened by loosening the through bolts that hold it together. Mark the motor sections before removing to be sure that they can be aligned exactly as they go back together. Then gently pull each end bell off and inspect the condition of the shaft where it enters the motor bearing. If it's gummy, a couple of drops of light oil will free it up and restore it to operation. Be sure that any spacers and washers on the motor shaft are reinstalled when the motor is reassembled.

Use a volt-ohm-meter to check for grounds before putting the fan back into operation. *SEE ALSO APPLIANCE REPAIR, SMALL.*

Electric Garage Door
[SEE GARAGE DOOR OPENER.]

Electric Hairsetter Repair

Electric hairsetters consist of a base with a heating element mounted under it along with a thermostatic high-limit switch for safety. When the unit is plugged in, the base begins to heat. The curlers slide on pins which are part of the base. The pin heats with the base, and transmits this heat into a metallic or heat-absorbing section within the curler itself. After the curler is heated, it can be removed from the base and will retain its heat for some time.

If the hairsetter does not heat at all, check the voltage to the receptacle by using a table lamp. If this checks okay the most likely fault would be at one of the wiring connections in the base of the unit. Inspect the cord carefully around the plug and the strain relief where it enters the base. If there is no problem here, remove the bottom panel after first being sure the plug has been pulled from the receptacle. The panel is sometimes held in place with small screws under or within the rubber feet on the bottom of the hairsetter.

Once the panel is removed, the thermostatic disc and the heating element are visible. Most hairsetters like this use the ribbon-type nichrome

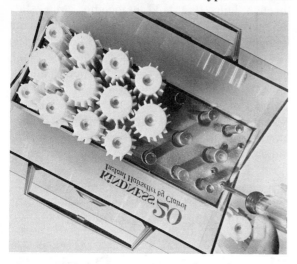

After unplugging hairsetter, remove base cover by finding and loosening retaining screws. These are located on top cover.

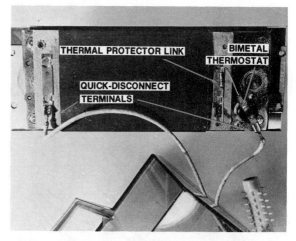

With cover removed, look for corroded or broken wire connections at terminals. The element in these units is usually not serviceable. If terminal is riveted, it can often be tapped back into place to provide a firm connection. Clean it thoroughly before tightening. Small button soldered into circuit is special link that melts if bimetal sticks and equipment overheats.

heating element, insulated by mica supports. A break in this element will often be visible, but is not repairable without replacing the element. Sadly, few repair parts are available for most of these hairsetters.

Look carefully at the base connection switch. Sometimes they can become loose and corroded. Since they are often riveted in place, careful cleaning followed by a tap with a punch or hammer can often restore the connection.

The bimetal high-limit used is an enclosed type and the fault here will not be visible. You will have to use a VOM or continuity tester to check it. It should check closed when the unit is cool, then it should open when it is heated by holding a match or cigarette lighter under it with the tester connected.

If the hairsetter overheats, it's a sign that the limit switch is not opening when it should. The unit should be taken out of service until this is eliminated. The same applies if you receive a shock from touching a hairsetter when it is plugged in. When reassembling it, be sure and check for grounds to the metallic housing of the hairsetter with the VOM.

Electric Heaters, Hot Water System
[SEE HEATING SYSTEMS.]

Electric Heating Systems
[SEE HEATING SYSTEMS.]

Electric Heating Troubles
[SEE HEATING SYSTEMS.]

Electrician's Test Equipment
[SEE ELECTRICIAN'S TOOLS & EQUIPMENT.]

Electrician's Tools & Equipment

The home craftsman will find that an assortment of electrician's tools and equipment are essential to any wiring job. Some tools, screwdrivers and pliers, for instance, are quite ordinary while others, like the conduit bender, are found usually on commercial wiring jobs. All are easy to use if their purpose is understood.

The cable ripper is often seen on commercial sites or where heavy wiring is being done. This flat, wedge-shaped instrument is used to separate the braided wire in a cable so that a splice can be made.

A tool used often in conduit work is the conduit bender. Semicircular in shape, the conduit bender is used to bend the conduit without crimping its thin wall.

The amateur electrician will need several types of screwdrivers. Among these are the electrician's screwdriver, whose narrow head makes it convenient for wiring switches and other tight places with deeply recessed screws. Because many appliances are put together with Phillip's head screws, the Phillip's screwdriver may also be needed. However, the No. 2 Phillip's will be the largest size needed. A screw-holding screwdriver is essential for hard-to-reach places. The head is magnetized so that a screw will not fall out while being started. For example, this screwdriver would be useful in screwing screws into a wall outlet. Insulation or plastic on all screwdrivers help prevent shock.

Some pliers that the home electrician will need are the electrician's pliers, the utility or mechanics pliers and needle-nose pliers. The electrician's pliers have rubber insulated handles, a blunt nose and a cutting edge, making them an asset to many heavy cable wiring jobs. The utility or mechanic's pliers will be the handiest because they are light, yet strong enough to make wire splices and loops for around-the-house wiring. These may be purchased at any hardware store. The needle-nose pliers do well in congested places like those found in electrical appliances. The long nose is tapered to a point much like a needle is tapered; hence the name "needle-nose."

For light wire cutting jobs, use diagonal cutting pliers. Shaped much like electrician's pliers, the cutting sides close completely to allow positive cutting action.

House wiring requires the use of two types of saws: the keyhole saw and the hacksaw. The keyhole is a tapered saw utilized in making holes in the wall for switches and outlets. The pointed end is sharp enough to bite into almost any wall except those made of concrete. The hacksaw is essential to extensive cable work. Its fine teeth quickly and easily cut through the metal of conduit and armored cable.

A variety of tapes are necessary for insulating and protecting wire splices. The electrician's tape or plastic vinyl tape is most often used.

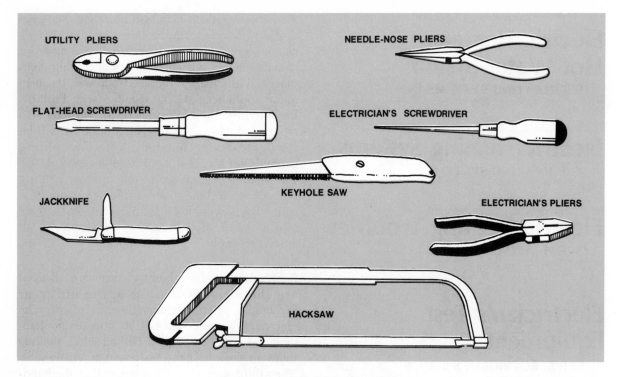

UTILITY PLIERS

NEEDLE-NOSE PLIERS

FLAT-HEAD SCREWDRIVER

ELECTRICIAN'S SCREWDRIVER

KEYHOLE SAW

JACKKNIFE

ELECTRICIAN'S PLIERS

HACKSAW

Basics for an electrician's tool kit.

However, rubber and friction tape are better selections in wet areas.

There are many different testers and test lights for checking the condition of a circuit. Many of these can be made by the home craftsman. For example, the circuit tester is made by connecting two lengths of wire to a small neon bulb. Insulated receptacles on the ends of these wires help minimize the possibility of shock. A closed circuit will light the bulb.

Much like the circuit tester, the clicktester verifies a closed circuit or an electrical charge in any conductor. The test prods make a clicking sound if current is flowing through the conductor. Since the intensity of electricity is not measured, the clicktester or circuit test is best suited for checking short circuits.

The volt-ohm-meter also measures electrical current flowing through a conductor. However, it is most often used in appliance or electric motor repair. These devices are very accurate in measuring the voltage and resistance of electrical wires.

Another essential item in appliance or electric motor repair is a soldering gun. Unlike soldering irons, the gun heats faster while the pistol grip allows for maximum control of the heating element. Soldering guns are used when solid contact is essential.

The home craftsman will find that these tools and equipment will enable him to do any electrical fix-it job in a more professional manner. *SEE ALSO HAND TOOLS.*

Electric Iron Repair

Electric irons take very much the same form and shape of their precedessor of many years ago — the old flat iron. This was simply a piece of heavy cast iron which was heated over an open fire. Today the plate is heated with an electrical heating element. In most modern irons this is an enclosed-type element that is built within the bottom casting of the iron and is not replaceable if it should fail. On some older irons it may be

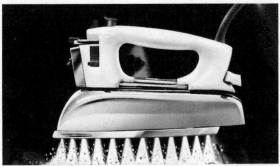

Courtesy of General Electric Company

GE's new self-cleaning irons help eliminate a problem.

made from a ribbon-like nichrome wire with mica insulators, and these may be replaced if they are still available.

The electric iron probably has a tougher life than most appliances. Even though permanent press clothing has greatly reduced the number of hours it must work each week, it is still used quite frequently. When it is in use, it is operating under conditions of high temperatures, and in the case of a steam iron, dampness and moisture as well. Also, it is moved back and forth vigorously as part of its operation. These things combine to create an atmosphere in which problems can arise.

The best way to prevent repairs with your iron is to use it carefully and properly. The water which goes into an iron will largely determine the service it will render. Where possible, use distilled water for this purpose. Distilled water of sorts can be obtained from ordinary rain water filtered through a cloth before putting into an iron. The water condensate from a humidifier is another good source of mineral-free water for the iron. In addition, several gadgets are made which contain a compound that helps filter and remove minerals from water that is used in an iron. These have proven to be of some worth. Any precautions you can take will be worthwhile, particularly if you use your iron frequently.

Minerals in the water cause a build-up when the water is evaporated since the minerals tend to remain. If this occurs, the iron must be com-

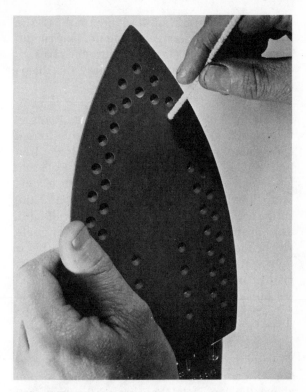

Spray openings in base of iron can sometimes be cleaned with pipe cleaner if they have become restricted from deposits. Use of distilled water or rain water after being filtered will help reduce this condition.

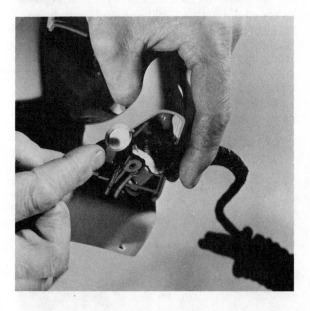

Cord can be reversed from right to left side on many newer model irons. Simply remove rear cover at terminal connection, switch side at which cord exits, and install special plug in opening.

pletely disassembled and cleaned. If the buildup is severe this is hard to do. One manufacturer, General Electric, has introduced a self-cleaning iron with a burst of spray that helps open the ports after each use.

The movement of the iron in use also tends to take its toll in wear of cords and helps loosen connections within the iron as well. If the iron fails to work, the cord would be the first place to look after checking the receptacle with a table lamp. Look closely around the plug and the strain relief at the iron. If all appears well here, unplug the iron and remove the cover plate where the cord enters the iron. Usually this is easily found, and once removed the terminal is visible for inspection. It's very possible to find the break at the terminal. If the terminal should be corroded, it must be cleaned and tightened thoroughly before putting the iron back into use.

Disassembling an iron can be a tricky proposition. If there is a trim used on the handle section above the top metal housing of the iron, pry gently around the edges to see if it snaps up. If so, there will usually be a large screw or nut that will facilitate removal of the handle. Once this is off, the studs that hold the top cover down can be loosened. If the iron is old, the studs may be corroded. Some penetrating oil or a drop of light machine oil will help to loosen them. A few drops of vinegar on the rusted studs will often

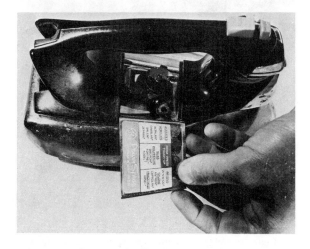

Begin iron disassembly by unplugging, then checking under trim plates for attachment nuts and screws.

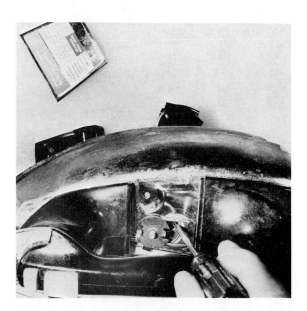

Temperature on this GE is accessible after removing trim plate. Exact temperature cannot be set without special equipment — try to compensate with control before attempting thermostat calibration.

help loosen the rust enough to remove the nut. Be sure and put oil back on the nut and stud before it is replaced.

Under the top cover you will usually see a bimetal thermostat unit anchored to the control. The thermostat contacts open and close rather slowly on most irons, so look at their condition carefully. If they are burned and pitted, they will have to be polished and burnished before they will make proper contact. To do this, use an automotive point file available from automotive suppliers or department stores that sell automotive parts. Clean the points, but only enough to remove the burned section. Once they are cleaned, polish them with a hardwood stick or a striking cover from a book of paper matches.

Under the thermostat, you'll find the heating element. The heat from this element causes the thermostat to operate, thus maintaining temperature. The heating element will rarely be open. It can be easily checked with a continuity tester or volt-ohm-meter.

Often the problem with an iron is due to a leaky or damaged steam tank or gasket. In a steam

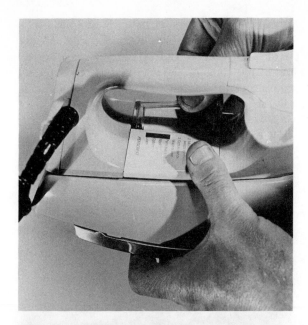

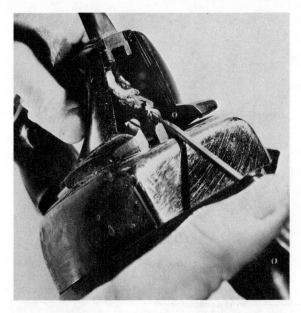

Removing cord terminal screws found under cover at rear of handle on most irons is usually one of the necessary steps prior to disassembly.

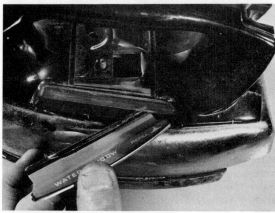

Indicator tube found on many irons can sometimes be pulled out of rubber retaining grommets. On some models plate under indicator is removed while indicator itself stays in position.

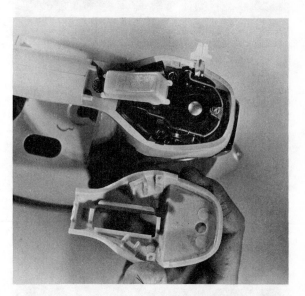

Next, unhitch steam mechanism from body. Top cover snaps off many units like this Penny's model. Look closely at linkages — make a sketch to remember their position.

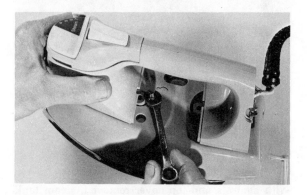

With plate removed, loosen any nuts that hold cap cover in place.

iron, the tank is under the top cover. At one end of the tank there is a metering valve which can be removed with the top of the iron. The valve is like a small meter that enters a tiny orifice or opening at the bottom of the tank. When it is in the raised position, it will allow a controlled

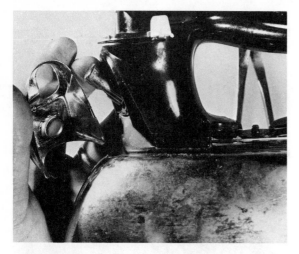

Fill opening can be snapped out of place on some models of steam irons to remove handle. On others it must be pried away and replaced with a new one when iron is reassembled.

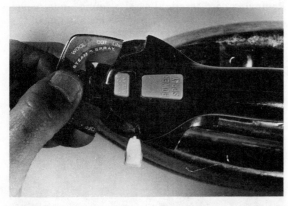

When removing control panel look for spring loaded clip such as this decorative trim on the GE iron shown.

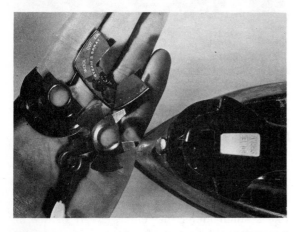

Once trim is removed, other components of control can also be pulled from position as shown above.

amount of water to enter the base casting, which has passageways cast into it. As the water strikes the hot surface, the steam is immediately forced out of the vents on the sole plate of the iron. Of course, at this point it must pass through the clothing under the sole plate.

If passageways become clogged with minerals from the water, they block the flow of steam. If the deposits are not too hard, they can often be cleaned by inserting a pipe cleaner up through the passageways. But even so it is often necessary to disassemble the iron and remove the covers on the sole plate to gain access to the

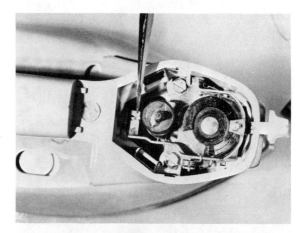

With control cover removed on this iron, it's necessary to open linkage before handle can be removed from top. Be sure to note exact position of all such linkages carefully to aid in reassembly.

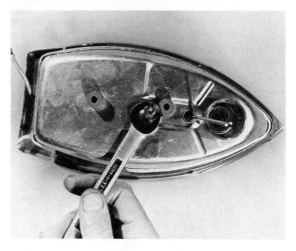

With controls and top cover removed, steam tank can usually be taken off after removing retaining nut.

passageways. This is another good reason for using care in the type of water you use in the iron.

When you have disassembled an iron, be sure to test it for grounds before putting it back into use. Do this by using a VOM or continuity tester and testing from each terminal of the plug to the housing of the iron. If continuity is indicated, there is a ground in the housing, possibly a wire pinched or a terminal touching the housing. Never operate an appliance in this condition. Using your volt-ohm-meter for this test, use the RX10,000 or the highest resistance scale provided for making the test.

When disassembling an iron, take special note of each part as it is removed. Pay particular attention to the control knob because often this determines the calibration of the thermostat. If a splined shaft is used without any key to retain the knob in a particular position, mark it with a dab of white paint or fingernail polish before removing. This allows you to align it precisely when the iron is put back together. *SEE ALSO APPLIANCE REPAIR, SMALL.*

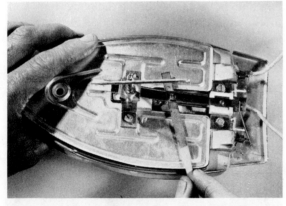

With tank and housing removed, control section is accessible for servicing. Here contacts are cleaned with automotive point file. Before reassembling, they will be burnished or polished using a hardwood stick or striking surface from a matchbook cover.

Electricity

Electricity is energy in nature created by friction. Electrons, transmitted through a network of wires at a rate of 6.28 billion billion per second, produce electrical current.

DIRECT AND ALTERNATING CURRENT

Direct current, DC, is one of two types of electrical current and flows in one direction from a power source to a point and back again in a continuous motion. Storage batteries and generators always produce DC.

Alternating current, or AC, reverses its direction sixty times a second at measured periods or cycles. Easier to produce, transport and utilize, AC is extensively supplied by power companies. Homes are powered by alternating current.

MEASURING ELECTRICITY

Electricity is measured in standards named after the men who discovered them. The coulomb is used to calibrate electrical current "flowing" through a wire. The ampere is used to calculate this flow. A current of 1 coulomb per second equals a current of 1 ampere, thus setting a simple and well-known standard. Amperages are found on specification plates of all electrical devices to insure safe usage.

The force of the current is calculated in volts. The ohm is said to be the amount of resistance that a conductor imposes on electrical flow. The rate of work produced by the current is known as the wattage. One thousand watts is defined as a kilowatt.

Any of these measurements may be calculated through simple arithmetic. For example, a conductor has the resistance of 1 ohm if it allows 1 volt to send 1 amp through it in 1 second. In order to find out the ohms of a wire, simply divide the volts by the amps.

Electric bills are computed in kilowatt hours. If the amount of amps consumed is multipled by the number of the line voltage, the wattage is known. The kilowatt hour is found by dividing the number of watts into 1,000. A device that consumes 2 amps on a line of 115 volts uses 230 watts or .23 kilowatt hours.

All service panels are equipped with meters that automatically compute the amount of electricity used. The clock meter has four dials that are read from left to right. The digital meter is easier to read because the numbers appear much in the same way as a digital clock. *SEE ALSO ELECTRICAL WIRING.*

Electric Knife Repair

Electric knives contain a universal motor which has a worm gear machined into one end of the shaft. The worm in turn causes a drive gear to rotate. Two pins are set into the side of this gear, one connected to each side of the blade socket. This drive setup imparts a reciprocating motion to the original rotary motion, causing the knife blade section to move back and forth.

The blade is made in two sections. They are held together by a rivet on one end and by the blade sockets on the other end, which are installed in the housing of the knife. The edges are serrated to give maximum cutting effect on the back-and-forth motion. This allows the blade to actually guide itself through the cut.

Electric knives come in both cordless and non-cordless models. In the non-cordless models, the power supplied to the housing is used to drive the motor. In the cordless model batteries provide a DC current which in turn drives the motor.

If you are encountering a problem with the electric knife, try to determine if it lies within the blade section or within the motor housing itself. If the motor housing is providing the proper reciprocating motion, you can eliminate that portion of the knife. If the problem lies within the blades, look at them carefully to try and determine if they have been bent or misaligned in any way. The blades should be replaced as a pair. In some cases they can be returned to the factory or to a distributor for an exchange replacement set.

If the motor unit fails to run it will be necessary to disassemble the housing. Be sure the knife is

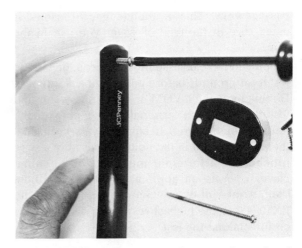

Look for hidden screws or retainers on the end and cover of electric knife body. Be sure that knives are unplugged and turned off when handling. Remove blades before servicing.

unplugged at any time except when you are cutting. When disassembling, carefully remove the blade and look for any screws that may help to open the housing. Sometimes these are located under decals or trim strips. Often they are located in the ends of the knife next to the blade socket and next to the point where the cord enters the housing. With the housing removed, motor and brushes are visible. Further disassembly would be necessary to check the gear train.

If the knife has been dropped, look carefully for broken connections and check around the

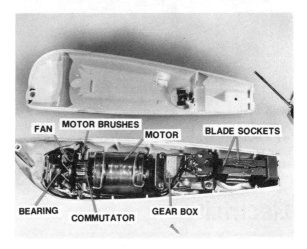

With covers split into two halves, the works of the knife are exposed for servicing. Gear boxes are to right, commutator at left in photo above.

brushes to make sure that they are making contact with the comutator. Sometimes a brush holder will become knocked out of place due to a fall and this will prevent the knife from operating. The motor drive is usually contained within a housing which is filled with grease to lubricate the gear train. By loosening several screws you should be able to remove the upper portion of this housing. Be sure and note particularly the position of any spacers or retainers that are used and reinstall them in exactly the same manner when putting the motor back in place.

If the problem is within the gear train, the motor will run, but the blade sockets will not oscillate. Redistribute or refill the gear box with lubricant

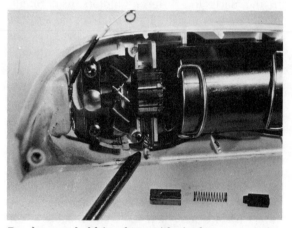

Brushes are held in place with single screw, acting as retainer for brush holder. Be sure that commutator is cleaned, if it's necessary to replace motor brushes.

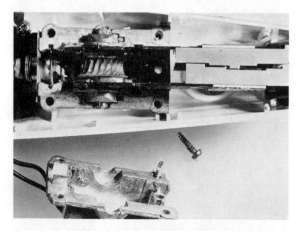

Removal of gear box cover shows how drive gear is connected. Worm from machine on motor shaft is underneath this gear.

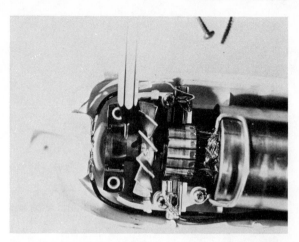

Bearing can be removed for cleaning and oiling after loosening screws and clamps that hold it in place. Most bearings are made of material with self-oiling properties.

of the same consistency originally found in it when putting it back together. Be sure that the cord is back in the same position as it was located when removed. This is often tight quarters, so there is the possibility that the housing won't fit until the cord is securely back in place. *SEE ALSO APPLIANCE REPAIR, SMALL.*

Electric Mixer Repair
[SEE FOOD MIXER REPAIR.]

Electric Motors

Electric motors greatly increase the work capacity of electricity in the home. The average household utilizes an estimated 25 electric motors for doing a variety of jobs from operating washing machines to playing records. Although motors differ in size and power, in accordance with load requirements, their operation is similar.

PRINCIPLE

Understanding magnetism is the key to understanding electric motors. The armature, a metal wire-wrapped bar, is balanced on an axle or rotor. Wire is individually wrapped around two rods (stators) placed at each end of the ar-

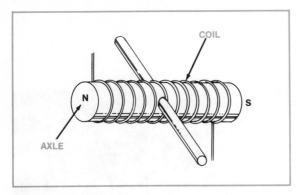

An armature is a cylinder wrapped in metal wire and attached to a rotor, or axle.

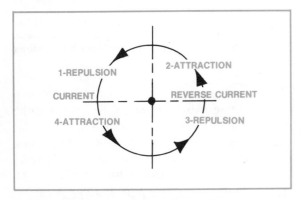

An electric motor works by the repulsion-attraction theorem of magnetism.

mature. By passing an electric current through these motor windings, two electromagnetic fields are created. The armature is set in these fields so that "like poles" face each other. These poles repel one another, forcing the armature around a quarter turn. The unlike poles then attract each other, turning the armature a second quarter turn. The electromagnetic field is then reversed by reversing the current. The poles repel, causing another quarter turn, with the final quarter turn being again caused by magnetism. Thus, by reversing the current, the armature is made to spin the rotor. The simplest example of this principle is the induction motor.

MOTOR TYPES

Electric motors fall into two categories: single-phase and poly-phase motors. Single-phase motors, those that develop less than one horsepower, are common to almost any household. These motors run by the induction of alternating current through the motor windings to start or run the motor. There are many groups of single-phase, AC induction motors, but the more common are split-phase motors and capacitor-start motors.

Poly-phase motors (frequently tri-phase) are so termed because they run on two or more phases of current. This type of current flows in a sequence with the "A" phase slightly ahead of the "B" phase, which is in turn slightly ahead of the "C" phase. Industry uses poly-phase motors because of their high horsepower torque capacity.

The main differences in the categories are found in the parts the different motors use. Single-phase motors usually have squirrel cage rotors, while poly-phase motors utilize brushes and commutators for keeping the rotor in motion.

Split-Phase Motor

The split-phase motor is one type that requires a squirrel cage rotor. This motor contains two sets of windings. The starting windings are set opposite from the running windings to compose a two-phase magnetic field. These windings are connected by a centrifugal switch. The displacement of the fields gives the rotor a great turning force, or torque. When the rotor reaches a certain speed, the centrifugal switch cuts the start-

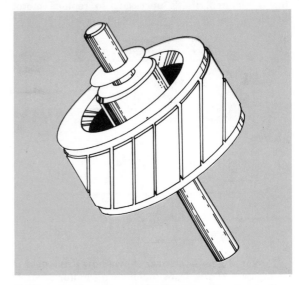

Eddy currents cause squirrel cage rotors to revolve.

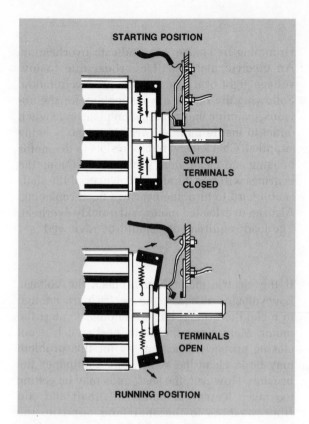

STARTING POSITION

SWITCH
TERMINALS
CLOSED

TERMINALS
OPEN

RUNNING POSITION

A split-phase motor incorporates a centrifugal switch into its starting system.

ing windings out of the circuit. At that point, the motor runs like a single-phase induction motor, with eddy currents keeping the rotor in motion by centrifugal force.

Capacitor-Start Motor

The capacitor-start motor works much like the split-phase motor but uses much less electricity. A capacitor has the ability to hold an electrical charge. Therefore, when placed in the circuitry of a motor, it reduces the amount of electricity consumed in starting by boosting the initial current. Because capacitor-start motors produce a higher torque, they are used in hard-to-start equipment such as air compressors.

Universal Motors

The universal motor is different from both split-phase and capacitor-start motors in two ways: these motors have wire-wound rotors, called rotor windings, and can use poly-phase current.

series or sequence — first through one, then the other. This particular circuitry, connected by brushes that constantly touch commutators, produces an enormous torque which in some instances may reach as high as 35,000 revolutions per minute. Although ideal for industrial plants, the home craftsman will also find universal motors in much of his home equipment. For instance, they run electric power tools, vacuum cleaners, electric blenders, etc.

The name, "universal", comes from the fact that the motor will operate on either alternating or direct current. The rotor and stator windings are set up so that the current flows through them in a

HORSEPOWER

Electric motors are rated in horsepower. Fractional-horsepower motors are those which produce less than one horsepower of torque, or twisting force. Specification plates usually represent horsepower in terms of the maximum torque capacity. For example, if a motor utilizes 3 hp. for starting but requires only $1/_4$ hp. to run, the plate will state the starting surge of 3 hp. If no specification is printed, it may be assumed that the torque is less than $1/_8$ hp.

MOTOR MOUNTS

Motors are kept in position by motor mounts. These may assume any of a number of sizes, shapes, styles and weights depending upon the size and location of the motor. The mount is attached to the motor and to a foundation known as the mounting block. This assembly stabilizes the motor while it is in operation.

MOTOR CARE & CLEANING

There are many mechanical problems in electric motors which may be solved by the amateur repairman — and often without dissassembling the motor.

If any trouble arises, always check the obvious first. Examining the plug, cord, fuse or circuit breaker may be all that is necessary. Also, some motors have thermostatically controlled overload switches. When the load becomes great enough to overheat the motor, the swtich automatically shuts the motor off. These

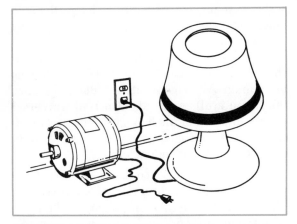

Always check the outlet if the motor does not start.

Overheating

Humming or smoke may indicate overheating. An electric motor will overheat due to low voltage, tight bearings or inadequate ventilation. Following the rule of always looking for the obvious, examine the specification plate and switch outlet to insure that the correct voltage is being supplied. Check the ventilation slots in the motor housing and clean them if necessary. Oiling the bearings will free the shaft. However, if the shaft is still hard to turn, the bearings need replacing. Also, an overloaded motor will quickly overheat. The load requirements should be reviewed.

Humming

If the electric motor hums, check the voltage. Low voltage will charge the electric parts enough to make them hum, but not enough to start the motor. Many times the centrifugal switch is not closing properly. The remedy for this problem may be to clean the switch and sandpaper the brushes. However, the shaft ends may be getting too much leeway. Examine the shaft and add fiber washers to the shaft end opposite the switch. This will reduce the leeway and allow the switch to close. At other times, the capacitor may fail. If so, take the capacitor to an electric motor shop to be tested, and/or replaced.

A motor is said to "lock" if the bearings are too tight. A humming sound is also a clue to this problem, which can be verified by turning the shaft by hand. If the shaft seems tight, oil it lightly. If the problem persists, the bearings need to be taken out and cleaned or replaced.

switches are sometimes geared to restart the motor when the windings cool. Another variation, such as those found in electric heating systems, must be manually started or "reset" by pushing a red button, usually found near the control panel.

Keep the motor clean and adequately oiled, as many troubles can be thwarted by simple cleaning. Vacuum cleaners or air pressure hoses do well on large motors, while a soft brush should be used for the much smaller ones. Excessive oiling will cause as many problems in electric motors as those caused by unnecessary neglect. Oil may seep into armatures or windings and mix with dust to clog these parts. A few drops of oil, periodically, will be enough to keep the motor well lubricated.

MOTOR REPAIRS

The amateur electrician should be able to replace most motor parts. Armatures and brushes, even windings, are sold at any electric motor shop. The mechanism diagram printed near the motor will help to locate these parts and to insure the safest and quickest means of installation. A cautionary word: Do not attempt to test capacitors or high-voltage motors without professional help. These require special test equipment not readily available to home electricians. The home craftsman is able to handle most simple motor malfunctions on low-horsepower motors.

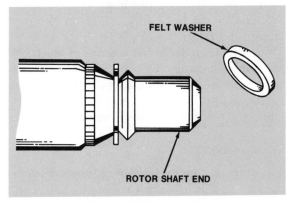

FELT WASHER

ROTOR SHAFT END

Placing a felt washer on the shaft end opposite the switch is a solution to the problem of end-play.

Clicking

Clicking is a sign of trouble with the brushes or commutator. If the brushes are not seated properly, there may also be sparks. The soft carbon portion of the brushes may have worn badly enough to allow the hard stub to rub against the drum. Or the brushes may be bumping against high mica insulation. The commutator and brushes may not be making proper contact. In cases where the brushes do not need replacing, light sanding and cleaning will usually solve the problem.

Electric Shaver Repair

Electric shavers may use either a small universal motor to drive a set of rotary blades or a vibrator type motor to cause the heads to oscillate thousands of times each minute. The heads are expendable and are replaceable as matched sets. They can be obtained from a dealer for the brand of shaver that you own. If the head or blades are damaged in a fall, don't attempt to straighten them. They require perfect alignment and the

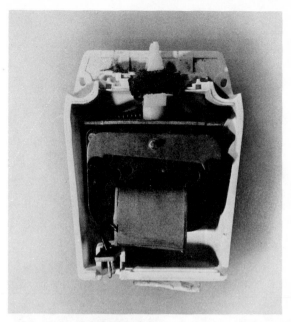

Vibrating arm on this shaver provides force to drive blades back and forth. Plastic pin at top attaches to blade to transmit motion.

only answer is to replace them as a set. The head of an electric shaver should be cleaned thoroughly after each use.

To disassemble the shaver, first remove the head and look under any felt seals for screws that hold the housing together. Some of these may also be located on the bottom of the shaver. After the housing is removed, carefully brush away any lint or particles that may have found their way into the shaver. Then determine which type motor it has.

The vibrator type motor simply uses a coil to create an electromagnet field. This field attracts an armature which is mounted and linked so that it imparts movement to the blade as it is pulled toward the field. When it reaches a certain point, a spring tension overcomes the force of the field and pulls the armature back. The process is repeated very rapidly.

A variation of this is the contact point motor. It uses a set of contact points to interrupt the circuit when the armature is moved past a certain point. Some contact motors have a small thumb wheel to put them into motion initially.

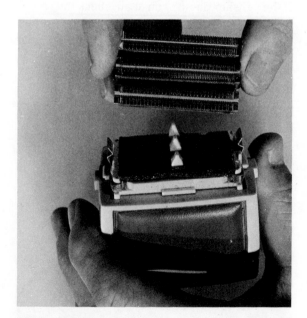

Shaver head is critical area. It should be replaced only as a matched set of blades available from dealer.

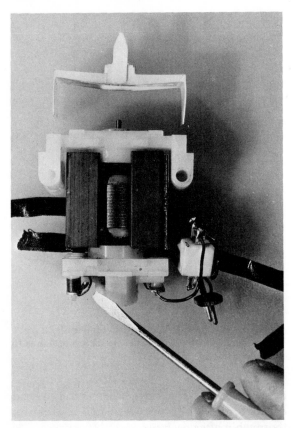

Rotary motion of motor is converted to reciprocating motion by the linkage on this shaver. Lead goes to motor brush, as indicated by screwdriver.

The universal type motor is a miniature high speed motor which is attached to the rotary head.Check the motor brushes when servicing and inspecting a universal motor.

In any type of shaver, all linkages must be free. The armature in the universal motor must be free to turn. A drop of oil in each linkage and a drop of light oil in each bearing point of the universal motor should clear up any problem that arises here.

Cordless shavers utilize a battery pack to power the shaver motor. The base that the shaver is stored in serves as a charger to charge these batteries. The nickel-cadmium batteries used in most of these units will last for many years, given proper care. Be sure that all battery terminals are clean and shiny and that the battery is making contact when it is in position.

Electric Shoe Polisher Repair

Electric shoe polishers look and operate much like an electric mixer, except that only one output socket is used with the brush or buffer pad. Like the mixer, the polisher uses a universal motor which has a worm gear machined into the rotor shaft. The worm turns a pinion to which the polisher brush is connected.

Most shoe polishers are disassembled by unplugging, then splitting the housing into halves by removing the upper and lower sections. The halves are usually held together by screws which pass through from the bottom side. Look into recesses to locate the screws. It seldom is necessary to remove trim strips to disassemble a shoe polisher.

With the top section removed, the switch and motor is readily accessible. Vacuum away all lint and dust before beginning a repair procedure.

If the polisher doesn't run at all, check the receptacle with a table lamp to see if power is reaching that point. If it is, check the cord around the plug and at the point where it enters the polisher. If all appears to be well here, the problem is likely to be in the motor itself.

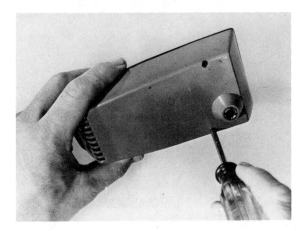

Look for screws on bottom of housing which hold housing together.

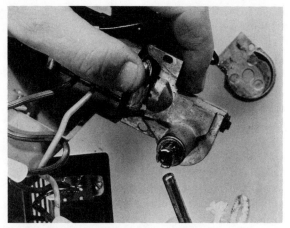

Shoe polisher is designed much like mixer with only one output socket.

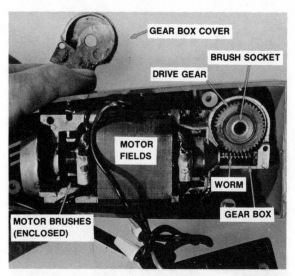

Note that only one drive gear is necessary to turn single polishing brush. Be sure that wires are in position before housings are put together again.

Since the polisher uses a universal motor, brushes are used to conduct the current from the field winding to the rotor. These carbon brushes are subject to wear and are an expendable part. If they are less than a quarter of an inch long, they should be replaced.

Shoe polishers aren't likely to have the brush caps on the outside of the housing, so disassembly is almost always necessary to reach the brushes. It is also often necessary to remove a sheet metal screw that holds the brushes in position. When purchasing new brushes for any appliance, be sure to take the old ones along. This insures obtaining the right size and shape.

Check the motor carefully for signs of loose or damaged wire and check the area around the switch contacts. If the switch contacts have become linted or dirty, they can be cleaned by spraying them with television tuner contact spray. This is available from most radio-TV parts suppliers.

If the motor runs but the brush will not turn, it is likely the pinion gear is damaged. To remove it, look for a retaining clip just outside the housing near the socket where the brush shaft is inserted. After removing the clips, the gear may be pulled upwards when the housing is removed. Use goggles or shatterproof glasses when handling these clips. The gear and socket is manufactured in one piece. If a socket becomes worn and will no

longer retain the brush, the gear will have to be replaced.

Check for grounds with a VOM before putting the shoe polisher back into service. When reassembling the housing, be sure all wiring is in correct position away from the motor shaft and any revolving parts. *SEE ALSO APPLIANCE REPAIR, SMALL.*

Electric Switches
[SEE SWITCHES & OUTLETS.]

Electric Switch Plates

Electric switch plates or wall plates conceal switch boxes and their switches and connections. The wall plate is fastened to the switch with two countersunk screws. If the screws are tightened too much, the plate will crack.

Electric switch plates are inexpensive and available in enough colors and finishes to harmonize with any decor. *SEE ALSO SWITCHES & OUTLETS.*

Electric Toaster Repair

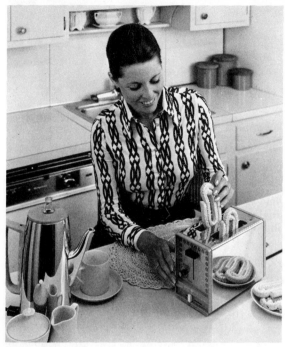

Courtesy of General Electric Company

Electric toasters are probably one of the most complex portable appliances in the average home. They are made with a number of heating elements, depending upon the number of slices the toaster will contain. One element is placed on each side of each cavity.

The carriage of the rack which supports the bread is springloaded to provide a "pop up" action. A trigger and latch mechanism is designed to hold the racks down during the toasting time. When the handle is depressed to lower the bread this latching mechanism takes over. At the same time, contact is made through a switch to turn the heating element on. The heat also acts upon a thermostat built into the toaster which acts as a timing mechanism. When the predetermined temperature is reached, the bimetal releases the latch and the bread rack springs upwards. As soon as it rises, the switch that controls the heating element opens and the elements turn off. A shock absorber or damper is built into the toaster and linked to the rack to prevent the toast from flying completely out of the toaster when it returns to the top.

Most toasters have a crumb tray underneath which can be removed for cleaning. Before opening it, unplug the toaster and with the crumb tray open shake all crumbs away from and out of the mechanism. It is advisable to use a small brush to brush away small stubborn particles. If a toaster doesn't work, first check the receptacle by plugging a table lamp into it. If the lamp does not operate the problem will be in the house circuit, probably a blown fuse or circuit breaker. Toasters consume quite a bit of power when they are on. If another appliance, particularly a heating appliance, is plugged into the same circuit, there is a possibility that it would overload the circuit and blow the fuse.

If the toaster still fails to operate, you will have to take a look at it. Unplug it and check the cord by inspecting it at the strain relief where it enters the toaster and at the plug itself. If this fails, you will probably have to go into the toaster.

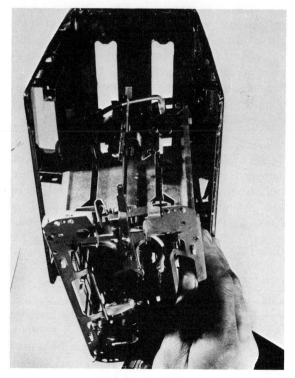

Inner works can be removed from "envelope" after front and rear covers are removed and attachment screws loosened.

Most toasters are built with an "envelope" cabinet. To remove it, first remove the knobs using a small screwdriver or phillips screwdriver as required. Next, open the crumb tray, removing any screws that secure the crumb tray to the bottom. Also, look for screws that retain the end panel while you have the bottom open. Then remove the end panels and remove the envelope. The end panels are often held at one end with strain retainers that just pull away from the envelope. With these out of the way, the shell can be removed from the mechanism. Don't hold the toaster upside down while removing the shell. The wires which hold the bread in place and support the bread on the side can fall out, and there are many of them to pick up.

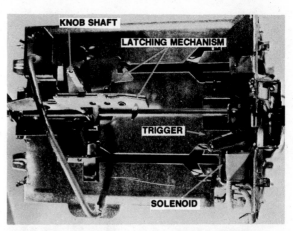

Front view of toaster mechanism shows latch and solenoid position. When bread rack is lowered, latch holds it in bottom position. When thermostat contacts close as correct temperature is reached, solenoid energizes and releases bread rack.

With the envelope removed you can depress the toaster and watch the action of the linkage in the toaster as it takes place. Any binding should be apparent. A single drop of oil on any rusty components or linkages should relieve the problem.

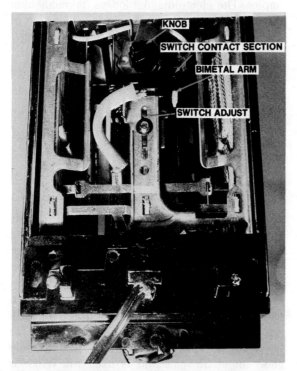

If lightness-darkness control won't provide correct range for your toasting needs, additional adjustment is often provided at thermostat mounting point. Look under bottom of toaster for knob or sliding switch.

With the shell removed, look closely for broken terminals and connections, particularly around points around a switch. Some toasters use a solenoid, which is a small electrical coil that acts as a magnet to release the latching mechanism of the toaster.

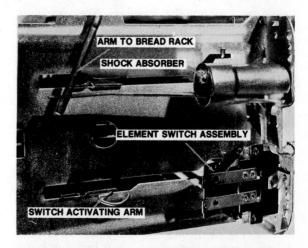

Rear view shows element switch and shock absorber. Shock absorber dampens spring return of bread rack, keeps toast from flying out of toaster when solenoid releases mechanism.

If a switch contact appears to be pitted, corroded or burned, smooth it with an automotive point file and then burnish it with a hardwood stick or a striking surface from a book of matches. This should restore it to operation. By operating the toaster with the power off, you will often be able

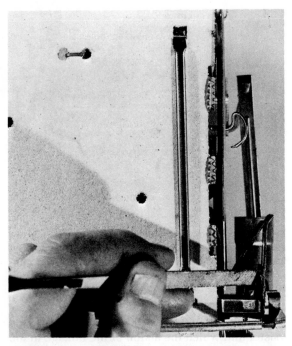

Burned contacts can often be cleaned using automotive point file. Hooked arm at top closes contacts when bread rack is lowered.

to see any problem that develops. Your previous diagnosis should give you some idea of the area in which the problem lies, whether it is due to a binding mechanism or an electrical problem with the heating element or the switches.

The heating elements of toasters are usually ribbon type with mica supports serving as insulators. These elements may appear identical but their wattages are often different. The outside elements are usually of a higher wattage than the inside ones. Be sure to obtain an exact replacement from the dealer which sells your brand of toaster if it is necessary to replace an element and be sure to specify which element is at fault. A break in an element can often be seen, but a good volt-ohm-meter or circuit tester will pin it down faster. Use a volt-ohm-meter on the highest resistance scale to check for any ground after the shell is placed around the toaster again. *SEE ALSO APPLIANCE REPAIR, SMALL.*

Electric Tools, Portable

[SEE PORTABLE POWER TOOLS.]

Electromagnets

An electromagnet is a core of soft iron wrapped with a coil of wire through which an electric current is passed to magnetize the core. When the current is turned off, most of the magnetism disappears.

A small electromagnet can be made by wrapping a large nail or bolt with fine magnet wire and then attaching the wire ends to a large dry cell battery. The nail is then magnetized and can be used for picking up loose bits of metal, tacks or staples. The electromagnet looses its magnetism and releases the attached material when one of the wire ends is disconnected from the battery.

A more complex electromagnet is used in electric motors to turn the armature which in turn spins the shaft.

Elm Wood

Elm wood is a firm hardwood used in making barrels, baskets, interior trim and the curved portions of furniture. Three unique features of this wood are that it bends easily, has a light grain pattern and contains pleasant light and dark shades. It lends an elegant accent when used with other woods. Because the pattern in the wood grain makes it almost impossible for the wood to split or cleave, elm is extremely good for chair seats and is used for Windsor chairs. The wood grain also makes elm one of the favorites of wood carvers since the exposed patterns are quite artistic.

There are three species of elm trees used as ornamental shade trees. The American elm, which is also called the white or gray elm, the slippery elm, also known as the red elm, and the rock elm, also referred to as the hickory or cork elm. The distinguishing feature of the elm is the leaves, which are oval with sawtoothed edges

and a rough surface and have the unique feature of one side being larger than the other.

In the days before metal was used in plumbing, elm wood was used for the water pipes and pumps. When shut away from air, elm wood pipes last indefinitely. *SEE ALSO WOOD IDENTIFICATION.*

Emery Cloth

An emery cloth is an abrasive cloth which removes rust and polishes unplated metals. Emery, the abrasive coated onto the cloth, is black in color, fine-grained with a sandpaper appearance, and has a slow cutting action which tends to wear out quickly. *SEE ALSO ABRASIVES.*

Emptying the System

Emptying a home water-supply system may become necessary from time to time, especially if the house is to be left unheated during winter months. If the system is installed correctly, pipes will tend to slant downward toward drain valves.

The first step in draining the system is turning off the water at the main supply valve. Then all toilets must be flushed and faucets and drain valves opened. Flush tank inlet valves in toilets and open faucets admit air to their supply pipes. When air cannot enter, a pipe acts as a vacuum, holding in water which may later freeze.

There should be a *relief valve* connected to the water heater in a hot-water system. Releasing water that is above normal pressure or approaching boiling temperature is the purpose of this valve. Thus, it helps to prevent damage to the system. At normal pressure the valve will remain closed.

A drain valve at the lowest point of a water heater empties it. When it is opened, all hot-water faucets in the house should be opened to clear the supply pipes. To put the system back in order, it should be filled with water before the heat source is turned on again. Water will run from these open faucets as an indication that the water-supply system is full. *SEE ALSO PLUMBING SYSTEMS.*

Emulsion Wood Stain

Emulsion wood stain is a liquid that is spread onto unfinished wood to accentuate the wood grain and give it a smooth surface. Emulsion wood stain accents the wood grain to a lesser degree than an oil-base stain. It is also thinner and easier to clean from the brush. *SEE ALSO WOOD FINISHING.*

Enamel

Enamel is an opaque varnish finish mixed with ground pigment which produces a smooth, hard film. There are varying kinds of enamel with different properties. To produce a good enamel finish, a smooth undercoat of flat paint or enamel leaving no brush marks is necessary. The two main types of enamel are interior and exterior. Interior enamels come in glossy, semi-glossy and flat finishes. Since dirt does not adhere to the surface, cleaning will not dull it. Proportions of pigment and binder vary in the glossy and semi-glossy types; more binder will produce a higher gloss. A dull, soft finish is produced by the flat enamel, which occasionally is used as an undercoat for glossy enamel. Interior enamels are used for furniture, woodwork and walls, particularly those in kitchens and bathrooms. Exterior enamels are made to be weather resistant and more durable than interior enamels. They are used on outside woodwork, such as porch floors, house trim, decks, boats and outdoor furniture. *SEE ALSO PAINTS & PAINTING.*

End-Cutting Nippers

End-cutting nippers, which are excellent for snipping wires of all kinds, have a fixed pivot and blunt nose. The jaws, even when completely closed, are approximately 1/8" apart and slightly off-center. Besides being useful when cutting nails off flush with the surface, this type of nippers is used for cutting tiles, especially small ceramic mosaics. *SEE ALSO HAND TOOLS.*

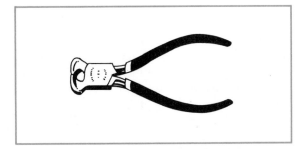

End-Cutting Nippers

End Grain

End grain is the pattern of the annual growth rings that is exposed when a piece of lumber is cut across the grain. The lumber may be sawed edge-grain, which means that the rings run at a 45 to 90 degree angle to the face of the piece, or flat-grain, meaning the rings run at less than a 45 degree angle to the surface. A combination of

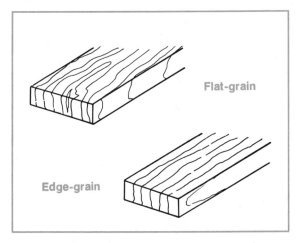

Flat-grain

Edge-grain

edge-grain and flat-grain is called mixed-grain lumber. In edge-grain timber, the rings on the face of the piece are spaced closely and evenly, while the spacing of the rings in flat-grain lumber varies. *SEE ALSO LUMBER.*

End-Lap Joint

An end-lap joint is a variation of the lap joint, found in may basic furniture pieces. The end-lap joint is commonly used in frame construction, and is made by first removing the same amount of stock from one end of two pieces of wood so that one piece fits into the other. The two pieces are then joined together by gluing. *SEE ALSO FURNITURE MAKING.*

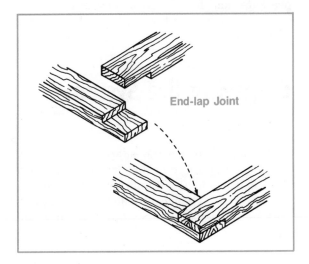

End-lap Joint

End-Matched Lumber

End-matched lumber is lumber with tongue-and-groove ends. *SEE ALSO LUMBER.*

English Bond

English bond is a bricklaying pattern formed by continuous layers of brick in a wall which adds

to the appearance as well as the strength of the wall. English bond is composed of alternating layers of headers, bricks laid crosswise, and stretchers, bricks laid end to end. This pattern is used in walls that are eight inches thick. Half-header bricks compose the staggered vertical joints, which help spread the weight of the bricks and/or other components over the whole wall, producing a stronger wall. *SEE ALSO BRICK & STONE WORK.*

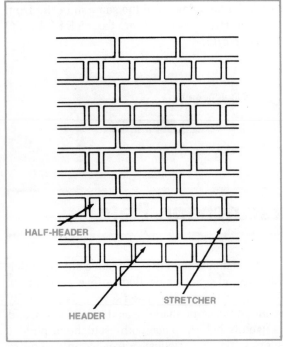

English Bond

Enlarging, Photographic
[SEE PHOTOGRAPHY.]

Entertainment Centers
[SEE RECREATION ROOMS.]

Epoxy Glue

Epoxy glue, the strongest kind of adhesive, is a two-part resin adhesive which comes in separate containers. The two materials, a resin and a hardener, must be mixed in equal proportions before application. Frequently epoxy glue is labeled "100% Solids", meaning it sets completely by a chemical process rather than solvent evaporation. This causes the entire mixture to solidify without shrinkage. Before the glue is applied, make sure that both surfaces to be joined are clean; and that nonporous surfaces have been roughened with sandpaper. Press the parts together and wipe away any extra glue. This glue is available in a clear form, which makes it good to use for glasswares. It also comes in a variety of colors.

The drying time varies with different brands. Normally, epoxy will set in two hours and cure overnight in regular room temperatures of 60° to 70° F. If a 250-watt infrared heat lamp is placed about 16 inches from the joint, the setting time can be cut by 20 minutes, making the curing time proportionately less. Small areas that are joined can be put in a kitchen oven which is heated to 150° for 90 minutes. There are also certain kinds of epoxy glues which will cure in five minutes.

When mixed and cured correctly, an area joined with epoxy glue will hold indefinitely. It is resistant to most alkalis and acids and also will resist boiling water, continuous freezing and thawing. When the heat resistance of the joint is the major concern, rather than its strength and flexibility (as with china and glassware that is exposed to hot water and steam), mix the glue with two parts resin to one part hardener.

Epoxy glue can be used for most any household repairs, as in repairing water pipe leaks, mending broken glasses or china and bonding fixtures to tile walls. China, glass, metals, plastics, porcelain, wood, masonry and leather can be joined by this glue. *SEE ALSO ADHESIVES.*

Epoxy Paints

Epoxy paints have a catalytic action which produces a cohesive bond to most any surface. They

will withstand rough wear and their resistance to alkali and acids is higher than other paints.

Epoxy paints consist of two coating components: a pigmented base and a hardener, which must be added before applying the paint. These are mixed and left to stand 60 minutes before application. The mix should be applied with either a nylon brush, a shortnap mohair roller or a spray gun. To clean or thin epoxy paints, use a special epoxy solvent. Thinner helps the paint to penetrate porous surfaces, such as concrete. Small jobs, such as kitchen appliance painting, may be done with a ready-to-use spray can.

Epoxy paints should be applied at temperatures above 60° F. and should not drop below this point for at least 72 hours after the paint is applied. Painting in unheated areas should be done during warm weather and during a time of year when an overnight drop in temperature is not likely.

Since the drying time is normally only one hour, dust does not present a problem with epoxy paints as it does with enamel paints. However, the final coat needs a longer curing time than standard paints. Before walking on a floor freshly painted with epoxy paint, one week of curing at 70° F. is recommended.

These paints were made originally to use on floors, but now they are used almost anywhere. For example, they can be used on old ceramic-tile kitchen or bath walls, on tables and counter tops to make them colorful and durable and on basement or garage floors which need a tough coating that will resist oil, grease and road salt. Since these paints are water-resistant, laundry wash tubs, basement walls, boat hulls and swimming pools can be painted with them also. Porous brick and concrete walls can be beautified and sealed by using epoxy paints which produce a glazed coating.

Because epoxy paints have a strong, lingering odor, some ventilation is needed for about 24 hours. Forced-air ventilation must be used in closed places to make the strong solvent evaporate more quickly. *SEE ALSO PAINTS & PAINTING.*

Escutcheon Pins

Escutcheon pins are small, decorative nails with sharp points and curved heads used for holding an escutcheon plate to a door. This is done by driving the pin with a hammer through the nail holes on the plate and into the wood. Escutcheon pins are usually made of brass or copper, but can generally be obtained in the same material from which the plate is made. *SEE ALSO FASTENERS.*

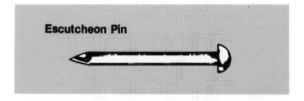

Escutcheon Pin

Escutcheon Plate

An escutcheon plate is a protective shield which fits around and is installed with a door knob. The escutcheon, also called a rose, is generally made of the same material as the door knob, and is usually held in place with escutcheon pins or screws. Some varieties, however, only require turning the interior and exterior escutcheons in opposite directions for them to fit tightly against

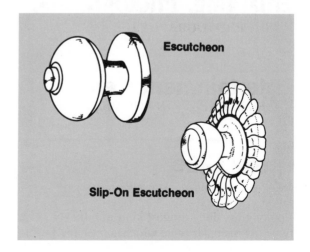

Escutcheon

Slip-On Escutcheon

the door. The more common escutcheon is round, has a flat, concave or convex surface which is molded into a rim approximately 1/2-inch long which fits against the door. Rectangular escutcheons have no rim so they are placed flat on the door surface. These escutcheons provide a larger protection area than round escutcheons, and are available with or without a built-in lock.

Slip-on escutcheons generally fit around the original escutcheon and are used primarily for decoration. These escutcheons are available in many styles, colors and materials to match the exterior architecture and size of the home and the interior room design. *SEE ALSO DOOR KNOBS & KNOCKERS.*

Excavation

Excavation is the process of grading dirt in preparation for the footings and foundation of a home or building. This is done with bulldozers, backhoes, scoop lifts and other earth-moving equipment. The top soil removed during excavation should be piled where it will not interfere with construction. It can then be used later for the finished grade when the building is completed.

In laying a basement foundation, excavate two feet beyond the building lines to permit clearance for formwork. The depth of an excavation can be determined by the vertical section views on the architectural plans. Excavations in cold climates should extend below the frost line to prevent the freezing of the wet soil under the footing, which would cause damage to the foundation wall. The excavation depth may also be controlled or limited depending on the slope of the site and the elevation of sewer lines. *SEE ALSO FOOTINGS & FOUNDATIONS.*

Expanding Cement

Expanding cement is a fast-setting cement designed for anchoring bolts, guard rails, banisters, fixtures and conduit. The homeowner, however, will probably use it more for patching cracks in walls, floors, masonry and other surfaces. Expanding cement usually sets in 15 minutes, has no rust-producing iron additives and expands to completely fill the gap. If the cement is used where it will be continuously exposed to water, apply an industrial water sealant over the cement to prevent erosion. Do this after the cement has cured for no less than seven days. Expanding cement generally comes in 1, 5, 25, 50 and 125 pound containers and is mixed with water to different consistencies for pouring or patching. For best results, follow the manufacturer's mixing directions and measure accurately. *SEE ALSO CEMENT PATCHING MATERIALS.*

Expansion Anchor

An expansion anchor, consisting of a bolt and shield, is used to fasten heavy objects to a wall. The shield expands inside the wall and remains there when the bolt is tightened. *SEE ALSO FASTENERS.*

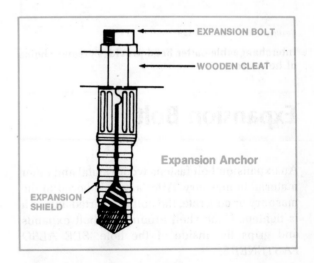

EXPANSION BOLT

WOODEN CLEAT

Expansion Anchor

EXPANSION SHIELD

Expansion Bit

A single expansion bit can be a helpful and economical tool in the home workshop as it

eliminates the need for a large assortment of auger bits. The bit is made with a cutter which can be adjusted to the desired hole width by means of a screw. The widths available are marked on some of the cutter tools. Some expansion bits have interchangeable heads which facilitate an even wider choice of hole sizes. *SEE ALSO HAND TOOLS.*

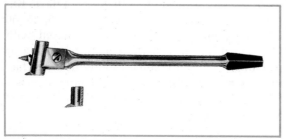

Courtesy of The Stanley Works

Solid-head Expansion Bit adjusts width by means of an adjusting screw.

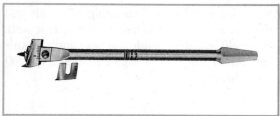

Courtesy of The Stanley Works

Interchangeable cutter head provides greater choice of hole sizes.

Expansion Bolt

An expansion bolt fastens wood, metal and other material to masonry. After a hole is bored in the masonry or concrete, the bolt is inserted and as it is tightened, the shell around the bolt expands and grips the inside of the hole. *SEE ALSO FASTENERS.*

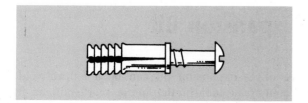

Expansion Joint

An expansion joint, also called a contraction joint, is the series of vertical or horizontal channels in driveways and sidewalks that prevent the slabs from cracking when they expand and contract. Expansion joints are formed by placing thin boards inside the framework so that they fit tightly against the sides. After the concrete is poured and dried, these boards are removed, leaving expansion joints. *SEE ALSO CONCRETE.*

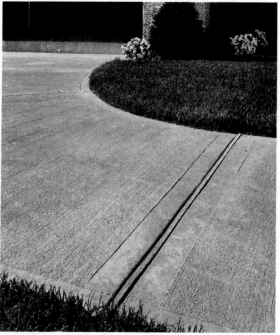

Courtesy The Homasote Company

An expansion joint in concrete prevents cracking of the slab.

Exposed Rafter

An exposed rafter is a rafter which extends beyond the wall frame of a home and is not covered with plywood or other materials on the underside. *SEE ALSO WALL & CEILING CONSTRUCTION.*

Extension Cords

An extension cord is used to increase the length of an electrical cord on an appliance. The extension cord is flexible with a plug on one end and a receptacle on the other end. Extension cords for home use generally contain only two wires, and should not be used to operate more than one or two small appliances, such as clocks, radios or lamps. The plug may be either the two-prong or three-prong grounded type, depending on the size and type of cord used and the job to be performed. The receptacle slots will also vary from one set of two-slot receptacles to three pairs of two-slot receptacles. Extension cords having three wires are used to operate outdoor appliances and electric power tools that need to be grounded. Thin extension cords have a low conducting capacity. Using the same cord to operate too many appliances will cause the cord to overheat, resulting in a fire hazard. Also, the size and type of the extension cord should be matched correctly with the size and type of the original cord. The length of the cord should also be considered, since a cord that is too long causes a drop in electrical current, and may impair the efficiency of the appliance. For this reason, combinations of extension cords should be avoided. Extension cords are available with plastic or rubber sheathing. *SEE ALSO PLUGS & CORDS.*

Extension Rule

A type of measuring and marking instrument, the extension rule has one end section that contains a calibrated slide-out brass extension for inside measurements, and all sections have a square end to seat squarely against a surface. Although most standard rules are graduated in inches and sixteenths, special models of the extension rule are made with feet divided into tenths and hundredths and with metric markings. This rule can also be used as a marking gauge. *SEE ALSO HAND TOOLS.*

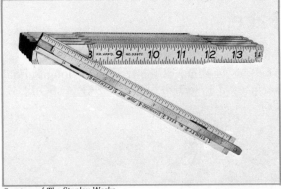

Courtesy of The Stanley Works

Extension Rule

External Threads

External threads are the spiraling grooves on screws, bolts and pipes that may be joined, without use of fittings and adhesive, to an object with internal threads. The external threads on fasteners such as screws, form their own internal threads in wood, metal, plastics and other materials to maintain a secure hold.

Eye Bolt

An eye bolt is a special, all-purpose combination fastener and holder. It has external threads and a square nut and its curved end forms a circle. This feature permits a variety of uses such as holding tools, stringing a clothes line and receiving the screen door hook. *SEE ALSO FASTENERS.*

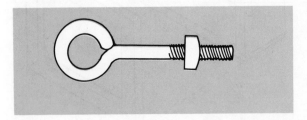

Eye Bolt

Face

The face is either of the two wider longitudinal surfaces of a piece of lumber. *SEE ALSO LUMBER.*

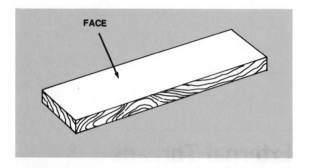

Facebrick

Facebrick is used for wall surfaces which are subject to weather exposure. It comes in two grades: SW (severe weathering), which is frost resistant, and MW (medium weathering), which is resistant to below freezing temperatures. Most face bricks have squared corners and sharp edges. They are available with smooth or rough surfaces, and may also be enameled. *SEE ALSO BRICK & STONE WORK.*

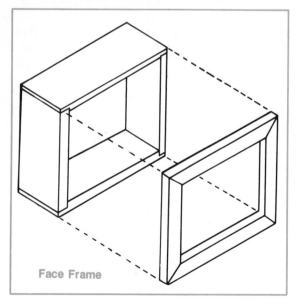

Face Frame

Face Frame

A face frame is an open wood frame that fits on the front of cabinets, shelves, chests, etc., to admit, enclose or support drawers and hinged or sliding doors. *SEE ALSO KITCHEN DESIGN & PLANNING.*

Face Nailing

Face nailing is a method of driving a nail through two board surfaces to join them together. The length of the nail for this type of nailing should be $3/16$- to $1/4$-inch less than the combined thickness of the two boards. When face nailing, lay the surfaces face-to-face, place the nail perpendicular to the wood and drive it in straight.

Faceplate

A faceplate is a metal disc that may be screwed onto the headstock spindle of a wood lathe. Long, columnar objects are turned on the lathe by inserting the piece of wood between the headstock and tailstock spindles. A faceplate attachment, however, provides a means for turning wide-diameter pieces that cannot be mounted between the two spindles, such as bowls or trays. *SEE ALSO LATHE.*

Fans
[SEE VENTILATION, HOME.]

Fans, Electric
[SEE ELECTRIC FAN REPAIR.]

Fascia

A fascia is a flat, horizontal strip of lumber used for the outer face of a box cornice. It is nailed to

the ends of the rafters and lookouts to hide and protect them. On some houses, the gutter is attached to the fascia. *SEE ALSO ROOF CONSTRUCTION.*

for strength and durability. The fasteners can range from thumb tacks to foundation wall anchor bolts. In each case the wise choice is a prime factor in doing a job right.

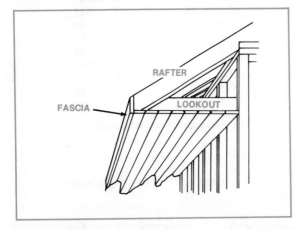

Fasteners

The vast number of assemblies in and about the home depend mostly on mechanical fasteners

Table Of Common Nails

SIZE	LENGTH	GAUGE	APP. # PER LB.
2d	1″	15	840
3d	1$\frac{1}{4}$″	14	540
4d	1$\frac{1}{2}$″	12$\frac{1}{2}$	290
5d	1$\frac{3}{4}$″	12$\frac{1}{2}$	250
6d	2″	11$\frac{1}{2}$	160
7d	2$\frac{1}{4}$″	11$\frac{1}{2}$	150
8d	2$\frac{1}{2}$″	10$\frac{1}{4}$	100
9d	2$\frac{3}{4}$″	10$\frac{1}{4}$	90
10d	3″	9	65
12d	3$\frac{1}{4}$″	9	60
16d	3$\frac{1}{2}$″	8	45
20d	4″	6	30
30d	4$\frac{1}{2}$″	5	20
40d	5″	4	16
50d	5$\frac{1}{2}$″	3	12
60d	6″	2	10

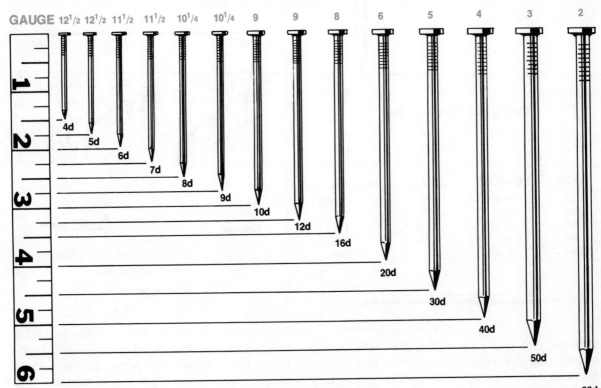

Common Nail Selection Chart

Finishing Nail Selection Chart

SIZE	LENGTH	GAUGE	APP. # PER LB.
10d	3″	11$\frac{1}{2}$	120
8d	2$\frac{1}{2}$″	12$\frac{1}{2}$	190
6d	2″	13	310
4d	1$\frac{1}{2}$″	15	600
3d	1$\frac{1}{4}$″	15$\frac{1}{2}$	870
2d	1″	16	1000

2D 3D 9D 6D 8D 10D

ACTUAL SIZE

Casing Nail Selection Chart

SIZE	LENGTH	GAUGE	APP. # PER LB.
16d	3$\frac{1}{2}$″	10	75
10d	3″	10$\frac{1}{2}$	95
8d	2$\frac{1}{2}$″	11$\frac{1}{2}$	150
6d	2″	12$\frac{1}{2}$	245
4d	1$\frac{1}{2}$″	14	480

Brad Selection Chart

LENGTH	GAUGE
$\frac{3}{16}$″	20-24
$\frac{1}{4}$″	19-24
$\frac{3}{8}$″	18-24
$\frac{1}{2}$″	14-23
$\frac{5}{8}$″	13-22
$\frac{3}{4}$″	13-21
$\frac{7}{8}$″	13-20
1″	12-20
1$\frac{1}{8}$″	12-20

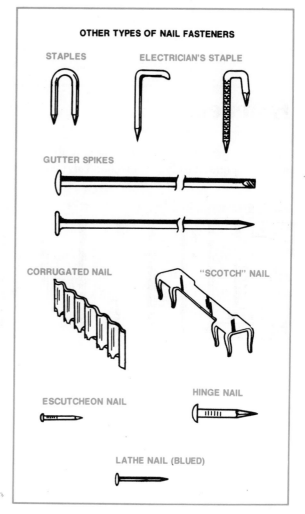

OTHER TYPES OF NAIL FASTENERS

STAPLES ELECTRICIAN'S STAPLE

GUTTER SPIKES

CORRUGATED NAIL "SCOTCH" NAIL

ESCUTCHEON NAIL HINGE NAIL

LATHE NAIL (BLUED)

The array of materials in this area would be bewildering if it were not for the fact that many fasteners can be identified by use. For example, there are finishing nails and casing nails — roofing nails and sheetrock nails — hollow and solid wall anchors — sheet metal screws — etc. Quite often, the selection in a particular category is made easier because of the material being fastened. Many wall panel manufacturers sup-

ply nails that are exactly right for the product, even to a matching color. Corrugated roofing needs nails that you would not use on shingles. You cannot drive a common nail into concrete. The latter calls for a nail that is specially hardened.

Whenever you are in doubt, describe the material and the job to your supplier, and he will produce the appropriate fastener.

NAILS

You can identify the length of a nail by the term "penny" (usually shown as a small "d") or in actual inches. The range of common nails is from 2d (1″) up to 60d (6″). There are exceptions but, usually, the diameter of a nail increases with its length. The length of the nail should be three times the thickness of the piece being secured. Thus, if you are attaching $3/4$″ stock to a 2 x 4 frame, the length of the nail should be $2^1/4$″ or 7d. This rule can't always be followed. It won't work, for example, if you are attaching $3/4$″ stock to $3/4$″ stock. In such a case you would use the longest nail possible to drive a too-long nail and clinch it on the back of the work, or maybe work with screws.

Common nails have great holding power because of their broad heads but they are not the best selection for "pretty" work. When appearance is important, finishing, or casing nails are used. These are driven in normal manner but only deep enough so the head is still above the surface. The final driving is done with a nail set, deep enough so the head is $1/16$″ to $1/8$″ below the wood surface. This, so you can conceal the nail by filling the hole with a wood dough or, in the

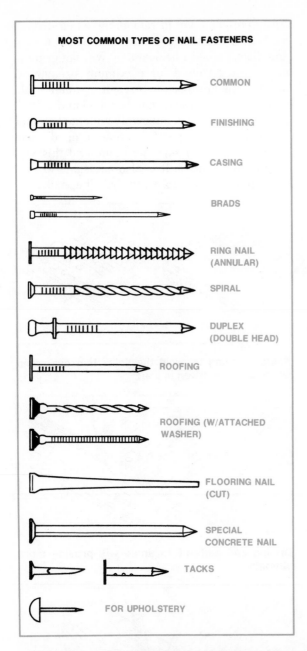

MOST COMMON TYPES OF NAIL FASTENERS

COMMON

FINISHING

CASING

BRADS

RING NAIL (ANNULAR)

SPIRAL

DUPLEX (DOUBLE HEAD)

ROOFING

ROOFING (W/ATTACHED WASHER)

FLOORING NAIL (CUT)

SPECIAL CONCRETE NAIL

TACKS

FOR UPHOLSTERY

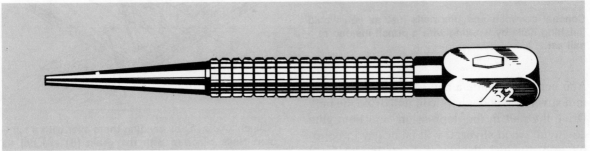

Nail sets come in different sizes. It's a good idea to have a complete set.

case of pre-finished wall paneling, a colored, wax crayon.

It is a mistake to use one nail set for all nail sizes. It's best to have an assortment of nail sets so you can choose one that most fits the size of the nail head. Common nails may also be set and hidden, but in this case, you would use a flat-face punch instead of a conventional nail set.

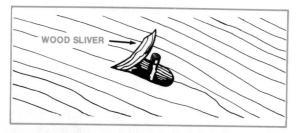

Do blind nailing by carefully lifting a sliver of wood with a chisel, driving the nail flush, and then gluing back the sliver.

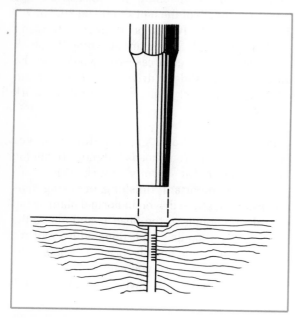

Conceal common and box nails just as you would finishing nails by working with a punch instead of a nail set.

Another way to hide a nail is to lift, carefully, a thin sliver of wood where you will drive the nail. Drive the nail in the depression, and then glue down the wood sliver. It will be nearly impossible to distinguish the sliver if you employ good craftsmanship.

An important point to remember when driving nails is to avoid heavy blows, which can split and distort wood fibers so they will not grip the nail as they should for maximum strength. A more gentle approach will result in a better job. Often, when it is likely that the wood may split, it pays to tap the nail point gently with the hammer to blunt it. Such a point will tend to bend wood fibers rather than separate them, and this will help to avoid splits. It is also advisable to drill small pilot holes before you drive the nails.

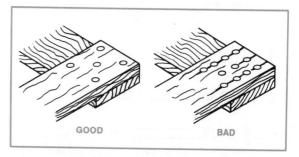

Stagger nailing to avoid the splits that can occur when nails are driven in line.

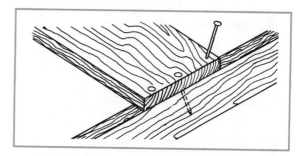

Driving end nails at an angle will provide more strength.

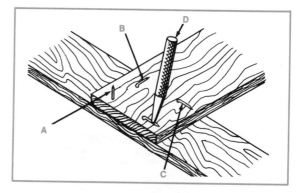

"Clinch" nails (A) by bending them over with a hammer. Nails clinched with the grain (B) are not as strong as nails clinched across the grain (C). Imbed the nail-end with a nail set (D).

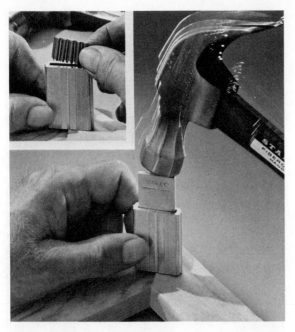

Nails and screws come in different finishes. If rust, which can lead to discoloration of areas adjacent to the fastener, is likely to occur, choose a fastener that is made of a rust-resistant material such as aluminum or copper — or fasteners that are galvanized. For example, if you are erecting shelves inside a garage, use ordinary nails. If the project is a fence, use galvanized nails.

SCREWS

Screws hold better and are easier to remove than nails, but they require a little more time to install. For all but the smallest screws, drill a pilot hole and a body hole and, when necessary, a countersink. The body hole matches the shank diameter of the screw. The pilot hole is relative to screw size and has to do with removing just enough wood so that the threads of the screw will cut and grip as they should.

A special device for corrugated fasteners is available. The fastener is dropped into a casing and driven home with a plunger. The plunger will set the fastener so it can be hidden with wood dough.

Screw Hole Drilling Chart

SIZES OF PILOT HOLES AND SHANK (BODY) HOLES

A = SIZE OF SCREW

B = SIZE OF PILOT HOLE TO DRILL IN HARDWOOD

C = SIZE OF PILOT HOLE TO DRILL IN SOFTWOOD

D = SHANK CLEARANCE HOLE

A	B	C	D
0	66	75	52
1	57	71	47
2	54	65	42
3	53	58	37
4	51	55	32
5	47	53	30
6	44	52	27
7	39	51	22
8	35	48	18
9	33	45	14
10	31	43	10
11	29	40	4
12	25	38	2
14	14	32	$1/4''$
16	10	29	$17/64''$
18	6	26	$19/64''$
20	3	19	$21/64''$
24	$1/4''$	15	$3/8''$

A good procedure is to drill the pilot hole through both pieces. Enlarge the upper portion to body size (often right through the piece to be

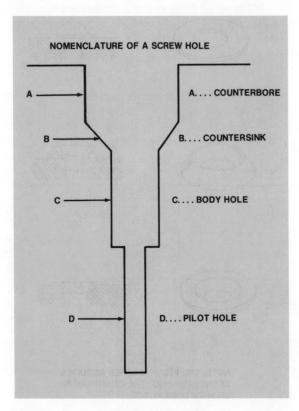

NOMENCLATURE OF A SCREW HOLE

A.... COUNTERBORE

B.... COUNTERSINK

C.... BODY HOLE

D.... PILOT HOLE

Parts of a screwhole

fastened) and then, if necessary, countersink. Unless the wood is very hard, the diameter of the countersink should be a shade less than the diameter of the screw-head, so that driving the screw will pull it down to be flush with the wood surface. If the wood is soft and the screw is small, drive a test screw to determine if it is possible to get by without countersinking. Generally, though, its a good idea to provide a seat for the head of the screw.

Counterboring is usually done when it's desirable to hide the screw. The counterbore forms a hole for a wooden plug that is glued in place after the screw is driven home. Always cut the plugs a fraction too long. Do this so that after the glue has dried, the plug can be sanded flush with adjacent surfaces. Sometimes the plugs are left long and rounded off to provide a decorative detail. This is seen quite often on Colonial style furniture.

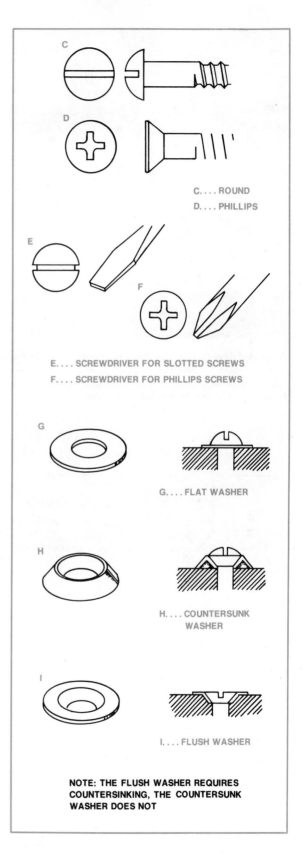

C.... ROUND

D.... PHILLIPS

E.... SCREWDRIVER FOR SLOTTED SCREWS

F.... SCREWDRIVER FOR PHILLIPS SCREWS

G.... FLAT WASHER

H.... COUNTERSUNK WASHER

I.... FLUSH WASHER

NOTE: THE FLUSH WASHER REQUIRES COUNTERSINKING, THE COUNTERSUNK WASHER DOES NOT

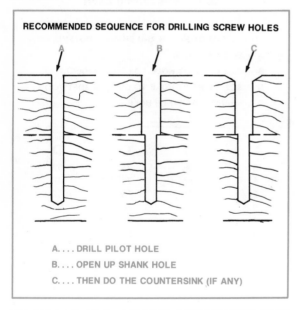

RECOMMENDED SEQUENCE FOR DRILLING SCREW HOLES

A.... DRILL PILOT HOLE

B.... OPEN UP SHANK HOLE

C.... THEN DO THE COUNTERSINK (IF ANY)

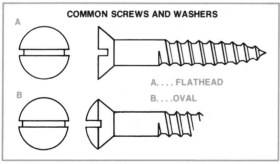

COMMON SCREWS AND WASHERS

A.... FLATHEAD

B.... OVAL

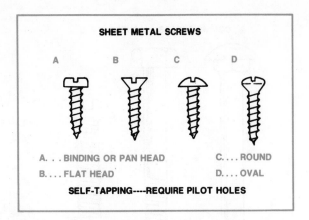

SHEET METAL SCREWS

A B C D

A. . . BINDING OR PAN HEAD   C. . . . ROUND

B. . . . FLAT HEAD   D. . . . OVAL

SELF-TAPPING----REQUIRE PILOT HOLES

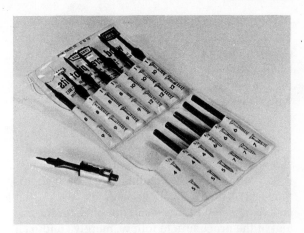

Special tools are available that form pilot hole, shank hole, countersink and/or counterbore in one drilling operation. Since screws come in many sizes, it's wise to buy such tools in sets.

The jobs described above can be accomplished with separate tools, or they can be accomplished with one-procedure tools that are designed for the purpose. These are available under different trade names, and they can be used with hand or power tools. They do come in different sizes for various screws so it makes sense to buy them in sets. By using them, it is possible to form pilot hole, body hole, countersink and, if needed, counterbore, in a single drilling operation.

Screw sizes are called out by both length and diameter. Just remember that in any particular gauge, it is possible to get different lengths to suit the work on hand. The general rule for selecting a screw length is to work for $2/3$ of the screw length to be in the base material. Again, as with nails, this rule can't always be followed. A secondary rule is to select a screw that is about $1/8$th inch shorter than the total thickness of the pieces being joined.

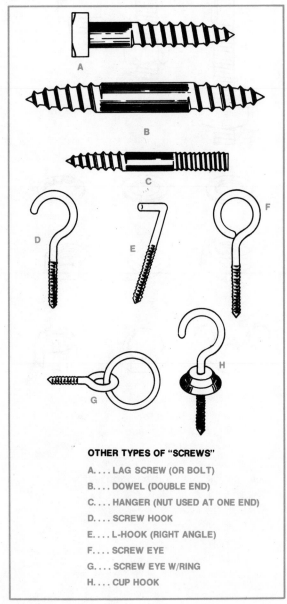

OTHER TYPES OF "SCREWS"

A. . . . LAG SCREW (OR BOLT)

B. . . . DOWEL (DOUBLE END)

C. . . . HANGER (NUT USED AT ONE END)

D. . . . SCREW HOOK

E. . . . L-HOOK (RIGHT ANGLE)

F. . . . SCREW EYE

G. . . . SCREW EYE W/RING

H. . . . CUP HOOK

Screw Length Selection Chart

Size	Length	Size	Length
0	$1/4$-$3/8$	9	$1/2$-3
1	$1/4$-$1/2$	10	$1/2$-$3^1/2$
2	$1/4$-$3/4$	11	$5/8$-$3^1/2$
3	$1/4$-1	12	$5/8$-4
4	$1/4$-$1^1/2$	14	$3/4$-5
5	$3/8$-$1^1/2$	16	1-5
6	$3/8$-$2^1/2$	18	$1^1/4$-5
7	$3/8$-$2^1/2$	20	$1^1/2$-5
8	$3/8$-3	24	3-5

Always select a screwdriver that fits the head of
the screw. When the driver is too narrow, it can
clip to damage the screw-head; damage can also
occur to the driver itself. If the driver is too wide
for the screw, it can damage the material into
which the screw is being driven.

Never start a screw by tapping it with a hammer.
This does nothing but distort the wood so the
screw-grip is less than efficient. When the wood
is soft or the screw is small or when both conditions exist, start the hole with an awl (often
called an ice pick). If ever in doubt about the extent of the procedure to follow, merely conduct a
test program in a scrap piece of the material
being worked with.

Often, and this occurs mostly in very hard
woods, the screw can be difficult to drive even
after you have followed all the good procedures.
A good solution is to coat the screw threads with
soap before driving. Using oil in place of soap is
not a good idea since the oil can stain the wood.
Another idea is to form a "tap screw". This is
done by filing a sample screw longitudinally so
that the result (in cross-section) is a half-screw.
Use the tap screw first; then remove it and drive
the permanent screw. The purpose of the tap
screw is to form threads so that the regular
screw will be easier to drive.

Washers are usually used to provide more bearing surface than can be obtained from the screw-
head alone. They also help to avoid marring of
the wood surface when driving the screw and on
those occasions when it must be removed. Flat
washers are usually used under round-head
screws. Flush type washers are used with either
countersunk screws or oval head screws. The
flush washer requires a countersink in the work.
The countersunk washer sits on the work surface and provides a seat for flathead or oval-
head screws. It does not require a countersink in
the work.

BOLTS AND NUTS

A bolt is usually a two-part device consisting of a
partially or wholly threaded shank with head
and a nut. Whatever is secured is gripped between the head of the bolt and the nut. Washers

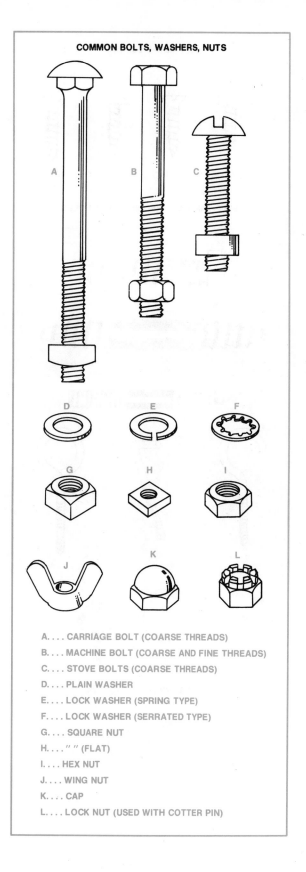

COMMON BOLTS, WASHERS, NUTS

A.... CARRIAGE BOLT (COARSE THREADS)
B.... MACHINE BOLT (COARSE AND FINE THREADS)
C.... STOVE BOLTS (COARSE THREADS)
D.... PLAIN WASHER
E.... LOCK WASHER (SPRING TYPE)
F.... LOCK WASHER (SERRATED TYPE)
G.... SQUARE NUT
H...." " (FLAT)
I.... HEX NUT
J.... WING NUT
K.... CAP
L.... LOCK NUT (USED WITH COTTER PIN)

may be used under the head, under the nut or in both places. The thread size of a bolt indicates the number of threads per inch. General categories are *coarse* thread and *fine* thread. Machine bolts are available in either, while carriage bolts and stove bolts are usually coarse. The work being done determines which way to go, and the *coarse* and *fine* titles are the key. A workbench assembly, for example, falls in the *coarse* category while the attachment of a speaker to the front panel of a cabinet will be more fitting in the *fine* category.

Bolt sizes are determined by both diameter and thread. An example would be a $1/4$-20 which describes a bolt that is $1/4''$ in diameter and has 20 threads to the inch. The length is also required. If a 3'' bolt is needed to fit the above description, ask for a $1/4$-20 x 3''. Exceptions would occur when the style comes in, for example, coarse threads only. Here, ask for a $1/4''$ x 3'' carriage bolt.

Many bolts require a holder both at the head and on the nut. The carriage bolt is a typical exception. It has a shoulder under the head that sinks into and grips the wood so that the bolt can't turn when taken up on the nut. This kind of design makes it possible to tighten the nut even when the bolt-head cannot be held.

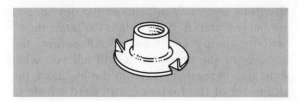

"Tee Nuts" are used to supply metal threads in wood

Washers are used under bolt heads (and nuts) for the same reason they are used under screws. When vibration in the project may cause the fastener to loosen, use a lock washer (either spring-type or toothed) under the nut. Special lock nuts are available for some bolts. These may be "distorted" so that they grip the bolt shank firmly, or they may contain unthreaded fiber inserts to accomplish the same purpose.

All bolts are set through holes that are drilled for them. The hole must not be so small that ham-

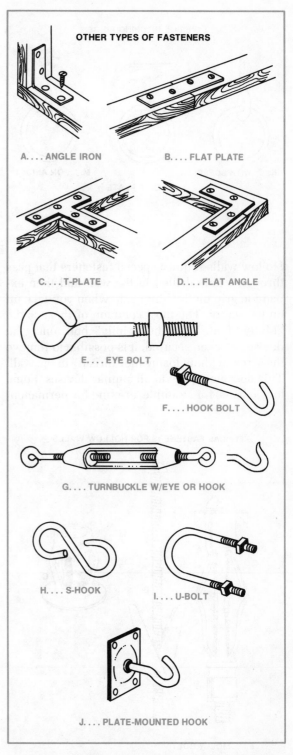

OTHER TYPES OF FASTENERS

A.... ANGLE IRON

B.... FLAT PLATE

C.... T-PLATE

D.... FLAT ANGLE

E.... EYE BOLT

F.... HOOK BOLT

G.... TURNBUCKLE W/EYE OR HOOK

H.... S-HOOK

I.... U-BOLT

J.... PLATE-MOUNTED HOOK

mering the bolt is necessary, or so large that the bolt wobbles. When in doubt, check the bolt diameter with a caliper, and drill the hole accordingly.

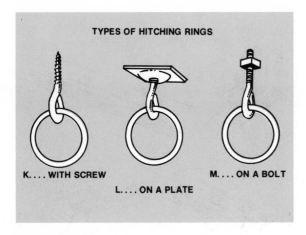

TYPES OF HITCHING RINGS

K. . . . WITH SCREW

L. . . . ON A PLATE

M. . . . ON A BOLT

FOR HOLLOW WALLS

Hollow walls require special fasteners that pass through a hole drilled in the wall and then expand to grip on the blind side when you take up on the screw. The most common of these is the "Molly" bolt. With the "Molly" bolt, once the devise has been secured, it is possible to remove the screw without losing the "thread" in the wall. This does not apply to all similar devises. Some toggle bolts, for example, are fine for permanent

TYPICAL FASTENERS FOR HOLLOW WALLS

A. . . . MOLLY BOLT

B. . . . TOGGLE BOLT

C. . . . JACK NUT IS GOOD FOR *THIN* WALLS —
HOLLOW CORE DOORS

installations, but if it is necessary to remove the screw, the securing device will fall down into the wall.

The size of the hole you drill for such items is very important because the manufacturers allow no room for guesswork. The right hole size is usually stamped on the item. Fasteners that fall into this category may be used through plaster, sheetrock, hollow concrete block, wood paneling, etc.

FOR SOLID WALLS

Fasteners for solid walls are usually in the expansion shield or anchor categories. The expansion type spreads when the screw or bolt is tightened to grip the sides of the hole that has been drilled for it. An anchor can work this way too, but many times the screw or bolt causes an integral part of the device to spread and grip inside the hole permanently. The latter is especially good for providing threads for machine bolts or threaded rod that may have to be removed on occasion. In a sense, it's like installing metal threads in a concrete wall.

All such items come in different sizes chosen according to the load they must carry. As with fasteners for hollow walls, be careful to note the hole size that is called for. If the hole is too small, it will be necessary to hammer the devise, and probably distort it. If the hole is too large, the fit will be sloppy and weak. Chances are, the package or the devise itself will tell you what hole size is needed. When in doubt, check the diameter of the fastener, and drill a hole to match.

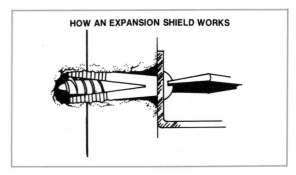

HOW AN EXPANSION SHIELD WORKS

Tightening the screw forces the shield against the sides of the hole

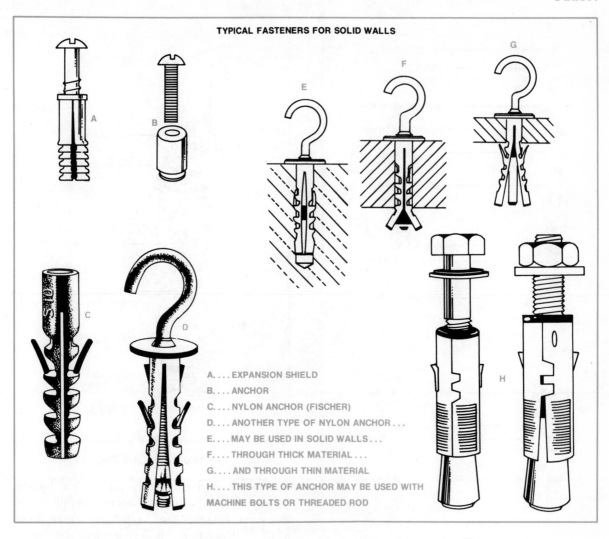

TYPICAL FASTENERS FOR SOLID WALLS

A.... EXPANSION SHIELD

B.... ANCHOR

C.... NYLON ANCHOR (FISCHER)

D.... ANOTHER TYPE OF NYLON ANCHOR...

E.... MAY BE USED IN SOLID WALLS...

F.... THROUGH THICK MATERIAL...

G.... AND THROUGH THIN MATERIAL

H.... THIS TYPE OF ANCHOR MAY BE USED WITH

MACHINE BOLTS OR THREADED ROD

Faucet

A faucet, which is a fixture for drawing liquid from a pipe, may be composed of many intricate parts, depending upon its type. There are several types including the deck, freezeproof, sill or outdoor, hot water, disc valve and one-handle faucets. Some common parts of a faucet are the handlescrew, handle, bonnet, bonnet packing, bib washer, spindle or stem, faucet washer, faucet screws, slip joint washer and brass friction ring.

The bonnet contains inside working parts of the assembly and, when loosened, allows the entire assembly to lift out.

Washers, made of plastic or rubber, are attached to the spindle or stem. Since the washer twists each time the handle is turned, it may wear out easily. However, some modern faucets are designed with washers which are pressed against the valve seat so they rarely ever wear

DISC VALVE FAUCET

There are some washerless faucets such as the disc valve. It is operated by one handle and is composed of discs which allow cold and hot water to mix. These discs are contained in a cartridge body along with the stem through

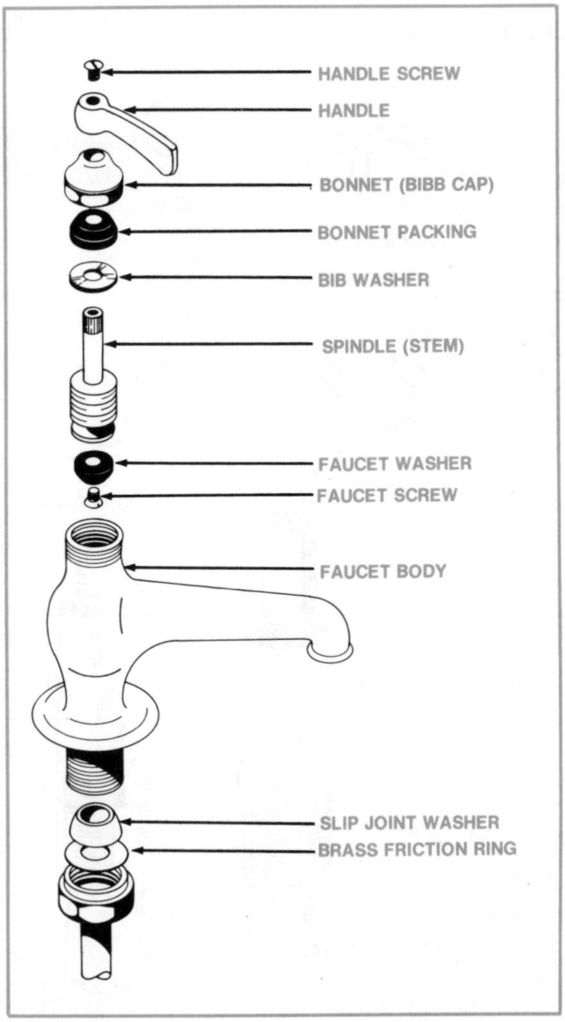
HANDLE SCREW
HANDLE
BONNET (BIBB CAP)
BONNET PACKING
BIB WASHER
SPINDLE (STEM)
FAUCET WASHER
FAUCET SCREW
FAUCET BODY
SLIP JOINT WASHER
BRASS FRICTION RING

Faucet Parts

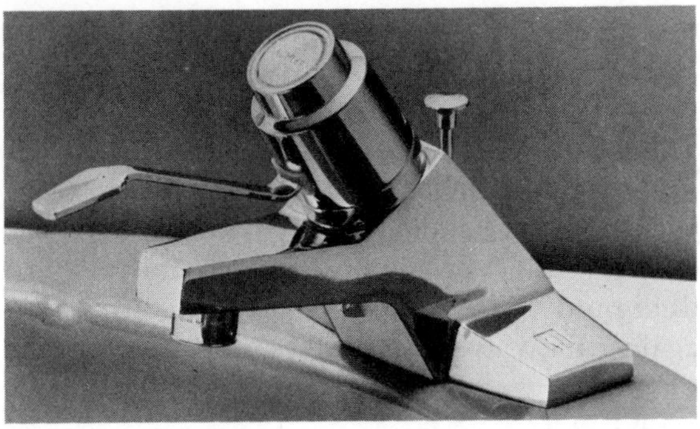

Courtesy of Kohler Company

Disc Valve Faucet

which water flows. At the bottom of this cartridge are cold and hot water inlet seals. Two large screws hold the unit together. When the

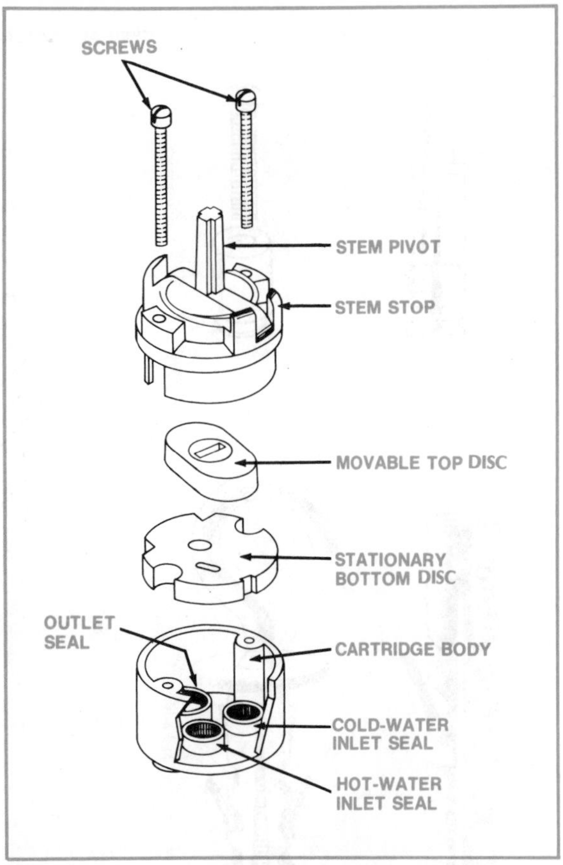
SCREWS
STEM PIVOT
STEM STOP
MOVABLE TOP DISC
STATIONARY BOTTOM DISC
OUTLET SEAL
CARTRIDGE BODY
COLD-WATER INLET SEAL
HOT-WATER INLET SEAL

Parts of Disc Valve Faucet

handle is turned, the top disc moves. The bottom disc is always stationary. Parts of this faucet will not wear out, but hard water can cause inner seals to deteriorate. An O-ring disc valve faucet allows water to flow through or prevents its flow, depending on the alignment of the discs.

Other one-handle faucets, like those used in modern showers, have complex workings such as steel-ball encapsulations, eccentrics and cams which are activated by the handle to blend hot and cold. The inner spindle is composed of neoprene O-rings. An O-ring may be restored to its original function by being turned over, although it can be easily replaced. The spindle may be removed by disengaging the faucet handle and taking off the keeper ring.

Most faucets today have an aerator, an attachment which breaks up the stream of water, to make an even flow. It is composed of fine screen

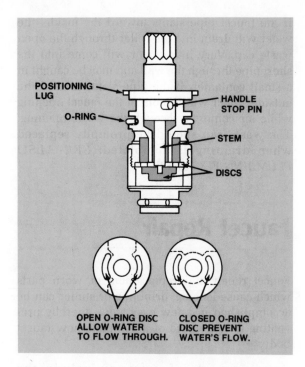

POSITIONING LUG

HANDLE STOP PIN

O-RING

STEM

DISCS

OPEN O-RING DISC ALLOW WATER TO FLOW THROUGH.

CLOSED O-RING DISC PREVENT WATER'S FLOW.

discs enclosed in a screw-on attachment. Water passing through the aerator produces a vacuum where air is drawn in through tiny holes around the fitting. When dirt accumulates in the screen, the water flow is cut down. To correct this, the nose at the end of the faucet may be removed. An old toothbrush is good for cleaning parts, which can easily be put back in place.

Deck Faucet

A deck faucet is equipped with two handles and a valve through which both hot and cold water flow. These parts are set on a faucet mounting

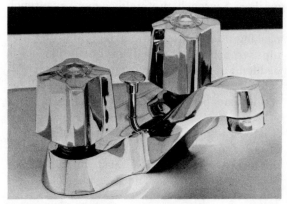

Courtesy of Kohler Company

Deck Faucet

which varies in sizes from four to six to eight inches between stems.

HOT WATER FAUCET

A hot water faucet is connected to pipes leading from the home's water-heating devices, such as the hydronic or forced hot water system. In this system, heat is transferred from the boiler through coiled tubing to the hot-water supply for the faucets. The boiling water and faucet water do not mix. Since the hydronic system is also used to heat the home in winter, shutting off the pump, that drives the boiler water to the radiator, enables the unit to heat the faucet supply in summer without heating the house.

Regular water heaters are used in homes which require large amounts of water. Depending on the fuel — oil, gas, or electricity — the unit takes a certain amount of time to recover, or provide a new supply after all hot water has been used.

If the house is to be left unheated, a hand-operated drain valve at the heater's lowest point empties it. Hot-water faucets should be opened during the emptying process to clear the supply pipes. To reactivate, have the system completely filled with water. Hot-water faucets should also be left open during the process of filling the water-heating system, as water will run from them when it's full.

FREEZEPROOF FAUCET

A freezeproof faucet may be used when the faucet is located outside basement walls. The handle, located outside the shaft of the faucet, continues inside to the valve. When the faucet is

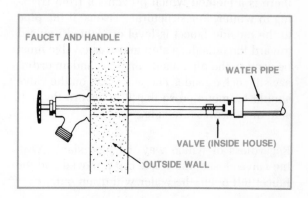

FAUCET AND HANDLE

WATER PIPE

VALVE (INSIDE HOUSE)

OUTSIDE WALL

turned off, water is shut off inside the basement and all water remaining in the faucet itself drains out. The warmth in the basement prevents freezing. This type of faucet may be left open all winter since it drains itself.

OUTDOOR FAUCET

An outdoor faucet, is often called a sill cock because it is mounted on the wooden sill of the house structure, is used primarily for the garden hose. The sill-cock supply pipe outside the house may have a special extra valve attached to it in cold areas. It is called the stop-and-waste valve and shuts off the water to the outside faucet. The stop-and-waste valve provides a vent to admit air to the intervening section of pipe to drain it and the outside faucet. A small brass cap on the side of the valve may be removed to open the vent.

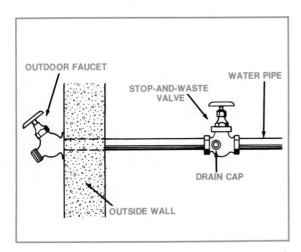

Outdoor Faucet

If the outdoor faucet is not a freezeproof one, there is a method which prevents it from freezing in winter. For structural reasons, if the pipe to the outside faucet is level or slanted upward toward the outside, a stop-and-waste valve must be used in the pipe inside the wall and an ordinary sill cock outside. The waste cap on the valve should be mounted so that it is toward the outside or non-pressure side.

Regardless of which way the pipe slants, with the valve closed, the waste cap removed and the faucet left open, the water will drain out.

If the faucet pipe slants toward the inside, the water will drain into the cellar through the open waste cap. Very little water will come into the short pipe through the wall and may be caught in a small container. If the pipe slants toward the outside, water will run out of the faucet opening while air comes in through the waste opening. The waste cap should be promptly replaced when draining is completed. *SEE ALSO PLUMBING FIXTURES.*

Faucet Repair

Faucet repair and replacement of worn parts which cause leaking, dribbling or stutter can be accomplished in a few easy steps, thereby preventing the purchase of a complete new faucet body.

Common parts of a faucet include the handlescrew, handle, bonnet, bonnet packing, bib washer, spindle or stem, faucet washer, faucet screws, slip joint washer and brass friction ring.

Problems in faucet leakage can usually be traced to a worn washer or worn packing around the stem of the faucet. A washer is the plastic or rubber portion of the faucet attached to the stem. Some less modern faucets have washers which twist each time the handle turns. This is the reason they wear out easily.

A few simple tools are needed to replace a worn washer. A wrench, preferably a monkey wrench or a crescent wrench, is needed to remove the packing nut, to prevent marring the fitting. If a pipe wrench must be used, be sure the surface is padded to protect the grooved or plated parts. A screwdriver is also needed to remove the large screws connecting the handle to the stem.

It is best to purchase an assortment of washers in order to get the right size. Washers come in different types also — the most suitable can be used for both hot and cold water faucets.

When replacing a washer, the first step is to turn off the water at the closest shut-off valve, usually

found directly below the sink. The handle is removed by disengaging the large screw attached to the spindle. The screw may be hidden under a chromium cap. After turning the handle clockwise, use a wrench to loosen the packing nut. With the nut removed, the spindle will lift out. The washer, located at the bottom of the spindle, will obviously appear flat, hard and out-of-shape if it is badly worn. Remove the old washer and put a new one in its place.

One of the older faucet types is the Fuller-ball type. To replace a washer for it, first loosen the packing nut, remove it and unscrew the stem while turning the handle clockwise. Loosen the screw at the bottom of the stem and take out the worn washer. Replace the parts in reverse order.

Old homes may also have faucets with antique china handles which project in four directions. Care must be taken in disassembling parts of these since they are delicate. The discs which indicate "hot" and "cold" are usually nickel-plated and set in the center of these handles. The discs have to be removed to unscrew the handles. When the handle is taken out of the shaft, a flat nut below it is turned to free the china covers over the faucets. When these are removed, two six-sided caps on the faucet are revealed — an upper one which tightens the packing and a larger lower one which removes the washer unit. Washer replacement is the same as on other models once these parts are removed.

If a replacement washer is too big, it can be cut down to size with a power drill. A small bolt and

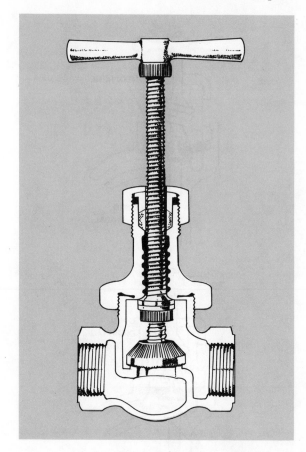

Faucet Reamer

nut are put through the hole in the washer's center. The washer is covered in abrasive paper, like sandpaper, and is spun by the drill until it reaches the proper size.

Sometimes washers wear out faster than normal, in which case it is very difficult to turn off the water flowing from the faucet. This can result when the faucet seat has uneven edges or is nicked in places. It can be restored by resurfacing it with a faucet reamer, which is an adjustable hand tool for smoothing rough edges. Some types of faucets have replaceable valve seats.

Most modern faucets have washers which press directly against the valve seat and require no twisting. These washers rarely wear out.

Modern washerless faucets, unlike the washer types, rarely cause trouble, although they occasionally do need repairs and replacements.

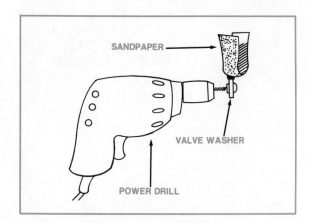

SANDPAPER

VALVE WASHER

POWER DRILL

Washer Size Readjustment

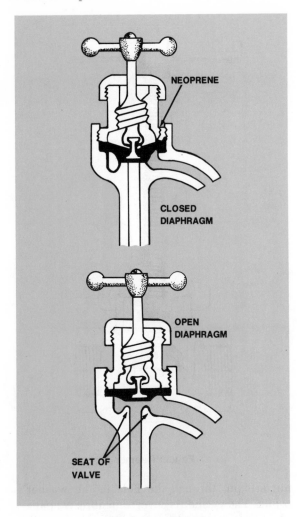

Diaphragm Faucet

Single-lever faucets, such as the tip-valve and sliding-port types, produce temperature variations when the lever tips to certain positions. In the sliding-port, the sleeve, controlled by the lever, lets in different amounts of hot and cold water.

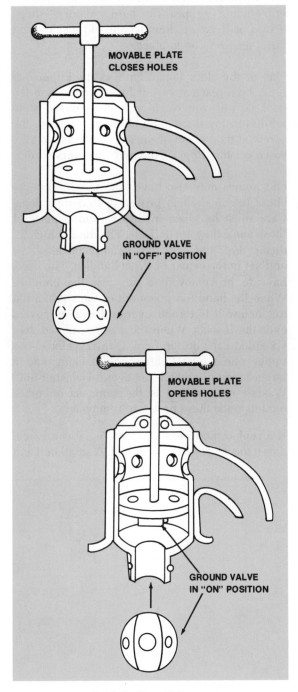

Hard Surface Valve

The diaphragm type of washerless faucet has either metal-plated discs, which work together to stop water flow, or a diaphragm made of rubber or similar material. These parts take the place of washers.

There is usually no packing in this diaphragm type. The assembly can be lifted out by unscrewing the stem. The diaphragm may be hard to lift out past the seals. Sometimes if tools do not work, the whole unit must be replaced. To replace just the diaphragm, press it on the end of the stem.

If a faucet drips in the diaphragm type, the cap and inner housing must be unscrewed and the neoprene diaphragm replaced.

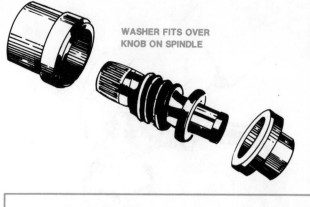

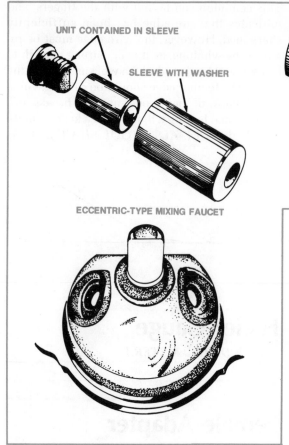

Faucet Variations

Replacement of the valves or sleeve in these faucets usually takes care of any problem in working order. This can be done by removing the plated covers and exposing the inner parts, as in older faucets.

Hard surface valve faucets, such as the disc valve type, have movable plates that turn against stationary ones. These plates, which come in specific models, may be replaced by using a specially designed repair kit. The shaft of this faucet is usually sealed with O-rings instead of packing. O-rings should be replaced whenever plates are replaced.

Stems in washerless faucets are generally dry and need lubricating with grease or petroleum jelly when they are removed. Oil can be used to free threaded parts of old antique-types. The china faucet mentioned earlier, as well as other faucets made of breakable or bendable material like brass, may also require lubricants.

If a faucet leaks around the stem, it is an indication of old, worn packing. This condition may be examined by removing the faucet handle and the cap or packing-nut.

The packing nut is the bonnet-shaped nut through which the stem protrudes. The packing under this nut is made of fibrous material such as soft cord. It is sometimes lubricated with graphite, a pliable, lustrous form of carbon, wound around the stem.

In many instances, a leak can be stopped by simply tightening the packing nut. If the tightening makes the handle difficult to turn or does not completely stop the leakage, the packing will have to be replaced.

To replace it, the water supply to the fixture must be shut off and the faucet handle removed. The cap-nut will then be exposed and should be unscrewed to show the packing underneath. A sharp-pointed object can be used to dig out the old material. Then the new packing is wound around the stem, and the parts replaced.

If a faucet vibrates loudly when it is partly opened, this is known as faucet stutter. It is caused by a loose washer. To remedy the stutter, remove the spindle and tighten the screw which holds the washer in place. Faucet stutter is more prevalent in sill cocks and utility outlets than in indoor fixtures. *SEE ALSO PLUMBING REPAIRS.*

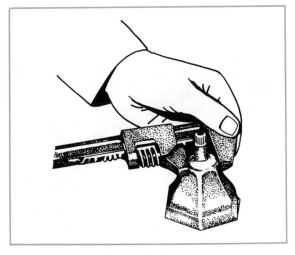

Cap Nut Located Under Housing.

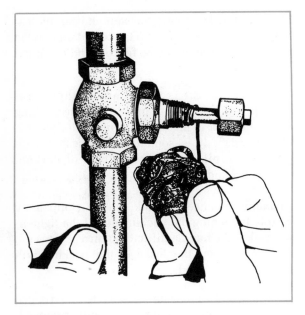

Loosen cap nut; wind packing material around stem.

Faucet Washers
[SEE FAUCET; FAUCET REPAIR.]

Feather Edge

A feather edge, or wire edge, forms on the extreme edge of a blade when this edge becomes very thin and curves back during sharpening.

This condition can be felt with the fingers, and indicates that the edge has been sufficiently sharpened. However, the wire edge must be removed by whetting, as it is not strong enough to be used and tends to dull the working edge of the blade. The feather edge should be rubbed with a small block of hardwood until it breaks off. Then, a final honing will produce a keener, more useful edge. *SEE ALSO TOOL SHARPENING.*

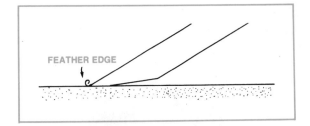

Feeler Gauge
[SEE DWELL METER.]

Female Adapter

A female adapter is a copper tube fitting. It is used to connect different sizes of pipes. Having internal threads, the female adapter receives the male adapter that has external threads. *SEE ALSO PIPE FITTINGS.*

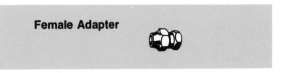

Female Adapter

Fences & Gates

A fence performs at least one of three functions: it controls the amount of sunlight or wind that reaches an area; provides a physical or visual barrier for an area or provides a decorative accent for an area.

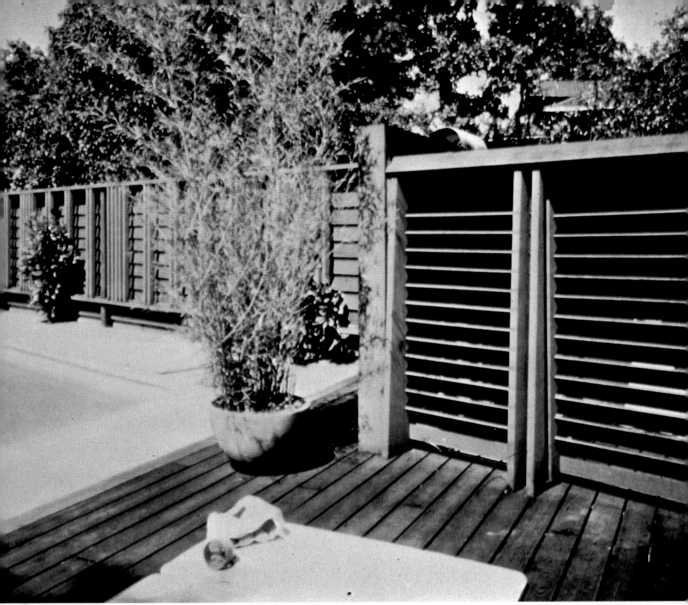

Wind control, a visual barrier, and a decorative background are all provided by this fence.

A homeowner planning a fence must consider not only the function the fence must perform, but also the legal boundaries & conditions and the site advantages and disadvantages.

Possible legal problems with fences are often due to building codes, property lines and attractive nuisances. Local building codes directly affect the materials, height, construction and location of fences. A building permit should be obtained before putting up a fence. If a boundary fence is to be built, care should be taken to locate the property lines. Fences built on another's property belong to that person. Neighbors may fre-

quently share the cost of a boundary fence, and such shared projects may do much to avoid the "over-the-line" problem. Finally, most communities have "attractive nuisance" ordinances covering items that may be alluring and dangerous to children such as swimming pools, guard-dog kennels, etc. These ordinances usually establish criteria for fencing to surround these areas.

The ideal site for a fence is a large, extremely level plot of ground, with no trees, rocks, walks, streams, easements or structures above the surface, and no rocks, covered concrete, pipes,

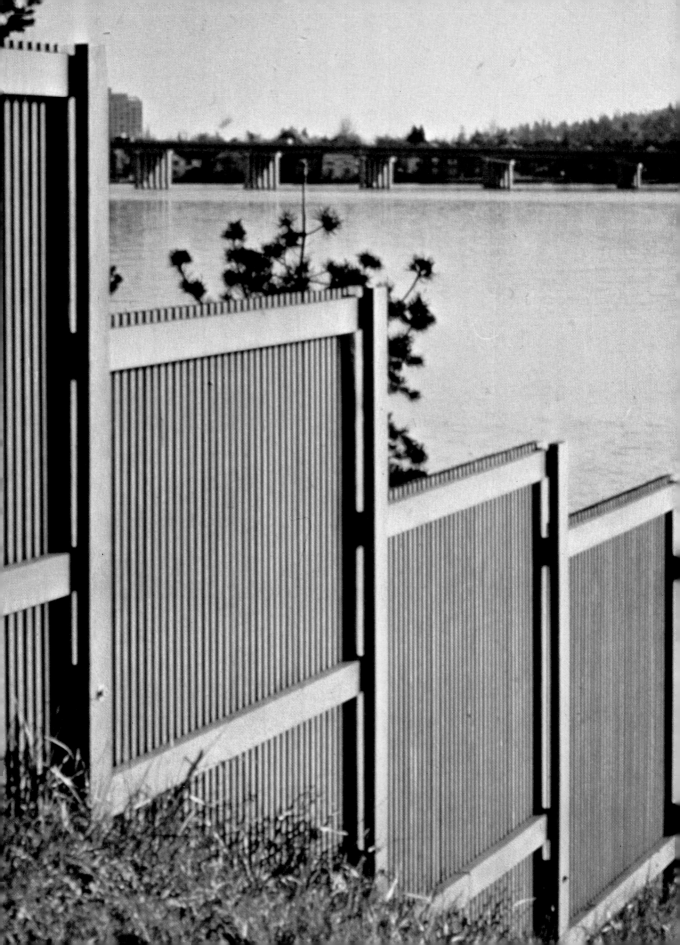

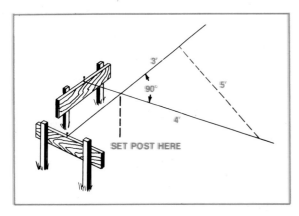

Use batter boards and strings to lay out an accurate fence line. Use Pythyagorean Theorem as shown to get accurate right angle.

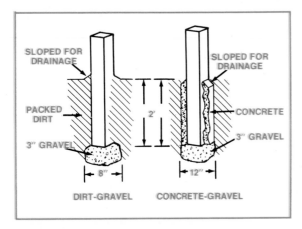

Two methods of solidly setting fence posts.

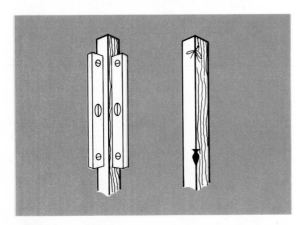

Make sure that the posts are plumb before and after setting.

Courtesy of Western Wood Products Association.

This fence answers many slope problems.

wires, tree roots or watersoaked clay below the surface. Such a site is rarely found. Usually a person must adapt a fence to local conditions such as hilly site, high winds, high noise level or objectionable view.

A hilly site presents problems in fence design. Rail fences and picket fences can adjust to ground contours with relative ease. Basket weave fences, panel fences, and similar designs made up of large, relatively inflexible units will

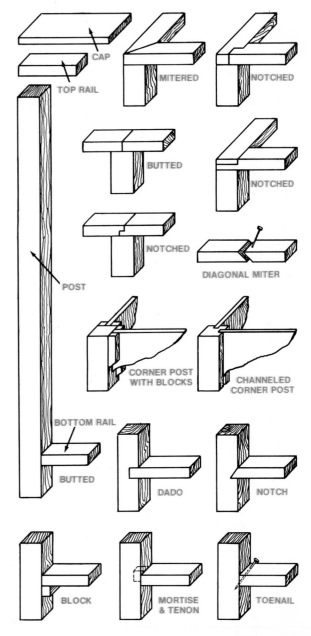

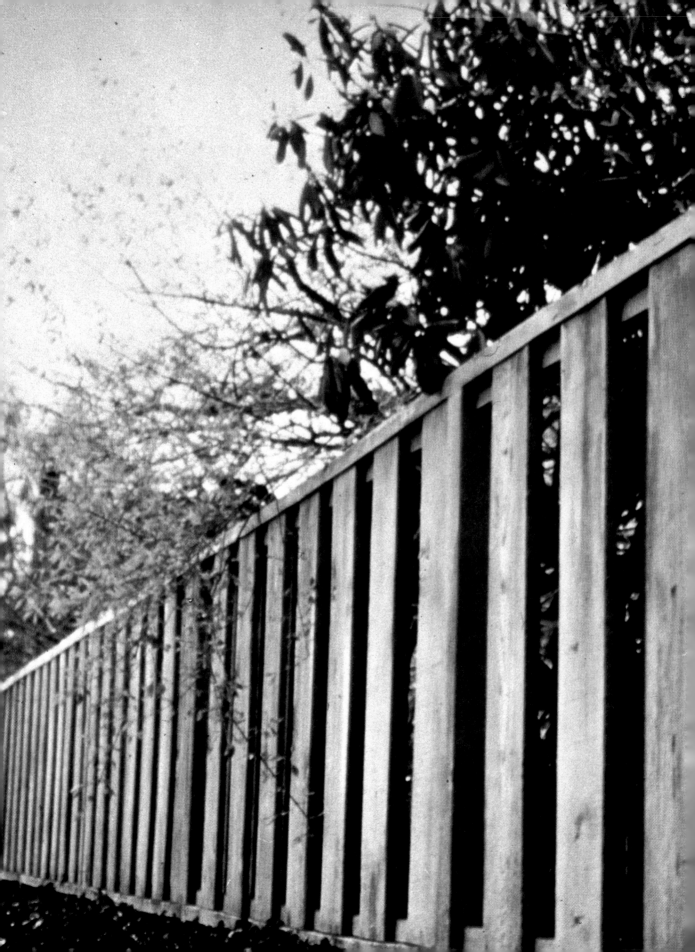

have to be stairstepped to adjust to ground contours. A design that cannot be adjusted or angled to allow for a sloping site is obviously eliminated for use on a hilly site.

A site subject to high winds poses two design problems. First, is the fence to serve as a wind break or a wind guide? Second, what additional strength must be added to the materials to withstand high winds?

If a fence is designed to serve as a windbreak, large solid panels extending to the ground are not the best solution. Wind blowing over such a barrier will create an eddy of air which could be uncomfortable or annoying. A 6″ space at the bottom of the fence would create an air flow that would disturb the complete development of the wind eddy. Useful designs for windbreaks include basket weave; solid plywood, fiberglass, plastic, or canvas panels and certain board-on-board designs.

If aiming, rather than stopping, wind flow is desired, a vertical or horizontal louvered fence is the answer. Some louver designs may also serve as windbreaks. Careful selection of louver angle can provide privacy as well as wind control.

The traditional framework of a wood fence is made up of corner and gate posts of 4″ x 4″ stock, line posts of 2″ x 4″ stock, doubled below ground, and cross rails of 2″ x 4″ stock. Line posts are cut about 2′ longer than the planned aboveground height of the fence (a 4′ fence needs 6′ posts). Corner and gate posts should be about one foot longer than the line posts, particularly if there is a high wind load. High winds also require larger stock sizes in fence framework.

Acoustic experts point out that complete noise suppression demands high and thick barriers. Few people want — or can afford — a reinforced concrete wall 10′ high and 3′ thick surrounding their property. However, a tall palisade fence of grape stakes or shaped 2″ x 4″ lumber, a tall

Courtesy of Western Wood Products Association

Board-and-board fences serve well as windbreaks, in addition to providing privacy.

board-on-board fence or a tall wood panel fence serving as backing for a tall, thick hedge will greatly lessen and deflect loud noises from a nearby source such as a busy street, a railroad line, etc.

An unpleasant view from a window or outdoor living area can be masked by fencing. The non-view may be completely masked by a palisade, basketweave, or panel fence, or it may be "camouflaged" by a more open fence, such as post and rail or picket, used as trelliswork for climbing shrubs or vines.

In selecting the materials to construct a fence, the homeowner will usually choose from four generally available materials: wood, plastic or fiberglass, metal or glass.

Wood is probably the most traditional fencing material. It can be used in a wide variety of fencing, from rustic post and rail to the most formal of plywood panels. Wood offers the home craftsman a wide range of possible materials: lath, dimensional lumber, rustic rails, dowels, plywood panels, railroad ties, pickets and combinations of these and other lumber forms.

Plastic and fiberglass panels can be used to make an attractive, colorful windbreak, privacy screen, or non-view screen. Framing for fiberglass fencing should fall with a 4′ x 4′ or 4′ x 8′ module, since fiberglass — like plywood and plastic — is frequently sold in 4′ x 8′ sheets. The fiberglass can either be fastened to lath or molding nailing strips attached to the fence framework, or be fitted in rabbets cut into the posts and rails of the fence. The variety of colors available in plastic or fiberglass make it possible to create colorful geometric designs in the fencing.

Metal fencing is most often used in two forms: expanded metal and woven wire. Barbed wire is not usually practical for suburban fencing. Expanded metal, which is usually found as sheets of grille material in hardware or home-improvement centers, can be used as a partial windbreak, as a view screen, or as a decorative accent panel set into other fencing. Woven wire fencing is possibly the most widely used and

least expensive utiliarian barrier fencing used in suburban and urban lots. Commonly known as *chain link, hurricane* or *cyclone* fencing, its utilitarian look can be easily masked with climbing shrubs or vines.

Clear or patterned glass can be used to make attractive windbreaks or screening fences. Clear glass is most useful in areas where a windbreak is needed that will not obstruct a view. Flowers and small trees planted behind panels of translucent glass will provide moving patterns of color

and shade. Whenever glass is used in fencing, it should be tempered or safety glass. Older construction using untempered glass should be protected with decals, simple railings, furniture arrangements, or plants to save the unwary from injury.

GATES

Gates must be provided when the home craftsman designs a fence. A wooden gate adaptable to most styles of fencing may be constructed and hung using the following procedures:

1. Establish opening size. Measure the top and bottom widths of the gate opening. If these measurements vary considerably, the gate posts may have to be aligned before the gate can be hung. Deduct one inch from the opening width to establish the gate frame size. This one inch will provide clearance for hinges to be attached and

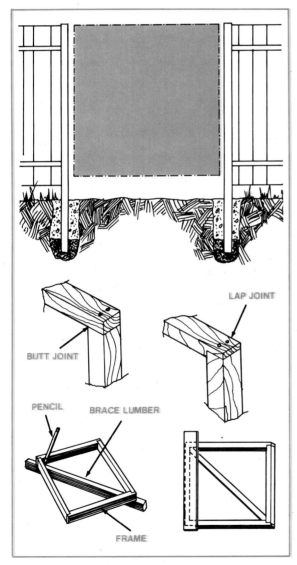

The basic steps in building a gate are shown: establishing size, building frame, bracing frame, sheathing frame.

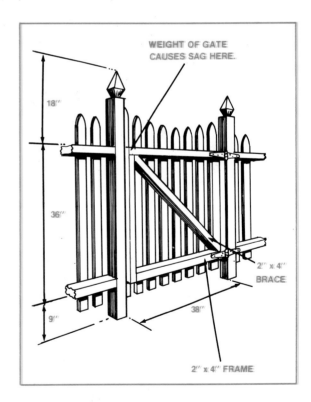

Many different styles of gate may be built on this frame.

Courtesy of Western Wood Products Association.

The louver fence allows for light, air and privacy.

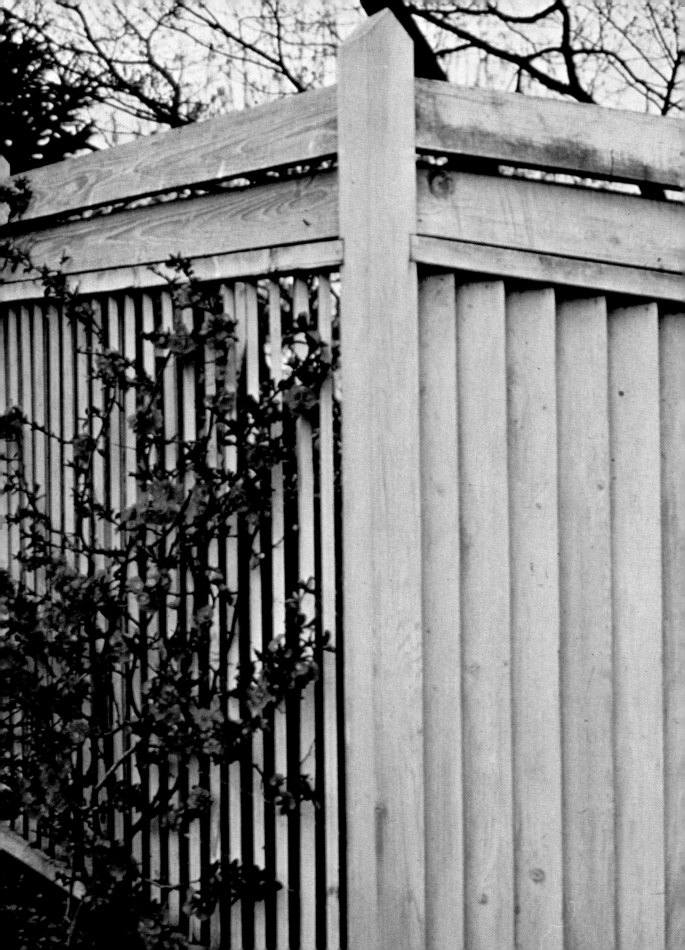

the gate to swing. A gate frame of extremely wide lumber may need additional clearance.

2. Construct the gate frame. Lay out and cut a square or rectangular frame on any convenient flat surface. Use butt, lap, or mortise joints to assemble the frame. Use a try-square to make sure the corners form right angles. Use galvanized or non-corroding fasteners for the gate.

3. Brace the gate. Place the frame diagonally on a 2″ x 4″ x 5′ or larger piece of lumber. Using the frame corners as guides, pencil in the cutting marks. For a tight-fitting brace, cut the brace outside the pencil marks, so the remarks will remain when the cutting is complete. Toenail the ends of the brace to the frame.

4. Attach fencing material. Fasten pickets, boards or panels to the gate frame, beginning at the hinge side. Board size or spacing may have to differ from the fence itself in order to get even spacing or a good appearance. If the completed gate would be too heavy to be easily manageable, the frame may be hung and then the fencing applied.

5. Fasten hinges to frame. To avoid splitting the framing, guide holes for nails and screws should be drilled. Use a drill that is slightly smaller than the fastener.

6. Check the fit. Hold or temporarily fasten the gate in the opening to check clearances. If the gate does not swing freely, trim the latch size of the gate until sufficient clearance is gained.

7. Hang the gate. Prop the gate in position with bricks, wooden blocks, etc. and attach the loose leaves of the hinges to the gate post.

8. Mount latch. Attach the chosen latch to the gate. Since the latch often takes a great deal of abuse, use long screws or throughbolts for a solid mounting.

FENCE PROJECTS

The following plans and information about picket, louver, post and rail, and screen fences are suggestive of the wide variety of designs

possible in fences. Once the basic frame for both fence and gate is constructed, virtually any material may be used as fencing material.

Picket Fences

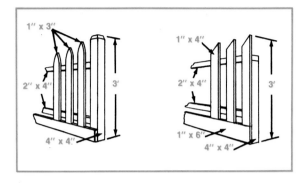

Angle-cut boards are simple do-it-yourself pickets.

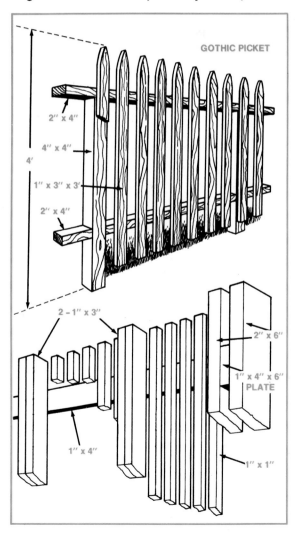

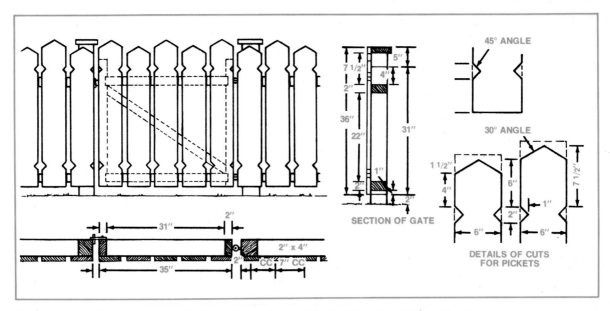

The wide picket fence is made with 1″ x 6″ boards on a 2″ x 4″ frame mounted on 4′ x 4″ posts. The pickets may be all the same height, or cut to 2 different lengths, as here. Use the first picket cut to each size to mark the remaining pickets.

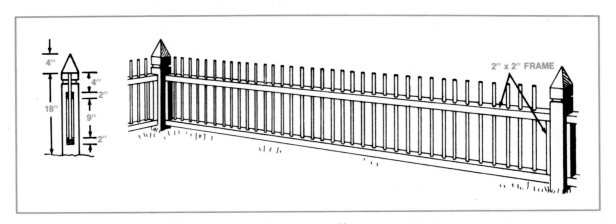

This low courtyard fence uses ³/₄″ dowels for pickets.

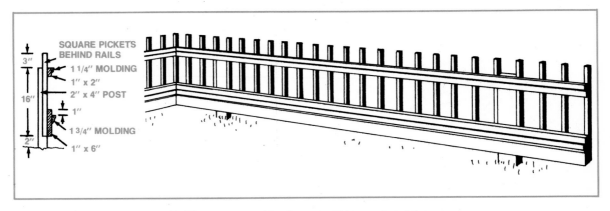

Moldings are used to dress up this courtyard fence.

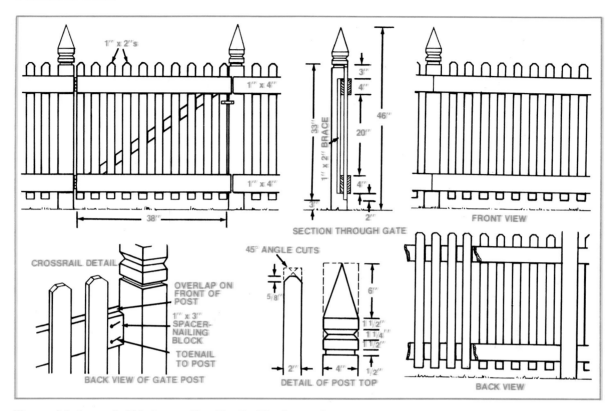

These pickets are held between 1" x 4" rails. The front rails are continous, overlapping and meeting on the front of the posts. The rear rails are butted to the sides of the post, and toenailed.

Louver Fences

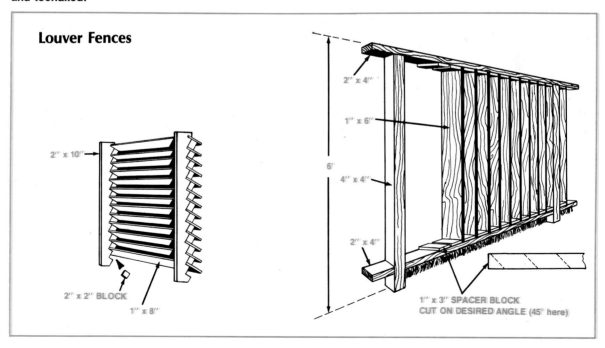

Louver fences can be both vertical and horizontal. Blocks are screwed between the horizontal louvers for support.

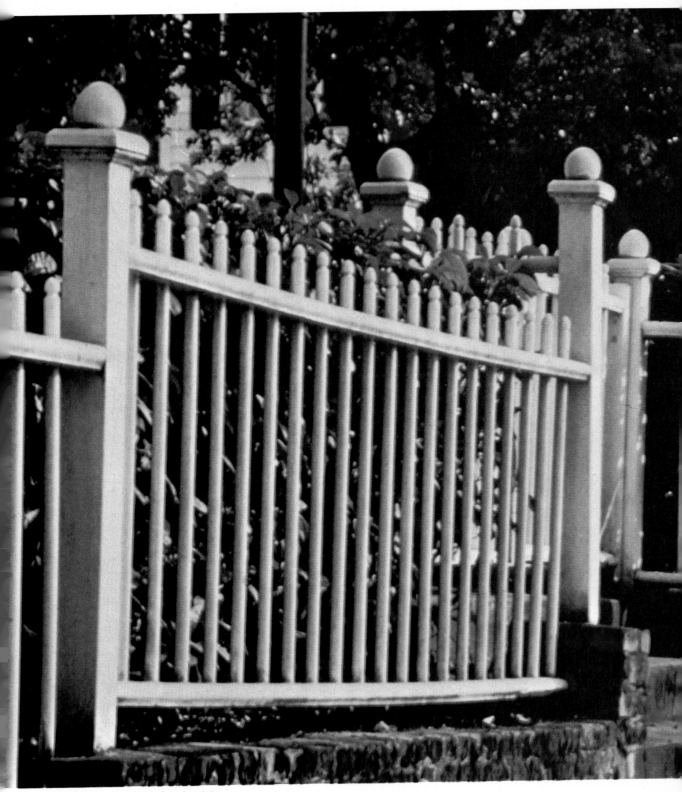

Courtesy of Western Wood Products Association

Picket fencing, combined with shrubbery, provides a decorative yet effective barrier.

Post & Rail Fences

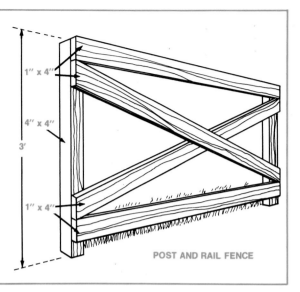

POST AND RAIL FENCE

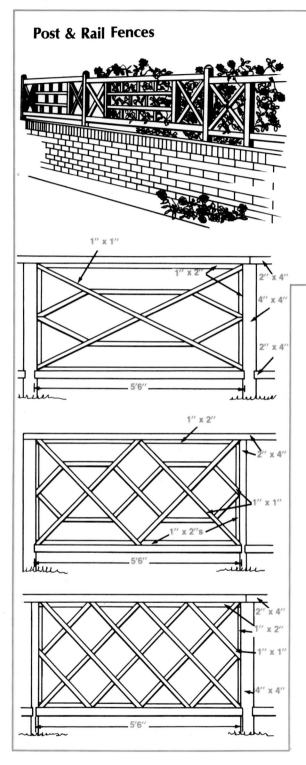

Screen Fences

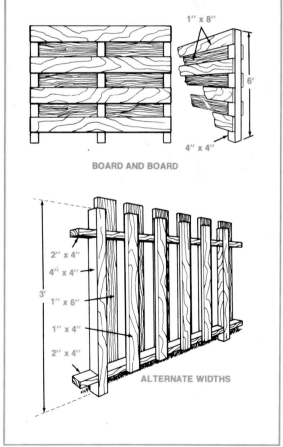

BOARD AND BOARD

ALTERNATE WIDTHS

Post and rail fences can vary from the very informal to the most formal. Thomas Jefferson's designs for the University of Virginia were the sources for three of these fences.

Courtesy of Western Wood Products:

Wooden railroad ties form an effective and rustic fence for this wooded area.

568

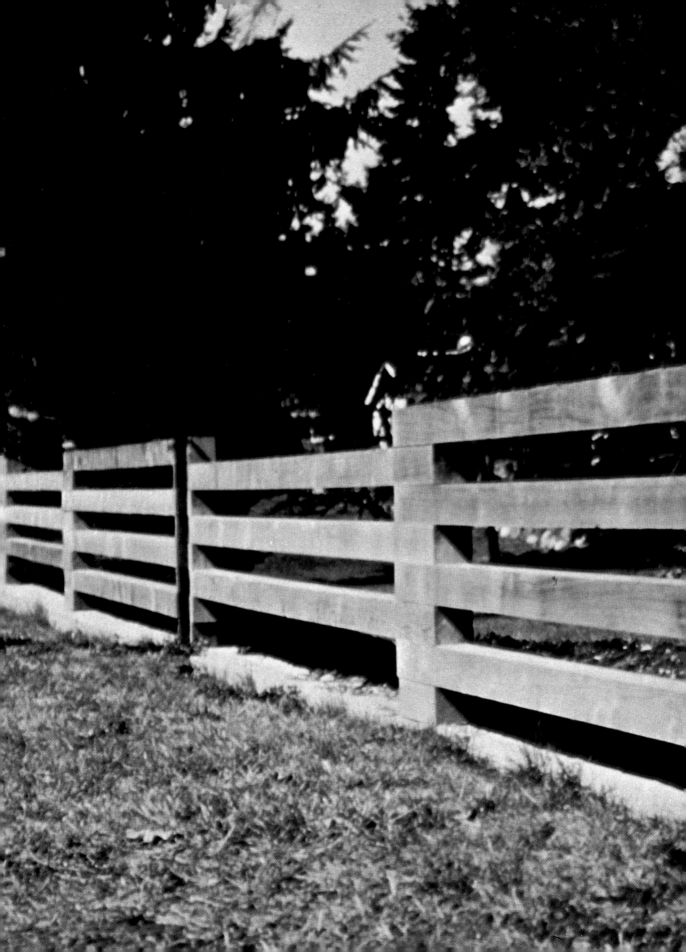

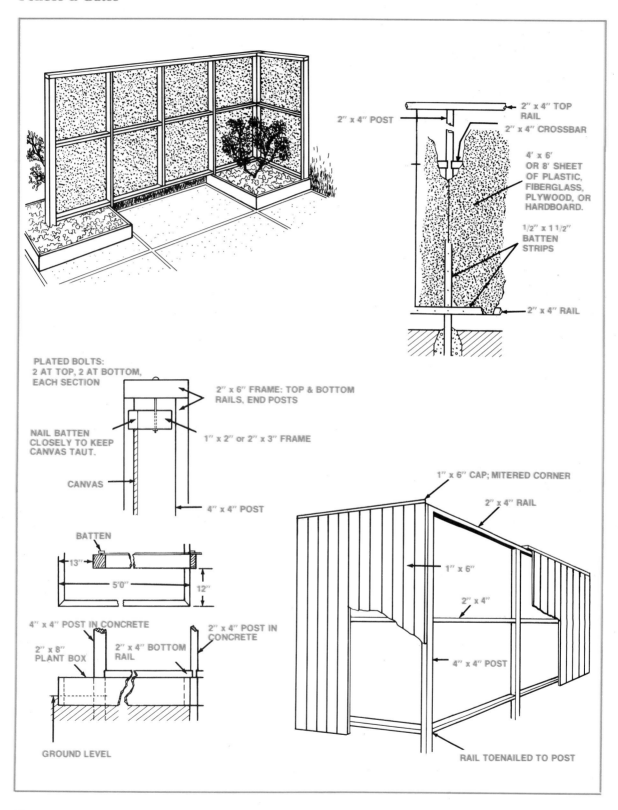

2" x 4" POST

2" x 4" TOP RAIL

2" x 4" CROSSBAR

4' x 6' OR 8' SHEET OF PLASTIC, FIBERGLASS, PLYWOOD, OR HARDBOARD.

1/2" x 1 1/2" BATTEN STRIPS

2" x 4" RAIL

PLATED BOLTS: 2 AT TOP, 2 AT BOTTOM, EACH SECTION

2" x 6" FRAME: TOP & BOTTOM RAILS, END POSTS

NAIL BATTEN CLOSELY TO KEEP CANVAS TAUT.

1" x 2" or 2" x 3" FRAME

CANVAS

4" x 4" POST

1" x 6" CAP; MITERED CORNER

2" x 4" RAIL

BATTEN

13"

5'0"

12"

1" x 6"

2" x 4"

4" x 4" POST IN CONCRETE

2" x 4" POST IN CONCRETE

2" x 8" PLANT BOX

2" x 4" BOTTOM RAIL

4" x 4" POST

GROUND LEVEL

RAIL TOENAILED TO POST

The central crossbar in the plywood fence is replaced by the canvas stretcher frame.

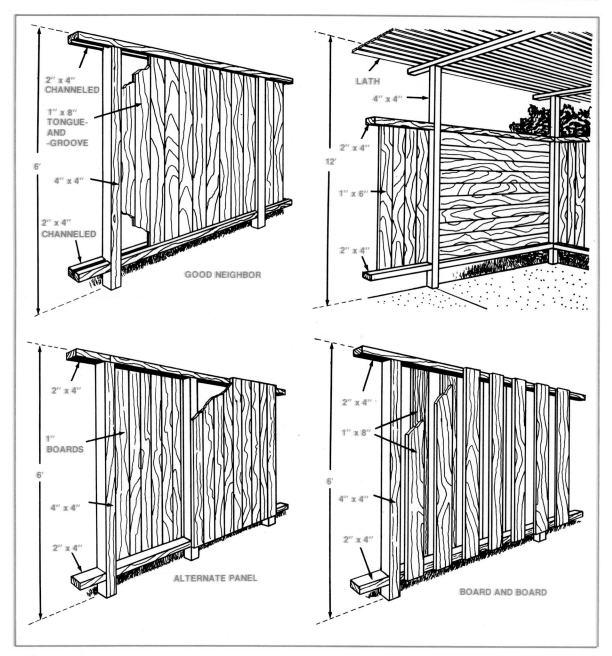

2" x 4" CHANNELED

1" x 8" TONGUE-AND-GROOVE

6'

4" x 4"

2" x 4" CHANNELED

GOOD NEIGHBOR

LATH

4" x 4"

2" x 4"

12'

1" x 6"

2" x 4"

2" x 4"

1" BOARDS

6'

4" x 4"

2" x 4"

ALTERNATE PANEL

2" x 4"

1" x 8"

6'

4" x 4"

2" x 4"

BOARD AND BOARD

Screened fences may be made of boards, canvas, or plastic. Garden shelters may be formed by extending the support posts of a screen fence. Examples of different screen fences are shown.

Ferroconcrete

Ferroconcrete is concrete that is reinforced with steel rod. The rod gives tensile strength to the concrete, preventing it from pulling apart under the stress of added loads or its own weight. For example, a concrete structure with both ends supported or attached tends to pull apart on the underside of the slab, so the rod reinforcement should be placed near the bottom of the slab. A beam or slab with middle support may tend to be

weakest along the upper surface, so the steel rod is placed near the top of the slab. A cantilever, which is an outward-projecting structure supported at one end only, such as a raised hearth, will also tend to break downward, calling for upper support. A concrete driveway or sidewalk has both end and middle support, so the steel rod is logically placed toward the middle of the slab. *SEE ALSO CONCRETE.*

Ferrule

A ferrule is a wide metal band on the end of the wooden handle of many tools, used for reinforcing the tool blade in the handle, and also to prevent the handle from splitting. A ferrule is also used to hold the bristles of a paint brush in the handle of the brush. Also, ferrules are the metal rings placed over the ends of furniture legs, for floor protection and to minimize wear on the legs.

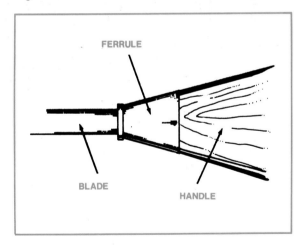

Fertilizers
[SEE LAWNS & GARDENS.]

Fiber Core Door

A fiber core door is a type of flush door which has various composition materials as its core.

The basic frame consists of softwood with face panels, called skins, usually made of plywood.

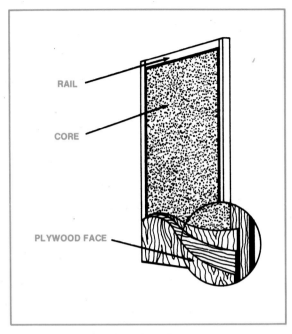

Fiber Core Door

Fiberglass & Acrylic Plastic Sheets
[SEE PLASTIC SHEET MATERIALS.]

Fiberglass

Fiberglass, which could be called today's miracle material, is glass in fibrous form and can be made into various products including insulation, yarn and compressed sheets. Fiberglass has many properties that make it a nearly perfect building material. First, it transmits light, while being translucent enough to provide both privacy and light when used as partitions or walls. Second, fiberglass is weather resistant, being almost unaffected by snow, strong wind, rapid changes in temperature and rain. Third, fiberglass needs little maintenance, as its smooth surface can be washed clean with household detergent and water. It is virtually shatter-proof.

Unless severely abused, it will not break, chip or peel. And finally, it is relatively inexpensive. All of these qualities make fiberglass a valuable material for the homeowner.

Parts of experimental as well as commercial automobiles are made of fiberglass. Because the material can take any form, entire body shells can be formed with great strength and durability as well as design.

FENCES & AWNINGS

The most common application of fiberglass is in the construction of fences and awnings, such as those found above and around patios and pools. The general rules to follow while working with fiberglass are the same as those working with most other building materials. Always drill nail holes before attempting to fasten fiberglass to support rails and stay within $3/8$ of an inch from the edge. Use neoprene washers when attaching panels to framing and remember that screws and other fasteners can be used instead of nails. Always caulk joints to avoid water leakage.

One of the most economical features of fiberglass panels is that they come in sheets up to 46 x 56 x $1/2$ inch thicknesses. Fiberglass can be cut by using any fine-toothed saw. If the thickness permits, even a sharp linoleum knife

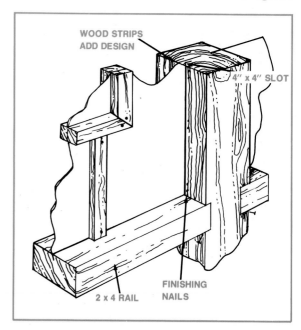

Detail of Fence Using Straight Fiberglass Panel

or scissors may be used to cut it. When determining dimensions, cut all sides $3/8$ of an inch smaller to allow for expansion.

Fences

Any fiberglass fence should be set in concrete for best results. The depth of the base will be determined by the conditions of the surrounding area. For example, a deeper base is necessary in areas with hard frosts and high winds. Four by four posts should be placed 8 feet apart, allowing less space if wind is a constant factor. A 2 x 4 bottom rail should be placed at least six inches above the ground. Corrugated panels are then toenailed to the post and rails. Cut a $1/8''$ x $1/2''$ slot to anchor the straight side of the panel and use finishing nails to fasten it in the final steps.

Another popular fence that adapts itself easily to fiberglass is the basket-weave fence. Twelve inch strips cut from straight panels are used for the weaving, and the effect can be heightened by using two or more colors. Fiberglass is easy to bend and can be woven between one inch wooden dowels spaced at one foot intervals. Use a flat head screw to fasten each strip to the dowel and complete the project with a strip of quarter round molding.

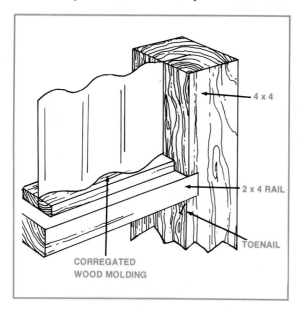

Detail of Fence with Corrugated Fiberglass Panel

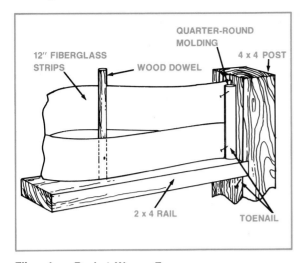

Fiberglass Basket-Weave Fence

Awnings

Fiberglass is also used for porch, carport, pool and patio coverings. The translucent panels provide a roof without blocking sunlight. Fiberglass, chosen in the lighter shades, helps to deflect sunrays, and coupled with the correct ventilation, produces cool protection against summer heat.

The procedure for installing a fiberglass awning is much the same when used to cover a carport or a pool. Design will differ according to individual tastes, but a general framework can be adopted for specific applications. The first con-

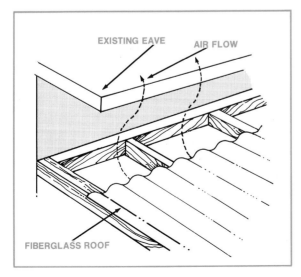

Proper Ventilation Using Original Eave

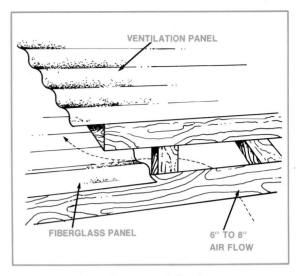

Ventilation Using Constructed Overhang

sideration is ventilation, because without it there is no control of condensation or coolness. There are two basic ways to ventilate a roof awning. If the eaves of a house protrude at least eight inches, the fiberglass roof may be built below it with an eight inch space left open next to the building. The overhang must be built before the covering is constructed beneath it.

The first step in the construction of the frame for an awning is the installation of the support posts, which are usually made of ornamental metal or 4 x 4 wooden posts. These can be secured to a concrete base by means of a concrete footing or by 8 inch angle irons.

The front headers are applied next. Either 4 x 4s or 4 x 6s are used for these, depending on the span of the covering. The header should be placed at least $7\frac{1}{2}$ feet high for proper ventilation once the covering is added. The rear header is installed to every stud of the adjacent wall structure with lag screws. Expansion bolts are used in attaching the back header to a brick structure.

The next step is the installation of the rafters, which should be notched to fit over the front and back headers. Rafters can be spaced by using precut braces. The panels are then nailed to rafters with weatherproof aluminum nails and

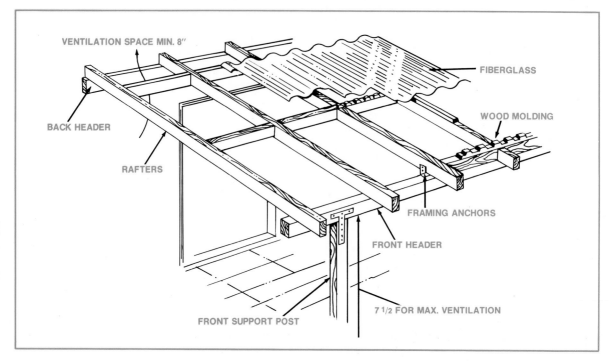

Basic Parts of a Roof Awning

neoprene washers. To avoid leaks later, nail only at the top of ridges and apply sealers over the nail heads.

Remember that these are only general directions. It is possible to obtain directions for many detailed projects from almost any dealer who sells fiberglass panels.

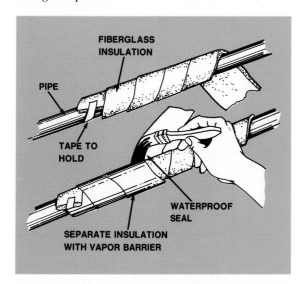

Fiberglass Insulation for Water Pipe

INSULATION

Fiberglass can be made into insulation blankets that fit within the studs of the house frame. It comes in widths to fit between studs spaced 12, 16, or 24 inches apart. These blankets have tough flanges that bend around and are stapled to the stud. Rigid board fiberglass insulation fits around and inside walls in crawl spaces.

Fiberglass sleeves or fiberglass insulation tape can be wrapped around pipes to prevent water condensation on cold pipes in hot, humid weather.

FIBERGLASS SCREENING

Fiberglass screening has become popular in the last few years. If it is used as screen for doors or windows, repairs of small tears and holes are easy to make. Cut a piece of screening to fit the tear and then cement it in place with clear epoxy glue.

Another use of fiberglass is in the repair of such things as rusted places in cars and leaks in boats. A kit may be purchased with all the items

necessary to make the repair. However, if a kit cannot be found the basic materials can easily be assembled. First, sand all of the rust from the edges of the hole and cut a piece of fiberglass large enough to cover it. Use the epoxy to secure it. Once the fiberglass has set, apply enough epoxy to fill in the entire hole. Wait 30 minutes for the epoxy to dry, and then sand the whole area. Give the patch several days to cure before attempting to refinish or paint.

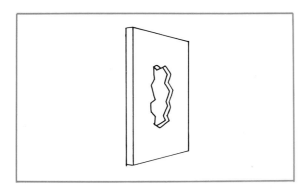

Sand the area around existing hole to bare metal.

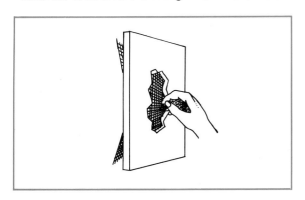

Attach screen with epoxy. Allow for 1/2″ overlap.

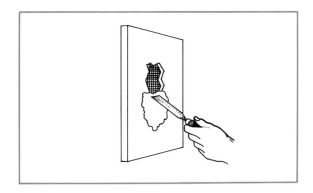

Put epoxy over screen.

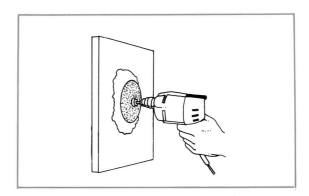

Sand epoxy smooth when dry.

HOW TO FIBERGLASS A WOODEN BOAT

Although adding a fiberglass coating on a wooden boat does not make it last as long as a fiberglass boat, it does add strength in case of impact. Be sure to follow the resin manufacturer's instructions carefully before fiberglassing a wooden boat.

All dirt, paint and other coatings must be completely removed before applying the fiberglass. Use a scraper, sander or chemical stripper to remove the materials rather than a blow torch to keep melted paint from penetrating the pores. Fill all cracks in the wood with ground fiberglass and resin or a resin and talcum powder mixture. Sand the surface until smooth.

Cut the fiberglass cloth with scissors so that it will fit the hull. Roll the cloth around a cylindrical object, such as a broom handle, to facilitate application to the boat hull. Mix the resin catalyst according to the manufacturer's directions and quickly paint on a coat of resin, using a brush or roller. If the wood appears dull, add more resin to the surface. Roll the cloth from the broom handle onto the hull a section at a time, immediately after the resin is applied. Smooth out any wrinkles with your hands, which may be cleaned later with a special cleaner. Do one area at a time, overlapping each section at least two to six inches. Apply a top coat of colored resin to the entire boat. Wait overnight and then trim off the rough edges, sand and add another coat of resin. Add a coat of wax to the boat after the final coat of resin is dry.

MAINTAINING FIBERGLASS

Fiberglass maintenance involves washing it down periodically with mild household detergents and water. If the surface is neglected and looks dull and lifeless, it should be washed completely and coated with a high-gloss fiberglass refinisher. Steel wool can be used to knock off rough surfaces before applying the resealant. *SEE ALSO PLASTIC SHEET MATERIALS; RECREATIONAL BOATS & BOATING.*

Fiber Pipe

Fiber pipe, available in various lengths, is commonly found in sections of eight and ten feet. Because better grades of fiber pipe are made with a coal-tar formula, this type of pipe is higher priced than the majority of its counterparts.

There are two types of fiber pipe. The first is a continuous pipe that conveys drainage material to disposal systems. The second type is a series of fiber pipes placed with space between them to permit the liquid flowing through to seep into the soil. This type usually is perforated with small, evenly spaced holes forming straight rolls.

The ends of fiber pipe are tapered to match the internal taper of couplings and fittings. To make a joint, push the coupling or fitting on the end of the pipe with some force. Place a block of wood over the fitting and hammer. Because of elements in the coal-tar, the friction created will fuse the fitting and the pipe.

When cutting a fiber pipe, a coarse-tooth saw, similar to a large frameless hacksaw, should be used to cut the pipe squarely. Since cutting fiber pipe removes the tapered end, some couplings are made to resplice it while others have an outer sleeve with metal bands to clip the joint to the cut ends.

Elbows, couplings and special couplings are fiber pipe fittings, as well as Y-branches and crosses. *SEE ALSO PLUMBING MATERIALS.*

Fiber Pipe Fittings

Fiber pipe fittings are usually secured to the pipe by forcing the pipe into the fitting. The friction created will fuse the coal-tar elements in the pipe to the fitting. The most common fiber pipe fittings are the Y-branch, tee, cross, bend, cast-iron adapter, joining sleeve, coupling and snap coupling.

The joining sleeve, coupling and snap coupling join pipes to form straight runs. A joining sleeve

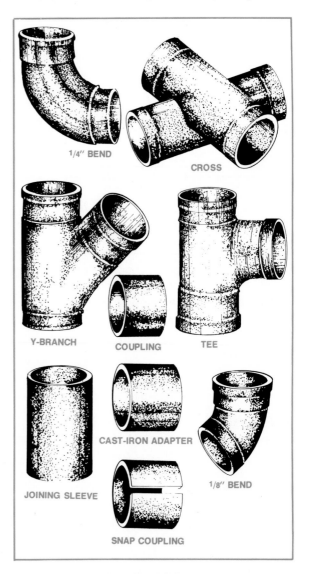

1/4" BEND

CROSS

Y-BRANCH

COUPLING

TEE

CAST-IRON ADAPTER

1/8" BEND

JOINING SLEEVE

SNAP COUPLING

Fiber Pipe Fittings

is longer to accommodate the tapered ends of the fiber pipe. A coupling or snap coupling is used to connect tapered or cut fiber pipe. The snap coupling has the distinct feature of being able to *snap* over the pipes.

The cast-iron pipe adapter joins a straight run pipe consisting of fiber pipe on one end of the fitting and cast-iron pipe on the other end.

A cross joins four pipes meeting at right angles. A tee joins a straight run pipe with a branch entering at a 90 degree angle. The Y-branch also joins a straight run with a branch angling into the joint.

A bend combines pipes to form turns or curves. Available in different sizes, the bend gently changes the direction of flow without seriously reducing the rate of flow. Bends are commonly found in the $1/4''$ and $1/8''$ sizes. *SEE ALSO PIPE FITTINGS.*

Fiber Saturation Point

Fiber saturation point refers to the stage at which the cell walls of wood are saturated but the cell caviities are free of water. The fiber saturation point is calculated by the oven dry weight and the degree below which shrinkage occurs. Saturation point is considered to be thirty percent moisture content.

Figuring Board Footage

A board foot is equal to the amount of lumber in a board 1 inch thick, 12 inches wide and 12 inches long. In other words, a board foot is equal to a square foot of lumber one inch thick. To figure board footage, multiply thickness in inches times width in inches times length in feet and then divide the result by twelve to get the number of board feet. Use the nominal thickness and width.

For example, a 2'' x 6'' x 12' piece of lumber will contain 12 board feet, while a 1'' x 6'' x 12' piece would contain only 6 board feet. *SEE ALSO LUMBER.*

File Card

The file card is a rectangular-shaped tool used in cleaning files. It has a wooden base with wire bristles that, when run across the file, remove excess wood or metal chips. *SEE ALSO HAND TOOLS.*

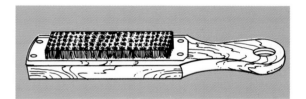

File Card

Files & Rasps

Shaping and smoothing wood or metal are achieved with files and rasps. Generally, files are for metal and rasps for wood, but some are dual purpose. The mill, half-round and crosscut files are the most common. *SEE ALSO HAND TOOLS.*

Fillister

A fillister is an adjustable rabbet plane. This tool makes a cut as wide as its base and descends into the groove as it cuts. Each stroke deepens the cut until a desired depth is reached. A fillister is excellent for cutting a recess groove along the surface edge of a board. Because of a sharp spur attachment, a fillister can be used for across-grain planing without tearing wood fibers. *SEE ALSO HAND TOOLS.*

Finger-Lap Joint

A finger-lap joint is commonly used for joining drawer backs and in other light furniture construction. The joint is made by cutting pre-measured fingers in the ends of two pieces of lumber so that they form a joint when the fingers lap together. Finger-lap joints can be glued together or joined with a dowel when holes are drilled through each of the fingers. If a dowel is used, the holes should not be greater in diameter than half the thickness of the stock. *SEE ALSO FURNITURE MAKING.*

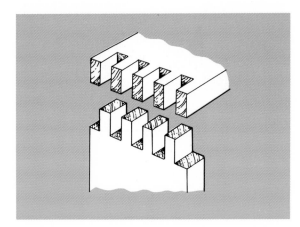

Finger-Lap Joint

Finial

A finial is an ornamental piece at the top of an arch or upright, such as a spire or lamp. It is usually the foliated section often seen in Gothic architecture.

Finish Flooring

Finish flooring is a term referring to materials used as the final floor surface. Among these are hard and soft woods, tile, linoleum, slate, brick ,

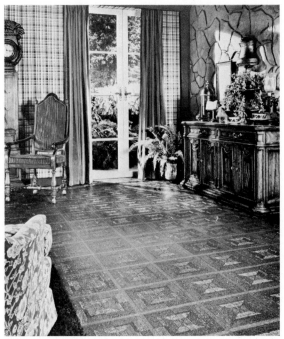

Courtesy Azrock Floor Products

A Mediterranian decorating motif is carried out in the parquet design of the floor tile.

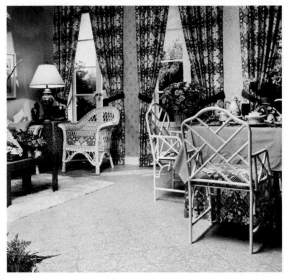

Courtesy Azrock Floor Products

Wicker, bamboo-turned furniture, ferns and a vinyl asbestos floor combine to create a cool, inviting area for entertaining.

flagstone and ceramic tile. The latter four are generally chosen for specific areas such as bathrooms, foyers and dens, while the others may be used in any area of the home.

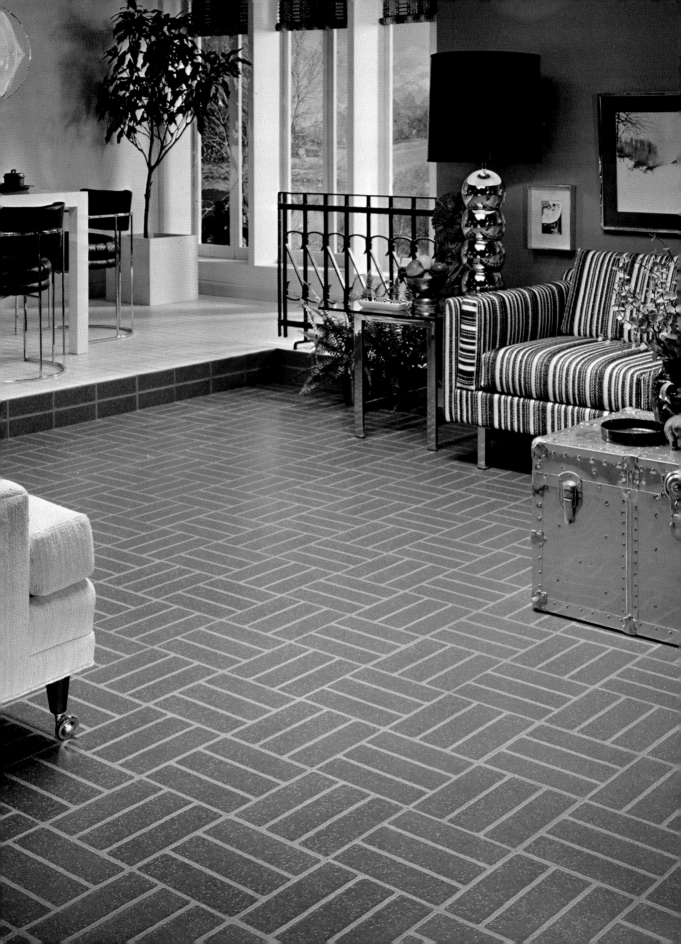

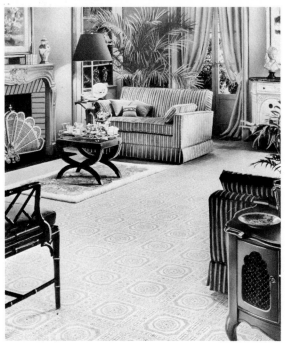

Courtesy Azrock Floor Products

Eighteenth century formality is expressed not only in the furniture and accessories, but also in the balanced pattern of the flooring.

RESILIENT FLOORING

Tiles and sheets of linoleum, asphalt, vinyl, vinyl-asbestos and cork are the most common forms of resilient flooring. Asphalt tile is moderately popular because it is inexpensive. However, vinyl-asbestos tile costs only a little more and offers more colors, requires little maintenance and resists grease. Vinyl is the most popular material used for flooring. A wide range of colors, textures and patterns make vinyl an extremely versatile material to use in any room. Textured vinyl conceals dirt better than flat surfaces so little maintenance is required. Cork tile is the only natural resilient flooring. Its rich color and soft texture add beauty to any room and, when a vinyl coat is spread over cork tile, it is easily cared for.

It is particularly important before installing a

Courtesy Azrock Floor Products

◀ **A brick pattern in an easy-care floor covering brightens this room.**

resilient floor to correct any problems in the subflooring. Any rough or uneven areas should be planed and smoothed to prevent irregularities in the appearance of the flooring. Because adhesives are used in laying resilient floors, the old floor must furnish an adequate bonding surface. This may be done by covering the floor with plywood or hardwood boards. Fill all gaps with filler and renail any loose boards. Remove all paint or oil by scraping, sanding or scrubbing.

If the tile is to be laid on a concrete floor, clean, dust, moisten and fill any cracks with filler. To avoid total resurfacing of badly worn concrete floors, a thin layer of latex underlayment may be first troweled over the entire floor surface. As with wood floors, oil and paint must be removed before the flooring is laid. Before installing any type of resilient flooring, read the directions thoroughly and follow each step carefully.

WOOD FLOORING

The three main types of wood flooring in houses are plank, strip and block. Plank flooring provides a casual atmosphere because the boards used are of different widths, making no definite pattern. Strip flooring is pieces of narrow boards cut to the same width and laid at random across the floor. Block, or parquet, flooring is made by placing small, thin wood blocks with their grain at right angles to the surrounding ones. The hardwood chosen most often for flooring is oak, although hard maple, walnut, chestnut, beech and birch may be used successfully. Soft woods like southern pine, Douglas fir, redwood and western red cedar all dent, chip and break more readily than hardwoods and are not recommended for flooring.

To lay a strip or plank floor in a new home, secure building paper over the subflooring, place the strips at a right angle to the flooring joists and nail them to the subflooring. A chalk line should be used to check for even alignment before laying the boards. If the strip or plank floor is being laid over concrete slabs, screeds must be used as risers so that the strips can be nailed to a wood surface.

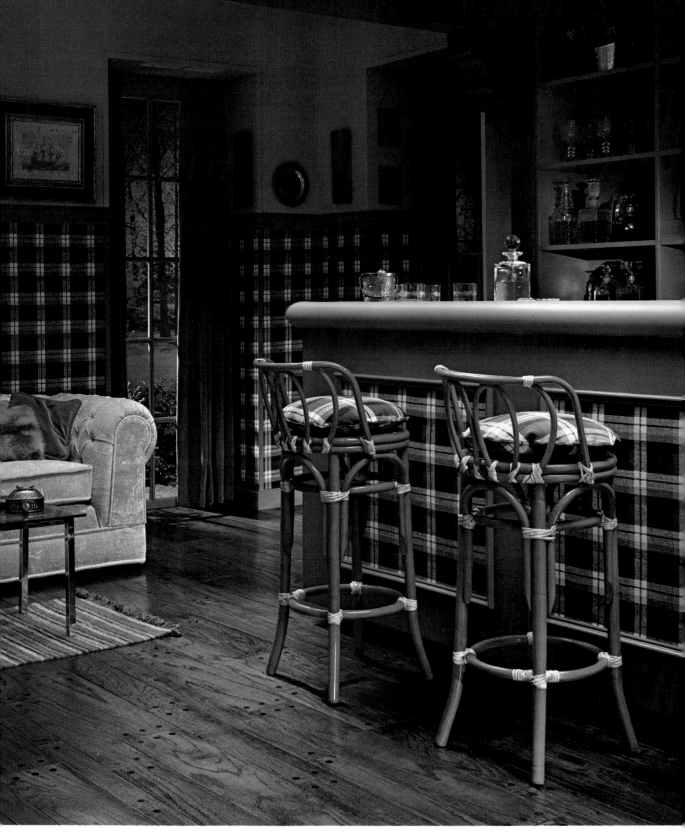

Pegged oak planks add to the informal, natural at-mosphere of an entertainment area.

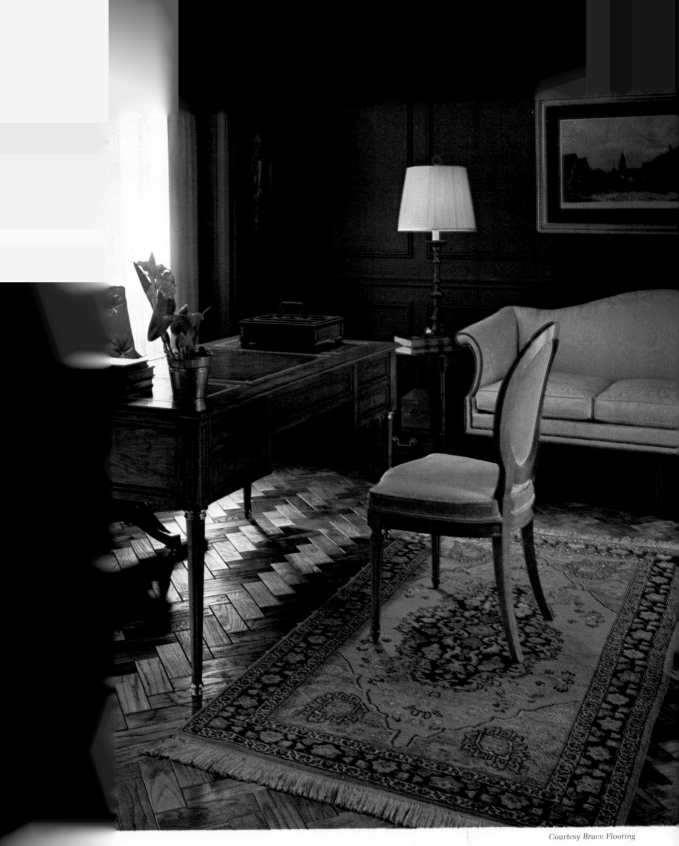

Courtesy Bruce Flooring

...ring in a traditional herringbone pattern blends with eighteenth century ...signs.

583

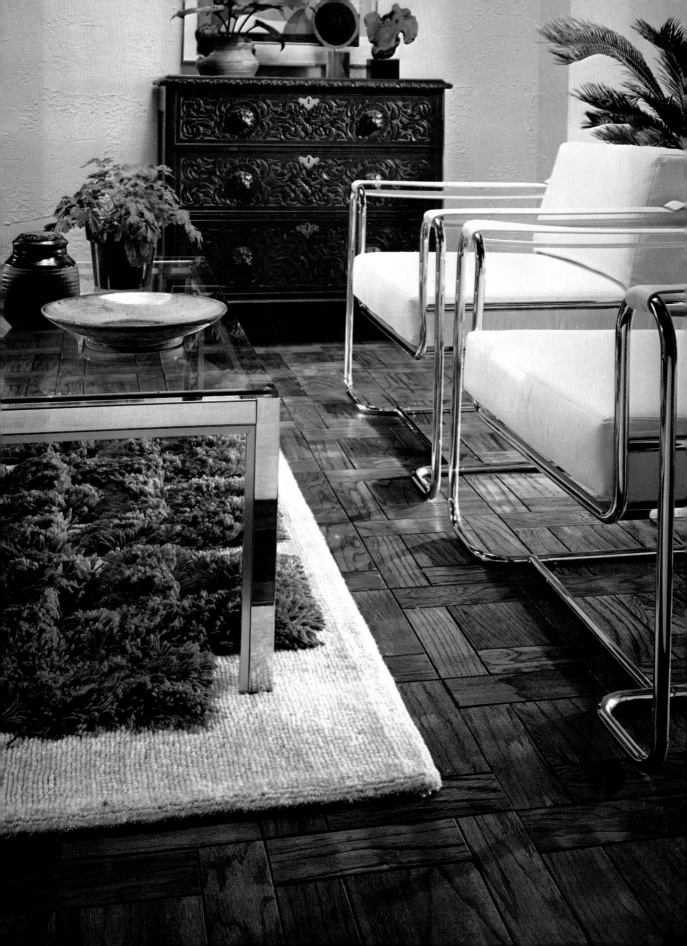

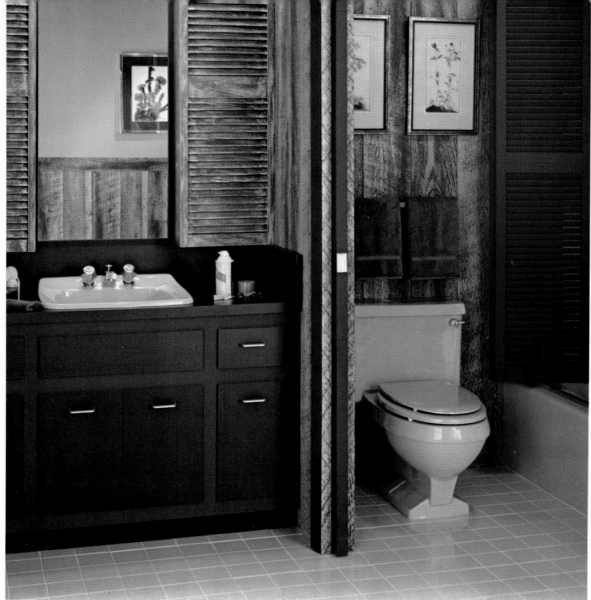

Courtesy of Eljer

Block floors are easily installed by nailing the blocks to the subflooring or by gluing them in place with a special mastic. As with strip and plank flooring, use a chalkline to insure accurate placement.

CERAMIC, BRICK & STONE FLOORING

Ceramic tile is more commonly used on bathroom and laundry room floors and kitchen

Courtesy Bruce Flooring

The crisp lines of modern furniture are blended with the ornate chest by the pattern of the wood flooring.

walls. These unglazed squares are available in a variety of colors that can be mixed and matched to accent the decor of the room. Ceramic tile is placed in mastic which secures it to the subflooring.

Brick, slate and flagstone finish flooring are more commonly used outside the home for constructing patios, porches and terraces. However, these materials can add an impressive look to foyers, sun rooms dens and even kitchens. The room area determines the method of installation and this should generally be left to a professional. *SEE ALSO FLOOR CONSTRUCTION.*

585

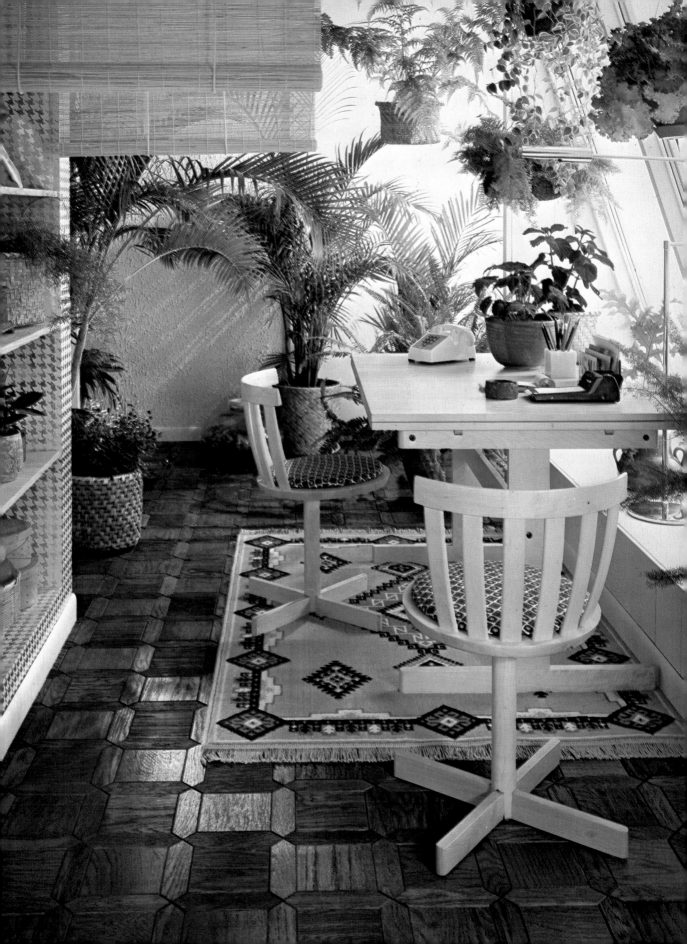

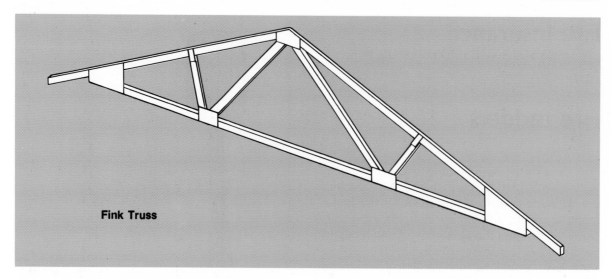

Fink Truss

Fink Truss

A fink or "W" truss is the most commonly used type of roof truss, which is the web-like wood or metal roof frame that supplies rigidity to the entire roof structure. The straight members of the truss are joined to form triangular units. Trusses also provide for open floor spans and serve as an economical means of support over wide floor spans, such as garages or hangars, eliminating the need for interior wall or post support. The truss is preassembled on the ground and then placed in the correct position in the structure. *SEE ALSO ROOF CONSTRUCTION.*

Fir

Fir is a softwood which is divided into two species: Douglas and White.

Douglas fir, one of the strongest of the softwoods, is a straight-grained wood with a white sapwood ring and orange-red heartwood. There is a marked difference in spring and summer

Courtesy Bruce Flooring

An informal home office plays modern furniture and natural greenery against a mitered pattern of dark oak flooring.

growth. It works well with hand tools, but machine sands poorly. Douglas fir is primarily used for trim, framing, doors and veneers.

White fir is a fine textured, fairly uniform sized cell wood. It has a very narrow summerwood band. Springwood is white while summerwood has a very slight reddish-brown tint, and there is little difference between heartwood and sapwood.

There is only a minimum danger of splitting white fir because of its softness. It is easy to work with and shapes well. It adapts well to paint, enamel or even stain and natural finishes. White fir can be used for furniture, plywood or general millwork. *SEE ALSO WOOD IDENTIFICATION.*

Firebrick

Firebrick is made of a form of fire clay which is capable of withstanding high temperatures. This brick will not crack when used to line the inside of fireplaces, furnaces, barbecues and other places of intense heat. Firebrick is normally larger than a standard brick and frequently is hand-molded. When older fireplaces which are built with regular bricks begin deteriorating, they should be replaced with firebrick.

Fire Insurance
[SEE INSURANCE PROTECTION.]

Fire Ladders

Fire ladders provide a safe escape route in houses with two or more stories. Fire ladders can be purchased or easily made in the home workshop. Before building or buying a fire ladder, keep in mind the ages of everyone living in the home, as a ladder with rungs rather than hand grips would be more practical for young children and older adults. For additional safety, a ladder should be installed in every upper-level bedroom, even in those which are not used very often, like guest rooms.

SINGLE-ROPE LADDER

The single-rope fire ladder is a piece of rope with wooden grips tied at intervals along it. One end of the rope is tied in a double half-hitch and drawn tightly around a lag screw that is fastened into the window trim. The plywood hand grips are usually triangular-shaped with rounded corners. A slot approximately one inch wide and four inches long is cut close to the bottom of the grip with a knot hole drilled directly above it. The grips are held in place by a knot tied on either side of this hole, and are generally spaced 15 inches apart.

To protect the ladder while it is not in use, an inverted can may be secured on the exterior window casing with a lag screw driven through a T-shaped hole in one side of the can and into the casing. A steel pin driven through one side of the lid and the opposite side of the can holds the ladder in the can. When the pin is pulled, the ladder falls to its full length.

An alternate method may be used for holding the ladder inside the house. Select a 1½-inch pipe that extends on either side of the window. Drill a hole that matches the diameter of the pipe into a pair of 2 x 4 wood blocks. Slide the blocks on each end of the pipe and place them just inside

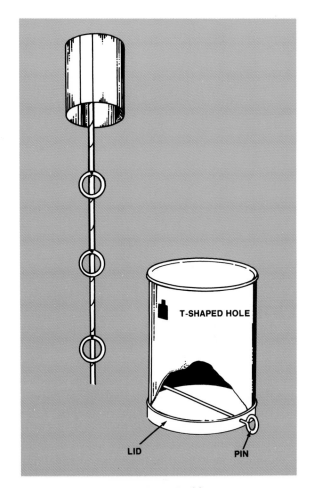

Single-Rope Ladder

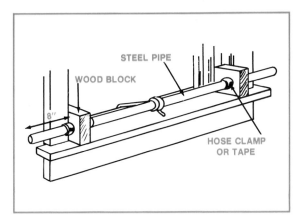

Alternate Method of Securing Single-Rope Ladder

the trim pieces of the window. They can then be held in position with either hose clamps or tape. Secure the ladder by tying a double half-hitch around the center of the pipe.

DOUBLE-ROPE & DOUBLE-CHAIN LADDERS

Double-rope and double-chain ladders equipped with rungs are more common and much safer than single-rope ladders. Both ladders can be stored either inside or outside the window.

The double-rope ladder is made by passing rope through drilled holes at each end of hardwood rungs and securing them in place with a knot on each side. If the ladder is to be stored inside, anchor it with lag screws and washers below the inside window. Tie a double half-hitch in one end of the rope, place a washer over the loop hole and drive the lag screw through the washer, loop hole and into the wall. Do the same with the second rope end and check for even alignment before fastening.

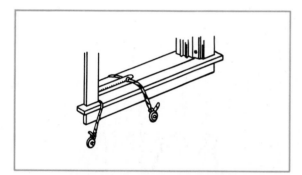

Placement of Anchored Ends of Double-Rope Ladder

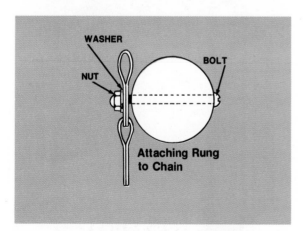

Since steel is not flammable, double-chain ladders have an advantage over rope ladders. However, the rungs are not as easily installed on a chain ladder as the rope variety. Run a bolt through the holes in the steel rung and through a

link in the chain. Then, fasten it in place with a washer and nut.

The double-chain ladder can be anchored inside the home like the double-rope ladder, or both can be fastened and stored inside the home under the window sill.

To do this, place a 2 x 4 board under the sill and drive two lag screws through the end of the ladder, through the board and into wall studs. Evenly place three nails along the top edge of the board and drive them in so that the shaft closest to the head is exposed about 1/2 inch.

A piece of canvas as wide as the board is long holds the ladder next to the house. The canvas should be doubled and sewn at each end for extra strength. In one end of the canvas, install three grommets so that they are in perfect alignment with the three nails on the board edge. The other canvas end is placed under the lag screws

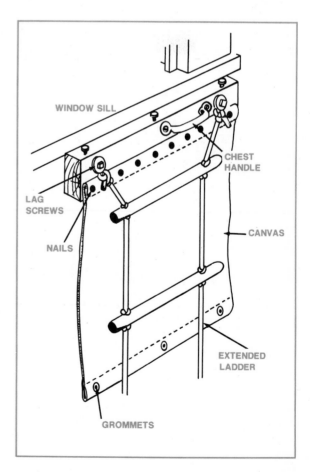

589

and secured with shingle nails. A canvas handle, attached with rivets, may be placed on the grommet end of the canvas.

To provide a proper hand hold for descending the ladder, a chest handle can be installed with screws to the left of the right lag screw and above the canvas end. For left-handed persons, a second handle may be placed on the left side of the board.

After the ladder has been installed, it is rolled up and placed inside the canvas with the grommets hooked over the nails. To release the ladder, pull up on the canvas handle and the grommets slip off the nails, letting the ladder fall down.

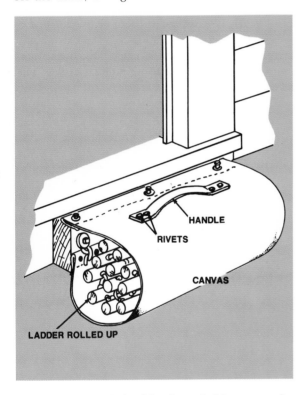

HANDLE

RIVETS

CANVAS

LADDER ROLLED UP

Double-rope and double-chain ladders may be kept inside the home in an existing or homemade window seat. One can be easily constructed from plywood and equipped with a hinged top for quick removal of the ladder.

Fireplace Construction
[SEE FIREPLACES.]

Fireplace Hood
[SEE FIREPLACES.]

Fireplaces

While an ordinary fireplace heats you by radiation alone, the circulator type adds warm air by convection. This salvages and makes useful much of the 80 to 90 percent of the heat that goes up the chimney when logs are burned in an ordinary fireplace.

The result is that a circulator fireplace adds significantly to comfort as well as pleasure in any house in any climate. Where the climate is mild and the house is small, a circulator fireplace may do the whole heating job by itself — especially in the case of a vacation house or cabin where automatic heating may be less in demand.

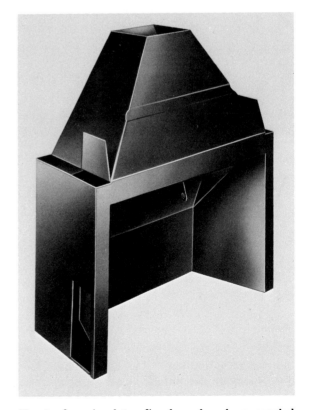

Heart of a circulator fireplace, largely concealed under masonry, is a heavy steel unit like this.

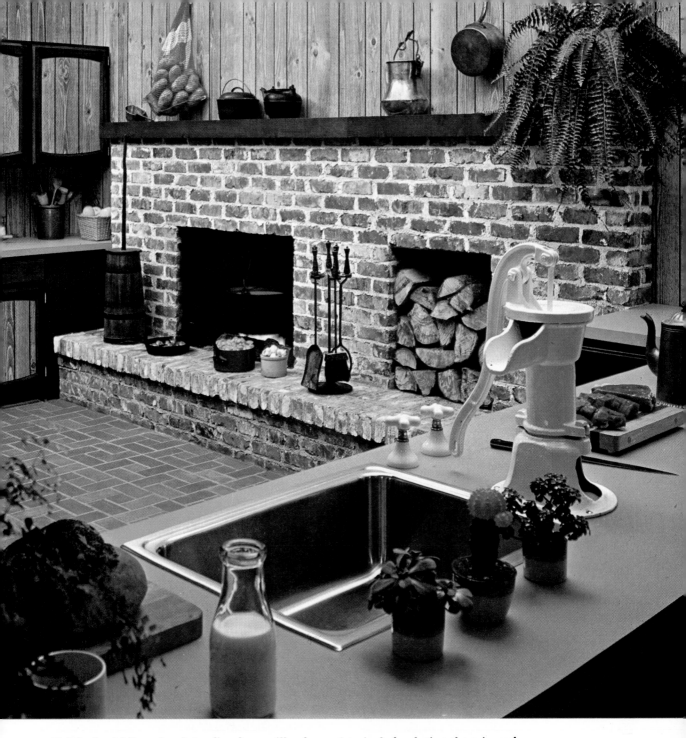

Tricks for hiding circulator-fireplace grilles from view include placing them in end walls and, in the case of outlets, horizontally on the top of a mantel like this one. Where the fireplace is on a partition wall, as here, all grilles may be placed in the other room and heat of the fireplace shared with it.

The efficiency of a circulator fireplace is produced by its hollow-steel construction. Essentially it is a double-walled unit, the walls being several inches apart. As this firebox heats up, air is pulled into it by convection through floor-level registers and flows out through grilles set into the wall at a higher level. One or more of these grilles may be placed in an adjoining room — usually behind the fireplace wall or directly above the room in which the fireplace is located.

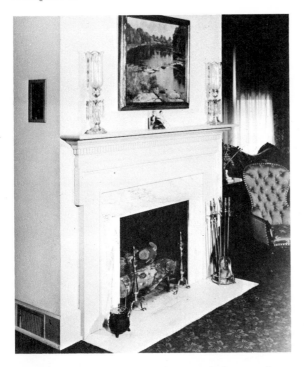

Classically simple fireplace for a period room places all grilles at the side where they do not detract from the historically accurate design.

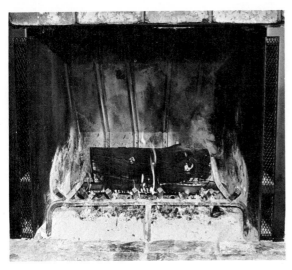

One way to create a circulator fireplace without using a circulator unit is shown here. A hollow steel firebox is inserted into an ordinary fireplace.

The circulating warm air only increases the proportion of the fire's heat made useful, but also circulates it throughout the house to produce more even heating. This effect can be increased by installation of electrically driven fans in the intake grilles; however, it has usually been found that ample circulation is produced by convection alone. Omit the installation of fans until use of the fireplace has indicated that they might be helpful, but wherever possible, build intake ducts in such a way that power for the fans can easily be supplied later. The fans themselves are mounted in frames that fit into the grille boxes supplied with the cold-air grilles.

A circulator unit contributes far more than warm-air circulation alone. Essentially it *is* the fireplace, guaranteeing a scientifically formulated shape and opening and smoke shelf — this last being the aspect that so often proves to have been neglected in ordinary masonry fireplaces that have smoke problems. When you build with a circulator core there are no design decisions about width, height and flue size for efficient and smokefree operation. A damper is also included and is already in place.

In choosing the steel core there are several options. To begin with, there are two types of construction, representing the philosophies of different manufacturers. Some units include the smoke shelf in their steel design. This speeds up the masonry work and guarantees proper smoke-shelf shape.

Another unit does not include a smoke shelf. Instructions are included to tell you just how to form it of concrete during construction. The manufacturer believes that this extra trouble is justified by the greater durability of the masonry smoke shelf, since this is the part of the fireplace subject to down-the-chimney rainwater that might cause rusting out. The manufacturer does, however, use the included-smoke-shelf pattern for its lower-priced model that emphasizes ease of construction as well as economy.

Where there is a choice of models at different prices, the difference usually lies primarily in durability. The longer-lasting units at somewhat higher costs would be the obvious choice for a main fireplace in a year-round home where frequent use is to be expected. For a secondary fireplace such as in a bedroom, for a summer cabin or for the economy construction in general, the lower-priced units are the wiser choice. In these

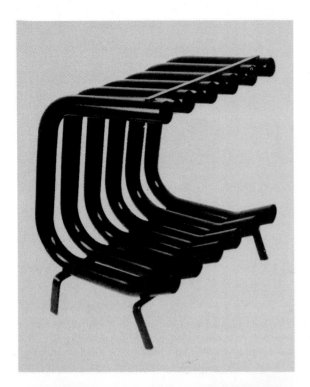

or other as well. Models that open through to permit viewing the fire simultaneously from two rooms are also available. These should be used with some caution, however, as through-opening fireplaces are subject to problems from drafts especially when placed opposite an exterior door.

Circulator units are offered in a variety of sizes, ranging from 28 to 54 inches wide which is the dimension of the finished opening with height and depth varying, but not in direct proportion. The table below gives the statistics for the circulator units of one leading manufacturer.

Finished Opening		Overall Dimensions			Approx. Flue Size	Ship Wt.
Wide	High	Wide	High	Deep		
28	22	34³/₄	44	18	8¹/₂ x 13	171
32	24	38¹/₂	48	19	8¹/₂ x 13	181
36	25	42¹/₂	51	20	13 x 13	224
40	27	47³/₄	55	21	13 x 13	243
46	29	55	60	22	13 x 13	302
54	31	63	65	23	13 x 18	400

In choosing size of unit to be used, make the decision on three grounds. Select a size that is appropriate to the size of the room, the size of

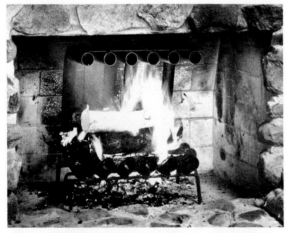

This is another way to convert a new or existing conventional fireplace into a heat-circulating model using a special hollow grate. Called Thermograte, it warms and circulates air by convection much as a full circulator unit does.

uses, the small sacrifice in efficiency and durability may be unimportant. In addition to being less expensive, these units tend to be lighter weight and squarer in shape, contributing to speed and saving in the construction work.

There is also choice between the usual front-opening style and units that are open to one side

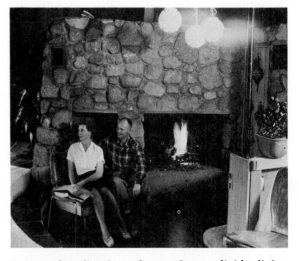

Freestanding fireplace of natural stone divides living room from entryway in the Pacific Grove, California, home. Air intakes are on back of wall; outlets ducted to ends of wall circulate warmed air to distant parts of room.

the wall and the use of the room. A large fireplace is more suitable to a large room or on a long wall, and is more appropriate for a living room than for a bedroom.

Cost and labor involved in building a fireplace are in relation to its size. It involves not only more costly unit, but larger concrete footings, bigger flue, and a larger chimney (though not a taller one).

In respect to function, size should depend not so much upon how much heat will be required as upon the size of firewood that is to be used. This, in turn, may depend upon the source of supply and also upon storage facilities. If there is a built-in woodbox beside the fireplace which is limited to holding 24 inch logs, that is probably the largest size you will burn regularly. A 36 inch wide fireplace will burn such logs more efficiently, that is, it will produce more heat in the room from them, than will a 42 or 48 inch one.

For situations where the need for heat is limited, the fireplace that is not a circulator may be preferred. This single-walled steel unit provides a form and damper around which to build a fireplace. It is a more compact, less costly outgrowth of the circulator idea, but as it is not hollow it does not draw room air through to produce heating efficiency greater than that of conventional fireplaces.

Since a large mass of masonry will be involved a fireplace will need a stout slab foundation. This may sit directly on a concrete footing extending 8 inches below ground level (further if local frost conditions require it) or it may be suspended above ground level with ashpit space between. In that case you will want an ashdump in the slab and a cleanout door outside.

Make the foundation at least as large as the area to be occupied by the fireplace unit and the masonry to go around it. For brick or thin stonework the foundation will have to be from 2 to 3 feet wide and half-again as long as the length of the firebox opening. For other kinds of masonry such as concrete block and fieldstone, plan more generously. The footing below should extend 6 inches beyond the foundation on all sides. To

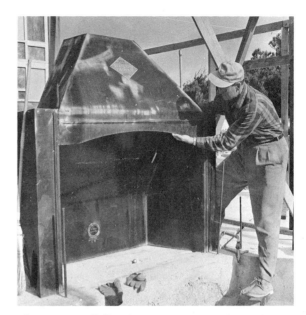

The stone-wall fireplace seen in the picture began like this as a new wing was added to a house. With gas kindler in place and reinforcing steel stubbed up to key with masonry, large unit was pushed into place.

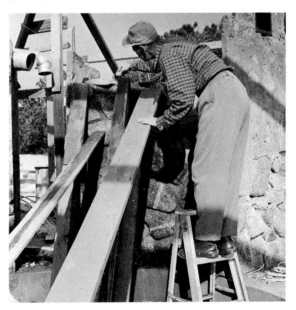

Fireplace was laid up with stone around the steel core, timbers in foreground serving to brace stones in place while mortar hardened. Warm-air grille can be seen in place at upper right.

key the whole masonry structure together, stub up at least two pieces of $\frac{1}{2}$ inch reinforcing steel from the foundation.

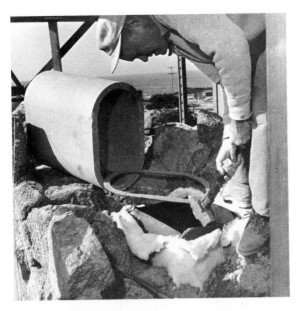

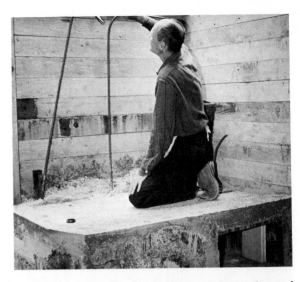

The job begins with a poured concrete base, elevated and faced with stone in this case to produce a raised hearth. The sloping lip helps to prevent logs from rolling out.

With stonework completed to top of circular core, it is time to place the first terra cotta flue section. Cardboard template seen here was cut to shape of flue to simplify shaping top of circulator to fit the flue. Note the insulating material surrounding the circulator.

For the part of the hearth that lies within the fireplace it is recommended that the foundation be finished off with a layer of firebrick large enough to hold the unit. Many builders, however, place a circulator unit directly on the concrete of the footing and slab.

Since fireplace circulation units are extremely heavy, it is often necessary to find some mechanical aid for getting it into place on its hearth. Water pipe can be used as rollers or with a raised hearth, then a lever arrangement, with timbers or a pulley may be required with any but the smaller units. If your design includes an extended or cantilevered hearth that has been poured so recently that the concrete has not fully cured, it may be necessary to use a pulley that permits easing the heavy unit very gently into place.

With the unit properly placed, lay up the masonry around it much as you might build a wall. With most types of brick and stone, which are comparatively costly, you will probably prefer to use inexpensive concrete block for all parts of the job that will not show.

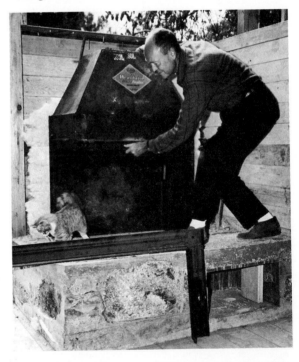

The unit is pushed into place. Angle steel seen in foreground will be placed horizontally with its corner supported by the post to hold the cantilevered masonry.

For a laid-up stone facing, choose your stones carefully for fit, shaping them with a mason's hammer when necessary. Set them in mortar

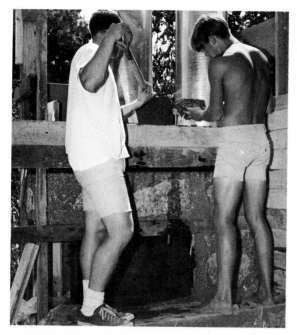

made by mixing one shovelful of portland cement with three of plaster sand and enough water for easy working. A hoe is a good mixing tool and a wheelbarrow is convenient to mix the mortar in. A brick facing is laid up in much the same way.

Fill behind the facing with concrete plus any spare rock or broken bricks. You may let the steel core act as a form, but remember that it must not support any weight except temporarily while the concrete is setting. Where gaps must be bridged put in pieces of reinforcing steel.

A roll of mineral wool will come with a fireplace unit. Use it to cover all steel surfaces before putting masonry against them, holding it in place while you work by daubing the steel first with a paste of cement and water. The wool acts as a cushion for expansion that otherwise might produce cracking when a fire is built.

The method described so far is the conventional one for constructing a masonry fireplace with a circulator core. An alternative shown in some of the photographs was originated to simplify the work and speed it up. This method uses wooden

Stone-in-poured concrete fireplace like this one is ordinarily constructed over a period of several days, with form boards removed and new ones added each day. Flue at right serves floor below.

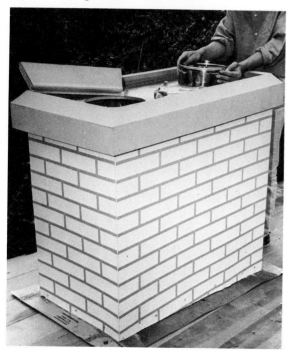

With flues extended through roof, chimney housing is cut to roof slope and placed over flashing. Large chimney housing needed to handle twin flues was later painted neutral gray to cover unconvincing brick pattern and to render it inconspicuous.

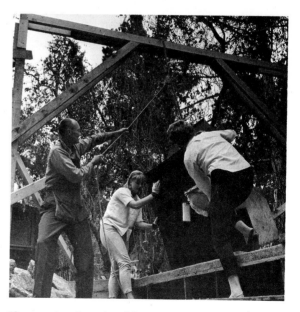

If your circulator is a big one, you may need levers, pulleys and helpers to get it into place. Problem here was a raised hearth so freshly poured that it could easily have been cracked.

forms to permit pouring concrete around stones instead of laying them up with mortar. The unit — properly decked with mineral wool — becomes the other form. This is actually an adaptation to circulator fireplace construction of the method used so much by the architect Frank Lloyd Wright to enable his unskilled apprentices to build magnificent desertstone walls.

While doing your masonry work by whichever method, you must provide ducts to the two air intakes and to the two outlets. How you place these will have a good deal to do with how attractive your fireplace will be and how efficiently it will produce heat. The rule for placement of intake ducts and grilles is simple: as close to the floor as possible. The idea is to recirculate the coldest air in the room. Intakes will often be less conspicuous if placed at the sides of the fireplace in cases where its surround extends into the room and makes this possible. One of the fireplaces illustrated was built in a freestanding section of stone wall, making it convenient to place the openings behind the fireplace.

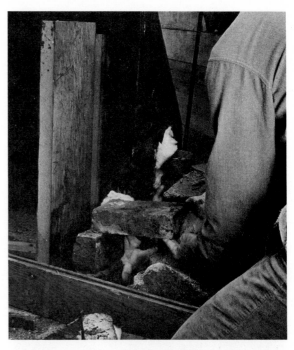

Any kind of scrap material, including old bricks and pieces of sheet metal, can be used to form the air-intake ducts. They serve merely to hold the concrete while it hardens.

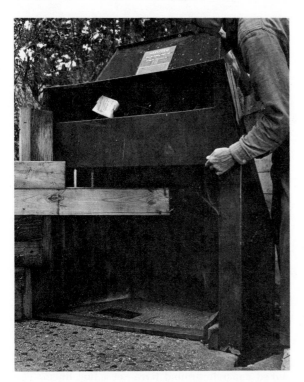

Begin the job by pouring concrete footing, foundation and hearth. Pebbles were floated into the surface of this exterior hearth for appearance.

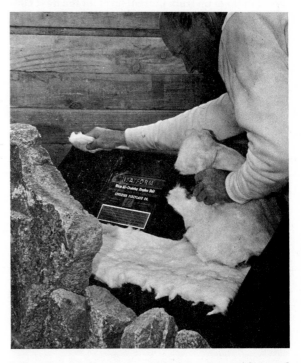

Mineral wool that comes with the unit must be used wherever concrete or mortar might come into direct contact with the steel of the unit. It forms a cushion for expansion that occurs when fires are built.

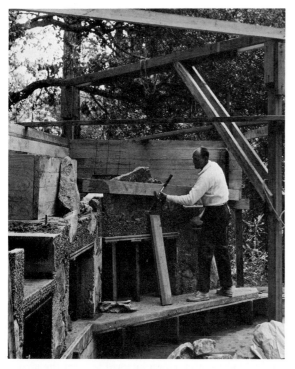

Back form at corner of house is seen here. The builder having pulled off forms at front, is now building them up from present level for the next concrete pouring. Openings cast already are for a barbecue, woodbox, and fireplace.

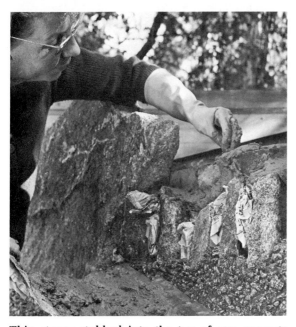

Thin stones stubbed into the top of one concrete pour are spaced to become a grille for warm air exhausted from the circulator. Bits of paper keep mortar from tumbling in during construction.

Warm-air outlets are usually placed just above the firebox, but anywhere above the openings in the unit is acceptable and more attractive, because less obvious, locations can usually be found.

In ordinary masonry, ducts are easily formed in the process of laying up the brick or stone. When the pouring method is used, temporary wood forms will do the work for making short ducts; longer ones can be constructed by using ordinary galvanized heating ducts of the kind that roll up and snap together like stove pipe which are left in permanently.

Use steel angle to reinforce and support the top of the fireplace opening. A piece of the correct size will ordinarily be available when you purchase the unit. If yours is a poured-concrete fireplace, use lumber to make a temporary form, setting the stones in a bed of reinforced concrete

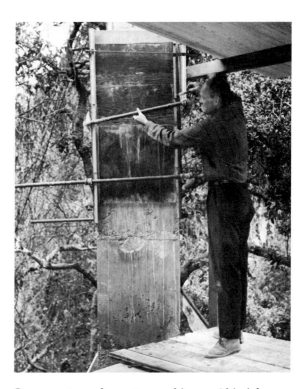

One way to make a strong chimney (this job was done in earthquake country) is by pouring reinforced concrete around terra cotta flue liners. The form is easily made by nailing together plywood sheets, then adding clamps for strength during pouring.

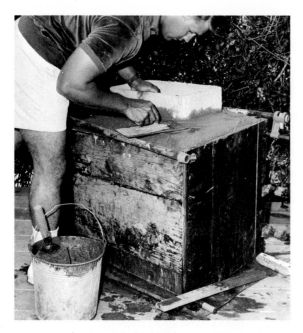

Poured chimney should stop several inches below the top of the last flue liner and should be sloped slightly away from it. This arrangement discourages downdrafts that might produce a smoking fireplace.

several inches thick. If the fireplace wall is large enough, you may want to include an integral woodbox.

Begin chimney construction by placing a length of terra cotta flue liner just above the opening in the top of the circulator unit. How this part of the job is shaped depends upon the type of unit chosen, but the instructions that come with the units tell what to do. Remember that the flue liner must always be supported by masonry, not by the steel unit. Continue upward, adding flue-liner sections as you go, until the chimney is at least 3 feet higher than the roof at the point it passes through and at least 2 feet higher than any part of the roof that is within 10 feet.

How you surround the flue liner to. make a strong chimney will depend upon the type of construction being used. The liner might be surrounded with 8 inches of concrete and stone, to carry out the method used for the rest of the fireplace. This should be reinforced with a vertical steel rod at each corner. Finish the chimney at the top by sloping the concrete upward from the face of the chimney toward the liner, letting the

flue extend about 2 inches above the rest of the chimney. These are precautions to drain off rain water while deflecting wind to discourage downdrafts that could cause a smoky fireplaces.

If you wish to compromise with full masonry construction, you have a time- and laborsaving option: you can use a prefabricated metal all-fuel chimney such as the stainless-steel type described in the entry on *Freestanding Fireplaces*. After securing the lowest section of this chimney in the concrete or mortar of the fireplace construction, continue upward just as you would with a freestanding fireplace and build the whole chimney within an hour or two. This was the method used with the non-circulator-core fireplace.

It is recommended that the concrete or mortar cure for two to three weeks before building the first fires.

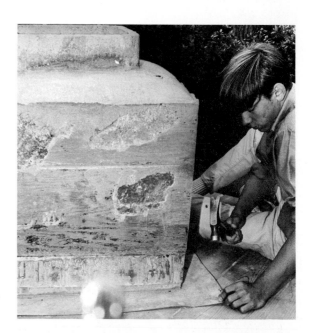

With chimney completed, metal flashing is nailed at upper edge in preparation for roofing. Barely visible is pipe coupling that has been inserted into wet concrete for possible future use in supporting an antenna.

Fireplaces, A-Frame
[SEE FIREPLACES, FREESTANDING.]

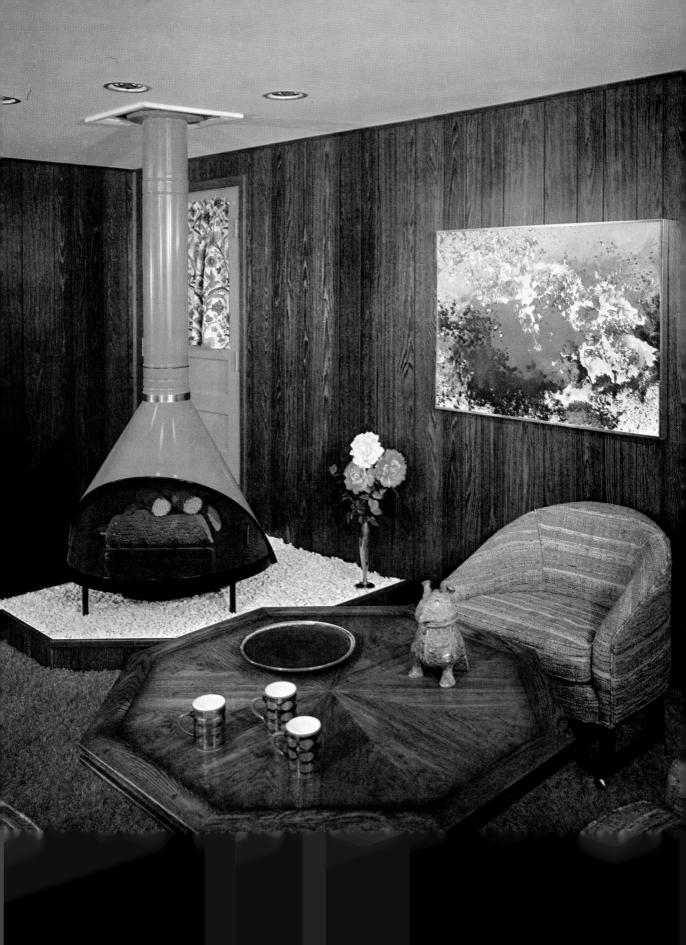

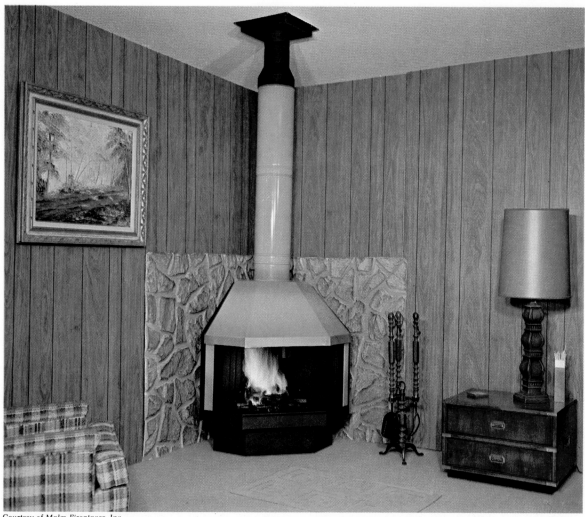

Courtesy of Malm Fireplaces, Inc.

This fireplace was chosen for its spacesaving corner installation.

Fireplaces, Freestanding

It is not unusual for two people without any prior experience to install a freestanding fireplace in a single afternoon and warm themselves by it the same day. Essentially, installation of a manufactured fireplace of this type consists of placing a hearth, assembling unit and chimney

Courtesy of Malm Fireplaces, Inc.

This is the most popular shape in the most popular color. This is an excellent example of the versatility of the freestanding fireplace.

and placing flashing around a hole cut in the roof. Installations that pass through a chimney as well, or those in the lower story of a two-story house, naturally take a little longer. But the procedure remains much the same. The choice of freestanding fireplace shapes and sizes and types and colors is so enormous that you could spend more time making your selection than putting it into place.

The most usual type is a cylinder, cone or rectangular box made of steel, finished either in plain matte black or in almost any color of brilliant porcelain. Most of these units sit on metal bases or legs, although a few are designed to be suspended by chains or hung on a wall.

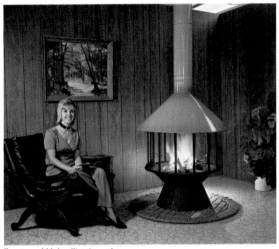

Courtesy of Malm Fireplaces, Inc.

This model is glass-enclosed for clean burning and for heating efficiency.

Several of the cone-shaped porcelain-enamel fireplaces are enclosed in glass to prevent loss of furnace heat up the chimneys. One has an additional feature of its own: it eats ashes. Without moving parts, baffles in the hood and an adjustable air intake in the door work together to create a spinning column of flame, an unusual sight to watch. This whirlwind of flickering fire burns so intensely and so efficiently that the wood or other fuel is fully consumed and about 90 per cent of the ashes are sucked up and out the chimney to be expelled in particles so small that they leave no residue on the roof or lawn.

A less complete answer to the ash problem but still helpful, is the feature called *silent butler* in some models. What is accomplished by the built-in ash dump in many masonry fireplaces is ap-

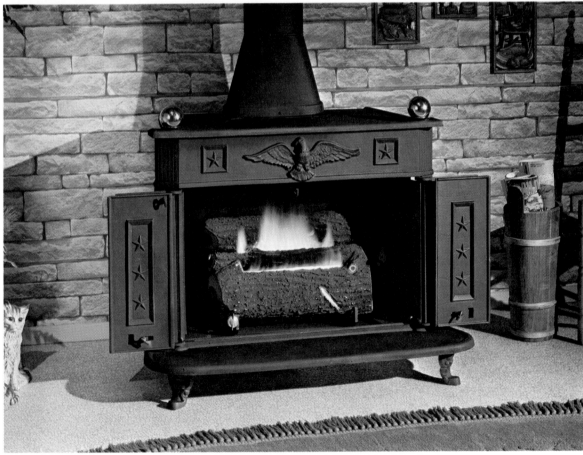

Courtesy of Georgia-Pacific

The Franklin stove is practical as well as decorative. The door closes to prevent heat escaping up the chimney.

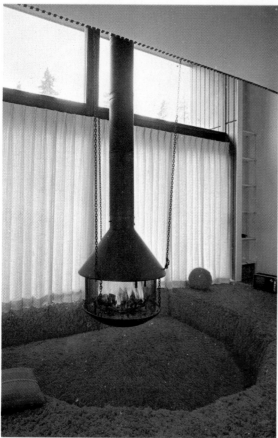

Courtesy of Malm Fireplaces, Inc.

This free-hanging fireplace needs no hearth, and adds an unusual decorative touch to a room.

proximated by the drawer beneath the firebox. Slide it out to empty it, eliminating the dusty chore of sweeping and shoveling out ashes.

As for the loss-of-heat problem, that is solved also by the modern versions of the old Franklin stove, which can be either built-in or freestanding. Close the doors of a Franklin stove, whether there is fire going or not, and the loss of furnace heat is put to an end. Open the doors and there is an open fire to watch. Some of these are brand-new on the market in this decade, yet in both form and function they go back to the days of the statesman-philosopher-inventor they are named for.

A modern stainless steel all-fuel chimney for use with ▷ any kind of fireplace. Other shapes of chimney housings and caps are available.

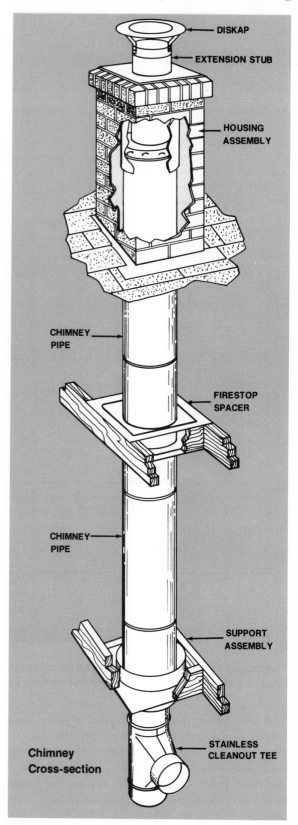

DISKAP

EXTENSION STUB

HOUSING ASSEMBLY

CHIMNEY PIPE

FIRESTOP SPACER

CHIMNEY PIPE

SUPPORT ASSEMBLY

STAINLESS CLEANOUT TEE

Chimney Cross-section

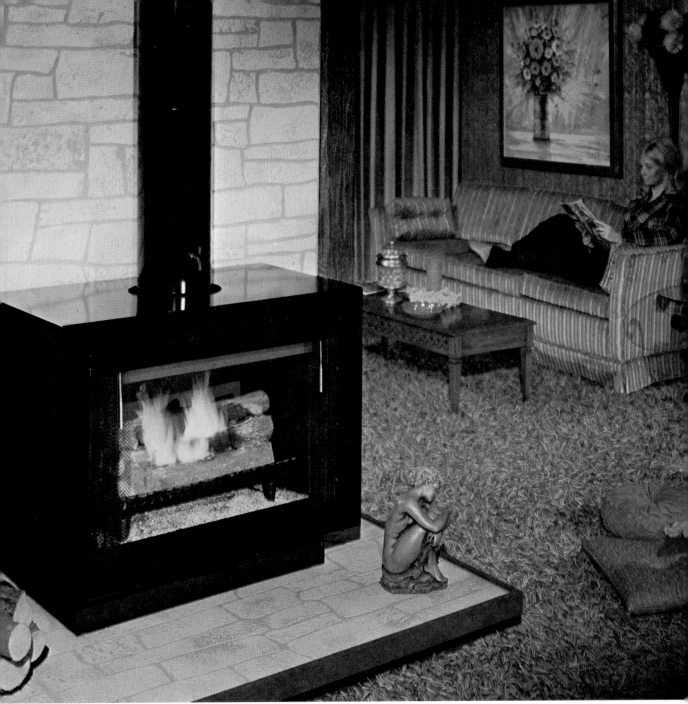

Courtesy of Martin Industries

The unique rectangular shape of this unit makes it suit most any room and many, difficult locations. It helps, too, that models are offered for rear venting as well for top.

The reasons for the jump in sales of these iron fireplaces are practical as well as sentimental. They use their fuel most efficiently since they have large radiating surfaces and full damper and draft control. They avoid the loss of room heat which is a real problem with an ordinary fireplace during the night after an evening's use.

A dying fire gives little heat, yet you can't close the damper on it for fear of smoke and gases.

The secret of the one-day installation that is often possible with today's freestanding units is the ready-made chimney. With most types, chimney sections and rooftop housings are

available from the manufacturers, and the fireplace and chimney may be purchased as a package.

The fireplace and chimney will be a custom-assembled package to allow for several of the conditions that vary from one house to another. Height is allowed for by the number and length of the chimney sections you purchase. Choose as many firestop spacers as you have ceilings or floors to go through.

Should you wish to make a freestanding fireplace yourself, or to have one made to your own design, you can still obtain a metal chimney assembly for it. The most usual type is sold to meet this need and also for use with manufactured freestanding fireplaces that do not come with their own chimneys. It comes as an all-stainless-steel, all-fuel chimney in sizes (inside diameters) ranging all the way from 6 inches to

14 inches, the largest being ample for a large fireplace, masonry, metal or ceramic.

These chimney sections come in 18-inch and 30-inch lengths that can be combined to produce just about any total height wanted. There are various support fittings, insulated tees and elbows, as well as metal rooftop housings finished to resemble brick or shaped as plain galvanized-steel cylinders. The pipe sections have threaded internal couplers that lock with a simple twist, making installation a one-person job with no special tools needed.

Such modern chimneys are made possible by new insulating materials. Having 17 times the insulating value of brick, they need be only 1 inch thick. Even a 14-inch flue is no larger in diameter than a 7-incher used to be.

For safety, all freestanding fireplaces must be placed not closer than some specified distance from a wall; and this distance will vary not only with the model of the fireplace, but also with the nature of the wall. For example, one of the fireplaces illustrated may be placed as close as 6 inches to a brick wall, but must be kept at least 16 inches from a combustible wall. If the same wall is protected by $1/4$ inch asbestos board with a 1 inch airspace behind it, clearance from the combustible wall may be reduced to 12 inches.

Another glass-enclosed model requires clearance of 42 inches from a combustible wall. Information concerning clearance requirements must be obtained in advance if a tight location is intended.

A second fire-safety requirement is that some kind of noncombustible hearth must protect the floor from coals or hot ashes. Where this is necessary it may often be solved most simply by placing the unit on a square of $3/8$ inch asbestos board. Brick is very often used to form a more interesting hearth, as is flagstone or slate. Generally, all safety needs to meet building codes are spelled out in the instructions that accompany the units.

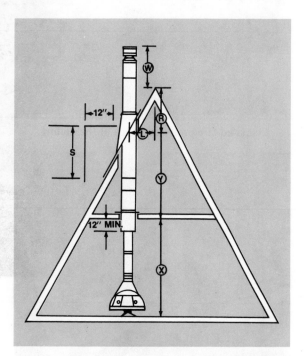

A typical freestanding fireplace chimney is fitted to the roof and ceiling structures in this manner. The use of firestops, roof flashing, chimney housings are included. The letters (R, L, W, X, S) are one manufacturer's way of designating the dimensions that you may need to know in ordering any fireplace unit and chimney.

HOW TO INSTALL A FREESTANDING FIREPLACE

Installation begins with laying a fireproof hearth and placing the unit at least 4 ¹/₂ inches from the wall behind it, 12 inches from wall beside it. Cut flue holes in the ceiling (if any) and the roof over the fireplace. The chimney parts go on the rooftop, one slipping over the other to form a modern, round chimney housing. The storm cap tops the flue. It is fastened with sheet-metal screws, and fends off rain and downdrafts. The flashing slips under the shingles above the chimney, and goes on top of those below to shed rain. The insulated section is fire protection at the ceiling. It must protrude 12 inches below the ceiling. The adjustable metal collar is now placed around the insulated section to cover the gap between it and ceiling. The hearth can be slate, stone, tile or asbestos board at least ³/₈ inch thick.

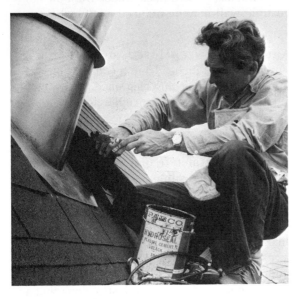

Chimney parts go on the roof.

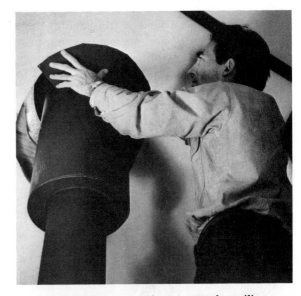

Insulated fire protection goes at the ceiling.

Flashing goes under shingles

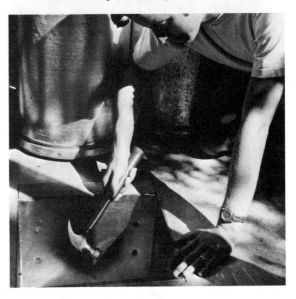

A box is necessary in a house with a second story.

HOW TO INSTALL A FIREPLACE CHIMNEY

Installation of a typical chimney in a house having a second story or attic above the room begins

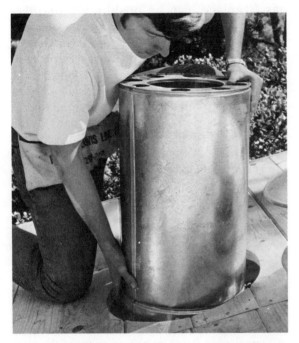

Rooftop flue section must be at least 2 feet above the roof.

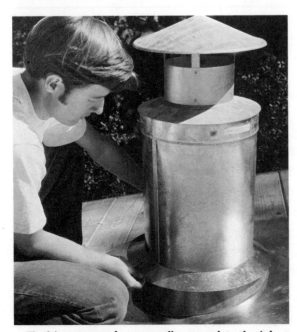

Flashing cap and storm collar complete the job.

with nailing in a box supplied for support. The color-matched or black chimney from the fireplace fits into steel flue sections, above, that snap together.

Last flue section continues above roof to required height—at least 2 feet above any near-by part of roof.

Fireplaces, Gas & Electric

An electric or gas-fired fireplace does not have all the primitive appeal of a crackling wood-burner, but there are situations where you may not want the inconvenience of wood-carrying and splitting and ash-removal or where an open fire might be dangerous. There are also conditions where installation of even the simplest woodburning units is too difficult to be feasible. Then the electrics and the gas-burners come into their own. They can do many of the things that wood-burning fireplaces do—and do them well.

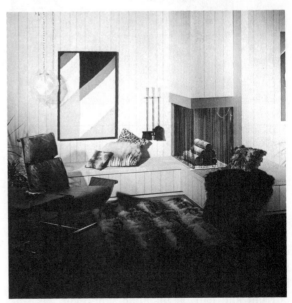

Courtesy of Masonite

Gas and electric fireplaces can go where a wood-burning unit would be out of place, possibly dangerous. Gas units use realistic ceramic logs that radiate heat.

A gas fireplace can be installed right on a wood floor without masonry foundation. If there is no existing flue you can put in a simple 6-inch metal gas vent, usually available from the maker of the fireplace.

This kind of fireplace can be styled any way you wish. The only safety requirement related to fire danger is 2 inches of noncombustible trim above the opening. The realistic set of gas logs that will come with the fireplace is so skillfully molded that it will look more like firewood than most real logs do.

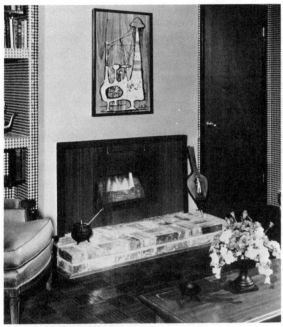

Courtesy of Majestic

This compact gas fireplace can be obtained with wide and high screen assemblies like this, to give the illusion of a large woodburning fireplace. This gives it a scale much more suited than ordinary gas models to use in a large room.

A special advantage of a total gas fireplace is that its automatic pilot can be turned on by remote control. Since the electricity this arrangement uses is generated by the thermocouple connected to the pilot light, it is not connected to household current and can be installed wherever gas (including liquid petroleum gas) is available without regard to the presence of a power line. The pushbutton can be located any where in the room. Thermostatic control is also available.

GAS CONVERSION

The same kind of ultramodern gas-log set may now be purchased by itself. You can use it to convert your existing fireplace to gas-fired, whatever type it may be. The conversion, like the gas fireplace, can be pushbutton or thermostatically controlled. A conversion of this sort need not be permanent, but can easily be done to meet some temporary need. A basket or tray of artificial logs replaces the grate and conceals the gas burner. This can be accomplished in a matter of minutes if a connection for a gas-fired kindler already exists, as it does in a great many of the woodburning fireplaces built in recent years.

If a gas line has to be brought to the fireplace so that the conversion is possible, this same line will be useful for a kindler if the fireplace is later converted back to woodburning by removal of the gas burner and logs.

ELECTRIC FIREPLACES

Under the most restrictive conditions—such as the lack of a flue and it is not feasible to install one, as with temporary use or a rented property,—an electric fireplace serves many of the purposes of a woodburning one.

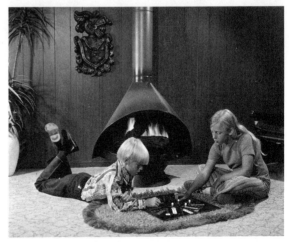

Courtesy of Malm Fireplaces, Inc.

This fireplace uses its matching pipe as a vent. In electric models resembling this one, the pipe is telescopic, has no function—but is used to give a realistic imitation of a conventional freestanding fireplace.

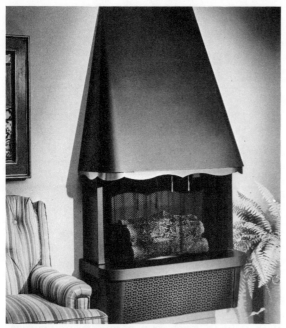

Courtesy of Majestic

This electric fireplace can be purely decorative, with its flickering fire effect the focal center of a room. With an optional heating element it becomes functional as well.

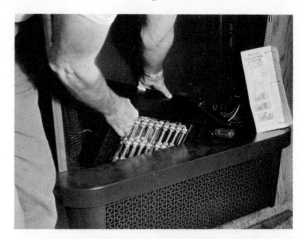

The heating element slips into place behind grille. Since this is the 240-volt type capable of producing 13,600 BTU, it requires a special circuit.

It provides a focal point for the room. It creates a pleasant, warm glow from a manufactured (but remarkably realistic) log. If it contains an electric heater, included with some, optional with some others, it can partially or entirely heat the room at the same level of cost and energy consumption as a conventional electric heater and, like any electric heater, it may be equipped with a thermostat.

All that is needed in order to install an electric fireplace is a source of electricity. With some models you will also need some free area of wall to hang it on, but other types are freestanding and can go anywhere. There are no clearance problems with most electric fireplace units. The hanging ones can go on any kind of wall and the conical metal freestanding ones can be placed where desired without requiring to be spaced away from combustible walls.

The electrical connection can be as simple as plugging into an existing outlet, if you are satisfied with a no-heater model or one that produces about 5,000 to 5,640 BTU per hour. The lat-

ter figure is the amount of heat produced by a 120-volt, 1,650-watt model. If there exists, or can be put in, a 240-volt circuit for an electric fireplace, much more heat is available. A typical model gives the choice of a glowing, flickering log alone—or either 6,800 or 13,600 BTU (at 2,000- or 4,000-watt settings) of thermostatically controlled heat.

GAS IN A WOODBURNER

Once gas has been piped to a fireplace, as when converting from woodburning to gas-fired

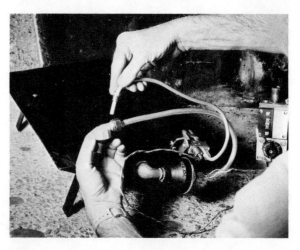

With the safety pilot kit shown, converting a fireplace to automatic gas operation is a matter of a few simple connections once the gas line has been brought in.

operation, the presence of gas can be put to good use if the fireplace is later converted back.

A log kindler or starter is easily made once gas has been brought in. The simplest method is just a length of $1/2$ inch (or $3/8$ or $3/4$ inch, if one of these is more convenient) gas pipe attached to the gas line by way of a shut-off valve for this purpose. The end of the pipe is plugged or capped and a series of small holes is drilled perhaps 2 inches apart along the part of the pipe near the center of the fireplace. Instead of drilling holes and capping the pipe, you may prefer to end it with a street el and then a cap—across the end of which you have hacksawed a slot for the gas.

Building codes usually require that in addition to the control used to operate a kindler, there should be a cut-off valve in the line. Then if the kindler valve fails there is still a way to shut off the gas without turning off the supply to the entire house. Most householders who have used gas starters come to consider them virtually indispensable. A kindler takes the place of kindling, makes careful fire laying unnecessary, and insures that a fire will continue to burn without attention for hours.

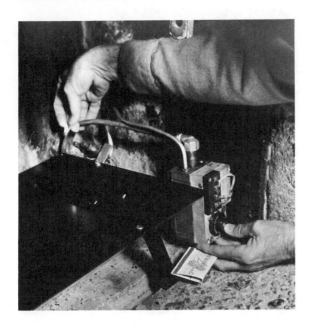

The gas pilot is lighted initially just as would be done with a gas furnace or water heater. Control is by a switch, which can be elsewhere in the room, or by thermostat.

Fireplaces, Zero Clearance
[SEE ZERO CLEARANCE FIREPLACES.]

Fire Protection
[SEE INSURANCE PROTECTION.]

Fire Stop

A fire stop is used in the construction of walls and floors for fire safety in a building. The spaces between studs are open and permit drafts. By tightly closing off these open spaces with lumber, brick or concrete, fire stops prevent the spread of fire and smoke throughout a building. In addition, fire stops add extra bracing and backing for floors and walls. *SEE ALSO FLOOR CONSTRUCTION.*

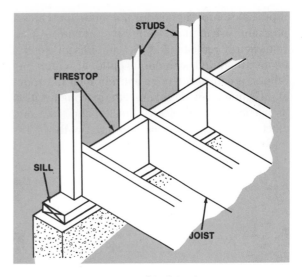

Fire stop used in floor frame.

Fire Wall

A fire wall is a wall made of a noncombustible material, such as concrete or brick, which is

used to restrict the spread of fire in a building. A fire wall usually separates two building sections and extends from the bottom floor to above the roof. Occasionally, automatic closing fire doors are included in fire walls.

Firmer Chisel

A firmer chisel has a thicker blade than the paring chisel. Having a plastic handle which is metal-capped makes the firmer chisel suitable for both medium and heavy duty tasks, such as paring, light mortising or heavy driving. This chisel may be driven by hand or with a mallet. *SEE ALSO HAND TOOLS.*

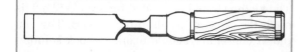

Firmer Chisel

First Aid

Knowledge of correct first aid measures are essential. These suggestions, however, are simply what is implied — *first* aid — and are to be used only until the injured person can receive proper medical attention. The seven major areas of first aid the homeowner should know are bleeding, blisters, burns, choking, foreign objects in the eye and mouth-to-mouth resuscitation.

BLEEDING

Pressure can be applied directly with a cloth pressed on the cut. The first thing to remember about bleeding is that a small cut takes 4 to 8 minutes with pressure to stop, and large cuts from 10 to 15 minutes with applied pressure. An important fact to know about stopping bleeding is the main pressure points. They are located in front of the ear, on the jaw, in the neck, behind the collar bone, inside the upper arm and the groin. Pressure should be applied directly to the

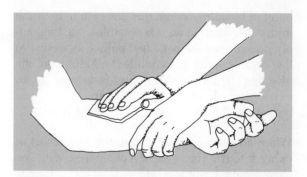

Apply pressure with pad directly over wound.

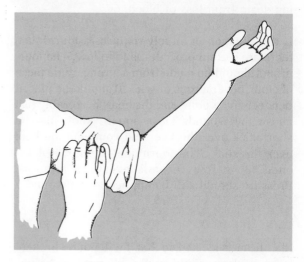

Pressure on inner arm will stop bleeding below this spot.

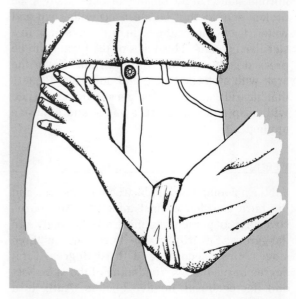

Pressure just below the groin will stop bleeding below this point.

point of bleeding. When this does not help or the injury is located in an inaccessible area, then apply pressure on the principal points, as well as to the injured part if possible to help stop the bleeding. If the bleeding point is located on an extremity, elevation of the limb, if it is not broken, will help to reduce the blood flow.

When all other measures fail, the last resort of using a tourniquet can be considered with extreme caution. Since a limb can be lost, a tourniquet should be used *only* in the case of impending death from loss of blood.

If the situation definitely requires a tourniquet, there are certain procedures to follow. The tourniquet should be made from a strong, *wide* piece of cloth, never a rope or wire. It should be placed between the wound and the heart preferably just above the wound. Tie a square knot, place a short stick over the knot and complete the knot over the stick. The tourniquet should be loosened for a few seconds every 15 minutes. Pressure should still be applied to the wound.

BLISTERS

If a blister is located so that it will not be broken, leave it alone. Fluid in the blister will be absorbed by the skin and the area will return to its normal state. Larger blisters or ones likely to be broken should first be cleansed with soap and water. Then, pierce the edge of the blister with a sterilized needle. The edges of the blister can be pressed gently to force out the fluid. Cover the area with a sterile gauze and adhesive. Blisters that have already been broken should be washed with soap and water and a gauze and adhesive applied.

BURNS

All burn patients should be treated for shock and the burn guarded against infection. Any burns covering 20 percent or more of the body are dangerous. Severity of the burns are in three stages: first, second, and third degree. First degree burns involve reddening of the skin. Second degree burns involve blisters. And, third degree burns may have some skin burned away or severely charred.

First degree burns can be held under cold water or apply ice until the pain dissipates. A sterile dressing can be substituted if cold water is not available. For mild cases, a cream, oil or petrolatum can be used to soothe the parched skin. Sunburns are usually first degree burns.

Second degree burns should be protected by sterile gauze held in place with a bandage. This degree of burn is more serious since the blisters may break and become open wounds. Never try to open the blisters. Cut clothing away from the area.

Third degree burns are the most serious of all. Do not attempt to remove any clothing sticking to the burned area. Cover the burned area with sterile dressings or a clean sheet will do.

The victim should be treated for shock. Shock is often the cause of death in burn cases. The victim, if conscious, should drink a shock solution to replace the lost body fluids. Mix $1/4$ teaspoon salt and $1/2$ teaspoon baking soda in one quart of water.

Chemical burns should be flushed thoroughly with water until all possible traces of the substance is removed. Then, treat the chemical burn as any other burn.

An electrical burn has a different set of precedents. The first step is to identify and treat if necessary, respiratory failure. After normal breathing has resumed, treat the burn according to procedures for first, second and third degree burns.

CHOKING

A foreign body can easily lodge in the throat or air passage way. It is essential that it be removed quickly, and if the victim stops breathing, to begin mouth-to-mouth resuscitation.

To remove an object from an adult have him lie on his side so that the head is lower than the trunk of his body or have him straddle a chair so that his chest rests on the back of the chair with his head hanging down. Sharply slap him between the shoulder blades. Clear the throat by

pulling the tongue forward and reaching in with the fingers to remove the object.

To remove a foreign body from the air passage way of a child, hold his head down over an arm or leg and sharply pat between the shoulder blades. Clear the throat and mouth with the fingers after the tongue has been pulled forward.

For a choking infant hold it by the ankles, thus allowing the head to hang straight down. Open the infant's mouth, pull the tongue forward, and allow the object to fall out. The child may need to be sharply patted on the back to dislodge the object.

FOREIGN OBJECTS IN THE EYE

A foreign object in the eye is not only irritating, but can also be dangerous. Flushing the eye with water can remove most objects easily. Pour a steady stream of water into the corner of the eye nearest the nose. This will allow the water to flush the particle out and not contaminate the other eye.

If no water is available and the particle is small, have the patient blink. The irritation will cause the eye to tear and possibly wash away the particle. If the object is under the upper eye lid, pull the upper lashes out and down over the lashes of the lower lid. If the object is located under the lower lid, pull the lid down with the thumb and remove the object with the corner of a clean, dampened handkerchief. If the particle cannot

be removed with any of the mentioned methods, cover the eye with gauze and take the patient to the doctor.

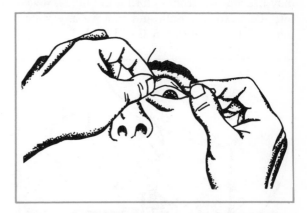

Second, examine inside of lid while the patient looks down.

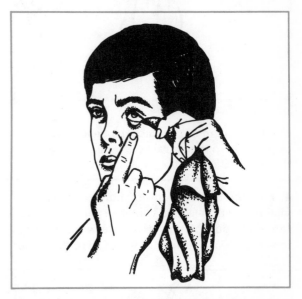

Third, gently remove object with moist, clean corner of handkerchief or other soft cloth.

MOUTH-TO-MOUTH RESUSCITATION

There are many situations where artificial respiration is required. This first aid measure is of utmost urgency. Do not wait for help or try to move the victim to a better location. If the victim has another first aid emergency, allow someone else to take care of that situation.

There are some simple steps to follow. Be patient; the process may take a long time.

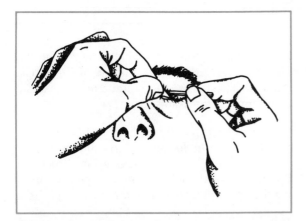

First, grasping eyelashes with fingers, roll eyelid around a cotton-tipped swab.

1. *Turn the victim on his back.*

2. *Clear the air passage way.* Any obstruction may prevent air from entering the lungs. Reach into the victim's mouth and remove any water, mucus, blood, food or artificial teeth.

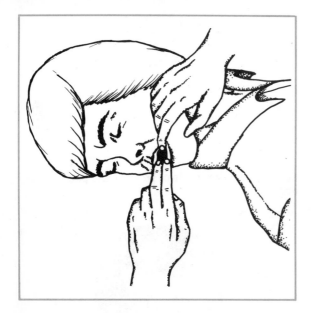

3. *Tilt the head back.* Place the head as far back as possible so that the skin is pulled taut over his throat.

4. *Pull the chin up.* Insert thumb between the victim's teeth near the center of the mouth and forcefully pull his lower jaw outward until the lower teeth are further outward than the upper

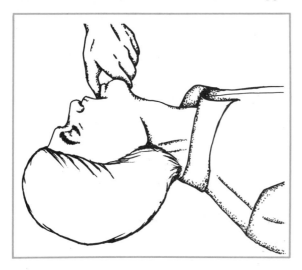

teeth. A piece of cloth can be wrapped around the thumb to prevent injury from the teeth.

5. *Close the nostrils.* Compress the nostrils with the thumb and forefinger of the free hand.

6. *Blow air into the victim's lungs.* There are actually two ways to do this. First is the mouth-to-nose method where breathing is into the mouth and nose. In this case the nostrils would not be compressed. This method is always used for a small child. The second is the mouth-to-mouth breathing. In this method the nostrils are compressed, the rescuer's mouth is placed over the victim's mouth and air is blown into the mouth. The air flow should be forceful for adults but gentle for children.

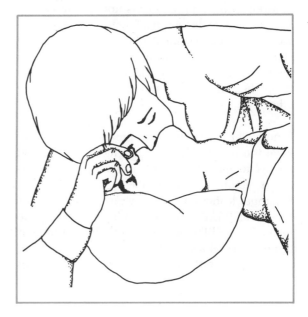

7. *Let the air escape.* One hand may rest on the victim's chest to indicate fullness of the lungs. After his chest rises, discontinue mouth contact and allow air to escape.

8. *Repeat steps five through six until the victim is able to breathe for himself.* As soon as the air escapes, breathe into the lungs again. Breathing into the lungs should take place 12 times a minute for adults and 20 times a minute for children.

POISONING

If possible, follow antidote directions on the

label in cases of poisoning. If there are none or the origin of the poisoning is unknown, induce vomiting immediately unless the poison is acid or alkali. First dilute the poison. Diluted poison enters the system slower and causes less damage. Soap water, salt water, baking soda water, lukewarm water or milk can be used in large quantities to dilute the poison. Vomiting is easier to induce if the stomach is full. Tickle the back of the throat with a finger to help initiate vomiting. Continue until the substance vomited is as clear as the substance being taken to dilute the poison.

If acid has been swallowed than administer any type of alkali, such as magnesia, baking soda, chalk, lime water or olive oil. Then, give milk or egg white and keep the victim warm.

If an alkali has been swallowed, then administer a very weak acid such as vinegar or lemon juice. Then, give the victim milk and keep him warm.

All cases of poisoning should also receive shock treatment.

SHOCK

Shock can often cause death from injuries that in themselves would not have been fatal. Shock in some degree can result from all but the most minor injuries. In serious injuries, treat the patient for shock even if symptoms have not yet appeared. Definite signs of shock include paling of the skin color, cold, clammy skin with perspiration beads on forehead and palms of hands, irregular and shallow breathing, a weak pulse that is either rapid or irregular, nausea, vomiting and trembling, apprehension or nervousness. These symptoms may appear slowly, but the danger is still present. The following measures should be taken:

1. Lie the victim down. The head should be lower than the rest of the body.

2. Keep the victim warm, but do not overheat. The object is to keep him from getting chilled.

3. If the victim is conscious and able to swallow, give him fluids. The solution of ¼ teaspoon salt,

½ teaspoon baking soda and one quart of water may help to prevent or delay shock. If this shock solution is not available, administer water, tea, coffee or cocoa. Do not attempt to give liquids if the victim is unconscious. Instead, place the unconscious victim face down with his head turned to one side.

The suggestions given are only to be used until the person can receive proper medical care. Every home and workshop should have a first aid book and an approved first aid kit for emergency use.

Fishing

Fishing is a technique of pulling wires through conduits or tight places when rewiring old houses. The *fish tape* is a flat, thin strip of metal with a hook on its end. By passing it through the walls in the desired wiring area and attaching it to the length of wire to be installed, the tape will snake the wire through places where the hand cannot reach. *SEE ALSO ELECTRICAL WIRING.*

Fish Joint

A fish joint is a wood or metal strip placed on one or both sides of a butt joint for reinforce-

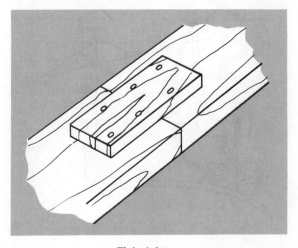

Fish Joint

ment. The fish joint is narrower than the width of the boards that form the butt joint, but it extends across each side of a butt joint. Fish joints are usually secured with nails or screws and are generally associated with furniture construction.

Fish Tape

Fish tape is a springy wire with a hook on one end. It is used to feed wires through a run of conduit or pre-drilled holes in the framework. After the tape has been snaked through the opening, the wires are attached to the tape and pulled through as the tape is pulled out. *SEE ALSO ELECTRICIAN'S TOOLS & EQUIPMENT.*

Fittings
[SEE PIPE FITTINGS.]

Fixture Boxes

Fixture boxes are round, square or octagonal metal outlet boxes used for mounting light fixtures in either walls or ceilings. The box has

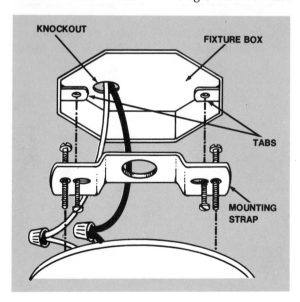

Ceiling Fixture Box

"knockouts" or clamps for incoming cable and tabs into which the fixture's mounting strap is screwed. Many fixture boxes also come equipped with a center hole for threaded fixture studs. Small holes in the back of the box permit direct fastening to ceiling joists or wall studs. Junction boxes may be used as fixture boxes. *SEE ALSO SWITCHES & OUTLETS.*

Fixture Wiring & Repair

The wiring and repair of a fixture vary with the area where it is mounted. But whether found on a ceiling or wall, incandescent or flourescent fixtures do have certain wiring and repair techniques in common. For example, always connect black wire of the circuit to the black wire of the fixture to avoid a short circuit which may result in fire.

WIRING & MOUNTING

Fixture studs or *mounting straps* are commonly used to attach or support fixtures to walls or ceilings. The stud is a threaded nipple that is attached to the center of the fixture box which may be anchored to the wall stud or ceiling joists with nails, screws or through other fasteners. Lamp sockets are held to the "studs" with *fixture hickey* or *collar*. The hickey will allow the cover plate (commonly known as the lamp socket) to adjust in height. The collar is a small nut that will hold the fixture cover to the hickey. For wall attachment, a knurled cap will support the fixture.

Since fixtures usually contain their own lead wires, connection to the circuitry of the house is achieved by simply splicing the black wires together and the white wires together. Fixtures often are wired with solderless connectors for fast wiring and easy replacement. Once the connections are made, push the fixture against the ceiling and fasten it there with the fixture collar or knurled cap.

REPAIR

An obvious sign of trouble in a home lighting circuit is a bulb that will not light. However, a bulb

that will not light may indicate either a burned-out bulb, a blown fuse, a dirty contact at the light socket base, loose terminal screws or more complicated problems, like broken wiring, an inoperative switch or a defective light fixture.

Both a dead bulb and a blown fuse are easily corrected. If the bulb burns out, it is probably because of its age; but a prematurely burned-out bulb may signify that the voltage of the circuit is producing more amperes than the bulb is using. Check the voltage and amperage of the circuit against the wattage and amperage of the bulb and replace the bulb if necessary. A blown fuse usually indicates an overloaded circuit.

Compare the total amperage of the electrical devices drawing power from the circuit with the blown fuse against the amperage capacity of the circuit and/or fuse. Remove enough of the electrical devices needed to relieve the extra load on the circuit before replacing the fuse.

At times, the flat metallic surface through which the bulb makes contact with the current may be dirty, not allowing the bulb to light. After turning off either the household power or the power to the circuit controlling the light fixture, examine the contact, using a flashlight for light. If the contact is dirty, a sharp screwdriver or filing paper may be used to sand the contact, making it bright and shiny. Lightly sand the metallic stem of the bulb until it shines, also. After it is replaced, the bulb should light when the power and switch are turned on.

If the problem is not a dead bulb, blown fuse or dirty contact, further investigation is warranted. Perhaps there is poor contact between the wire and the light switch terminal screws. To check for this, remove the light switch cover and touch the terminal screws with a circuit tester. If the tester does not light, tighten the terminal screws with a screwdriver and test again. If it still does not light, the wires between the light switch and fixture may be broken or worn. With the current off, splice new wires to the existing wires. When the old wires are pulled out of the wall, the new wires are fished back into the same route.

When tightening the terminal screws or replac-

ing the switch-to-fixture wiring does not eliminate the problem the light switch should be examined. If the light switch has a toggle, the clicking sound made by this toggle may mean an inoperative switch; i.e. a dead clicking sound may mean a dead switch. After turning off the electricity to the circuit, remove the switch cover plate with a screwdriver. Then, remove the screws that hold the light switch to the receptacle box and pull the switch away from the wall. One by one, loosen the terminal screws and remove the switch from the bare wire ends. Reconnect the wire ends to the terminal screws of the new switch and push it back into the receptacle box. Replace the screws that hold the switch into the receptacle box and put back the cover plate.

Replacement of the light fixture is complicated but sometimes necessary. Remove the lamp cover if there is one. There will be a point marked "PRESS" at the base of the light fixture. By putting pressure on this point, the light fixture will be released from the receptacle box. However, some light fixtures are fastened to the receptacle box by fixture straps, fixture studs or both. When mounted this way, light fixtures are removed by removing the screws on the strap or by removing the knurled cap or fixture collar. Some modern light fixtures may have solderless connectors which can easily be removed so that the fixture may be released from the bare wire connections. Connect the black wire leading

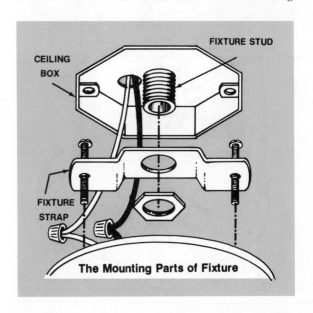

The Mounting Parts of Fixture

from the light receptacle box to the black wire of the new light fixture; connect the white wire to the white. Push the light fixture back into the receptacle and fasten it according to the type of mounting used. Be sure that there is a bulb in the socket. After the circuit is turned on, the bulb should light. *SEE ALSO ELECTRICAL WIRING.*

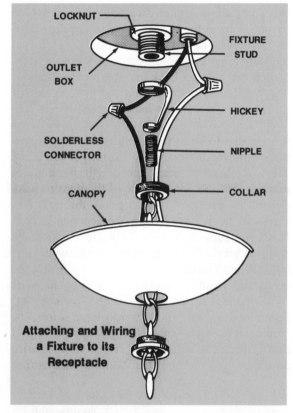

Attaching and Wiring a Fixture to its Receptacle

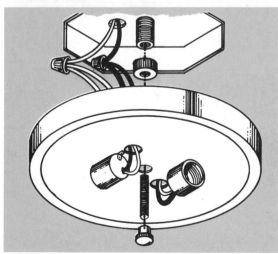

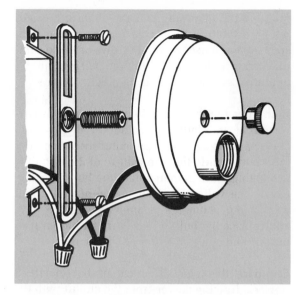

A fixture may be mounted on either ceiling or wall.

Flagstone

Flagstone is a hard stone which is stratified evenly and split into flat pieces. This rock is used for paving patios, terraces, walks, paths and other areas.

Flagstone Paving

Flagstone paving is now a fairly simple operation almost any homeowner can do to improve the appearance of a porch, terrace, patio or garden walk. Conventional flagstone paving requires a lot of time, labor and money; the dry method of flagstone paving can be done in a few hours by one person with only a very few household items.

To use the dry method, level the area where the flagstone will be laid and cover it with cinders. Fill the area with a two-inch layer of sand and smooth it with a rake or board so that there is a slight pitch for water drainage. Place the flagstones close together to cover the sand, but leave at least a 1/2 inch gap between stones. Work the stones into the sand so that the flat surfaces

are level, and support any high points by packing sand underneath the stones. Wet the stones and sand and allow the stones to dry before pouring the cement.

If a rough surface is desired, use three parts coarse sand to one part cement. For smooth results, mix two parts fine sand to one part cement. *Do not add water.*

Pour the dry cement-sand mixture onto the flagstones and sweep it across with a broom until the areas between the stones are filled and level. Then brush the stones clean with the broom. Wet the area with a fine spray of water from a garden hose until the mortar has absorbed all the water possible without any left standing on the surface. Repeat every 15 minutes until the mortar is thoroughly wet. No troweling is necessary. Keep the area damp for several days by sprinkling frequently or covering with plastic. *SEE ALSO BRICK & STONE WORK.*

Flagstone Sealers & Stains

Knowledge of sealers and stains is essential in the maintenance and preventative care of flagstone. The sealers act as a preventative measure while the removal of stains is necessary for proper maintenance.

SEALERS

Flagstone sealers are needed to help prevent stains from adhering to and water from penetrating the stones. Usually applied with a paintbrush, sealers are normally a clear, transparent silicone. These sealers also help to prevent a wearing away process called stone dusting.

STAINS

Soot, mortar, grease and efflorescence are only four of the many stains that affect masonry. Before attempting to remove any stain, the handyman will need a pair of rubber gloves, an eye shield and a stiff-fibered brush.

To remove mortar from flagstone, use muriatic acid. Scrubbing with soap and water and a stiff-fibered brush will remove efflorescence stains. There are many excellent commercial stain removers available at a masonry or building supply store. Oil and grease stains are best removed with a commercial cleaner whose main ingredient is trisodium phosphate. *SEE ALSO BRICK & STONE WORK.*

Flakeboard

Flakeboard, also called particle board and chipboard, is a type of hardboard made of wood chips, flakes and shavings bonded together with adhesives. Then it is pressed, producing a composition board which ranges in thickness from $1/4$ inch to $1^7/_{16}$ inches. The standard size board is a 4 x 8 sheet with a $3/4$ inch thickness. Various sized wood chips make up the layers of board; in the middle are large ones which provide strength and on the outer surface are fine ones which provide smoothness. Flakeboard makes an excellent base for plastic laminates and also is used as a core for plywood. It is better to use flakeboard than plywood for sliding and cabinet doors, counter tops and other areas that need stability because flakeboard is very stable and does not warp easily.

Flanging Tool

A flanging tool or flaring tool is an instrument used to enlarge the end of plastic or copper pipes so a second pipe can be inserted and clamped into place. The flanging process is used in instances where soldering techniques are hazardous or inappropriate because of the pipe material. The cone or pointed end of the flanging tool is inserted into the pipe and pressure is applied to mushroom or flare the pipe enough to allow insertion of the second pipe. A flare fitting is then placed over the juncture to hold the pipes securely.

619

The simplest flanging tool is a bullet-shaped instrument that is struck by a hammer. Several of this type of flanging tool would be needed since they are not adjustable in size. A more versatile model has an adjustable ledge containing holes for various tube sizes. Turning the handle at the top of the instrument screws the conical point into the pipe. The pointed cone is allowed to penetrate only as much as the hole allows. *SEE ALSO PLUMBER'S TOOLS & EQUIPMENT.*

Flaring Tool

A flaring tool or flanging tool is an instrument used to enlarge the end of plastic or soft metal pipes so a second pipe can be inserted and clamped into place. The simplest flaring tool is a bullet-shaped instrument that is struck by a hammer. More than one of these would be needed since they are not adjustable in size. The more versatile model provides a tray containing holes for various tube sizes. Turning the handle at the top of the instrument screws the conical point into the pipe. The pointed cone is allowed to penetrate only as much as the hole on the tray allows.

The flaring process is used in instances where the soldering techniques are inappropriate because of the pipe material or hazardous because of the flame. The cone or pointed end of the flaring tool is inserted into the pipe and pressure is applied to mushroom or flare the pipe enough to allow insertion of the second pipe. A flare fitting is then placed over the juncture to hold the pipes securely. *SEE ALSO PLUMBER'S TOOLS & EQUIPMENT.*

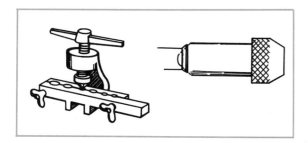

Flaring Tools

Flashers

Flashers are types of lighting devices, such as blinkers, that are used during the day or night to indicate trouble. These flashing or blinking lights on highways will caution approaching traffic to prevent any collisions. Dry-cell battery-powered flashers or blinkers which plug into the cigarette lighter socket can be used. *SEE ALSO DRIVING SAFETY & AUTO INSURANCE.*

Flashing

Flashing is used to seal and waterproof the joints between two parts of the house, for example, between chimneys and roofs or dormers and roofs, where two sections of the roof come together in valleys or ridges, between plumbing vents and roofs or between exterior walls and the tops of doors and window frames. Flashing diverts the flow of water and prevents leakage into the house by forcing water to flow over it from a higher level.

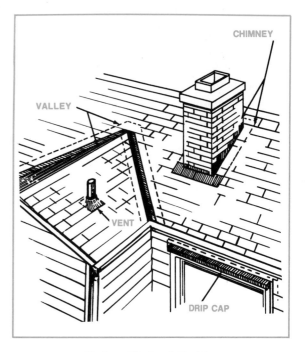

Various Kinds of Flashing

Flashing is made of sheets of galvanized steel, copper, lead, aluminum, plastic, asphalt roll roofing, felt, or rubber, depending on the specific flashing joint to be installed or repaired. *SEE ALSO ROOF CONSTRUCTION.*

Flat File

The flat file, which is tapered in width and thickness, is generally used by machinists for smoothing metals. The flat file will range in length from four to eight inches and, unlike some files, is available in only three cuts — bastard, second and smooth. *SEE ALSO HAND TOOLS.*

Flat Finish

A flat finish in painting refers to a finish which lacks gloss or sheen. Flat finishes are used on walls and ceilings of living areas because they reduce glare by reflecting less light to the eye than glossy finishes. The vinyl types can be washed, but not scrubbed like semi-gloss or high-gloss enamel and are, therefore, not recommended for woodwork or hard-use areas. *SEE ALSO PAINTS & PAINTING.*

Flat-Nose Pliers

Flat-nose pliers are also known as duck-bill pliers. Their smooth jaws make holding fine or flat bits of heated metal easy, without scarring the surface. *SEE ALSO HAND TOOLS.*

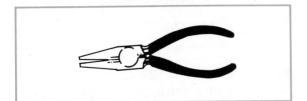

Flat-Nose Pliers

Flat Roof

A flat roof is any roof which is either completely flat or only slightly pitched to provide proper water drainage. These roofs are more common on skyscrapers and office buildings than on homes. *SEE ALSO ROOF CONSTRUCTION.*

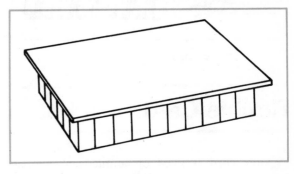

Flat Roof

Flat Varnishes

Flat varnishes are durable, nonglossy varnishes which give a rich, satin finish without the work of sanding and waxing the final coat. They also eliminate the need for sanding between coats of varnish.

Flat varnish is not as clear as glossy varnish, but the difference is hardly noticeable so that two coats of it can be used without dulling the finish. However, three coats of flat varnish may mean the loss of transparency. *SEE ALSO WOOD FINISHING.*

Flexible Armored Cable

Flexible armored cable, usually referred to by the trade name BX or Flexsteel, is an easily installed cable, widely used in either concealed or surface interior wiring. It cannot be exposed to moisture or weather. This cable consists of two or three insulated wires wrapped in heavy

paper and then enclosed in a spiraled steel armor. This armor permits flexibility and makes the cable a grounding conductor. Also enclosed in the cable is a small uninsulated grounding wire which the handyman may discard or ignore. *SEE ALSO WIRE SIZES & TYPES.*

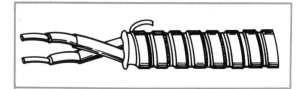

Flexible Armored Cable

Flexible Cord

Flexible cord is used on appliances such as lamps, radios, vacuum cleaners, shavers, power tools, etc., that will be plugged and unplugged frequently. For flexibility, the cord is composed of many strands of fine copper wire covered with a layer of cotton which prevents the insulation from sticking to the copper wire. The outer covering on flexible cord can be made of rubber, cotton, rayon or plastic.

There are several kinds of flexible cords with different thicknesses of insulation depending on the use of the cord. The major kinds are Type SPT, Type S and Type HPD.

TYPE SPT

Type SPT is most commonly used for radios, lamps and other small appliances. Its copper wires are embedded in flexible plastic. There is a groove in the insulation to permit separation of the two wires where a connection is made. Type SPT is durable, inexpensive and available in several colors. The same kind of cord known as Type SP has rubber insulation instead of plastic.

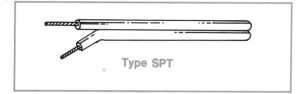

Type SPT

TYPE S

Type S can withstand more wear and tear than Types SPT or SP and is water resistant for use with garage and workshop equipment. In Type S, each wire is rubber insulated, then twisted together and rounded out with jute or paper twine and finally covered with a layer of high grade rubber. Type SJ is similar, but the outer layer of rubber is much thinner. If neoprene is used instead of rubber for the outer covering, Types S and SJ are designated SO and SJO, which means that they are oil resistant.

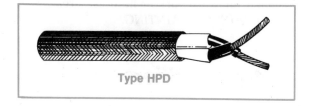

Type S

TYPE HPD

Type HPD, or heater cord, is used with irons, toasters, portable heaters and other appliances that generate large amounts of heat. Its copper wires are covered with rubber and a layer of asbestos before being twisted and wrapped in a final covering of either cotton or rayon. If this type wire has an outer layer of rubber it is called Type HSJ.

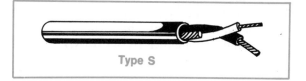

Type HPD

The National Electric Code prohibits the use of flexible cord as a substitute for permanent wiring, specifying also that it cannot be spliced or tapped. *SEE ALSO PLUGS & CORDS.*

Flint Paper

Flint paper is a cheap sandpaper with an abrasive or grit of soft quartz. It is used for sanding off old paint or for working on waxy or resinous surfaces, because it cuts slowly and

clogs easily. For these reasons flint paper should be discarded frequently. Flint paper is not suited for work on good, unpainted wood, because it is not sharp enough and dulls too rapidly. *SEE ALSO ABRASIVES.*

Float, Bull
[SEE CONCRETE AND MASONRY TOOLS.]

Float, Darby
[SEE CONCRETE AND MASONRY TOOLS.]

Floating Shelves
[SEE SHELVES & SHELF CONSTRUCTION.]

Float Valve

A float valve is the toilet water inlet valve which extends from the float arm. Besides refueling the toilet tank after it has been flushed, this valve also shuts the water off.

The float valve's function follows a series of movements in the flushing process. After the flush valve, located in the bottom of the tank, allows water to rush into the toilet bowl, the float ball, attached to the opposite end of the float arm and lifted by the handle's turn, drops. This movement opens the float valve. Through it, fresh water comes into the tank. When the float ball in the water reaches a certain level in the tank, the water is automatically shut off by this valve. The float valve brings in water more slowly than the flush valve, thus making the filling process longer than the flushing process.

There are two types of float valves: the vacuum breaker and the non-vacuum breaker. A vacuum breaker has bonnets and air inlets an inch or more above the water overflow level, while a non-vacuum breaker is beneath the water flow. The vacuum is preferred because it prevents toilet tank water from mixing with the home's water supply. *SEE ALSO TOILET.*

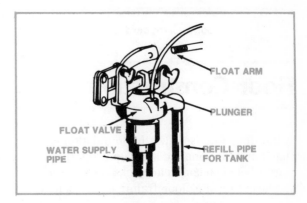

Float Valve Connection

Flock

The term flock is used to describe both stuffing and a decorative finish. When used as a padding, flock is scraps of cotton or wool used to stuff furniture or mattresses. It is also a very short or pulverized fiber used as a protective covering on metal or a decorative pattern on cloth or paper. The very popular flocked wallpaper has a paper backing with short fibers attached by an adhesive forming a set pattern.

Floodlamp
[SEE PHOTOGRAPHY.]

Floor & Clapboard Chisel

A floor and clapboard chisel has a narrow blade and a long shaft. Its most common size is 18 inches. The main purposes of this tool are to remove clapboards, cut nails, pry in depth and open crates. *SEE ALSO HAND TOOLS.*

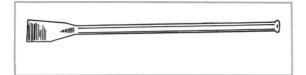

Floor & Clapboard Chisel

Floor Construction

In building a house after the foundation is completed and the concrete is set up properly (or the mortar between concrete blocks is set), work can be started on the floor framing, also called the platform or deck.

In many areas local codes or conditions require that a termite shield of sheet copper, aluminum or galvanized steel be fitted on top of the foundation under the sill. This strip of metal is wide enough to cover the top of the foundation and projects a couple of inches on either side. There is some question about the effectiveness of termite shields, as even the originator of the device has expressed doubts as to whether it really keeps out termites. A more certain protection is to use pressure-treated lumber that is toxic to the insects and also is rot-resistant. Another method is to poison the soil under and around the foundation with chlordane or other chemical. In this time of ecology and conservation such poisoning is not popular, as the chemical stays in the soil for many years before leaching out from rain.

If a termite shield is used, it is drilled or punched to fit over the anchor bolts (J-bolts) in the foundation and the mud sill fitted over it. The term *mud sill,* incidentally, originated from the practice of using a mortar mud under the sill to assure a flat, true surface on the foundation for the sill. A 2 x 8 generally is used for the sill and it is positioned so its outer edge is the thickness of the sheathing from the outer edge of the foundation. If a brick or masonry veneer is to be applied, the foundation will be wider than normal at that point and the sill is set back to allow for the thickness of the masonry plus the sheathing; sometimes an air space is specified by the architect and this would require an additional setback of the sill.

The sill is positioned with its end flush with the end of the foundation, and against the anchor bolts. A square is used to draw a line along each side of the bolts, then the sill is removed and holes drilled between the lines, spaced from the edge as determined by the factors described. The holes are drilled $1/4$ inch oversize to allow for adjustment of the sill. Replace the sill on the foundation (a strip of resilient sill-sealer may be fitted under the sill to assure an airtight seal), fit washers on the bolts, turn on the nuts and snug them up. Check for any spaces under the sill and use wedges to keep the sill flat and level. Tighten the nuts on the bolts.

Because the average home is too wide for a single length of floor joist to provide adequate strength, it is necessary to have one or more girders the length of the foundation to support the joists between the foundation walls. In a building with a crawl space, the girders are supported on piers. The piers can be solid cast concrete, or a footing on which concrete-block are assembled and mortar is used. The height of the piers is determined by the kind of girder used, which can be wood or steel. Local codes generally will specify the size and kind of girder, and the architect will specify it on the blueprints and in the materials list.

A wooden girder can be a solid timber, such as a 4 x 6, 4 x 8, etc., but since such heavy timbers are expensive and getting more difficult to obtain, girders usually are made by spiking lengths of 2 inch lumber together. Thus, a 4 x 6 girder would be two 2 x 6s.

In a structure with a basement, the girders would be supported on wood or steel columns or, occasionally, on a masonry partition. These columns are set on concrete footings poured before the floor is poured.

If wooden columns are used (steel is more common), a short pier is poured to project a couple of inches above the floor. This assures that moisture will drain away from the bottom of the column. A steel bolt or pin cast in the pier fits in

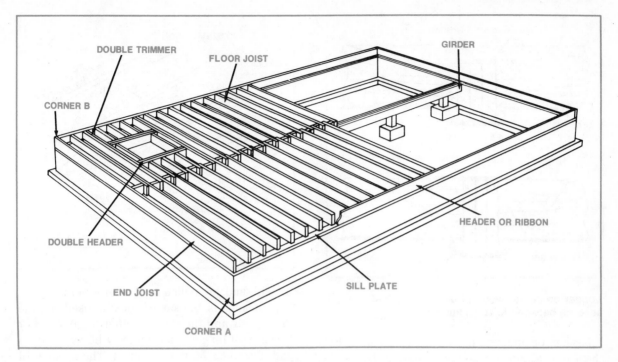

DOUBLE TRIMMER
FLOOR JOIST
GIRDER
CORNER B
HEADER OR RIBBON
DOUBLE HEADER
END JOIST
SILL PLATE
CORNER A

Typical Floor Framing

a hole in the bottom of the column to keep it in position. Steel brackets also can be used at the bottom of the column to hold it in place and assure drainage. The top of a wooden column is attached to a wooden girder with angle brackets or other device. Steel columns will have caps that fit under a wood or steel girder.

When a wooden girder is used, the columns or piers are a height that locates the top of the girder flush with the top of the mud sill. If a steel girder is used, its top should be flush with the top of the foundation. When a piece of 2 inch lumber is bolted to the girder it will be flush with the sill. The ends of a joist are fitted in notches cast or formed in the foundation. If the wood is untreated there should be a $1/2$ inch clearance all around to allow air circulation. In areas where termites are a problem, the recess generally is lined with metal.

While the simplest floor-joist framing has the joists setting on top of the girder, greater headroom can be provided (from floor to ceiling in the basement) by using ledger strips on the joists to support the inner ends of the floor joists. This permits raising the girder several inches. A

solid tie between exterior walls is created by nailing notched joists together. Joists must bear on the ledgers, not on top of the girder. In some methods a scab connects the two joist ends and provides a nailing surface for the flooring. A steel strap can connect the joists when the beam and joist tops are level. In a situation where space is required for a heat duct in a partition over a girder, a spaced wood girder can be used. Blocking is used between the girders where space permits.

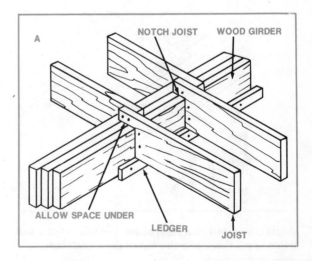

A
NOTCH JOIST   WOOD GIRDER
ALLOW SPACE UNDER
LEDGER
JOIST

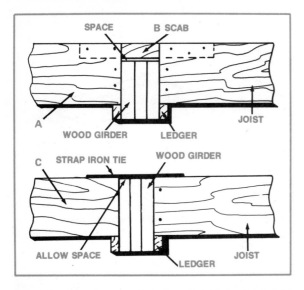

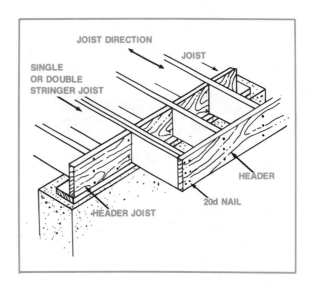

Ledger on center wood girder: A, Notched Joist; B, scab tie between joist; C, flush Joist.

Joists can be attached to a steel girder somewhat the same as on a wooden girder. A ledger is bolted to the beam and the ends of the joists rest on it. The joists can rest directly on the lower flange of the beam, which must be an "H" beam rather than an "I" beam, because the latter has too much slope on the flanges. Because there is no way to attach the joists to the flange of the beam, blocking is used between the joists to prevent them turning over.

A joist header (ribbon or boxing board) is positioned on edge around the foundation on top of

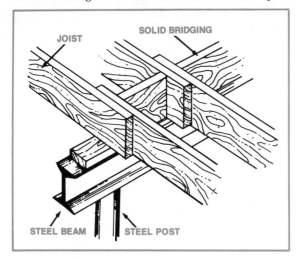

Joists supported on a steel beam. The top of the steel beam is set flush with the top of the foundation wall.

the sill, and toe-nailed to it with 8 penny nails. This header is the same stock as used for the floor joists and the size, whether 2 x 6, 2 x 8 or larger, will be governed by local building codes and described on the blueprint. The spacing of the joists is marked by the header, with single vertical lines. An X is marked on the side of the line to which the joists are located. When joists are overlapped on the girder (and the overlap should be at least 8 inch, the Xs on the opposite header are marked on the opposite side of the lines to allow for the offset created by the overlapping.

Standard construction calls for the joists to be spaced 16 inches on center. A new construction method called *Mod 24* has been developed by the Western Wood Products Association, and floor joists and wall studs are spaced 24 inches on center. The wider spacing calls for top-grade lumber and tighter quality control, but it does save lumber (and cost) which makes it worthwhile in this time of lumber shortages and rapidly rising prices. Local building codes will determine whether Mod 24 can be used, or standard 16 inch spacing. Both spacing methods accept standard 4 x 8 ft. sheets of plywood subflooring or underlayment, or other panel materials. When you lay out the joist spacing, start with the joist header, so that the edge of a 4 or 8 ft. panel of flooring material will locate on the center of a joist. This will provide nailing surface.

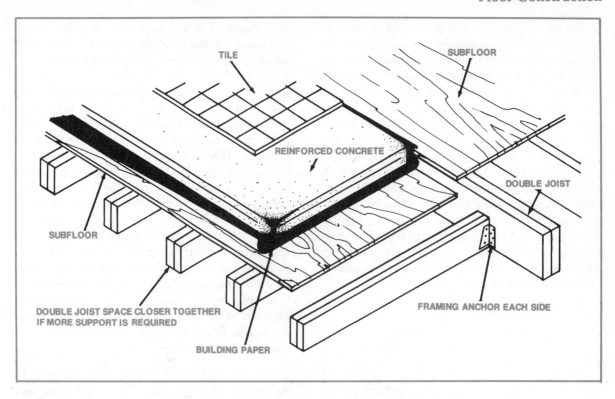

Lowering the floor frame to accommodate a concrete base for tile or stone surfaces.

Follow the architect's blueprints carefully to determine in which direction the floor joists run (usually across the narrow width of the foundation, but not always); what the spacing should be and where openings are located. Also check for locations of partitions; a double joist is used under partitions. Where wiring, water or drain pipes and heating ducts are to be run, the double joists are spaced to allow for easy installation of these items. Walls or partitions that have pipes or ducts in them usually are built from 2 x 6s rather than 2 x 4s, so the joists under these walls should be spaced accordingly.

Joists also are doubled around openings in the floor framing for stairways, chimneys and fireplaces. These doubled joists are called *trimmers* and support the headers that carry the tail joists. Lay out the standard joist spacing on the headers and add for any doubled joists and trimmer joists needed along the opening. Where regular joists will become tail joists, change the Xs on the header to Ts so you don't inadvertently install full-length joists at these locations.

Double joists are spiked together with 16 penny nails spaced about 1 foot apart near the upper and lower edges. Start by driving several nails straight through and clinching the ends to draw the joists together, then finish with 16 penny nails driven at an angle, so they do not go all the way through and also will hold better. Be sure that the ends of all joists are cut square and true and that joists are full length. Poor fits and short pieces will reduce the strength of the floor platform considerably, and a building inspector could require you to tear out the framing and redo it to meet specifications. Floor loading usually is figured at 30 to 40 pounds per square foot.

Use straight lumber for framing openings. Where a joist has a slight crown in it, position the crown upward; a normal floor load will force the joist level. If a joist is really curved, cut it at the high point of the crown and use the shorter pieces for another part of the framing where the curve will not matter.

627

When an assembly of tail joists and headers is small, the pieces sometimes are nailed together first, then the assembly is fitted in place and nailed to the other joists. In most cases the headers are installed first, then the tail joists are nailed to them. One of the tail joists can be nailed to a header to accurately locate the header and hold it while it is being nailed. Be sure to check the blueprints for areas where a foundation will be required for supporting a concrete slab on which tile for a fireplace hearth or bathroom will be located. In such cases you use narrower joists, doubled to support a floor below the regular floor. Note that joist hangers are used for these smaller doubled joists. Similar metal hangers can be used for holding the inner ends of joists and attaching them to wooden girders.

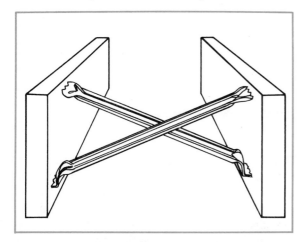

Metal bridging between joists.

Cross-bridging or solid bridging often is used in house construction in floor framing. The bridging can be strips of wood, fitted at an angle from near the top of one joist to the bottom of the adjacent joist, or manufactured metal devices that are hammered into place. Solid blocking is just short lengths of wood and the same size as the joists and nailed between them. Research has shown that bridging or blocking does little good in adding structural strength to floor framing, but many building codes require it, specifying a spacing of no more than 8 ft. Solid blocking can be located to provide nailing surfaces for the ends of plywood flooring. Because the pieces of blocking are staggered to permit nailing into them through the joists, alternate blocking will

be a couple of inches back from the edge. A second piece of blocking every other set of joists will provide nailing surfaces if required.

Plywood is the most commonly used subflooring today. In some instances 1 inch lumber is nailed diagonally across the joists, but this takes more time and costs more for material than the plywood. Where a second flooring is to be installed, a $1/_2$-in. plywood can be used, as under hardwood strip flooring. For kitchens and bathrooms where a resilient floor tile or sheet flooring is to be used, $5/_8$ inch plywood is installed. It generally has a tongue or groove on all four edges to assure a strong, tight floor. Flooring should be described on the blueprint, Fig. 18 and listed on the materials list. Some accommodation must be made to position the top of the plywood to be flush with the top of the finished hardwood floor. This will be described on the blueprints.

Sheets of plywood are installed with the grain of the outside plies at right angles to the joists, and staggered so the ends of adjacent panels fall over different joists. Nail the panels with 8 penny nails spaced 6 inches apart along the edges and 10 inches apart across the joists. Where plywood is both subfloor and underlayment as in a kitchen or bath, nails are spaced 6 inches along the edges and across the joists.

FRAMING AT WALL PROJECTIONS

Floor framing under projections beyond the foundation, whether on the first or second floor, consists of extensions of the floor joists. These may be with the projection in line with the joists or with the projection at right angles to the joists. Metal hangers can be used in the latter case to assure a strong, riged assembly. The subflooring is extended flush to the edges of the projecting framing members.

Projections are right angles to the floor joists should be no more than 24 inches and the width should be kept to a minimum. To reduce the load on such a projection, very often the roof rafters are carried on a heavy header over the opening in the wall. The weight of the roof then is carried mostly by the header.

The floor framing described is the *box sill* or *western*. *Balloon framing* seldom is used today, but differs from box-sill framing by having the wall studs run full-length from the floor of the first story to the ceiling of the second story. The disadvantage of balloon framing, other than the need for very long studs, is that the spaces between the studs have no natural fire stops, as does the platform framing described.

The regular framing creates a platform for the first floor on which the wall studs are positioned, and a second platform for the second floor. An alternate floor-framing method coming into use more with the shortage of lumber, is the truss-joist system. In this system a 2 x 4 is used for the top and bottom members that are spaced by short pieces of 2 x 4. Reinforcement is by wood or metal members that create rigid triangles between the upper and lower 2 x 4s.

When applying the plywood decking to the floor framing if there is a chance that snow or rain will fall on the flooring, use plywood rate exterior grade or waterproof. Interior plywood may buckle, warp or delaminate when wet.

Floor Drain

A floor drain is a cast-iron soil pipe fitting. Its function is to receive liquid from a floor level surface and allow it to flow through a p-trap and into the drainage system. A metal screen is placed over the upper portion of a floor drain to prevent objects from falling into it. *SEE ALSO PIPE FITTINGS.*

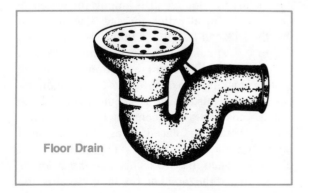

Floor Drain

Floor Finishes

Floor finishes for wood floors must be durable and have a pleasing, suitable appearance. The finishes used for floors, such as varnish, shellac, lacquer or polyurethane, are basically the same finishes used on other wood, although the method of application for floor finishes may differ somewhat.

Penetrating wood finishes, which are generally considered the best, supply an in-the-wood finish. These materials have a hardening effect on the wood, make it more wear-resistant, and give the finished floor a lustrous sheen. They are also the easiest to apply, and are easily repaired if a spot becomes worn.

Shellac is used most often on floors than on any other surface. It is economical, flexible, and dries quickly. Shellac is also "patchable." A worn spot on a floor can be feathered in with new finish for a patch that is hardly visible. Although not very water resistant, shellac becomes very durable with a good wax covering it.

Varnish is very resistant to abrasion, although it does not penetrate the wood very deeply after the first coat. Varnish finishes must be allowed to dry for 24 hours.

The main advantage of a lacquer finish is its ability to dry quickly. Two or more coats of lacquer can be applied in a 24 hour period.

Oil-modified urethanes, or polyurethanes, are *air-drying* finishes. A film is left on the floor by the evaporation of the solvents. *Moisture-cure* urethanes do not actually "dry". The film left by the material cures and hardens as it takes up moisture from the air. These finishes must be used in areas with sufficient ventilation. Polyurethanes are the best materials to use for an in-the-wood finish, and are available as satin or semi-gloss. Moisture-cure urethanes have the highest degree of resistance to wear.

The first step in floor finishing is to remove the old finish. A new floor should be sanded clean and dry before finishing. The old finish is best removed with a good floor sander, which may be rented from a hardware store. Final hand sanding on spots the sander cannot reach, such as in corners and close to the walls, gives best results.

There are three stains which are generally used for most floor coloring: penetrating wiping stains, water stains and nongrain-raising stains. Pigmented wiping stains must be continually stirred, for they have solid pigments suspended in them. They are used under varnishes or penetrating finishes.

Water stains work like cloth dyes, permanently coloring the wood fibers. They are very economical, produce intense colors, and uniformly penetrate the wood. Nongrain-raising stains use little or no water and do not act to soften the wood grain. Either of these stains are good for use under lacquer, shellac, or spirit varnish top coats.

Nongrain-raising stains use little or no water and do not act to soften the wood grain. Either of these stains are good for use under lacquer, shellac, or spirit varnish top coats.

Wood fillers, for smoothing open pores in flooring materials, are not used as often today as in the past. Filler is used when a very smoothly varnished floor is desired. The filler should be completely dry before the top coat is applied.

The new finish is applied in two by six foot sections, parallel to the floor boards. A first layer of the finish is applied with a varnish brush, followed by a second application with a lamb's wool applicator. The floor should be burnished between coats, using a floor polisher containing a steel wool pad. The floor should be vacuumed after burnishing.

A layer of good paste wax on the finished floor will protect the surface, thus reducing maintenance time. Wax is applied with an electric buffer-polisher, containing a fine floor pad. The wax should be applied by two to three foot square sections, following application directions on the container. If a damp cloth applicator was used, any moisture should be removed from the floor and the paste should be smoothed out evenly before polishing. Some paste waxes are colored to darken a light or uneven stain. *SEE ALSO WOOD FINISHING.*

Floor Framing
[SEE FLOOR CONSTRUCTION; FRAMING]

Floor Jack

A floor jack, or jack post, is an adjustable device used to level or support sagging floors. The sag may be caused by heavy loads, inadequate post support, faulty house construction, or excessive settling of foundations or basement floors, which could result in sinking posts and twisting girders. The floor jack is composed of two steel tubes; one tube moves inside the other, and is raised to the needed height and then secured with a locking pin inserted into a hole in the outer tube. Plates are attached to the top and bottom of the jack, and the top plate is raised or lowered by a heavy screw. Floor jacks are available in lengths up to eight feet. Larger jacks, used on sagging floors over basements, are called jack columns and will adjust to the standard floor-to-ceiling height.

Check floors for sagging by placing a straight-edged board over the suspected droop, or by rolling a marble across the floor to determine any recurring sloping. It is important to locate the exact point at which the sag is greatest, so that the jack can be applied under this spot from the crawl space, room or basement below. Establish a stable base for the bottom plate of the jack by stacking two or three 2 x 6 boards on the bottom-level joists. This is not necessary if the jack is to be based on a concrete floor. A similar bridge should be placed across the overhead joists for load distribution. The jack is then placed between the two levels, and the screw is turned so that the top plate fits snugly against the

overhead bridging. Make sure that the jack is exactly plumb, and then nail or bolt the top plate to the boards to prevent sliding. It is important that the sag is corrected gradually — raising the jack too rapidly may cause damaging rupture in the floor structure. The jack should be tightened approximately one fourth inch each day until the sag is sufficiently corrected. A slight over-raise is advisable, to account for slight settling of the

floor due to removal of the jack. To make sure the sag does not recur, the corrected joists should be reinforced by spiking a few two-inch planks to the joists while the jack is still in place. These planks should be the same width as the joists. If the sag is not too pronounced and the load the floor must bear is not too heavy, one plank for each joist should suffice.

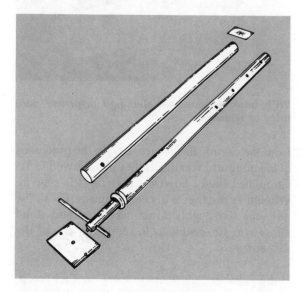

Floor Jack

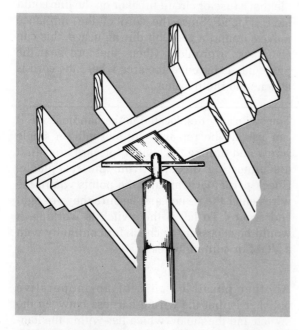

2 x 4 boards placed under sagging joists provides for load distribution.

Floor Joists

Floor joists are the backbone supports on which a floor, or platform, rests. Joists are made of wood, steel or concrete, and are usually placed 16 inches apart. The ends of the joists are placed on the sills, or on girders, which are intermediate joist supports. *SEE ALSO FLOOR CONSTRUCTION.*

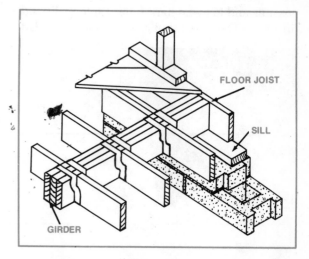

Floor Joists

Floor Plans

A floor plan is a detailed, cross-sectional drawing of a building, horizontally crossing all openings, regardless of the opening height. The floor plan denotes the outside shape of the building, the size, shape and arrangement of the rooms, the type of materials used, and the length and thickness of building walls. The plan also tells

the location and width of doors and windows, and the location of utility installations and stairways. *SEE ALSO BLUEPRINTS.*

Floor Polisher Repair

Most floor polishers that are used around the home are powered by a universal motor with a double shaft. A worm gear is machined into the ends of this shaft. This drives a pinion gear which in turn drives the brushes. The gear train serves to reduce the rotation of the motor to a usable speed and also to increase the torque that is necessary to drive the brushes. It also serves to turn the brushes at a right angle to the direction of motor rotation.

It's important to keep the polisher as clean as possible and to avoid hard bumps into walls and furniture. The motor and gear train are shielded

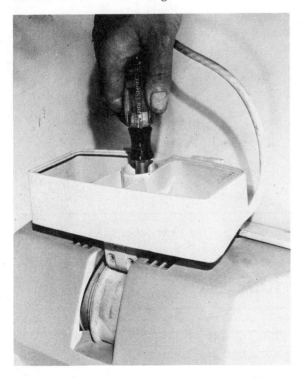

Floor polishers can be deceivingly simple in appearance. To disassemble, first remove handle assembly and look closely at attachment points for hidden nuts. A nut driver is used to remove base so that housing from motor unit can be removed.

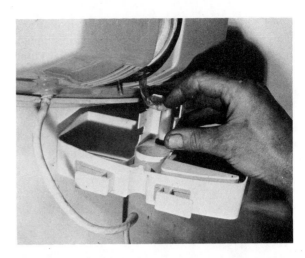

With housing loosened, shampoo dispenser hose must be removed.

from the chemicals that are used in the processes of cleaning and waxing. If they are allowed to accumulate heavily, however, they can still seep in. When they do, they will cause damage. Clean the polisher thoroughly after each use and don't allow wax or chemicals to remain in any of the dispensers.

If the polisher fails to operate, try another receptacle which is known to be operating. It's possible that a fuse or circuit breaker on the line could have tripped. Since the cord of the appliance moves around a good bit during usage, this can also cause a problem. Check the cord near the plug and also around the area where the cord is attached to the polisher.

The switch is often located in the handle itself. It can usually be removed by loosening a single screw and pulling the switch forward after first disconnecting the plug from the receptacle. Check particularly around the points where the wires enter the switch and be sure they are tight and secure. To tell if the switch is working, it would be necessary to check for continuity with a VOM or continuity tester.

Another possible cause of an inoperative polisher is that the wiring harness between the switch and the motor, which lies within the handle, may be old. It should be checked for a break here also.

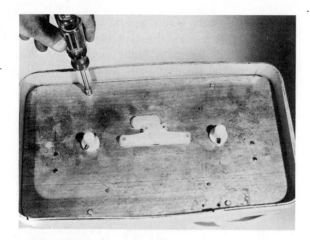

Base is loosened by removing screws from around outer circumference.

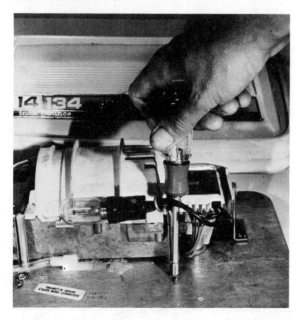

With housing removed, gear cover retaining plates are loosened from base.

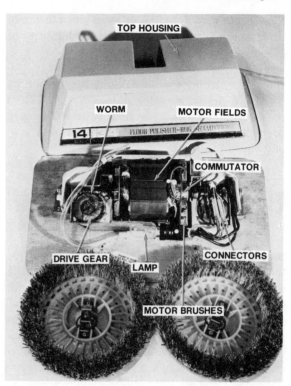

Finally cover plates are removed, exposing gear drive mechanism, motor bearings and motor brushes.

Most polisher motors use carbon brushes. If they become worn they can prevent the motor from starting. To check them, remove the motor shield and remove the motor brush covers by loosening the cap or retaining screw. If the brushes are less than a quarter of an inch in length it's time to replace them.

Motor damage is often visible. Look for loose or broken wires around the armature and the field of the motor.

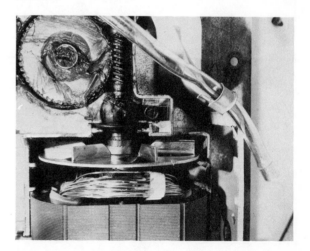

Close-up of drive mechanism shows how worm turns driving gear which turns brushes. Fan on motor shaft provides cooling for field winding.

Worn or broken gears are easily replaced. Most polishers have left and right side gears, with the teeth cut in different directions. When obtaining a replacement be sure and specify which side you need.

633

Most gears use "C" clips or snap rings to retain the gears in place. Wear goggles or shatterproof glasses when removing them.

Check for grounds with a VOM before putting the floor polisher back into service. When reassembling the housing, be sure all wiring is in correct position away from the motor shaft and any revolving parts.

Floor Squeak Repair

Squeaks in floors are usually caused by sags or loose boards. There are several cures for a squeaky floor: applying graphite powder or oil, or bracing with strips of wood, screws, nails and wooden shingle strips. The simplest way to eliminate squeaks in hardwood strip or block floors is to apply powdered graphite or commercial oil to the squeaky area. If the floor is properly finished, the oil will not leave stains when the excess oil is removed.

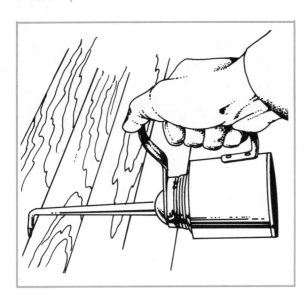

Oil a squeaky joint with commercial lubricants

When graphite or oil fail to stop a squeak, nails may be used. Place two 8d finishing nails approximately one inch apart and, while applying downward pressure on the board, drive the nails at opposite angles toward the squeak. Pilot holes may be necessary when nailing in hard floors, such as oak, to prevent the nails from bending or splitting. Drill the pilot holes slightly smaller than the nail shank diameter.

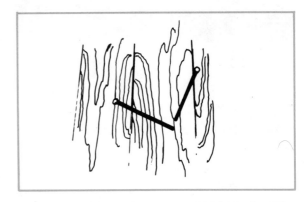

Nails driven at opposite angles may stop a squeak.

If the squeak still persists, go down to the basement or under the house and drive a wooden shingle wedge between the top of the joist and the bottom of the subflooring. Hammer in the wedge so that it fits tightly, but does not strain the subflooring. This may be done at several points on the adjoining joists until the squeak is eliminated.

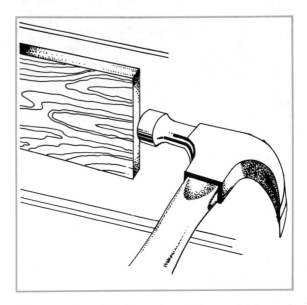

Drive wooden shingle wedges between joists and subflooring to eliminate squeaks.

Another method of floor squeak repair is to nail a 1 x 4 or 1 x 6 lumber cleat at the squeaky point.

To do this, cut a 2 x 4 post an inch or two longer than the distance between the subflooring and the basement floor or ground. Use the post to slightly lift the subflooring while nailing the cleat to the joist. When nailing is completed, remove the post.

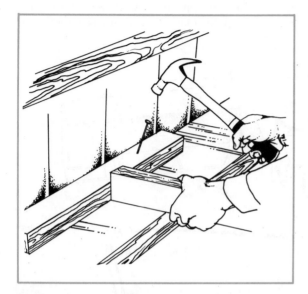

Squeaks may be stopped by nailing a cleat to a joist at the squeaky area.

Squeaks in floors covered with resilient tile or sheet metal are caused by sags in the subflooring. This can be corrected with the shingle wedge or brace methods previously described. If

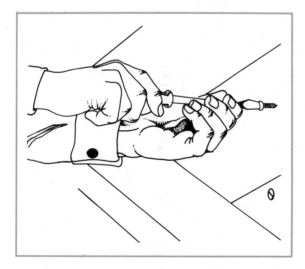

Screws driven into the bottom subflooring are good for curing squeaks in tile-covered floors.

neither of these work, remove the finish material around the squeaky area and drive nails at the squeaky spot. Be sure the nails are driven flush before replacing the flooring. When access to a basement is available, resilient floor squeaks may be corrected by drilling wood screws through the subflooring and into the hardwood. Pilot holes can be predrilled and the screws coated in glue to provide more holding power after the screw is driven into the wood.

Floors, Seamless
[SEE SEAMLESS FLOORS.]

Flue

A flue is a passage in the chimney which allows gases and smoke to pass from the chimney. There should be 15 to 16 inches of flue area for each square foot of fireplace opening.

Flues should remain the same size and run as straight as possible to the top of the chimney. Sharp setbacks or steps should be avoided. If offsets or turns are impossible to avoid, they should be gradual with no narrowing of the passage way. Round flues provide easier cleaning and less resistance to spirally moving gases than square or oblong flues.

Flues should be lined with a fire-resisting material. Local codes will specify type and size of lining. The simplest method of lining a flue is to use a commercial flue liner. This is usually installed as the chimney is constructed. There should be at least four inches of masonry on each side of the flue. *SEE ALSO FIREPLACES.*

Fluorescent Lighting

Fluorescent lights improve the efficiency of lighting while adding a natural quality to the illumination. These lamps last as much as 15 times

longer and produce many more lumens, or "light power", than incandescent bulbs which use the same amount of current and produce much more heat.

Most fluorescent lamps require a starter with an automatic switch. However, there are some rapid-starting types that do not need a starter.

Both types operate similarly. A small transformer, two filaments, a mixture of gas and mercury vapor and an inner lining of phosphors compose the rest of the lamp's working parts. The current first flows through a filament, the ballast, the starter, and then through a second filament at the opposite end of the tube before producing light. Once the circuit is completed,

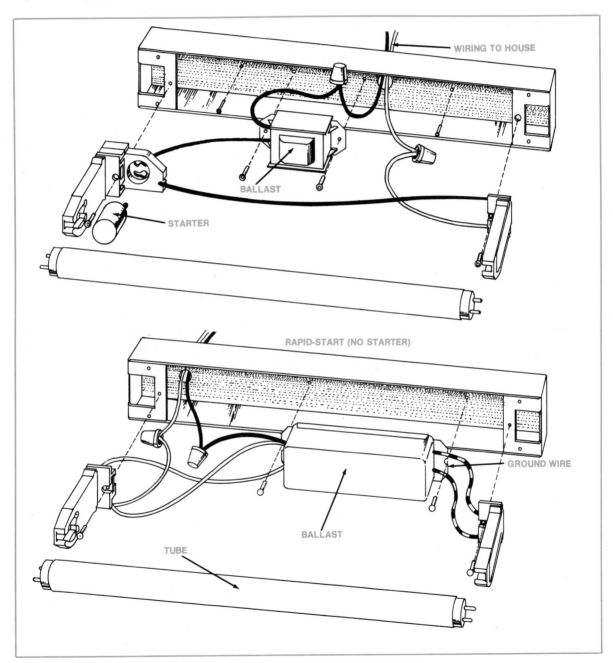

WIRING TO HOUSE

BALLAST

STARTER

RAPID-START (NO STARTER)

GROUND WIRE

BALLAST

TUBE

Fluorescent lamp with and without starter.

the starter switch opens and the ballast produces a surge of electricity to make the filament send an arc of ultra-violet light through the mercury and gas vapor. This arc creates a glow which filters through the phosphors, creating the bright light of the lamp. Once started, the arc will continue without the extra power surge. The ballast then acts as a step-down transformer to control electric current.

The fluorescent light was once solely used in industry, particularly for plant lighting because its long cylindrical shape and usually naked bulb made the lamp aesthetically unpleasant in the home. However, many architects have since found that the advantages of fluorescent lights (long life, more light for less electricity and heat, etc.) make them assets to the home. These bulbs are now being inserted into many panel-type lighting fixtures, creating a natural quality to home lighting and cutting down on electrical bills.

There are two forms of fluorescent lights: decorative and utility forms. Any permanent fluorescent fixture, regardless of its use in the home, should be connected with heavy-duty BX cable.

The utility form has a rectangular box with several knockouts, or holes about the size of a quarter, for easy wiring. There are simple mountings for the bulb, also. Both make mounting the utility lamp on ceiling joists an easier job. After mounting the light, connect it to the desired circuit with BX cable. Either a pull chain switch or wall switch is acceptable for activating the lamp.

The decorative form may be installed in a number of ways. For example, living room areas may require recessed fixtures while kitchen lamps would need only a short clear plastic covering. The procedure for mounting is the same as for utility form. However, where multi-outlet raceway systems are involved, there are special snap-in units that are inserted into the raceway itself.

There are clues (for instance, a flash before a steady glow) to look for in determining the condition of the lamp or its efficiency. As with all electrical devices, the voltage should be checked first.

A lamp will flash due to low voltage, while exposure to high voltage will result in dark spots close to both ends of the bulb. The lamp that has a brown tinge at the ends is burning normally. Black ends signify starter trouble. The decision to replace the starter or replace the entire lamp would depend on the age of the lamp.

Frequent on-off switching will damage a bulb. The starter capacity may not be suited to the bulb size, possibly resulting in a prematurely burned-out bulb. The capacity, printed on the side of the case, should be examined and a correct lamp size installed, if necessary.

A lamp that does not light may mean several things, one of which is a blown fuse. Check all fuses and circuit breakers. If the problem is not in the circuit, chances are that the starter, tube or ballast needs replacing.

A bulb that is not properly seated will blink on and off. Determine if the prongs at each end of the tube are straight. If not, sand and straighten the pins or clean and then sand the socket contacts.

A humming sound may mean ballast trouble. Usually the connections are loose. There is a low-noise type ballast available that will eliminate the hum by making a closer contact. *SEE ALSO DECORATING; ELECTRICAL WIRING.*

Flush Door

A flush door is even at all surfaces and angles, and lacks any trim. There are two main types of flush doors, the solid core, which is made by gluing narrow board blocks of different lengths inside the frame work, and the hollow core, which weighs about one third less than solid core type because they have spaced braces. Both the solid and hollow core doors are covered with thin sheets of material on each side to conceal the framework.

To construct a flush door, join the side pieces to the top and bottom rails with a mortise joint, and apply a strong adhesive to keep the joint secure. If a hollow core door is being made, space boards inside the frame vertically between the top and bottom rails and glue them in place. When a solid core door is made, boards may be placed both vertically and horizontally. After the core is laid, glued and dried, a solid sheet of plywood or other material is nailed and glued to each side of the frame. Plane and sand later to achieve level surfaces and corners. The door may then be finished in any way desired.

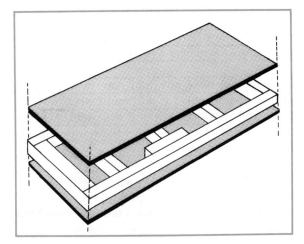

Hollow-Core Flush Door

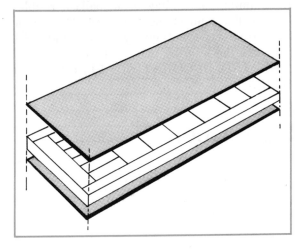

Solid-Core Flush Door

Flush Mechanisms
[SEE TOILET.]

Flush Tank Mounting

The flush tank of a toilet is mounted against the bathroom wall after the bowl is secured to its drain. Making this connection properly is important since the flush tank is considered the most widely used fixture for water supply to the water closet. Its fixed volume of water and gravity feed to the bowl gives it constant pressure.

The floor drain should be positioned close enough to the wall for the tank to be mounted soundly. It is better to have too much space between the drain and wall than too little, since it can be closed in by wood fittings. Re-adjustment is a big problem, however, when there is not enough room for the tank fixture to fit correctly.

Dimensional diagrams for new toilets called templates show how far a drain opening should be from the wall. Usually flanges, attached to the bowl base over the drain pipe, allow enough movement for correct alignment. Even so, the bowl should not be moved repeatedly because this could wear down the flange.

Before installing a used toilet, full-scale positions of the drain opening should be drawn off to make sure of ample space.

There are different designs in flush-tank mounting. Tanks positioned on the top rear of the bowl are sealed at the connecting water passage by a rubber gasket. A *spud* or chrome-plated pipe may connect other tank and bowl units. This pipe is placed several inches above the bowl. A spud wrench should be used for tightening rubber gaskets between the two parts.

Some flange-types of screws used for mounting the tank and those for fastening down the bowl are similar. One end resembles a bolt; the other end is threaded. Two nuts are tightened together on the bolt-threaded end when putting these screws into wood. The upper nut is turned with a small wrench when the wood-screw is driven into the floor or wall. The locked nuts can be removed when the wood-screw threads are in all

the way. Two wrenches might be needed for locking and unlocking. Screws and washers to match may be purchased.

When a toilet is mounted on a cement floor, the parts should be arranged so that the fastenings can be set into the cement in their proper places.

If this has not been done, masonry bolts may be used. *SEE ALSO TOILET.*

Flush Tank Repairs
[SEE TOILET REPAIRS.]

Flux

Flux is a substance used to dissolve the non-metallic oxide film on surfaces to be soldered. If this film is not removed, a layer of corrosion will be formed on the surfaces as they are soldered.

There are two types of flux. The acid flux, often used when soldering large objects, leaves potentially dangerous corrosive residues. These residues are capable of absorbing moisture from the air and can become electrical conductors. Once this happens, the residues can cause an electronic system to be short-circuited. Acid flux is good for soldering materials other than those used in electrical work.

The other type is rosin or resin flux. This is the one that should be used when soldering electrical wiring. Only corrosive when molten, rosin flux becomes a plastic-like, inert electrical insulator after cooling. Rosin flux is available in a solder wire so that as the solder liquifies, the correct amount of rosin flux will be applied to the area. After the solder solidifies in the joint, the oxide residues along with the rosin harden on the surface.

Fly Cutter

The fly cutter or circle cutter, referred to as a circle inscriber when used as a hand tool, is used

with a drill press or portable hand drill. The fly cutter is used for forming holes approximately 12″ in diameter or as small as ¹/₂″. The center pilot drill bit has a single cutter which is a special side-cutting device that revolves at the end of an adjustable arm.

Much like the pencil compass that draws a circle, the fly cutter inscribes and cuts a circle. When cutting, allow at least ⁵/₃₂″ for blade width. *SEE ALSO DRILL PRESS.*

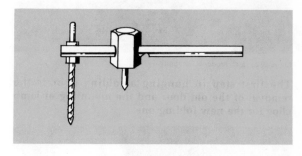

Fly Cutter

Folding Doors

Folding doors have three principal uses, each of them important in home planning and home improvement. They replace ordinary hinged doors where it is important to save the space that swinging doors use when opened or closed. They divide rooms, so that one room becomes two and then one again, as use changes. Finally they turn spaces, such as the ends of rooms, into full-access closets. Both accordion-fold and bi-fold doors serve these purposes, although the bi-fold kind are limited to situations where maximum compactness is not essential.

Most folding doors are made of either vinyl or solid wood, although a few are wood slats. Vinyl ones are very durable, easy to clean and attractive; and some of the more elegant woodgrain versions are acceptable in any room.

The first sequence of photographs shows how to install a typical inexpensive vinyl accordion-fold door in an ordinary doorway. It is used on a

bathroom, where the colorful vinyl seems appropriate.

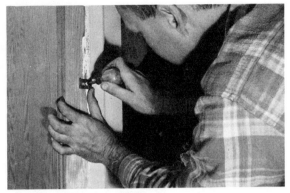

Courtesy of H. C. Products Company

The first step in hanging a folding door is the removal of the old door and the mounting of jamb clips for the new folding one.

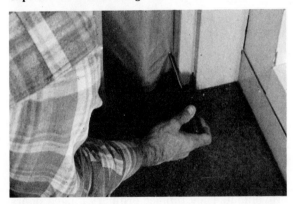

With the overhead track fastened by screws, the jamb side of the new folding door is attached to the clips just installed.

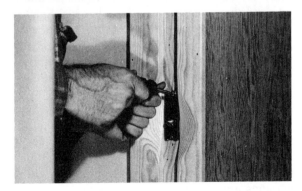

On the opposite side of the doorway goes the strike plate for the latch. Some types are mortised in, others surface-mounted. Trim was needed in this installation to cover the scars left by removal of the old hinges.

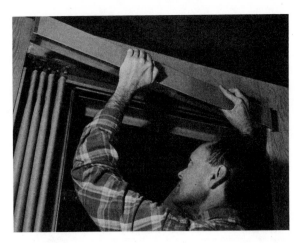

Decorative cornice is pushed into place and held by clips inserted between frame and roller track. This completes the installation.

The other photo-sequence shows the use of a solid walnut door to create new space by inclosing the end of a room. Walnut, with natural finish, was chosen for this study-bedroom to match existing woodwork. This is a natural use for a large folding door since, without taking up appreciable space, it converts the end of a room into a fully accessible closet. When the additional closet space is no longer needed in this house, the owner plans to use the area for a home office by building in a desk and file and cupboard space. The advantage of the folding door for this use is that it opens fully when the office is needed, closes instantly to hide all clutter when office use is over.

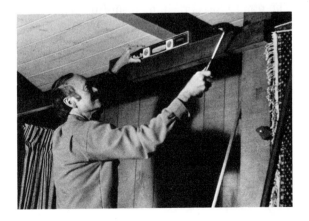

Before installation, a frame must be provided unless the opening is already framed to size. The beam to take the door track should be level.

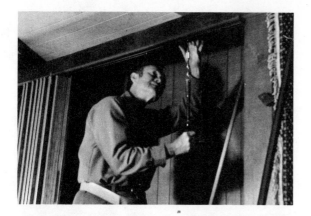

Track is first slipped over door glides, fastened to frame at one end and then the other.

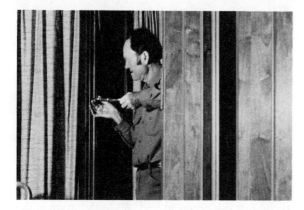

The trim consists of matching wood strip channeled to take end of door. One screw sets the magnetic latch.

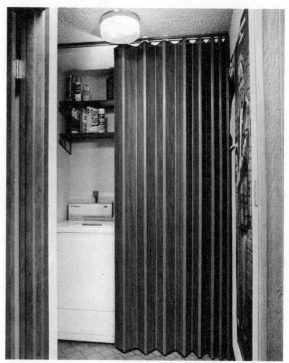

Courtesy of Woodfold-Marco Manufacturing Company, Forest Grove, Oregon

This Woodfold door of natural walnut, elegant enough for any room, turns a niche into a closet.

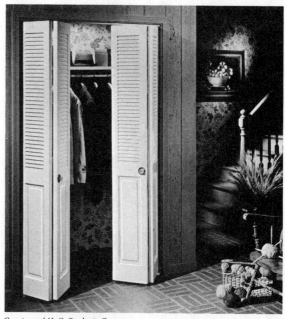

Courtesy of H. C. Products Company

Though less effective at saving space than accordion folding doors, bi-fold installations are much more compact than swinging doors and offer full access to closets as sliding doors do not.

Some of the places in a typical home where the space-saving and flexible-use qualities of a folding door are valuable are wardrobes, room dividers, creating family room, separating a dining area, hiding utility areas, surrounding a heating unit, preventing drafts, at kitchen-dining pass-through, to close off basement areas, and for temporary closures anywhere.

More than one-third of the space used by a swinging door is saved when it is replaced by a bi-fold and even that space requirement is cut in half with an accordion-fold door. When a swinging door is eliminated and a folding door is installed, enough space can be saved to permit adding a home office or a dressing table because a swinging door uses more than seven times the space of one that folds.

TYPICAL PROCEDURE FOR INSTALLING ACCORDION-TYPE VINYL DOORS

If the door is too long it may be shortened before installation by following these steps. Lay door flat. Peel back the vinyl 1/2 inch above point where you wish to cut. Mark the core stock where cut is to be made. Cut through the core stock using tin shears or razor knife, being careful not to cut vinyl.

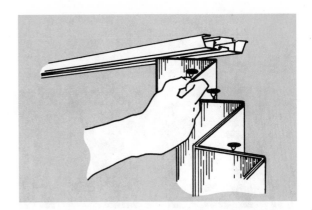

With a hacksaw or finishing saw, cut off end of lead post and anchor molding 1/2 inch longer than core stock. Reglue the vinyl with household glue and trim the vinyl even with bottom of lead post. Be sure to leave 1/2 inch of vinyl below core stock.

Now proceed with installation.

Fit the Track to the Opening. Measure the width at top of the opening and cut the track with a hacksaw to fit. If the opening is to be filled with a pair of doors meeting at center, an equal amount should be cut from each track.

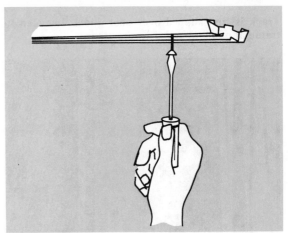

Holding the track against the top of the opening, mark the location of each screw hole. Set the track aside and make the starter hole for a screw with a small nail or drill.

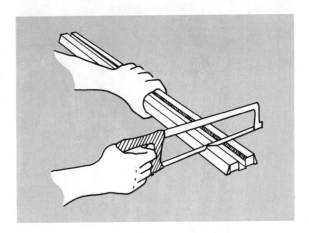

Slide the Door in the Track. Slide the nylon hanger glides into track slot. Make certain all glides are in place prior to mounting the track.

Install the Track. Stand the track up in the opening. Stack the door at one end while installing

screws at the opposite end. Slide the door to the fastened end of the track and install the remaining screws.

Attach the Fixed Jamb. Stack the door at the jamb and mark the location of the anchor flap. Spot tack the flap with the 3/4 inch nails which are furnished. Hold the anchor molding in position and drill the pilot holes. Fasten the anchor molding with short screws.

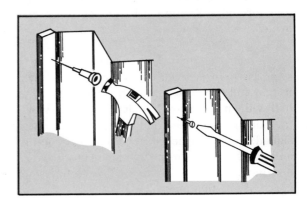

Lead Adjustment. If leading edge of door does not hang straight, adjustment may be made after the final installation. Each glide on an adjustable twinstile post hanger must be adjusted the same. Use the special wrench provided.

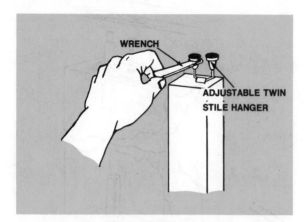

Attach the Latch Strike Plate. Close the door. Mark the top and bottom of the nylon latch insert on jamb (A). Set the escutcheon (B) and mark the screw holes. Make pilot holes. Insert nylon strike (C) in escutcheon (B) and attach to jamb with screw. Optional: to lock from other side, reverse the lock lever (D) by removing the screw. The strike assembly may be mortised into jamb if desired.

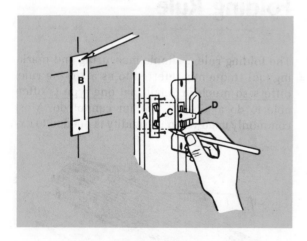

Pair of Doors. When installing a pair of stock doors in a single opening it will be necessary to remove the handle of one door to replace the latch lever and retainer plate with the strike. The latch and strike are interchangeable inserts. Escutcheon plates are not used on a pair of doors

and may be discarded along with the surplus latch lever and retainer plate.

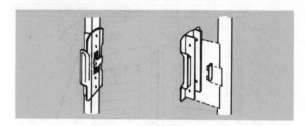

TYPICAL PROCEDURE FOR INSTALLING BI-FOLD DOORS

Step 1: For 4-panel opening, locate a top pivot assembly (spring loaded) in top of pivot panel, and in top and bottom of guide panel. Locate a bottom pivot assembly (screw adjustable) in bottom of pivot panel only. Fasten assemblies with $1/2$ inch screws provided. Caution: Over-tightening will strip threads.

For 2-panel opening, proceed as above for one pivot panel and one guide panel only.

Step 2: Fasten top track to header, approximately $7/8$ inch back from front of opening (allows for trim), using the $1^1/2$ inch screws provided.

Step 3: Place bottom pivot sockets in each end of bottom track before mounting.

Step 4: Fasten bottom track to floor directly in line with the top track, using the $1^1/2$ inch screws provided. Plumb to insure alignment between top and bottom tracks.

Step 5: Place top pin of pivot panel in track pivot bracket hole; lift panels (compressing spring), and seat bottom pivot in the bottom pivot socket hole. Repeat for other pair of panels, for 4-panel opening.

Step 6: Locate slide guide over top panel pin; then swing panel in line with track while compressing spring of pivot. Release pressure so slide guide seats into track.

Step 7: Install pivot glide cap bushing on bottom

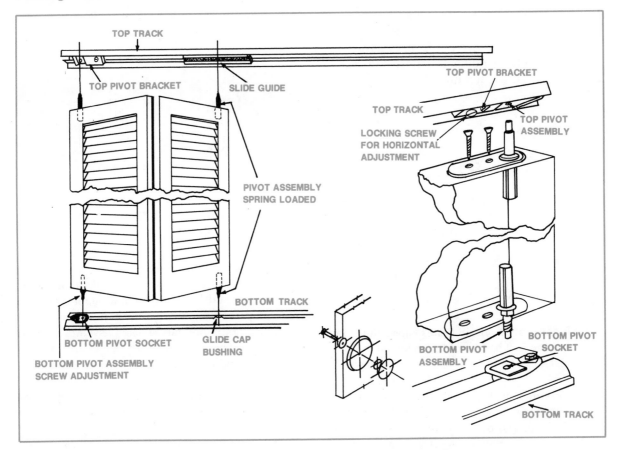

pin of each guide panel; compress spring and align bottom of panel with track. Release spring so pin and glide cap bushing seat in track.

Step 8: To adjust horizontally, use wrench to reposition top pivot brackets and bottom pivot sockets (in tracks). To adjust vertically, turn hex-head bolt on bottom pivot to raise or lower panel.

Step 9: Attach door knobs. Locate on guide panel of each pair, 34 inches above bottom of panel, and 1$\frac{1}{2}$ inches from hinged edge. Drill $\frac{3}{16}$ inch hole from back side of panel. Fasten knob and escutcheon plate.

Note: The above instructions also cover six and eight panel doors. A six panel installation consists of one 4-panel unit and one 2-panel unit. An eight panel installation consists of two 4-panel units.

Step 10: If doors bend inward at hinged joint; place a self-sticking felt button on the door edge within the open space of each butt hinge.

Folding Rule

The folding rule, a simple measuring and marking tool frequently referred to as a zig-zag rule, differs so much in detail that one type is often able to do a job that another cannot do. Most commonly used when its rigidity is needed to ex-

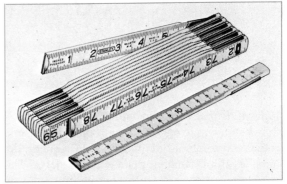

Courtesy The Stanley Works

Folding Rule

644

tend across wide openings such as doorways and stairwells, the 24″ folding rule is the most popular. This rule folds into a 6″ length, easy to tuck into a pocket. Often made of boxwood, it is now also available in white nylon which is impervious to moisture and humidity. Its hardware is stainless steel. Gradations are very distinct and easy to read. *SEE ALSO HAND TOOLS.*

Food Mixer Repair

Food mixers use a small universal motor, a speed control, and a drive train to turn two beaters. These are designed to give practically foolproof results in mixing, beating, and blending food. There are two primary types of food mixers: portable types which are hand-held and used in any type of food bowl, and the table type or stand type which generally has its own bowl and sits on a revolving turntable. As the food is mixed, the turntable revolves to feed more food into the beaters.

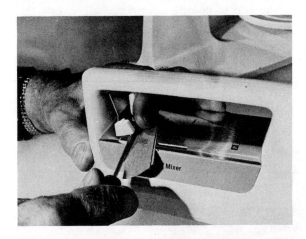

Begin mixer disassembly by unplugging, then removing the knobs. If it's necessary to pry against housing, use protective cloth or heavy paper as shown above.

From the standpoint of trouble-shooting the appliance, the primary difference is not in the types but in the motor speed-control systems. Otherwise units are basically the same. One method used to control the speed of the motor uses a tapped field winding. The coil that forms the electromagnetic field that turns the motor is tapped at several points. The resistance varies, depending on the portion that is energized. This alters the magnetic field and changes the speed of the motor. This method is found primarily in small portable type units.

Another commonly used method and one often found on heavy-duty stand-type units is the governor control. In a governor control, a small centrifugal governor is used on the revolving motor shaft. Flyweights are incorporated into this governor so that the faster the shaft turns, the farther out the flyweights tend to swing. This gives a mechanical motion that can be used to open and close a set of contacts. The contacts are wired in series with the motor windings. As the speed increases, the flyweights pull out and open the contacts. Immediately the rotor slows down. As soon as the speed decreases, the contacts again close. By altering the distance of the contacts from the governor, the speed can be made higher or slower. Of course, this results in a rapid opening and closing of the contacts, but at all times that the motor is energized, it is also operating at full torque. A capacitor is often used across the contacts to reduce radio and television interference.

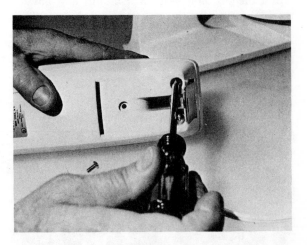

Next, look for screws under bottom or housing and remove them. This should release top housing.

The universal motor uses brushes. There are small carbon rods that serve as conductors between the field and the armature which is in series with the stationary field. These brushes are subject to wear and should be checked at any

time that the mixer fails to operate. On some models they are accessible from the outside by removing two caps found on the housing of the mixer.

The brushes can also serve as a means of speed control. By shifting the position of the brushes around the field of the motor, a type of speed control is gained. This occurs because the magnetic field between the armature and the field is altered. Mixers that use this type of control usually have a geared connection to the control knob from the plate upon which the brushes are mounted.

If it's necessary to disassemble a mixer, unplug it and remove screws from housing. The type of speed control used would be rather obvious. Look for the geared brush plate to determine if it is a brush-shift type speed control. Look for numerous wires (the exact number depends upon the number of speeds) connected to the speed control switch from the motor windings, which will denote a tapped field type speed control. On the governor-type control, the centrifugal governor and the contact plate are obvious.

Often the problem with brush-shift and governor speed controllers is stuck linkages. The

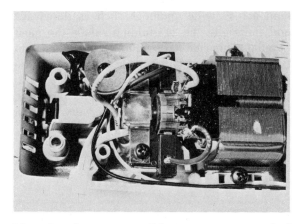

Motor brushes are accessible at commutator end of motor. After long use they may have to be replaced.

dust, crumbs, etc. from getting into the mixer. It is not an easy job, since many mixers have cooling fans which pull air across the motor. Brushing the openings around the housing once a month or so can help. Check for this type of problem if the mixer operates but the speed controller doesn't work or if it operates at a constant speed.

If the mixer doesn't operate at all, check the voltage at the receptacle by plugging in a table lamp. If this checks all right, look carefully at the cord at the plug and at the place where it enters

When housing is removed, motor, control, and drive mechanism are exposed. Note position of contact plate in this governor-controlled system.

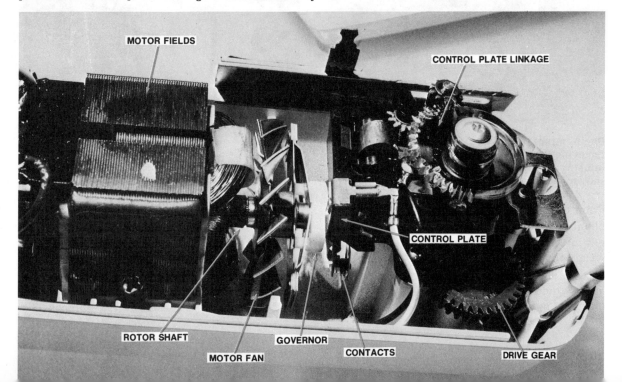

MOTOR FIELDS

CONTROL PLATE LINKAGE

CONTROL PLATE

ROTOR SHAFT

MOTOR FAN

GOVERNOR

CONTACTS

DRIVE GEAR

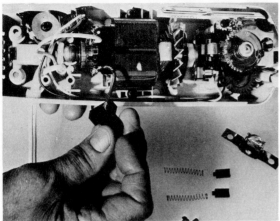

Bearing plate and brush holder are removed in this photograph. Lubricate bearing with single drop of oil when repairing motor. Replace brush tension springs when it's necessary to replace brushes.

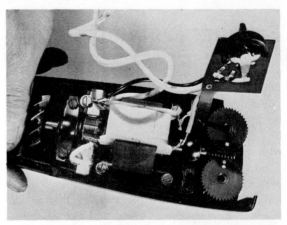

When replacing plastic gears found in many units, be sure that timing marks are aligned properly. In this mixer mark one goes opposite mark two. This prevents beaters from striking each other in use.

the body. If brush caps are visible on the outside of the housing, they will appear as two small plastic caps, usually with a slot and somewhat smaller than the size of a dime. They will be located opposite each other. Remove the caps and remove the brushes and springs. If the brushes are less than a quarter of an inch long, it's time for them to be replaced.

If brush caps aren't visible, it will be necessary to disassemble the mixer. On most newer mixers the body is made in two sections, upper and lower. Remove any knobs, then turn the mixer upside down and look for recessed screws which can be loosened to separate the two halves. On mixers with a speed control knob at the rear, remove the knob to gain access to the mixer body. With the mixer disassembled, look for the circle of copper bars on one end of the motor armature. The brushes will lie against this bar. Often the brush holder is held in place with a single screw if brush caps were not used. Removing this screw will allow the brush spring to be loosened. Replace it in the same manner. Often these brushes are visible and can be inspected without removing the brush holder.

If there is much flour or dust within the mixer, vacuum it as thoroughly as possible with a vacuum cleaner and dusting brush. Check all wiring connections and contact conditions carefully.

If the mixer operates but is noisy or the motor operates but the beaters don't turn, look for a problem in the gear train. In most mixers the end of the motor shaft is machined into a worm gear. Two pinion gears, one on each side, are turned by the worm gear. In many mixers (especially portables), the gear and socket for the beater are all contained in a single piece.

In many mixers the two gears are identical, but they'll have different timing marks on them, often marked with a 1 or 2. When reassembling a mixer or when replacing the gears, be sure and assemble the timing marks opposite each other. This insures that the beaters will not touch when they are turning. When replacing gears, lubricate them with the lubricant recommended by the manufacturer.

In some mixers removal of "C" clips may be necessary to remove the gears. You can purchase a special tool which holds them apart. Lacking this, they can usually be pried apart, but use care — they can fly off creating a hazard to your eyes. Sometimes mixers are put to uses for which they are not intended. Be sure to use them only as directed, and use particular care to keep utensils, spoons, etc. away from beaters for safety's sake as well as for the good of the appliance.

If a shocking condition occurs, take the mixer out of service until it can be checked with a VOM and the problem remedied.

Footings & Foundations

Before the excavation for the footings or foundation is made, the condition of the subsoil should be determined. This can be done by test borings or by examinig houses nearby. If they have water problems because of a high water table, or if rock formations were found that required expensive blasting or special excavating equipment, it may be more practical to change the plans from a basement to a crawl space or concrete slab.

The building site must be cleared of brush and trees (specific trees can be marked and saved if they are not too close to the foundation) and the ground leveled and graded. The plot should be surveyed by a surveyor and the corners of the plot marked by posts. The surveyor also should roughly mark out the location of the house. The position of the house on the lot will be determined by local codes, and the setback from the street may be partially determined by the locations of houses already built on adjacent lots. Spacing for the side yards (distance from the lot line) will be specified by the building code. A plot plan is a requirement in most areas for getting a building permit, so the location of the house on the lot must be determined before you apply for the permit.

After determining the location of the house, lines and grades are figured. Usually the high point of the lot is used for figuring the height of the foundation, which should be above the finished-grade level to keep siding well clear of the soil. This assures that ground moisture will not contact the wood members to cause rot, and termite tunnels can be seen if these insects attack the house.

Stakes are first driven into the ground at the four corners of the foundation with a nail driven into the top of each one to accurately locate the outside of the foundation walls. The diagonals now are measured to make sure the foundation is square. You also can use the 3, 4, 5 method of squaring: three units are measured along one

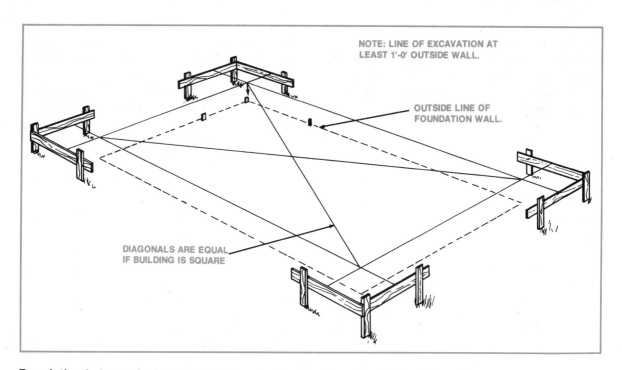

NOTE: LINE OF EXCAVATION AT LEAST 1'-0' OUTSIDE WALL.

OUTSIDE LINE OF FOUNDATION WALL.

DIAGONALS ARE EQUAL IF BUILDING IS SQUARE

Foundation is located with use of stakes, batter boards and taut string. Diagonals are measured or 3, 4, 5 method is used to assure foundation is square.

side, four on the adjacent side, then a diagonal should have five units. This could be 9 and 12 feet, with the diagonal 15 feet. Batter boards next are nailed to three stakes driven into the ground outside the foundation stakes and cord stretched tautly from the boards over the tops of the nails in the stakes. A plumb bob will help in accurate alignment. When the strings are in line, cut grooves or notches in the batter boards so the strings can be replaced in the correct position if they are moved or broken during the excavation. Remember to double-check the squareness of the strings and their position after the excavation

is made, in the event either the string or batter boards have been moved.

Basement walls can have a height of 8 feet, as with upstairs rooms, and the minimum height should be 7 feet 4 inches. There will be less headroom under girders, of course.

Excavation for basements or crawl spaces can be done quickly and efficiently with power equipment. Topsoil should be scraped or dug up and piled to one side of the lot so it can be replaced after backfilling around the foundation is done,

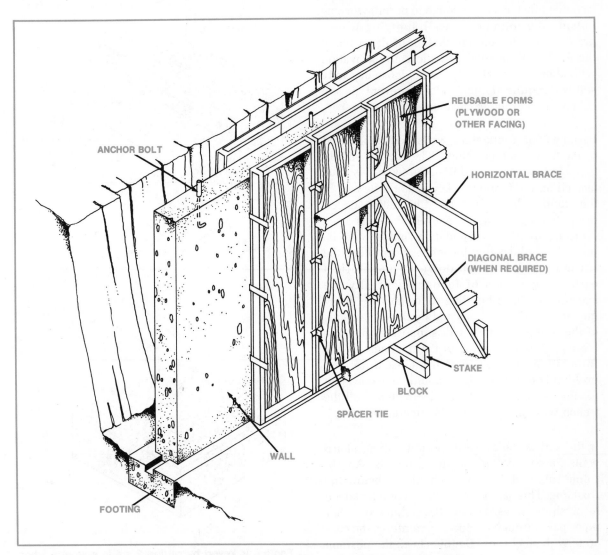

Poured-concrete walls require reusable forms of plywood reinforced with lumber, steel panels or assembled planking. Forms should be well braced against weight of liquid concrete.

and all construction is complete. There will be extra topsoil and it can be used to create proper drainage away from the foundation.

Excavation should be taken down only to the top of the footings or the bottom of the basement floor, because some soils will become soft on exposure to air or water and easily collapse. Final excavation for footings should be made just before you are ready to pour the concrete. If form boards are used, this precaution is not necessary. In some soils, form boards are mandatory because of lack of support by loose soil. The excavation must be large enough to permit working outside the foundation wall applying waterproofing and for the installation of drain tile at the footing. Firm soils will allow an excavation with almost vertical walls, while loose or sandy soil will require sloping walls to prevent the soil collapsing into the excavation.

Basement or foundation walls can be poured concrete or concrete block. The footing should be poured concrete, and if a poured wall is to be located on the footing a "key" should be cast in the footing. The key is formed by setting a 2 x 4 in the footing when it is poured. Footings are a critical part of the foundation and should be poured on solid soil. If the lot has been filled, the fill must be excavated down to undisturbed earth. Dimensions of footings generally are specified by local building codes and are determined by soil conditions and by the dimensions of the foundation they will support. Depth of a footing should be equal to the thickness of the foundation wall; at least 6 inches thick and preferably 8 inches thick. Should the excavation for the footing be made too deep, do not fill the trench with earth, fill it with concrete.

If the soil is too loose to permit cutting sharp walls for the footing, use form boards. An absolute rule is that footings should be below the frost line. This can be as much as 4 or 5 feet deep in northern areas. Where sewer lines or other pipes pass through the footing, reinforce the concrete with steel rods. Double-check the position of the form boards for the footing by dropping a plumb bob from lines stretched across the batter boards. The location of the forms for a poured-

concrete wall or for a built-up block wall also is checked by dropping the plumb bob from these points.

Footings for piers, posts or columns should be square and have a pedestal cast integral with them. A steel pin or bolt is set in the pedestal to anchor a wooden column, while bolts for attaching the bottom plate of a steel column are cast in

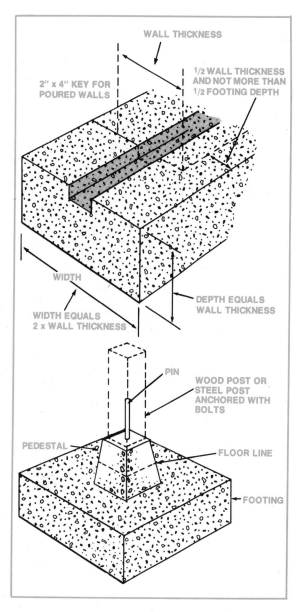

Footing is keyed by setting 2 x 4 in concrete when footing is poured. Footing for piers or columns is square, has pedestal cast integral with it with pin to hold wooden column, bolts for plate of steel column.

the pedestal. Pedestals should project three inches above a poured-concrete floor and 12 inches above finish grade in a crawl space. Footings for fireplaces, furnaces and chimneys are poured at the same time as other footings.

Stepped footings may be required where a lot slopes. The vertical part of a stepped footing should be poured at the same time as the horizontal section. The footing must be below the frost line at all points and each run of footing should be horizontal. A vertical step should be at least six inches thick and just as wide as the footings. Some foundations may require more than one step; each step should be limited to a drop of 24 inches.

Foundation drains are required where ground water is a problem. The tile is placed at the bottom of the footing on a bed of gravel 2 inches deep. Lengths of 4 inch drain tile are placed end to end, spaced 1/8 inch apart. The top of each spaced joint is covered with tar paper, then 6 to 8 inches of gravel is poured over the tile. Dry wells may be used to catch water from a foundation drain, but this will depend on soil conditions and local codes. While allowed in some areas, most building codes will forbid draining a foundation line into a municipal sewer. Frequently a well is used (or sump) cast in the basement floor and a pump is used to lift the water and drain it onto the soil outside the foundation. Check local codes before starting construction of the foundation.

Walls for a basement or crawl space will be either poured concrete or concrete block. Treated-wood foundations also are being used in some areas. Wooden foundations, even made with treated wood, may not sound very permanent, but they can last 30 years or more. The walls of block or concrete will vary in width from 8 to 12 inches depending on building height, local codes, soil conditions and other factors. These specifications should be on the blueprints, having been determined by the architect. If you are using ready-made plans, the specifications for the footing and foundation must meet the local building code.

Poured-concrete walls require forms of lumber,

plywood braced with lumber or metal panels. Most walls are poured in reusable forms. With any type form, ample bracing and reinforcement should be used to assure the forms do not shift or buckle under the weight of the fluid concrete. Forms for windows, doors and girder pockets are fastened inside the forms. Concrete should be poured continuously when pouring is started. Any interruption in the pouring will cause a joint that may leak under the pressure of ground water.

Forms are not removed until the concrete has set solidly, which means at least 48 hours. This should be longer in cool or freezing weather. When the temperature is below freezing a special mix is used with antifreeze in the water and straw or other material should be used to cover the concrete to prevent freezing. Poured-concrete walls are water-proofed with a coat of hot or cold asphalt or tar applied to the outside from the footings up to grade level.

Concrete-block walls require no formwork and are set on flat footings (not keyed). The blocks are laid with 3/8 inch mortar joints in common bond. The wall is capped with 4 inches of solid masonry blocks or concrete reinforced with steel mesh. Anchor bolts for sills are fitted in the top two rows of block and are L-shaped or have a large washer at the bottom to anchor them in the poured concrete that fills the two rows of block. If a block wall is to be used as a finished wall in a basement room, the stacked bond can be used. This type bond requires metal reinforcement every two courses, as it is weaker than common bond. Block walls are waterproofed by applying a coating of mortar over the outside of the wall with a cove at the footing. A coating of asphalt is applied over the dried mortar. For added waterproofing in damp soils, a membrane of roofing paper or other material is applied with hot tar.

Crawl-space foundations are used where conditions dictate that a basement would not be practical, or where building cost is a consideration. Foundation walls for a crawl space are made much the same as for a basement, but generally no waterproofing or foundation drain is required. The area inside the foundation should be

cleared of all scraps of wood and other material, leveled and covered with about 4 inches of gravel. A watertight membrane of sheet plastic is placed over the gravel and run up the wall 6 inches and sealed to the wall. Joints in the plastic should be lapped at least 4 inches and sealed. This arrangement permits using the crawl space as a heat or air-conditioning plenum. If it is not used as a plenum, then ventilating louvers are installed in the walls. The louvers are metal devices set in openings cast in a concrete wall or formed in block walls. These louvers can be closed in cold weather, opened in warm weather to assure ventilation in the crawl space and remove moisture.

Anchor bolts are cast in the top of poured-concrete walls to hold sill plates. Although a poor construction technique, some builders eliminate the sill plate and use steel straps embedded in the concrete to tie the headers and end joists to the concrete. This is not accepted practice in high-wind areas, and is not good construction in any situation. The use of a sill plate is the best method. Where a sill plate is used, a sealer strip of special material may be placed under the sill to seal it against irregularities in the concrete.

Where a concrete porch, planting box or the like is not poured at the same time as the foundation, reinforcing rods are set in the foundation wall to later provide attachment. Concrete-block walls for porches and planting boxes are built at the same time as the foundation wall, on footings poured at the same time as the foundation footings. Metal reinforcing strips sometimes are used between a foundation wall and adjoining walls for porches and other attached structures. Reinforcing rods generally are not used in concrete foundation walls except over window or door openings. For concrete-block walls a precast concrete lintel reinforced with steel rods, or a steel beam, is used over openings.

When masonry veneer is used against wood-frame walls, the foundation wall must be about 5 inches wider than a regular foundation. This provides a 1 inch space between the sheathing and masonry, which aids in laying the brick or other masonry, and also provides an insulating dead-air space. A flashing is used under the masonry course that is below the bottom of the wall sheathing and weep holes are provided in the masonry to permit draining condensation from between the walls. The weep holes are formed by eliminating mortar in vertical joints or by setting short pieces of pipe or tubing in the mortar joints. Metal ties are nailed to the sheathing of the wall, then bent to fit between the courses of masonry to tie the masonry and framing together. The ties are spaced about 16 inches vertically and about twice that distance horizontally.

CONCRETE SLABS

Because heating and air-conditioning units, as well as hot-water tanks, have become smaller and more efficient over the years, they no longer have to be located in the basement. This permits elimination of that excavation, unless the house is in a tornado area where a basement can be a storm shelter.

With no basement required, a home can be built on a concrete slab if soil and grade conditions permit. Sloping areas or places where ground moisture is a problem are not good for slab foundations because the necessary structural and drainage requirements would make the costs too high. Some split-level houses will have part of the foundation poured as a slab; this takes advantage of the features of a slanting lot.

At one time the objection to a concrete slab was that it was cold and uncomfortable and that moisture sometimes condensed on the floors and on the lower part of walls in cold weather. Improved construction has eliminated such problems, but has also added to the cost. Heat loss through floors and foundation walls are what caused slab floors to be cold, and moisture migrating up through the concrete caused them to be damp. Plastic sheets or other material now is used as a vapor barrier under concrete slabs to seal out moisture. Suitable insulation between the floor and the foundation as well as heating ducts around the edges of the floor, eliminates cold floors. Radiant-heating systems in the floor with hot water pumped through pipes is another method of assuring a warm floor.

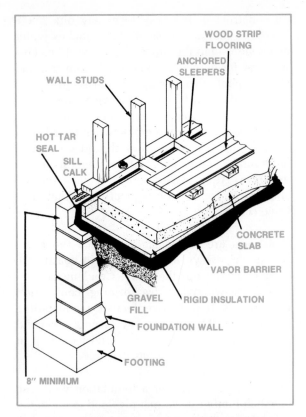

WOOD STRIP
FLOORING
ANCHORED
SLEEPERS
WALL STUDS
HOT TAR
SEAL
SILL
CALK
CONCRETE
SLAB
VAPOR BARRIER
GRAVEL   RIGID INSULATION
FILL
FOUNDATION WALL
FOOTING
8" MINIMUM

Best floor for slab construction is hardwood strips on scabs or sleepers attached to slab. Vapor barrier should be installed between flooring and the slab.

In warm climates a combined slab and foundation can be used where frost is not a problem. Soil conditions also must be favorable. The foundation wall should be at least 12 inches deep and set on solid ground.

Where frost is a problem, the walls of a house must be set on foundations or piers that extend below the frost line. In this case the slab and foundation are separated by rigid insulation.

Some years ago concrete slabs were polished and painted for a finished floor, or were covered by asphalt or other resilient tile or sheet flooring. These materials were cold and never provided a satisfactory floor. Parquet or wood-tile flooring is better, but best is a strip-wood flooring nailed to sleepers that are anchored to the slab. In all cases a vapor barrier is painted on the concrete slab, or sheet plastic or other material is used to prevent any chance of moisture migrating up through the wood flooring.

Force Cup

The force cup, also called a plumber's friend or plunger, is the main tool needed for clearing clogged drains. It frees clogged material by forcing it up or washing it down the drain. Force cups are designed specifically for sinks or toilets. However, there is a two-way variety plunger, which has a flange that folds out for toilet use, that may be used for both. The best kind of plunger to use has a wide, flat face, making it possible to have good contact with the bottom of the fixture.

When using the force cup, fill the basin with one or two inches of water. If there is a stopper, be sure to remove it. Seal off the overflow opening with a folded washcloth to keep the plunger pressure concentrated on the clogged area. Apply petroleum jelly to the cup's rim to assure a tight grip. As the force cup is immersed, tip it to let the air out and then put it directly over the drain. To maintain a tight seal during the up and down plunging, do not tip the cup again. Begin pumping the cup down and pulling it up firmly to build up the force. To draw or break up the clogged matter, pull the force cup off the drain. *SEE ALSO PLUMBER'S TOOLS & EQUIPMENT.*

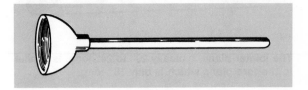

Force Cup

Forced Draft

A forced draft is created when a furnace blower forces air through a heating unit and up the chimney. This differs from a *natural* draft in which air is unassisted as it goes up the chimney and the *induced* draft where air forced up the

chimney causes air to flow through the heating unit.

A forced draft results in better performance from the heating unit and lower fuel consumption rates in a one-story house. A complete forced draft system needs no help from a natural draft to aid in combustion and expelling combustion up the chimney. *SEE ALSO HEATING SYSTEMS.*

Fore & Jointer Planes

Two of the most important planes in the home workshop, the fore and jointer planes are the best choices for edge-straightening. Although they range in length from 18 to 24 inches, their features are similar to the jack plane. When it is necessary to true up edges of boards prior to fitting them closely together, the jointer plane is used. The fore plane, a shorter type of jointer plane, is sometimes preferred because of its light weight. *SEE ALSO HAND TOOLS.*

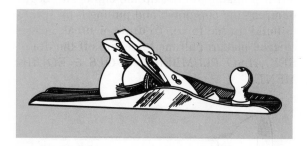

The jointer plane, typically 20″ to 24″ long, is similar to the fore plane which is only 18″ long.

Forms

Forms are constructed to enclose the area into which concrete will be poured for driveways, sidewalks, porches and walls. Forms should be made of sturdy materials and fastened to stakes with double-headed nails. Oil should be applied to any surface on the forms where the concrete will touch to prevent sticking. A level will be needed to check the work.

To construct a driveway form, lay out 2 x 6 boards so that the forms are three inches wider on all sides than the finished drive will be. This way the forms can be placed on even ground. Nail all joints together tightly and secure 2 x 4 wood stake reinforcements every three feet along the boards and near corner joints. Use a level to check the alignment between boards and joints. Temporary dividers should be placed horizontally and nailed at 10 feet intervals inside the form. After the concrete has been poured and cured, remove these boards so that they leave contraction joints.

Walkways are constructed in much the same way as driveways, except that 2 x 4 boards are used in laying out the form. Cracking is controlled in walkways by forming contraction joints every four to five feet or by installing wood joints. This is done by placing a second divider board close to the first and leaving it in place after the concrete has dried.

To construct a form for a foundation wall, use one inch lumber or ³/₄ inch plywood to make the sides. Support these with 2 x 4 studs placed at two foot intervals; brace each stud with a 2 x 4 strip. A wall higher than four feet should also be supported horizontally. To tie the forms together, drill holes at two foot intervals in the

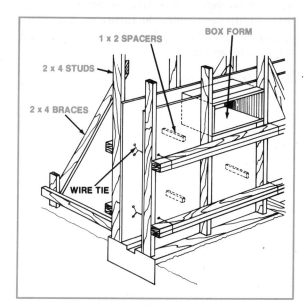

Concrete Foundation Wall Form

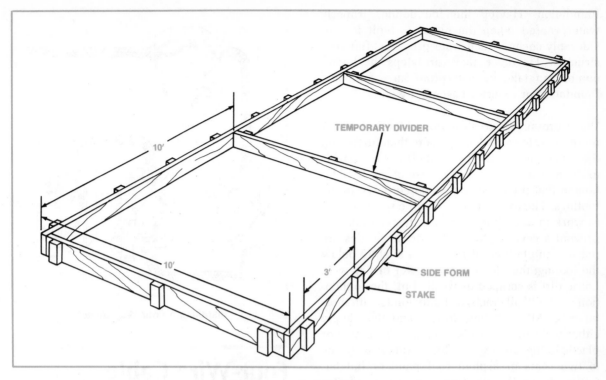

Driveway or Walkway Form

plywood sheet above and below the horizontal braces. Run soft wire through the top and bottom holes. around the brace, and twist the two wire pieces together so that they form an X in between the side forms. 1 x 2 spacers cut to the length of the width of the area between the side forms are placed at two foot intervals between the side forms to keep them in shape. The spacers are removed as the concrete is poured. Allow for basement windows by building a wood box into and between the spacers. *SEE ALSO CONCRETE.*

Foundation
[SEE FOOTINGS & FOUNDATIONS.]

Foundation Wall

A foundation wall is a concrete, rock, brick or stone wall located below the grade of a building

which supports the entire upper structure. *SEE ALSO FOOTINGS & FOUNDATIONS.*

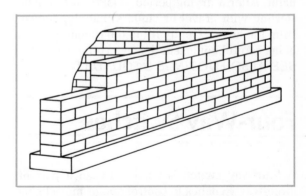

Concrete Block Foundation Wall

Foundation Waterproofing

Foundation walls must be waterproofed because constant exposure to water weakens the entire

foundation. Having the foundation properly waterproofed when the house is built is considerably cheaper than waterproofing after construction. However, there are steps the homeowner can take to waterproof an established foundation or exterior basement wall.

Water pressure is greatest around footings and is more likely to cause leakage here than further up the foundation wall. The most effective repair is to dig a trench down to the base of the foundation so that it can be waterproofed down to the footings. The excavation should be wide enough to work in and shored up with heavy timber to prevent a cave-in. Next, clay drainage tiles are put into the bottom of the trench slightly below the footing; the tiles run to a sewer or dry well. Loose dirt is scraped or washed off the foundation wall. Fill all cracks or faulty joints with mortar mix. Allow it time to dry and then apply either waterproof mastic, asphalt roof cement or plastic to the clean wall. This is followed by one to two coats of asphalt roof paint or hot tar. Cover the wall with asphalt paper or plastic, overlapping it at least six inches and extending it high enough to prevent water from running down under it. Finally, apply a coat of asphalt paint. After a drying period, backfill the trench, starting with gravel or cinders that slope away from the house. Gently fill in the remaining dirt, being careful not to tear the waterproof covering. *SEE ALSO FOOTINGS & FOUNDATIONS.*

Four-Way Switches

A four-way switch is used between a pair of three-way switches to control one or more lights from three different locations. For instance, one may be used to control a kitchen light from switches on both sides of the room and from a room adjoining the kitchen. A four-way switch looks like an ordinary wall switch but its lever is not lettered "on and off". An additional four-way switch must be added for each new control location. For example, to obtain control from four locations, two four-way switches must be used; for five locations, three four-way switches are used. *SEE ALSO SWITCHES & OUTLETS.*

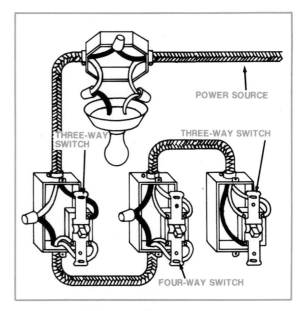

Installing a Four-Way Switch

Four-Wire Cable

Used in the wiring of four-way switches, four-wire cable is not always available from electrical suppliers. In its place, two separate strands of two-wire cable can be used. In either case, the ends of any white wire used as a switching wire should be painted black. The white wire is left white only when it is carrying the grounded side of the circuit. *SEE ALSO WIRE SIZES & TYPES.*

Framing

The completed floor platform provides a convenient surface for assembling the wall framing. This includes primarily the vertical studs and horizontal members such as sole plates, top plates and headers over windows and doors, in both the exterior walls and the interior partitions. The framing provides nailing surfaces for exterior siding, interior paneling or plasterboard and it also supports ceilings, upper floors and the roof framing.

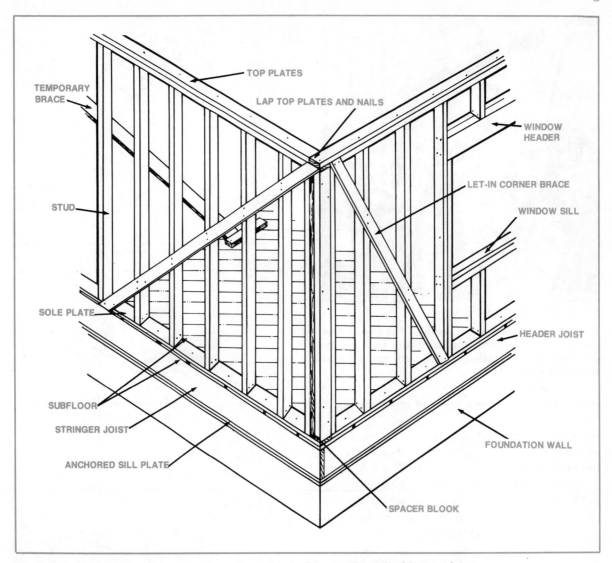

TOP PLATES

TEMPORARY BRACE

LAP TOP PLATES AND NAILS

WINDOW HEADER

STUD

LET-IN CORNER BRACE

WINDOW SILL

SOLE PLATE

HEADER JOIST

SUBFLOOR

STRINGER JOIST

ANCHORED SILL PLATE

FOUNDATION WALL

SPACER BLOOK

Platform construction has wall framing setting on top of the subfloor. Double top plates overlap at the corners of the framing to tie the walls together, and let-in bracing makes the corners of the framing rigid.

Generally the spacing of the members, mostly 2 x 4s, is 16 inches on center. In some cases the *Mod 24* system created by the Western Wood Products Association can be used (depending on local building codes) and considerable time, material and cost can be saved.

One method of making wall framing is to build the frame on the floor platform, then lift the framing to a vertical position. If several helpers are available, the full length of the wall framing can be built and lifted into place. If there is only one helper or just yourself, the framing is built in shorter sections, then spiked together when in the upright position. Some builders preassemble the wall almost completely, nailing on the sheathing and even installing doors and windows.

The usual practice is to assemble just the framing, with precut studs, window and door headers and short-length studs under windows and windowsills. The studs are nailed to the top plates and sole plates with 16 penny nails. Where required, let-in bracing should be installed. This requires notching the top and sole plate as well

657

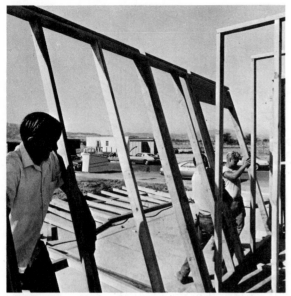

Courtesy of Western Wood Products Association

Wall framing generally is assembled flat on the floor platform, then is lifted into place and braced temporarily until the ceiling joists, roof framing and sheathing are in place.

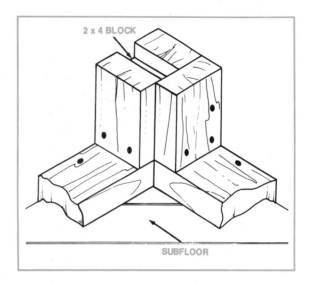

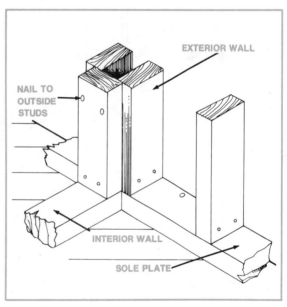

Two methods of providing solid attachment of interior partitions with exterior wall framing and also providing nailing surfaces in the created corners.

as the studs to accept a piece of one inch stock.

An alternate method to building the complete wall framing on the platform is where only the top plates are nailed to the studs. The sole plate is spiked to the floor, then the framing assembly is lifted vertically on top of the sole plate and toenailed to it. A temporary brace of one inch stock is tacknailed to one or more studs and to a block nailed to the floor.

In areas of high wind the wall framing sometimes is anchored to the sill plate by steel straps. The straps are run under the sill plate and spiked to its inner edge, and to the outside face of the header joist during construction of the floor framing.

The outside corners of wall framing are assembled to provide nailing surfaces inside for plasterboard paneling or other wall covering. One method is the use of 2 x 4 blocks to space a 2 x 4 stud to provide the necessary nailing surface.

Interior partitions must be well fastened to exterior walls where they contact, and provide nailing surfaces for wall-covering materials. One

method is to double the outside studs at the inside wall. A second method utilizes a 1 x 6 or 2 x 6 nailer held on blocks between adjacent studs. A similar assembly is used in the framing of interior partitions where they are joined.

After all wall frames are set up vertically, a second top plate is spiked to the first top plate, overlapping at the corners to provide added connection between adjacent framing. These top

plates also can be partly attached when the framing is assembled horizontally on the floor. On one end of the wall the top plate projects the width of a 2 x 4, while on the other the plate is short by that width, to accept the top plate of an adjacent wall frame. Top plates are assembled with 16 penny nails spaced 16 inches apart. The temporary braces that hold the framing assemblies vertical are left in place until the sheathing has been applied to the outside of the framing and the ceiling and roof framing have been spiked in place to assure a rigid overall assembly.

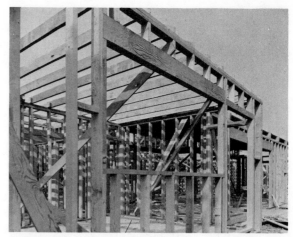

The wider an opening, the heavier the lumber used for headers. Note the difference between the doubled 2 x 4 over the door and the much wider stock over the long window.

inch thick strips of wood which are all nailed together. The ends of the headers are supported on the inner studs of double stud framing at the sides of openings in the wall framing. For very wide openings, trussed headers, usually prebuilt in a shop, are required, as they will have much more strength than regular timber.

Framing around window and door openings should be sized for the specified rough opening indicated by the maker of the millwork. The rough openings also may be indicated on the blueprints; the architect may specify a particular door or window and give the required opening for the specific units.

Interior partitions in a house of conventional construction provide support for ceiling joists as well as being room dividers. These load-bearing walls or partitions are at right angles to the ceiling joists; partitions parallel to the joists generally are not load-bearing walls. Framing for interior partitions can be assembled on the floor in the same manner as exterior walls, then lifted into place. Be sure to check blueprints for doors, pass-throughs and other openings that should be framed into interior partitions. Most interior walls are assembled from 2 x 4s in the same manner as the exterior walls, but 2 x 6s or 2 x 8s may be used for a wall in which plumbing or heating units are fitted. Be sure to have nailing

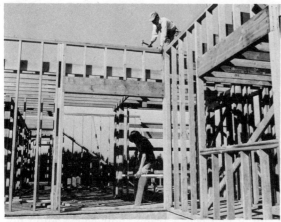

Doubled 2 x 6s, 2 x 8s or wider stock spaced by strips of wood ³/₈ inches thick are used as headers over door and window openings in the framing of exterior walls.

Balloon construction, seldom used today, differs from platform framing mostly at the floor line. In balloon framing, both the floor joists and wall studs rest on the sill and are toenailed to each other and to the sill. The ends of the second floor joists are set on a 1 x 4 which is set in notches cut in the full-length joists. The joists also are nailed into the studs. Building codes will usually require that firestops be installed between the joists in balloon framing to prevent the spread of fire and smoke through the natural chimneys that the studs make through the full height of the structure.

Headers or lintels are used over door and window openings in wall framing. Headers usually are lengths of two inch lumber spaced with ³/₈

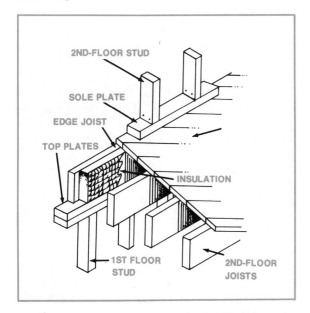

Labels on diagram:
2ND-FLOOR STUD
SOLE PLATE
EDGE JOIST
TOP PLATES
INSULATION
1ST FLOOR STUD
2ND-FLOOR JOISTS

An added touch for quality building is the use of insulation inside the headers and end joists where second floor meets the exterior wall framing.

surfaces in the corners of all joining partitions to accept paneling, wallboard or other covering. Two top plates are used on all interior walls, the same as for exterior walls.

If there is a second story, framing for the second floor is attached to the floor platform the same as for the first floor. End joists and headers are spiked to the double top plates on the framing of the first floor. The insulation inside the headers or end joists adds weathertightness that is important in conserving energy.

For the same reason that double 2 x 4s and other assemblies are used for the inside corners of wall framing to provide nailing surfaces for wall-covering materials, a method must be provided for nailing ceiling material to inside corners. Ceiling joists can be located adjacent to the edges of the top plates of the wall or partition framing to provide nailing surfaces for the ceiling.

Framing Chisel

The framing or mortising chisel was once used

for heavy-duty mortising of building framework. Because of modern construction methods, that practice has vanished and it is not likely that you will have much need for this chisel. Hardware stores rarely carry them anymore. *SEE ALSO HAND TOOLS.*

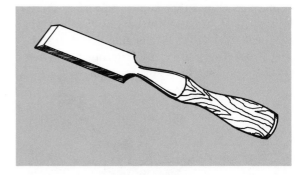

Framing Chisel

Framing Pictures

Picture framing is an art in itself and selecting the proper frame for a picture is important to the painting's effect. A frame, however, should not be more noticeable than the picture it surrounds. It should enhance the picture and bring it into harmony with the surroundings.

The frame should be designed to relate directly to the character of the picture. For example, when pictures are to be set against a patterned wallpaper, frames should be heavy and wide enough to separate the picture from the designs on the wall. Pictures with black and white contrasts usually take a narrow frame. It is better if pencil drawings, water colors and pastels are matted and under glass. Oil paintings do not need a glass cover. A deep frame is used when the subject has depth while flat or abstract subject matter can use a narrower strip-type of frame.

The size and color of the mat covering the area between the frame and picture are important. The outer or inner edge may be painted gold to highlight the picture within. If the entire frame is

gold, warm colors will go best with it, while silver enhances cool colors.

Frames selected for a room setting do not necessarily need to be of the same style. It is more interesting, in fact, to have a variety of styles. Also, the frame does not have to be the same shape as the picture it contains. Good effects may be produced by combining shapes, such as rectangular frames with square pictures. The important thing is that the picture catches the eye and that the frame allows the viewer to make an adjustment between the picture and the wall.

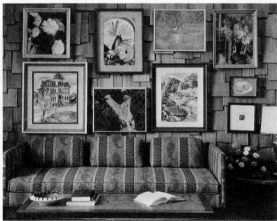

Courtesy of Western Wood Moulding & Millwork Producers

To unify an art gallery setting, make sure upper and lower lines are level.

Some pictures should be matted or mounted. A mat is stiff paperboard on which the picture is placed. The mat board is white inside and white or colored on the outside. A window, smaller than the picture size, is cut in the board. A mat may be covered with silk, linen or other fabrics.

Mounting board is cheaper and more practical than mats. Though mats conceal dirty or ragged edges of a picture, mounting is better when the painting or picture is extended to the edges.

Mats and mounts come in many colors, mostly in light, neutral or off-white. Mats or mounts should be used when only a certain part of a picture is to be revealed, when the frame is to be a different shape and when pictures of different sizes with the same size frames are to be hung.

Mats or mounts solve the size adjustment problems.

MAKING FRAMES

There are assorted styles and widths for frames in wood or metal which come packaged in pairs, one for horizontal and the other for vertical length. They are easily put together. Making frames for pictures is a money-saver as well as a unique hobby for one who enjoys working with wood. It is, however, time-consuming and rather tedious since even little imperfections are conspicuous when the frame is hung.

A rabbet or right-angle recess, cut out of the edge of wood along its length, is the kind of molding used for making picture frames. This kind of molding is bought specifically for framing. Wood molding might be purchased from a lumberyard. It can be adapted by adding a strip of wood $1/4$ inch from the inside edge of the back molding. The wood should be deep enough for the backing and glass used, with space left for brads or glazier's points to be added without stripping the wood.

Tools necessary for making frames include a light hammer, nail set, ruler, fine toothed saw, small nails, corner fasteners, pencil, sandpaper and glue. A miter box is needed to cut a 45-degree angle when mitering the frame corners.

The first step in frame making is to glue the molding strips that make the frame complete.

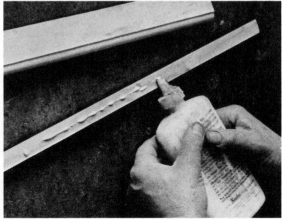

Courtesy of Western Wood Moulding & Millwork Producers

1. Glue molding strips.

Clamp or weight them until the glue sets, then saw off the molding at 45 degree angles.

Measure the edge of the picture and cut, adding $1/8$ inch to the total. Transfer the measurement to the molding, starting from the edge of the miter at the point where the picture inserts into the frame. Cut a 45 degree miter opposite the one just cut. Since another piece will be needed for the top, the second piece should be measured from the first to make the lengths the same.

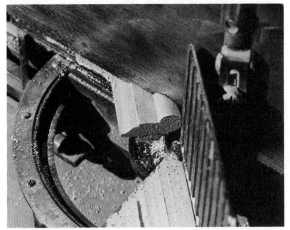

Courtesy of Western World Moulding & Millwork Producers

2. Cut corners at 45-degree angle.

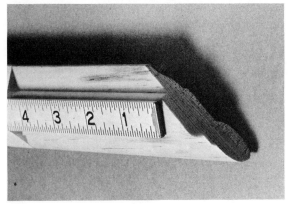

Courtesy of Western World Moulding & Millwork Producers

3. Measure along rabbet.

After measuring the side edge of the picture, two pieces of molding should be cut. Add the extra $1/8$ inch and measure the second piece from the first side piece. To assemble the frame, take a side piece and bottom piece and coat the ends with glue. Place in a corner clamp. Tighten the clamp

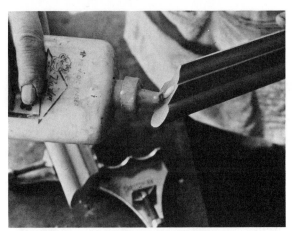

Courtesy of Western World Moulding & Millwork Producers

4. Apply glue to both surfaces.

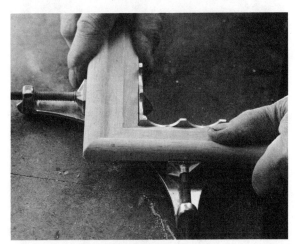

Courtesy of Western World Moulding & Millwork Producers

5. Clamp corners tightly.

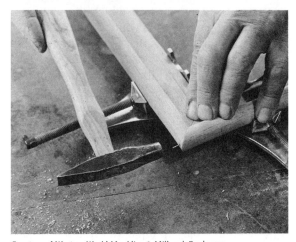

Courtesy of Western World Moulding & Millwork Producers

6. Nail from both edges.

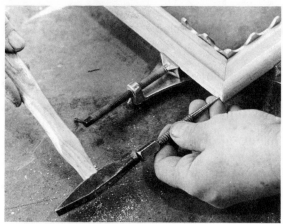

Courtesy of Western Wood Moulding & Millwork Producers

7. Set nail heads below surface ¹/₁₆ of an inch.

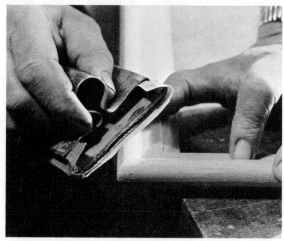

Courtesy of Western World Moulding & Millwork Producers

8. After glue sets, sand lightly.

when the corner is correctly aligned so the pressure will be heavy enough to hold the pieces rigid. Then nail the corner together.

Drive brads or finishing nails through the corners from the sides, allowing the heads to protrude slightly. Finish the brads with a small nail set so that the heads are ¹/₁₆ inch below the frame's surface.

Fill the nail holes with wood putty or fine sawdust from the cutting mixed with glue. Let the mixture dry and use fasteners to secure the joint. Do the same for the other three corners.

In addition to glue, one of three methods of fastening joints can be used to secure

them: blind doweling, brads or finishing nails and corner fasteners.

FINISHING FRAMES

When the glued frame is completely dry, it should be sanded lightly with fine sandpaper. Decide whether the frame is to be finished natural, stained, painted, textured or treated in another way. For a natural finish, frames should be sanded lightly after each of several coats of white shellac. They are buffed then with paste wax. For staining, the shellac and wax treatment is done after the stain is thoroughly dry.

A frame is glazed or textured when it needs to match the tone or texture of the picture it contains. This is done before the paint, of a cool, gray heavy-bodied or warm type, is brushed on. When dry, the surface is colored with thin paint, applied with a cloth. Colors should be chosen to blend with the picture. Buff on good paste wax when the color dries.

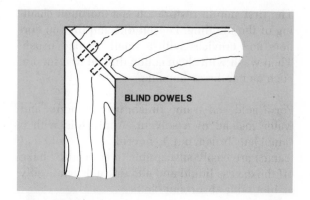

Blind doweling is very strong; recommended for large frames.

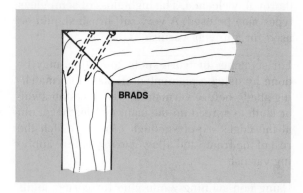

Small brads hold corners together more securely.

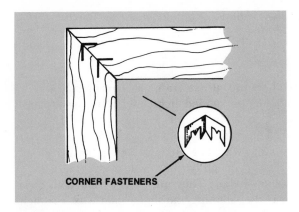

Corner fasteners may have a special countersink attachment to be used for a concealed joint.

REFINISHING AND REPAIRING OLD FRAMES

Handle old picture frames carefully by avoiding scrubbing or using harsh treatments with strong solvents. Test cleaning materials on an undetectable part of the frame.

The first step in restoration is a thorough cleaning of the molding. Loosen dirt and dust in corners and crevices with a small bristled brush. Then wash with clean cotton dipped in a solvent such as naptha or benzine.

For a gold leaf frame finish, use ammonia and water instead of a solvent. Apply this with a camel hair brush, but do not rub it in as gold leaf frames are easily susceptible to abrasion. Shake off the excess liquid and allow it to dry naturally or blot with absorbent cloths.

Clear varnish may be applied when the frame is thoroughly cleaned. The high-gloss of semi-gloss types may be used. A very soft brush should be used for applying varnish.

For scratches or worn spots, touch-ups may be done by using a pigmented oil stain in a matching shade before varnishing. Use a cotton swab or cloth to spread on the stain and feather it out at the edges. Apply enough coats to match the rest of the frame and allow it to dry before applying varnish.

Using non-staining white glue for corner joints that have worked loose. Apply from the back side with a pallet knife or thin putty knife. It may be best to disassemble the entire frame to do this.

If carved frames have chipped places or missing sections of molding, they may be patched by using powdered water putty, wood plastic or prepared spackling paste. Use a knife blade or spatula to put the compound into the crevice, shaping it to match the original carving. The compound may need to be smoothed down after it has hardened with steel wool, sandpaper or some similar material.

Gilt frames which have been damaged may be touched up with ready-to-mix gold paint or a brighter luster paint if preferred. A substitute method may be gilt powder which is sold in a wide range of colors.

FRAME TYPES

A frame may be made for a wall chart, such as a map, from a piece of surfaced wood 1 x 2. The wood is joined at the corners with a glue joint and glue pin. Heavy cardboard, plywood, etc., may be used for backing. Wire brads of $1/2$ inch will hold the backing in place. Oak, cherry or walnut are good woods to use for a natural finish; yellow poplar for a painted frame.

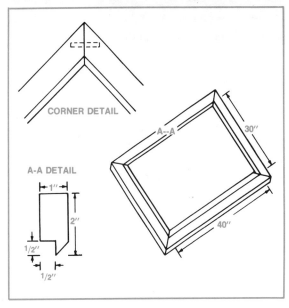

Frame for a Wall Chart

One attractive frame consists merely of two pieces of glass. The glass is cut at the top and bottom and a picture sandwiched in between so that it appears to float in the frame. This type of frame is good for modern art.

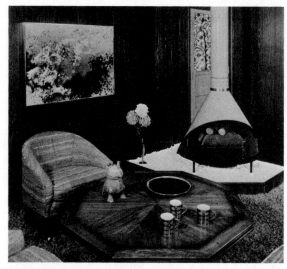

Courtesy of Masonite Corporation

Framing Square

The framing square (also called a carpenter's or rafter square) is a flat piece of L-shaped steel. The body measures 24 by two inches, and the tongue is 16 by one-and-one-half inches. Graduations and special tables are marked on both the body and tongue to aid in measuring

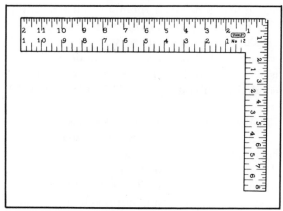

Courtesy of The Stanley Works

Framing Square

and cutting braces and rafters, calculating proportions, converting timbers from squares to octagons and figuring board measure. The framing square can also be used for finding the circumference and center of a circle and laying out ellipses, miters and hopper joints and is considered to be the most important and useful of all squares. *SEE ALSO HAND TOOLS.*

Franklin Stove

A Franklin stove is a cast iron heating stove that resembles an open fireplace except that it has doors. It is designed to fit anywhere in a room. With the doors open, the Franklin stove provides the pleasures of an open fire or fireplace, but with the doors closed, the unit serves as a heater, stove or small incinerator. Since it stands free of the wall, the Franklin stove can radiate heat in all directions including into adjacent rooms. With its doors closed, the Franklin stove prevents the loss of room heat because furnace heat is not drawn up and out its chimney. The Franklin stove, invented by Benjamin Franklin, was a familiar household fixture in colonial times and in recent years has enjoyed a renewed popularity.

The Franklin stove requires a noncombustible floor for support with a space of 24 to 36 inches

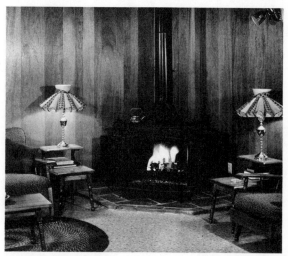

Courtesy of Martin Industries.

Franklin Stove

665

between it and a combustible wall. It can be vented by connection to an unused flue in an existing chimney or by stovepipe to a prefabricated metal chimney. *SEE ALSO FIREPLACES.*

Freezeproof Faucet

When a faucet is located directly outside a basement wall, a freezeproof faucet may be used to prevent freezing. The faucet shaft, connected to the faucet handle outside the building, extends to the water supply pipe inside the wall. The water valve in a freezeproof faucet is enclosed in the faucet shaft near the place where it connects to the supply pipe. When this faucet is turned off, water is shut off inside the basement, and the water left in the faucet fixture drains out. Freezing is prevented since it is warm in most enclosed basements. The freezeproof faucet may be left open all winter.

A freezeproof faucet may not be used when the supply pipe for an outdoor faucet must run under an unheated porch or through an unheated crawl space. In both situations, an ordinary sill faucet is used. *SEE ALSO FAUCET.*

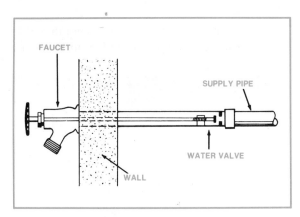

Freezeproof Faucet

Freezers

There are two types of standard freezers: chest types and uprights. On uprights, the evaporator

tubing forms a shelf for most if not all the shelves within the freezer compartment. The freezer usually has to be defrosted about once a year which is somewhat less than a normal refrigerator because of the reduced number of door openings. You will probably notice on an upright freezer that the upper shelves become more frosted than the lower ones. This is because the warm air that enters when the door is open also contains the moisture. When the door is closed the air tends to rise towards the top of the freezer. Also the top shelves are usually the first ones in the refrigeration circuit as the refrigerant enters the evaporator shelving. The first coils tend to run somewhat colder, so some frost is transferred to that section by sublimation.

The door gaskets on freezers are changed in the same manner as they are on refrigerators. Problems with door gasket leakage will likely show up quickly on standard freezers. If a heavy, soft snowy frost buildup appears very quickly it is a good indication that the door gasket is allowing air to enter or that the door has been left ajar.

Chest-type freezers usually have the evaporator tubing attached to and behind the liner that forms the outer edges of the compartment. Again, frosting is heaviest toward the top of the unit for the same reasons as it is on the upright freezer. However, chest freezers do have an advantage in efficiency since cold air is heavier than the warm air in the room. If the lid is left open, the cold air can't fall out so readily and there is less transfer between room air and that within the freezer itself. Another device often employed on chest freezers is using the outer cabinet as the condenser. The condenser tubing is welded into the inside of the outer wall, and condensation is also reduced to a lower level.

Frostless freezers are found primarily in upright types. They operate very much like frostless refrigerators except that the evaporator is designed to provide the lower temperatures necessary in a freezer. The evaporators in such freezers often cover an entire wall at the rear of the freezing compartment. A cover is used, making this wall a plenum or mixing chamber for the

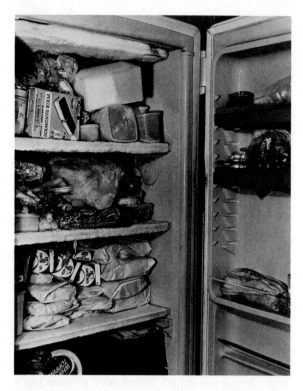

Note frosting pattern on the shelves of this upright model. Most frost will collect near top where coil surfaces are colder and where warmer, moisture-laden air tends to migrate.

warmer air from the freezer and the frigid air immediately surrounding the evaporator. Again, a fan is used to force air over and through this chamber and back out into the cabinet.

Fin-and-tube evaporators are also used on frostless freezers. Sometimes these have a radiant heater enclosed in a glass sheath which attaches directly in front of the tubing. Replacement of the heater simply involves unplugging the old one and plugging a new one in after the cover is removed. Of course, power must be turned off before service is performed.

The timer used on most freezers is of the 24-hour type and is set to defrost the freezer once every 24 hours, usually during the early morning hours. Of course, the timer must first be set to the correct time of day. This is often indicated by a notch on a small knob which protrudes through the front of the timer cover.

To care for a freezer correctly, follow the same

general rules that apply to refrigerators. Wipe up any spills immediately, keep the condenser coils clean and investigate any condition that produces frost buildup immediately. Set the control to maintain a temperature level of approximately 0 degrees within the cabinet. And finally, remember that home freezers are a storage system rather than a fast-freezing system. Don't fill over 10 percent of the capacity of the freezer with warm food. Doing so provides more of a load than the system can handle and temperatures go up substantially within the entire freezer. Add small amounts at a time and your operating characteristics will be much improved.

French Polish Finish

A French polish finish is a luxuriously deep shine in a wood finish. To obtain such a shine requires time, but the work is relatively simple. It may be beneficial for the handyman to practice the rubbing motion needed in obtaining a French polish finish. This can be done on a piece of scrap wood or on an area of the object to be finished that is not easily visible.

Before the actual polishing process is done, sand the surface, if necessary, or remove any accumulated wax. Wax removal may be accomplished with mineral spirits or turpentine. Any desired staining should be done before beginning the shellac applications. White shellac can be used to obtain an orange-brown finish.

One of two types of applicators must be used when applying the shellac. One type is a small bag made by wrapping cotton wool in linen and tying the edges together. Before closing the bag, thinned shellac and a few drops of boiled linseed oil are poured on the cotton wool. The second type of applicator is a $1/4$ inch pad made from washed cotton such as old white shirts. Wet this pad with boiled linseed oil and squeeze out the excess liquid. Either type of applicator can be used in the finishing process.

Rub the applicator hard in a continuous movement of straight strokes or figure 8's with the

figure 8 being the preferred rubbing motion. Apply shellac evenly to the entire surface, allow it to dry and repeat the process until the desired depth of shine is obtained. When using a pad applicator, the handyman may find it better to allow the shellac to dry thoroughly, sand lightly and then repeat the procedure. This sanding process eliminates the possibility of brush marks. The finish may also be rubbed down with rottenstone and oil after the final drying. *SEE ALSO WOOD FINISHING.*

Friction Tape

Friction tape has a cloth base, making it very good insulation for a wire splice in changeable weather conditions. At one time friction tape was used on any wiring job. Now it is more often seen in outside wiring as a sealant and protector for the softer, more pourous rubber tape. *SEE ALSO ELECTRICIAN'S TOOLS & EQUIPMENT.*

Frieze

A frieze is a member of a cornice assembly on a building. The frieze is a wide, horizontally laid board which is placed flat against the wall of a building, under the extension of the roofing boards. It acts as a base for the crown molding, a molding directly under the eave. *SEE ALSO MOLDING & TRIM.*

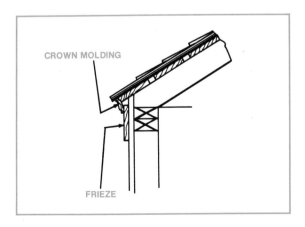

Frost Line

The frost line, which varies according to geographical location, is the depth to which frost penetrates the ground in cold climates. Footings and foundations of a building should be constructed below this line, for the foundations may be forced upward by the freezing of the moist soil, causing damaging cracks in the structure.

Frozen Pipes

Frozen pipes call for a two-step repair process: thawing the pipe and keeping the freezing from recurring.

Along with the use of an electric iron or heating pad, the simplest and safest way of thawing a pipe is to wrap the pipe with a heating cable, an insulated wire that heats electrically. Wrapping the pipe with heavy cloth and pouring boiling water on the cloth is another effective and widely used procedure. Only if the pipe is entirely clear of any potentially flammable materials and all faucets are left open to release steam pressure can a propane torch be used. Leaving the non-working faucets open also allows the pressure of the water moving in the pipe to help speed the thawing process and to let the worker know when the water is running freely. It is important not to get the pipe too hot. If it is warm to the touch, the heat is sufficient to travel along the pipe for a considerable distance.

After the pipe has been thawed, the next step is to try to prevent freezing from happening again. Wrapping the exposed pipe with insulating materials will hinder further freezing. If pipes are located in a hard-to-reach area, lining the walls or surface around it with insulation will be beneficial. If it is impossible to insulate the pipe or the area around it, focusing a heat light on the wall at the spot where freezing usually occurs is recommended. Chances of pipes freezing within the house will be reduced if doors to rooms are

left open so warm air can circulate. *SEE ALSO PLUMBING EMERGENCIES.*

Fruitwood Stain

Fruitwood stain is a pigmented wiping stain. For natural fruitwood staining, the substance is clear, but in order to stain other woods to appear as a fruitwood, the substance must be semi-opaque with tints added.

Simulated fruitwood stain is suitable for any wood and sometimes metal, and is applied in two steps. First, equal amounts of furniture varnish and mineral spirits are mixed to which a heaping teaspoon of burnt-sienna color, ground in oil is added. Apply this mixture to the wood surface in wood figure lines with a feather to simulate the wood grain, and allow it to dry for twenty four hours. Next, mix a cup of white paint and $1/3$ cup of mineral spirits tinted with raw-sienna colors ground in oil. Apply the mixture and then wipe it off. After allowing it to dry for six hours, apply a coat of clear varnish or shellac. The above procedure can be used on real fruitwood with the omission of the drawing of figure lines.

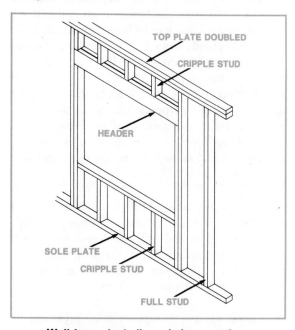

Wall frame including window opening.

Full Stud

A full stud is a structural part of a wall or partition frame which runs the full length of the wall from sole plate to top plate. When a full stud is cut because of an opening, such as a window, it becomes a cripple stud. *SEE ALSO WALL & CEILING CONSTRUCTION.*

Furniture Making

Furniture making is the assembly of legs, boxes, and panels into items of furniture. Such a system of component construction will work with such pieces as a Shaker table and a canopy bed. Using component construction, any home craftsman can build furniture.

PLANNING

The first step in furniture making is design selection. A large number of well-designed plans are available from tool manufacturers, from craft plan companies and in a variety of published books. Plans from these sources are tested before sale, and, if followed carefully, will result in well-designed sturdy pieces of furniture.

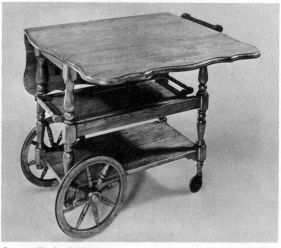

Courtesy The Stanley Works

This tea cart is typical of the designs available for the home furniture maker

669

If commercially available plans do not fit the particular need of a home craftsman, he should design his own piece. Designing is not too difficult at task, if the concept of legs, boxes and panels is kept in mind.

Any furniture design should have visual balance, style compatability and functional form. With visual balance, a piece of furniture looks in proportion.

With style compatability, the pieces of furniture fits the rest of the furniture in the room, for instance a carved, chintz-ruffled chair would not be suitable in a room which has leather and plastic furniture. With functional form, the parts of the piece of furniture are shaped with their ultimate function in mind. Planning for function usually creates simple, efficient lines that blend well with most furniture styles.

MATERIALS

Select materials by matching the necessary strength or flexibility required with the suitability of its appearance. For example, wood and acrylic plastic, the two materials most used in furniture making, both serve well as cabinet doors. The acrylic plastic, however, would look out of place on an Early American dry sink.

To work with wood, select from solid softwood and hardwood lumber, from plywood, and from hardboard. Each has advantages in use for furniture making.

Solid Woods

Softwood, such as pine or fir, is one of the easiest materials for the beginning craftsman to use. It is worked easily with hand tools; it nails, glues, and paints well and it also takes a natural finish well.

Hardwoods, such as maple, walnut or oak, have long been used in the making of fine furniture. These woods can provide the home craftsman with virtually invisible joints, sharp detailing, and satin smooth finishes. Pilot holes must be drilled before driving nails or screws in hardwoods to lessen the danger of splitting the wood.

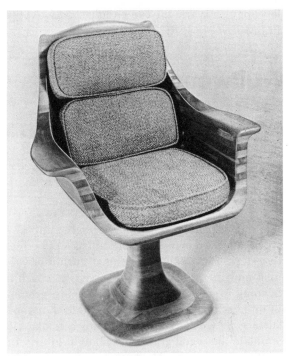

Courtesy of Stanley Works

This modern chair, laminated of walnut, is available as a home workshop plan. Patience in shaping the blanks will result in a similar professional-looking result.

Plywood

Plywood was once thought unsuitable for fine furniture. However, advances in manufacturing processes, plus the use of both fine hardwoods and exotic woods as surface veneers, have made plywood suitable for many furniture projects. Plywood has certain advantages over solid wood. Since the sheets are laid down with the grain of each ply perpendicular to the preceding, expansion and contraction of plywood is less, and the strength greater, than solid lumber. Plywood is also more flexible and more resistant to splitting.

Plywood is available in two types; exterior and interior. Exterior plywood is laminated with waterproof glue, and will not delaminate if left outdoors continuously. Interior plywood is formed using water-resistant glue, and should not be used for outdoor projects.

A special plywood, lumber-core plywood, is often used in fine furniture projects. This

plywood has a center core of edge-glued lumber, rather than several layers of veneer. Lumber-core plywood eliminates much of the problem of special treatment in the finishing of plywood edges.

One of the disadvantages of plywood is that the laminations of a piece of plywood show in the edges. This edge may be difficult to smooth, and may not add to the appearance of the piece of furniture, particularly if an appearance of solid wood is desired. Plywood edges may be concealed in several ways. Edge joints may be mitered, molding or thin strips of wood may be glued to the edge, or adhesive-backed veneer tape may be applied to the edge.

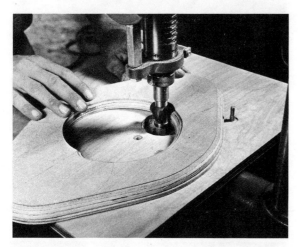

Laminations visible along the edge of a piece of plywood often make an opaque finish necessary, particularly when the edge is shaped as here.

Hardboard

Hardboard is another useful high-density wood product. Formed of wood fibers bonded into sheets by heat and pressure, hardboard is used in furniture making for drawer bottoms, chest or bookcase backs, and, in the thicker grades, upholstered chair bottoms.

Perforated hardboard, or pegboard, is an extremely useful material for the home craftsman. In addition to large-scale storage applications, perforated hardboard may be used in furniture pieces needing ventilation such as bathroom hampers or stereo cabinets.

Acrylics

Acrylic plastic is manufactured in rigid, resilient sheets that are available colorless, in transparent tints, in translucent and opaque colors and in smooth and textured finishes.

Acrylic sheets may be used in building such diverse furniture items as lighting diffusers, cabinet sliding doors, wine racks, cube tables, display pedestals, occasional tables, shelves, book stands, picture frames and magazine racks.

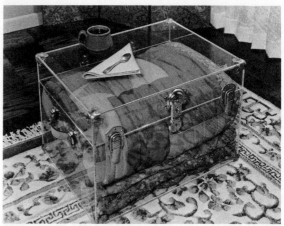

Courtesy of Rohm & Haas Company.

The old fashioned trunk takes on a modern look when it is built with Plexiglas acrylic plastic sheet.

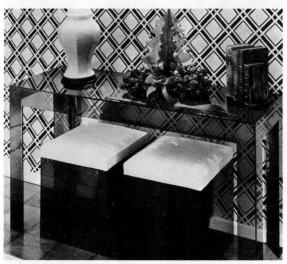

Courtesy of Rohm & Haas Company.

A Parsons table made of transparent bronze Plexiglas is an eye catching addition to an entryway. The simplicity of the table's design will enable the home craftsman to scale it for a variety of locations.

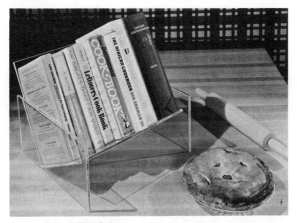

Courtesy Rohm & Haas Company.

A cookbook collection rack may be built using acrylic plastic sheet. Welded joints using liquid solvents add to the attractiveness of the completed item.

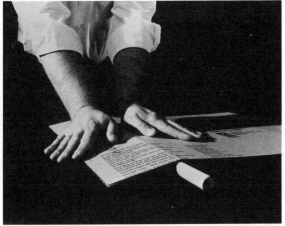

Courtesy of Rohm & Haas Company.

Acrylic sheet plastic can be easily cut by scribing and breaking. First mark the line to be cut, then scribe along it for several times. Place a 3/4'' dowel beneath the scribed mark, and press down.

Techniques used in working wood or soft metals can be applied to acrylic sheet. The plastic may be cut and drilled with both hand and power tools. Acrylics may be fastened together with nuts and bolts if desired; however a much stronger joint is obtained by chemically welding the parts with liquid or jellied solvents.

ASSEMBLY

The key to professional looking furniture is taking the time to perform each step accurately and

carefully. Allowing sufficient time is particularly important when measuring and cutting.

Accurate measurement is extremely important for tight, well-formed joints. Study the plan carefully to make sure that the dimensions are laid out correctly on the work. Remember that saw cuts, or kerfs, use up fractional inches of the lumber and make sure that the cuts are made on the waste side of the cutting line. If the kerf is not on the waste side, the length of the cut piece will be off a fraction of an inch, causing an improper fit when assembling the piece.

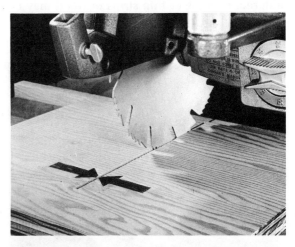

A saw kerf takes space. Be sure to allow for this waste space when laying out pieces for sawing.

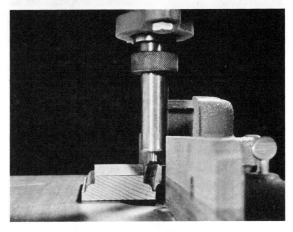

If power equipment is available in the home shop, moldings may be made rather than purchased.

Careful cutting is equally important. In more complex joint assemblies, such as locked miter or mitered rabbet, the need for accurate layout of

angles is matched by the need for accurate cutting if a smooth, hairline joint is to be achieved. Careless cutting will cause loose or over-tight joints. Loose joints will not hold together of themselves, and will place additional strain on the adhesive used to fasten the joint. Overtight joints that must be force-fitted together may split the wood, particularly if the joint is glued.

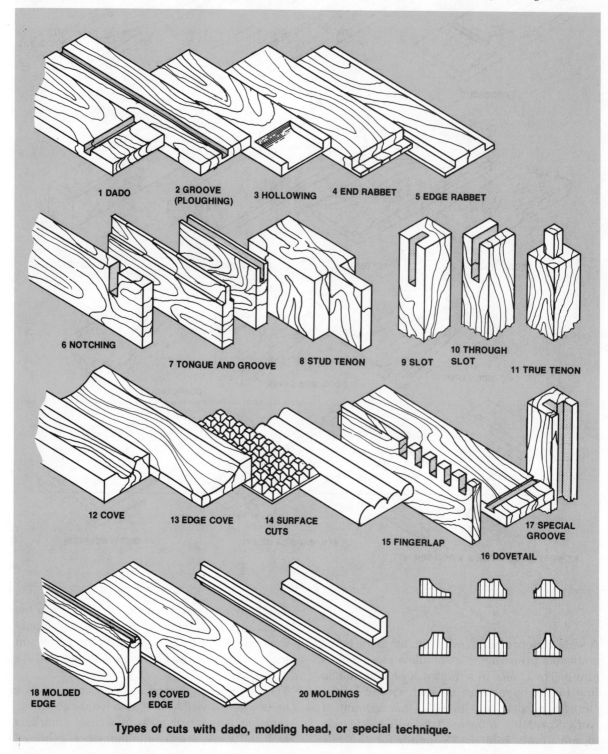

1 DADO 2 GROOVE (PLOUGHING) 3 HOLLOWING 4 END RABBET 5 EDGE RABBET

6 NOTCHING 7 TONGUE AND GROOVE 8 STUD TENON 9 SLOT 10 THROUGH SLOT 11 TRUE TENON

12 COVE 13 EDGE COVE 14 SURFACE CUTS 15 FINGERLAP 16 DOVETAIL 17 SPECIAL GROOVE

18 MOLDED EDGE 19 COVED EDGE 20 MOLDINGS

Types of cuts with dado, molding head, or special technique.

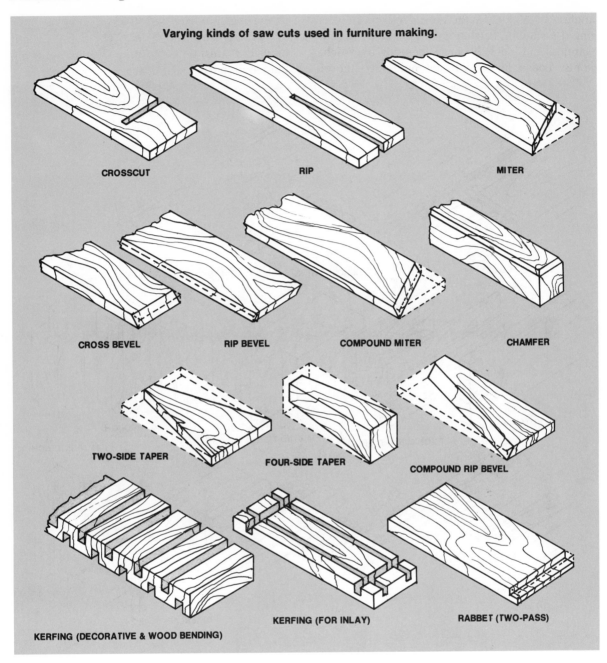

Varying kinds of saw cuts used in furniture making.

CROSSCUT   RIP   MITER

CROSS BEVEL   RIP BEVEL   COMPOUND MITER   CHAMFER

TWO-SIDE TAPER   FOUR-SIDE TAPER   COMPOUND RIP BEVEL

KERFING (DECORATIVE & WOOD BENDING)   KERFING (FOR INLAY)   RABBET (TWO-PASS)

Joints

A wide variety of joints are available to the home craftsman preparing to assemble a piece of furniture. The choice of a joint will be determined first by the appearance desired, second by the strength needed, and third by the amount of work acceptable to the craftsman. A good guide to selecting a joint is "Strength for the job; simplicity for the craftsman." In addition to the basic *butt joint,* there are five joints commonly used in furniture making; miter, mortise and tenon, dowel, lap, and groove (dado and rabbet).

The *miter joint* is used at the corners of box units where a visible end grain would not be acceptable. A square to measure angles, a marking tool, and a saw are the minimum tools required

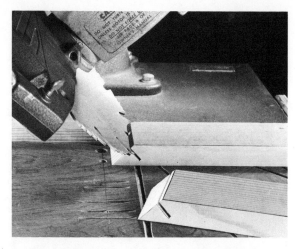

A spline will increase the strength of a miter joint. Dowelling the joint will serve the same purpose.

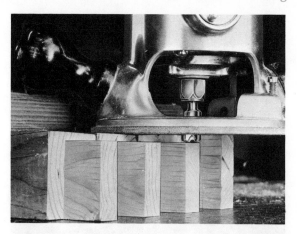

When a number of similar cuts or joints must be made, gang cutting is an efficient method of making them.

to cut miter joints. A home-made or commercially available miter box is a help in cutting accurate angles. An unsupported miter joint is susceptable to shear breakage; adding dowels or splines increases the strength of the joint. If the inside of the joint is concealed by a chair seat or table top, glue blocks will also strengthen the joint.

The *mortise and tenon joint* is a traditional furniture making joint. The mortise is a recess or groove; the tenon is the tab or projection that fits the recess. This joint is most often used to join legs to box units, or rails to legs. Tenons can be cut either with a backsaw or with power tools. Mortises are usually formed by drilling a series of overlapping holes of the proper depth, then

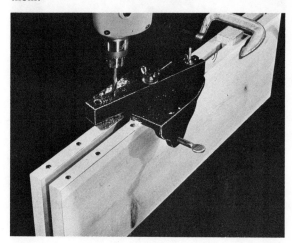

A commercially available jig insures accurate drilling for dowel joints.

chiseling the sides smooth and the corners square. In cutting mortise and tenon joints, chamfer one or two edges of the tenon to allow space for excess glue to escape.

Dowel joints may be defined as two mortises holding a common tenon. Most simple joints, such as the butt joint, for example, may be strengthened by inserting a dowel. (Dowels are wooden rods of varying diameters sold in building supply stores — or at lumberyards.) Dowels should be notched or grooved, much like a tenon, to allow excess glue to escape.

Lap joints are also used in joining rails. There are actually two types of lap joint; the *half-lap*

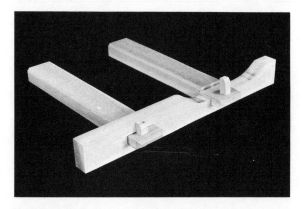

In rustic furniture, a pegged mortise and tenon joint is not only very strong, but also an attractive design feature.

and the *cross-lap*. The half-lap is formed at the ends of two pieces of wood, and is often the joint used to create very long rails or beams. The cross lap occurs anywhere other than the ends of the board, and is quite literally where two boards lap where they cross. To make either type of lap joint, plane the wood on each piece to one half the width of the board. The resulting areas of half-thickness are fastened together to form the joint.

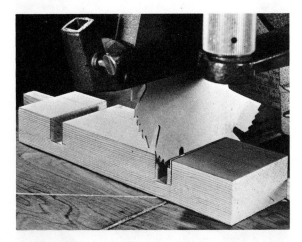

If a dado cutter is not available, repeated passes with a power saw or cuts with a hand saw will also form the joint.

Two joints formed by grooving are the *dado* and the *rabbet*. The rabbet is a groove formed along the edge of a piece of wood, forming a ledge or lip. The *dado* is a groove cut somewhere other than the edge of the piece of wood, forming a ledge area to support a shelf, lock a side together or the like.

Drawer Construction

Selection of joints is important in the building of drawers. A drawer is essentially a box which slides on cleats. The area of greatest strain in a drawer comes at the joint which fastens the front to the sides. Locking joints, such as the dovetail, provide the strength needed to keep the front fastened to the drawer after repeated use. The simplest way to fasten a bottom to a drawer is to cut a dado about 1/4 to 1/2 inch from the bottom of all four sides of the drawer. Assemble the front and the sides, slip the bottom into the dadoes, then attach the back.

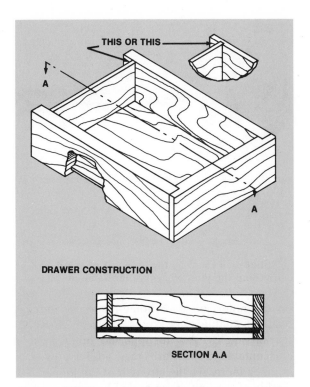

DRAWER CONSTRUCTION

SECTION A.A

Dadoes provide a simple way to fasten parts of a drawer together.

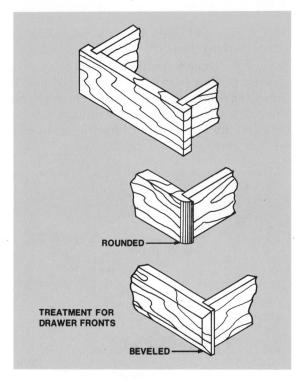

ROUNDED

TREATMENT FOR DRAWER FRONTS

BEVELED

Simple joints for fastening drawer sides and fronts. Note varied treatment of drawer fronts.

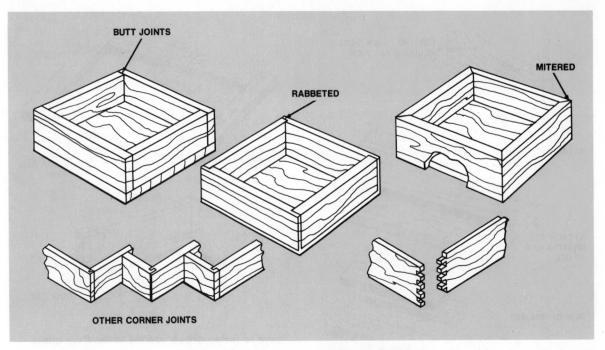

BUTT JOINTS

RABBETED

MITERED

OTHER CORNER JOINTS

Several joints that may be used with drawers.

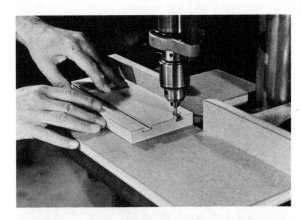

Dovetail joints can be formed by either power tools or hand sawing and chiseling. Here the angled dovetail cut is being used to form a locking dado.

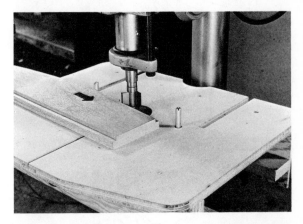

Rabbets such as these may be used to form drawer fronts, to serve as door stops, or to form ledges for shelves and drawers to rest on.

Drawer guides may be either commercial units or home made. The simplest home units are dadoes cut into the drawer sides which are next to the guides. Cleats on the sides of the case fit the dadoes and guide the drawer.

Standard Furniture Dimensions

In adapting or designing furniture designs, the home craftsman should use generally accepted

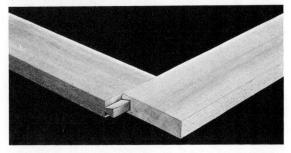

Anytime a locking lip can be cut in a joint, it will increase the strength of that joint.

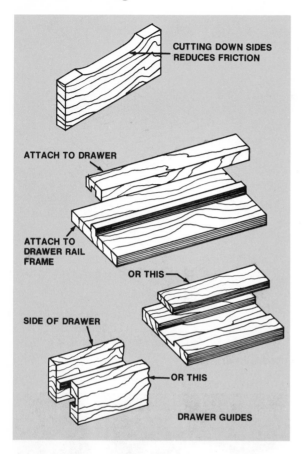

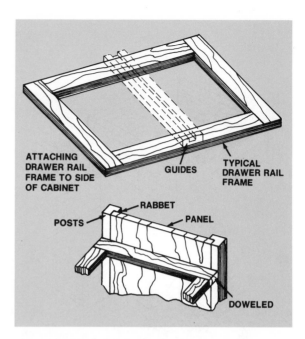

Several ways to handle drawer sides to provide drawer guides.

Ways to fasten drawer guides to furniture cases.

measurements for table heights, chair heights, and bed widths. By staying within accepted dimensions for major pieces of furniture, the project will be in proportion with the other furniture in the house.

Beds are built to fit standardized mattress sizes. Lengths will vary between 78 to 84 inches. The widths of the various mattress sizes are as follows: Twin, 42 inches; double, 54 inches; queen, 60 inches and king, 72 inches (minimum).

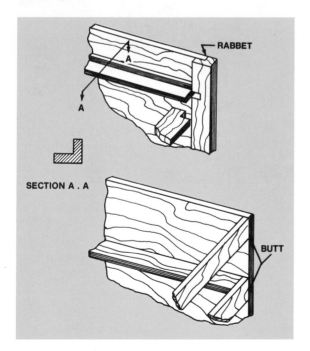

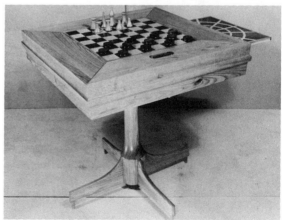

Courtesy The Stanley Works

A multi-use game table is formed of simple components assembled in a home workshop.

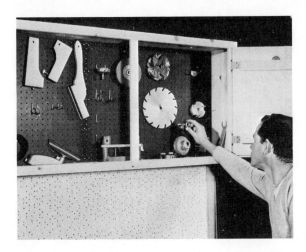

Perforated hardboard provides useful storage at the back of a cabinet.

The top of the mattress should be about 24 inches from the floor.

Chests of drawers can vary greatly in size. Drawer widths are usually 24 to 36 inches and depth are 18 to 21 inches. Chests of drawers range from 36 to 54 inches in height. Colonial highboy reproductions may be taller, but their top surfaces are not intended for use.

Table sizes vary greatly, depending upon the planned use of the article.

Table Chart			
Table Dimensions			
Type	**Height**	**Width**	**Length**
Coffee	12-18	17-38	31-79
End	22-26	17-20	12-21
Dining	29	36-48	56-121

While table legs may be angled slightly for improved appearance, great care must be taken not to use an angle that will weaken the support, nor cause the legs to extend from beneath the table.

Desks need a minimum area of 14 by 22 inches. A maximum useful size for a desk is determined by the front to side reach (arm length) of the person who will use the desk. An average writing desk should be 29 to 30 inches high; for comfortable use, a typewriting desk should be about 27 inches high. For comfort the minimum legroom in the kneehole should be about 22 inches wide, 21 inches deep, and 25 inches high.

When building bookcases, estimate 9 average books for each running foot of shelf space. Excluding the larger size books, 1 x 10 planks spaced 9 inches apart will store most books.

The design of an actual chair can be somewhat complicated. The beginning craftsman should probably limit himself to prepared chair plans. However, certain dimensions are relatively standard for all chairs. Seat height should be about 18 inches; average seat depth should be about 18 inches also. The top of the seat back should support the back at about the level of the armpit, or approximately 18 inches above the seat. The seat back should slant to the rear about 3 inches.

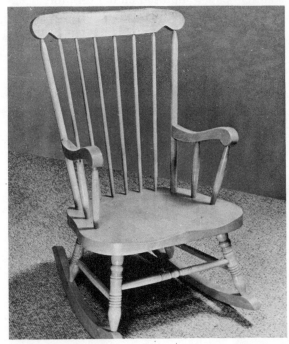

Courtesy The Stanley Works

A traditional Boston Rocker can be made in the home workshop, using readily-available plans.

FINISHING

Once the article of furniture is completed, it must have a protective finish. The most common finishes used are paint and varnish. Craft stores, or artist's supply houses, have supplies of decals that may be applied to painted furniture. Color-

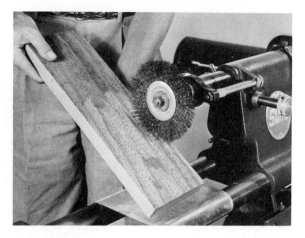

Wire brushing is a quick way to obtain a weathered or distressed finish on wood.

ful applique designs may be cut from contac-adhesive paper and used on the furniture. Contact adhesive paper in leather or wood-grain designs may be applied to the item of furniture, and then sealed with a plastic finish. *SEE ALSO: BLIND DOWELING, CABINETMAKING, UPHOLSTERY, WOOD FINISHING, WOOD JOINTS.*

FURNITURE PLANS

The following plans for a colonial table, a rustic table, and a modern chair are supplied by the Educational Department of Stanley Tools.

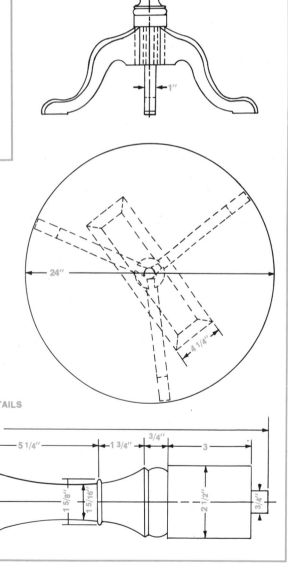

Colonial Table

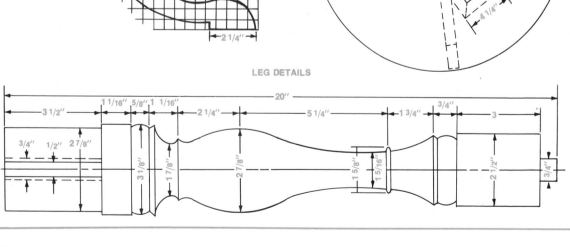

FOOT DETAILS

3 3/8"

GRAIN

1/2" sq.

2 1/4"

LEG DETAILS

24"

4 1/4"

20"

3 1/2"   1 1/16" 5/8" 1 1/16"   2 1/4"   5 1/4"   1 3/4" 3/4"   3

3/4" 1/2" 2 7/8"   3 1/8"   1 7/8"   2 7/8"   1 5/8" 1 5/16"   2 1/2"   3/4"

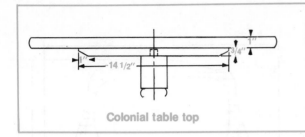

Colonial table top

MATERIAL LIST
Colonial Table

Part Name	No. of Pc.	T	W	L
Top	1	1	24	24
Leg	1	$3\frac{1}{8}$	$3\frac{1}{8}$	20
Foot	3	1	$8\frac{1}{2}$	11
Cleat	1	$\frac{3}{4}$	$4\frac{1}{4}$	$14\frac{1}{2}$

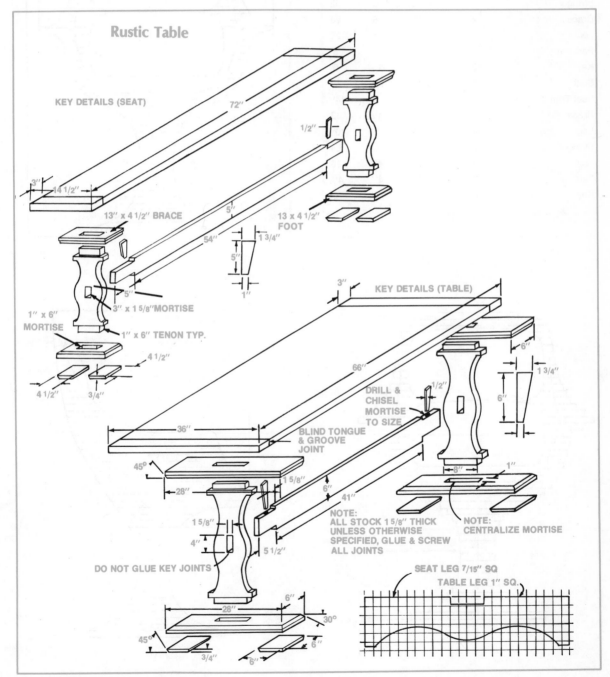

Rustic Table

KEY DETAILS (SEAT)

72"

14 1/2"

3"

13" x 4 1/2" BRACE

5"

13 x 4 1/2" FOOT

1 3/4"

54"

5"

5"

1"

3" x 1 5/8" MORTISE

1" x 6" MORTISE

1" x 6" TENON TYP.

4 1/2"

4 1/2"

3/4"

KEY DETAILS (TABLE)

3"

66"

6"

1 3/4"

6"

DRILL & CHISEL MORTISE TO SIZE

1/2"

BLIND TONGUE & GROOVE JOINT

36"

45°

28"

1 5/8"

6"

41"

1 5/8"

4"

5 1/2"

8"

1"

NOTE: CENTRALIZE MORTISE

NOTE: ALL STOCK 1 5/8" THICK UNLESS OTHERWISE SPECIFIED, GLUE & SCREW ALL JOINTS

DO NOT GLUE KEY JOINTS

28"

6"

30°

45°

6"

3/4"

8"

SEAT LEG 7/15" SQ

TABLE LEG 1" SQ.

681

MATERIAL LIST

Rustic Table

Part Name	No. of Pc.	T	W	L
Top	1	$1^5/_8$	36	60
Top Trim	2	$1^5/_8$	3	36
Leg	2	$1^5/_8$	11	24
Stringer	1	$1^5/_8$	6	52
Brace	2	$1^5/_8$	6	28
Foot	2	$1^5/_8$	6	28
Pad	4	$3/_4$	6	6
Key	2	$1/_2$	$1^3/_4$	6
Seat	2	$1^5/_8$	$14^1/_2$	66
Seat Trim	4	$1^5/_8$	3	$14^1/_2$
Brace	4	$1^5/_8$	$4^1/_2$	13
Leg	4	$1^5/_8$	5	$10^1/_2$
Stringer	2	$1^5/_8$	5	64
Foot	4	$1^5/_8$	$4^1/_2$	13
Pad	8	$3/_4$	$4^1/_2$	$4^1/_2$
Key	4	$1/_2$	$1^3/_4$	5

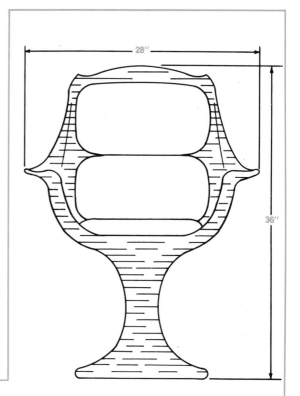

Modern Chair

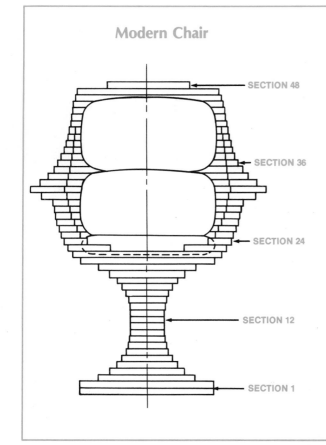

SECTION 48

SECTION 36

SECTION 24

SECTION 12

SECTION 1

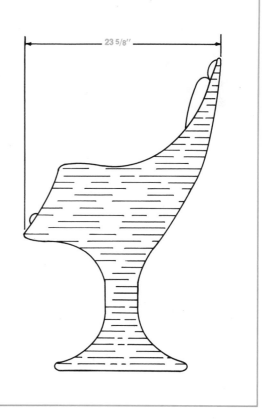

MATERIALS LIST

Section No.	No. of Pc.	T	W	L	Section No.	No. of Pc.	T	W	L
		Modern Chair					Modern Chair		
1	1	³/₄	16	16	25	1	³/₄	17³/₈	20⁵/₈
2	1	³/₄	16	16	26	1	³/₄	17³/₈	21³/₁₆
3	1	³/₄	11⁵/₈	11⁵/₈	27	1	³/₄	17³/₈	21¹¹/₁₆
4	1	³/₄	9	9	28	1	³/₄	17⁵/₁₆	22
5	1	³/₄	7¹/₄	7¹/₄	29	1	³/₄	17⁵/₁₆	22⁵/₁₆
6	1	³/₄	6	6	30	1	³/₄	17⁵/₁₆	22¹³/₁₆
7	1	³/₄	5¹/₈	5¹/₈	31	1	³/₄	17⁵/₁₆	25⁵/₈
8	1	³/₄	4¹/₂	4¹/₂	32	1	³/₄	17⁵/₁₆	28
9	1	³/₄	4¹/₄	4¹/₄	33	1	³/₄	8¹/₈	26
10	1	³/₄	4	4	34	1	³/₄	6¹/₄	23⁷/₈
11	1	³/₄	4	4	35	1	³/₄	5¹/₄	22⁹/₁₆
12	1	³/₄	4	4	36	1	³/₄	4⁷/₁₆	21⁵/₈
13	1	³/₄	4	4	37	1	³/₄	3¹³/₁₆	20⁷/₈
14	1	³/₄	4¹/₄	4¹/₄	38	1	³/₄	3³/₈	20³/₁₆
15	1	³/₄	4¹/₂	4¹/₂	39	1	³/₄	3	19⁵/₈
16	1	³/₄	5¹/₈	5¹/₈	40	1	³/₄	2¹¹/₁₆	19¹/₄
17	1	³/₄	6	6	41	1	³/₄	2¹/₂	18⁷/₈
18	1	³/₄	7¹/₄	7³/₈	42	1	³/₄	2¹/₄	18⁵/₈
19	1	³/₄	9	9³/₈	43	1	³/₄	2	18³/₈
20	1	³/₄	11⁵/₈	13¹/₂	44	1	³/₄	1¹¹/₁₆	18¹/₈
21	1	³/₄	16	16⁷/₈	45	1	³/₄	1³/₈	17⁷/₈
22	1	³/₄	17⁷/₁₆	17³/₄	46	1	³/₄	1⁵/₈	17¹/₂
23	1	³/₄	17¹/₂	19	47	1	³/₄	1³/₄	16⁷/₈
24	1	³/₄	17³/₈	20	48	1	³/₄	1³/₄	9¹³/₁₆

Acrylic Plastic Wine Rack

The plans for the acrylic wine rack and the accompanying shaping heater are supplied by Rohm and Haas Company, manufacturers of Plexiglas acrylic sheet.

Without removing the masking paper, cut an 18 by 33 inch rectangle from ¼ inch Plexiglas. Buff the edges to transparency. Next, make pencil marks on the still-unremoved masking paper to

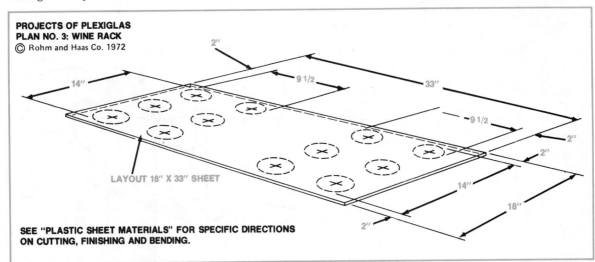

PROJECTS OF PLEXIGLAS
PLAN NO. 3: WINE RACK
© Rohm and Haas Co. 1972

2″
14″
9 1/2
33″
9 1/2
2″
2″
14″
18″
2″

LAYOUT 18″ X 33″ SHEET

SEE "PLASTIC SHEET MATERIALS" FOR SPECIFIC DIRECTIONS ON CUTTING, FINISHING AND BENDING.

mark the centers of 3½ inch holes for wine bottles. (These holes should be marked as groups of six in each 9½ by 14 inch end section.) Cut the holes with a sabre saw, jig saw, or fly cutter, then buff the edges of the holes to transparency.

Remove the masking paper from the Plexiglas. Using a Blaisdell china marker, draw lines across the sheet 13 inches from each end. Using the strip heater described below, make the two 90° bends 13½ inches from each end.

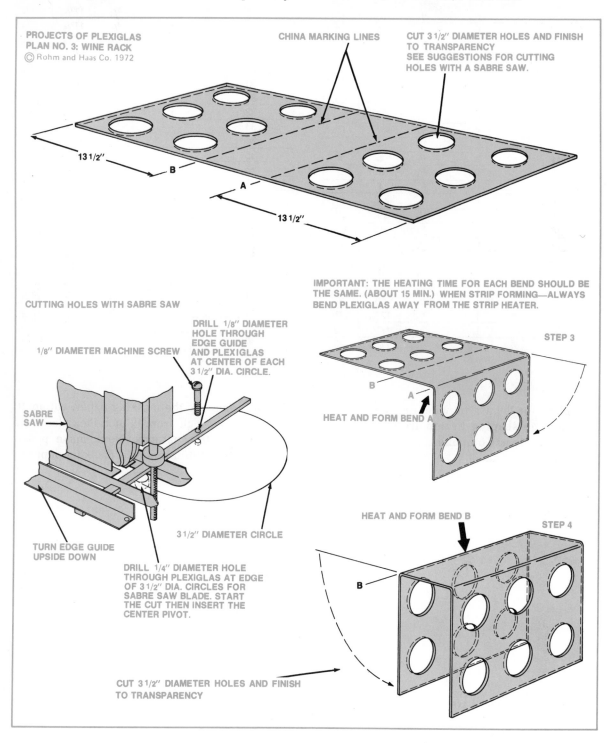

PROJECTS OF PLEXIGLAS
PLAN NO. 3: WINE RACK
© Rohm and Haas Co. 1972

CHINA MARKING LINES

CUT 3 1/2″ DIAMETER HOLES AND FINISH
TO TRANSPARENCY
SEE SUGGESTIONS FOR CUTTING
HOLES WITH A SABRE SAW.

13 1/2″

B

A

13 1/2″

CUTTING HOLES WITH SABRE SAW

1/8″ DIAMETER MACHINE SCREW

DRILL 1/8″ DIAMETER
HOLE THROUGH
EDGE GUIDE
AND PLEXIGLAS
AT CENTER OF EACH
3 1/2″ DIA. CIRCLE.

SABRE
SAW

TURN EDGE GUIDE
UPSIDE DOWN

3 1/2″ DIAMETER CIRCLE

DRILL 1/4″ DIAMETER HOLE
THROUGH PLEXIGLAS AT EDGE
OF 3 1/2″ DIA. CIRCLES FOR
SABRE SAW BLADE. START
THE CUT THEN INSERT THE
CENTER PIVOT.

CUT 3 1/2″ DIAMETER HOLES AND FINISH
TO TRANSPARENCY

IMPORTANT: THE HEATING TIME FOR EACH BEND SHOULD BE
THE SAME. (ABOUT 15 MIN.) WHEN STRIP FORMING—ALWAYS
BEND PLEXIGLAS AWAY FROM THE STRIP HEATER.

STEP 3

B

A

HEAT AND FORM BEND A

HEAT AND FORM BEND B

STEP 4

B

684

Note: the suggestions and data contained in this plan are thought to be reliable by the manufacturer. They are offered in good faith, but without guarantee, as conditions and methods of use of these products are beyond the manufacturer's control. It is recommended that the prospective user determine the suitability of the materials and suggestions before adapting them on a commercial scale. Suggestions for the uses of these products or the inclusion of descriptive material from patents and the citation of specific patents in this publication should not be understood as recommending the use of these products in violation of any patent or as permission or license to use any patents of the Rohm and Haas Company.

Shaping Heater

The wine rack is formed by bending Plexiglas acrylic sheet. This bending is accomplished by spot heating the acrylic. Because of fumes given off by the heated plastic, such heating must be done in a well-ventilated area, *not the kitchen oven.* A simple heating unit may be constructed as follows: Cut a strip of 1/2 inch plywood 6 inches by 42 inches. Next, cut two 1/4 inch plywood strips, 2 5/8 inches by 36 inches. Leaving a 3/4 inch channel down the center line of the base, nail the two strips to the base. Cut two pieces of heavy duty aluminum foil 6 inches by 36 inches, then fold and fit in the center channel. Attach a ground wire to the aluminum foil using a nail. (The ground wire should be long enough to reach a common ground, such as a cover plate screw for an electrical outlet.) Cut two pieces of asbestos paper 6 1/4 inches by 36 inches. Fold paper to fit on top of foil in channel on base. Staple paper and foil to side strips of base. Lay the Briskeat heating element in the channel. Drive a nail 1 1/2 inches from each end of the base along the center line. Tie the end strings of the heating element to the nails. Assemble the plug; fasten ground wire to common ground; and plug in heating unit.

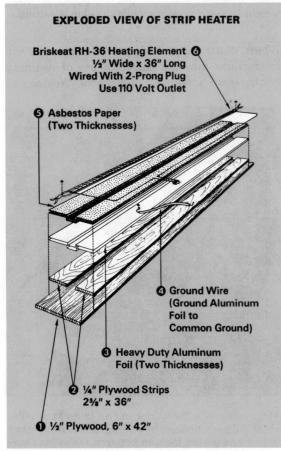

EXPLODED VIEW OF STRIP HEATER

Briskeat RH-36 Heating Element ❻
½" Wide x 36" Long
Wired With 2-Prong Plug
Use 110 Volt Outlet

❺ **Asbestos Paper**
(Two Thicknesses)

❹ **Ground Wire**
(Ground Aluminum
Foil to
Common Ground)

❸ **Heavy Duty Aluminum
Foil** (Two Thicknesses)

❷ **¼" Plywood Strips**
2⅝" x 36"

❶ **½" Plywood, 6" x 42"**

Courtesy Brisco Manufacturing Company and Rohm and Hass Company

DINING TABLES FROM FLUSH DOORS

An unusual way to build a dining table is by using a stock slab door as the top. Such doors are mass produced in attractive kinds of wood, at surprisingly modest prices at lumber dealers everywhere.

All the ideas for table building shown here are so simple that they require only hand tools, though several of them can be accomplished more quickly with a few power tools. A screwdriver, hammer and saw will do most of them, and even the most difficult will require you to add only a square, a chisel and a brace and bits.

Since slab doors come in a wide variety of woods and an equally wide choice of width, it will probably be easy to find one to suit your taste and requirements. One kind of door that is well suited for a dining table is a solid-wood-core type with hardwood veneer. Less expensive, but no less attractive, is one of the Philippine mahogany slab doors now most frequently encountered. If a hollow-core door is chosen for

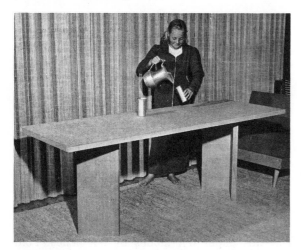

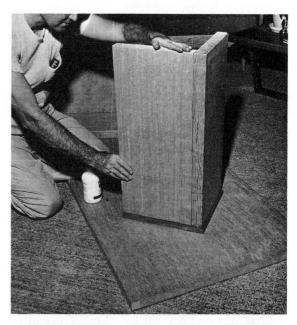

This design for an unusual table can be built in an hour or two. Instead of using legs the top is supported by joining two pairs of plain lumber rectangles into V-shaped troughs.

Materials: Slab door, 3 feet (or narrower) by 6 feet 8 inches. 10 feet of 2 x 12 lumber. 12 x 14 inch piece of 1-inch lumber. Screws or finishing nails.

Center the troughs 8 inches from the ends of the door and glue into place. Unless you are using contact cement to make this joint, pile on books or other weight to apply pressure while the glue is setting.

Where dimensions of leg parts are given in the instructions they are based on use of ordinary lumber-yard softwood, such as the Western or

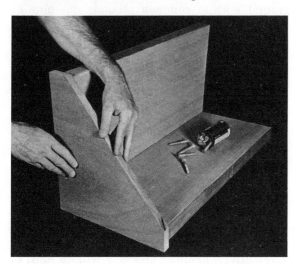

Cut the 2 x 12 into four 28-inch lengths and rip an amount equal to the thickness of the lumber (about 1½ inches) off two of them. Assemble into matching troughs, and glue to triangles like this, cut from the 1-inch lumber.

its low price and light weight, you will have to use glue to fasten the door to underpinnings, or confine screws to areas near edges.

For a utility table or for a breakfast or dining table to be finished with enamel or pigmented lacquer (black lacquer can be striking) a low-priced hardboard door can be used.

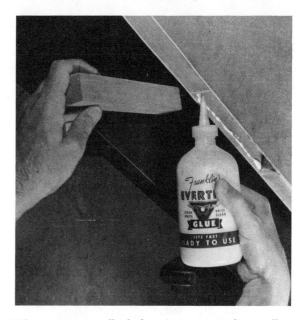

When you saw a flush door in two to make smaller tables, fill open hollows by cutting blocks from scrap lumber and gluing them in between the veneer surfaces.

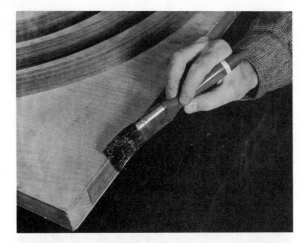

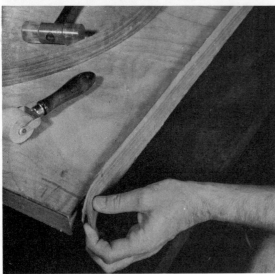

purpose, or it can be thin strips of lumber cut from a hardwood plank. Wider edging strips may be used it you wish to increase the size of your table somewhat beyond the dimensions ordinarily available in stock flush doors. The standard exterior door, 3 feet wide and 6 feet 8 inches long, can become a rather magnificent dining table 40 inches wide and 84 inches long.

A clear finish will preserve the natural beauty of the hardwoods used in manufacturing flush doors. One of the wipe-on sealers or oil finishes

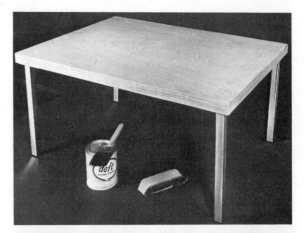

To conceal lumber edges of flush doors, use strips of matching veneer, now widely available in lumber yards, or strips of wood. To apply, brush a coat of contact cement onto the edge of the door and one side of the strip. After 30 minutes, apply a second coat. When it is dry, place strip exactly in position and press firmly. Trim flush with a plane and sanding block.

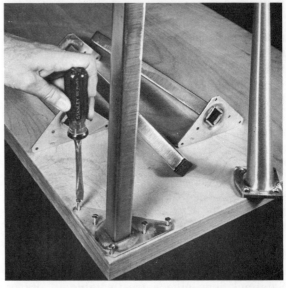

other pines, Douglas fir or redwood. So 2 x 4 means actual dimensions of $1^1/_2$ by $3^1/_2$ inches, the dimensions you will use if you cut the parts from hardwood.

Many doors are so nicely edged that you may be satisfied to use them as they come, after giving the edges a good sanding. More deluxe treatment will involve adding edging by use of contact cement. This can be veneer edge strips sold for this

Quickest way in the world to create an attractive table is by fastening one-piece brushed brass legs to a piece of edge-trimmed plywood or a slab door or part of one. Tapered round leg displayed at right is an alternate design; like the square type, round legs may be had in heights suitable for coffee or dining tables.

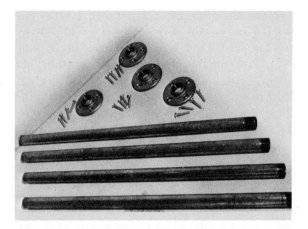

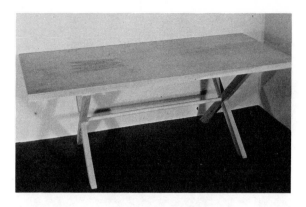

This kit, made up of stock plumbing parts, can be used to turn a slab door, sheet of plywood or three cleated-together redwood or pine 2 x 12s into a fine table that can be quickly taken apart for storage. The floor flanges are fastened into place near the corners of the top with screws and the four equal lengths of galvanized water pipe (³/₄ inch or 1 inch, except for a very small table) are twisted into the flanges. Note that threads are needed at only one end of pipes.

can be applied so quickly that you can finish your table in a single afternoon and use it the next morning.

Designs shown are easily modified in height. The most desirable height for a dining table is 28 to 30 inches. The same height is usual for a table to be used as a desk, but you should consider first the chair most likely to be used with it. If it is a living-room side chair, it will probably be lower than the usual desk chair, and the desk should be made correspondingly lower too. For a table to hold a typewriter, the standard height is 26 inches, but here again allowance should be made for chair height. Usual coffee-table height is about 15 inches; vary this a little if the table will be placed near a couch that is unusually high or low.

Trestle (Sawbuck) Table

Sawbuck legs give a trestle table its Early American air. To mark both ends of legs for cutting at 45 degree angle, first find exact width of the 2 x 3. Measure that distance from a corner and then 38³/₄ inches from there and also from other corner.

Cut two braces 31³/₁₆ inches long from a 1 x 4. Arrange the legs in an X and mark both of them for cutting, making sure that each leg is level when marking.

Saw both legs of each pair just halfway through at the lap marks, then chisel out the wood between. Additional saw cuts between the marks make wood removal easier.

Drill a hole the same diameter as the pole in the center of the lap on each of the two leg pieces that will go to the inside. These will face each other. Drill and countersink screw holes 1¹/₄ inches and 3 inches from both ends of each brace. Center the legs on braces and secure with glue and 1¹/₂ inch screws. Also glue the lap joints and reinforce them with two oval-head screws.

Glue in the pole and assemble the trestles to the underside of the door, using glue and four screws in each.

MATERIALS LIST:

Slab door, 3 feet by 6 feet 8 inches.
14 foot 2 x 3 cut into four 38³/₄ inch legs with ends at 45 degree angles.
6 foot 1 x 4 cut into two 31³/₁₆ inch braces.
4 or 5 feet of closet pole
4 No. 8 oval-head screws 1¹/₄ inch;
16 No. 8 flathead screws 1¹/₂ inch.

Hollow-Square Table

A pair of open-square frames support this attractive dining table. Wedge-shaped corner blocks

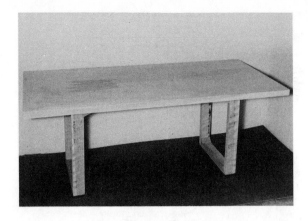

reinforce the frames, while concealed triangles keep everything strongly braced.

Cut square joints half the thickness of the wood at the ends of the legs and braces. Drill and countersink a pair of screw holes at the ends of the braces, starting 1$\frac{1}{2}$ inches in and slanting to corner. Fit two legs and two braces together to make each support. Glue the joints. Put screws through the holes in the braces and into the legs.

Cut four triangles the width of the lumber and about 8 inches long. Cut eight triangles making them as long (3$\frac{1}{2}$ inches) as the lumber is wide. Glue the small triangles into the corners where the legs and braces meet. While the glue dries, hold them tight with C-clamps, finishing nails or ropes. Drill and countersink two screw holes in each large triangle. Glue and screw them to the legs. Drill and countersink screw holes near each end of each top brace. Center the supports on the door about 14 inches from the ends, with triangles toward inside. Glue and screw top brace of each support to the solid-core door.

MATERIALS LIST:

Slab door 3 feet wide, 6 feet 8 inches long.
20 feet of 2 x 4 lumber cut into four 28$\frac{1}{4}$ inch legs and four 22$\frac{1}{2}$ inch braces.
Scraps to make triangles.
28 No. 12, 2 inch, flat-head screws.

Furniture Refinishing
[SEE ANTIQUING; WOOD FINISHING.]

Furring

Furring is used to prepare an existing wall for a new paneling material. The wall may be unsightly, abused, uneven, or exposed masonry units in a basement or to give a room a new look even if the existing walls are sound. All such situations fit in this area of remodeling.

Furring consists of strips of wood that are secured to the wall to provide a nailing surface for the new facing. The wood does not have to be the best grade, but it should be sound and easy to nail. An occasional tight knot is not objectionable, but do avoid wood that has loose knots, an abundance of blemishes or splits. The fact that the furring is a mount-method and will be concealed does not justify the use of inferior grades. Most professionals prefer a pine that falls somewhere between the shelving grades and clear stock. The wood must be dry and free of wind and excessive warp. Judgments can be made by

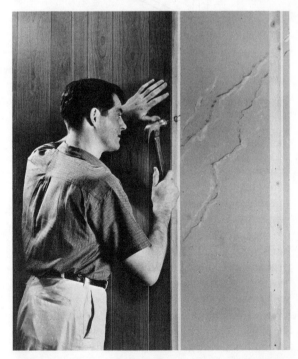

Furring is applied over existing walls to provide nailing surface for a new cover. Whether the furring is applied vertically or horizontally — or both ways — depends on the material.

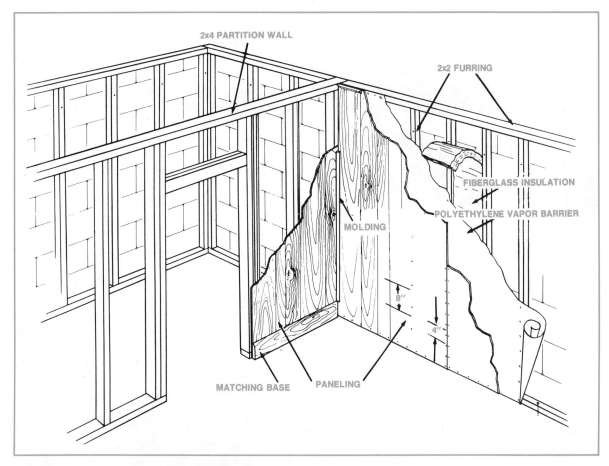

2x4 PARTITION WALL

2x2 FURRING

FIBERGLASS INSULATION

POLYETHYLENE VAPOR BARRIER

MOLDING

8″

4″

MATCHING BASE

PANELING

One method of covering a masonry wall.

viewing the stock in a local lumber yard, or just ask for furring and you will get a good material for the job.

Whenever possible, get strips that are long enough for one-piece coverage to minimize the number of end joints. If you are applying furring vertically, you want pieces that run from floor to ceiling. If the furring pattern is basically horizontal, then the length of the wall is the prime dimension. The strips can be as narrow as $1^1/_2$ inches, but many professionals prefer to work with wider material, as much as 3 inches, since this increases the available nailing surfaces. The choice is between saving a few dollars on material and greater work convenience.

Whether you apply the furring vertically or horizontally and how much of it you use, depends on the cover material. For example,

material that is very thin and flexible requires more backing than a $3/_4$ inch tongue and groove lumber paneling. The latter has rigidity in itself, the former will acquire it in direct relation to the amount of backing provided. Do not, for example, attempt to mount $3/_{16}$ inch thick panels that are 4 feet wide on furring that is spaced 4 feet on-centers. You will certainly get bows and bulges and the feel of the wall will be anything but assuring. It is not necessary to overdo the furring, but do not make the mistake of using too little.

Start the job by locating a stud. This you can do by tapping along the wall with a hammer until you get a solid sound. If you have trouble working this way, then drill a series of small holes or drive a number of nails on a horizontal line until you hit a stud. Drill or drive only as deep as you must to penetrate the wall in order not to inter-

fere with wiring or plumbing that may be in the wall space.

Mark the center of the stud and then measure out in each direction and make pencil marks every 16 inches. Use a plumb bob or a level to extend the marks from the floor to the ceiling. Assume that the studs are vertical and spaced correctly. Some errors might exist and, if so, you will have to compensate when nailing the furring.

Use box or common nails in a length that is three times the thickness of the furring. It is a good idea to add to this the thickness of the existing wall. Thus, if the furring is $3/4$ inch thick and the wall is $1/2$ inch thick, the nails should be $2 3/4$ inches long.

Start the job by securing one strip at the floor and another at the ceiling. Strips between should be spaced 16 inches on centers. Start at the bottom and work toward the top. Chances are that the last strip will not have the recommended spacing but that will not matter. Just mark or note its location so you will know where to nail when nailing the paneling.

The edges of all panels should have nailing surface. So, assuming panels that are 4 feet wide, apply vertical furring across the wall 4 feet on centers. Many times, this vertical furring is put on *every* stud.

Vertical furring *only* may be the best way to work. This is especially true when the new covering will be something like a horizontally placed, solid lumber, board paneling. In all situations, check the face of the furring to be sure it is level. To do this stretch a line across the material or use a level. If necessary, use slim wedges (pieces of shingle are fine) to compensate for wall errors. Should you find a spot that is high, work it down with a hand plane or a belt sander. Be sure that you frame around all door and window openings. Nail all furring ends securely. If you must join pieces end-to-end, be sure that the joint occurs over a stud.

The general caution is to be sure that all ends and edges of the new wall covering will have

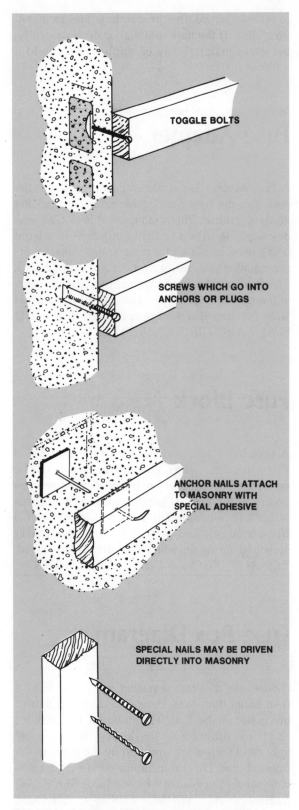

TOGGLE BOLTS

SCREWS WHICH GO INTO ANCHORS OR PLUGS

ANCHOR NAILS ATTACH TO MASONRY WITH SPECIAL ADHESIVE

SPECIAL NAILS MAY BE DRIVEN DIRECTLY INTO MASONRY

Four ways to attach furring to masonry walls.

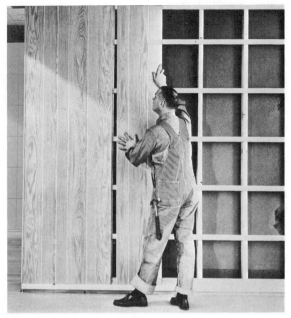

Courtesy of Marlite Random Plank

Material being installed here is Marlite Random Plank — a plastic-surfaced hardboard that has a handsome woodgrain. Note that this is a "stud" wall erected to form a partition.

nailing surface. Be sure that you check the material in relation to the position and the amount of furring to be used.

Many modern wall paneling materials have special installation procedures that require a particular furring pattern. Some are applied with adhesives; some with special metal clips. It is even possible to attach some directly to a sound, smooth wall without going through the furring procedures. These factors should be checked in advance and any special manufacturer's instructions should be followed.

MASONRY WALLS

Masonry walls require special attachment considerations that include specially hardened nails that can be driven directly into masonry, toggle bolts, anchors, and mastic-applied nail-pads. Refer to the FASTENERS entry for specifics that relate to this situation.

A caution — if the masonry wall is very rough, it would be wise to erect a new stud wall instead of using furring. This can present the opportunity

to take waterproofing precautions and to install insulation. If the new stud wall is done carefully, the cover material may be applied directly to it without furring.

Fuse Adapter

A fuse adapter is permanently screwed into the socket of the fuse panel, making the fuse socket nontamperable. The nontamperable socket was developed to prevent a high-amperage fuse from being used in place of a lower-rated fuse, an error which could result in a serious fire hazard. The fuse adapter will accept only a fuse of a certain amperage, therefore creating definite socket sizes for the various ampere ratings. *SEE ALSO FUSES AND CIRCUIT BREAKERS.*

Fuse Block

A fuse block is a device which carries or holds fuses in a fuse panel, and is removed from the panel by a handle. As a block is removed the power to the circuits supplied through its fuses is cut off, allowing for safe replacement of a blown fuse. The power is automatically switched on again when the block is replaced. *SEE ALSO FUSES & CIRCUIT BREAKERS.*

Fuse Box Diagram

A fuse box diagram is pasted to the inside of a fuse panel door, and shows the organization of the fuses in the box. The diagram is really an electrical diagram of the house, telling what lights and outlets are supplied by the fuses in the fuse cabinet. This information makes it easier to determine the cause of a blown fuse. *SEE ALSO ELECTRICAL WIRING; FUSES & CIRCUIT BREAKERS.*

Fuse Cabinet

A fuse cabinet is the main distribution panel directing the current coming from outside to all the branch circuits throughout the house. It contains fuses, which protect the circuits from overload, and a switch which disconnects all household power easily before repairs and immediately in emergencies. The service panel must be located no more than one foot from where the cable enters the building from outside, and should be near rooms where the most electrical current is needed, most often the kitchen. In most modern cabinets, the fuses are contained in removable blocks. When a fuse is blown in a certain block, the block is pulled out by a handle, cutting off power to the fuses it supplies. The fuse may then be replaced while the block is out, and the current is automatically restored when the block is replaced. *SEE ALSO FUSES & CIRCUIT BREAKERS.*

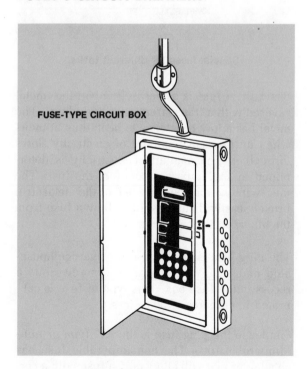

FUSE-TYPE CIRCUIT BOX

Fuse, Cartridge
[SEE FUSES & CIRCUIT BREAKERS]

Fuse, Plug

A plug fuse is a thin strip of metal which softens and breaks when an overload of current passes through it. A plug fuse is made in 30 or less ampere ratings, and is most commonly used for household wiring systems. It screws into the fuse panel like a light bulb screws into a socket, although it must never be screwed into a bulb socket, or into a socket formerly housing a lower-rated fuse. A blown plug fuse is revealed through a transparent mica window covering the fuse. The broken strip may be visible through the window, or metal vapor may cause the window to be discolored or fogged. *SEE ALSO FUSES & CIRCUIT BREAKERS.*

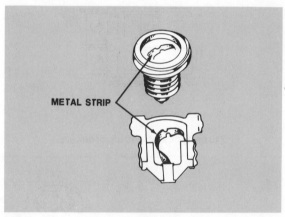

METAL STRIP

Plug Fuse

Fuses & Circuit Breakers

Fuses and circuit breakers protect household wiring by "blowing" when too much electricity runs through them. Some of the conditions that could activate a fuse or circuit breaker are these: a circuit has shorted out from bare wires touching; the circuit is overloaded because too many appliances are drawing electricity from it; or, a motor is overloading it. In any case, do not

replace the fuse or reset the circuit breaker until the problem has been discovered and solved.

Most fuse boxes carry a diagram of the house wiring system in which they are installed. Such a chart, known as the *fuse box diagram,* allows the homeowner to find the cause of his blown fuses in less time.

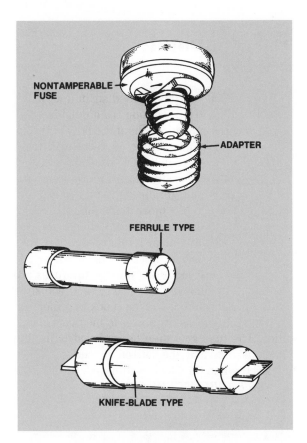

Special fuses for different tasks.

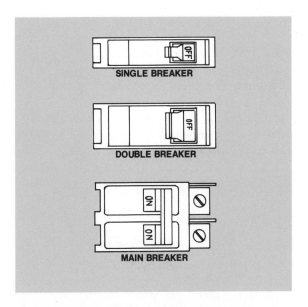

Three types of circuit breakers.

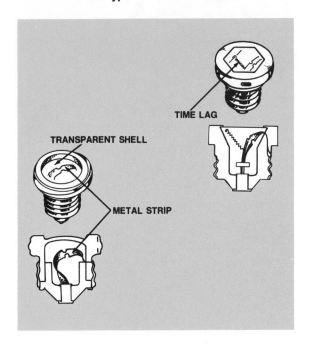

A cut-away view of a fuse.

Basically, a *fuse* is a piece of ribbon-like metal covered with a transparent mica "window". The metal has a low resistance to heat; thus, it melts when an excessive amount of electricity flows through it. The amount of electricity is determined by the ampere capacity of the fuse. The mica window may be darkened or the metal strip broken, easily distinguishing a blown fuse from the others in the fuse box.

The *plug fuse* is common to the average household and is so called because it screws into a recess in the fuse box. This type of fuse is calibrated in amperes of 30 or less.

Similar to the plug fuse is the *"S" type or nontamperable* fuse. The nontamperable fuse has an adapter that will allow only a fuse with a certain ampere rating to be plugged into it. This type of fuse decreases the possibility of a high amperage fuse being inserted into a low amperage circuit, thus avoiding an overload.

Cylinder-shaped *cartridge fuses* come with either metal caps or flat, blade-like terminals that protrude from the end. The ferrule, or metal cap type, are rated at 60 amps or less and snap into spring-clip terminals in a fuse panel. The knife-blade type are similar in shape and in means of connection, but are rated at 60 to 600 amps.

The *time-lag* or *time-delay fuse* is used in circuits to support a short-term overload. Although an electric motor may use only five amps while running, it may draw as much as 25 amps in starting. The design of the time-lag fuse can tolerate this initial overload thus allowing the motor to start without blowing the fuse.

Circuit breakers, which do the same job as fuses, are found in most modern installations. The advantage of the circuit breaker is that it is reset rather than replaced. If the circuit becomes overloaded, a sensitive switch automatically breaks the circuit. To reset the circuit breaker switch, flip it to the "on" position.

Modern installations may also provide a safety device known as the *fuse block* to help in replacing fuses. This device can be removed from the wiring, allowing the homeowner to replace his fuses without fear of shock.

There are certain precautionary measures to take when removing or replacing a fuse. Take a flashlight in case the lights are off where the fuse panel is located. Wear rubber-soled shoes in basement areas. Some older fuse panels may have exposed hot wires. In such cases, rubber gloves may help prevent shock. Keep one hand free while replacing fuses to avoid shock that could be fatal. *SEE ALSO ELECTRICAL WIRING.*

FUSE BOX

CIRCUIT BREAKER

Fuse box and circuit breaker panel.

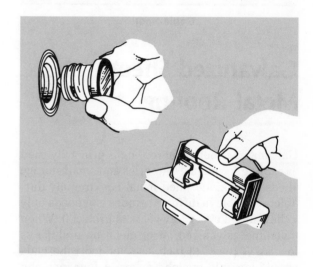

Installing a fuse or circuit breaker.

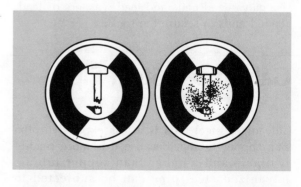

Blown fuses may be discolored, or the metal strip may be visibly broken.

Gable Roof

A gable roof is a two-sided sloping roof that forms a gable at one or both ends. The simple design of a gable roof plus its relative low cost make it popular in residential construction. *SEE ALSO ROOF CONSTRUCTION.*

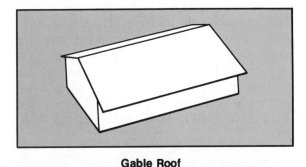

Gable Roof

Galvanized Sheet Metal Roofing

Galvanized sheet metal roofing is primarily used as roofing for plants, foundries and small storage sheds. This zinc-coated metal is extremely durable, available in different grades and needs only to be painted every few years to protect it. When installing galvanized sheet metal on a slope as low as $1/8$ pitch, (3 inch rise per foot) the ends should lap at least eight inches. A four inch end lap is sufficient on those roofs with a $1/4$ pitch. Use galvanized nails and lead washers or lead-headed nails to secure the roofing.

Galvanized Steel Pipe

Galvanized steel pipe is a less expensive pipe than copper tubing. Because it is more readily available and tougher than copper tubing, galvanized steel pipe can be subjected to mechanical work, especially in areas where it may receive rough treatment such as acciden-

tally being hit in the workshop. Galvanized steel pipe can be purchased in lengths of 21 feet with both ends threaded and a coupling screwed on one end. Those with no threaded end or couplings are called pipe nipples and are available in lengths up to six feet. They are used for small jobs. Size of the pipe is determined by its outside diameter. *SEE ALSO PLUMBING MATERIALS.*

Galvanized Steel Pipe Fittings

The most common galvanized steel pipe fittings are the elbow, tee, union, reducer, coupling, hose adapter, bushing, plug and cap.

Elbows gently curve or bend to join pipes meeting at angles. While most elbows have only internal threads, street elbows have one end with external threads and the other end with internal threads.

A tee joins straight run pipe with a branch entering at a right angle. A reducing tee works the same way except that the pipe diameter is made smaller on the straight run portion. With both ends having internal threading, a reducer connects two pipes of different diameters in a straight run. Serving the same purpose as a reducer, a bushing differs only in design. The large externally threaded end fits into the larger pipe while the smaller internally threaded opening receives the smaller of the pipes.

A coupling joins two equal sized pipes in a straight run. Although it functions the same as a coupling, a union secures the joint by not only twisting the pipe into the ends of the fitting, but also tightening the outer rim by hand or with a wrench to securely fasten the pipes together.

The only difference between a union and a hose adapter is that a union has external threading and a hose adapter has internal threading. A plug and a cap function alike, only the method of securing the result is different. A plug screws into a pipe to end the line while a cap screws

over the end of the pipe to end the line. *SEE ALSO PIPE FITTINGS.*

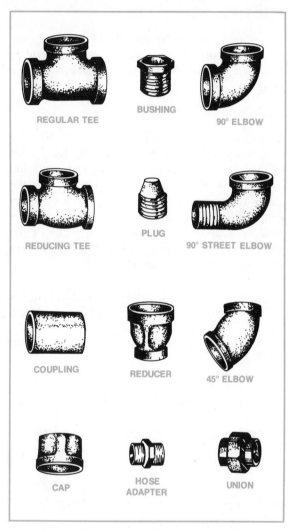

Galvanized Steel Pipe Fittings

Galvanizing

Galvanizing is the process of coating iron or steel with zinc. This zinc coating protects the material from the atmosphere, preventing corrosion. A properly applied zinc covering will seal the material from the atmosphere for 15 to 30 years or longer. The two methods of zinc application are the hot-dip method and the cold or electrogalvanizing method.

Gambrel Roof

A gambrel roof is similar to a gable roof with each slope broken into two sections. The upper section has a slight pitch, while the lower section has a steep pitch. The framing element where the two sections are attached is called the purlin. This type of roof offers more efficient use of a second floor and is common in colonial styles. *SEE ALSO ROOF CONSTRUCTION.*

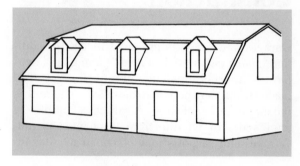

A Typical Gambrel Roof

Game Room
[SEE RECREATION ROOMS.]

Gang Box

The purpose of the gang box is to provide a receptacle for a group of two or more wiring devices. These devices may be either switches or outlets. To make a gang box, remove the side plates of two or more outlet boxes and join them

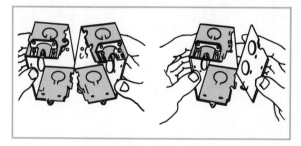

Making a gang box.

together. Replace the original screws in the top and bottom of the new receptacle. *SEE ALSO SWITCHES & OUTLETS.*

Garage

[SEE GARAGE & CARPORT CONSTRUCTION.]

Garage & Carport Construction

Garages and carports are car shelters. In addition, man's ingenuity has made them boat, lawn-mower, sport equipment and junk shelters. The basic difference between these two shelters is the amount of enclosure. A garage is completely enclosed and weathertight; a carport is not. Garages and carports may be constructed as integral parts of a house, as additions to a house or as completely detached structures.

CONSTRUCTION PLANS

These plans detail how to build a one-car attached carport. Suggestions on how to modify this carport into a one or two-car garage are also included.

Foundations and Slab

Excavate trenches for the footings and foundation walls to the depth required by local frost conditions. Construct the forms and pour the foundations. (Note concrete proportions and the foundation estimating procedure.) To compensate for the lower wall plates, make sure that the exterior rear and side foundation walls of the storage unit are poured 1 $5/8$ inches higher than the inside walls and the wing wall.

Pour and cure the slab, installing the bolts for 2 x 4 wheel stop if desired. (A 16 x 14 foot by 4 inch

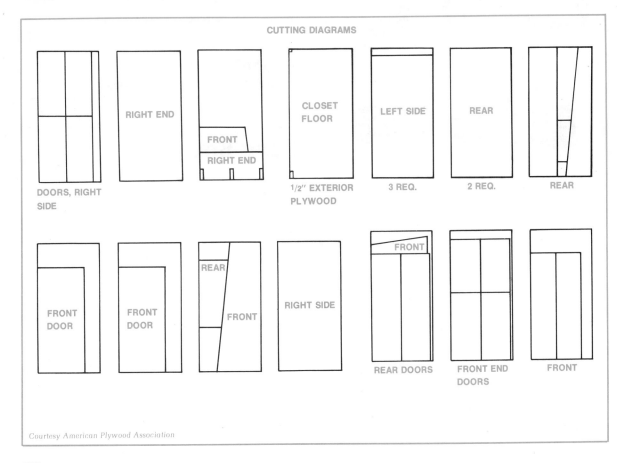

CUTTING DIAGRAMS

DOORS, RIGHT SIDE

RIGHT END

FRONT

RIGHT END

1/2" EXTERIOR PLYWOOD

CLOSET FLOOR

LEFT SIDE
3 REQ.

REAR
2 REQ.

REAR

REAR

FRONT DOOR

FRONT DOOR

REAR

FRONT

RIGHT SIDE

FRONT

REAR DOORS

FRONT END DOORS

FRONT

Courtesy American Plywood Association

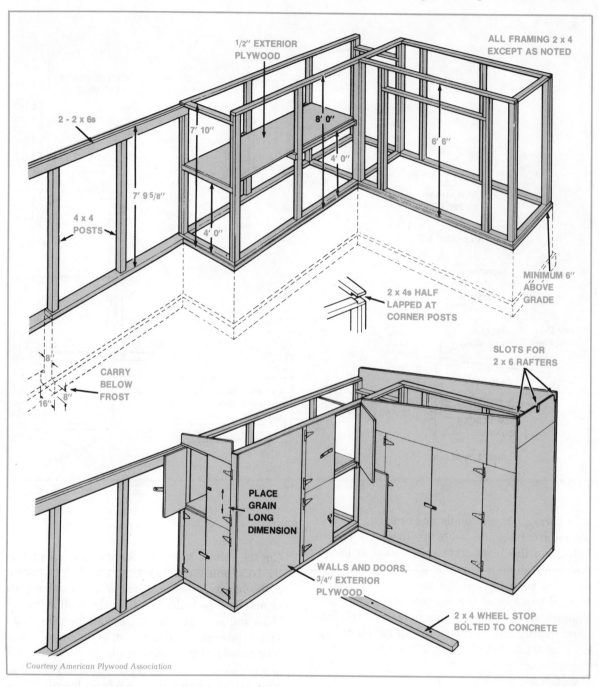

1/2" EXTERIOR PLYWOOD

ALL FRAMING 2 x 4 EXCEPT AS NOTED

2 - 2 x 6s

7' 10"

8' 0"

6' 6"

4' 0"

4 x 4 POSTS

7' 9 5/8"

4' 0"

MINIMUM 6" ABOVE GRADE

2 x 4s HALF LAPPED AT CORNER POSTS

8"

CARRY BELOW FROST

8"

16"

SLOTS FOR 2 x 6 RAFTERS

PLACE GRAIN LONG DIMENSION

WALLS AND DOORS, 3/4" EXTERIOR PLYWOOD

2 x 4 WHEEL STOP BOLTED TO CONCRETE

Courtesy American Plywood Association

slab will require about 2¹/₂ cubic yards of mixed concrete and 224 square feet of 6 x 6 No. 4 reenforcing mesh.)

Drill holes for the anchor bolts in the foundation walls, and set all the bolts and the lower wall plates in place as shown in plans.

Cabinet Structure

Cut the framing to size for the walls, including the wing wall. Assemble each wall section on the cured slab, using 10d or 12d common nails, then raise the assembled section into place. Brace if needed with a 2 x 4 temporarily nailed at an out-

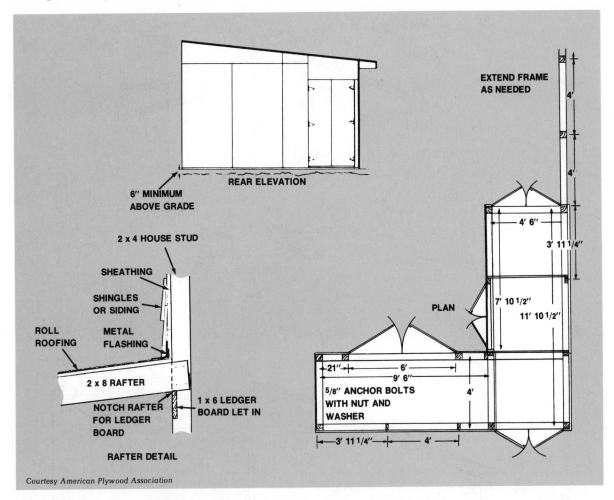

REAR ELEVATION

6" MINIMUM ABOVE GRADE

EXTEND FRAME AS NEEDED

4'

4'

2 x 4 HOUSE STUD

SHEATHING

SHINGLES OR SIDING

ROLL ROOFING

METAL FLASHING

2 x 8 RAFTER

NOTCH RAFTER FOR LEDGER BOARD

1 x 6 LEDGER BOARD LET IN

RAFTER DETAIL

4' 6"

3' 11 1/4"

PLAN

7' 10 1/2"

11' 10 1/2"

21"   6'
9' 6"

5/8" ANCHOR BOLTS WITH NUT AND WASHER

4'

3' 11 1/4"   4'

Courtesy American Plywood Association

side corner. As the walls are erected, the rear plates are fastened with the in-place anchor bolts, and the front plates are nailed to the already installed lower plates. Offset the front plates ³/₄ inch toward the inside of the unit to form doorstops at the bottom of the opening. Plumb the framing with a carpenter's level, then permanently nail in place. Install the shelf supports in the left cabinet.

Cabinet Sheathing

Lay out the plywood walls and doors following the cutting diagram. Adjust the panel sizes to fit the locations specific dimensions, then cut. Install the shelf, and the inside partitions. Nail the exterior panels in place, using 8d casing nails spaced 6 inches apart at the panel edges. Be sure the upper panel of the right end is notched for rafters.

Roof Construction

Cut the rafters to length. Remove sufficient siding from house wall to let in a 1 x 6 ledger board. If the house is of brick veneer or masonry construction, attach the 2 x 6 to the wall with lag bolts and suitable anchors. Install the rafters, 24 inches on center, nailing them to the house studs (see detail). If the house studs are 16 inches on center, provide blocking as necessary for the stud nailing. Apply the 1 x 6 fasia board. When the framework is complete, apply the roof sheathing of ¹/₂ inch exterior plywood, using 6d common nails spaced 6 inches at panel edges and 12 inches on intermediate rafters. When the sheathing is complete, apply roll roofing running the length of the carport. Begin at the eaves and complete with metal flashing at the wall-roof joint.

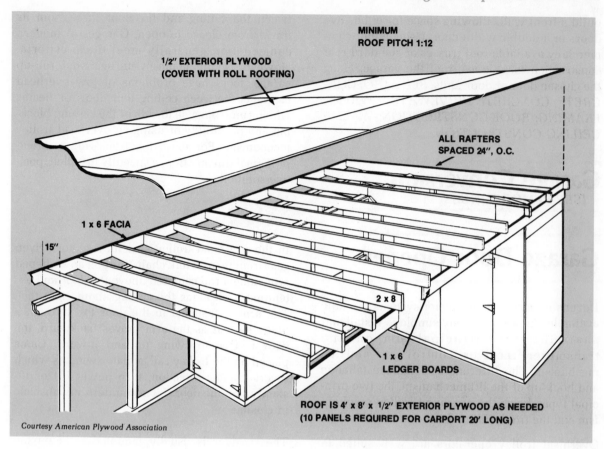

MINIMUM
ROOF PITCH 1:12

1/2" EXTERIOR PLYWOOD
(COVER WITH ROLL ROOFING)

ALL RAFTERS
SPACED 24", O.C.

1 x 6 FACIA

15"

2 x 8

1 x 6
LEDGER BOARDS

ROOF IS 4' x 8' x 1/2" EXTERIOR PLYWOOD AS NEEDED
(10 PANELS REQUIRED FOR CARPORT 20' LONG)

Courtesy American Plywood Association

Door Construction

Pair the unhung doors. Fasten a 1 x 2 doorstop on the inside meeting edge of one of each pair of doors. Attach 6 inch T-hinges (or more ornamental equivalent hinges, if desired) to the jamb edges of the doors. Fit and hang the doors.

Finish

Stain or paint the carport to match or complement the colors of the house. Use at least two coats of an opaque oil stain, or a primer coat plus two coats of a good quality house paint.

ONE CAR GARAGE CONVERSION

This carport is easily converted into a one-car attached garage. If the storage unit is set away from the house wall, use standard framing techniques to build an enclosing wall from the right end of the storage unit to the house wall. An exterior door may be installed in this wall to provide convenient access to the back of the house.

A wall of standard framing is built across the front of the carport, allowing a 10 foot wide opening for the car. This opening should be offset to the right to allow for the wing wall storage unit. Either hinged or overhead doors may be used. A plastic sheathed overhead door unit provides a lightweight closure for the opening and provides illumination for the interior.

If a detached unit is desired, a fourth wall may be added to the structure. This wall should be approximately 10 feet tall to provide proper pitch for the roof. Standard framing methods should again be used in construction. One or two windows installed in this wall will provide additional light.

TWO-CAR CONVERSION

To expand the one-car detached unit plan into one for a two-car garage, double the width of the slab. Build two storage units on the back corners, reversing the plans. Using standard techniques,

build a front wall, allowing space for either two doors or a double width door. Using either commercially available roof trusses or standard roof construction techniques, roof the garage. Hang the chosen door or door units. *SEE ALSO: CONCRETE; CONCRETE DRIVEWAYS & WALKS; FRAMING; ROOF CONSTRUCTION; WALL & CEILING CONSTRUCTION.*

Garage Conversion
[SEE REMODELING.]

Garage Door Opener

Dozens of garage door opener systems are now available. All are relatively simple to install and share the same principal components: transmitter, receiver, control unit and lift mechanism. The differences lie in the installation and hook-up of the lift mechanism, the two principal types being the *overhead trolley mechanism* and the *track-riding direct-pull mechanism.*

Overhead trolley operators are well suited to hinged, sectional roll-up doors and one piece pivot doors, but require that the ceiling be clear of obstructions between the operator and its attachment point at the top of the door. There should be a clearance of from 4 to 10 inches be-

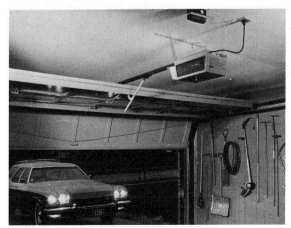

Courtesy Nutone Division of Scovill

Overhead trolley operators are fastened to one-piece garage doors through a door-connecting arm.

tween the ceiling and the door throughout its travel from closed to open. Garages of modern construction generally meet these criteria. However, many homes with sectional roll-up garage doors have problems of low overhead clearance between ceiling and door, or beams which run from side to side of the ceiling, blocking any possibility of using an overhead trolley mechanism. For these the *track-riding direct-pull mechanism* offers a speedily installed, positive solution.

OVERHEAD TROLLEY MECHANISM OPERATION

In the overhead trolley system, a motor-driven gear train turns a link chain, pulling an L-shaped arm along a rail centered above the door and extending back along the ceiling about eight feet. The arm is fastened to the door top through a pivot, so that as the arm moves backward, the door is free to swing up and inward. Cams placed on the trolley rail actuate switches which reverse motor direction, turn power off or instantly stop the door if it encounters any obstacle in closing.

The receiver is usually mounted right on the motor unit, as is a garage light. A time-delay relay within the unit holds power on the light for about one minute after the motor has stopped running.

TRACK-RIDING LIFT MECHANISM OPERATION

The motor unit of the track-riding mechanism is joined to the door through a pivot, but is also supported by a friction drive comprising two rollers (one metal, one rubber) which pinch the door track between their surfaces. The metal roller fits inside the track, the rubber roller bears against the track undersurface. The receiver and control box mount on the wall and connect to the motor by flexible cable.

When an open signal is received, the control box switches power to the motor, which turns the rubber roller. The friction drive pulls the motor up and along the track and the pivotally attached door obediently follows along. Sensor switches controlling up and down limits are activated by

cams secured to the door track and operator motor.

INSTALLING AN OVERHEAD TROLLEY MECHANISM

The procedure for installing all sectional doors or one-piece doors with track hardware where the door path is a straight line first involves making two measurements: the center of the door, and one-half inch above the highest point of door travel. Mark these, and at the intersection of these two lines, mount the front wall bracket.

With the door closed and the power unit resting on the floor, raise the front of the trolley rail and

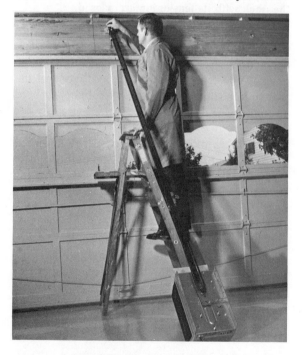

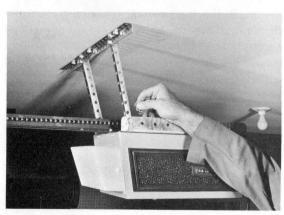

secure it to the front wall bracket. Raise the power unit to the height required for the door to clear the trolley rail during opening and closing. Hang the power unit at this height, securing to brackets attached to ceiling.

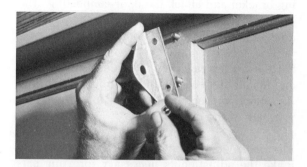

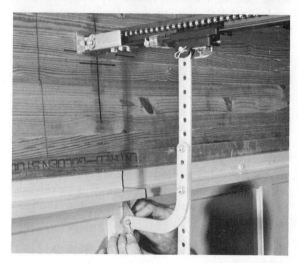

Assemble the door-connecting trolley arm and attach it to the carriage and the door. When the arm is vertical and the door is fully closed, the front trolley rail clamp should be directly in front of the carriage. The rear trolley rail clamp should be directly behind the carriage when the bottom of the door is even with the door header. Install the radio receiver on the ceiling, close to the operator. Mount the pushbutton near the door into the house.

For one-piece doors with jamb or pivot hardware (in other words, those with an irregular door path) the installation is essentially the same, but in a different sequence. First, secure the power unit at a height even with the lowest point of the opened door. The trolley rail is supported by the door. Then, by closing the door,

raise the trolley rail to the angle required to clear the highest point of door travel by at least one-half inch. The front wall bracket should be mounted at this point and the front end of the trolley rail secured to it. Secure the door-mounting bracket and attach the door-connecting arm. You will find that by lengthening the arm, the door will operate more smoothly.

Set the trolley rail clamps as described earlier and install the receiver and pushbutton. Refer to the manufacturer's instructions for proper adjustment of the operator.

The final step, no matter what type of door, is to make the adjustments necessary for your particular installation. (The specific instructions for the operator model you have chosen should be followed.) This means making sure the limits which set the level of pressure required to stop the motor if the door encounters even slight opposition are properly adjusted. A preliminary safety adjustment has usually been made at the factory; however, the final adjustment must be made to correspond to the operating characteristics of your garage door. When the adjustments have been made, the convenience accessories should be installed, such as an outside key switch or outside key-operated manual release.

INSTALLING A TRACK-RIDING LIFT MECHANISM

This unique lift mechanism works where a conventional trolley mechanism will not fit, and is also simple to install. This operator is installed so that the motor applies power to the door by actually riding on the same overhead track that the door does (on one side only). The motor drive unit is attached to the top corner of the door with a special bracket that replaces the original roller-holding bracket on the top of the door on that side so that as the motor moves along the track on its way up or down, it pulls or pushes the door in the same direction.

The motor is propelled along the track by two rollers: a metal one that fits inside the track just like one of the regular door rollers, and a hard rubber roller that fits under the track directly

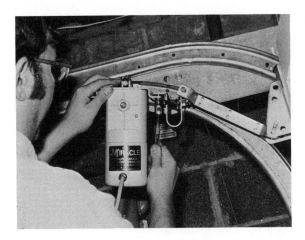

The operator should be straightened and locked into the track with its tensioning arm closed.

under the metal one and is kept tightly pressed against the track by a special spring tension device. The track is thus pinched between the two rollers (one metal and one rubber) to hold the motor firmly in place as it rolls along.

When the motor is activated, power is supplied to the rubber roller and this moves the entire assembly along the length of the track. In doing so, it pulls the door open or pushes it closed.

It is essential that the door be well-lubricated and well-balanced so that it opens and closes freely before installation is begun. If yours is not working well, check the hardware on doors and tracks for tightness and grease only the inside surfaces of the door tracks (*not* the under-surface where the operator's rubber roller will grab the track).

To install the track-riding mechanism, remove the topmost original roller bracket from the door on the left or right side. (Choose the side that is closest to a power line outlet.) Slide out the door roller and engage it in the track. Mate the special bracket mentioned earlier to the U-shaped fitting, called a *down-limit sensor,* and slide these onto the roller's axle. Fasten the bracket to the door where the original bracket was fitted.

If the overhead clearance of the garage door is very low, chances are there will be double tracks on each side. Contact the manufacturer for a

special kit of parts which instantly adapts the mechanism to double tracks.

Mount the operator (motor unit) on the track by releasing its spring-loaded tensioning mechanism and fitting its metal roller into the track. Move it forward so that the holes on "ear" of the operator can be fitted over the two threaded studs on the rear of the U-shaped sensor. Straighten the operator and lock it to the track by pulling its tensioning arm closed. Secure the operator to the sensor studs with two nuts.

The down-limit sensor is a switch activated by the "push" of the motor when the door meets opposition. The *U* compresses and contacts close, turning off power to the motor and preparing it so that the next time power is applied the motor will turn in the reverse direction, pulling the door open. The operator comes from the factory wired for installation on a right-hand track. For a left-hand track installation, a simple reversal of wires is needed so that the motor will run in the proper direction for open and close commands.

To set the maximum opening point of the door and tell the operator when to shut off, two sets of cams are installed at the rearmost track end. Install the first, about 20 inches forward of the track end; the second, about 17 inches behind the first. Below the second cam is a *dead-end* clip that acts to prevent the operator from overrunning the track should the two cams fail to shut off the motor. (This last possibility is very slight, but the dead-end clip is a sensible precaution.)

The cams are adjusted so that they depress the upper leaf of a pair of switch contacts when maximum rearward travel of the motor has occurred. This shuts off power and programs the motor to reverse direction on the next cycle.

The control unit and receiver mount together, on wall or ceiling, nearby the travelling operator. Flexible cables interconnect all components and the control unit power cable simply plugs into the 120-volt power line outlet. Be sure it's a grounding-type outlet so that the motor frame is safely grounded, as all such appliances should be.

Garbage Disposal Repair

Garbage disposals come in two basic types: batch-feed and continuous-feed models. Actually, the units themselves are basically the same. The major difference is that the batch-feed type has a switch to turn the unit off and on which is located in the sink flange. You put a special stopper in place and turn it to turn the disposal on. With the continuous-feed model, the switch is located on the wall; you flip it on manually when you are ready to turn the disposal on.

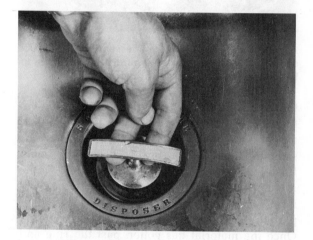

This batch-feed disposal has special stopper which must be turned to correct position before disposal will operate.

Disposals are capable of handling all wet garbage that you'll have around the household. They even digest steak bones with no problem; in fact, it is good for them. But they cannot handle metallic objects or glass. By using the disposal to handle food scraps and bones and using the garbage can for paper, cans, metallic objects and glass, your garbage-emptying chores are reduced considerably.

To put the disposal into operation, the food is put into a hopper, which is the upper housing of the disposal. The hopper is bolted directly to the bot-

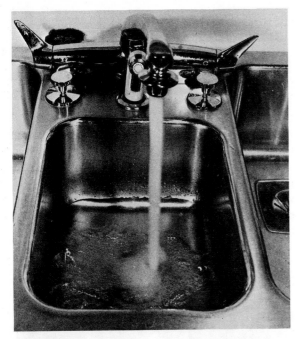

A good flow of cold water is essential to disposal operation. This keeps greases hard, allowing them to be chewed up and passed through drain line.

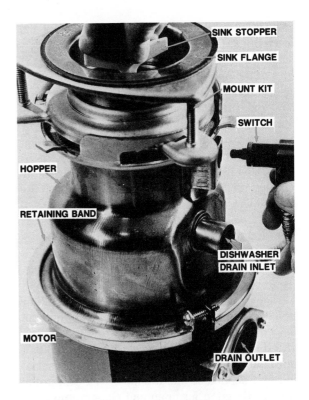

A view of this GE disposal shows how the hopper assembly is attached to motor unit with retaining band. The switch being removed is operated by stopper on this batch-feed model.

tom of the sink. When the disposal is turned on, the motor drives a rotating disc or ring at the bottom of the hopper. Cold water is supplied at the same time that the disposal is turned on to help flush away particles as they are ground. As the revolving disc drives the food to the outer edge, it runs into a cutter ring, which shreds it into fine particles before it is allowed to pass through. Once the material has gotten past the ring and into the drain line, it is so fine that it causes no problems with the drain lines themselves so long as plenty of cold water is supplied.

This cold water flow is important. It not only helps to flush food particles down the drain, but it also prevents grease and other food soils from liquifying. If hot water were used, grease would be a liquid at the disposal but would then solidify farther down the drain line as it cooled. This could cause a clean-out problem over a period of time. It is a good idea to keep the cold water running for ten or fifteen seconds or longer after the disposal has been turned off.

Basically, the works of a disposal consist of the housing, a switch, a motor, the disc and cutting

ring and a seal to prevent water and food from passing between the disc and motor assembly. It is a simple and reliable appliance and given proper care will last for many years. If problems do arise, you can often remedy many of them yourself.

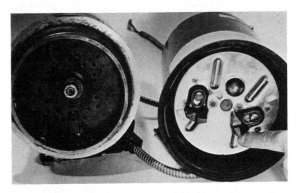

Two common designs of impellers in garbage disposals are shown here. A porcelain coated, fixed blade type is used on the model at left; the stainless steel blade on the model on the right is free to swivel. Both finishes prevent corrosion.

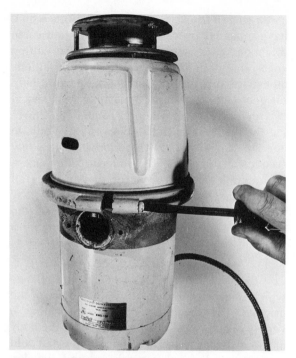

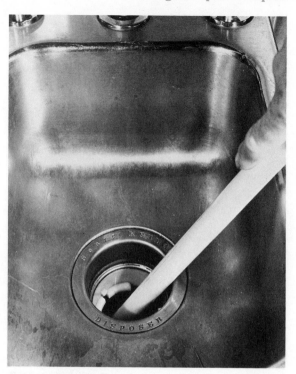

A retaining band sometimes holds two sections of disposal together. Others use locking tabs. New gaskets should be used whenever a disposal is disassembled.

If it is necessary to attempt to unjam disposal, be sure that it is unplugged and that all power is removed before sticking any screwdriver or pry bar into mouth of hopper. One of the best tools for unjamming is a broomstick. Insert it into hopper and pry against the ears on disc.

If a disposal fails to operate, check to see that the switch has not blown or that the circuit breaker has not tripped. If the disposal is a plug-in model with a receptacle located under the sink, you can check this by simply plugging a table lamp into the outlet with the disposal. Otherwise, you will have to check the fuse or circuit breaker manually. Be sure and pull the switch before removing a fuse and turn off all power before inspecting or servicing the disposal.

On most disposals there is an overload protector built into the base of the motor. This is usually on the bottom of the unit. It has a button that must be manually pushed in before the disposal can be put back into operation. This protector will likely pop out if the disposal jams or if it is overloaded for any reason. A third possibility is that the switch itself, either at the sink flange or on the wall, is defective. You will need a continuity tester or volt-ohm-meter to check this after first having turned off all power to the circuit. Sometimes the flange switch simply needs adjusting. Usually this can be inspected underneath the sink without removing the disposal.

If a disposal jams, it will likely trip the overload protector or the circuit breaker. If after restoring a tripped circuit breaker the disposal fails to operate and only buzzes, it is likely that something has jammed the impeller. Remember, never attempt to service a disposal without first making sure that all power has been turned off. Even so, it is a good idea never to stick your hand into the mouth or hopper of the disposal.

To unjam a disposal, look around the edges of the cutter disc by shining a flashlight directly into the mouth of the unit. Metallic objects are particularly obvious. Some disposals have a small wrench like a set screw wrench that can be inserted into the motor shaft at the bottom of the disposal. Using this wrench, the rotor of the motor can be turned backward and forward, often helping to dislodge an object.

Some disposals have reversing switches which can be manual or automatic. If an object should

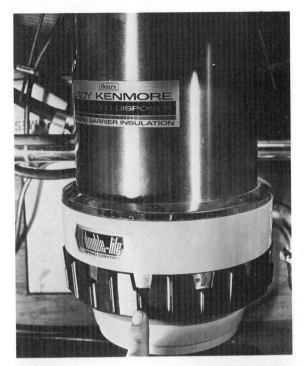

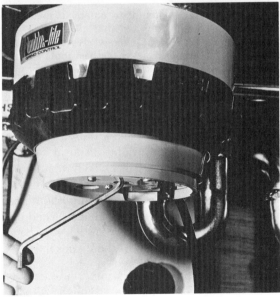

Reversing switches can often be used to help free a jammed disposal. If yours does not have one, see if setscrew wrench is provided for bottom of motor shaft.

become lodged in the cutter it will switch to the opposite rotation. Often this will dislodge the object. In normal operation, the motor reverses rotation each time the disposal is used. This helps to keep the cutting edges of the disc and

cutter ring sharpened. On reversible units which have a manual switch it is a good idea to reverse directions each week to help keep the cutting edges sharp. Unless the manufacturer cautions otherwise, this feature can also be used to help dislodge an object simply by turning the disposal off, reversing the direction of rotation and turning the disposal on. If the disposal still fails to operate, leave it turned on no longer than a few seconds. If all else fails, you can often use a broomstick or a large screwdriver inserted through the mouth of the hopper to force the disc to turn and dislodge the object. If you can see the object near the edge of the disc, it can sometimes be pried away.

The disposal mounts to a special sink flange which is inserted through the sink in place of the original. The mounting system usually has a variety of hooks and screws which hold the body of the disposal in place. If one of these should loosen, the disposal can vibrate and develop other noises. Should this occur, turn off the power and inspect the mounting system under the sink. If it shakes easily, it is a sign that the system may be at fault. Look closely for any loose nuts or screws that could be the cause of the problem.

A leaking sink flange can also be responsible for a leak that appears to be coming from the disposal. Check and be sure that it is tight, but don't overtighten as this can crack porcelain in the sink. Another cause of a leak could be the seal itself. The entire unit would have to be disassembled to replace this. It is also imperative that the motor be thoroughly dried before putting it back into operation. A seal leak may have allowed water to reach the motor windings.

Keep in mind that a disposal is part of the plumbing system of your house and is subject to the same sort of problems. If water will not flow through it, it is possible that the line in front of the disposal, and possibly the disposal itself, is stopped up. If so, it is usually caused by using insufficient water over a long period of time while grinding with the disposal. To remove the problem, you will probably have to remove a section of the drain line or the trap. Clean it by

using a brush, rod, or plumbers snake if the blockage is located more than a few feet away.

It has been the custom of some homeowners and even service technicians to run a soda pop bottle through a disposal about once a year. Don't do it. While the theory behind this has some merit (it helps to remove the buildup of citric acid) the problems that it can cause far outweigh any advantages. It can damage plastic seals and covers in many newer disposals. It can also build up within the plumbing of your home's drainage system. If steak bones or other bones from food are occasionally run through the disposal, this tends to take care of any buildup in a much more satisfactory manner.

There is little maintenance involved in using a disposal. Most motors are self-oiling and require no regular checkups. Just follow the manufacturer's instructions for the amounts and types of food to be placed in it and use plenty of cold water while it is in operation. When you do this, it is likely to be many years before it requires the attention of a professional technician. *SEE ALSO APPLIANCE REPAIR, MAJOR.*

Gardening
[SEE LAWNS & GARDENS.]

Garden Planters
[SEE PLANTERS.]

Gardens
[SEE LAWNS & GARDENS.]

Garden Shelters
[SEE LAWNS & GARDENS.]

Garden Steps
[SEE BRICK & STONE WORK.]

Garden Tools & Equipment
[SEE LAWNS & GARDENS.]

Garden Tool Sharpening
[SEE TOOL SHARPENING.]

Garden Walks
[SEE LAWNS & GARDENS.]

Garnet Abrasive

A garnet abrasive is a piece of material coated with granulated garnet for abrasive purposes. Sandpaper is the most common example of a garnet abrasive. Garnet usually lasts five times longer than flint abrasives, is relatively inexpensive, produces excellent results during fine sanding and is considered by many to be the hardest natural abrasive. *SEE ALSO ABRASIVES.*

Gas, Natural

Natural gas, a combustible mixture of methane and hydrocarbons, comes from natural or bored openings in the earth's crust. Although it is often used without being treated, natural gas can be processed to remove hydrocarbons, carbon dioxide and sulfur compounds. Chiefly used as a raw material, natural gas serves as a fuel.

Gas & Oil Heaters
[SEE HEATING SYSTEMS.]

Gauges

There are several gauges, but most are used to control the depth, length or angle for drilling and cutting in wood or metal. The most useful gauges are the marking gauge, butt gauge and depth gauge. *SEE ALSO HAND TOOLS.*

Generators, Portable Electric

[SEE PORTABLE ELECTRIC GENERATORS.]

Girder

A girder is a heavy beam that supplies intermediate support to floor-spanning joists when the area between the outside walls is too great to be covered by a single joist. A girder may be composed of several beams nailed together, or it may be a solid wooden, steel or concrete beam. Girders bear a large portion of the entire building weight, and are supported by the foundation walls. *SEE ALSO FLOOR CONSTRUCTION.*

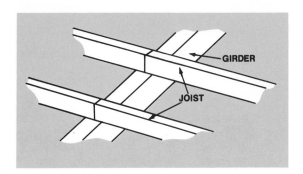

Girder Loads

Girder loads are the amount of weight a girder can support. The safe load can be increased up to four times when the depth of the girder is doubled. Tables are available specifying normal girder loads. *SEE ALSO FLOOR CONSTRUCTION.*

GIRDERS	SAFE LOAD IN LBS. FOR SPANS FROM 6 TO 10 FEET				
Size	6 Ft.	7 Ft.	8 Ft.	9 Ft.	10 Ft.
6 x 8 Solid	8,306	7,118	6,220	5,539	4,583
6 x 8 Build-Up	7,359	6,306	5,511	4,908	4,062
6 x 10 Solid	11,357	10,804	9,980	8,887	7,997
6 x 10 Build-Up	10,068	9,576	8,844	7,878	7,086
8 x 8 Solid	11,326	9,706	8,482	7,553	6,250
8 x 8 Build-Up	9,812	8,408	7,348	6,544	5,416
8 x 10 Solid	15,487	14,732	13,608	12,116	10,902
8 x 10 Build-Up	13,424	12,768	11,792	10,504	9,448

Standard Safe Girder Loads

Glass Adhesives

Glass adhesives are used to glue glass to various materials. Four different types of glue may be used. Epoxy glue is used to glue glass to brick, concrete, metal, plaster, plastics, stone, glass or china. To adhere glass to rubber or laminated plastics, use a contact cement. Glass may be attached to paper, cardboard, fabrics or cork using a rubber base cement. Plastic cements are sometimes used to glue glass to vinyl, glass, china or metal. *SEE ALSO ADHESIVES.*

Glass Block

Glass block, which reached its height of popularity in the 1940's and 50's, is still used today in both commercial and residential construction. It has two outstanding properties that make it useful in the home: insulation and light direction. Because glass block is made of two hollow glass forms fused together on an open side, with air left between, it insulates against excessive

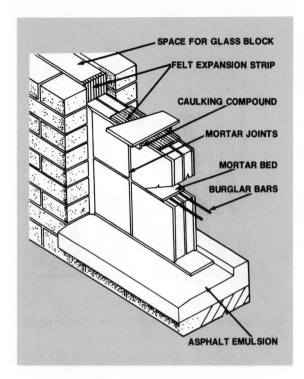

Installation of glass block in brick wall.

heat and cold, aiding air conditioning and heating units. In this aspect, it also helps prevent drafts and softens harsh, distracting noises. Inside the home or office, glass block can add a decorative touch providing both privacy and continuity of surrounding areas. Glass block is versatile in appearance; it is available in either transparent or translucent design and can either diffuse or direct light.

Glass block is made in three standard sizes: 8 x 8, 12 x 4, and 8 x 4, all are 4 inches thick. It is installed similarly to brick, using most of the common masonry tools a home handyman might have in his workshop. Glass block can be laid to any height without any special means of support. This characteristic of glass block, combined with its relative ease of installation, makes it a popular material. For example, when measuring a window opening for installation, allow $\frac{3}{4}$ inch per block for the mortar (i.e., for 12 x 4 block, work with the measurement of 12 $\frac{3}{8}$ x 4 $\frac{3}{8}$). If the blocks fall short or exceed the measurement of the window, do not attempt to cut the block. This will produce a messy appearance and will eliminate the insulation quality. Instead, build a

frame around the top, bottom and sides of the opening so that the blocks will fit.

Use white mortar when installing glass block and plan for about $\frac{1}{4}$ pound per block. Although the courses of blocks may extend to any height, if the glass wall is to go only half way up, a wooden shelf should be placed between the top layer of block and the rest of the wall. When building an outside construction such as a window, first cover the sill with a heavy coat of asphalt roof paint. An expansion strip of thick felt on each side of the frame may be useful. After the first course of block has been laid, steel reinforcement bars placed between each course will make the window burglar-proof. Continue laying the block using the $\frac{3}{8}$ inch white mortar beds until the area has been covered. The final touch is a caulking compound applied to all areas where the glass block and the original wall or frame meet.

Glass Cutting

Glass cutting begins with a new sharp cutter. Cutters, which are relatively inexpensive, should be bought packaged and should be tested before purchase. Skips or rough places in a piece of cut glass indicate that the cutter is worthless. Store the cutter in a glass jar with a cloth saturated in kerosene in the bottom. The pad protects from nicks; the kerosene from rust.

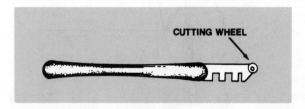

Glass Cutter

The glass to be cut should be placed on a thick pad of newspapers or a blanket. Clean the glass with mineral spirits since grit will impede the cutting. Place a straightedge on the glass along the proposed cut, holding it firmly against the glass with one hand. With the glass cutter in the

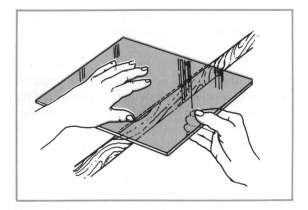

A piece of glass may be snapped at the score line by placing it on the edge of a table top.

other hand, make a smooth stroke along the glass surface pressing the cutter firmly against the straightedge. A good cut makes a ripping sound. This stroke is for scoring the glass, not to cut through it. Never go over the cut to make sure it is continuous since this would result in a break. To make the break, place a pencil under the score line, and press down on each side of the cut. If the glass is to be broken twice, score lines and break separately. Frosted or patterned glass should be cut on the smooth side.

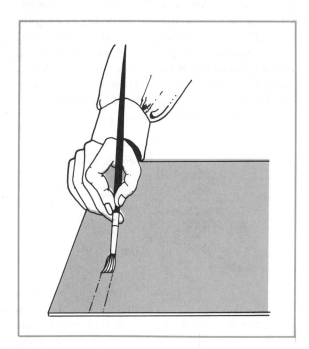

Paint mineral spirits on glass to clean it and prepare a path for the cutter.

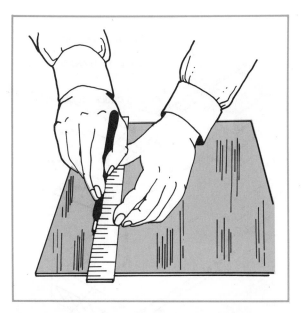

Hold the cutter at right angles to the glass to score a line.

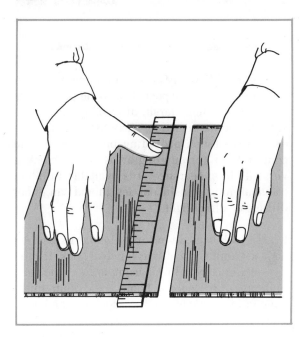

Place the glass over a guide and snap downward.

Wire-reinforced glass may be cut just like ordinary glass but the wires must be separated by working two pieces up and down until the wire breaks or by cutting the wires with side-cutting pliers. Follow the same procedure with heavier glass except apply lubricating oil on the line to be cut.

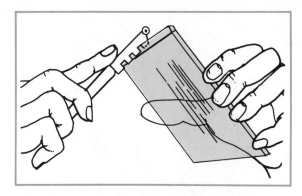

For removing narrow strips, score and fit the notched edge of the cutter over glass. Snap downward.

Use a dull cutter wheel for figured or textured glass. Though it takes more pressure, a sharper wheel would cause too much crazing. Colored cut glass, if bowed, should be scored on the concave side; mirrors on their unsilvered surface.

Large glass tubes and bottles may be cut by scoring a line around the circumference with a glass cutter and applying heat. Another method is to cover the bottle with wet paper very close to both sides of the score line, and then apply a blow-pipe flame along the gap. One method which eliminates scoring is to fill the bottle with motor oil to the desired height and plunge into it a heated tiny iron rod. The bottle will break cleanly at the oil level.

To make a hole in a sheet of glass, score the diameter marks. Score a second circle about an inch inside the first and make radial scores between the two. Coat the glass outside the first circle with a black substance and expose it to an infrared heating lamp. When it becomes hot, break out the center, then the ring.

To cut a disc from a sheet of glass, clean the glass and apply oil along the cutter path and on the cutter wheel. With a beam-type cutter wheel, score a circle. Turn the glass over and press along the circle to see if the cut is clear through. At the narrowest edge, score a line just outside the circle to the outer glass edge. Bend at this point and separate. The disc will fall free when the scrap edge springs away from the circle.

A homemade circle cutter may be used in place of a beam cutter. This device consists of a $1/_2$ inch angle-iron arm which turns on a 3 inch suction cup. The head of an ordinary cutter can be used for it. The cutter may be assembled with brackets or it may be welded. Two long angles are laid upside down and anchored by using a bottom clamp-plate held in place by a C-clamp. Two shorter cross angles are welded onto it.

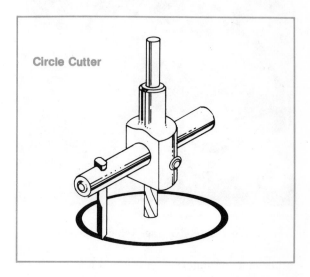

Circle Cutter

Oilstone may be used to smooth the edges of glass to be used for shelves or table tops. Dip the oilstone in water and graze it back and forth over the glass at a 45 degree angle. *SEE ALSO GLASS INSTALLING.*

Glass Doors
[SEE SLIDING DOORS.]

Glasses, Safety

Safety glasses or goggles should be worn when doing any operation that may endanger the eyes. These protective glasses, which prevent sparks or chips of metal from flying in the eyes, should be worn anytime grinding, drilling or buffing is being done. Wear special glasses or a shield when welding, when using paint remover or

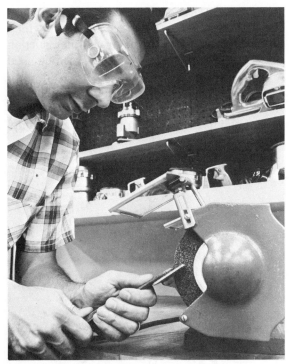

Courtesy of Power Tool Institute, Inc.

Wear Safety Glasses Where Needed

other caustic materials and when a job calls for working overhead.

Regulations require that a safety lens must withstand the blow of a $1/8$ inch steel ball dropped from a height of 50 feet. In addition to safety glasses, ample light should be provided for the job being done to lessen eye strain. *SEE ALSO SAFETY.*

Glass Installing

Installing a glass window pane to replace one that is broken or cracked, can be a relatively simple process. It is important that a good glass cutter be used for the process. A good cutter makes a steady ripping sound when scoring glass.

To replace a pane for a wooden sash frame, cut the glass to its correct size, lay it aside and remove the shreds and remains of broken glass from the window frame. This is probably the most difficult step in the installation process.

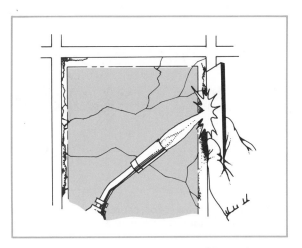

Soften the old putty for removal with a propane torch.

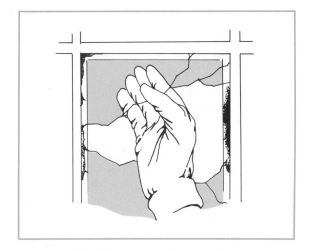

Carefully remove broken glass.

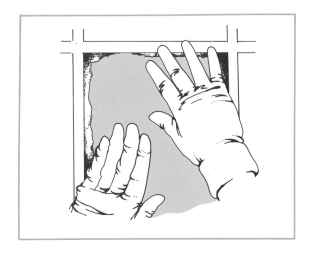

Measure opening for the new pane and center it.

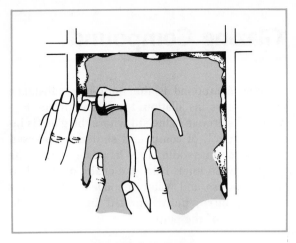

Drive in glazier's points.

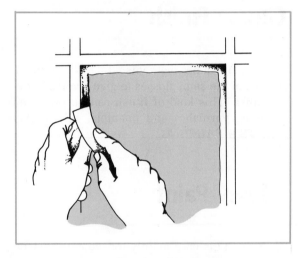

Place putty around the edges.

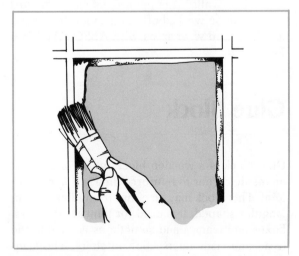

Paint for appearance and to keep the new seal from shrinking.

Wear heavy gloves to lift out the glass. If the putty around the frame has hardened, a soldering iron or electrical paint remover may provide heat to soften it. While it is warm, it can be easily scraped away. Remove the old glazier's points with pliers when scraping the putty.

Coat the groove, where the glass is to be set in the frame, with linseed oil. Then place putty, about 1/8 inch thick, around the groove. The putty should feel like dry dough. If it is tough, linseed oil will soften it. When putty has been placed all around the window frame, insert the glass with two glazier's points on each side to keep it in place. Center the pane in the opening with equal allowance on all sides. Press it down until the putty oozes out slightly along the inside edges.

Insert the glazier's points with a chisel, sliding it along the edge of the frame. Then apply more putty along all four sides, using the fingers to press it against the glass. Use a putty knife or chisel to scrape away the excess, leaving a firmly sealed glass pane. Use a slow troweling movement in scraping for the smoothest bevel. Paint with an oil base may be applied over the putty. The paint should extend just barely on the glass to seal it. Masking tape applied to a fraction of the exposed glass will make the edge neat.

Metal storm windows, mounted in rubber or vinyl gaskets, have small screws at their corners which must be removed to open their frames for glass replacement. When the frames or storm windows are put back together, the mitered corners must go together tightly.

Metal windows used in basements may be removed by lifting them out of the slotted brackets which support them. Casement windows are hinged and more difficult to remove for replacing broken glass.

Glass for both metal and casement windows is replaced in a similar manner. The broken glass is removed like that in wooden sash windows. Metal clips which hold the glass in place, can be either pressed down or pryed up for removal. There may be glazing in place of clips. Putty

should not be used for metal windows, instead use a special glazing compound recommended for them. Do not let the glass in a metal window come into direct contact with the metal. Be sure it is protected by glazing compound. Single strength glass is suitable for wood windows, but double strength should be used for metal windows.

Replacing insulating glass is often not practical. Cost of the glass may be more expensive than purchase of an entire sash unit.

Glazed Tiles

Glazed tile is ceramic tile that has had a thin veneer of glass fired onto the surface. Glazing makes the porous ceramic material waterproof and makes the surface easier to clean.

Glazier's Points

Glazier's points are small pieces of metal, usually triangular-shaped, that hold a glass pane into the window frame. After putty has been applied inside the groove of the frame and the glass set inside, glazier's points are placed flat between the pane and the frame. Using a tack hammer or a chisel, drive the points in just far enough to keep the glass from moving without straining any wood or glass areas. *SEE ALSO GLASS INSTALLING.*

Glazing

Glazing is the professional term used to mean the installation of glass. It is also used to refer to the process of adding a thin glass veneer to ceramic items such as tile, brick or art objects.

Glazing Compound

Glazing compound is the putty-like substance used in glass installation. It is placed in the bottom of the groove in the sill where the glass is installed. A roll of compound should be pressed against the glass after it is in place to lock the pane into the joint. This also cushions the glass against stress and water seepage. Given a few days to cure, paint should be applied to weatherproof the putty.

Glossy Finish

A glossy finish has pigments which break up the surface of the semi-glosses to give a velvet-looking finish. This kind of finish can be produced by using varnishes and enamels. *SEE ALSO PAINTS & PAINTING.*

Glossy Paint

Glossy paint is used mainly for woodwork, trim for windows and doors, furniture and bathroom or kitchen walls. This paint does not show dirt easily, can be washed off and is, therefore, good to use in hard wear areas. *SEE ALSO PAINTS & PAINTING.*

Glue Block

Glue block is a wooden block which is glued at an inside corner to reinforce the right-angle butt joint. This block may be either triangular- or rectangular-shaped. It is used for joints in drawers, boxes and frames and sometimes is used at the tread and riser intersection in stairs. The standard triangular kind is satisfactory for box corners and the rectangular type is used in framing

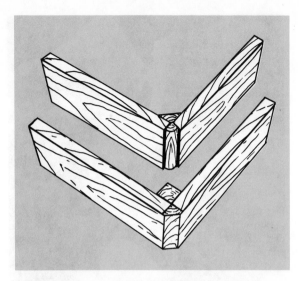

Triangular- and rectangular-shaped glue blocks

to stiffen the joints. Since glue blocks are unexposed, they do not have to match the wood or material in the visible areas. *SEE ALSO FURNITURE MAKING.*

Glues & Gluing

A good construction or repair job requires selection of the right adhesive, or one of the right ones, from among the more than 100 distinct chemical types now on the market. But the job begins with preparation of the joint and ends with clamping or other provision for holding the pieces together while the glue sets.

HIDE GLUES

At one time the only glue a craftsman would consider for woodworking was genuine hide glue. This is an animal glue that is made from hides and sold in flakes. To use it, it must be heated with water and kept hot so that it remains a thin liquid until used. Hide glue is still a good adhesive for general woodworking purposes, with its light color and good gap-filling characteristics, when the quantity of woodworking being done justifies the trouble of mixing the glue and keeping it hot. It is inexpensive and can be brushed on very rapidly when properly thin and hot. However, the fact that the glue joint is

not waterproof and the nuisance of using hot glue have made this adhesive a comparative rarity today.

Chemical treatment (using acetic acid) can turn hide glue into a product that remains liquid at usual temperatures, and hide glue is now used primarily in this form. It will not adhere well if used cold, however, so it should be used at room temperatures or even warmed slightly so that it flows freely. A good liquid hide glue is tough, light in color, resists heat and mold and is easy to use. It has good gap-filling qualities and so gives strength to even rather poorly fitted joints, making it suitable for furniture and general cabinet work. Its usefulness is limited, however, by its poor weather resistance. An additional drawback for some uses is that it requires about 12 hours to set up properly, compared to 4 hours for its leading competitor, white glue.

HOW TO REGLUE FURNITURE

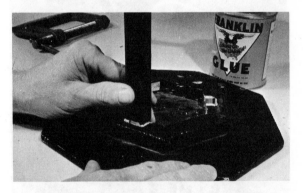

Test the joints for fit. If the fit is poor and cannot be improved, use a glue, such as casein or hide, which is recommended for its gap-filling qualities.

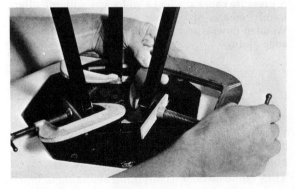

Clamp the joint or otherwise hold it securely while glue sets.

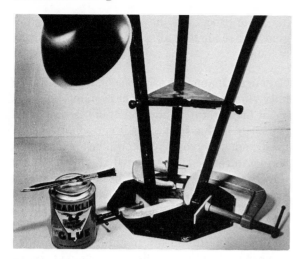

Let the joint dry, using heat (such as this heat lamp) if quick set is wanted. Note that overtight clamping is as bad as loose; it squeezes out too much glue and produces a "starved" joint.

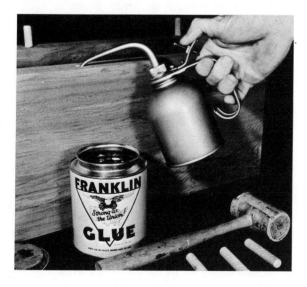

A pressure can, excellent also for use with oil, offers handy means of putting glue into dowel holes. Wooden dowels add strength and help alignment in edge-gluing.

WHITE GLUES

White polyvinyl glues have taken over most wood gluing jobs in the home and home shop. They set up comparatively fast, are nonstaining and can be used at any reasonable temperature. They come as near as anything available to being general purpose adhesives. Work with small tile mosaics is often done with white glue, as is

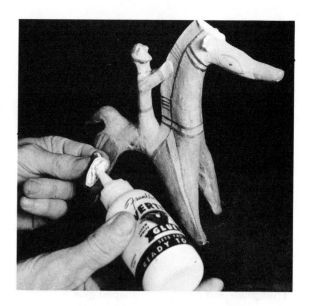

Porosity is the test: use white or other wood glues for porous objects, super-glues, contact cements and epoxies for nonporous.

wallpaper repair and mounting of maps and pictures. For this use, thinning the glue with water makes the job easier and more economical. One way to convert a glass window into a translucent one for privacy or sun protection is by covering it with four to six inch slightly overlapping squares of tissue paper that have been dipped into white glue thinned with water. Since white glues become virtually transparent as they dry, they can be used to give a protective coating to such things as the address on a package to be mailed. Mixed with sawdust from a woodworking job, they form a tough, nonshrinking, quick-drying plastic putty of a matching color for filling cracks, defects and nail holes.

ALIPHATIC RESINS

A general-purpose adhesive, sufficiently similar to white glue to be frequently confused with it, is the aliphatic resin type. With about twice the strength of white glue, this is probably the strongest general-purpose adhesive. (It should be noted, however, that any good wood glue is so strong that the wood glued will break before the joint will, so that comparative strength of glue is not a factor in most work.) It is useful with any porous material, including cloth, paper and plastic laminates, spreads easily at temperatures

between 45 and 110 degrees F., will not burn, stain or produce toxic vapors. In a warm room, clamps may be removed after 30 minutes, although overnight drying is required for full strength. Like the white glues, aliphatic resins are not waterproof.

CASEIN GLUES

Made from milk, casein glues are now used much less than they used to be in shop and home use, partly because they require mixing with water and a slight delay before use. These glues work in cool locations, fill joints well and have a moderate degree of water resistance. Since they add low cost to these other virtures, they are widely used in laminating beams where a large amount of adhesive is called for. Another characteristic of casein glues, which is both an advantage and a drawback, is that they react uniquely to certain kinds of wood. With acid woods, of which redwood is the most common, they produce a heavy purple stain or other discoloration that can be highly objectionable in woodworking. On the other hand, caseins work well on such oily woods as teak, yew and lemon that are sometimes a problem with most types of glue. The moisture-resistant qualities of casein glues makes them useful under moderately damp conditions, but they are not sufficiently moisture-resistant to be suitable for making or repairing outdoor furniture.

As casein glues are not at all sensitive to shop temperatures, thay are an especially good choice where work must be done outdoors (but not left exposed to rain) or in a cold shop.

PLASTIC-RESIN GLUES

Like the caseins, the plastic-resin or form-aldehyde glues come in the form of a light tan powder that must be mixed for each use. At one time, they constituted one of the most popular of wood glues, but the greater convenience of white glues has pushed them aside in recent years. They have other disadvantages, too. They do not fill gaps well, so are not suited for use with any but well-fitted joints. Since they are not at all sticky in nature, joints made with them must be tightly clamped as well as closely fitted. Wide

joints tend to be brittle. They are not suited for use with oily woods.

Against all these drawbacks, powdered-resin glues offer an advantage not found in most other wood glues: they are highly water-resistant. At one time, they were classified and labeled as waterproof; but the term has since become moisture-resistant, therefore these glues should not be used in damp conditions without a previous test in that situation.

An example of a typical test of a glue is one in which a piece of redwood lawn furniture, with joints secured solely by a plastic-resin glue, was immersed for a week in a swimming pool, held under water by weights. It was found at the end of the period that when the chair was pushed, pulled and twisted until it broke, the breakage was in the wood itself and not in the glued joint. Further testing should involve cycles of wetting and drying and perhaps a variety of temperature conditions, but it was possible to conclude that plastic-resin glue has a substantial degree of resistance to water.

RESORCINOL GLUES

Most brands of this product are sold under names that include the words *resorcinol* and *waterproof,* since their best quality is an almost total resistance to moisture in any form. It is also strong, nonflammable and reasonably quick-setting: and it works better than many glues do with poorly fitted joints. You can use it with porous materials, such as cork, cardboard and paper, as well as with wood.

Resorcinol glues come in the form of a powder and a liquid (a catalyst and a resin) that must be mixed for each use. Because of this and the fact that the glue is dark in color and can easily stain the work, resorcinol glues are not commonly used except where their waterproof qualities are required. They are the best choice on boats, wooden sinks, vehicles and outdoor furniture.

CONTACT CEMENTS

Contact cement was developed for gluing down counter tops of plastic laminate. It quickly prov-

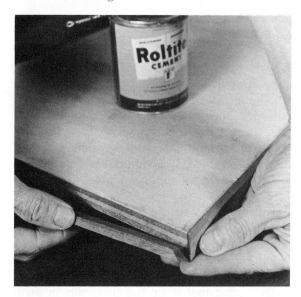

Edge-gluing of narrow trim strips is quickly done without nails or clamps by the use of double coating contact cement.

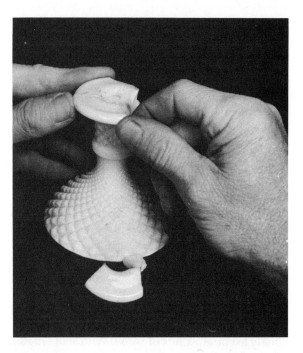

A perfect candidate for repair with super-glue is an object that is valuable (these glues are costly) and needs fast-setting adhesive because its shape makes clamping difficult.

ed to be equally useful for putting up wall paneling without the use of nails. Its virtue for both of these uses is that it holds instantly, making it unnecessary to use nails or fasteners, weights or clamps.

The greatest drawback to contact cement should be mentioned at once: it is highly flammable during application and has caused many fires. It should be used only where ventilation is good and also in the absence of any possible flame or spark, as from smoking, from a pilot light on a glass appliance or from any electrical appliance. Some serious fires have resulted from the spark produced when the thermostat of an electric refrigerator turned on the unit near a sink counter spread with contact cement. The problem is not that contact cement is inherently more dangerous than many other products containing similar volitile solvents, but rather that the cement is often used over a large area, releasing a considerable volume of fumes at one time.

To prevent this danger, one manufacturer now offers an alternate form of contact cement with a water base. Although it has somewhat less strength (seldom a problem where large areas are concerned), it is slower in application, takes longer to set and costs about one-third more than

the flammable kind, its use is very much to be recommended where there is the slightest possibility of fire danger.

The beauty of this many purpose, quick-hold adhesive is that it will stick almost anything, porous or not, (metal or wood or glass or fabric) to almost anything without the benefit of clamps. It should not, however, be used in the place of wood glues discussed above if a bond of maximum strength is required. It is not that strong, and it must not be used like ordinary glue. It must dry before the joint is put together.

Contact cement, except the water base kind, is composed of synthetic rubber and resins in a volatile solvent. When the solvent evaporates, a pressure-sensitive adhesive coating remains on both surfaces. It is of a kind that will stick together and they will hold instantly. Other materials however, will not readily adhere to a dry film of contact cement. The basic technique for using this adhesive is simple enough. Spread the cement on both surfaces, give it 30 minutes to dry (usually 60 minutes with the water-based

type) and then press the surfaces accurately and firmly together.

Contact cement also handles such hard-to-glue substances as metal and glass (including mirrors), various types of molded plastics and plastic sheets. When it is possible to do so without damaging the work, it is well to roughen the surfaces of such nonporous substances before applying the cement. It is also well to clean them with a solvent such as lacquer thinner, and to be sure that both the materials to be bonded and the cement itself are at ordinary room temperatures.

To get the comparatively heavy coat desirable with contact cement, spread it with a notched trowel if you are covering a large surface. Such trowels can be purchased where contact cement is sold. By holding the trowel so that its teeth are at a right angle to the surface, it is possible to put on the unusually heavy coating of cement that is desirable with porous sufaces including softwood, plywood, untempered hardboard and most kinds of wallboard. Porous materials will usually require a second coat after the first has dried, as will most vertical surfaces.

Allow at least 30 minutes drying time for each coat; anything up to two hours should be safe. To make sure that the surfaces are tacky, but not wet, before you join them, press a piece of wrapping paper lightly against them. It should come away without lifting any of the cement.

It is essential to join the surfaces accurately the first time, since you will not be able to move the parts once they touch. This is likely to be a major problem only with large sheets of material, such as plastic laminates. The solution is to place a sheet of wrapping paper so that it covers most of the adhesive area, slipping it out only after accurate contact has been produced where cemented surfaces touch. If you fail to get a good bond in some area, or there are indications that the joint is not bonding as it should, the cement may have been permitted to become too dry. You can reactivate such cement with heat from a heat lamp or an ordinary light bulb, but *never* flame. Warm the area and then press the two materials together, holding or weighting them until they

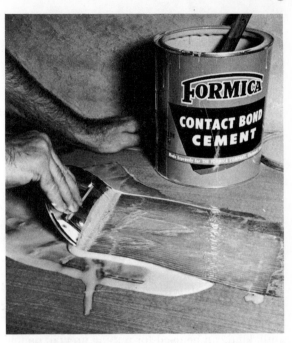

For accurate spread of contact cement, use a trowel designed for the product. On porous surface, turn trowel over.

have cooled. Such reactivation of cement is usually possible up to perhaps three days after initial application.

PANEL & CONSTRUCTION ADHESIVES

Similar in chemical makeup to contact cements, but much thicker in consistency, are the construction adhesives that come in tubes for use in calking guns. These have a multitude of uses in building and remodeling and in home maintenance. One major use of construction adhesive is for making the stiffest possible floor where plywood rests on wooden joists.

Panel adhesives differ from the kind labeled as construction adhesives, mostly as they are available in smaller tubes and in a greater variety of types. Some are interchangeable with construction adhesives; for example, one manufacturer suggests their use for replacing loose shingles, laying subfloors and sealing thresholds and sills.

In their primary use, most types of panel adhesive are squeezed onto framing or furring,

then drywall is pressed into place. Whether it is also necessary to swing the panel out and in again and to form a hinge with a few nails along the top edge will depend upon the type of panel adhesive. Because of this variation in behavior, which is produced by the fact that some panel adhesives are essentially mastics while others behave more like contact cement, it is important to read the instructions on the tube, preferably before purchase.

Various mastics are used in construction, special types being offered for wallboards, different kinds of tile (both floor and wall), and for carpets and the like.

Most come in bulk, in quart and gallon cans, and can be spread with a stick or a trowel as specified on the can. Many are interchangeable with construction adhesives in tubes; that is, the bulk kind can be used for putting up wall panels and the panel kind may serve very well for laying ceramic floor tile on either a concrete slab or plywood subfloor. Although black mastics have long been used for fastening furring strips to masonry walls (as when putting up prefinished plywood paneling in a basement-recreation room) the newer construction adhesives in tubes speed up the job and do it at least as strongly and permanently, although at a somewhat higher cost.

HOUSEHOLD & PLASTIC CEMENTS

Household cements and liquid solders are quick and easy to use on almost every type of surface, but cannot usually produce a very strong bond. They work with relatively nonporous substances, including glass and china, as well as with porous ones like wood and cloth.

Satisfactory bonding of plastics will often require a special adhesive obtained for the specific plastic, if known. Most common are the solvent types that work by dissolving the surfaces of the two pieces of plastic so that they melt together.

A late development in this field is a true superglue that makes remarkably strong bonds for materials not satisfactorily glued together until

now. This type of adhesive may be identified under its chemical name *alphacyanoacrylate*. In the absence of any generally accepted generic name, it is sometimes misleadingly named contact cement. It is most easily recognizable by the size of the tube it is sold in (very small) because the ingredients are costly or by warnings on it to keep it out of the hands of children. After some initial sale, adhesives of this family were taken off the market for a period but were allowed to return when adequate warnings were printed on the packages.

These costly instant cements are most satisfactory with nonporous materials, just the ones most difficult to bond with other adhesives. It is necessary merely to put a thin coating of the transparent adhesive on one or both surfaces, then press together almost instantly, maintaining pressure for perhaps a minute.

The principal precaution suggested in using these cements is to keep them off the fingers so far as possible (they will quickly cement fingers together, too) and especially to keep them away from the eyes. A careless move could result in bonded eyelids followed by surgery. Obviously such effective adhesives should be kept out of the hands of children unless constant supervision is maintained.

HEAT-MELTED GLUES

Adhesives that come in the form of crayon-like sticks that must be melted in a glue gun at the time of use are a development of the 1970's, so far as regular home use is concerned. Their most attractive characteristic is that since they set by cooling, they typically have a setting time of perhaps half a minute. This makes it feasible to form joints without using clamps or clamp-substitutes by merely holding the parts together by hand while the glue hardens.

Glues of this kind have a moderate degree of water and weather resistance, combined with medium strength. They can be used with plastics, metal, masonry and tile as well as wood and porous materials. The same gun, and sometimes the same glue stick, can also be used for caulking.

EPOXY ADHESIVES

Epoxies are a last-resort adhesive. They require accurate mixing, they must be used very quickly, they are rather costly and they are difficult to clean off of anything that they get on, including hands and clothing. They make little sense for uses where other adhesives exist, including wood gluing, especially.

Where nothing else will serve however, epoxies are invaluable. What other adhesive could be relied upon to hold a steel guide to a concrete floor when a sliding garage door has been installed? To repair a metal gutter? To stop a pressure leak in a water pipe for which no suitable fitting can be found? Epoxies are also waterproof.

For most adhesive uses you can buy epoxy in the form of two small tubes. Equal amounts should be squeezed out of each tube and mixed together thoroughly. For repairs requiring a product with more body, use liquid epoxy (readily available where auto-body repair products are sold) supported by glass cloth.

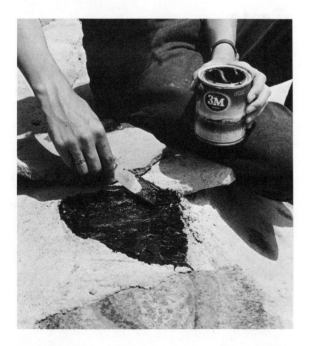

Black mastics and epoxies are two good adhesive choices for such outdoor jobs as cementing this loose flagstone.

Gold Leaf

Gold leaf is a very thin sheet of gold which may be used in gilding. It is available in roll form and in layers with conveyer or wax paper between the leaves. There is a process of gold leafing which is a kind of decorative furniture finish.

To begin gold leafing, first varnish the surface and let it set from 30 minutes to one hour, not long enough to completely dry. Place a sheet of gold leaf over the varnish and let it settle; then gently press it down with a cloth. Any furniture varnish which is diluted with an equal amount of thinner and brushed on sparingly, will work satisfactorily, however, special varnishes are available for this type of finishing. The gold leaf normally will crack when it is applied, so in this case, place another small section of gold leaf on the area where the surface is visible. Then press it down and blow away any excess which does not stick to the varnish.

On mirrors the gold leaf foundation is normally polished plaster which has a very smooth finish. It should be polished 24 hours before applying the gold leaf. Any of the rough spots will polish out as the gold is settling. To polish, use a flannel cloth.

Gold leaf is often laid on antique white French furniture which has carving and is left cracked. To produce a Chinese red that will show through the cracked areas, first paint the carving with varnish, and then place the gold leaf on top in the regular way.

Gold leaf should be protected, especially if the furniture gets much wear. Varnish, shellac or lacquer may be used. To achieve a more perfect film, use a spray can.

Gooseneck Ripping Bar

A gooseneck ripping bar is used for wrecking, prying and heavy nail pulling. The overall length

ranges from 18 to 36 inches. This bar has tremendous leverage due to the deep hook on one end, but it requires a long swing which limits its uses. *SEE ALSO HAND TOOLS.*

Courtesy of The Stanley Works

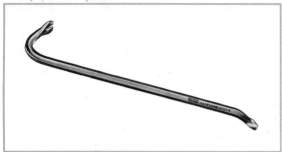

Gooseneck Ripping Bar

Gooseneck Scraper

Gooseneck scrapers are for scraping the interior of surfaces, such as the inside of a wooden bowl, which would be practically impossible to do with any other type of scraper or knife. *SEE ALSO HAND TOOLS.*

Gouge Chisel

A gouge chisel is a tool which is rounded with a hollow-shaped cutting edge. For different jobs, the blade has three degrees of curvature which are flat, medium and regular. This chisel is used to shape, make grooves and cut hollows. It may be operated by hand or with a soft-face hammer or mallet. *SEE ALSO HAND TOOLS.*

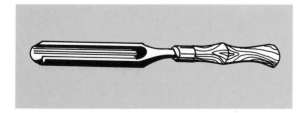

Gouge Chisel

Grading

Grading is the process of altering the lay of the ground by excavation. This may be both leveling an area or filling a crevice or ravine with earth. Bulldozers and backhoes are the two primary machines used in grading.

Grain

Grain refers to the pattern and texture of a piece of wood produced by the annual growth rings, rays and knots.

Graining
[SEE ANTIQUING; WOOD FINISHING.]

Grate

A grate is a frame made of parallel or crossed bars forming a latticework and used to block passage of materials, such as a grate over a drain. In addition, a grate is a barred frame used for cooking over a fire or holding wood or coal in a fireplace.

Gravity Heating Systems
[SEE HEATING SYSTEMS.]

Grease Trap

A box usually made of concrete or wood, which collects grease in the pipes coming mainly from the kitchen sink and dishwasher, is called a

grease trap. These traps are normally found in septic tank systems where there is no city sewer. As the water from the house flows into the trap, grease floats to the top and is stopped by a wooden block. The remaining water exits the trap at the bottom while the grease stays in top of the trap.

Grease traps should be placed in a convenient location easily accessible for cleaning. To clean a grease trap, remove the cover, scoop out the grease which has accumulated and dispose of it in a garbage can. *SEE ALSO CLOGGED DRAINS.*

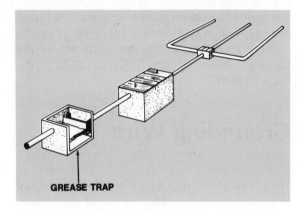

GREASE TRAP

Greenhouses

A greenhouse is a glass-enclosed building that regulates environmental conditions for growing plants. Greenhouse gardening can be enjoyed all year, in any season. Chrysanthemums, asters, orchids, roses, african violets and begonias (to name a few) can be grown at any time by controlling the humidity and temperature of the greenhouse.

For the gourmet cook, the greenhouse offers an additional bonus. Some fresh vegetables, such as cucumbers and tomatoes, as well as fragrant herbs like basil, sage and chives, can be grown the year round.

Although most early greenhouses were self-supporting structures built away from the house,

there are a variety of kits and design plans that attach the greenhouse to the home. When this is built as an addition, it is called a *conservatory.* Growing plants indoors causes two things to happen that are healthful to the homeowner: it raises the house humidity and purifies the air (on a small scale) since plants give off oxygen.

Although greenhouses are usually framed with glass, more and more structures are being built with fiberglass and certain types of plastics. Plastic has several advantages over glass: it does not weigh as much as glass, and unlike glass, it can be cut with a fine-toothed saw or linoleum knife, depending on the thickness. Also, plastic can be tacked to the frame using finishing nails or cement staples. The main disadvantages are that plastic scratches quite easily and does not last as long as glass. *SEE ALSO LAWNS AND GARDENS.*

Grommets, Insulated

Insulated grommets are rubber washers that protect electric cords where they pass through metal coverings. Used especially in lamp mountings and electric motors, the grommets protect the cord from rubbing against the sharp sides of a hole in the metal housing, eliminating wear and possible electrical shock. *SEE ALSO ELECTRICAL WIRING.*

Groover

The groover is a tool used in masonry work for making control joints in concrete slabs. It has a rectangular body with a handle on one surface and an extension in the center of the other surface. The extension makes the grooves by running the groover back and forth across the concrete area. This is usually done against a straightedge, such as a 2 x 4, to keep the grooves aligned. For sidewalks, make joints every four or five feet; 10 to 15 feet on driveways, patios and floors. *SEE ALSO CONCRETE & MASONRY TOOLS.*

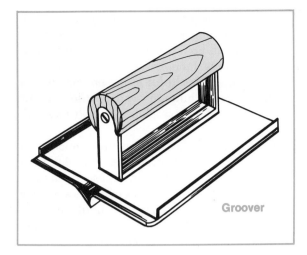

Groover

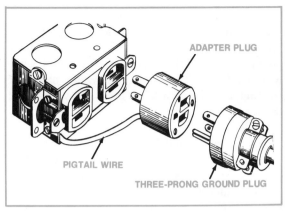

An adapter plug.

Grounding

Grounding is a safety measure incorporated into all wiring systems to reduce the possibility of shock due to shorts or fire.

Conduit or armored cable are "automatic grounds" for wiring systems because their metal sheathing provides a continuous path for electricity.

Systems that do not implement conduits or armored cable should be grounded with a bare metal grounding wire. Connected through the circuit by ground terminal screws, the grounding wire provides a continuous ground to the fuse box. The fuse box has a grounding cable running to an underground water pipe system or to a metal rod driven into the earth. Thus, if a short circuit or lightning should occur, the current will go directly through the grounding system.

Many electrical appliances and tools have their own grounding systems that are connected to the house grounding system through a three-prong plug. If the outlet is not equipped with a three-prong slot receptacle, an adapter may be obtained. This adapter looks much like a two-prong plug except that it has a three-prong receptacle face and a neutral wire, usually color-coded green, leading from the back of the plug. The adapter is inserted into the two-prong receptacle

plate and the pigtail wire is attached to the screw that holds the cover plate to the wall. A three-prong plug may then be inserted into the adapter, thus, grounding the appliance to the house grounding system. *SEE ALSO ELECTRICAL WIRING.*

Grounding Wire

The grounding wire is a bare metal wire running from the entrance panel to either an underground water pipe system or a metal grounding rod. House circuitry color codes the grounding circuit as the white wire. The intent of the grounding is to form a continuous route for household current from outlets, switches and all exposed metal through the grounding terminal at the service entrance to a point under the earth.

The grounding point may be either a water pipe system or a grounding rod. If the water pipe is less than ten feet under the ground, use both methods to insure a well-grounded circuit. The grounding wire should be over eight feet long and buried at least ten feet into the earth. Connect the rod to the circuit with a bare wire leading to a grounding terminal, or clamp, located about two feet below the ground.

Electrical appliances, also, have a grounding system that is connected to the house ground when the appliance is plugged into the outlet. Should some "live" metal component touch the metal housing of the appliance, the ground

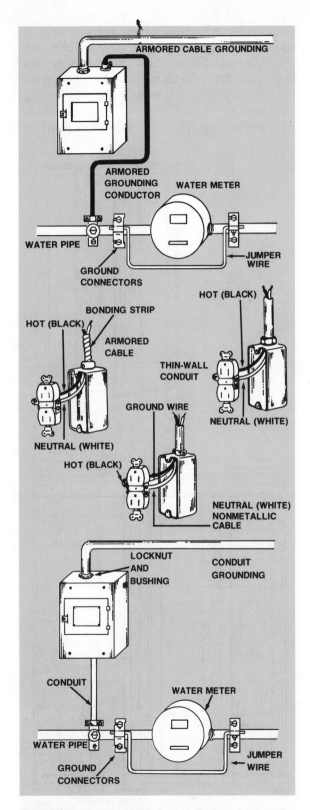

Grounding systems must be continuous from outlet to water pipe in city grounding.

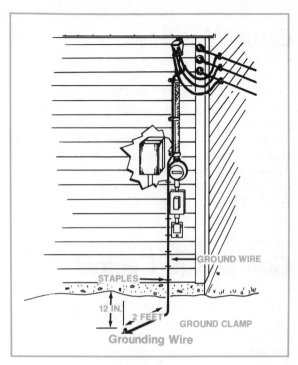

Use of Ground rod.

system will provide the quickest possible route to the earth for the current. *SEE ALSO ELECTRICAL WIRING.*

Grout

Grout is a thin cement mortar that comes either in the form of a powder that is mixed with water or in a premixed paste. It is used around tiles to make them watertight.

There are also types of grout made of epoxy resins or vinyl which are more flexible and elastic and so minimize cracking.

Guide Bar

A guide bar is a support on which a drawer slides. Usually made from metal or steel, a guide bar steers the runner attached to the drawer bottom to properly align the drawer within the framework of a structure.

Gum Wood

Gum wood, a fairly strong, close grained hardwood, is referred to as sweet gum or red gum. Its pinkish-white sapwood is used for veneer panel cores. The reddish-brown heartwood is used in making fine furniture and cabinetmaking. Although it warps easily, gum wood stains, glues and sands well. *SEE ALSO WOOD IDENTIFICATION.*

Gun & Rod Cabinet

To begin construction, glue up the pieces that are needed for the top, sides, back, partition, shelves and other parts. After the glue has dried, the pieces can be cut to exact sizes.

Dado the sides and partitions for shelves and bottoms $3/4''$ wide by $3/8''$ deep. Leave 1'' margin on the front edges of the sides for doors. The cabinet back butts against center partition. Dado sides for header $1/4''$ wide by $3/8''$ deep by $1 1/2''$ (width of header). Notch sides (front and back) for frame base strips $1 1/2''$ wide by $3/4''$ deep. Make sure all rabbets have been made before beginning to assemble cabinet.

Fit ends of header and butt mullion to header, then screw door block to the mullion and header for rigidity. Miter both ends of front base and one end of side base; shape lower edges 6'' from ends of front piece and 4'' from end on side pieces. Notch partition at top for triangular block block and at floor, trim 1'' from front half of width.

Rabbet edges of the door frames for panels and glass $1/2''$ wide by $3/8''$ deep. Also rabbet wood panels the same amount on the front side and bevel the inside edge slightly. Install glass with glass bead.

As doors close over drawers, allow $1/4''$ clearance when setting shelves or figuring drawer lengths.

Simplified construction of the two drawers is achieved through the use of drawer slides which keep drawers aligned and with an even margin all around. Sizes for dados on sides of drawers and sizes of slides are identical and will need to be planed and sanded slightly to prevent sticking. Paraffin or graphite will help allow drawers

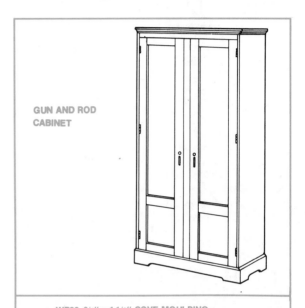

GUN AND ROD CABINET

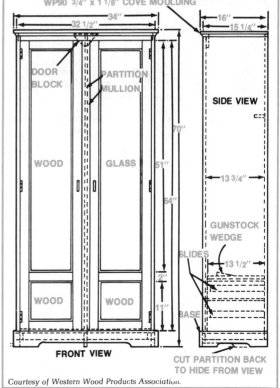

Courtesy of Western Wood Products Association.

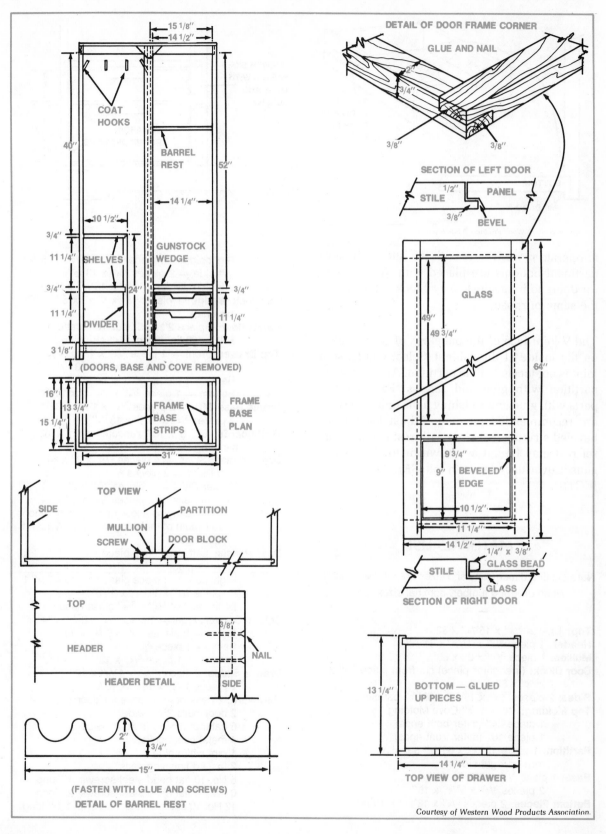

DETAIL OF DOOR FRAME CORNER

GLUE AND NAIL

SECTION OF LEFT DOOR

STILE   PANEL

BEVEL

GLASS

BEVELED EDGE

GLASS BEAD

STILE

GLASS

SECTION OF RIGHT DOOR

BOTTOM — GLUED UP PIECES

TOP VIEW OF DRAWER

COAT HOOKS

BARREL REST

GUNSTOCK WEDGE

SHELVES

DIVIDER

(DOORS, BASE AND COVE REMOVED)

FRAME BASE STRIPS

FRAME BASE PLAN

TOP VIEW

SIDE

MULLION SCREW

PARTITION

DOOR BLOCK

TOP

HEADER

NAIL

SIDE

HEADER DETAIL

(FASTEN WITH GLUE AND SCREWS)

DETAIL OF BARREL REST

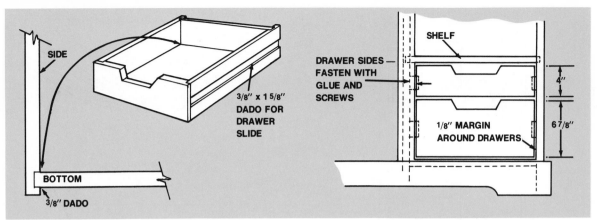

Courtesy of Western Wood Products Association

to operate more freely. Both left and right compartment bottoms are placed with $1/4''$ showing for doors to hit against. Door block at top serves the same purpose.

The V-joint face of the paneling, of course, goes on the inside of the cabinet. Select widths so a joint is not located at the partition. Attach back to partition with glue and screws. Fasten other parts with glue and finishing nails unless screws are recommended on plan. Adjust location of beveled strip so that stock will rest evenly. Barrel rest may be cut as shown or to fit owner's guns. Cover the edge with felt. *SEE ALSO PROJECTS.*

MATERIALS LIST

Note: Cutting dimensions and sizes are all given exact. When ordering lumber, nominal sizes are used.

Top: 1 piece $3/4'' \times 15^1/4'' \times 32^1/2''$
Header: 1 piece $3/4'' \times 1^1/2'' \times 31^3/4''$
Mullion: 1 piece $3/4'' \times 2'' \times 66^1/8''$
Door Block: (triangular piece) cut from piece $3/4'' \times 2^7/8'' \times 6''$
Sides: 2 pieces $3/4'' \times 15^1/4'' \times 69^1/2''$ paneling
Top Molding: $3/4'' \times 1^1/8''$ Cove Molding
    1 piece 34'' (miter both ends)
    1 piece 16'' (miter front ends)
Partition: 1 piece $13^3/4'' \times 69^1/2''$ paneling with pattern on right side
Base: 1 piece $3/4'' \times 3^5/8'' \times 34''$
    2 pieces $3/4'' \times 3^5/8'' \times 16''$
Bottom Pieces: 2 pieces $3/4'' \times 13^1/2'' \times 15^1/8''$

Shelves: Right side — 1 piece $3/4'' \times 13^1/2'' \times 15^7/8''$
    Left side — 2 pieces $3/4'' \times 13^1/2'' \times 10^1/2''$
    Left side divider — $3/4'' \times 13^1/2'' \times 23^3/4''$
Gunstock Wedge: 1 piece $5/8'' \times 1^1/8'' \times 5'' \times 15''$ (beveled)
Barrel Rest: 1 piece $2'' \times 15''$ cut from pattern
    Felt — 28 lin. inches $3/4''$ stripping
Top Drawer: Front — 1 piece $3/4'' \times 4'' \times 14^1/4''$
    Sides — 2 pieces $3/4'' \times 4'' \times 13''$
    Back — 1 piece $3/4'' \times 4'' \times 13^1/2''$
    Bottom — 1 piece $3/4'' \times 12^1/4'' \times 13^1/2''$
Frame Base Strips: 2 pieces $3/4'' \times 1^5/8'' \times 32^1/2''$
    2 pieces $3/4'' \times 1^5/8'' \times 13^3/4''$
Backboards: 6'', 8'', 10'' random width x $66^3/8''$ paneling for width of $31^5/8''$
Door Frames: Stiles — 4 pieces $3/4'' \times 2'' \times 64''$
    Top Rails — 2 pieces $3/4'' \times 2'' \times 14^1/2''$
    Center Rails — 2 pieces $3/4'' \times 2'' \times 14^1/2''$
    Bottom Rails — 2 pieces $3/4'' \times 2'' \times 14^1/2''$
    Note: Lengths allow for mortise or tenon full width of matching member. Adjust if doweled.
Door Panels: Left door — 1 piece $3/4'' \times 11^1/4'' \times 49^3/4''$ 1 piece $3/4'' \times 11^1/4'' \times 9^3/4''$
    Right door — 1 piece glass $11^1/4'' \times 49^3/4''$ 1 piece $3/4'' \times 11^1/4'' \times 9^3/4''$
    24 lin. feet of $1/4'' \times 3/8''$ glass bead
Bottom Drawer: Front — 1 piece $3/4'' \times 6^7/8'' \times 14^1/4''$
    Sides — 2 pieces $3/4'' \times 6^7/8'' \times 13''$
    Back — 1 piece $3/4'' \times 6^7/8'' \times 13^1/2''$
    Bottom — 1 piece $3/4'' \times 12^1/4'' \times 13^1/2''$
Drawer Slides: 2 pieces $1/2'' \times 1^5/8'' \times 12''$
    2 pieces $1^1/8'' \times 1^5/8'' \times 12''$
Hardware: 2 desk drawer locks for doors
    2 door pulls $2^1/2''$ wide
    6 cabinet hinges (butt) 2'' wide
    4 metal coat hooks
    1 pint white glue
    2 lbs. 6d finishing nails
    6 No. 10 flat head steel screws, 1'' long
    6 No. 10 flat head steel screws, 2'' long
    12 No. 10 flat head steel screws, $1^1/4''$ long

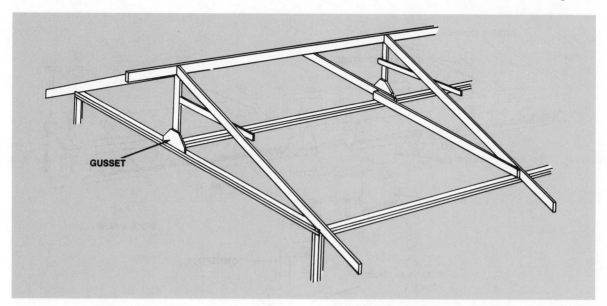

GUSSET

Gusset

A gusset is a small wood or metal plate bolted or riveted at corners of frames or trusses to stiffen the intersection and add strength. *SEE ALSO ROOF CONSTRUCTION.*

Gutters & Downspouts

Gutters and downspouts are important, though inconspicuous, rain-carrying devices attached to the house. Gutters, tucked into eaves or roof edges, appear to be part of the house trim.

Gutters are important because they prevent erosion which is caused by rainwater coming off the roof; they prevent water from dripping annoyingly off roof edges; and they keep water out of the basement.

There are two basic designs for gutters; half-round and K-style or ogee. The K-style has a square back and curved front. Downspouts are round or rectangular with rounded corners, sometimes simple; sometimes with paralleled ridges.

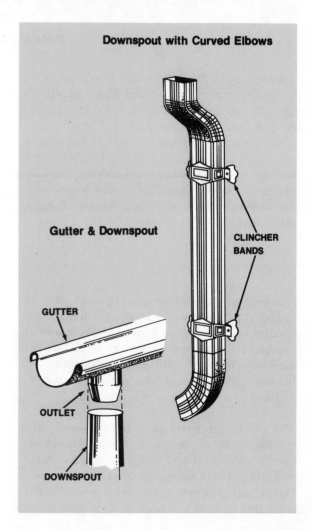

Downspout with Curved Elbows

Gutter & Downspout

GUTTER

OUTLET

DOWNSPOUT

CLINCHER BANDS

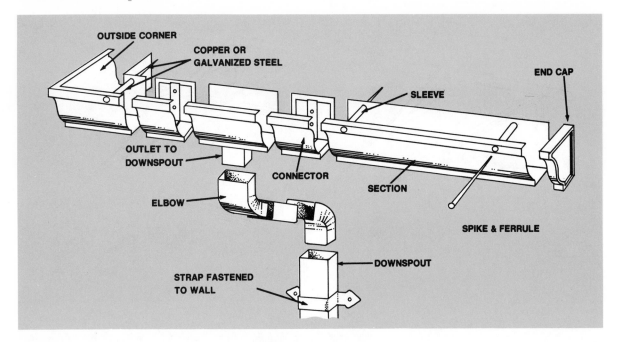

Parts of a Gutter Run

Materials used for gutters and downspouts include aluminum, galvanized steel, plastic or vinyl, copper and sometimes wood (for gutters only). Aluminum is considered the best material to use because it is lighter in weight and easy to work with and install. It is good, too, because it does not rust out or corrode. Wooden gutters are difficult to repair, should they wear down or rot. It is best to replace wooden gutters with metal rather than try to repair them.

COMPONENTS OF RAIN-CARRYING EQUIPMENT

Elements of rain-carrying equipment may be bought separately when replacement parts are needed. Gutters and downspouts come in lengths of 10 feet and longer, up to 30 feet. All parts slip together with special fasteners. All damaged parts, needed for replacement, may be obtained at a building supply company.

Often wooden parts may be replaced with another type of material. Metals, however, should never be mixed with galvanized iron elements because of the resulting excess corrosion. This wearing down is caused by electrolysis, when iron or steel is connected to another metal.

TYPES OF GUTTERS

Wooden gutters are mostly found on older homes, but are still installed occasionally. They require careful, regular maintenance. Repair for rotted wood is difficult and often a whole new run of gutter must be installed to replace it. New wooden gutters require preventive maintenance by lining them with fiberglass or putting several coats of linseed oil on them. The gutter should be cleaned as thoroughly as possible before lining. Resin, which may be bought along with fiberglass, should be applied before fiberglass cloth is put down. The resin is then reapplied when surfaces are dry. Linseed oil, a less expensive form of maintenance, should be applied annually. Painted gutters should be repainted annually, preferably in the fall.

Of metal drainage systems, galvanized steel is probably the most popular. If the zinc coating wears off, it causes the steel to rust. This can be temporarily prevented by metal primers which should be redone at the first signs of rust. When the gutter is reprimed and painted, all its parts should be inspected for corrosion. Every two to three years, galvanized steel gutters need to be coated with metal paint or roofing compound.

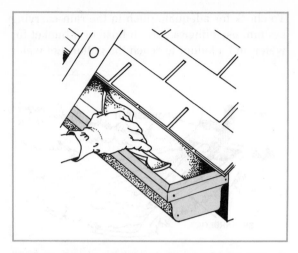

Wooden gutters should be painted annually. Prior to repainting, all debris should be cleaned out and the interior surfaces sanded.

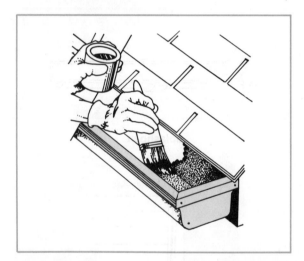

Next, apply paint thinner to the interior followed by asphalt roof paint. A few days later, apply a second coat.

Always clean the gutter and hose it down before applying coating.

The more expensive *aluminum* gutters, because they are not susceptible to rust and corrosion, do not require protective coating, but may be painted to match house trim. When new, aluminum and galvanized steel gutters cannot be painted. They must be allowed to oxidize for several months.

Copper gutters are maintained with the use of steel wool for polishing and spar varnish for

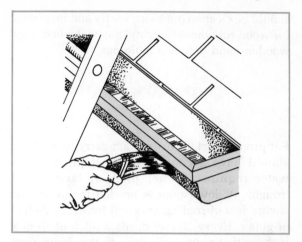

Sand the outer gutter surface and remove scaling paint. Apply paint thinner and exterior house paint, preferably two coats.

coating. Oxidation tends to turn unprotected copper into a dark green color. Copper does not rust, but requires regular cleanouts of debris to function properly.

Vinyl drainage systems are newer and fairly easy to maintain. The only metal connected with them is in the brackets and hangers which need painting every two years. These metal parts can be easily replaced also. Vinyl drainage systems

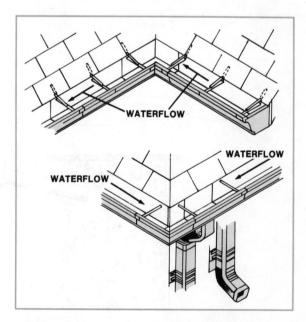

Gutters, with the proper sloping, drain toward corners where downspouts are located.

should be cleaned out twice yearly and inspected for wood rot where the vinyl meets the fascia, or wooden band between moldings.

GUIDELINES FOR RAIN-CARRYING EQUIPMENT

For proper working order, rain-carrying systems should have a good downward pitch. More water requires greater pitch or larger eave troughs. A downspout is needed for every 500 square feet of roofing area and for every 20 feet of gutter. Every 20 feet needs a pitch of 1/2 to 1 inch so that water will flow to the downspout rapidly enough to prevent run-over. It should have quick water movement for carrying out dirt and dust and to eliminate standing pools after the rain. Excess water left in the gutter run hastens rust and corrosion. Downspouts should have as few bends as possible to lessen chance of clogging or water blockage. Underground piping, grading off and splash blocks take water away after it leaves the downspout. Underground piping may lead into a drywell, a large hole in the ground filled with rocks through which water seeps.

To check for adequate pitch in the rain-carrying system, use either a garden hose or a bucket for water and a ladder to reach the gutter. Let water

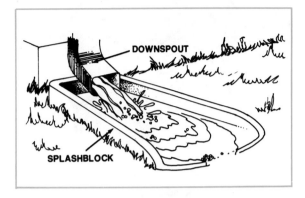

Splashblock

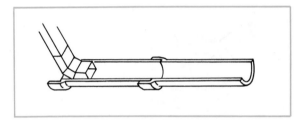

Splashpan

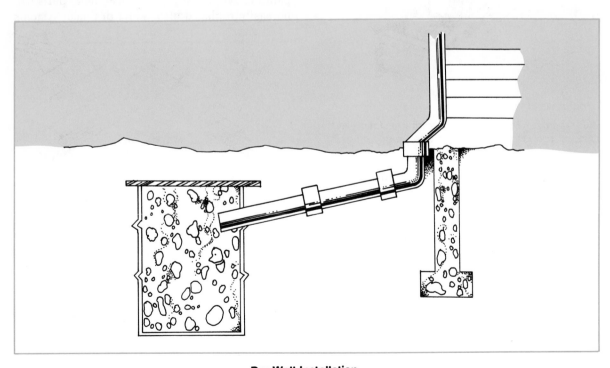

Dry Well Installation

from the hose or bucket go into the gutter at the highest end, opposite the downspout end. When a run is longer than 20 feet, usually downspouts are located on either side with the high spot in the middle. When a run is 40 feet or more, there may be three downspouts, one on each end and one in the middle. The high spots for this run would be located halfway between the middle downspout and the downspouts on each end.

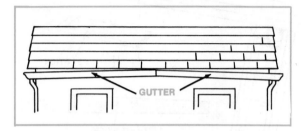

When a gutter run is longer than 20 feet, it should be pitched to a downspout on each end.

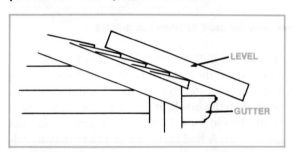

Check to see that the roof line is level when laying out gutters.

Check for water puddles during this process and raise the gutter run at places where water is left standing. Hangers have to be repositioned when the gutter is raised. To do this, first remove nails in the sagging area. Then raise the hangers or increase their tension, depending on design. The sags can be detected by laying a 1 x 2 or 2 x 2 lumber in the trough. The sag will show beneath the board.

HANGERS

Gutter hangers are spaced about 32 inches apart. The basic types are the fascia clip or bracket hanger, the strap hanger and the spike and ferrule. The spike and ferrule is easiest to use. The

ferrule is a metal tube used to mold the gutter edges and get the proper spacing. The spike should fit into a rafter end.

A strap hanger fastens directly to the roof, independent of eave design. It fits under a shingle.

The fascia clip fastens to the fascia board at the eaves. It is easy to adjust up and down on the board for the proper pitch.

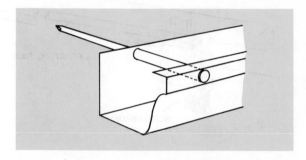

Spike & Ferrule. The ferrule fits within the gutter and the spike goes into the roofboards.

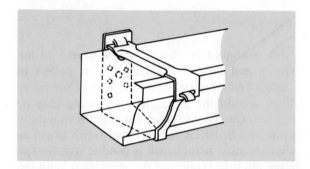

Bracket Hanger. The bracket attaches to the fascia board below the roof.

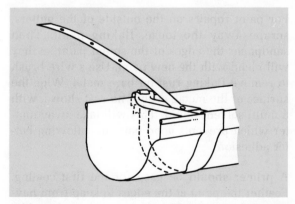

Strap Hanger. The strap is nailed to the roof under the shingle.

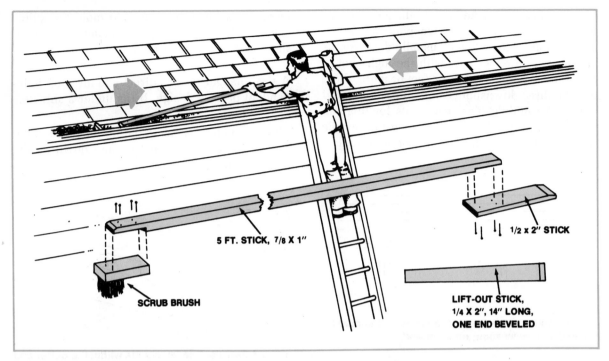

5 FT. STICK, 7/8 X 1"

SCRUB BRUSH

1/2 x 2" STICK

LIFT-OUT STICK, 1/4 X 2", 14" LONG, ONE END BEVELED

A simple double-ended stick, such as the one shown above, may be used to clean out gutters.

MAINTENANCE

Gutters should be cleaned twice yearly, in the spring and fall since leaves tend to collect in them when trees are shedding. If there are many trees around the home, more cleaning may be needed. One way to clean gutters is with a putty knife and brush. A stiff-bristled scrub brush or short-bristled paint brush is good to use. Scrape mud and other collected particles away with the knife and sweep this out. Then water down the gutter with a hose.

For paint repairs on the outside of the gutters, scrape away the loose, flaking paint. Then sandpaper the edges of the sound paint so they will blend with the new paint. Use a wire brush to remove flaking rust on bare metal. Wipe the surface of the metal, even if no rust shows, with a multi-solvent liquid. This will take away matter which prevents good painting, allowing better adhesion.

A primer should be used for the first coating. Feather the paint at the edges to keep from having an abrupt line. This first paint coat should be latex house or trim paint.

Inspect the gutters when they are clean for rust and to see if they are properly coated inside with paint or roofing compound. If paint repair is needed on the inside, it is best to use asphalt roof paint. Inside rust is related to protection, not good looks. A bad corrosion problem may develop in a gutter in just a season if it has not been properly cared for in the beginning. Rust inhibitors are used on most modern gutters and should be maintained with good paint on the outside and continuous film on the inside. If the metal has weakened from rust, three things can remedy this: the area may be patched with metal and cement, the damaged part may be replaced or the entire part of the gutter which is corroded may be replaced.

To patch a rusted area of a gutter, get a piece of metal the same kind, style and size as the gutter being repaired, about 12 inches longer than the part to be patched. Trim the edges so the piece will be in the shape of the gutter. Press the patch in the proper place, allowing it to nest inside the gutter. A few adjustments may be necessary for this. Drill holes for sheet metal screws to hold the patch in place. Remove the patch and smear the area with gutter cement. Replace the patch

and drive sheet metal screws from the outside on the front and bottom, from the inside on the back. Finally, coat the edges of the patch with cement.

To insert a new piece of gutter, take a hacksaw or tinsnips to cut out the old length of gutter. Buy a larger piece of material than that cut. Slip the new piece too far into one end, sliding it back into the other end until spacing on both ends is even. Then use sheet metal screws or rivets, and gutter cement.

To replace an entire unit, remove all screws, rivets and nails. Put the new length in place by using cement and fastenings in the same place as the old.

INSTALLATION OF A NEW GUTTER

The first step to installing a new run of gutter is taking down the old equipment and carefully assembling it on the ground, preferably on a walk, driveway or level lawn. Compare the new material to the old in order to get the proper length and outlet spaces. Join pieces of the new material together with the necessary tools and adhesives. When installing the new run, use any easy-to-attach hangers.

To establish pitch (of at least 1/2 inch for each 20 feet) attach a nail on the fascia or rafter at the high end of the run. Then tie a length of stout cord, such as mason's line, to the nail. Move the cord to the low end, pulling it tightly. Use a line level on the cord, making adjustments until the

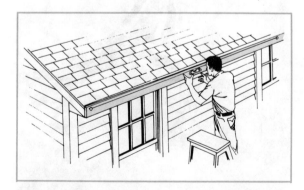

A chalk line tied to a nail driven into the fascia board helps determine the correct slope for gutters. Use a line level for checking alignment.

bubble in the line level is centered correctly. Sags should not be a problem if the cord is pulled tightly enough. Measure an inch down from where the level is correct and tap on nails and mark places to show the slope of the gutter along the boards. This is the correct slope line for the edge of the gutter to follow.

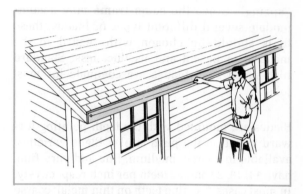

To mark a line on the board, pull the chalk line and snap it when it is at the desired slope.

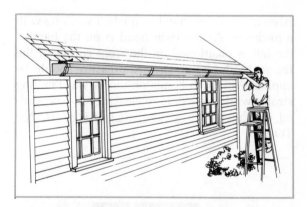

A circular wire held by a nail will keep one end of the gutter span in suspension while replacing.

Gypsum Wallboard

Gypsum wallboard is a panel used instead of plaster in wall and ceiling construction. The wallboard consists of a fire-proof core made of gypsum rock which has been specially treated and spread between sheets of treated paper. Some gypsum wallboards are covered on one side with an additional layer of plastic or aluminum foil. *SEE ALSO DRYWALL.*

Hacksaw

The hacksaw, a special tool for cutting metal, has a rigid frame to permit adequate tension on the blade with no chance of blade-slackening "spring". Since the same frame may accommodate several different types of blades, these tools should be chosen with regard to the material to be cut and its thickness. Standard high-speed steel blades are adequate for most jobs.

Blades are mounted with the teeth pointing forward to cut on the push stroke. Blade varieties, available in coarse, medium, fine and very fine, have 14, 18, 24 and 32 teeth per inch respectively. In most cases, use fine teeth on thin metal, coarse teeth on thick metal. The 18-tooth medium blade is best for general shop work.

Always use a two-hand grip when working with a hacksaw. As the right hand is on the handle, the left is positioned on the front corner of the frame. Moderate downward pressure should be applied with both hands on the forward cutting stroke, while almost no release pressure is needed on the return stroke. *SEE ALSO HAND TOOLS.*

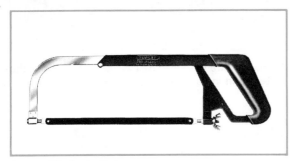

Courtesy of The Stanley Works

Hacksaw

Hair Dryer Repair

Hair dryers are found in two basic types. One is the hand-held unit and another is the bonnet type, which also includes the tabletop hairdryers. These operate by passing air over the heating element, then forcing it through the bonnet, out the nozzle or through the perforations in the hood.

There are three principal component parts to these hair dryers. One is the heating element itself, the second is a small shaded-pole fan motor which turns the blower wheel and the third is the control switch which selects the heat range or no heat at all if desired. Many of the heating elements have a small bimetal arm that is part of the element assembly. This will open and break the circuit to the element in case air flow becomes blocked or if the element should otherwise overheat.

Always unplug the hair dryer before attempting to service it. To service tabletop models, look under the bottom for any screws that hold the cover in place. These may be located under the rubber feet that support the base of the unit. For hand-held models, it is usually necessary to split the housing. You will have to look for hidden screws, especially under trim plates and decals.

With the housing off, look closely around the wiring connections to be sure that they are tight. If a wire is broken or corroded, polish it until it is bright and shiny before attempting to solder or fasten it back into place. A break in the heating element will often be visible also since these use

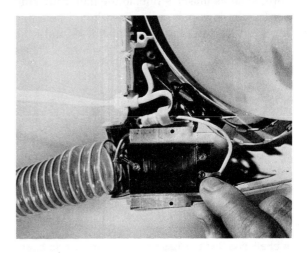

Heating element is located in air outlet. Bimetal safety limit is part of element assembly.

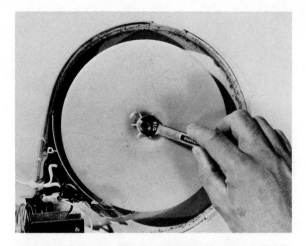

Clip or nut that holds the blower in place can be a source of noise problems. Be sure that it is tight.

an open-type element. However, a new element assembly will have to be obtained — they can't be repaired if there is a break in the element.

While the hair dryer is apart, vacuum away any lint or hair that may be in the blower. A loose or out-of-balance blower is often the cause of a noise problem in this type unit. It's easily remedied by cleaning the blower wheel and tightening connections.

When reassembling the hair dryer, be sure that heat shields which surround the heating element are back in place. *SEE ALSO APPLIANCE REPAIR, SMALL.*

Half-Round

Half-round is a simple molding with a semicircular shape or cross section. It is used to cover joints between wall and ceiling panels. *SEE ALSO MOLDING & TRIM.*

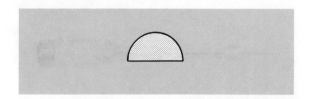

Half-Round Molding

Half-Round File

The half-round file, which is available in different lengths and degrees of coarseness, can be used for fast filing on both metal and wood. Its rounded back is suitable for smoothing concave parts and flat surfaces, while the flat side of the half-round is used mainly on the flat areas. *SEE ALSO HAND TOOLS.*

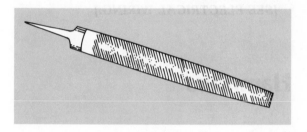

Half-Round File

Half-Round Shoe Rasp

For the shaping of wood, leather and soft metals, filing slots or fitting tenons, a half-round shoe rasp can be used. Being half-round, this rasp has a flat side and a rounded side. From the center to one end both the flat and rounded surfaces have rasp teeth for fast, rough filing. From the center to the other end, again on both the flat and rounded surfaces, there are file teeth for final smoothing. Half-round shoe rasps are primarily used in the manufacture and repair of shoes. *SEE ALSO HAND TOOLS.*

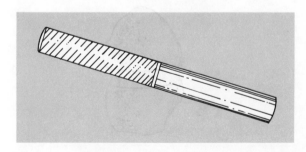

Half-Round Shoe Rasp

Half Story

A half story is the top floor of a house in which the upper portion of the front wall is formed by the roof. Front windows are usually contained in dormers.

Hallway Wiring

[SEE ELECTRICAL WIRING.]

Hammers

Hammers can be used for driving nails, ripping boards apart or pulling out nails. The ones considered to be "standard" are the bell-faced, ball-peen and sledge hammers. *SEE ALSO HAND TOOLS.*

Hammer Stone

Hammer stone is an archeological name for a specially chosen hard stone that was used as a hammer by Stone Age man. The stone usually had one hollowed side to provide a thumb grip. Later, man cut a groove around the head of the stone so it could be lashed to a handle.

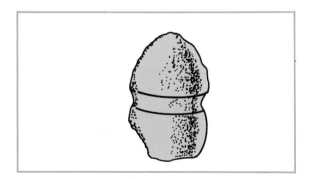

Hammer Stone With Grooved Head

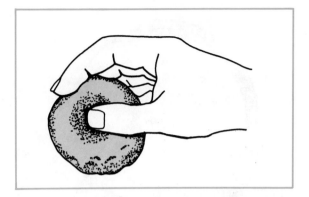

Hammer Stone With Thumb Grip

Hand Drills

Hand drills are hand-powered tools used for boring holes in wood, metal and plastic. The crank-operated hand drill provides plenty of speed for drilling in wood or metal, but can be slowed to prevent overheating a bit in metalwork. A breast drill is larger than a hand drill and can accommodate auger bits. Most breast drills have two speeds and some models have an adjustable ratchet on the spindle to provide a clockwise or counter-clockwise motion to the bit for drilling in small areas. A bit brace provides

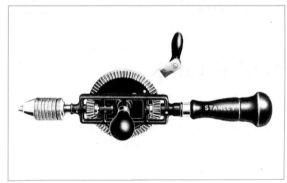

Courtesy of The Stanley Works

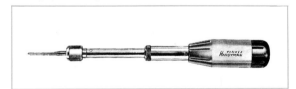

Courtesy of The Stanley Works

Two Types of Hand Drills

greater turning leverage than the hand and breast drills because of its large "sweep diameter" (the area in which the handle turns). The push drill is operated by pushing down on the handle of the drill with one hand and holding the work with the other. When pressure is released from the handle, a spring forces it up for the next push. *SEE ALSO HAND TOOLS.*

Hand Grinders & Flex Shafts
[SEE PORTABLE POWER TOOLS.]

Handrail

Handrail is a type of molding, usually made of wood, that is attached to balusters and posts for grasping with the hand as a support. *SEE ALSO MOLDING & TRIM; STAIR CONSTRUCTION.*

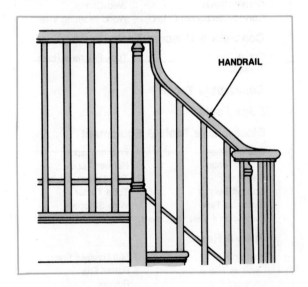

Handsaws

Very few home building and repair jobs can be adequately undertaken without the use of a handsaw. Although power sawing has become quite popular, the dozen or more varieties of handsaws available still have an important place in any tool collection.

Knowing how to select, use and care for saws is essential. Basic design factors, often too small to notice, determine each saw's suitability for a specific job. For example, blade length and number of teeth per inch should be two of the major considerations when selecting a saw. In addition, there are two blade patterns from which to choose: the straight-back and skew-back. One of the main advantages of the straight-back pattern is that the upper edge can serve as a line marker. Even though the skew-backed saw is not suitable for marking, this type is preferred by some because of its flexibility. Unlike most other tools, a handsaw generally needs professional sharpening. *SEE ALSO HAND TOOLS.*

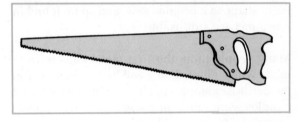

Handsaw

Hand Scrapers

The hand scraper is a thin piece of tempered steel that has no frame or handle, permitting

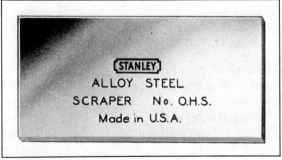

Courtesy of The Stanley Works

Hand Scraper

741

easy work in corners. To use the hand scraper, hold it at a 45° angle and apply pressure according to how deep of a cut is desired, and push it away from you. Most hand scrapers are five or six inches long with blade widths of two-and-one-half or three inches. *SEE ALSO HAND TOOLS.*

Hand Tools

Hand tools are the most commonly used tools among carpenters, gardners and metalworkers. Though most people do not realize it, many hand tools were invented thousands of years ago and are not relatively modern conveniences.

Saws date back as far as 130,000 years when the Neanderthal man used this tool much the same way carpenters do today. These saws were similar in shape to a pruning saw, and some found in museums are still usable.

Many people think the first metal chisels were made with a pointed tang and had no handle. But the earliest examples of chisels with and without handles were found in Bologna and are approximately 2,000 years old.

Metal-framed planes were invented by the Romans in 50 B. C. It was not until 1827 that planes with metal bodies were made.

The hammer dates back to stone age man, who used a rock with one hollowed side to provide a thumb grip. For attaching a handle to the rock, the rock had a grooved head so cord could be bound to the rock and lashed to the handle. The Romans were responsible for the claw hammer, even though it resembled a cross between a ripping and curved-claw hammer.

The carpenter's square was originated by a Vermont blacksmith in 1812. He made the first metal carpenter's squares from worn-out pit saw blades and stamped the scales on by hand. These squares became so popular that the blacksmith closed down his shop, obtained a patent for his square, opened a factory to manufacture them and later retired, independently wealthy.

Hand tools should be chosen for their quality and properly maintained for prolonged use. The chart below lists many of the thousands of hand tools in use today. Each are discussed individually throughout this encyclopedia.

Carpenter's Tools & Equipment

Carpenter's Apron	Chalk Line
Carpenter's Level	Plumb Bob
Carpenter's Square	Plumb Line

Chisels

Butt Chisel	Pocket Chisel
Cape Chisel	Ripping Chisel
Cold Chisel	Round-Nose Chisel
Firmer Chisel	Skew Chisel
Floor & Clapboard Chisel	Socket Chisel
Framing Chisel	Spear-Point Chisel
Gauge Chisel	Tang Chisel
Mill Chisel	Turning Chisel
Paring Chisel	Wood Chisels

Clamping Tools

Clamps & Vises

Band Clamp	Miter Clamp
Bar Clamp	Spring Clamps
C-Clamp	Vise Pipe
Corner Clamp	Web-Clamp
Curved-Component Clamp	Wood Working Vise

Concrete & Masonry Tools

Corner Trowel	Tuck Pointer's Rake
Trowels	

Convertible Tools

Edge Tools

Electrician's Tools & Equipment

Cable Ripper	Friction Tape
Circuit Tester	Rubber Tape
Clicktester	Test Lamps & Light
Conduit Bender	Tube Tester
Electrical Tape	Wire Strippers
Electrician's Test Equipment	

Files & Rasps

Bastard File	Mill Bastard File
Cantsaw File	Rattail File
Crosscut File	Rifflers
Curved-Tooth File	Round File
File Card	Single-Cut Files
Flat File	Square File
Half-Round File	Taper File
Half-Round Shoe Rasp	Three-Square File
Horse Rasp	Triangular File
Lead Float File	Wood Rasp

Flaring Tools
Garden Tools & Equipment

Aerator
Curved-Blade Pruning
  Shears
Edger
Garden Hose Care
Lawn Mowers
Lawn Sprinklers
Lawn Tools

Leaf Blower
Pruning Saw

Pruning Shears
Rake
Scythes
Sickles
Yard Tools

Gauges

Butt Gauge
Contour Gauge
Depth Gauge

Marking Gauge
Wood Marking Gauge

Hammers

Ball-Peen Hammer
Bell-Face Hammer
Chisel Mallets
Claw Hammers
Hatchets
Magnetic Hammer

Mallets
Mash Hammer
Nail Set
Plain-Face Hammer
Ripping Hammer
Sledge Hammer

Knives & Scrapers

Adze
Drawknife
Gooseneck Scrapers

Hand Scrapers
Linoleum Knife
Putty Knife

Layout Tools

Measuring & Marking Tools

Bevel Square
Boxwood Rule
Claiper Rule
Center Square
Combination Square
Compass Pencil
Dividers
Extension Rule
Folding Rule
Framing Square
Homeowners Square
Inside Try Square
Level
Level Transit
Line Level
Miter Square

Outside Try Square
Rafter Square
Rough Measuring
Scribers
Sliding T Bevel
Straight Edge
T-Bevel Square
Tape Measure
Trammel Points
Transit
Torpedo Level
Try Square
Wing Dividers
Yardstick
Zig-Zag Rule

Metalworking Tools

Dies & Taps

Planes

Block Plane
Circular Plane
Combination Plane
Dado Plane
Filister
Fore & Jointer Planes

Jack Plane
Plow Plane
Rough Plane
Scrub Plane
Smooth Plane
Spokeshave

Pliers & Cutters

Bolt Cutters
Combination Pliers
Curved-Nose Pliers
Diagonal-Cutting Pliers
End-Cutting Nippers
Flatnose Pliers
Lineman's Pliers
Locking Plier Wrench
Needlenose Pliers
Nippers

Parallel-Jaw Pliers
Pinking Shears
Scissors
Shears
Side-Cutting Pliers
Slip-Joint Pliers
Snips
Straight-Blade Shears
Tweezers
Wire Cutters

Plumber's Tools & Equipment

Auger
Basin Wrench
Blow Torch
Caulking Iron
Clean-Out Auger
Flanging Tool
Flaring Tool
Force Cup

Pipe Cutter
Pipe Reamer
Pipe Threader
Pipe Tools
Propane Torch
Seating Tools
Snake, Plumber's
Vise, Plumbing

Prybars & Ripping Bars

Crowbar
Gooseneck Ripping Bar
Jimmy Bar
Lining-Up Bar

Nail Claw
Straight Ripping Bar
Stripping Bar
Wrecking Bar

Punches

Center Punch
Line-Up Punch
Pin Punch

Self-Centering Punch
Starter Punch

Saws & Saw Blades

Backsaw
Bowsaw
Blades
Blade Teeth
Carbide-Tipped Blades
Chain Saw
Compass & Keyhole Saws
Coping Saw
Cordwood Blade
Crosscut Saw
Dado Blade
Docking Saw
Dovetail Saw
Egyptian Saw

Hacksaw
Handsaws
Hole Saw
Miter Box Saw
Rip Blade
Rip Saw
Scroll Saws
Shaping Saw
Skewbacked Saw
Stab Saw
Straight-Backed Saw
Timber Saw
Tree Saws

Screwdrivers

Clutch-Head Bit Screwdriver
Offset Screwdrivers
Phillips Screwdriver
Ratchet
Ratchet Screwdrivers

Reversible Screwdrivers
Screw-Holding Screwdrivers
Spiral-Ratchet Screwdriver
Yankee Screwdriver

Staple Guns

Stapling Tools

Tools For Boring Holes

Awl	Long Shank Straight Bit
Auger Bit	Multi-Bore Bit
Beading Bit	Ogee Bit
Bit Brace	Scratch Awl
Bits	Screw Bits
Boring Bit	Screwdriver Brace & Bit
Breast Drill	Shear-Cut Bit
Carbide Bits	Single-End Bit
Chamfer Bit	Single-Flute Router Bit
Chip-Groove Bits	Small Shank Bits
Combination Screw Bits	Spade Bits
Core-Box Bit	Straight Deep-Cutting Bits
Counterbore	Threading Bits
Countersink	Twist Drill
D-Bits	Whimble Brace
Doweling Jig	Wood Bits
Expansion Bit	Yankee Push Drill
Hand Drills	

Upholstery Tools & Equipment

Woodcarving Tools & Materials

Wrenches

Adjustable Wrench	Nut Drivers
Allen Wrench	Open-End Wrench
Box Wrenches	Setscrew Wrench
Chain Wrench	Slip & Lock Wrenches
Flare-Nut Wrench	Socket Wrenches
Hex Wrench	Spud Wrench
Key Wrench	Stillson Wrench
Monkey Wrench	Strap Wrench

Hanger

A hanger gives support to objects such as pipes, gutters and electrical boxes or accessories. A pipe hanger is usually used in conjunction with wood or light metal block. The hanger wraps

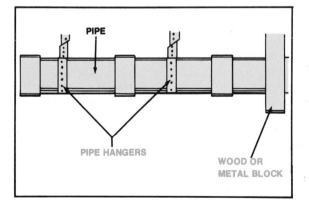

around the pipe and is secured to a stationary joist or beam by means of a conventional fastener.

An adjustable hanger is usually used when installing an object such as a ceiling box, ceiling fan or chandelier. They allow these items to be fastened directly to the ceiling by means of interstructural support.

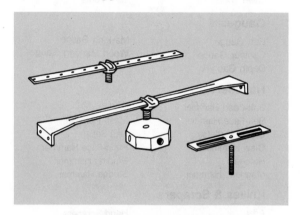

Various types of adjustable hangers

Another common use for hangers is in the installation of gutters. There are three main variations of gutter hangers. The first is the spike and sleeve type which fits a spike through a sleeve in the gutter. It is then nailed into the side of the roof.

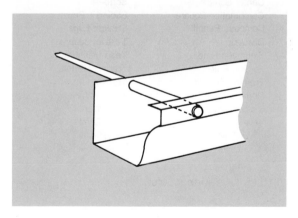

Spike and Sleeve Hanger

The second type is referred to as a bracket hanger because a bracket fits around the body of the gutter and is secured to the fascia directly below the roof. Screws or nails can be used with this type of hanger.

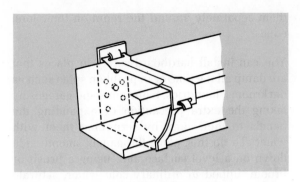

Bracket Type Hanger

Finally there is a strip option which is fastened under the shingle of the roof. It should then be covered with a clear sealant for weatherproofing.

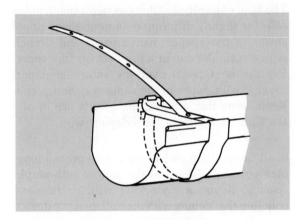

Strap Type Hanger

All these gutter variations of hangers should be placed every 30 inches in a straight run of gutter and at each corner joist. *SEE ALSO FASTENERS.*

Hardboard

Hardboard used to mean merely an inexpensive, brown building sheet that was put onto unimportant walls or cut up for the backs of chests and cupboards. Today it is a versatile craft material, which is used as a prefinished wall paneling in woodgrains and textures and simulations of brick, cork and tile, a shower wall, an exterior siding.

Hardboard is a product which uses sawmill wood residues as well as logs with nothing thrown away. Hardboard is made from wood chips converted to fibers which are permanently bonded under pressure and heat into a panel. The panel is then sawn to size, and the trimmings are recycled. In manufacture, the wood fibers are combined with natural and synthetic binders and other additives, giving a variety of types of hardboard for different uses.

A close relative of hardboard and often confused with it is particleboard. This material is also made now in woodgrain and other impressively patterned finishes for wall paneling. For many uses, but not all, it is an alternative to hardboard. It is, however, made not from fibers but from chips and particles, and it is made by a dry process.

WORKING WITH HARDBOARD

Hardboard sheets, siding and paneling can be sawed, drilled and shaped with normal woodworking tools. The tempered variety, which is also used to make the highly durable plastic coated paneling, is more abrasive than ordinary hardboard. Since plastic coated paneling will tend to dull blades, carbide-tipped ones are desirable. Hardboard takes nails and screws well, but the precaution should be taken to predrill for nails which will be driven very close to an edge.

Hardboard can sometimes be susceptible to damage from moisture — for instance, the ordinary kinds are not suitable for use in high-moisture bathroom areas, for which special plastic coated types are recommended. Some of these may even be used in showers and around tubs. Ordinary hardboard wall paneling of the prefinished type is now so resistant to damage from moisture that it is recommended for basement recreation rooms and other below-grade installations.

Hardboard siding is specially formulated to resist all extremes of weather. Preprimed hardboard takes paint easily and holds it longer. It offers some other advantages over metal siding; it is not noisy in wind, rain or hail; it is

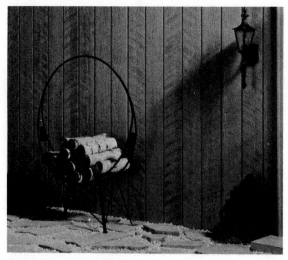

Courtesy of Masonite Corporation

With texture and appearance of rough cedar boards, this hardboard siding comes 4 feet wide, 8 or 9 feet long. It can be had prefinished, primed for painting or unprimed for staining on the job.

electrically nonconductive and it will not produce sounds from expansion and contraction as the temperature changes. However, hardboard will swell and shrink with changes in humidity. Proportionately, the possible change is not great.

Because it is most often used in big sheets, hardboard expands forcibly. Dry sheets fastened closely together with tight fitting joints will start buckling during high humidity. Long panels mounted between the floor and ceiling with no spare space at the ends create a worse situation. Hardboard expands in proportion to its length — the longer the panel, the bigger the problem. A sliding door that fits its track on a dry day may bind on a damp one.

The usual solution to this problem is a simple one. Before installing it allow the hardboard to condition itself to the expected humidity of the area in which it will be used and allow a little room for expansion.

OVERCOMING EXPANSION PROBLEMS

To condition panels for any normal use, just allow them to stand for two days in the room in which they will be used, or in some area of comparable humidity. Unwrap them first and stand

them separately around the room on their long edges.

You can install hardboard safely in places that are damp all the time or in problem spots such as darkrooms, laundries, bathrooms and garages by taking the extra precaution of expanding the panels to their limit by scrubbing them with water. To do this, place the panels smooth side down on a level surface and, using a brush or broom dipped in ordinary cold water, saturate them until their color darkens. Stack them back to back and cover the whole pile with a tarpaulin, heavy paper or a piece of polyethylene sheeting for 24 to 48 hours. Install them while the moisture is still in them.

The kind of hardboard that has two smooth sides calls for slightly different treatment. Place single sheets of newspaper over a panel and drench with a sprinkler can or a hose set for fine spray. Lay the next panel over the saturated paper, cover it with paper in the same way and wet it. Keep doing this until all the panels are in one stack and cover them for a day or two.

In all cases, along with conditioning precautions, plan your installation of the panels with ample spacing. If you are working with prefinished paneling that comes with a small spacing device in each package, be sure to use it. In any case, avoid jamming panels tightly together at joints; even where no increased humidity is to be expected and panels have been preconditioned by standing for 48 hours, light contact between panel edges is enough. One way to provide slight spacing at joints while maintaining uniformity of appearance is by using nails as temporary spacers.

When you are applying panels to masonry walls, especially in basements, provide a vapor barrier between the walls and the paneling. One easy way to do this is with a layer of polyethylene sheeting over the wall, held by the furring strips required for the paneling installation. Another, with additional advantages, is the use of insulation that contains a vapor barrier and is placed between the furring strips.

As with most paneling installations, hardboard

paneling should not press tightly against the ceiling. A quarter-inch of space obtained by resting the panels on a temporary shim should be left between panel and floor. It will be covered by base molding or other trim or by carpet edge.

PROJECT MAKING WITH HARDBOARD

Rules for cutting hardboard are the same as for all other sheet materials that require a saw rather than scoring and breaking with the exception that with hardboard, unlike plywood, there is no grain direction to consider. With a handsaw, cut with the good side (the side to be most exposed to view) up. This is the rule also for cutting with a radial-arm saw used in crosscutting position. However, when the radial saw is in rip position, panels should be cut face down, and this also applies to all cuts made with a portable circular saw or with a sabre saw. If this seems too complicated to remember, just apply the rule that the direction of the saw, whatever its type, should be into the face of the panel to prevent splintered edges.

In use, hardboard edges that are exposed require some kind of protection. Often this is merely beveling with a plane or rounding off with sandpaper.

It is possible to use hardboard panels as sliding doors in cabinets or as drawer or shelf partitions without framing. But usually hardboard is supported on a frame, the size of the material depending on the project. It will usually range from 1 inch square to 1 x 2 inches for small cupboards and cabinets to 2 x 2 and 2 x 4 for such things as garage doors or closet walls.

Generally, all hardboard joints must be supported by a continuous frame. Nails, screws, bolts or glue can be used to fasten the hardboard to supporting material. If finishing nails are used, the heads can be set and the holes filled. (When nails are used with prefinished hardboard, as in paneling, this nuisance can be avoided by the use of colored nails, often obtainable from the same source as the paneling in matching colors.) No method of fastening should come closer to the edge than $1/4$ inch. Nails and screws should usually come no further than 4

inches apart, and nailing should usually begin near the center of the panel, with edges done last.

BENDING HARDBOARD

Compound curves cannot be made with hardboard, but simple, one-direction bends are easily done. If the curve is to be supported by framing of some kind, the bend can be made dry unless the curve is very sharp. For unsupported bends and very sharp curves, hardboard must be dampened. To do this, scrub water into the backs of panels with a broom. If several panels are used, place them in pairs, back to back, with wet newspaper between. If the job calls for only one panel, then cover it with wet newspaper or cloth. Let dampened panels stand, at least 24 hours for standard hardboard to as long as 72 hours for tileboard and patterned types.

After the panels have become evenly damp, fasten them to the framing or to the shaping form that is constructed of wood. Let the panels dry thoroughly before removing them from the form. The radius of the shaping form for making a bend that will be unsupported should be slightly less than the finished curve wanted. This will allow for a small amount of spring-back when the form and panel are parted.

PANELING WITH HARDBOARD

If you are considering whether to do a wall-paneling job with hardboard, there are certain questions you are likely to ask.

Some of the advantages of hardboard over plywood panels or wood are that there is a wider selection of patterns and woodgrain finishes from which to choose. Hardboard paneling is better in terms of maintenance ease, resistance to wear and abuse and freedom from checking, splitting or cracking. Hardboard paneling is also easier to work with and apply as well as having exceptional smoothness, durability and strength.

Prefinished hardboard panel patterns are reproduced photographically from the best sections of board from a given species. Each panel can be exactly matched, because it is uniform in

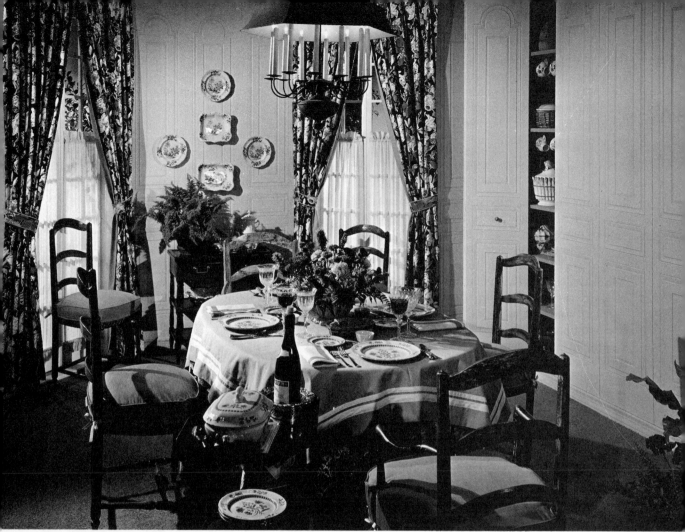

One of the reproductions of period panelings now made in hardbooard here carries the spirit of the French countryside. Same panels, cut twice to give 16 inch strips, cover the bifold doors.

color and in texture while wood and plywood panels commonly reflect natural variations in grain and color as well as any imperfections in the tree itself.

Some of the various woodgrain and pattern panelings available are walnut, pecan, butternut, wormy chestnut, teak, oak, cherry, birch, elm, maple and rosewood. There are also panels which are authentic reproductions of the painted wood walls, cork, brick and other natural materials.

Pattern surfaces include: marbelized, fleeces, burlap, louvered, cane, striated, embossed, plain, speckled and decorator colors, lacey prints, metallic flecks, rich fabric textures, simulated tiles and murals.

Hardboard paneling has superior resistance to damage. The prefinished surface is washable and the panels are not affected by food and beverage stains or by normal impact from toys.

Hardboard paneling is generally $1/8$ inch or $1/4$ inch thick in 4 x 8 sheets. Ordinary carpenter tools are all that are needed to work with hardboard. Good results are obtained by using a crosscut saw for straight cuts and a coping or sabre saw for curved cuts. If desired, beveled or rounded edges can be made with a carpenter's plane, sandpaper or beveling tool. Hand power tools work well on hardboard also.

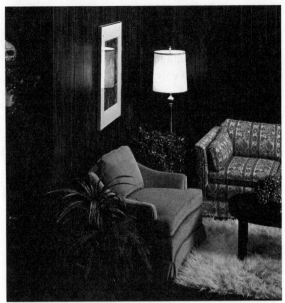

Courtesy of Evans Products Company

For the look of traditional deeptoned wood paneling, hardboard appears with a photographically reproduced surface on sheets that go up fast.

To install hardboard panels, nails or a panel adhesive may be used. Adhesive, which comes in a tube to be inserted into a caulking gun, permits faster, better and nail-less application. The procedure is quite simple. Just apply thin ribbons of adhesive. Then press panels into position and hammer two nails at the top of the panel. Continue to apply panels following the manufacturer's spacing recommendations. After about 15 minutes, return to the first panel for the final set, using a padded block and mallet.

To finish the inside and outside corners of walls or where the panels meet the ceiling and floor, use color-coordinated, or contrasting prefinished moldings and trim which can be applied with adhesive or by nailing. There is also a selection of color coordinated nails and putty sticks to add a further finished look if necessary. All of these should be available from the paneling dealer.

Prefinished 1/4 inch hardboard paneling helps overcome sound transmission. The American Hardboard Association had sound transmission tests made at a well known, independent acoustical laboratory. These tests definitely prove prefinished hardboard paneling is a superior barrier against the transmission of sound through a wall. Tests on a dozen different wall systems have given partitions faced with prefinished hardboard panels ratings equal and better than those recommended by the Federal Housing Administration (FHA) for through-the-wall noise transmission between rooms.

SIDING

Hardboard's extremely hard surface is highly resistant to damage. Unlike metal sidings, hardboard is not easily dented. Hardboard siding also has the sound deadening quality of hardboard.

Hardboard does not require electrical grounding as it is a good electrical insulator.

There is a much wider selection of finishes available than you can get with any other type of siding. Hardboards come factory preprimed which makes painting easy. Horizontal or vertical sidings can have a tough finish applied at the factory. These colors are long lasting and retain their appearance for years.

There is also a broad choice from deep embossed patterns through a variety of textures including the popular rough-sawn appearance.

Some of the styles of hardboard siding which are available are: the conventional lap siding with

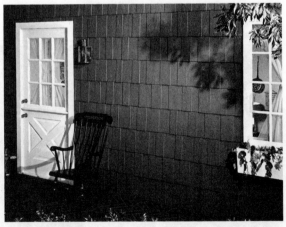

Courtesy of Masonite Corporation

Looking like cedar shakes but applied like lap siding, this Masonite hardboard product comes 1 foot wide, 16 feet long, may be had prefinished

deep shadow line, from 8 inches up to 12 inches in width and in lengths up to 16 feet, a contemporary verticle panel siding with square cut grooves on either four inch or eight inch centers, traditional panels with $1/2$ inch wide V-grooves on $5^1/_3$ inch centers and reverse board-and-batten panels. Ungrooved sidings are usually applied with batten strips. Some panels have shiplap edges which provide better weather protection and makes installation easier.

Even in severe climates, hardboard is less affected by temperature changes than many other sidings. They do not get brittle or soft as do some synthetic materials. The application instructions, which manufacturers recommend, will insure a weathertight exterior for long life and service.

Hardboard siding has to be painted less often than many other sidings. It should be years before a repainting might be required. An infrequent hosing normally will keep the siding fresh looking.

Hardboard sidings which are prefinished at the factory have an exceptionally long life. They include both liquid and film-laminated finish systems. Some finishes are guaranteed for up to 30 years.

If the primed siding cannot be painted right after it is installed, you have nothing to worry about. Preprimed siding can be left exposed for up to 90 days. This gives sufficient opportunity to do the job when the weather is more favorable or the time is more convenient.

Except when doing it on a comparatively small wall area, the installation of siding is quite a sizeable undertaking and, unless the homeowner is quite skilled, a professional should do the actual installing. However, only ordinary carpenter tools are required to cut, fit and apply the siding. The material itself is easy to work and can be cut and fastened by conventional methods as can the various coordinated accessories such as starter strips, outside and inside corners, drip caps and battens.

There are many other practical applications for hardboard siding, where its durability, strength and toughness serve excellently. Hardboard is used for soffits on the undersides of eaves and porches; for breezeway and carport ceilings. Use it too for fascia, eaves and rakes and for decorative insets below windows. Hardboard also makes attractive decorative fencing. There are many attractive and distinctive fence designs shown in manufacturers' literature, with instructions on how to build them. Use hardboard for patio screens, windbreaks, flower boxes, sand box enclosures, storage sheds for lawn mowers, snowmobiles, snow blowers and even cabanas at the swimming pool.

Prefinished Hardboard Paneling: Woodgrain and Texture

Courtesy of Masonite Corporation

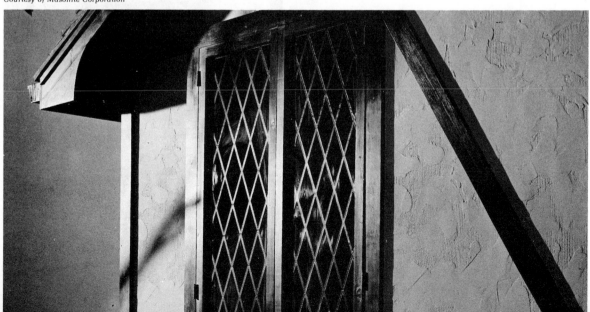

Hardware

Exclusive of fasteners like nuts and bolts, screws and nails, hardware is a wide range of items such as hinges, catches, brackets, handles, pulls, shelf brackets and desk supports. In each category of products there is a wide variety in color, style and even material. It may be a bit difficult to accept, but some "hardware" like hinges, handles and pulls are made of plastic or wood.

Craftsmen today are lucky because manufacturers cater to any and all buyers. Any well-stocked hardware store or do-it-yourself "home center" displays hundreds of items usually including instructions on how the item should be used or installed.

Very often the project determines the kind of hardware to be used. A classic piece of furniture, such as a French-provincial table, will require hardware to match. A simple decor with paint and wallcovering looks best with wooden knobs painted to match the wood. For natural woodwork and paneling, small brass pulls fit the decor. Mediterranean, early-American and contemporary designs all call for hardware with a matching theme.

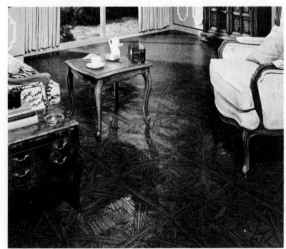

Courtesy of Armstrong Cork Company

A French-provincial table requires ornate pulls to suit its styling.

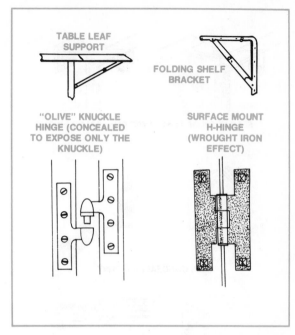

The amount of difficulty involved in installing hardware generally depends on whether it will be surface-mounted, semiconcealed or completely hidden. Hinges attached to a surface are no problem because you only need to drill starting holes, then drive screws. A butt hinge requires cutting a mortise in two edges, and a concealed hinge requires mortising or drilling or both. The pull on a door or drawer is easily mounted on the surface, but one that is flush with the surface requires cutting a mortise to recess it. In most cases there is a choice of whether to use a surface-mounted or flush pull, but for some projects such as a sliding door, the pull must be recessed into the door to keep it clear of the door that slides across in front of it.

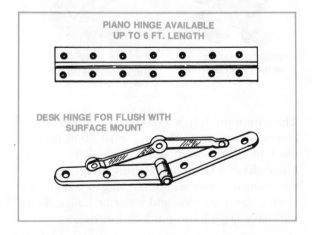

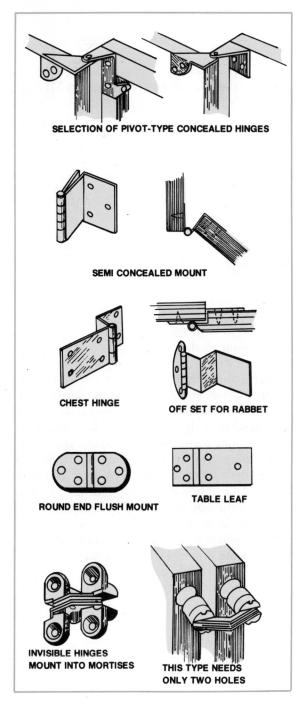

SELECTION OF PIVOT-TYPE CONCEALED HINGES

SEMI CONCEALED MOUNT

CHEST HINGE

OFF SET FOR RABBET

ROUND END FLUSH MOUNT

TABLE LEAF

INVISIBLE HINGES MOUNT INTO MORTISES

THIS TYPE NEEDS ONLY TWO HOLES

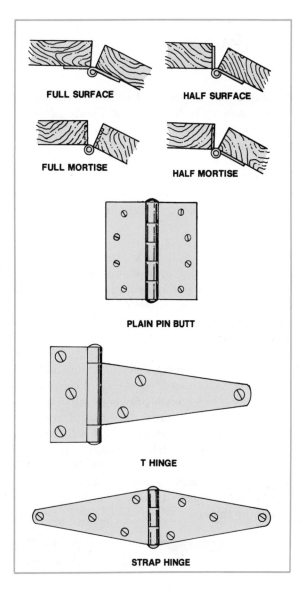

FULL SURFACE

HALF SURFACE

FULL MORTISE

HALF MORTISE

PLAIN PIN BUTT

T HINGE

STRAP HINGE

The common hinge consists of two folding leaves and a pivot. The one most often used is the type that lies flat when it is opened. Some hinges have a loose pin. Pulling the pin permits removing the door without having to take off the hinges. Both interior and exterior house doors will have large loose-pin butt hinges.

The strap hinge has long narrow leaves and is always attached to the surface. Generally it is a heavy duty hinge for use on gates, heavy outside doors as on barns and similar applications.

The T-hinge has one long leaf and one short one; sort of a combination butt-and-strap hinge. This type hinge comes in large sizes also, for gates and the like. Smaller versions of both the strap and T-hinge are used on cabinets when a rustic or early-American look is desired.

Ornamental hinges come in a wide variety of types, sizes and finishes. Wrought iron is popu-

lar now, but bright and antique brass are also widely used and even chrome-plated are occasionally used. Functioning somewhat like a hinge, but not used for doors, are items like supports for a drop-leaf table and those used for folding shelves.

For holding doors closed you need a latch, lock, catch or similar device. Most ordinary cabinets do not need a lock. Catches such as inexpensive simple spring-type catches are usually all that are necessary. Magnetic catches cost more, the price depending on the strength of the magnet. A modern catch is the touch latch that opens a door when you push against it, latches it shut when you push again. No pull is required on a door when a touch latch is used, as the latch causes the door to spring open when you push on it.

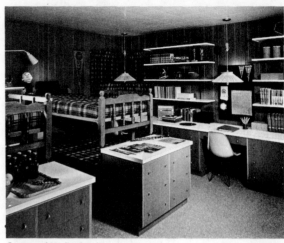

Courtesy of Marlite Paneling

Natural-wood cabinets call for small brass pulls on doors and drawers.

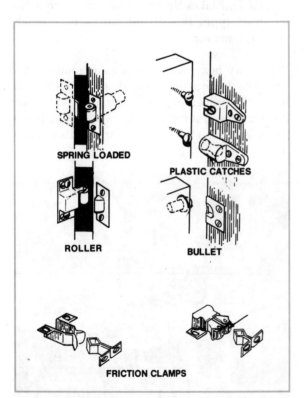

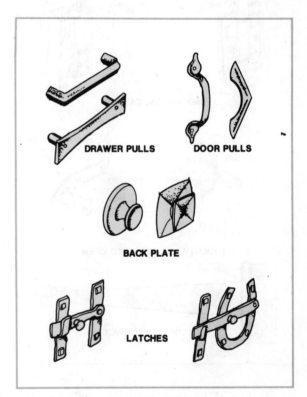

A thumb latch can be combined with a handle. Depress the latch which releases the catch. Then pull on the handle to open the door.

Handles for doors and drawers should be chosen to fit the project. They should also be functional for the job.

Sliding doors are used on closets and on small cabinets. For closets the hardware will be an overhead track with rollers attached to the top of the doors to fit in the tracks. Metal or plastic guides are screwed to the floor to keep the doors from swinging and to assure easy action. Sliding doors in cabinets slide in grooves cut in the top

753

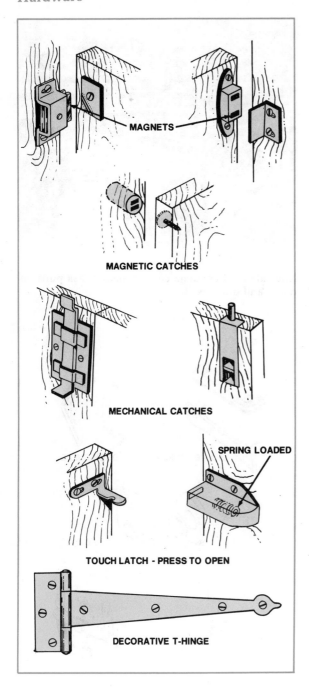

MAGNETS

MAGNETIC CATCHES

MECHANICAL CATCHES

SPRING LOADED

TOUCH LATCH - PRESS TO OPEN

DECORATIVE T-HINGE

edges of the pairs of doors moving parallel to the door opening of the closet.

One kind of modern and much-appreciated hardware is the type used to support drawers and make them roll in and out easily. One half of the pairs of guides is screwed to the sides of the drawer, the other two pieces to the cabinet opening. In most cases the opening must be 1 inch wider than the width of the drawer, to allow a $1/2$ inch space on each side for the slides. Ball-bearing rollers are used in this hardware and the drawers move almost effortlessly. These slides are available in sizes which can handle weights of two or three hundred pounds and small enough to handle just a few pounds.

A second type of drawer slide fits under the drawer and takes up less space than the side-mounted type. It will not support as much weight, however.

For a very heavy door, such as a framed-glass unit, a continuous, or piano, hinge will do the job better than several individual hinges. This type hinge comes in several widths, and in lengths up to six feet. It can be cut to shorter lengths to suit a job.

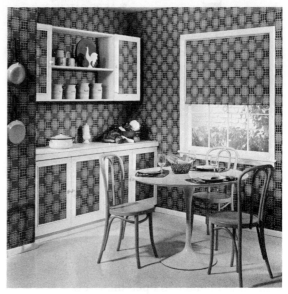

Courtesy of Wallcovering Industry Bureau

Simple wooden knobs are used as pulls on doors and drawers when cabinets are painted and accented with wallcovering.

and bottom of the opening, or in metal or plastic tracks that are slipped into those grooves.

Bi-fold doors on closets use a combination of hinges and tracks. Rollers on the top corners of the inside doors run in a track attached overhead, while the pairs of doors are hinged together. Guides on the floor keep the two inside

For the ultimate in kitchen-cabinet hardware, miniature automatic door closers are available. If you want a cabinet door fitted with one of these closers to stay open, swing the door all the way open.

Hardwood

Hardwood comes from the broadleafed, leaf-shedding trees such as oak, maple, birch, walnut and mahogany. Hardwoods cost more than softwoods but are stronger and last longer. Many hardwoods, however, are no harder than some of the softwoods. In the home, hardwood is used for molding, doors, floors, cabinets or furniture. *SEE ALSO LUMBER.*

Hatchet

A hatchet looks like an axe, but unlike the axe, which has a curved blade, the hatchet has a straight triangular blade with a slot in it to pull nails. The hatchet's flat side may be used as a hammering tool. Hatchets with their short handles are good chopping and driving tools for lawn and garden jobs, and are also used in splitting shims, shangles and boards down to size.

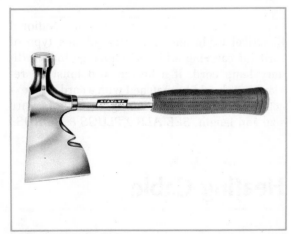

Courtesy of The Stanley Works

Hatchet

The hatchet most useful in the home is the half hatchet which has an extra thin blade. It also comes with a single or a double bevel. The single bevel is used with the right hand only. The double bevel is the all-purpose hatchet. *SEE ALSO HAND TOOLS.*

Header

A header is a wooden load-supporting member laid either horizontally over or surrounding an opening, such as a window or door, or an opening in a roof or floor. The joists run at right angles to headers. A header may be two pieces of lumber nailed together and placed on edge, or one piece of four-inch thick board. *SEE ALSO WALL & CEILING CONSTRUCTION.*

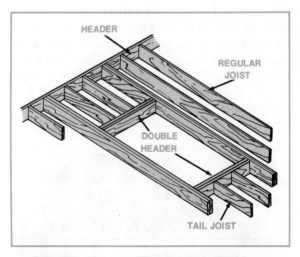

Headers and joists framing a floor opening.

Headlights
[SEE SYSTEMS, AUTOMOTIVE.]

Headroom

Headroom is the clear space between the floor line and ceiling of a building. In stair construction, the headroom extends from the front

border of the stair tread to the header or surface above. Local building codes generally regulate this distance. FHA minimum requirements are six feet, eight inches for main stairs and six feet, four inches for service or basement stairways. *SEE ALSO STAIR CONSTRUCTION.*

Hearth

The hearth is the floor of a fireplace which generally extends into the room a few inches to protect the flooring from hot, popping ashes. The hearth is usually made from brick, tile, slate or other materials that can withstand the heat of a fire.

The hearth is supported by building temporary supports and forms and using reinforced concrete no less than $3^1/_2$ inches thick. If there is sufficient space beneath the hearth, an ash pit and clean-out door may be installed. When the floor construction is concrete slab, the ash pit may be built next to a raised hearth. This is a practical design for fireplaces located on an outside wall. *SEE ALSO FIREPLACES.*

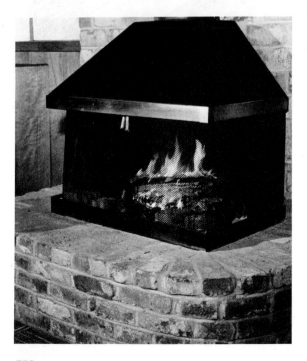

Heartwood

Heartwood, the core of a tree, is older, harder and more durable than the tree's outer rings, or sapwood. As the tree gets older and larger, the inner sapwood ceases to carry sap and becomes heartwood. Heartwood is usually darker and more resistant to fungi than sapwood because of the gums and resins it contains. *SEE ALSO LUMBER.*

Heat Distribution Systems
[SEE HEATING SYSTEMS.]

Heater Cord

Heater cord, or Type HPD, is asbestos-insulated cord used with irons, toasters, portable heaters and other appliances that generate large amounts of heat. It contains two conductors made of fine, stranded copper wire covered first with a layer of cotton and then with rubber insulation. The conductors are then covered completely with a layer of asbestos before being twisted and wrapped in a final covering of either cotton, rayon or rubber.

Because of its asbestos insulation, the National Electrical Code allows the use of this type of cord for carrying a higher amperage than ordinary lamp cord. If a heater cord must be replaced, it should be matched with a cord with exactly the same outer covering, insulation, wire size and length. *SEE ALSO PLUGS & CORDS.*

Heating Cable

Heating cables are cables placed in the ceiling to produce radiant electric heat. These electric

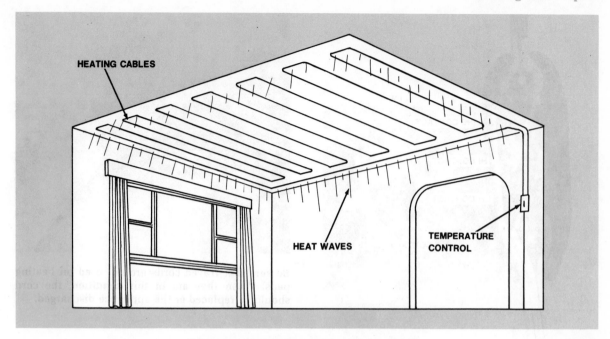

Heating cables embedded in a plaster ceiling.

heating cables may be embedded in the plaster or placed between layers of plasterboard. After the wires are fastened, the ceiling may be painted. In new construction, heating cables are preferred over panels with heating elements factory-installed. Heating cables are also used on roofs to keep ice from sticking.

Heating, Forced Warm Air
[SEE HEATING SYSTEMS]

Heating, Gravity Warm Air
[SEE HEATING SYSTEMS.]

Heating Pad Repair

Heating pads consist of a soft, flexible, resistance heating element that is woven be-

tween several layers of cloth to provide warmth to a small area. This is usually a dual-element device with one side having twice the wattage of the other.

Several heat ranges can be applied by a single switch. The low wattage element is energized for low heat, the higher wattage element for medium heat and both elements for a high position.

If a heating pad fails to operate, check the receptacle first with a table lamp. If this fails check the cord carefully after unplugging it, particularly around the points where it enters and leaves the switch. By removing the cover of the switch (usually an in-line type with two screws holding it together) you can check the contacts and wiring inside.

Many faults in heating pads arise with the connection of the wiring in the switch itself. On some units this is attached permanently with a terminal. On others it is held in place by a screw. If this wire should break, trim the insulation back and clean both terminal and wire before retightening. If the contacts have become corroded or dirty, you can clean them by brushing them and/or by applying television contact cleaner.

757

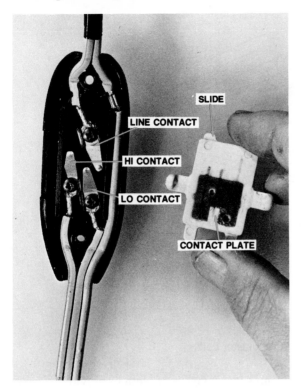

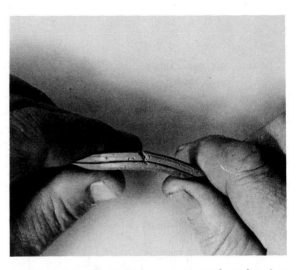

Be sure that frayed cords are not used on heating pads. When they are in this condition, the cord should be replaced or the appliance discharged.

Switch on heating pad is usually in-line type and is accessible by removing screws which hold two halves of housing together. Clean the switch, using television tuner spray, if it has become extremely linted. Otherwise make sure that contacts are making firm connections and that wire attachment points are tight.

If the pad is not heating at all and the switch contacts check okay, the problem is likely within the pad section itself. In addition to the two elements there is also a thermostat to shut the unit down if it should overheat. It's not advisable to make repairs inside the pad, and replacement parts for this type of repair are not generally available.

If the pad is heating only partially, it may be due to an open element. In this case it would heat on one or two of the settings but not on all. Don't overlook the possibility that the switch may be at fault. Disassemble and inspect the contacts and connections before condemning the pad.

If one element should prove to be open, it's very possible the pad may still be usable, though only on the one heat setting. Consider this before throwing it away. Should any fault develop in

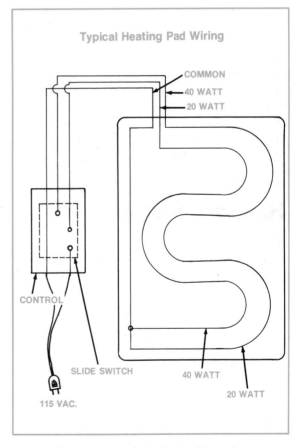

Wiring diagram is typical of circuit used on many heating pads. Slide switch completes circuit to either or both elements as required for three-heat-level control.

the wiring or cords connecting the switch and the pad, the cord should be replaced at once. Don't use a lamp cord. Use only a heat-resistant type cord specified for this type use. *SEE ALSO APPLIANCE REPAIR, SMALL.*

Heating Systems

Heating systems for the home range from the simple to the complex. The most simple system is the fireplace or the room space heater. Central heating systems may be classified into three general categories: forced air, hot water and steam. Home heating systems are generally dependent on three sources of fuel or power: fuel or heating oil, natural gas and electricity. Research is being done to make solar heating economically feasible. *SEE ALSO HOME HEATING SYSTEMS.*

Heating Tape

Heating tape is most commonly used to wrap outdoor water pipes and faucets to keep them from freezing. This electrical heating tape should be wrapped around the faucet and pipe leading to it, from the frost line up. A thermostat, which comes with the tape, should be connected to a weatherproof outdoor outlet and placed near

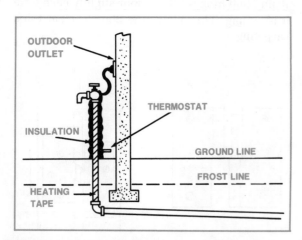

Outdoor faucet protected with heating tape

the faucet. In addition, use insulation on all above ground sections.

Heating tape also refers to the tape or cables put on concrete steps, garage sills, roofs and hotbeds to prevent ice build-up. Be sure to buy the correct type of heating tape for your purpose as most types are not interchangeable. Follow manufacturer's instructions carefully to avoid a short.

Heavy Load Wiring
[SEE ELECTRICAL WIRING.]

Hedges, Evergreen
[SEE LAWNS & GARDENS.]

Hemlock

Hemlock is a softwood that is reddish-brown with slight purple casts. The eastern hemlock is known as a hemlock spruce or spruce pine and the western hemlock is referred to as Alaska fir, Alaska pine or gray fir.

Although light in weight, hemlock is moderately hard, straight grained and has an excellent weight/strength ratio. It glues, stains and finishes well and is easy to work and shape. Hemlock is used for exterior construction, pulpwood, small containers and plywood core stock. *SEE ALSO WOOD IDENTIFICATION.*

Hex Nut

A hex nut is a rounded edge hexagon with internal threads. It is used on screws and bolts for tightening and securing a position. *SEE ALSO FASTENERS.*

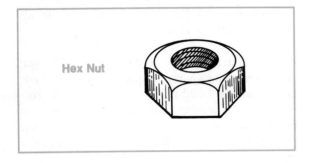

Hex Nut

Hex Wrenches

The hex wrench is probably one of the best tools to use in getting a strong, nonslip grasp on many-sided fittings and nuts. The jaws of the hex wrench are smooth, so they won't mar chrome-plated finishes; and they are narrow so they can fit into small spaces. Although some hex wrenches come in sizes that will take a nut up to 3 inches, the wrench that will handle 1^1/$_2$ inch bathtub and sink drain nuts is the best size to own. The hex wrench also comes in an offset design that works well in tight places. *SEE ALSO HAND TOOLS.*

Hickory

Hickory, a North American hardwood, is tan in color, splintery and hard to work with. Cutting hickory with the grain shows the pores as long channels. Hickory is used in furniture making for the larger bent sections such as backs of Colonial chairs. Windsor chair backs are made from either hickory or brown ash. *SEE ALSO WOOD IDENTIFICATION.*

Hi - Fi Systems
[SEE STEREO SYSTEMS.]

High Fidelity
[SEE STEREO SYSTEMS.]

Hinges

Hinges are paired, pivoted plates or cylinders used to support a movable panel such as a door or lid. There are nineteen different types of hinges.

A butt hinge can not be taken apart. It can be used on left- or right-handed doors.

Loose-pin hinges are the most common door hinge. The door can be removed by simply extracting the pin.

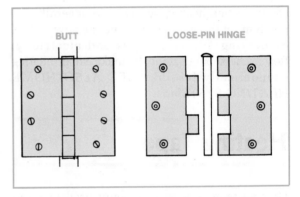

Loose-joint hinges are much like a loose-pin hinge. To separate the hinge simply lift it enough to clear the immovable pin. Loose-joint hinges are often used on portable typewriters, record players and similar cases.

Rising butt hinges lift the door slightly each time it is swung. This allows the door to clear thick carpeting.

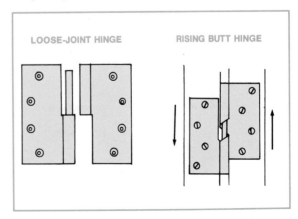

Ball-Bearing hinges are used on exterior-opening heavy doors. This hinge is permanently lubricated.

Knuckle hinges are decorative. The knuckle is the only portion of the hinge showing when the door is closed.

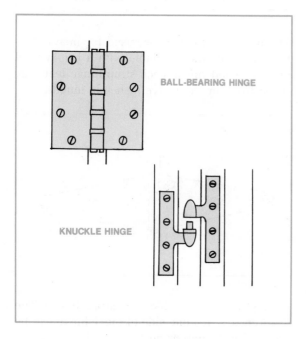

Flush door hinges are used when the majority of the hinge is to be concealed. When the door is closed, the only part of the hinge showing is the barrel.

A pivot reinforced hinge does not require a door frame. This feature makes the hinge useful on overlay, flush and recessed doors.

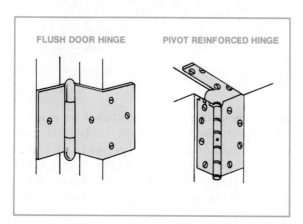

Used on hall or louver doors that must swing both ways, gravity pilot hinges often have a hold-open stop.

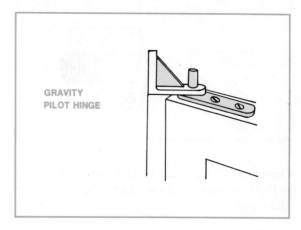

A double-acting hinge allows folding doors to swing both ways.

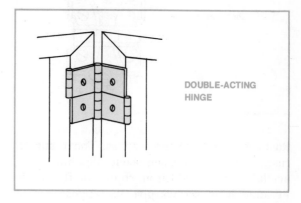

Used on screen or storm sashes, offset blind hinges allow full opening without hindrance from the hinges.

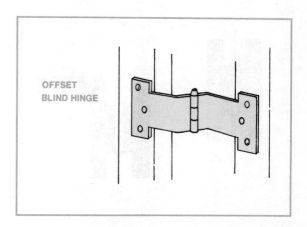

Spring-loaded hinges are used on heavy screen doors and will automatically close an open door.

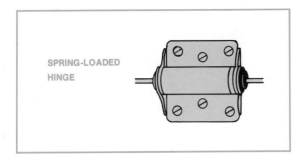

Ornamental hinges are used when their design will blend in or enhance the cabinet or door style.

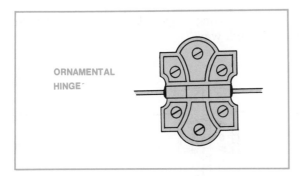

Rustic hinges have three styles. The rustic H, rustic H-L and rustic semi-concealed hinges are available in wrought iron, copper or flat black. Pyramid head screws give the appearance of handmade nails.

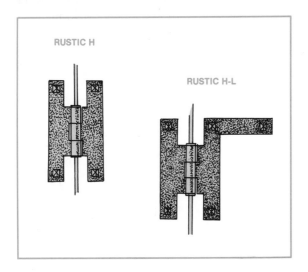

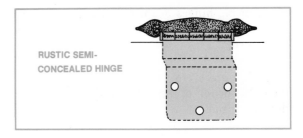

The large strap hinges are used for heavy double-folding doors. Available with a bright steel or zinc-plated finish, each strap hinge leaf may range from one to twelve inches in length.

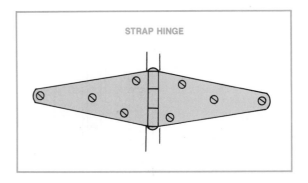

T hinges are much like the strap hinge. The difference is that one side of the T hinge can be fastened to a jamb or post.

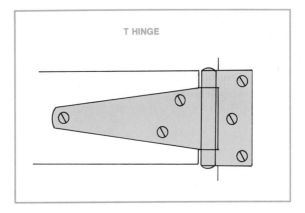

A continuous or piano hinge is used for extended support. Used for various kinds of lids or doors, continuous hinges are made of brass, aluminum, nickel or steel. Available in lengths up to 84 inches, the hinge plates contain holes approximately two inches apart countersunk for flathead screws.

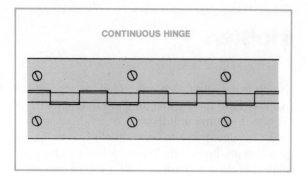

CONTINUOUS HINGE

Hip Jack

A hip jack is a shortened common rafter that runs at right angles from the wall or rafter plate to the hip rafter, the rafter connecting the wall plate and the ridge at the corner of the plate. *SEE ALSO ROOF CONSTRUCTION.*

Hip Rafter

A hip rafter is a hip roof member which extends from the corner of the top wall plate to the ridge of the roof frame. *SEE ALSO ROOF CON-STRUCTION.*

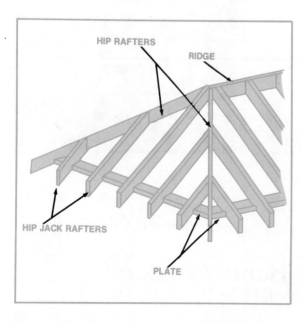

HIP RAFTERS

RIDGE

HIP JACK RAFTERS

PLATE

Hip Roof

A hip roof has four sides sloping toward the center. The adjacent sides of the roof are joined by hip rafters. This type of roof provides a protective overhang on end walls, in addition to the overhang on side walls. *SEE ALSO ROOF CON-STRUCTION.*

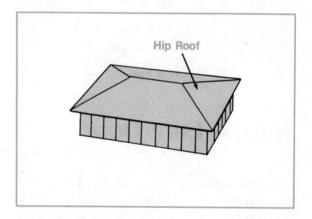

Hip Roof

Hobby Workshop
[SEE WORKSHOPS.]

Hole Saw

A hole saw is an attachment which is used with a power drill or drill press to drill holes as large as 3″ in diameter. There are a variety of types, one of which contains a mount (mandrel) and a blade. The mandrel fits into the chuck and the blade of the desired size is attached to the mandrel. These are sometimes sold in sets with an assortment of blade sizes. Another type is a single, adjustable tool. (This one usually comes equipped with two blades, one for wood work and one for metal.) Hole saws of specific sizes may also be purchased.

A good hole saw will cut through most any sort of building material. Some are even able to cut

through plumbing fixtures. One good use for a hole saw is drilling lock set cavities in doors. *SEE ALSO HAND TOOLS.*

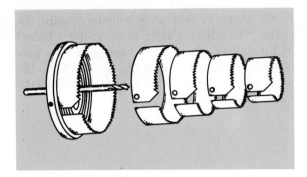

Hole Saw

Hollow Core Door

A hollow core door is one which has spaced braces for an internal frame. These braces are placed horizontally inside the frame between the side pieces and the upper and lower rails. Additional board braces are placed where the lock, knob and hinges are to be installed for extra support. Hollow core doors are approximately 30 to 40 pounds lighter than solid core varieties and are primarily used inside the home.

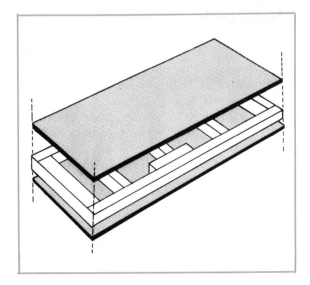

Hollow Core Door

Holsters

Holsters usually fasten onto a belt or around the waist to hold tools when they are not being used. The more common holsters are made of leather and can accommodate from one to five tools, depending on the design. Some varieties of holsters may contain a *T* chain to hold a roll of tape, and harness snaps for carrying small tools. A canvas carpenter's apron, which holds a variety of tools, may be considered a holster. Holsters are more commonly used in situations where several tools are needed frequently, such as in house construction, than in the home workshop.

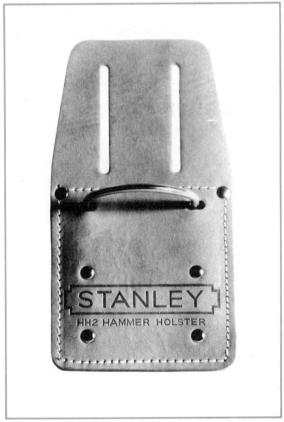

Courtesy of The Stanley Works

Hammer Holster

Home Additions
[SEE ROOM ADDITIONS]